THE HISTORY OF BLACK BUSINESS IN AMERICA

Capitalism, Race, Entrepreneurship

Twayne's

EVOLUTION OF MODERN BUSINESS SERIES

Kenneth Lipartito, University of Houston, Series Editor

JULIET E. K. WALKER

THE HISTORY OF
BLACK BUSINESS IN AMERICA

Capitalism, Race, Entrepreneurship

MACMILLAN LIBRARY REFERENCE USA
An Imprint of Simon & Schuster Macmillan
New York

PRENTICE HALL INTERNATIONAL
London   Mexico City   New Delhi   Singapore   Sydney   Toronto

Twayne's Evolution of Modern Business Series

The History of Black Business in America: Capitalism, Race, Entrepreneurship
Juliet E. K. Walker
Copyright © 1998 by Twayne Publishers

Macmillan Library Reference
An Imprint of Simon & Schuster Macmillan
1633 Broadway
New York, NY 10019

Library of Congress Cataloging-in-Publication Data
Walker, Juliet E. K., 1940–
    The history of Black business in America : capitalism, race, entrepreneurship / Juliet E. K. Walker.
       p. cm. — (Twayne's evolution of modern business series)
    Includes bibliographical references and index.
    ISBN 0-8057-1650-5 (alk. paper)
    1. Afro-American business enterprises—History.   I. Title.
II. Series.
HD2344.5.U6W35   1998
338.6′422′08996073—dc21   98-23170
                                      CIP

Printed in the United States of America

For my sons,
James Edward Walker II
and
Jeffrey Edmond Walker

Contents

Tables

Foreword

The history of African-American business is an untold story. Juliet E. K. Walker has brought this hidden side of the black experience to light for the first time. It is a timely story, one that will make us rethink what we believe about business, race, and success in American history.

Beginning her story in precolonial Africa, Walker demolishes Eurocentric myths that for too long have portrayed Africans as passive victims of Western commerce and expansion. Pulling no punches, she shows how the supply of slaves to the New World rested on a well-developed network of trade and marketing with a long history on the African continent, implicating Arabs, Jews, Muslims, Christians, and Africans themselves in this traffic of human misery.

The victims came to America as slaves, but also as men and women with long traditions of African commerce and entrepreneurship. For nearly two centuries, much of this business expertise was put to use on plantations and in cities, where Africans made important contributions to American agricultural and artisanship. In contrast to free laborers and indentured servants, slaves were forced to expend their talents and human capital in service to others for their entire lives. Still, a surprising number were able to accumulate capital, albeit capital they had to expend to purchase their own freedom and the freedom of family and friends. The entrepreneurial determination of enterprising slaves to make money in order to buy freedom is a compelling story of the expression of human will to succeed despite oppression and hardship.

The end of slavery left African-Americans free for the first time to take the full value of their skills, capital, and investments for themselves. Many did so by acquiring land and becoming commercial farmers. But with segregation and racism following close on the heels of slavery, few were able to rise far in the desperately poor southern economy. Many were forced back into dependency as landless sharecroppers. Even as America was opening its doors to enterprising immigrants from Europe, black Americans were falling ever more deeply into the trap of poverty in the Jim Crow South. Cut off from the mainstream economy and denied capital by banks, black entrepreneurs found success in building enterprises to serve the black community. Until the Civil Rights era, this economy thrived, particularly in northern cities. There it underpinned new ideologies of liberation, self-help, and autonomy to counter the prevailing weight of white racism and oppression.

Business success in the black community provided a key source of money and leadership for the Civil Rights movement in the twentieth century. Through political equality, African-Americans began to gain greater access to entrepreneurial opportunity, as the walls of segregation that had divided the black economy from white sources of capital came down. Some black businesses grew to national and international scale. But the end of segregation also had wrenching effects on the old segregated economy. As middle-class blacks left the ghetto, they deprived black businesses of crucial patronage, draining the economic life from black urban areas. The return of high levels of immigration in America since World War II has produced greater competition for black-owned business in these areas.

By recounting the long history of African-American business, Juliet E. K. Walker has made it impossible for anyone ever again to blame racial problems on the supposed lack of a black entrepreneurial tradition. She has shown that African-Americans, like all other Americans, have defined themselves as people of business and have sought the goals of success through business.

KEN LIPARTITO
Series Editor

Acknowledgments

This book began with my study of Free Frank (1777–1854), who through his business activities as both a slave and a free man, purchased 16 family members, including himself, from slavery for a sum approximating $15,000. Free Frank began his business career as a slave who hired his own time from his owner. He established a saltpeter manufactory during the War of 1812. In analyzing Free Frank's business activities, I described him as a *slave entrepreneur*. With the initial publication of Free Frank in 1983, there was objection to the application of this term to the business activities of slaves. The term has now entered literature on African-American history, however, for slaves established enterprises, advertised, granted credit, developed innovative production techniques, and were creative in generating markets for their products or services. They assumed risks and were innovators in various phases of their business activities. Free Frank was not the only antebellum slave entrepreneur. So began the next stage of research into the history of black business activity and entrepreneurship.

At various stages of my research, support has come from several sources that enabled me to pursue and complete this study as it expanded to become the first comprehensive history of African-American business. I wish to acknowledge my gratitude for the National Endowment for the Humanities Fellowship for Independent Study and Research; for the Albert J. Beveridge Grant for Research in American History; from the American Historical Association; to the Radcliffe College Mary Ingraham Bunting Institute for a Berkshire Fellowship in History; to the Rockefeller Foundation; and also to both the University of Illinois Center for Advanced Study and the Harvard University W. E. B. DuBois Institute for appointments as a research associate. A Princeton University Shelby Cullom Davis Center Fellowship and a Senior Fulbright Fellowship enabled me to conclude this study and to begin a new area of research looking at the business activities of African-Americans in South Africa, as well as research in a comparative study of black business in the United States and South Africa. The research board at the University of Illinois funded research assistants and travel in the early stages of this project.

Documentation for this study was derived from many sources from the Atlantic to the Pacific and from Lake Michigan to the Gulf of Mexico, as I searched countless records in state archives, historical society libraries, and special collection holdings at university libraries. I am especially indebted to the librarians, archivists, and other staff at the Harvard University Baker Business Library, Rhode Island Historical Society, Boston Public Library, Newport Historical Society, New York Public Library Schomburg Center for Research in Black Culture, Philadelphia Library Company, Historical Society of Pennsylvania, Charles A. Blockson Collection at Temple University, University of Pittsburgh, Lancaster County

(Pennsylvania) Historical Society, Chicago Public Library Vivian Harsh Collection, Tulane University Library, Library of Congress, National Archives, Amistad Research Center, Fisk University Library, Howard University Moorland-Spingarn Research Center, Ohio Historical Society, Western Reserve Historical Society, New Orleans Office of Deeds and Records, University of California Bancroft Library, University of California at Berkeley, and Louisiana State University. At Tuskegee University, archivist Daniel T. Williams was especially helpful and encouraging of my research.

Over the years, my research in African-American business history has been supported and encouraged by friends, family, and colleagues. Since I began the study of Free Frank's business enterprises, my dissertation advisor at the University of Chicago, John Hope Franklin, has encouraged the development of my work in black business history. Also, since the 1980s, Barbara J. Flint, Edna Medford, Margaret Burnham, Alexa Benson Henderson, Janice Sumler-Edmonds, Sylvia Jacobs, Bettye Gardner, Christopher Reed, Robert Weems, Richard Blackett, Glenn Loury, Peter Berger, Paul Pryde, Shelley Green, Thomas Daniel Boston, James Cash, Gena Rae McNeal, Ishaq Shafiq, A'Lelia Bundles, and George Fraser have in various ways supported my work in black business history. I especially want to acknowledge Nell Painter, John Sibley Butler, and Julianne Malveaux for their sustained interest, encouragement, and support.

Several colleagues at the University of Illinois have also supported my research on a topic considered by many others to be insignificant and peripheral to the black historical experience. I gratefully acknowledge the encouragement from William Widenor, Ronald Toby, Keith Hitchens, Robert McColley, John Pruett, Carolyn Hibbard, Elizabeth Pleck, Sharon Michalove, Lillian Hoddeson, John Lynn, John McKay, Kevin M. Doak, and former colleague Geoffrey Parker. Chester Fontenot, Bill Berry, Christopher Benson, Rosemary Stevenson, Jane Wiles, Bernice Barnett, and William Trent, too, have encouraged my research in black business history, as did Bruce Murray at the University of Witwatersrand in Johannesburg during my study of blacks and business in South Africa. I express my deepest appreciation to former colleague Paul Uselding for his support from the beginning of my study in antebellum black business. And a special thanks to Ralph A. Austen, Willard Gatewood, and Edwin J. Perkins.

Former students, now university history professors, have also provided research assistance in various stages of the book, including Sundiata Cha Jua, Sundiata Djata, Clause Meyer, and David Krugler. And, in the final stages, several undergraduates who now plan careers as historians provided assistance, including Oluwatoyin Caldwell, Geneen Wright, Quincy Mills, and Timothy Steil. The history department office staff—Sandy Coclasure, Stanley Hicks, Jan Langedorf, Aprel Orwick, and Pat Prothe—was always helpful. A special thanks to Kenneth Lipartito, editor of Twayne's Evolution of Modern Business Series, who carefully commented on the manuscript, raising questions and providing insights to sharpen its focus. I also thank Robert L. Harris for his suggestions and support of the manuscript. I am especially grateful to the staff members of Impressions Book and Journal Services for their perceptive and careful editing.

Family and friends have sustained me with love and encouragement, and I thank them for their faith in this project. Ernest and Edwina Beavers, Elia Sandoval, and my "sisters" Vera Mitchell and Melodye Wehrung deserve special acknowledgment and thanks for their friendship and support of my work. My two sons, James and Jeffrey Walker; my daughters-in-law, Stephanie and Faye; my brothers, Allen and David Kirkpatrick; my sisters-in-law, Deloris and Lorraine; and my numerous nieces, nephews, and cousins have been there for me from the beginning, as was my sister, Marye Alberta Kirkpatrick Taylor, who died in 1995. Once again, I acknowledge my greatest indebtedness to my mother, Thelma Elise Mcworter Kirkpatrick Wheaton, who remains my strongest supporter in believing that my work has importance.

And, to Zachary, Brianna, and Bryce, I look forward to your comments.

Introduction

This book is the first to provide a comprehensive history of black business in America. Beginning in the 1600s, Africans in America, slave and free, seized every opportunity to develop enterprises and participate as businesspeople in the commercial life of a developing new nation. While they established a tradition of black business participation in colonial America, slavery and racism defeated attempts by blacks to develop enterprises competitive with those established by whites. Black American business activity, as a result, is distinguished by a sequential establishment of small enterprises. Consequently, the historian's duty requires specificity in the documentation of the existence of these enterprises. Each chapter in the book focuses on the recovery of identity of African-American businesspeople and on the diverse enterprises established by them. This study, then, moves beyond vague, depersonalized accounts of amorphous groups of nameless blacks, whose commercial activities are viewed as limited only to personal service and small craft enterprises. The book also illuminates the entrepreneurship of those blacks who, despite establishing businesses that paralleled mainstream American business enterprises, remain noticeably absent from the historical record.

Despite the historic continuity of efforts by blacks to develop competitive mainstream businesses, service-sector enterprises continue to dominate the African-American business picture, a situation that raises a significant historical question. Why, after almost 400 years, do we find black business activity in the late twentieth century existing at virtually the same level of industry participation as it did under slavery? Formulating theoretical constructs that emphasize why businesses established by African-Americans remain small and/or fail, however, is not the purpose of this study. Proceeding from this perspective would limit the study's focus and content to an extensive analysis of multiple forms of racism and degrees of business undercapitalization, rather than to the reconstruction of a history of black business activities.

At the same time, theoretical constructs that proceed from a class analysis of the black experience do not form the basis of this study. An emphasis on social class defeats reconstruction of the reality of the history of black business in America. Race, not class, accounts for the historic, economic, legal, and societal subordination of people of African descent in America. Even before blacks became a numerically significant population in colonial America, options for freedom and economic mobility were virtually nil. As historian Edmund S. Morgan emphasizes, the status of a person of African descent "in the community was proclaimed by his color and maintained by a tyranny in which white men of all ranks and regions consented and approved. The consensus on which colonial society rested was a racist consensus."[1]

Even for those African-Americans who achieved wealth before and after slavery, seldom did class intersect with race when it came to the exercise of power. America's second president, John Adams, could claim that "power follows property." Proceeding from the construct of Max Weber, however, power includes the ability to exercise one's will in the face of virtually insurmountable obstacles.[2] For wealthy antebellum blacks, especially large slaveholders with expansive plantation agribusinesses producing sugar and cotton, their substantial property holdings, both real and chattel, never translated into power. Although men of property, as people of African descent confronting a "racist consensus," they had no power.

There was one exception. America's first black millionaire, William Leidesdorff (1810–1848), was San Francisco's first city treasurer. But he passed for white. After his death, when his racial origins were discovered, Leidesdorff was relegated to obscurity. Yet prosperous black planters and other wealthy antebellum blacks, despite holdings in excess of $100,000, which placed them in the top one percent of the nation's wealth holders, never achieved freedom from the racial constraints that subordinated people of African descent and denied them equality with whites.[3] Wealthy black entrepreneurs today are as limited as their antebellum counterparts in exercising power to eradicate race-based institutional and societal constraints that continue to relegate a comparatively disproportionate number of blacks to the back of the line when seeking capital and other means of achieving business success.

Race, not class, accounts for these societal and economic disparities. First, slavery from the colonial period to 1865 and, then, debt peonage that lasted into the first half of the twentieth century, forced most black Americans into labor-intensive agricultural employment under white control. Moreover, the deliberate, systematic, and institutionalized actions of whites to exclude blacks from free access to and participation in the American business community during the age of slavery—almost 250 years—contributed a great deal to the myth that people of African descent lack a historic tradition of business participation.

As a theoretical construct, "the myth of Negro business," was formalized in the work of E. Franklin Frazier, an African-American and one of the nation's leading twentieth-century sociologists. Frazier's construct proceeded from the premise that black business, with its minimal profits, was limited in providing the capital necessary for the economic salvation of African-Americans. This black business "myth," he said, was propagated by a black bourgeoisie, including black intellectuals, the black press, and especially William E. B. DuBois and Booker T. Washington. In contradistinction to early-twentieth-century black nationalist economic thought, Frazier's position was that a viable black-group economy finds little hope of succeeding, based as it is on the reality that black businesses earn only negligible support from black consumers.[4] Validated by a solid foundation of data from the early 1900s to the 1950s, Frazier's denunciation of the myth of black business was advanced in the work of subsequent theorists on the black experience, including Nathan Glazer and Daniel Moynihan. They also emphasized that black businesses lacked markets in their own communities and attributed the failure of blacks to support their own businesses to the absence of racial clannishness.

Frazier's construct of the "myth of Negro business," however, was dual in focus and conceptualization. It was based not only on the failure of blacks to support black businesses but also on what he claimed was the absence of a historic tradition of business participation. The difficulty encountered by blacks in their attempts to develop successful business enterprises, either on a small or large scale, as Frazier also emphasized, was to be understood within the context of a "simple but fundamental sociological fact that the Negro lacks a business tradition or the experience of people who, over generations, have engaged in buying and selling."[5] Frazier's construct was never successfully challenged in the scholarship of the black experience. Again, Glazer and Monyihan proceeded, as had Frazier, without documentation to assert that slavery precluded blacks from the development of a business tradition. As slaves, they explain, blacks had no experience with money. They further claim that, because of their exclusion from the southern business community, slaves were denied opportunities to develop skills in financial planning, business organization, and management.[6]

Yet, to their credit, Frazier, Monyihan, and Glazer, conceded that racism, prejudice, and discrimination have locked blacks out of both capital and consumer markets, which consequently limited their access to financial resources, credit, and venture capital. Still, Glazer and Moynihan insist that blacks must stand accountable for the lack of venture capital needed to establish business enterprises; they emphasize that "In the end, the most important factor is probably the failure of Negroes to develop a pattern of saving."[7] But what is the historical reality? Have blacks failed to develop a pattern of savings? Or has the government failed by not insisting that the private sector employ black Americans at wages that allow them to save?

While the government has failed blacks, blacks have not failed themselves. Even with minimal resources, black Americans have had a long tradition of saving for both individual and cooperative group enterprises, beginning with African-slave secret burial societies established in the 1600s and continuing with free-African mutual aid societies founded in the 1700s. Indeed, the emergence of free blacks during the age of slavery was, to a great extent, the result of their savings, especially those of slave entrepreneurs. From the 1600s to the Civil War, they saved money to expand their businesses and increase their profits, which, in turn, were saved to purchase freedom for themselves, their family, and friends. Black churches, colleges, and universities were built as the result of savings, as was the acquisition of land by blacks from the colonial era to the present. What national minorities in the United States, despite the size of their wealth, have built an institutional infrastructure as extensive as that of the African-American community? If black financial achievements seem inconsequential, it is not that blacks have failed to save, but that the capital available for saving has been unconscionably circumscribed by race.

The pattern of black savings, while important, is not the significant issue that challenges theoretical constructs supporting the "myth of Negro business." Neither the failure of black consumers to support black business nor even the absence of a historic tradition of business participation is the determining factor in the comparatively low business participation rates and business receipts of blacks. In America, government support, both direct and indirect, is critically important for business success. Simply put, in America, white businesses and government have been inextricably linked since the colonial era.

Government policies supported and protected the nation's slave economy. Before the rise of post–Civil War industrial capitalism, American exported commodities, tobacco, rice, and cotton, produced by slaves on plantation agribusinesses, propelled the national economy, while the value of the slaves' labor was absorbed in the profits of slaveholders. Congressional legislation, Supreme Court decisions, and executive mandates also supported a probusiness fiscal and monetary policy. As foreign investment in America's private sector propped up the nation's new businesses, protective tariffs shielded America's infant industries and encouraged the expansion of manufacturing. The nation's banking system and trade policies also favored business investors and developers. Government support, moreover, funded the private-sector creation and maintenance of an infrastructure. Even before the coalescence of the nation's military-industrial complex, the building of America's railroads by private enterprise in the nineteenth century illuminates government subsidization in the private sector. Government support of white American business included not only land grants but also farm subsidies, oil subsidies, and military contracts.

Theorists and policy analysts who formulate constructs that emphasize the poor performance of black business somehow fail to acknowledge that white business in America has succeeded because of government support. This historic reality, however, stands in direct contravention not only to Adam Smith's eighteenth-century idea of the "invisible hand" and to nineteenth-century laissez-faire classical economic theories but also especially to theories propagated by the late-twentieth-century descendants of classical liberalism, America's new libertarians. Their assessments particularly have failed to acknowledge the extent to which the government provided a foundation as well as continued support for white America's spectacular economic success in business and industry.[8] Racism in both the private and the public sectors has limited the full expansion and success of black business activity in America. Yet theoretical constructs critical of black business performance proceed from one basic premise: that black American businesses fail not because of racism or the historic failure of the government to support them as it has white businesses, but because African-Americans lack a tradition of business participation.

One has to wonder why, despite the agency of blacks in attempting to forge their own economic liberation through business activities and entrepreneurship since the 1600s, that reconstruction of the African business tradition continues to evoke only limited historical interest, compared to that given to the servile-labor contributions of blacks in the development of the American economy. Within the voluminous literature that examines the broad scope of the African-American experience, historical assessments of black business activities have remained at the periphery of American scholarship. Is it because slavery has ended and the nation can congratulate itself on the advancement of liberty, while the continued poor performance of black businesses underscores the extent to which racism has persisted in the economic life of black America?

It is not enough to emphasize the existence of wealthy blacks in post–Civil Rights America as an example of black economic advancement. There were wealthy blacks in pre–Civil War America who had to contend with not only racism but also slavery. Moreover, just as human capital in the development of personal service skills in occupations such as barbering, tailoring, and catering accounted for a substantial number of wealthy blacks before the Civil War, human capital skills in the arts, entertainment, and sports account for a significant number of wealthy blacks in post–Civil Rights America. And in both historical periods, there were the black entrepreneurs, the "capitalists" and the financiers, who used money to make money.

There is a propensity in American culture to view the social and economic condition of blacks as one of failure, as opposed to acknowledging that the government has failed blacks. Consequently, theorists and analysts continue to establish theoretical constructs of blacks as a failed people. Beyond acknowledgment of an African-American cultural resilience for survival, they fail to consider the strengths and successes of African-Americans. While histories of plantation slave labor and studies of the status of the black underemployed and unemployed are invaluably important to document the continued pattern of racism in American life, reconstruction of the history of black business allows for the development of new theories that emphasize the historic continuity of black attempts to succeed in this nation. As George Fraser stated, "success runs in our race."[9]

Perhaps, it is not incredible then that only at the end of the twentieth century is black business history emerging as a distinct field important enough to warrant historical inquiry. What black Americans need now, after almost four centuries of existence in this nation, are theoretical constructs that factor in the strength and success that have distinguished blacks in their attempts to survive racism in America; what they do not need are theories that emphasize failure.

While it is a matter of record that blacks have achieved limited economic success, most blacks whose earnings have exceeded the average low income of other blacks have been business proprietors. That black America has not achieved success in business comparable to that of white America, however, can no longer be attributed theoretically to an absence of a tradition of business participation. My purpose in this book is to document that, despite racism, African-Americans have a history of business participation in America. Reconstruction of that historic tradition provides a basis to challenge those theories of black business failure that proceed from a premise that blacks lack a tradition of business participation.

In this comprehensive history of black business in America, information is provided that documents the historic continuity, diversity, and multiplicity of black business activity, as opposed to providing the details of one or two examples in each historic period. It is a matter of record that black businesses have difficulty surviving.[10] But do we know the extent to which blacks, from the colonial era on, have attempted to participate in all areas of the American business community? Those whose interest in black business history is limited to the pursuit of studies of flawed theoretical constructs, consequently, must go elsewhere. Simply put, in the reconstruction of black business history, theoretical constructs that rationalize the failures of blacks in business can no longer stand as a substitute for the reality of what occurred in the past.

Moreover, because slavery and racism have limited the full expression of black business activity, it would also be absurd to expect that black business history can achieve legitimacy only if it contained success stories that matched those of America's great white entrepreneurs in the accumulation of their wealth. There are no black DuPonts, Morgans, Rockefellers, Carnegies, Fords, Kennedys, Krocs, Waltons, and Gateses. But black entrepreneurs presented in this study—William Leidesdorff, Stephen Smith, Albin and Bernard Soulie, François and Julien Lacroix, Maggie Lena Walker, Madame C. J. Walker, Annie Turnbo-Malone, Anthony Overton, Herman Perry, Sarah Spencer Washington, S. B. Fuller, Arthur Gaston, John H. Johnson, George Johnson, Robert L. Johnson, Herman Russell, Berry Gordy, Naomi Sims, Edward Gardner, Earl G. Graves, Edward Lewis, Clarence Smith, J. Bruce Llewelyn, Reginald Lewis, W. Don Cornwell, and Oprah Winfrey—established or acquired black businesses that paralleled mainstream American businesses.

African-American entrepreneurship and business activity cannot be ignored simply because the financial activities of most black businesses fail to compare with those of the financial giants listed among the *Forbes* 400 or of the megacorporations that comprise the *Fortune* 500. Consequently, an emphasis on race, entrepreneurship, and the tradition of the "creative capitalist" voiced by Joseph Schumpeter characterizes this historic assessment of black business. As creative capitalists, these black men and women, all of whom became millionaires in the twentieth century, were propelled as much by profit as by "the will to conquer, the impulse to fight, to prove oneself superior to others, to succeed for the sake, not of the fruits of success but of success itself."[11] As Reginald Lewis, the first African-American to acquire a billion-dollar business, TLC Beatrice International Holdings, said

"Why should white guys have all the fun?"[12] Blacks are Americans. And black business-people, as Americans, have internalized the capitalist ethos of seeking profit.

Still, the history of black business in America is primarily one of small enterprises. It is patently absurd, then, to dismiss the specificity and significance of black business history on the basis that black business activities fail to replicate white American business activities. At the same time, some people presume that when black business interests do not differ substantially from white business activities, their activities can be subsumed within the context of American business history, a view that is ahistorical. The salient quality of history is specificity, rather than generalization. When black businesspeople respond to the same social, economic, and political forces as white Americans, as during World War I, their business activities are important for historical specificity.

Until America becomes "one nation indivisible," the black business experience cannot be subsumed and generalized within the context of the white experience. Also, when black businesses fail, it is not enough to dismiss their existence or the reasons for their failure by emphasizing that white American businesses also fail, as if race and racism are not significant variables that must be included among the reasons for the failure of black businesses. Economic institutions and political and social systems based on race in America, as opposed to class, have limited black Americans from achieving economic equality throughout the history of this country. For America's black entrepreneurs, unlike for their white counterparts, racism must be factored into any analysis of their business activities.

African-Americans have a tradition of business participation. The focus of this book, then, proceeds from several themes distinctive to the history of black business in America. First, the origin of the African-American business tradition has its basis in the survival of a commercial culture that existed in precolonial West Africa during the transatlantic slave trade. Second, despite their forced settlement, Africans, slave and free, developed enterprises in colonial America that contributed to the commercial life of the nation during the age of slavery. Third, from the colonial era, when free blacks first developed businesses, to the late twentieth century, limited access to credit has been a major factor in the difficulties of blacks in expanding and succeeding in their business ventures. Fourth, from the colonial era to the end of the twentieth century, venture capital for black businesses has come mainly from blacks, reflecting the self-help tradition that distinguishes the history of black business activity in America. Fifth, since the antebellum period, African-American business activity has paralleled mainstream American business activity, except that with few exceptions, blacks have never been successful as manufacturers in heavy industries or as retail merchants. Sixth, in the twentieth-century expansion of African-American business, there have been three waves in the rise of black corporate America.

In addition, within the broader stream of American business history, several themes have distinguished African-American business history. First, literally from the beginning of black settlement in America, laws were constructed to discourage black business activity. Second, from the post–Civil War era to the post–Civil Rights era, whites have attempted to usurp successful businesses developed by blacks. In the late nineteenth century, whites in the new South pushed blacks out of the trades, which not only had been dominated by slaves but also was a major area of self-employed enterprise for free blacks. In the post–Reconstruction North, the emerging white hotel industry pushed blacks out of catering, a significant source of wealth for antebellum free blacks. In the twentieth century, the black hair care products, cosmetic, and recording industries were subjected to fierce competition from white companies. Third, black business owners in twentieth-century urban black business districts have secured only a limited share of the black consumer dollar. Fourth, in the post–Civil Rights era, governmental affirmative action programs, which were provided white businesses since the colonial era to encourage and assist in their development, were extended, in a limited way and only for the first time, to black businesses. Fifth, even in post–Civil Rights America, despite the increasing business success of the nation's new immigrants, white racism continues to plague America's minorities in both the public and private sectors. Despite these conditions, African-American businesspeople have generated financial resources in the only national homeland they have known in the modern world.

These themes find support in this historical reconstruction of African-American business activity in all its multiplicity and diversity, which is the conceptual framework that forms the basis of this study. Each chapter in this book provides an industry-by-industry discussion of black business activity to emphasize not only the multiplicity and diversity of African-American business endeavors but also their persistence and continuity. Participation in commercial real estate speculation, rural and urban land development, and building construction are examples of black business activity that has continued from the seventeenth century to the present. African-Americans also have been involved in finance and investment activities in corporate America, municipal bonds, international trade, and hair products manufacturing since before the Civil War.

This assessment of black business, then, proceeds from the premise that the post–Civil Rights era of black business activity marks the continuation, rather than the beginning, of a historic tradition of black American business that had its origin in precolonial West and West Central Africa. Also, the history of black business prior to the 1960s, which had been limited primarily to small enterprises, is as important as the history of the third wave of black corporate America in the late twentieth century.

Still, this introductory study, while comprehensive, is not inclusive. The history of black business activities in America is broad and deep. Many areas of black business activity, especially that of the black church, with its long tradition of business involvement dating to the late eighteenth century, are not detailed. As black business history develops as a field, monographs focusing on individual black entrepreneurs, businesses, organizations, and institutions, will provide a substantive base for conceptualizing valid theoretical constructs based on historic reality as opposed to historic myths. Also, with an increasing number of studies, historians will be able to assess such specific issues as capital mobilization, market strategy, and the organizational structures of black business prior to the twentieth century.

Ultimately, however, the issue for black-American business history today is more than the question of the existence or nonexistence of a black business tradition, the size of black businesses, or even whether or not all black enterprises operate in a separate and/or internal group economy. With few exceptions, black-American businesses have remained small enterprises. This situation would be tolerable if those enterprises were competitively profitable. Small enterprises have always existed at the core of American business life, and they have been especially important for providing employment for a large segment of the American population. Even with the rise of industrial, managerial, and finance capitalism, small enterprises have remained as much a part of the fabric of the nation's formal economy as large businesses.

Much more compelling than the issue that most black businesses are small enterprises, however, is an understanding of the significance of the black consumer dollar. Within the broader context of American business history, what would be the economic and social impact on white America if more black dollars went to black business? Moreover, what would be the impact if this substantial amount of money found reinvestment in the black community, rather than being used to finance ventures in the white and new immigrant communities? Racism in both the private and public sectors continues to account for limited access to venture and development capital for black business. And racism must be acknowledged as the singularly most important factor contributing to the low participation rates of and profits earned by black businesspeople.

Quantitative data that are limited to measuring the growth of black business from the 1950s to the present have obscured the historic reality of the advancements made in business by blacks from slavery to the present time. The historic reality is that while there has been an increase in the number of blacks in business since the Civil War, the rate of business participation of blacks in post–Civil Rights America remains virtually the same as it was for free blacks before the Civil War. The total number of businesses owned by free blacks at the start of the Civil War has been conservatively established at 2,000. Given the demographics of the free-black population, the distribution of commercial activities and residential patterns in antebellum urban areas and towns, and the occupational distribution of free blacks, that figure is not inclusive. In the nation's preindustrial economy before the Civil War, human capital factors as the basis for black participation in the crafts, personal service enterprises, and various marketing activities must also be considered.

In antebellum America, opportunity for free blacks to participate in business was limited, more so in the North than in the South. Free blacks concentrated in northern urban ghettos were also confronted with virulent racism. Because of this, self-help activities were crucial for their economic survival. Indeed, African-Americans cornered the secondhand clothing and furniture market until the massive late-nineteenth-century influx of European immigrants.

It is probably safe to assume that before the Civil War, a typical black business would have an average of 100 black customers in order to survive and to provide poor blacks with the most basic goods and services. Based on this general proportion, the number of small black businesses in the North was probably close to 2,500. Moreover, given the pattern and kind of goods and services provided by blacks, the data suggest that, in the 15 slave states alone, the rate of free-black business participation would be higher than 2,500 enterprises. With the nation verging on war, the 1860 census no doubt underrepresented the number of businesses run by self-employed blacks, while being more careful about counting black enterprises that provided goods and services to white consumers. In 1860 there were about 500,000 free blacks, with slightly more than half living in the South. With an estimated 5,000 businesses established, the free-black business participation rate would approximate 10 businesses per 1,000 blacks. The 1987 business participation rate per 1,000 blacks was 14.6, an increase from the 11.3 participation rate per 1,000 blacks in 1982.

Yet what has not been calculated is that, in addition to the businesses established by antebellum free blacks, almost 3 percent of the slave population participated in the southern economy as self-hired bondmen and women. Many were self-employed as business proprietors and owners, including hucksters, peddlers, food vendors, and market women, as well as those slave entrepreneurs who established general stores, craft and dressmaking shops, and manufacturing and transportation enterprises. With the slave population in 1860 at almost 4,000,000, their business participation rate per 1,000 would be higher than that of free blacks. Consequently, the combined business participation rates of blacks before the Civil War roughly approximate or exceed the participation rates of blacks per 1,000 in the post–Civil Rights period.

In the antebellum South's preindustrial economy, the income that accrued to slaveholders from the profits made by their self-hired slaves who operated their own businesses allowed for the existence of slave business activities, despite the fact that this practice was illegal. Ironically, the southern state governments allowed the practice of slave entrepreneurship to continue because the elected officials represented slaveholders and other southern business leaders who would benefit most from the practice. As Max Weber would explain, "The limitation of successful legal coercion in the economic sphere lies in the relative proportion of strength of private economic interests on the one hand and interests promoting conformance to the rules of law on the other. The limitation to forego economic opportunity simply to act legally is obviously slight."[13]

Antebellum blacks, primarily slaves, in addition to being business owners, also participated as managers (intrapreneurs) in urban, industrial, and agricultural enterprises in the South's business community. In contrast, from 1865 to 1965, few blacks worked as managers in white businesses. It was not until the Civil Rights period that blacks were again employed as managers in white corporate America. Also, in antebellum America, the most successful black businesspeople were those who established enterprises that paralleled mainstream American businesses. The consumer base of these black entrepreneurs was generally white. But not until the post–Civil Rights period did black businesses, buttressed by government initiatives, again begin to tap a white consumer market. From the post–Civil War period to the post–Civil Rights period, however, black businesspeople relied principally on a black consumer market.

In several ways, as this study shows, the business activities of African-Americans before the Civil War, paradoxically, have more in common with those of blacks in the post–Civil rights Era, than they do with the business activities of blacks during their first century of freedom. In the antebellum South, government-private sector complicity allowed for the participation of slaves as entrepreneurs and intrapreneurs in the mainstream business community. In the post–Civil rights era, private-sector compliance with government affirmative action mandates also encouraged the expansion of mainstream black business activities. But at the same time, the limitations of black business expansion during this time, reflected efforts in both public- and private-sectors to dismantle federal affirmative actions mandates, are also underscored by the historic reality that (to repeat Max Weber) "The limitation to forego economic opportunity simply to act legally is obviously slight." In the late twentieth century, then, are we at a point where the declining governmental support for black business finds parallels in post–Reconstruction America?

The major issue for black business in the twenty-first century, then, goes far beyond whether or not black business can capture the purchasing power of the black consumer. If black business is to become competitive, it must also produce for and develop national as well as international markets, for both the nation's increasingly multicultural population as well as for an expanding global economy. The persistence of racism, which prevents any significant competitive advancement in black business activity, ultimately affects this reconstruction of black business history. The "visible hand" of the government, then, is critical for a much needed revolution in African-American business. For the twenty-first century, African-Americans in business must build on their historic tradition of business participation, rather than continue to repeat it.

AFRICAN DIASPORA COMMERCIAL SURVIVALISMS IN COLONIAL AMERICAN PLANTATION COMMUNITIES

Aiye l' oja, oja, l' aiye (The world is a market, the market is the world.)

—Yoruba proverb

If there had been no poverty in Europe, then the white man would not have come and spread his cloths in Africa.

—Asante proverb

But I must own, to the shame of my own countrymen, that I was first kidnapped and betrayed by some of my own complexion, who were the first cause of my exile and slavery; but if there were no buyers there would be no sellers.

—Ottobah Cugoano, 1787

Introduction: African-American Origins, a Business of Kings, Rich Men, and Merchants

The West and West Central African victims of the transatlantic slave trade to the Americas came from complex, organized, and structured market economies in which they participated as producers, traders, brokers, merchants, and entrepreneurs. While seldom emphasized by scholars of the American experience, trade and marketing were economic activities in which all Africans either participated or held an interest, regardless of their societal status or where they stood on the occupational hierarchy. They either produced market goods, were producer-traders, or brokers or merchants. Africans brought to America, then, did not live in subsistence-oriented economies. Rather, precolonial African political economies were based on surplus production, accumulation, and redistribution through trade and marketing. Moreover, the production of goods and trade and marketing activities in West and West Central African states were propelled by a high degree of both individual and communally based profit-oriented entrepreneurial activities.[1]

Moreover, Africans exported to America in the transatlantic slave trade were not "stolen people." Rather, most were sold by powerful African businessmen to agents of European cartels. Robin Law said that, as the transatlantic slave trade developed, "Indeed, it is impossible to separate slave marketing from other commodities, either for the internal trade or for the external trade."[2] In one of the many instructional books about doing business in Africa published during that period, John Barbot noted the kinds of commercial transactions made while he was a slave buyer on the Guinea coast from 1678 to 1682. In it he described the Africans who traded in slaves as commodities, emphasizing, that "[t]he trade of slaves is in a more peculiar manner the business of kings, rich men and prime merchants, exclusive of the inferior sort of Blacks."[3] A mercantile agent for the French Royal African Company, Barbot could have applied his commentary equally as well to the Portuguese, Spanish, English, French, Brandenburg Germans, Danes, and Americans. They, too, were kings, rich men, and merchants whose investments financed the Western world's first multinational enterprise, the transatlantic slave trade.

The three-part focus of this chapter is to provide an assessment of the commercial culture that existed in precolonial West Africa during the transatlantic slave trade period, an assessment that provides a basis not only for debunking the stolen people myth but also for establishing the African origin of the African-American business tradition. The precolonial African propensity for trading and marketing constituted a business ethos, which survived the Atlantic passage and consequently provided the foundation for the origin of the African-American business tradition. If there is to be a substantive intellectual basis for contextualizing the African origin of this business tradition, the commercial life, market forces, and trading patterns in precolonial West Africa and West Central Africa during the transatlantic slave trading period require examination.

Aside from recognizing the predominance of Africans as plantation field laborers, discussions of African occupational expertise in colonial America, however, have been limited to the preferences for Africans by slaveholders, a subject that is also briefly reviewed in this chapter. The perspective on how the labor capacity of Africans could to be used to advance their own economic and societal interests, as opposed to those of the slaveholder, has been generally ignored in other scholarly discussions. This chapter, then, illuminates the independent economic activities developed by African plantation slaves in colonial America. The historical significance of colonial African-slave economic initiatives is that, notwithstanding their subordinate legal and societal status, enslaved Africans in America forged a business tradition derived initially from their African commercial heritage in trade and marketing.

Precolonial African Markets

Trade existed at three levels in precolonial West and West Central Africa: local, regional, and international. Small markets dealing in a variety of general goods operated daily in villages, while bigger markets were periodically held in larger towns, where a wider variety of goods was available. Trade in these markets was for both wholesale and retail distribution.

The market structure was quite specialized on the highly urbanized precolonial Gold Coast. Inland towns in the seventeenth century had populations of 5,000 to 20,000, while the coastal towns averaged around 5,000.[4] In Dahomey's larger towns and cities, there were several kinds of markets in operation, including small daily produce markets; large periodic produce and goods markets (twice a week); large periodic goods markets (three times a week); large periodic produce and goods markets (once a week); large daily produce and goods markets; large periodic produce markets (once a week); and large periodic goods market (once a week).[5]

The diversity and regularity of these markets underscore the extent of surplus production in precolonial Africa, which could not operate without the markets. The extensive market activity and diversity of goods in the imperial city of Benin in 1688 was noted by William Bosman, chief factor for the Dutch West Indies Company in the late seventeenth century; he wrote that the city was "at least about four Miles large. The Streets are prodigious long and broad, in which continual Markets are kept, either of Kine, Cotton, Elephant Teeth, European Wares; or in short, whatever is to be come at in this Country. These Markets are kept in the Fore and Afternoon each Day."[6] In the late eighteenth century, the slave dealer John Adams also noted the extensive urban population in Benin: "The town is large and populous, and contains probably 15,000 inhabitants."[7]

The merchants and traders were predominantly men who engaged in the market distribution of goods obtained in regional, long-distance, and international export-import trade. But there were exceptions. Women traders and merchants could be found in the larger markets. As part-time traders, however, they predominated in the daily markets held in the smaller villages, where the bartering and selling of agricultural surplus and craft goods produced in the domestic sphere took place. As brokers at the local level, women purchased goods in quantity at village markets and then sold them either wholesale or retail in periodic markets in the larger towns. These women also purchased goods in quantity at wholesale prices at regional markets for retail sales in daily village markets.

In the markets of the large towns, goods were sold in a spacious square or along the streets by a large number of traders, some in mat-covered stalls, others on the open streets. Stalls and displays were highly portable because they had to be dismantled at the end of the day. In some places, stalls were located throughout the market area, while permanent business establishments were tightly crowded along narrow paths through which prospective buyers were forced to pick their way. Also, entertainment was very much a part of market life, with bands of musicians playing their drums and gongs.

Markets in West and West Central Africa were supplied through long-distance trade operations that linked local economies with each other and with those outside their region or nation. International trade operated at two levels. One was long-distance trade that was carried out by merchants from "stranger nations," the Hausa, Mande, Mossi, and Akan, often referenced as Djibula. The other level on which long-distance trade operated involved "middleman nations," which controlled trade that moved through their territory from inland regions to the coast. Long-distance traders, including those from the stranger nations, invariably passed through several of these middleman nations before reaching the coast. Conflict sometimes resulted since these nations demanded payment of transit tolls and market fees. States used armed force to ensure compliance by traders reluctant to pay. States controlled the markets at Accra and in the Lower Niger and Niger Delta at Bonny, and at Loango. Also, because of "their technical accomplishments," the Asante, Fanti, Accra, and Yoruba established themselves as intermediaries between "inland producers of raw materials and the overseas buyers of these goods."[8]

The regularity and infrastructure of precolonial West and West Central African market operations provided for both the distribution of as well as access to surplus commodities. Their existence also underscores the complexity of the political economies in those African societies. Yet, as slavery progressed in America, one of the major arguments in its defense was that Africans had lived as uncivilized people in their homelands and lacked a tradition of the complex economic responsibilities of free people, which left them incapable of understanding freedom, much less participating in a market-driven society.

Trading Organizations

In precolonial West and West Central Africa during the transatlantic slave trade, merchants performed multifunctional roles in trading and marketing. The intermediary who facilitated the exchange of goods between producer and consumer was the trader. In local markets, traders invariably were producers, illuminating the importance of the local marketing activities of women, especially where there were few, if any, professional traders. In regions such as the Niger Valley, there were many professional traders involved in both interregional long-distance and international trade. With professional merchants, trade was a full-time activity. Unlike traders, however, professional merchants were not involved in production, except when goods were produced by others under their management. Also, when commodity exchanges were controlled by professional merchants, they "bought and sold commodities for profit."[9]

On the Gold Coast, the Akani trading organization exemplified the complexity of commodity exchange that existed in precolonial Africa. The organization existed prior to 1600 and lasted as a cohesive and powerful business organization until the first decade of the eighteenth century. It was under the control of the Denkyira people as a state-administered mercantile organization that controlled not only commerce and trade but also the "army, the courts, and the revenue system."[10] As a corporate trading group, the Akani not only secured a near monopoly of internal commodity exchanges on the Gold Coast but also control of gold exports, and thus of the international gold trade. Some two-thirds of the gold exported by Europeans in the mid-seventeenth century was sold by the Akani trade organization.[11]

The corporate structure of mercantile operations was organized hierarchically. It was headed by men who functioned as merchants, investors, captains, and executive officers; they were also political leaders. They financed trading enterprise by purchasing inland goods and imports. At the second level in the Akani trading organization, the chief operating officers were caravan merchants who transported goods from the coast inland and back. Caravan personnel usually included from 150 to 300 porters (male and female), about 20 to more than 100 merchants, and over 100 servants, in addition to military guards.

Brokers represented the third level, trading in both coastal and inland towns, while transacting business for caravan leaders as well as trading for themselves. The commercial activities of brokers were diverse because, operating as subsidiaries, they also "had their own corporate organizations, or captaincies, each of which was headed by a senior merchant broker." Consequently, within the corporate structure, each captain had a chief merchant-broker under his authority who commanded varying numbers of ordinary brokers, from 10 to more than 50, in addition to numerous apprentices, who received their training under the master broker. The apprenticeship system assured generational continuity of the Akani in the control of commerce.[12]

In the early eighteenth century, the militarily powerful Asante gained control of the Gold Coast with their defeat of the Denkyira, which Bosman recorded with a celebratory note:

"Thus you see the towering Pride of the Dinkira in Ashes, they being forced to fly before those, whom they not long before thought no better than their Slaves, and themselves being now sold for slaves."[13] It seems very unlikely that the Denkyira, when sold to slavery in America, would forget their participation in these kinds of trading operations. With the Denkyira defeat, the Asante military, the *awurafram,* took control of the Gold Coast and also "brought their organising genius to bear on trade."[14]

The Asante introduced their trading guild, the *galli,* a "society powerful enough to move freely abroad when other Ashanti were killed on sight."[15] Although the principal export commodity of the Asante was slaves, guns became an important exchange commodity and also symbolic of the necessity of trade as a basis for defending the state. On the Gold Coast, all citizens were required to defend the state. The ownership of a gun was imperative. Rulers provided gunpowder, but it was the responsibility of the masses to obtain their own guns through trade: "the ideal was to encourage everybody to take part, and rulers therefore at times provided capital for up-and-coming captains for economic and political reasons."[16]

The Akani trading organization was perhaps the most extensive cooperative merchant association or trading guild that existed in precolonial Africa, and the Asante *galli* represented the most militaristic of trade operations. There were, of course, other merchant and trader associations. In the Kongo long-distance trade was an extended-family enterprise, with the kinship head assuming management responsibilities in determining trade commodities and those who were sent out as traders and merchants, while he "invested the profits in slaves and stockpiled goods for future communal consumption—at funerals, for instance." With the Vili of Loango, commerce was facilitated by credit sales, backed by a money-lenders' guild that also enforced payment of debts.[17]

The Yoruba established trading guilds that maintained closed shops prohibiting the participation of nonmembers, who were fined and their goods confiscated. Some merchant associations or trading guilds and associations operated as secret societies to advance the economic interests of their members, as was the case with the Calabar Egbo society of the Efik and Ekoi, which developed into a trading society.[18] In Nigeria, the *ekpe* secret society, founded in the late sixteenth century, "was the best known on the African continent." After 1725 it emerged as a powerful force in Nigerian trade operations, especially in regulating credit and the measures taken to recover debts. Membership was open to everyone. It was headed by a president and had a hierarchy composed of nine ranks, including slaves, who usually remained at the bottom. The top ranks were reserved for direct descendants of the Efik founders. Fees were required for entry into each rank.

On the Bight of Biafra in the Niger Delta at the city-states of Brass and Bonny, trading associations or guilds were known as "bloodbrother alliances with commercial motives" that, in the interest of trade, were stronger than family ties. Bloodbrother trading associations were also organized in the Upper Congo and in Angola among the Chokwe.[19] In each organization, traders who acted as brokers had technical knowledge of the market and linguistic skills that were used in an advisory capacity, either in supervising a trading expedition or accompanying inexperienced traders breaking into international trade.

In trade with Europeans, African brokers, rather than the principals, were often used to close important sales contracts. In the Congo, brokers who negotiated sale transactions for Europeans in the coastal and inland trade were called "lingsters" or "bush lingsters," since they served in the capacity of interpreter, legal adviser, and sales agents. They worked on a commission basis and also hired subagents. The broker system was used along the Guinea coast in Gambia, the Gold Coast, Accra, Dahomey, Benin, and Loango.[20]

As trade with the Europeans on the Gold Coast increased in the eighteenth century, commercial relations changed, requiring additional expertise. In the Bight of Biafra, as Captain Adams noted, exposure to Western culture in a formal setting was not unusual: "Many of the natives write English, an art first acquired by some of the traders' sons, who had visited England, and which they have had the sagacity to retain up to the present period. They have established schools and schoolmasters, for the purpose of instructing in this art the youths belonging to families of consequence."[21] Invariably, "families of consequence" were those involved in trade and commerce.

With the precolonial West African facility in mathematics, a Western education was not needed to learn the financial aspects of trade, a fact that was emphasized by Bosman in his discussion of trade on the Slave Coast : "They are so accurately quick in their Merchandise Accompts, that they easily reckon as justly and as quick in their Heads alone, as we [Europeans] with the assistance of Pen and Ink, though the Summ amounts to several Thousands; which makes it very easie to Trade with them."[22] Algebraic numeration in trade transactions was used in precolonial West and West Central Africa but differed with ethnic groups. The system used by the Yoruba was based on 20, using subtraction in calculations: $45 = (20 \times 3) - 10 - 5$; or $106 = (20 \times 6) - 10 - 4$. In West Central Africa, a 5 and 10 base were used, either adding or subtracting from those numerals for preciseness in determining sums: $17 = (5 \times 3) + 2$; or $50 = (20 \times 2) + 10$.[23]

Traders and merchants were essential to the economic life of precolonial West and West Central Africans, facilitating commodity exchanges of surplus goods from the agricultural sector, extractive industries, and craft manufactures. In the eighteenth century, then, highly complex commercial structures and organizations facilitated trade. These trader and merchant organizations and guilds influenced the quantity, quality, and volume of goods distributed. They are important in illuminating the professionalism of the precolonial African merchant and trader as a businessperson and entrepreneur, as well as demonstrating the extensiveness of marketing and trading during the transatlantic slave-trading period.

Craft and Merchant Guilds

In precolonial West and West Central Africa, artisans specialized in producing metalware, primarily implements, jewelry, and weapons; pottery for cooking and carrying water; textile manufacturing for clothes; and woodworking for construction, household utensils, and agricultural implements. The location of these craft activities was determined by access to natural resources and ethnic group proclivities. In large states, with some degree of urbanization, artisans practiced their crafts as full-time specialists. In smaller states, craft participation was by families or as a communal undertaking and was part-time or seasonal.

Iron was used throughout West and West Central Africa, but it was not always produced locally. Itinerant professional smiths brought both their product and skills to regional and long-distance markets, but few villages or towns were without a blacksmith who worked with either locally produced or imported iron to manufacture hoes, knives, spears, and other armaments. Increasingly, some artisans became skilled gunsmiths. Also, most African blacksmiths knew how to smelt gold.

Usually, craft specialists, jewelers, goldsmiths, iron makers, weavers, potters, carpenters, blacksmiths, silversmiths, woodworkers, brass smiths, ivory carvers, drum makers, miners, brewers, salt workers, medicine makers, and even minstrels and dancers were organized in guilds. Guild membership was often determined by households and kinship groups, as skills were passed from one generation to the next.[24] Invariably, kinship heads were also heads of craft guilds. They determined entrance requirements, production, standards of workmanship, quantity of goods produced, prices, and marketing.

Guild masters also had authority to discipline members who violated production, distribution, and price norms. In some guilds members had a degree of autonomy in matters of production or marketing. Guild membership provided the advantages of a protected monopoly, particularly in regulation of prices, which nonetheless remained competitive not only among guild members but also among merchants who retailed their craft products because "sellers were reluctant to close a sale by accepting an offer below the customary price."[25]

Failure to maintain price levels would subject both guild members and merchants to craft or merchant guild disciplinary measures, including ostracism and the resulting loss of benefits derived from guild membership; one of them was that "[g]uild members helped one another in sickness and one another's families in the event of death."[26] States also regulated craft production. Some precolonial West African states held a pecuniary interest in supply and price regulation and also intervened in controlling the guilds; craft specialists and merchants who failed to comply were subject to punishment.

In some states, not only the status of craftsmen varied but also access to guild membership and the practice of a specific craft determined class status. With the Asante, slaves were prohibited from participation in certain crafts.[27] In some societies, craftsmen were subjected to contempt if they were descendants of conquered peoples or if they practiced certain crafts. Wolofs considered ironworkers a despised class, but in West Central Africa they were held in esteem. Also, guild membership was not always exclusionary. Outsiders could apply and serve an apprenticeship before admission. Craft production met household needs, satisfied local market demands, and allowed for trade in long-distance markets to secure items not produced locally.

African Cooperative Work Ethic

The production of goods and trade and marketing activities in West and West Central African states was propelled by a high degree of both individual and communally based, profit-oriented entrepreneurial activities. The motivation to accumulate wealth was quite complex, involving the individual, his or her kinship group, and the community. While the latter was paramount, societal and economic imperatives that drove the precolonial African commercial world were also inclusive of hierarchical classes that encouraged the individual pursuit of wealth. The economic successes of individuals, then, were inextricably tied to the kinship group, which determined one's social and political standing, but "differences in wealth and prestige inevitably emerged as heads of households and lineages strove to become 'first among equals.' "[28] Simply put, inherent in the precolonial African economic imperative was the cultural dictate that "It is not enough to be born 'more equal than others'; the problem is to stay that way."[29]

Under precolonial African customary law, the ownership of natural resources was vested in the group but was not exclusive of the usufructuary right of each person to have access to the profitable development of his or her own individual holding.[30] In a discussion of precolonial Gold Coast agricultural practices, which applies as well to other states in West and West Central Africa, Kwame Dakuu emphasizes that while land was communally held it did not mean that "every member of the society had an equal right to every piece of the society's land. But every member of the community possessed a right by virtue of his membership of the community to be given land on which he could work privately for his own use."[31] Yet, the myth remains that "[u]ntil the Europeans, West Africans had little concept of the ownership of private property."[32]

Usufructurary rights in the private development of one's land remained undisturbed as long as customary obligations were met, which included taxation in the form of allocations of surplus to the immediate head of the group, usually the kinship leader, who had an obligation to his immediate head, subchiefs, or chief.[33] While land could not be sold, one could lose access to the right to their holdings by pledging it as security for debt. Among the Aja and Yoruba, creditors had the use of the debtor's land until the debt was paid: "But the pledge was always redeemable and therefore alienation, at least in theory, was never permanent."[34]

Prior to European contact, African practices in the cultivation of tropical crops were diverse and innovative, with a variety of land cultivation methods: shifting cultivation; permanent cultivation; tree cultivation; flood land and irrigated farming, mixed farming, rotational bush fallow; and rotational plant fallow. Both men and women were involved in agriculture. In the sixteenth century, West African expertise in subtropical agriculture and the extractive industries was quite advanced.[35] The most common African agricultural method of land cultivation was a system of shifting-hoe culture, often referred to as "a women's farming system."[36] New fields of one to two acres in a forest or bushland were cleared once or twice a year. After two or three crops had been produced, the field was left fallow for 15 to 20 years or sometimes abandoned.

In mountainous areas intensive hoe agriculture was practiced along with crop rotation. Organic fertilizers were used and irrigation was used in the production of some crops, including rice, as Bosman noted in his description of slave and free workers on the Grain Coast: "The Inhabitants of Cabo Monte [what is now the coast of Liberia] are industrious to the last Degree. Their Employments chiefly consist in planting of Rice."[37] In areas with shallow topsoil, hoe cultivation was much more practical than deep plowing, which would have increased the rate of soil erosion. Also, manure was used for fertilizer.

Crop production was a three-stage process. Men were involved in the initial heavy land-clearing activities, felling trees, burning scrub, removing stones. Women followed by breaking the soil, planting seeds, and weeding throughout the growing season. Harvesting was done either by men or women or both, depending on the crop cultivated. In some societies, such as Dahomey, Yoruba men worked the fields and women assisted in planting, weeding, and harvesting. Farm work in Dahomey began at daybreak, lasted three or four hours, ceased during the hottest part of the day, 11:30–2:30, and then continued until dusk. While Yoruba farmers in Dahomey worked their land as individuals or in family groups, the Aja farmed cooperatively.[38] While work was regarded as a cooperative enterprise with Africans, "Pride in the efficiency of good team-work was balanced by an awareness of what each individual worker had contributed to the whole: effective unity thrived on internal competition."[39]

A variety of grain, vegetables, legumes, and root crops was cultivated. On the western Guinea coast, yams, plantains, and rice were staples, in addition to okra, onions, and peppers. The English slaver Captain John Adams said that in supplying slave ships for the transatlantic voyage, Europeans purchased food provisions from Africans on the Guinea coast, while "on the Windward Coast they procure rice; on the Gold Coast maize; at

Wydah, Ardrah, and Lagos, maize and calavancies; at Benin, Bonny, Calabar, and Cama-roons, yams; but on the coast of Angola, the natives have no superfluity of provisions to sell."[40]

The cultural ethic that guided cooperative family, kinship, community, and ethnic groups in both small village states and the larger complex kingdoms in precolonial West and West Central Africa can be summarized by such questions as "Why do we work together? But isn't this our land? Aren't we brothers? Are we not as one man?" In observing work activity on the Gold Coast, William Bosman said everyone was constructively involved in some sort of labor and that unemployment was unknown: "What is most commendable amongst the Negroes is, that we find no poor amongst them who beg."[41]

Mutual assistance for the people was available through the extended family kinship group. Inherent in the cultural dictates of precolonial African societies was the idea that the well-being of all of its members and the commitment to cooperative enterprise incorporated social welfare measures. The infirm, ill, and aged members of the community, unable to sustain their own material well-being, were always provided assistance. Cooperation was requisite, expected, and inherent in the general kinship relationships of reciprocal obligations, as opposed to its being contingent on request, whim, proclivity, partiality, or disposition.

Mutual aid societies, savings organizations, and cooperative work associations were prevalent. In Dahomey two kinds of economic associations existed among the Fon, Weme, and Yoruba. As a mutual aid association, the *tontines* required its members to make "regular payments into a common treasury, administered by a set of officers. Each member in turn received the contributions of the group, and most often used the funds for funeral expenses, purchase of ritual cloth, and other ceremonies."[42] In the *donkpe* cooperative work association of the Fon, the young men of a community, headed by a special chief, were required to participate at all times in projects that required collective efforts, such as preparing fields or building houses. The cooperative work group of the Mossi was the *sosose,* which produced an agricultural surplus specifically designated for sale in the markets.[43]

Communal activities, such as clearing new ground, roofing a house, or building a compound, city walls, or other public works, required large-scale labor resources beyond that of the family. These activities were reserved for larger village groups usually organized on the basis of age. Among the Nupe of Nigeria, the large cooperative labor unit in agricultural production was called the *egbe* and was operative when the extended family needed assistance or "simply because its ambitious program demands larger cooperation than is at its disposal."[44] The building of a house or a compound required several levels of craft specialization, often determined by ethnic specificity, the kinds of material available, and architectural design. Men performed heavier or more dangerous construction tasks, while women wove and braided grass and palm leaves for the walls and roof.

Innovation in commodity production is also evident in tree crop cultivation, including the kola tree, shea tree, and particularly the palm tree. In addition to the manufacture of raffia cloth, which resembled velvet in texture, products made from the palm tree included branches woven for building walls and roofs, palm wine, and palm oil used for food preparation and in cosmetics, all of which had economic value.[45] Palm oil, combined with banana leaves and wood ashes, was used to make soap, as indicated by Bosman in his discussion of Benin: "Negroes here make Soap, which is better than any all over Guinea: And by reason this washes very well, the Negroes Cloaths are very clean."[46]

He also noted that in Benin women used palm oil as a hair pomade to enhance their hair styles: "Some divide their Hair into twenty or more Pleats and Curls, according as it happens to be either thick or thin. Some Oyl it with the Oyl which they Roast out of the Kernels of Oyl-Nuts, by which means it loses its black Colour, and in process of time turns to a sort of Green or Yellow, that they are very fond of."[47] The slave trader Joseph Hawkins said that palm oil was used both as a skin lotion for "annointing their bodies" and as a fuel for "feeding their lamps."[48]

The textile industry in precolonial West and West Central Africa was extensive, with professional weavers, spinners, and dyers found among the important craftspeople. Cloth manufacturing usually existed as part of the domestic economy, but in some states textile manufacturing had commercial significance, as with the Asante, Yoruba, and Nupe, who produced for market distribution. In the textile industry in Loango, large quantities of cloth were also produced by weavers for the market, as opposed to production solely for household self-sufficiency.[49] Bosman noted that textile manufacturing was one of the important industries on the Slave Coast: "their Manufactures are spinning of Cotton, weaving of fine Cloaths."[50]

Cotton cultivation and indigo production were auxiliary industries to textile manufacturing; in Benin, Bosman emphasized that "[t]he inhabitants are very well skill'd in making several sorts of Dyes, as Green, Blew, Black, Red and Yellow. The Blew they prepare from Indigo, which grows here abundantly; but the remaining Colours are extracted from certain Trees by Friction and Decoction."[51] Traveling in the Gambia region in the 1790s, the Englishman Mungo Park noted that in the cultivation of cotton and indigo, "The former of these articles supplies them with clothing, and with the latter they die their cloth of an excellent blue color."[52] Also, raffia cloth was made from palm bark by softening a long strip of bark in water, which was then beaten by a mallet until it flattened out as a single supple piece of cloth several times larger and wider than the original piece of bark.[53] In Ghana both kente cloth and bark cloth were manufactured.

A livestock economy also existed. Goats and sheep were raised in most of West and West Central Africa, but cattle raising was limited primarily to the western Sudan and the savanna, which offered pastureland free from the tsetse fly and cattle disease such as trypanosomiasis. The Senegambian Fulani were herdsmen, and there were cattlemen in Hausaland, northern Ghana, as well as in the Angolan highlands where cattle was raised by the Ovimbundu; while lagoon cattle were raised in Dahomey. Livestock was used for the production of both meat and dairy products, and for clothing made from animal hides and sheep wool. Few pigs were raised in West Africa, even before the Moslem influence. On the Gold Coast, livestock dealers became quite rich from the cattle trade.[54] The large livestock-trading ports on the Gold Coast were at Axim, Accra, and Great Ningo.

Development of the land also included the extractive industries. The mining expertise of Africans, however, was valued more by the Spanish and Portuguese in their colonies than the English in theirs. Gold, iron, salt, and copper mining were among the major extractive industries in precolonial West and West Central Africa.[55] Copper was mined in Loango in the Lower Congo and Angola, and was used in Benin and Yorubaland, where there were extensive "artistically productive bronze-casting industries."[56] The gold-mining industry also required working in specialized occupations as miners, carriers, washers and smiths to maintain mining tools in good condition. A foreman directed the mining operations, arranged for food supplies, and sold gold to goldsmiths and traders.[57] In West Africa, gold was mined in three principal regions: the Bambuk mines in Senegal, the Bure gold mines in the Upper Niger, and the Tano fields and Akan mines on the Gold and Ivory coasts.

Gold was panned, quarried from pits dug to a depth of 150 feet, or mined by the use of vertical shafts with underground tunnels. In the Gold Coast gold mines, a minimum of

40 people was needed to work a pit that was 20 to 30 feet deep, while a pit from 70 to 100 feet deep required at least 100 workers; larger goldfields had more than 100 pits per acre. Agricultural towns surrounding the goldfields provided foodstuffs for miners who lived in mining towns. On the Gold Coast, production was highly specialized, and slavery emerged as the principal form of labor in the fifteenth century. From 1475 to 1540, African gold merchants purchased some 12,000 slaves, primarily from the Portuguese, to work the mines. By the seventeenth century, free laborers, who retained half of their production, worked the goldfields, which were owned either by the state or sole proprietors. Until the eighteenth century, gold was the major Gold Coast export. With the escalation of the slave trade, labor shortages marked the decline of the gold industry.[58]

Iron was mined throughout West and West Central Africa, usually by excavating shallow pits or quarries; in West Africa, shafts and underground tunnels were occasionally excavated for mining ore.[59] Kilns were used for smelting, with heat supplied by wood and charcoal; further processing was done in forges by blacksmiths. Major centers of iron production in West Africa included the southern Ivory Coast, southwest Nigeria around Oyo where specialized iron-mining and manufacturing villages developed, and among the Mandingo who, according to Park, used kilns 10 feet high and 3 feet in circumference with seven vents at their base.

The fishing industry in precolonial West Africa was extensive along the Gulf of Guinea coastal areas from Senegambia to the Congo, as well as in the inland waterways and lakes. Nets, fishhooks, gaffs (spears and harpoons), traps, and poison were used in both fresh and saltwater fishing. In the seventeenth century, Bosman reported that in Ghana, "Five or Six hundred Canoes which went a Fishing every morning."[60] Depending on the ethnic group and its access to the development of other food resources, fishing was either a full-time or part-time occupation. On the coastal lagoons of the Niger Delta states, before their profitable and substantial involvement in the slave trade, fishing was the major occupation. In Dahomey, a significant minority of the population was engaged in fishing, including weir fishing, in which ditches were dug on floodplains to trap fish, which were then scooped up in baskets.[61] Processing included salting, smoking, and sun drying fish for local and long-distance trade.[62]

Women in Production and Trade

Women in precolonial West and West Central Africa participated in the economy at four levels: agricultural production; cottage industry craft manufacturing; market commodity trading; and common labor. On the coast of El Mina and Axim, women were often involved in placer mining in the mountainous areas and rivers, especially after heavy rains. In a description of their activities, Bosman said, "Each of these women is furnished with large and small Troughs or Trays, which they first fill full of Earth and Sand, which they wash with repeated fresh Water, till they have cleansed it from all its Earth; and if there be any Gold, its Ponderosity forces it to the bottom of the Trough."[63] The types of production, trading, and labor activities women were engaged in, then, were first determined by location and the resources available.

Most African women were involved in domestic production and trade at the local levels. In food production activities, whether in a monogamous or polygamous marriage, a woman and her children formed an economic unit, with access to fields allotted by her husband. Unmarried women in matrilineal societies also were allotted land. If a couple divorced, the woman still maintained those rights, compared to women in patrilineal societies, whose ties to the land were contingent on their husbands' land rights. In these societies, divorce or widowhood closed off a women's direct access to the land; she had indirect access, however, through her sons, whose membership in the kin group entitled them to land allotment.[64]

Food production, processing, and preparation were the most important economic activities for precolonial African women, but their efforts extended beyond providing merely for family meals. Processed foods prepared by women and sold in the markets included shea butter, palm oil, kola nuts, flour ground from maize and millet, and *gari* ground from manioc. Also thread spun from cotton, raffia cloth, and other textiles were sold at markets, along with clothing, pottery, baskets, and mats. On the Slave Coast, both beer making and food preparation were activities carried out by women; as Bosman noted, "Women are not idle; they brew, or rather boil Beer, and dress Victuals, which they carry to Market to sell together with their Husbands Merchandize."[65] A seventeenth-century Dutch trader on the Gold Coast also noted that wives of fishermen sold their husbands' catch at local markets, while other women purchased fish in large quantities and then would "carry them to other townes within the land, to get some profit by them, so that the fish which is taken in the sea, is carried at least an hundred or two miles up into the land."[66]

Women's economic activities in precolonial Africa were also determined by their age. In Dahomey, younger women undertook the most strenuous gender-based activities, while older women were involved in preparations of medicinal herbs. In his discussion of the processing of herbs, Bosman emphasized their effectiveness in treating tropical health problems and diseases that afflicted both Africans and Europeans, noting, " 'tis much to be deplored that no *European* Physician has yet applyed himself to the discovery of their Nature and Virtue; for I don't only imagine, but firmly believe, that they would prove more successful in the practice of Physicks than the *European* Preparations."[67]

Taxation and Exchange Media

During the transatlantic slave trade, the media of exchange for tax payments, duties, tolls, and other government imposts, as well as for commercial payments, included gold, copper, iron bars, salt, textiles and, the ubiquitous cowrie shell, "that currency propelling the exchanges of West Africa from Senegal to Lake Chad."[68] Fees and custom duties were based on the value of goods transported and also included road and ferry tolls, a practice so pervasive from Senegal and Gambia to Sierra Leone, the Gold Coast, the Niger Delta, Loango, and Angola, that Lars Sundstrom said in precolonial West and West Central Africa it "must be assumed to be of African origin rather than inspired by European fiscal policies."[69] In Accra, Ghana, Sundstrom noted that salt was the currency medium and with the exchange rate, "1 handful of salt bought 1, or even 2 slaves in the back country [since] salt was beyond the means of many slaves and even warriors." In Liberia, however, "1 slave was worth 100 salt sticks, or 10 baskets of salt."

In precolonial West and West Central Africa, the method of distribution, whether by barter or sale, and the accepted medium of exchange were based on ethnicity and the geographical location of the market. The first level of exchange took place through barter.[70] In Dahomean markets, the cowrie shell was the principal exchange medium, with the prices of some goods predetermined at the producer's level. In the Ewe market system in the inland states of Ghana, bartering existed but the cowrie was the principal exchange medium used to purchase goods, while "[f]oodstuffs were sold at fixed prices; in contrast, buyers and sellers of livestock and articles of craftsmanship, such as pottery, mats, and cloth always haggled, especially foreign traders."[71]

In the monetary systems of some states, various kinds of cowrie shells were in circulation. They were durable and could not be counterfeited, although their value responded to the cowrie "money market." In a 1592 report from Angola, one European trader wrote, "this *zimbo* [cowrie] has such great value in this Kingdom, that, when I was in the village of Loanda, a huge amount of gold coins was sent to Congo for ransoming a number of slaves, but they were rejected by the sellers, who said that the true money and [their] gold was the *zimbo* of Loanda, which made them rich."[72] Still, gold was always valued as a medium of exchange. In Benin in the mid-1550s, English traders were warned not to attempt to cheat the town's traders: "They are very wary people in their bargaining, and will not lose one sparke of golde of any value. They use weights and measures, and are very circumspect in occupying the same."[73]

Iron was also a common medium used in commodity exchanges for slaves, gold, ivory, textiles, and foodstuffs.[74] Copper in the form of bars or bracelets, manufactured from copper and brass, were also popular as exchange media. Ethnic preferences and class differences determined the value of these items since "the number of ornaments worn reflected the social status, and only indirectly the riches of the person or persons involved; ornaments were used as a form of hoarding wealth."[75] Salt and textiles served as media of exchange on two levels: as "small change" to pay for low-cost items, such as foodstuffs; and as "big money" to obtain commodities of large value, such as gold, slaves, ivory, and cattle, and to use for large-scale wholesale exchanges of such items as cloth and cola nuts.[76] The "big money" exchange rate for textiles also differed by region or state: at Goree, off the coast of Senegal, "5 pieces of indienne [cloth] . . . were equivalent to one slave," but further south along the Guinea coast, "1–2,000 Cape Verde cloths bought 100–150 slaves." In the Congo and Angola, Liberian cloth had intrinsic practical value as wearing apparel and was also a medium of exchange, until its monetary function became paramount and the cloth became highly negotiable symbolic money.[77]

In precolonial West and West Central Africa, taxes, duties, fees, and tolls were levied on income, exports, imports, access to and the use of roads and ferries, and even for permission to settle land, illustrating the complexity of the economic and commercial culture that existed during the transatlantic slave trade period. In the larger nation-states especially, taxation and impost policies were quite extensive. Sales taxes were collected in Ghana. In Nigeria and the Congo, death taxes were collected but payment differed. Among some Nigerian ethnic groups, the heirs paid the debts for the estate; in the Congo, the king paid if the decedent was destitute.

Also, heads of state were granted the right to levy taxes on an entitlement basis because they were the ultimate owners of the land, with rights to its productivity. Tax collections began at the lowest level of government in small villages and towns, then progressed to the provincial level, with all taxes ending up as tribute to the king. Often, the right to collect taxes at the village and provincial level was obtained by giving gifts to the king. Also, authority to collect taxes was obtained by the highest bidder and then "half of the taxes might be kept by the lower fiscal ranks."[78]

In noting the king's revenue in Benin, which was obtained from a tax collection process that began at the village level, Bosman said, "The King hath a very rich Income; for his

Territories are very large and full of Governors, and each knows how many Bags of Boesies (the Money of this Country) he must annually raise to the King, which amounts to a vast Sum, which 'tis impossible to many any Calculation of." Everyone paid. Although payment in kind might differ, all payment had value for the king. As Bosman indicates, the "meaner rank" paid its taxes in the form of livestock, poultry, yams and cloths, which meant simply that the king did not have to buy anything "on that account, and consequently he lays up his whole Pecuniary Revenue untouch'd."[79]

As in most societies, precolonial Africans were reluctant to part with their surplus, especially for taxation purposes, and various means were used to hide their wealth, a practice that Bosman noted occurred in Benin: "Wherefore those who are out of Power, and have no Share in the Government, always pretend to be poorer than they really are, in order to escape the rapacious Hands of their Superiors. This obliges them all to a cunning sort of mutual Civility, in order to avoid Accusers: . . . their Profession are very rarely sincere, but only feigned."[80] Fiscal policies required that taxes collected be redistributed, which were used for community development. The Asante used taxes to subsidize crafts and promote trade.[81]

African Commercial Culture and Ethics

During the transatlantic slave trade, commentaries written by blacks and whites establish the pervasiveness of trade and marketing in precolonial West and West Central Africa. These sources note the regional and ethnic differences in African business practices. In comparing trading activities on the Gold Coast with those on the Slave Coast, William Bosman asserts that men and women on the Slave Coast pursued profits more vigorously and were more competitive in business activities, which in his view accounted for the differences in wealth between the two areas. On the Bight of Biafra Slave Coast, he noted, "both Men and Women here are employed in getting of Money, and each zealously strives to outdo the other. Hence it is that they live very splendidly, and not as the Blacks on the Gold Coast."

Bosman's commentaries, it must be admitted, are sometimes suspect and, at times, even contradictory. But while he might often misinterpret traditional precolonial African business practices, activities, motivations, and ethics, his observations as a whole are still singularly important. For example, Bosman claimed that women in their public economic life on the Slave Coast worked much more diligently than Gold Coast women, since they were motivated to accumulate money: "Women [on the Slave Coast] are so vigorously Industrious and Laborious that they never desist till they have finished their Undertakings; and are continually endeavouring after [more] Work in order to get Money."[82]

The accumulation of wealth, primarily through trade, was encouraged, particularly in the large nation-states, such as with the precolonial Asante, for whom "[m]oney—gold dust—was equated with wealth. Wealth was equated with power."[83] Yet while the accumulation of individual wealth was encouraged by the state, the community also benefited from the commercial activities of its traders and merchants through the system of inheritance taxes. With the Asante, "One mode of the good citizen was the *sikani*, that person who had accumulated wealth through his or her own efforts whether privately or in public service, but from which the state was ultimately the beneficiary."[84]

Although displays of wealth were important, precolonial African merchants and traders were quite circumspect in their business affairs, especially when it came to concealing the extent of their financial successes. Dissimulation was perhaps the most distinguishing characteristic of the African merchant and trader. In the larger states, subterfuge was raised to the level of an art by the most successful merchants and traders in order to escape the scrutiny of public officials, who were often their business competitors. Under African customary law, some merchants were often vested with the authority to collect taxes for the state. With the heavy taxes on income in conjunction with the power given tax collectors, even Bosman admitted that merchants and traders, known as "big men," had some justification for failing to provide full disclosure of their profits.[85]

In the transatlantic slave trading period, European and American slavers on the Guinea coast were more than cognizant, even respectful, often grudgingly so, of the African commercial system and expertise. Bosman's commentaries are also quite revealing of the commercial practices involving commodity exchanges between Europeans and the African traders. In a discussion of merchants in the city of Great Benin, he emphasized the importance of timely payments in all commercial transactions made with Africans: "They are very prompt in Business, and will not suffer any of their antient [ancient] Customs to be abolish'd; in which, if we comply with them, they are very easy to deal with, and will not be wanting in anything on their Part requisite to a good Agreement."[86]

That same advice was also given one century later by the English slave captain John Adams in his advice to whites on how to do business with Africans. He emphasized that his authority was based on his trading experiences from Cape Palmas on the Ivory Coast to the Zaire (Congo) River. In discussing the necessity for prompt payment as the basis for establishing successful commercial relations with Africans, Adams advised: "In trading with the Africans, punctuality is of great importance, paying them to the last farthing whatever is their due, and in all transactions with them, it is not only just but politic, to deal honourably with them, never taking an unfair advantage of the ignorance of any individual, by which means their confidence is acquired."

Particularly, Adams stressed that saving face was quite important for the African trader and merchant, especially in any transaction with Europeans, and cautioned: "A trader once overreached by an European, becomes an object of ridicule to his townsmen, and will not easily be induced to traffic again with the same individual, particularly if he can obtain from another, such goods as he may required in barter for the commodities he has for sale."[87] Based on their long experience with European traders, Africans considered themselves more ethical. As one European slave trader, John Hewton, said in 1788, "When I have charged a Black with unfairness and dishonesty, he has answered, if able to clear himself, with an air of disdain, 'What! do you think I am a White Man?' "[88]

The business ethic that was deeply entrenched in the economic life of precolonial African states can be seen in the cultural beliefs and world view of wealth and poverty that distinguished those societies and in their traditions and folklore. Although the aphorisms on trade, wealth, and poverty in table 1.1 are Asante in origin, given the widespread marketing and trading activities of men and women in precolonial West and West Central African states, there is no doubt that other ethnic groups had similar proverbs and wise observations.

The economies of these societies, then, did not function in accordance with principles that are characteristic of traditional self-sufficient societies. Such a perspective is ahistorical and implies the existence of static, traditional societies that remain isolated and immune to

TABLE 1.1   Asante (Ashanti) Aphorisms on Trade, Wealth, and Poverty

1. "Money does not go out to earn its livelihood and come back empty-handed" (162).
2. "Wealth (is) beyond everything, nothing is beyond that again" (163).
3. "Gold dust is like unto a slave, if you do not look after it well, it runs away" (163).
4. "Fame of being noble born does not spread abroad, it is the fame of riches that spreads" (118).
5. "The Akusapem people say, when you get wealthy, 'Mischievous fellow!' and when you have nothing, they say, 'Unlucky one!' " (125).
6. "When some really big business is on hand, no flag is flown" (187).
7. "Where the gold dust is, that is where the women like to be" (133).
8. "When the women say (to You) 'You are a handsome fellow,' that means you are going to run into debt" (133).
9. "When a woman is beautiful, it is from her husband she gets her beauty" (133).
10. "When a man is wealthy, he may wear an old cloth" (164).
11. "When you are rich, you are hated; when you are poor, you are called a bad man" (164).
12. "Poverty is stupidity" (158).
13. "Poverty is madness" (159).
14. "When a poor man is decked out in gold, people say it is brass" (160).
15. "If the poor man has nothing else, he at least has a tongue with which to defer the payment of his debts" (160).
16. "If any one invokes a fetish against you, saying, 'Let this man die,' he is not harming you as much as he would were he to say 'Let poverty lay hold on him' " (161).

Source: Compiled from R. Sutherland Rattray, *Ashanti Proverbs* (Oxford: Clarendon Press, 1916).

change. Ultimately, the precolonial African economic order, inextricably intertwined with the social system, was built on reciprocal kinship relationships, which required maintaining equanimity, peace, and harmony within the group and the community. As kinship groups competed with each other in the pursuit and accumulation of wealth, with kinship heads pursuing their own individual economic interests, the rich and powerful found it imperative not only to mediate kinship obligations but also to respond to community dictates and sensibilities in their business practices. Among the Bambara, witnesses to sales contract [usually kinship members] were held liable if the principals did not fulfill their agreement.[89]

The community was very much involved in the economic life and affairs of its members, especially when it came to debtors who failed to meet their obligations by willful neglect. According to Joseph Hawkins in his observations of debtor-creditor relationships among the Ebo of Nigeria, the decision concerning the disposition of the debtor was based on preservation of the community and the survival of its members: "As they say the community should not be made to suffer by the knavery or idleness of one man, who has rendered himself unworthy by neglecting the duty he owed his own children, his wives, and himself."[90]

The general attitude toward work and the accumulation of wealth through surplus production was based on cooperative effort for the advancement of the individual, the family, the kinship group, the community and the nation. Kinship groups were involved in the business activities of its head, since all members had a vested interest in his economic success. In private transactions, creditors had the right to seize all of the dependents of the debtor, even his relatives, which forced an outcry of public opinion against the debtor to encourage him to meet his obligations. The underlying principle was "group responsibility for the actions of individual members."[91]

16

Debunking the "Stolen People" Myth

The African supply side of the transatlantic slave trade has engendered controversy. Most of the victims were kidnapped or prisoners of war who were sold by Africans as commodities to the Europeans. The trade was complex and slave-marketing activities developed within the context of African business practices. Europeans established trading posts, called factories, which were actually heavily fortified forts or castles that served as entrepôts of the African-European trade. They were constructed only with permission of the local African state and only after the payment of fees and rents in addition to taxes and custom duties. Beyond the coastal areas in West and West Central Africa, most African states refused Europeans entry, which prevented them from establishing trading posts in the interior forest belt and savanna.

In West Central Africa, Europeans were not even allowed to build forts on the coast but were forced to remain on shipboard, where they conducted the purchase of slaves. In Loango, Phyllis Martin notes: "Africans were wholly in charge of the buying, collecting, and holding of slaves until the arrival of the European ships in the harbors."[92] On the Bight of Biafra, John Adams details the African supply-side mechanism of the Atlantic slave trade. In the interior, he said slave markets operated with regularity: "Fairs, where the slaves of the Heebo nation are obtained, are held every five or six weeks at several villages, which are situated on the banks of the rivers and creeks in the interior, and to which the traders of Bonny resort to purchase them." Trading trips took six days from the seacoast to the interior markets and back.

Substantial outlays of capital were invested by African merchants to finance slave raids and equip slave caravans. The trading canoes of Bonny merchants carried up to 120 persons, in addition to merchandise obtained from European slavers, often on credit. On the return to the Guinea coast, the canoes traveled in fleets that carried from 1,500 to 2,000 victims, who were sold to the Europeans for transport to slave markets in the Americas.[93] In large African states, slave sales "remained a royal monopoly." In others the principal slave dealers were private merchants, as in the small states of the Niger Delta, where "it fell into the hands of strong groups of African businessmen."[94]

In noting the extent of the African supply side in slave-trading activities from 1786 to 1805 at the port of Bonny, Adams said: "This place is the wholesale market for slaves, as not fewer than 20,000 are annually sold here; 16,000 of whom are natives of one nation, called Heego [Ibo], so that this single nation has not exported a less number of its people, during the last twenty years, than 320,000." Also, an additional 50,000 Iboes were sold in the slave markets of New and Old Calabar.[95] Based on Adams's figures, 370,000 Iboes, in addition to 20,000 Africans from other ethnic groups were sold to Europeans from 1786 to 1805. An estimate of the number of Africans brought to the United States in the period after the end of the American Revolution, 1781 to 1807—when African slave trade to the United States was made illegal—is 36.5 percent, or 219,000, of the total of 600,000 individuals.

Ultimately, African merchants required state approval not only to engage in the international slave trade but also to secure state-authorized military protection for slave coffles transported from the interior to the coast. From the early eighteenth century, African slave trading with the Europeans was controlled by the state, and the major players, as in any complex political economy, were the elite, the ruler/politicians, wealthy merchants and businessmen, and the military. More specifically, during the transatlantic slave-trading period, the expansion of the state was high on the agenda of African rulers. While warfare "threatened the security and profitability of merchant operations," trade routes could not be secured or maintained in places under siege.[96] Warfare within Africa and the collusion of African slave-trading states with European slave traders, then, operated to provide most of the captives sold to the European slavers.

The American Joseph Hawkins, on a slave-trading expedition to Africa in 1794, underscores the collusive commercial relations between European and African slavers as a prime example of the supply mechanism for the transatlantic trade. In one instance, Hawkins, informed that prisoners of war were available for purchase said, "the Ebo and Golo Kings had been at war, the latter of whom having been defeated, and a great part of his army [700] had fallen into the hands of the conqueror.... [our African advisers who have] ... furnished us with further directions and assured us of a certain and good trade [in slaves]."[97] The military power of large African states enabled them to limit European incursions into the interior as well as to force their compliance with African trade policies.

By the early eighteenth century, as Bosman said, Africans had access to thousands of guns and superior manpower. He goes on to explain how the Africans acquired the guns: "Perhaps you wonder how the Negroes come to be furnished with Fire-Arms, but you will have no Reason when you know we sell them incredible quantities, thereby obliging them with a Knife to cut our own Throats. But we are forced to it; for if we would not, they might be sufficiently stored with that Commodity by the English, Danes, and Brandenburghers."

Was there really an alternative for the European slavers? As Bosman said, if they did not supply the guns, private arms dealers would "abundantly furnish them," thus cutting off the supply of slaves to Europeans. He emphasized the dilemma, noting that from the mid-seventeenth century on, guns and gunpowder were "the chief vendible Merchandise here, we should have found but an indifferent Trade without our share in it."[98] While the desire to trade in gold, textiles, ivory, and foodstuffs had brought the Europeans to Africa, trade in Africans for the transatlantic slave markets was the principal objective of the Europeans from the sixteenth until the nineteenth century.

In Africa, as elsewhere, warfare has always been the basis for securing victims for enslavement. From the sixteenth to the nineteenth century, powerful African states had the capacity not only to wage war against each other but also to defend themselves against European military intrusions. The African victims of the transatlantic slave trade, then, were not defeated by European military force and then dragged from the battlefields to the Guinea coast for transport to the Americas. That supposition does not take into account the existence of powerful precolonial West African states with sophisticated political economies that controlled slave trading on the African continent.

Had African slave-trading states been unable to repel European military aggression, the African victims of the slave trade would indeed have been "stolen people." Rather, warfare between Africans, kidnapping by Africans, and the judicial process in Africa provided most African victims sold to the European slavers. Historic assessments of the transatlantic slave trade, however, seldom confront the volatile market responses that drove African slave-trading states and their leading merchants to meet the gargantuan demands of New World slave markets. Instead, after cursory examinations of the seventeenth-century transatlantic slave trade, most scholars of American history ignore Africa in their historic reconstruction of the African diaspora.

Persistence of the stolen people myth, however, obscures the realities of the complex political economies and highly developed commercial structures that existed in the powerful precolonial West and West Central African states between the sixteenth and the mid-nineteenth centuries. Even before contact with the Europeans, a marketing system and social structure was in place in West Africa that facilitated the trans-Saharan Arab slave trade. The existence of an established mechanism for the "selection," trade, and marketing of slaves cannot be ignored as separate and distinct either from the precolonial African hierarchical class structure or, even more, from the African commercial world as it existed during the transatlantic slave trade period. As Robin Law said, "Indeed, it is impossible to separate slave marketing from other commodities, either for the internal trade or for the external trade."[99]

Proceeding from this contextual and historical imperative demands a reformulation in African diaspora historiography of African participation in the transatlantic slave trade, particularly within the context of the ethics of its commercialization of people as commodities. A sophisticated commercial culture distinguished the economies of the Guinea coastal states of precolonial West and West Central Africa during this time. Consideration must be given not only to the marketing mechanisms that drove Africans to supply slaves as commodity exports, but also to the societal and moral imperatives that sanctioned the institution of slavery in precolonial West and West Central Africa during the slave-trading period.

The Transatlantic Slave Trade

Within the 3000-mile stretch along Africa's Atlantic coast, there were eight major regions from which Africans were shipped to the New World. African regional proportions in the transatlantic trade, however, changed over time, often depending on the availability of groups and sometimes on the ethnic or national preferences of buyers.[100] Of the total number of Africans sold to America, most in the eighteenth century, only 13.3 percent arrived from Senegambia at American ports after 1690. European slavers and American slaveholders referred to them as Mandingoes, Fulas (Fulani or Fulbe), Seneganbians, and Senegalese. Today, the Senegambia region is comprised of portions of the states of Senegal, Gambia, Mauritania, and the western part of Mali.

About 16.9 percent of the total number of Africans brought to America were from the Upper Guinea coast, i.e., Sierra Leone and the Windward Coast, the geographical area of what is now Liberia, Sierra Leone, Guinea, and Guinea-Bissau. Some 43.5 percent originated from the following three regions: the Gold Coast, which is present-day Ghana; the Bight of Benin or the Slave Coast, which is now Togo, Benin (Dahomey until 1975), and western Nigeria; and the Bight of Biafra, today's eastern Nigeria and Cameroon. Including Senegambia, 73.9 percent of Africans brought to America were from West Africa. Africans from West Central Africa, Angola/Congo, now Angola and part of Zaire, constituted 24.5 percent of the total number of slaves brought to North America. The political economies of West Central Africa, then, are crucial in establishing African survivalisms as the basis for the black-American business tradition, as are those of West Africa.[101] In addition, 1.6 percent of Africans brought to North America were from Mozambique and Madagascar. The trade and marketing patterns of these societies are also important in establishing the diverse African origins of business practices reflected in the transculturation of New World Africans.

The transatlantic slave trade began in 1444 with the shipment of 235 Africans taken directly from the Guinea coast to Portugal where they were sold.[102] In 1501, Africans were taken as slaves to the Americas for the first time, but it was not until the seventeenth century that the Atlantic slave trade was established on a massive and systematic basis. The social and commercial infrastructure that facilitated the African side of the slave trade with Europeans, however, was well-established in West and West Central Africa before contact with the Europeans. Through the trans-Saharan trade, Guinea coastal and Sudanic nations provided sub-Saharan Africans as slaves to the Maghreb (present day Morocco, Algeria, Tunisia, and Libya) and Mediterranean markets several centuries prior to the Atlantic trade.

From 650 to 1500, an estimated 4,390,000 sub-Saharan Africans were victims of the Arab slave trade. Even during the transatlantic slave trade from 1500 to 1880, some 3,020,000 Africans were sold as slaves in the Arab markets.[103] Consequently, while the European trade in slaves made a substantial dent in Mediterranean slave markets during the Atlantic slave trade era, Arab middlemen maintained their control over the trans-Saharan slave trade to Islamic markets, an influence that remained powerful into the late twentieth century.[104] In addition to the Islamic Arabs, North African Jews also participated in the trans-Saharan slave trade, which also included ivory, pepper, beeswax, and gold.[105]

With the development and expansion of both the Spanish and Portuguese colonies in the Americas in the sixteenth century, demand for African slave labor intensified. Europeans themselves could not meet the demand for the labor that was needed, either in numbers or expertise, and still profit from their exploitation of New World resources. Consequently, in addition to the Portuguese and Spanish, the Dutch, French, English, Danes, Swedes, Brandenburger Germans, and, finally, the Americans participated in a multifaceted international trade that reached four continents: Europe, Africa, North America, and South America. From the sixteenth century until the mid-nineteenth century, Africans constituted the principal commodity in African-European trade. With the virtual decimation of the Native American population by the seventeenth century, particularly in the South Atlantic region, a new supply of labor was needed.[106]

Most Africans were exported to the Spanish and Portuguese colonies in Latin America, with some 52.4 percent, or 6,133,000, of them taken from 1701 to 1800.[107] Less than 6 percent of the total, almost 600,000, were brought to the United States, most after 1700. In the four-century Atlantic slave trade, an estimated 11,863,000 Africans were exported as commodities of trade to the Americas. Considering an estimated death rate of from 10 to 20 percent during the Middle Passage, probably only 9,600,000 to 10,800,000 Africans survived to reach the Americas. In 1896 America's first black Harvard Ph.D., William E. B. DuBois, published the initial systematic and scholarly study of the Atlantic slave trade. He estimated that some 50,000,000 Africans were victims.[108]

Patrick Manning, using statistical means to measure demographic changes resulting from African supply-side mechanisms, estimates that from 1700 to 1850 a possible 21,000,000 Africans were victims of the Atlantic slave trade both in Africa and the New World: 7,000,000 became slaves in Africa; 5,000,000 died within one year of capture; and 9,000,000 became slaves in the New World.[109] Manning includes not only the total number of African slave exports but also estimates of population losses in Africa during this time. In addition to 14,000,000 Africans who survived as slaves in both Africa and the Americas during that period, an additional 4,000,000 were exported in the 1500s and 1600s. Manning also considers the estimated population growth rate in Africa had there been no slave trade. He found not only that the Atlantic slave trade resulted in a population decline in Africa but also that there was a concomitant increase in the incidence of slavery in Africa. Consequently, given Manning's previous figures—that 21,000,000

Africans were victims of the slave trade from 1700 to 1850, with 4,000,000 in the sixteenth and seventeenth centuries, in addition to the 50,000,000 population loss from 1700 to 1850 because of the trade—it appears that from 1500 to 1850, Africa suffered both real and potential population losses of up to 75,000,000.

The losses were greatest in West and West Central Africa. Manning's findings, then, not only corroborate but also surpass DuBois's estimates on African population losses as a result of the Atlantic trade.[110] The consequent long-term impact on the socioeconomic and political structures of this region cannot be understood as anything but catastrophic. Europe and white America profited, but African human-capital costs were tremendous in its loss of productivity and labor.

Marketing African Occupational Expertise in Colonial America

The first Africans in North America were contraband, according to John Rolphe, chief operating officer of the Virginia Company of London. In 1607, as a profit-making venture, this joint-stock trading company had established Jamestown in Virginia for commercial development. In a financial report prepared for the company, Rolphe indicated that the Africans had been seized as plunder by a Dutch privateer from a Spanish slaver and ignominiously dumped at Jamestown's makeshift harbor: "About the last of August came in a Dutch man of warre that sold us twenty negars."[111] The commercialization of Africans as commodities of labor in America began, then, with the entry and settlement of these first blacks at Jamestown in 1619. Presumably, only their labor was sold. But they cannot be regarded as indentured servants, whose term of service was limited to five to seven years. Several of the first blacks eventually secured freedom.

The "sale" of the first Africans reflected practices in colonial America that allowed non-free white labor to be treated as commodities, as indentured servants. Unlike whites, however, people of African descent in the colonies became slaves because of societal presumptions, which became increasingly supported by judicial decisions and statutory enactments.[112] From the colonial era on, race in America determined one's legal status on a continuum from unfree to free. In the 13 colonies, only the labor of whites was sold and, then, only for a limited period of time. Various colonial laws and judicial decisions in the country's first century of settlement protected whites from a lifetime of forced hereditary servitude; unlike blacks, "there was never any such thing as perpetual slavery for any white man in any English colony."[113]

Yet in the agriculturally based economy of preindustrial America, the distribution of African slave occupations differed little from that of the white population, a condition that was, of course, limited by their status as people of limited freedom. From the time they settled in America, however, Africans capitalized on their slave occupations in attempts to develop property-accumulating enterprises, despite their subordinate status, institutional racism, and the brutal and atrocious punishment inflicted on them by whites, legally and with impunity.[114]

As a point of fact, the first Africans at Jamestown were company men and women, as were many of the first whites in that settlement. As a result, their labor, initially, was charged off to resident executives of the Virginia Company of London, some of whom held newly created positions in the first colonial government of Virginia. In the history of American slavery, corporate as well as public ownership of slaves existed, first with colonial government bodies. Even after the American Revolution, slaves were owned by state, county, and municipal governmental bodies, in addition to industries that owned slaves as their labor force.

In the 1620s, the first Africans in New York were contraband seized from either Spanish or Portuguese warships by the Dutch and then made company employees in much the same way as Jamestown's first black and white settlers.[115] Africans in New York were owned by the Dutch West Indies Company and, as at Jamestown, worked at clearing and cultivating land, in addition to performing unskilled labor as street cleaners, ditchdiggers, and cartmen or draymen. They were also put to work in occupations requiring craft skills. Africans contributed to the initial building of New York's infrastructure. They not only built fortifications but also assisted in armed defense of the colony. Eventually, some achieved a degree of freedom.

Even though they accomplished a great deal, only 20,500 Africans were brought into the American colonies before 1700, compared to the massive importation that took place in the eighteenth century. Also, many of the first Africans in seventeenth-century America were not direct imports from Africa, but had lived in Spain, Portugal, England, and the West Indies. In colonial America, the agricultural competence of Africans, their expertise in livestock raising and the extractive industries, and their proficiency in various crafts can be attributed to African survivalisms that proved singularly invaluable not only in contributing to the development of the American colonies but also in providing the basis for the emergence of African business practices.

The need for labor, particularly African slave labor, was especially critical in the early development of all of the English colonies. In the Massachusetts Bay Colony, the brother-in-law of the esteemed Governor John Winthrop expressed those views in a 1645 letter that emphasized the necessity of acquiring Africans as slave labor: "I doe not see how wee can thrive untill wee get into a stock of slaves sufficient to doe all our business. . . . And, I suppose you know verie well how we shall mayntayne 20 Moores [Africans] cheaper than one Englishe servant."[116]

In the seventeenth-century founding, settlement, and development of the American colonies, an unfettered freedom to pursue wealth was as important as the desire for religious and political freedom or societal reform. Developing a multifaceted transatlantic trade in slaves and slave-produced commodities was recognized as the linchpin of the economy of the Massachusetts Bay Colony, established in 1630. Among the Puritans, the accumulation of great wealth symbolically affirmed the greater blessings of God. In one instance, Governor Winthrop expressed his belief that prosperity from the slave trade and slave-produced commodities affirmed one's godliness as a Christian: "it pleased the Lord to open to us a trade with Barbados and other islands in the West Indies."[117]

While the occupational diversity and agricultural expertise of precolonial West and West Central Africans, in addition to their work ethic, made them invaluable as slaves, whites developed negative images of them to justify the brutality of slavery.[118] Contemporary accounts document the denigration of Africans. Newly arrived Africans were labeled primitive savages. The first African women imported to New York under the Dutch were described as "Angola slaves, thievish, lazy and useless trash."[119] As the marketing and selling of Africans became professionalized, however, not only health, strength, and moral fiber but also intelligence and occupational capacity, often based on geographic and ethnic origin, were established as standards for evaluating newly imported Africans.

In New England, while Africans from the West Indies were preferred because they survived the seasoning process, "unseasoned" Africans also found a ready market, despite their reputation for truculence. Consequently, while New England slave dealers advertised Africans from the West Indies as "brought up to do housework" or "skilled in the trades," they also stressed the special work characteristics of Africans exported directly from the Guinea coast. New England advertisements carried such announcements as "Choice Gold Coast Negroes."[120]

Africans from the Gold Coast were not only preferred in New England but also by planters from South Carolina . They were in demand because of their reputation for "vigor and intelligence."[121] Still, it was difficult for slaveholders to reconcile the advantages of their labor with the disadvantages of forced, involuntary servitude. The Coramantees of the Gold Coast were highly esteemed as slaves because "their spirit of loyalty made them the most highly prized of servants." Some whites acknowledged a "Spartan fortitude" in Coramantees, but it was also acknowledged that Gold Coast slaves were "frequently instigators of slave conspiracies and rebellions."

There was also a strong preference for Senegambians among planters in the American slave markets. Wolofs, Fulas, and Mandingos were seen as having a "strong equestrian and cattle-raising tradition," as were Angolans. They were especially desirable because of their expertise in the open grazing of cattle, a practice unfamiliar to the Europeans who, with a scarcity of land, grazed their cattle in enclosed pastures. Indeed, the colonial American cattle industry, initially developed in the seventeenth century, had its foundation in the transculturation of African pastoral practices. Slave holders in Latin America also prized the Senegambians, who were the first *vaqueros and ganaderos.*[122]

With the initial open grazing of cattle by Africans in seventeenth-century South Carolina and Louisiana, Africans emerged not only as the nation's first American cowboys but also "African-American herders played a prominent role in the spread of live-stock production across Louisiana, as they did in South Carolina and other plantation colonies."[123] Although Senegambians were the planters' slaves of choice in that colony, as Charles Joyner notes, "Certainly, any effort to explain the planters' preference for Senegambian Africans must take into account the prevalence of rice culture in those areas."[124]

The Senegambians' expertise in rice tillage made them particularly desirable as slaves when the cultivation of this commodity became big business in the eighteenth century, earning substantial profits in international markets. Rice cultivation contributed not only to the economic development of South Carolina but also Louisiana. It was African initiative that launched rice cultivation in colonial Louisiana, where most of the slaves were from the Senegal River region; as Daniel Usner said, they "soon were planting rice along the seasonally flooded banks of the Mississippi." Rice was not the only grain crop introduced or cultivated by Senegambian slaves in colonial Louisiana. Some of them, who came from the upper Guinea coast, "where a vast majority of Louisiana's slaves originated in the eighteenth century, were generally more familiar with maize than were their European contemporaries."[125]

African survivalisms could also be seen in the agricultural and mining activities of slaves in New England, where, as William Piersen said: "Africans were skilled with their short hoes and refused to give up hoe agriculture despite their masters' insistence on Euro-American plow techniques so destructive to the humus of the thin soil of the tropics." African slaves who worked the iron beds and forges of Hope Furnace and Cranston also used African mining and smithing skills and techniques. Their expertise in the extractive industries perhaps explains, as one contemporary said, why it was a slave and not a European who "discovered the copper deposits of nearby New Barbados Neck, New York, in 1710."[126]

In his assessments of African ethnic preferences among North American planters, Joseph Holloway emphasizes that the planters had a sophistication not generally attributed to them, as compared to West Indies planters. American planters, as he found, not only knew that rice, cotton, and indigo were produced in Africa but also they were "often able to relate the various African ethnic groups to the types of cultivation found in Africa."[127] The planters preferred certain African ethnic groups for work in four general occupational groups. For house servants, planters expressed a preference for Mandingo, Yoruba (Nagoes), Dahomean (Fon), and Fanti. For slave artisans, Bambara, Melinke, Whydah, Paw-paw (Popo), and Coromantee (Asante-Fante) were desirable. For rice cultivators, planters preferred Temne Sherbro, Mende, Kishee (Kisi), Papel, Goree, Limba, and Bola Bolante. For field slaves, planters sought Africans from the Niger Delta, the Congo, and Angola.[128]

Despite these preferences or prejudices, availability, regardless of ethnicity or point of origin, was the ultimate factor that determined the marketing of Africans in colonial America. The commonality of living in an agriculturally based economy marked by surplus production, trade and market relations, and commercial activities, that existed throughout West and West Central Africa, obviates the necessity of delineating African economic activities by ethnicity.

In the American colonies, this economic initiative was expressed in the development of independent African-American slave activities, despite the ethnic or national origin of the slaves or the occupations forced on them by planters. The attempts made by African slaves to pursue independent economic activities, then, transcended ethnicity or national origin and were based on the commonality of their production, marketing, and trading experiences in Africa, whether as free people, slaves, or slaveholders.

Colonial African-American Slave Provision Grounds

With an abundance of undeveloped land available to them, it was not unusual for slaves in colonial America to have extensive provision grounds, which allowed not only for food production for themselves but also for surplus production. With their initial settlement in the Americas and throughout the South Atlantic plantation system, Africans had access to land for self-provision. This land was acquired through the allocation of the planter, planter/slave negotiation, or self-appropriation. Even when planters provided food, the rations were never adequate in quantity, quality, diversity, or nutritional levels. Depending on their location, slave provision grounds consisted of extensive acreage or small garden plots; and it was not unusual for slaves in the South to have several acres of land under cultivation for such commercial crops as rice, tobacco, indigo, and cotton. Indeed, in some places, African slaves were " 'given as much land as they can handle,' on which they planted corn, potatoes, tobacco, peanuts, sugar and water melons, and pumpkins and bottle pumpkins."[129]

Provision-ground crop production was African in origin in two ways. One was through the usufructuary rights that Africans were granted in their homeland, by which they were allocated land for production, provision, and profit. What they produced on their land was theirs to be used in whatever way they wished. Second, in some parts of precolonial West and West Africa, African slaveholders, both large and small, allocated land to their slaves to grow their own food. These plots were known as provision grounds, land set aside for the slave and his family on which to grow crops for their own sustenance. Provision grounds were ubiquitous in African slave societies. Yet, where slaveholding units were small, the lifestyles of slaves and their owners were similar, and the economic activities of slaves paralleled those of free people. At the most fundamental level, slaves performed the same agricultural, domestic, and craft work as free people.

Yet the extent to which slaves in Colonial America profited from the limited time to work their fields depended more than only on their degree of initiative. Provision-ground activities were invariably constrained by the labor time appropriated by the slave owner, as well as by his idiosyncrasies. Plantation field slaves worked under two kinds of systems. Under the task system, used especially in rice cultivation, slaves were assigned one job. After completing that task, usually by early afternoon, slaves had the remainder of the day to work their provision grounds, which often consisted of "5 or 6 acres of ground, allowed them by their masters, for planting of rice, corn, potatoes, tobacco, & c. [calabashes, probably] for their own use and profit, of which the industrious among them make a great deal. In some plantations, they have also the liberty to raise hogs and poultry. . . ."[130]

Under the gang-labor system, the traditional practice allowed slaves a part of Saturday and all of Sunday to pursue self-sustaining activities, which included food production. There were always exceptions, harvest time for example, when field slaves were required to work every day. House slaves were on call literally every moment for both domestic work and field work. Only the very large plantations had specialized labor that allowed for full-time domestic slaves.

In addition, there were communal provision-ground activities much like those that existed in West African places known as slave villages. In colonial Louisiana, 153 slaves worked on the Company of the Indies plantation. They produced rice, tobacco, and indigo and also raised a herd of 70 cattle for their Paris-based owners. While the home of the manager and the plantation fields were located upriver, the slaves lived in a village compound downriver. It contained about 20 cabins in which 40 nuclear families lived. Daniel Usner notes that "[b]ehind their quarters, 'surrounded by stakes, roofed by Palmetto' like a distinct village, were fields of which the slave families cultivated their own food."[131] In eighteenth-century French Louisiana, the racial demographics of its African majority population was similar in composition to the English colonies of South Carolina and Georgia. Usner explains that in all three locations "the enslaved black workers themselves quickly adapted their own traditional economic practices to colonial life, turning to small-scale farming and frontier exchange to mitigate their bondage in America."[132]

While it is generally assumed that the only food available to the slave was provided by the owner, the reality is that slaves produced a good portion of their own food. In one report from the early eighteenth century, an individual "was so impressed by the way in which Carolina slaves used their 'little piece[s] of land' to grow vegetables, 'rear hogs and poultry, sow calabashes, etc.' that she thought they cultivated them 'much better than their Master[s].' "[133] Yet inadequate storage facilities meant that during the winter months, food supplies were not only limited in quantity but also inadequate in nutritional value to sustain energy levels.

Until recently, historians of American slavery usually emphasized that the only benefit that slaves derived from small garden plots was self-sufficient food production, more so than surplus food production for marketing in a cash system. Some scholars even insist that the provision-ground system of small garden plots provided a unique opportunity for slaves to learn to work independently. Eugene Genovese is one who holds this view: "The gardens nonetheless played an important role in the slaves' lives. Even on a small scale they gave the slaves a chance to learn to get along without a master."[134] Obviously, Genovese fails to consider the viability of African survivalisms in self-directed economic activity that provided the basis for the provision-ground system, which was initiated by slaves and persisted into the nineteenth century.

Despite cultural intrusions from American slaveholders, the development of the provision-ground system was shaped by African slaves and their descendants. In theory and practice, American slavery was not predicated on encouraging the economic independence of Africans. Rather, as whites capitalized on African expertise in exploiting their labor, at the same time slaves also tried every means possible to use their skills to their own economic advantage. It was only inevitable that African-American slaves would produce a surplus for trade and marketing with an eye to earning a profit. Adding support to this view is the fact that in precolonial West Africa, an independent slave economy existed. As Manning noted, slaves with provision grounds also "maintained a sort of familial exchange among themselves, and they participated in the local market system to the extent that time and their minimal wealth permitted."[135]

Provision-ground cultivation by African slaves in colonial America was also motivated by the need for money, which could be earned from the sale of surplus commodities, so that they could purchase food to supplement the monotonous reserves of corn meal and salt pork supplied by their owners. Even with these economic activities, most slaves did not earn enough to prevent them from existing at near-starvation levels. Also, as demand for slave-produced commodities intensified on international markets, whether they labored in a gang-labor system or under the task system, slaves found it imperative to capitalize on whatever free time was allowed to augment their subsistence-level standard of living. Despite the arduous labor, self-provisioning was in the best interests of the slave. Whether working under the task system or the gang system, slaves had no alternative but to capitalize on their available time in the production of foodstuffs.

They, of course, brought with them a knowledge of food production based on their African heritage.

Colonial American Slave-Trading and Marketing Activities

The allocation of provision grounds to the slave by owners was mutually rewarding. Slave owners found it economically advantageous to allow slaves to produce as much food for themselves as possible, thus reducing maintenance costs of the slaves. Planters could also profit in other ways from slave provision-ground production. Some planters purchased these commodities for resale at a profit. Most important for the planter, however, was that greater productivity could be expected from slaves allowed to cultivate their own crops, especially when they profited financially from the sale of their provision-ground products. Generally, African slaves marketed numerous items in colonial America: provision-ground commodities; poultry and farm animals; processed food; herb-based medicinal products; and goods produced from both household handicraft activities and by skilled artisans. Slaves also owned canoes and boats and valuable property in horses, cattle, hogs, and sheep.

In some instances, the provision-ground activities of slaves were encouraged. In the Louisiana slave village, the manager-overseer indicated "the inclination among slaves to satisfy personally their own subsistence needs and eating tastes." So, in a report to the absentee owners, he recommended the allocation of provision land to the slaves and also that they be permitted "to cultivate it for their own profit." The manager also advised the owners to "purchase their produce ... upon fair and just terms."[136]

It was not unusual that plantation owners became the initial purchasers of slave-produced commodities. In the Carolina and Georgia lowlands, several sales of commodities by slaves to their owners were recorded: in 1728, "a slave was paid L1 10s for eighteen fowls; a female slave [was] paid L8 for hogs she raised; 1736, 22 slaves [were] paid L50 for rice; 1750s slaves [were] paid L124 for 290 bushels of corn." In the 1760s, one slave owner "not only purchased his slaves' provision goods, consisting of corn, fowls, hogs, and catfish, but also their canoes, baskets, and myrtle wax."[137]

Slaves, however, preferred to market their own production, thus maximizing their profits by eliminating their owners as middlemen. The marketing of their products at adjacent plantations, small farms, and nearby towns allowed them mobility and a brief chance to escape the monotony of plantation life. Slave provision-ground commodities were available for sale and/or barter and trade on three levels: through sale to their owners; within the internal slave community; and by slave marketing in local towns and villages. The last system allowed slaves to begin to operate in a cash system. For example, the slaves in the Colonial Louisiana slave village marketed their goods in New Orleans on weekends.

Market towns throughout the colonies, even the northern colonies, provided places where slaves could sell their goods. The Catherine Market in New York City was noted for the trading activities of country slaves from Long Island and New Jersey. They would "journey to the market with loads of cracked eggs, roots, berries, herbs, fish, clams, and oysters to sell for pocket change." Most striking was the way in which they carried their goods to market: "Peddling these wares in baskets which they balanced on their heads, these Negroes became familiar figures in the city's markets."[138]

Even in New England, the marketing activities of the slaves reflected their attempts to replicate the commercial activities practiced in their homelands: "Elderly slaves and others with free time helped support themselves by using old African ways to spin yarn, to build toy drums as well as traps and snares for small game, to make baskets and recane chairs, to dispense herbal medicine, and to cook."[139] In describing slave activities on rainy days on the southern plantation where he lived, Charles Ball said: "At such time they make baskets, brooms, horse collars, and other things, which they are able to sell amongst the planters."[140]

The impact of African survivalisms on slave marketing practices was still evident two hundred years after the arrival of the first Africans to America. In 1819, Benjamin Latrobe, an engineer and architect, described the marketing of food in New Orleans, emphasizing that "everything had an *odd* look." The hawking and trading of goods in that city no doubt resembled the activity of markets that existed in precolonial West Africa. Latrobe also emphasized the phenotypical diversity of the slaves, whom he described as "black negroes and negresses," "mulattoes, curly and straight-haired," and "quarteroons of all shades, long haired and frizzled," all of whom were dressed in what he viewed as outlandish attire. He went on to describe further the colorful activities:

> Along the levee, as far as the eye could reach to the West and to the market house to the East were ranged two rows of market people, some having stalls or tables with a tilt or awning of canvass, but the majority having their wares lying on the ground, perhaps on a piece of canvass, or a parcel of Palmetto leaves. The articles to be sold were not more various than the seller, [foodstuffs as well as] trinkets, tin ware, dry goods, in fact of more and odder things to be sold in that manner and place, than I can enumerate.... I cannot sup-

pose that my eye took in less than 500 sellers and buyers, all of whom appeared to strain their voices, to exceed each other in loudness.[141]

In addition to the marketing of traditional products, there was also trade in goods ingeniously and furtively appropriated (although, the value of any goods "stolen" by slaves was hardly equivalent to the value of the unpaid labor expropriated from them).[142] For example, Usner notes that "[r]unaway black slaves, whose West African background made them more familiar than Indians with cattle, appear to have been the most numerous and skillful rustlers in the Lower Mississippi Valley."[143]

Despite their limited freedom to develop profit-making enterprises, African slaves as traders producing for a market, established themselves in the business community of colonial America. Yet the slave provision-ground and marketing system that developed in the American colonies is sometimes viewed as an economic initiative instituted by planters to provide opportunities for Africans to develop experience in market practices. In his discussion of the provision-ground marketing system, Robert Fogel emphasized that it "nourished independence because it permitted slaves to make their own decision about what and how much to grow, about how to dispose of their product, and about what to buy with the money earned from their sale."[144]

Yet these were business decisions distinctive to trading and marketing operations in precolonial African cultures, in which surplus production for the market and trading were economic activities as pervasive as agricultural labor for both slaves and free people. The three weeks or three months it took to transport Africans to the American colonies in the eighteenth century did not obliterate their memory of these activities, which were reinforced by their acculturation to their new land. Most important, they passed along this trading and marketing heritage to their nineteenth-century descendants.

Slave Property Ownership

In colonial America, the most important factor in the slave acquisition of property was derived from the cultural propensity and know-how of Africans to capitalize on natural resources in the development of enterprises. The property accumulated by slaves was acquired primarily through the trade and marketing of their provision-ground surplus production. In the colonial Louisiana slave village mentioned earlier, the provision-ground production of its 153 slaves was carefully stored for processing and subsequent marketing, as indicated in the overseer's report: "In several barns belonging to different negroes, 'an inventory taken on January 24, 1738, found eighty-six barrels of rice, twenty-five barrels of beans and four barrels' in addition to grains that 'have not been threshed.'"[145]

The right of slaves to own property was established quite early in the American colonies through both statutory legislation and the judicial system, and this right remained virtually unassailable through the colonial era. In 1771, Chief Justice Hutchinson of Massachusetts observed that anyone might have "property in goods, notwithstanding he is called a slave."[146] In the New England and Middle Atlantic colonies, customs and traditions developed that supported the right of slaves to own property. In the northern colonies, as Edgar McManus notes, slaves "could own and transfer property, receive and bequeath legacies"; and he emphasizes that the "master's property in the slave did not automatically entitle him to the property of the slave."[147]

Also, property legally willed to slaves could not be transferred by owners who attempted confiscation. Slaves were protected under a form of action known as *prochein ami,* whereby masters who arbitrarily seized a slave's property could be sued by a legal proxy for the slave. In one court case, a widow attempted to seize the property bequeathed to a slave by her husband, but she was required by the court to pay the slave for the property. The irony of this rule underscores one of the many incongruities of slavery in America. Slaves had no legal right in the protection of the property inherent in themselves as chattel. Paradoxically, while slaves could find no protection under the law for their own lives, their rights to property ownership were legally sanctioned and protected by law. From reviewing court decisions on slave property ownership, McManus notes:

> The numerous legacies that they received make it clear that their right to own property was taken for granted. Such legacies would have been made contingent on the right of enjoyment if there had been any chance that they might be taken by the masters. That testators with firsthand knowledge of slavery did not take this obvious legal precaution is convincing evidence that it was not necessary. Sometimes the slave themselves made wills leaving their possessions to relatives and friends."[148]

The legal precedent for protecting the rights of slave property ownership is not clear. Perhaps the concept of the inalienability of private property was so entrenched in the colonial free-enterprise system that it included protecting the rights of slaves in owning property, just as it protected the rights of slaveholders in owning their chattel property, even if it resulted in the destruction of the lives of their slaves. Yet slaves were valuable property and their labor was invaluable, which perhaps were the most important economic incentives that impelled slaveholders not only to allow slaves to profit from property ownership but also to protect their rights to property ownership.

While provision-ground economic activities enabled slaveholders to save food costs for their slaves, more important, slave owners early recognized that, with family ties and property ownership, most slaves were less inclined to attempt to escape. In one instance, while a slaveholder in 1800 expressed concerns about the disappearance of several of his slaves, he also indicated that he "was convinced these runaways would not go far, being connected at home, and having too much property to leave."[149] Also, while the provision-ground activities of slaves provided the basis for their marketing and trading activities, their agricultural expertise also resulted in the early utilization of slaves in the management of their owner's property.

In their duties as plantation managers, slaves developed both intrapreneurial and entrepreneurial profit-making activities, which further increased their access to property. The economic activities of the slave Francis Payne to secure his own and his family's freedom in Northampton, Virginia, took place from 1643 to 1656. In 1643, he was given full management/intrapreneurial responsibilities for producing a tobacco crop. A contractual agreement was negotiated between Payne and his owner, another incongruity of the American slave system, since slaves were legally prohibited from making contracts. Under the terms of this contract, Payne managed a tract of his slaveholder's land as the price of his freedom.

As a plantation manger, Payne made "all decisions concerning the crop" in the production of 1,500 pounds of tobacco and six bushels of corn. The profits he earned from the sale of tobacco were to be used by him to purchase three indentured servants, who would serve the owner for six years. Payne was urged to go about his business as a plantation manager "quietly," but his activities became common knowledge. It took six years before he was able to deliver the white indentured servants. Then seven years later, after his manumission, Payne, who remained on as the plantation manager, produced another 3,800 pounds of tobacco, which paid for his wife and children.[150]

There were other reported cases of slave intrapreneurs who were promised freedom in exchange for the purchase of indentured servants from the tobacco crop they produced for their owners. But, as T. H. Breen and Stephen Innes note, the practice reveals an incongruity: "It is illuminating that no one seems to have been bothered that a black slave purchased indentured servants to obtain his own liberty."[151] Payne's negotiations with his owner are significant, demonstrating that whites in midseventeenth-century Virginia found that profitable exploitation of African labor in producing cash crops could be made only under conditions of reciprocity.

Simply put, Africans did not acquiesce passively to a lifetime of forced servitude, despite the brutal reality that impelled the economic initiatives of slave owners and the institutionalized process that sustained the subordination of blacks. As Edmond Morgan said, "In order to get work out of men and women who had nothing to gain but absence of pain, you had to be willing to beat, maim, and kill. And society had to be ready to back you even to the point of footing the bill for the property you killed."[152]

Through provision-ground allocations, a reciprocal and informal negotiation system developed by which slaves determined the allocation of the quality of labor they would provide. Using their expertise in the production of subtropical agricultural commodities and their African work ethic, and capitalizing on the scarcity of skilled white labor and management expertise, some slaves negotiated discretionary economic opportunities. Payne's intrapreneurial ability to manage a tobacco agribusiness for profit reveals that some whites very early recognized African commercial expertise. His example also underscores that the failure to acknowledge that potential by many other whites was a major obstacle to the free participation of Africans in the colonial economy. Had those abilities not been suppressed by the institutions of slavery and racism, there would have been successful competitive achievements by Africans in the colonial American economy.

Conclusion

Obviously, the whole panoply of the West and West Central African commercial infrastructure could not be replicated in the Americas, including merchant guilds and trade specialists (brokers and merchants). African slaves also did not have access to regional and international markets. Ultimately, then, what was retained in America by Africans of their commercial culture was a propensity to trade, which transcended attempts to disperse African ethnicity or even the lack of a large critical population threshold necessary for retaining cultural practices. In his discussion of the difficulties in establishing the ethnic origin of African survival practices in New England, a discussion that can also be applied to the American colonies as a whole, William Piersen said, "The cultures of the African peoples along the coast from Senegal to Angola were similar enough to give a certain unity to the cultural heritage of New England's African immigrants, a unity that was reinforced by the general experience of northern slavery and a common bond from the Atlantic crossing."[153]

With the African diaspora, recognizable ethnic and cultural differences were revealed. Yet there were similarities that extended beyond variances in language patterns, religious beliefs, and aesthetic expression. A point made by Mechal Sobel in a discussion of African survivalisms in African-American religious activity also has application for African-American economic activities. As he notes, the geographic dispersion of African ethnic groups in America "hastened the destruction of separate black world views but abetted the creation of a single quasi-African world view. It did not lead to the destruction of all earlier values, as has been previously assumed."[154]

At the height of the transatlantic slave trade in the eighteenth century, Africans sold to America came from economies that produced surpluses for local, regional, and international markets. African survivalisms in trade and marketing were reinforced by the increasing number of American-born Africans, who, by the Revolutionary War, constituted the majority of blacks in the country. Moreover, for many victims of the eighteenth-century slave trade cultural fusion, a reciprocal process had begun when Europe met Africa in the commercial world of international trade on the Guinea Coast. There, precolonial West and West Central African commercial practices had provided the basis for trade with the Europeans.

The survival of African culture and heritage depended on the extent to which those cultural expressions enhanced not only the integrity and humanity of the slaves but also their survival at a more basic level. Africans in the Americas quickly found that their survival beyond mere sustenance, as well as any improvement in their material lives, would depend on their own initiative. The provision-ground system and the trade and marketing activities developed by African slaves in America, most of whom were field hands, point to the ubiquitousness and resilience of African-based independent economic activities. Within this context, then, the memory of their role as producers and traders in marketing their surplus production in Africa was not obliterated in the transatlantic passage, leaving the slaves with only a conscious imprint of just one aspect of the African economic culture—their expertise as skilled laborers in agricultural production.

As it was, that same commercial impetus and work ethic so pervasive in the African heritage, which provided profits for whites, also provided the basis for the initial expression of the independent economic activities of plantation slaves. The provision-ground system developed by plantation slaves provided an alternative structure for survival for those who refused to be degraded and dehumanized by their involuntary servitude and subordinate status. While their profits were limited, often negligible, independent slave-initiated enterprises were much more extensive than the historical record shows, particularly as seen in the property owned by slaves.

Invariably, those blacks who did participate in the burgeoning colonial business community, first as slaves and then as freemen, emerged as traders, craftsmen, and small businessmen or developed successful agribusinesses, including large plantations. In colonial America, then, the African economic initiative expressed in the development of independent slave activities provided the basis for the significant entry Africans would subsequently make in establishing a niche for themselves, as free blacks, in the developing American business community in all the colonies. The inauguration of profit-making business activities in colonial America by African agriculturists in the production of surpluses for trade and marketing has historical significance in providing the foundation for the origin and development of the African-American business tradition.

2

FREE BLACK BUSINESS ACTIVITY
IN COLONIAL AMERICA

The gentlemen in the country have among their negroes as the Russian nobility among the serfs, the most necessary handicrafts men, cobblers, tailors, carpenters, smiths, and the like whose work they command at the smallest possible price for nothing almost. There is hardly any trade or craft which has not been learned and is not carried on by negroes.
—Johann D. Schoef, *Travels in the Confederation,* 1783 – 1784

Those Negroes who keep shops live moderately, and never augment their business beyond a certain point. The reason is obvious: the whites ... like not to give then credit to enable them to undertake any extensive commerce nor even give to them means of a common education by receiving them in to their counting houses.
—J. P. Brissot de Warville, *New Travels in the United States of America,* 1788

Introduction

As enslaved Africans became free in colonial America, they used their slave labor activities to their own economic advantage, the initial step in the development of the African-American business tradition. The entrepreneurial motivation of the first African-Americans to participate in the colonial business community by establishing for-profit enterprises underscores the persistence of an African business ethos, the diversity of craft and occupational activities, and a commercial culture paced by trade and marketing that survived the Middle Passage. The extent of the occupational diversity that existed in precolonial West Africa is shown in table 2.1. While acculturation shaped the form and expression of black business activities in colonial America, an African culture that emphasized trade and marketing should not be underestimated as a factor that propelled an increasing number of free blacks in colonial America to establish business enterprises.

Consequently, despite virtually insurmountable obstacles, Africans in America were involved in almost all areas of the colonial American economy as businesspeople. Their business activities and enterprises included their ownership in property, participation in craft activities, and providing of personal services. Free blacks in colonial America established craft enterprises and opened small stores. They also developed enterprises by

TABLE 2.1   Precolonial Gold Coast Town Occupations of Africans,
Seventeenth Century

Astrologers	Doctors	Masons
Bead makers	Ferrymen	Mat makers
Blacksmiths	Fishermen	Pilots
Bricklayers	Goldsmiths	Potters
Canoemen	Grave diggers	Priestesses
Carpenters	Hammock carriers	Stonecutters
Charcoal burners	Hat and cap makers	Thatchers
Common soldiers	Hawkers	Water carriers
Coopers	Lime makers	Water sellers
Day Laborers	Low-ranking priests	Woodcutters
Diviners	Market sellers	

Source: Compiled from *Ray A. Kea, Settlements Trade and Polities in the Seventeenth-Century Gold Coast* (Baltimore: Johns Hopkins University Press, 1982), 41,

exploiting personal service niches. They established catering enterprises in the early eighteenth century and made profitable incursions into hair care services as barbers and hairdressers before the end of the century (see table 2.2). Few differences existed between occupations of Africans on the seventeenth-century Gold Coast and those of Africans in colonial America. Even in colonial America, Africans were "common soldiers," called upon to join the English in their various colonial wars, first against the Dutch, then against the French and Spanish and their Indian allies. Instead of being "hammock carriers," in colonial America, Africans were coach drivers and draymen.

Yet the three major enterprises that generated wealth in colonial America—large plantation agribusinesses, the transatlantic slave trade, and the mercantile trade in slave-produced commodities—however, were closed to blacks; although a class of black slaveholders did emerge in the mid-seventeenth century. In colonial America, participation in business proceeded within the context of race, class, and labor. That relatively few free black businesspeople achieved success comparable to their white counterparts can be attributed neither to any lack of business acumen or entrepreneurial expertise nor to a failure of acculturation to the American business community. Rather, slavery and racism precluded all but a few blacks from tapping into the business social system that existed in the colonies.

All American laws governing slaves and free blacks specifically pertained to anyone of African descent, including mulattoes, quadroons, and octoroons. Anyone with African ancestry, however remote, was defined as black societally and legally in America.[1]

Beginning in colonial America, whites found it necessary to make these distinctions to maintain white supremacy and an enslaved black society. The economic advantage to whites was enormous. The enslavement of African women, in particular, ensured the reproduction of a slave labor force, regardless of the race of the father.[2] In 1776, while African-Americans constituted over 21 percent of the American population, not more than 5 percent of the black population was free in the new 13 states. By then, most blacks in the United States were born in America.[3]

While the question of the legal status of Africans is important, the more basic issue is the degree of freedom that could be manipulated from the system by blacks, both slave and free. As racial constraints became entrenched in the customs, mores, and common law in colonial America, only one right granted to free Africans remained virtually unchallenged: their access to property, a right that became the basis of black business activity. Even this

TABLE 2.2   Business Activities of Free Blacks in Colonial America

I. Black Property Ownership and Development
Real property ownership by free blacks
   Rural: Commercial farming
   Urban: Rental use, real estate speculation, business use
Town proprietorships
Black settlements
   Agriculture
   "Racial Islands"
   Frontier
Chattel (slave) property ownership
   By free black businesspeople
   By free black commercial farmers and planters
Personalty ownership

II. Craft Specialization Enterprises

Construction	Metalworking	Clothing industry
Bricklayers	Blacksmiths	Cobblers
Brick makers	Coppersmiths	Dressmakers
Brick moulders	Goldsmiths	Shoemakers
Carpenters	Gunsmiths	Tailors
Caulkers	Silversmiths	Tanners
Glaziers		
Plasterers		
Transportation	Woodworking	
Carriage and dray makers	Carpenters	
Ship carpenters	Furniture makers	
Shipwrights	Utensil makers	
Wheelwrights		

III. Urban Personal-Services Enterprises
Arts/entertainment enterprises: music schools, portrait painters, sculptors
Food service enterprises: caterers, restaurateurs, bakers, butchers, street vendors
Hair care enterprises
Health care enterprises: medical and herb doctors, nurses
Psychic enterprises: fortune-telling, conjuring, divination
Shopkeepers, merchants, traders, hucksters.
Tavern and innkeeper enterprises, liquor distilleries
Transportation enterprises: boatmen, dray and carriage drivers

right would be challenged when black economic initiative threatened the institution of slavery or placed blacks in a competitive position with whites.

Free-Black Property Ownership

Free Africans in America began to acquire property in the various colonies by the mid-1650s. Eventually, black-held property in colonial America fell into three categories: in rural areas blacks acquired land and buildings; in towns and cities they acquired houses and lots; as founders and proprietors of newly established communities, they owned blocks, lots, and public spaces. Beginning in colonial America, Africans acquired land in five ways:

through purchase; the government's head-rights system and land grants; leaseholds; private land grants, often on manumission; and gifts such as inheritances.

In Virginia's first recorded slave manumissions in 1645, a will showed that the former slaveholder of freed blacks "left them land."[4] In New York, even before "half-free status" was granted to Africans, the minutes of the Directors of the Dutch West Indies Company show that property was acquired by a black, "Domingo Antony, who owned parcels of land."[5] The land granted Africans in New Netherlands with half-free status was located outside of New York City in a swampy area known today as Greenwich Village and Washington Square; it was populated by other blacks well into the nineteenth century.[6] In Connecticut, the owner of John Wham and his wife freed them in 1646 and "settled them on a farm."[7]

Free blacks in the northern colonies also acquired real estate in the form of town lots and houses, in addition to farmland. In Dorchester, Massachusetts, Bostian Ken ("Bus Bus") acquired not only "a house and lot in that town but also four acres and a half of land planted in wheat" from 1656 to 1662. More typical of black landholding in urban areas of colonial New England was the real estate owned by a former Boston slave named Angola. On his death in 1675, he willed his house and lot to his wife, with provisions that the property would go to their children on her death. Angola's freedom had been purchased by Bostian Ken. African women also acquired property. In 1670 Zippora Potter, the free daughter of a slave, purchased a lot, 28 by 60 feet, with a house for the price of "forty Six pounds currant Mony of New England in hand paid."[8]

The earliest record of extensive agricultural holdings by a free African family in colonial America is that of the Anthony Johnson family of Northampton, Virginia. During the 1650s, three family members secured property under the head-rights system. Johnson was brought to Virginia as a slave in 1621. Sometime in the 1620s, he took a wife, who was perhaps the first African woman in Virginia. The couple had four children. Eventually, they were manumitted, and by the 1640s, "the Johnsons acquired a modest estate," which included extensive livestock operations.[9] Their economic success in their agribusiness enabled them to take advantage of the head-rights system to increase their landholdings. Under the head-rights system, land was granted to any person who paid the passage of a new immigrant to the colonies. In the mid-1600s, the Johnson family acquired 900 acres under the system for importing 18 people as servants and slaves. In addition, African Benjamin Doyle of Surrey County imported 6 persons into Virginia, for which he received a head-rights grant of 300 acres. Emanuel Cambew of James City County imported 1 servant for 50 acres of land.[10]

Africans also acquired land for development through leaseholds. In the mid-1660s, Emanuel Driggus, who purchased his freedom, negotiated a leasehold of 145 acres. He raised livestock for sale and subleased a 50-acre tract to a white tenant to finance the transaction, which required that Driggus pay 7,500 pounds of tobacco. The terms of the sublease were for 2,000 pounds of tobacco. Driggus held the rights to the land for 99 years. He engaged in several other transactions in leasing and subleasing land. His farm operations, as well as his property holdings were extensive: "'houses, outhouses, orchards, gardens and appurtenances.'"[11] At the same time, Driggus was also buying his children from slavery.

In a few instances in colonial America, blacks and whites formed business partnerships. African Philip Mongum, who farmed his own leasehold, added to his holding by going into partnership with two whites. The three men leased a 300-acre plantation in joint tenancy. Mongum subsequently increased his holdings by securing another 200-acre leasehold.

The agribusiness activities of these and other colonial African-American landholders in Virginia included extensive livestock raising and tobacco cultivation, which assured a steady source of income. Tobacco was produced for export but prices fluctuated, determined by international supply and demand. Free black landholders often realized profits from the sale of their produce and livestock as well as from land speculations with each other and with whites.

Despite their early economic success, some of Virginia's free blacks left Virginia's Eastern Shore and moved west. In the early 1660s, the Anthony Johnson family left Northampton and settled the Maryland frontier, where once again they were able to secure cheap, productive land. Yet by the end of the century, their descendants, members of one of the first free black families of Virginia, then into the third generation, dropped out of the property records of those colonies.[12] Before the end of the seventeenth century, the racial climate changed in Virginia and Maryland. The number of landless whites increased and, with a rapidly expanding African slave population, free blacks became increasingly suspect in a society that had legalized racial restrictions as opposed to those based on class differences.

Competitive incursions by free blacks into the economy were discouraged. Their access to land had provided the basis for the profitable development of their agribusinesses. With the closing of the Maryland and Virginia frontiers, that road to economic freedom was closed, as well.[13] Easy access to the land by blacks was precluded by white community cohesiveness and unity and by being excluded from the full privileges and rights of citizenship, a condition determined by race not class. With the closing of those frontiers, cheap public land under lenient government land-grant policies was no longer available. Also, institutionalized racism in the economic sector limited opportunities for free blacks to earn the necessary funds to purchase land through private transactions.

Black land occupancy patterns in colonial America, however, extended beyond the possession of urban and rural holdings and included the establishment of towns and agricultural settlements.[14] Abijah Prince, a former slave who owned 100 acres of farmland in Guilford, Vermont, in 1764 was also "one of the original founders of Sunderland in the same colony. As one of the first petitioners and grantees, Prince drew an equal share of the lands in all six divisions of the new township."[15]

The late eighteenth century also marked the emergence of isolated rural communities founded by free people of African descent, which E. Franklin Frazier termed "racial islands," communities established by blacks of mixed Indian and white ancestry who sought isolation from both blacks and whites. Many of these inhabitants considered themselves racially distinct and claimed being of Indian heritage or descended from Spanish Moors. The Gouldtown settlement in southern New Jersey, established in the mid-1760s, provides the first recorded instance of this form of community settlement in a rural area. By the late eighteenth century, Gouldtown had expanded into an agricultural settlement of small farms. With the establishment of an African Methodist Episcopal Church in 1816, the settlement would not have been considered a racial island.[16]

The most historically significant settlement founded by a black in colonial America was the fur-trading post established on the present site of Chicago by Jean Pointe Baptiste DuSable in 1779. It was located on the banks of the Chicago River on what is now North Michigan Avenue. DuSable (c.1750–1819) was from Santo Domingo. His settlement was noted by the British commandant at Mackinac in a report dated 4 July 1779: "Baptiste Point DeSaible, a handsome negro, well educated, and settled at Eschikagou [Chicago], but much in the French interest." The market for DuSable's trading post extended more than 200 miles into what later would become Michigan, Indiana, and Wisconsin, and the post serviced fur traders from the Mississippi River valley.

The trading post included a five-room house, a horse mill, bake house, dairy, smokehouse, poultry house, workshop, stable, and barn. DuSable also had extensive farm holdings. After the Revolutionary War, his trading activities expanded. The site became increasingly important after Fort Dearborn was established and the Indians were defeated at the Battle of Fallen Timbers in 1794. White settlers, especially from the South, began to move to the site and capitalize on its trading advantages.[17] Competition from whites and repressive laws, which subordinated blacks by limiting their freedom and discouraging their settlement on American frontiers, finally forced DuSable to leave. In 1800 he sold his trading post and landholdings for less than their market value and moved to St. Joseph, Missouri, where he died in poverty and virtual obscurity, much like the Johnsons and other blacks on the early Virginia and Maryland frontiers.[18]

From the beginning of black settlement in America throughout the period of slavery, the pattern was established that economic opportunities for blacks were tied to property ownership. The property-holding patterns and social climate on the nation's undeveloped frontiers that characterized the Johnson family in the seventeenth-century South and DuSable in the eighteenth-century North were not unique for blacks, either to time or place. Rather, their experiences served as a precursor of the conditions of frontier life that would be experienced by successive generations of slave and free blacks in the American West. Still, various government land-grant policies would afford blacks access to cheap public land.[19]

Slave Ownership by Free Blacks

Africans in America obtained ownership of slaves in the seventeenth century through purchases, gifts, and inheritances from both whites and blacks. Some black slaveholders owned slaves for the same economic reason as did whites—to make a profit by the utilization of unpaid workers. Slaves represented a capital investment in both property and labor. Other black slaveholders owned slaves for benevolent, fraternal, and humanitarian reasons. The most important of these was to subvert laws that required newly manumitted slaves to leave the state, thus forcing separation of families and friends. Then, too, a few black slaveholders were themselves slaves. As American common law developed, anyone, including slaves, could own a black person as a slave.

In New England, the first purchase of a slave by a black person was made in Massachusetts on 6 February 1656, by Bostian Ken. He had purchased his own freedom and then purchased the slave Angola and manumitted him for humanitarian reasons. Since he lacked money for the full purchase price, Bostian Ken "mortgaged his own house and land . . . in payment for Mrs. Keayne's Negro man, Angola. The price was thirty-two pounds, sixteen of which [Bostian Ken] agreed to pay in wheat, peas and barley." While the remaining 16 pounds was to be paid in three installments over a period of two years, Bostian Ken discharged the balance before the year's end. Court records dated December 1656 showed that " the mortgage is cancelled by order of Mrs. Keayne."[20]

The existence of black slaveholders has generated extensive debate and controversy on why they, who themselves held a subordinate status because of race, kept others of their race in slavery. One explanation is that kinship and extended family ties formed the basis of slave ownership by some free blacks.[21] As has been noted, other free blacks owned slaves for commercial reasons. In some instances black slaveholders held slaves for both kinds of reasons.[22] The concepts of transplantation and acculturation provide a basis for understanding this phenomenon.[23] Given the social hierarchies that existed in precolonial Africa, where class, status, and wealth were based on the number of one's dependents, can the preservation of African cultural heritage be ignored as a factor that possibly influenced the pattern of African slaveholding in seventeenth-century colonial America?

The subordination of members of one's own race, even of one's own ethnic group, was not alien to some precolonial West and West Central African societies. But was the inclination of blacks to purchase slaves based more on their rapid acculturation of early English-American colonial life? The Johnson family of Virginia, who had an unmixed African ancestry, has the distinction of being among America's first black slaveholders.[24] In the 1640s, as soon as they secured their freedom, they began purchasing Africans as slaves. In mid-seventeenth-century Virginia, free Africans had access to two kinds of servile laborers to work their land and increase their wealth. They owned both white and black indentured servants, as well as slaves. For the Johnson family, transplantation, as much as rapid assimilation, explains their striving to achieve ownership of property and labor, a goal that was certainly a common one in their new land.

The financial capacity of Africans to underwrite the transport costs of white indentured servants, who would be subordinate to them, underscores their economic initiative. Using profits from their agribusiness activities to purchase indentured servants served two purposes for the first black property holders in colonial America. This system provided an avenue for them to increase their land holdings, while at the same time assuring them of labor to work their land. The legal system, moreover, protected blacks in their right to own property in the form of slaves. In the mid-1650s, Anthony Johnson went to court to reclaim his slave John Casor, who attempted to secure his freedom by claiming that he entered the colony as an indentured servant and had served the maximum term.

Initially, the court found for Casor but, on appeal by Johnson, reversed its decision, which rested foremost on the protection of private property. Yet a precedent was also established that would preclude Africans from suing for freedom on the grounds that their entry into the colonies was as indentured servants. That decision was strengthened by colonial legislation that limited the period of servitude for indentured servants, but only those from Christian nations. Then, to ensure that whites would not be made subordinate to blacks, a 1670 Virginia law prohibited blacks from holding white indentured servants.[25] It was a response to the economic initiative of free blacks who purchased the labor contracts of white indentured servants, thus becoming their masters.

In the eighteenth century, while free-black slaveholding was limited, it existed throughout the colonies and new states. In 1785 the black slaveholder Abraham Jackson left a will stipulating that "his plantation would be worked by his slaves and that sufficient income would remain to pay his debts and provide money to several of his relatives."[26] One of the largest black commercial slaveholders in the eighteenth century was James Pendarvis, who lived in the Charleston district. The 1786 tax lists him as having "paid taxes on 113 slaves and a plantation which contained 3,250 acres of land." The 1790 census listed Pendarvis as a white man with 113 slaves, but he was the son of a white planter and his African-born slave, leaving no doubt of his African heritage. The Duke de la Rouchefoucault Liancourt "referred to him as a free Negro and not as a mulatto."[27] There was also the Gideon Gibson family, whose property ownership in land and slaves and the lightness of their skin enabled some of them to be accepted into the white planter class.

Next to planters, the largest occupational group of free black slaveholders consisted of artisans. In 1771 a black Charleston bricklayer, who owned three slaves, requested that they be sold after his death with proceeds divided equally among his five children. In 1787 another Charleston bricklayer, William Rapper, had nine skilled slaves, four of whom were employed in his construction business; they were valued at "466 pounds sterling, 8 shillings, and 9 pence," who, at his death, were bequeathed to family members.[28] The ownership of slaves by black craftsmen in the South would continue until the Civil War. Some blacks justified their slaveholding as a response to the failure to secure the labor of whites, who refused to work for them. With the impoverished status of most free blacks, it would appear that they would have provided an available labor force, but free black craftsmen determined that their employment would not have been as profitable as that of a slave.

Wages for free labor were an ongoing expense, whereas the purchase price of a slave craftsman could be easily recouped by hiring the slave out. Slaves were also an investment and could be resold, even for a profit. Ownership of slaves by craftsmen was profitable in that it allowed them to expand their job commissions. Free black bricklayers George Gardiner and Thomas Cole also owned slaves.[29] Facing competition from slave-owning white craftsmen, free black craftsmen needed slave ownership to have any chance of success. In a slaveholding society, was there an alternative to unpaid labor?

Free-Black Craft Enterprises

Craftsmen and artisans comprised the largest occupational group of free black businesspeople in colonial America. They also represented the largest occupational group among slaves who purchased their own freedom. The tradition of free-black-owned craft enterprises, established in the seventeenth century, developed from the participation of African slaves in the crafts in colonial America. In the 1670s, a free African craftsman in Massachusetts was the owner of a chair-making enterprise.[30] Other black craftsmen were also furniture makers, cabinet makers, wagon and carriage makers, wheelwrights, coopers (barrel makers), and carpenters. Africans also became blacksmiths, silversmiths, and coppersmiths. They made domestic utensils, farm implements, and luxury items.[31]

The craft skills that some Africans brought into the colonies as slaves accounted for the rich diversity of labor that they exhibited in preindustrial manufacturing areas right up until the Civil War. In the lumber industry there were slave sawyers. Slaves also produced naval stores, including tar, pitch, and turpentine; and in the shipping industry, they were ship carpenters and shipwrights. In the building trades, there were slave carpenters, brick molders, brick makers, bricklayers, lime makers, plasterers, whitewashers, painters, glaziers, caulkers, and architects. There were also black gunsmiths.

While many of the first black craftsmen who secured freedom had learned their trade in Africa, increasingly apprenticeships provided the basis for a slave's or free black's entry into the crafts. When bound out to white artisans, blacks were considered as serving a formal apprenticeship. If they learned a craft under a black slave artisan, the apprenticeship was considered informal. The distinction implied that the white artisan was a professional and consequently more skilled. Also, the period of apprenticeship under whites was longer.[32] In addition to slave craft apprenticeship, some free black children were apprenticed out by their families to craftsmen, both white and black, and sometimes apprenticed out by the county courts.

In Winchester, Virginia, the free black craftsman Cyrus purchased his freedom after he had "served his master, Reuben Triplet, near thirty years, to whom he paid fifty pounds for his discharge." Cyrus was "discharged" from slavery in 1796, but during the previous 30 years, he had won recognition for his decorative skills in woodworking, as indicated in a 1796 newspaper advertisement: "This is to acquaint the public, that all kinds of wooden *TRAYS* and *LADLES* are manufactured by *CYRUS*, a black man, who by indefatigable industry during his servitude, acquired a sum sufficient to liberate himself, by making and vending the above-mentioned articles."[33]

Colonial black craftsmen knew the value of their skills. They also composed a significant segment of the fugitive slave population. After escaping, many of them would settle in a new location, pass themselves off as free, and establish a business, as indicated in a newspaper advertisement for a runaway slave that said he "would endeavor to leave the Province, or get to the Back Parts and follow the Business of a Tanner, Shoemaker, Sadler, Carpenter, or Wheelright."[34] Start-up costs for craftsmen were minimal; even tools and materials were available at cost. Also, craft enterprises were small businesses, and black colonial craftsmen conducted their business the same way as their white counterparts. They "opened and operated the shop, purchased tools and raw materials, designed the product, instructed the apprentices, supervised journeymen, procured commissions for work, and . . . sold ready-made goods over the counter."[35]

Successful free black craftsmen used their profits to purchase property, including slaves, which meant that their craft enterprises paid off not only because of their skills but also because of their business expertise. James Mitchell, a free black carpenter in Charleston who established a construction business, initially ran his enterprise out of the first floor of his two-story house. As his business prospered, Mitchell made plans to move to the outskirts of the city to acquire more space, as indicated in an advertisement he ran in the newspaper: "A Place in the suburbs, with a little Garden," which also included outbuildings and a stable. Mitchell's property holdings also included slaves who worked as employees in his construction business.[36]

Still, free black craftsmen did encounter financial difficulty, even those who had achieved some success. The South Carolina craftsman John Williams, who was a carpenter and joiner, owned two town lots and 400 acres on the Santee River, with a warrant for an adjoining 200 acres. Yet a 1763 newspaper advertisement for the sale of his property explained that "he had recently met with some discouragement and was intending to depart from the province."[37]

A major problem faced by most businesspeople is the collection of debts; with many, it precludes extending credit. At the same time, a limited cash flow makes it difficult to secure credit for the purchase of supplies needed in the ongoing operations of the enterprise.[38] For free black craftsmen, however, these and other financial problems that confronted all colonial craftsmen were compounded by race. Free black craftsmen encountered financial difficulties not only with whites but also with each other, sometimes for their inability to pay for materials purchased from each other or for subcontracting work done for each other. In either case, the difficulty was usually due to their inability to collect from their customers, most of whom were white. Free black craftsmen, moreover, operated at a comparative disadvantage in gaining opportunities that would enable them to advance their skills, particularly in the northern colonies.

White craftsmen in the northern colonies attempted to improve their skills, as well as their social status, by professionalizing the trades. Continuing education for the ambitious was imperative, and the most enterprising attended night schools where courses were offered in bookkeeping, geometry, trigonometry, surveying, gunnery, and navigation. Indeed, the rise of private evening schools in colonial America was a response to craftsmen to provide their apprentices with education. New York City opened the first trade school in 1690. Others were also established in Philadelphia, Newport, Rhode Island, and even Charleston. In the eighteenth century, Boston craftsmen had the opportunity to study under the distinguished "Isaac Greenwood, A.M., who drank his way out of the Hollis Professorship of Mathematics at Harvard, [and] for several years after 1738 kept a private school where white Boston apprentices and artificers could learn applied mathematical." Also, private libraries contained collections of books on "building, iron-works, cabinet-making, surveying and the useful arts." Since many craftsmen belonged to the Freemasons, they also could organize with other member craftsmen to protect their interests.[39]

While free black craftsmen were excluded from formal instruction in the colonial trade schools, training under the apprenticeship system, although not always provided at the highest levels, afforded educational advantages that were denied most free blacks in colonial America. In Virginia, for instance, a free black indentured servant bound out as an apprentice in 1729 was to receive training described in court records as follows: "David James's free Negro was bound to James Todel, who is to teach him to read the bible distinctly, also the Trade of a gun Smith." Free blacks also apprenticed themselves out for training in a craft, a practice that continued through the colonial period, such as in 1774 when "Stephen Jackson, a free mulatto, voluntarily apprenticed himself to a hatter."[40]

With their skills and even some degree of formal education, in addition to their income as business owners, black craftsmen were in the upper class of the free-black social hierarchy as it developed in colonial America. Their position and status, however, engendered anxieties that went beyond their competitive economic incursions into the colonial business world. Would they, like their white counterparts, emerge as leaders of discontent? In the American Revolution, white craftsmen—led by the printer Benjamin Franklin and the silversmith Paul Revere, both of whom had few ties to the Anglophile colonial aristocracy—"had leadership as well as organization. From their ranks they produced a number of clear-thinking and bold captains, who crystallized their discontents, formulated plans, and joined with other groups in precipitating the revolutionary movement."[41]

In much the same way, black craftsmen, slave and free, with their skills, knowledge, and a confidence developed by successful economic participation in the colonial American business community, represented an occupational group that had the capacity to seriously damage the institutions of slavery. In the New York slave conspiracy of 1741, which had as its objective the burning of the city and the murder of its inhabitants, most of the leaders and participants were black craftsmen.[42] Shortly after the birth of the nation in 1792, a slave revolt was put down on the Eastern Shore of Virginia. Some 900 blacks participated and were backed by a substantial armory, which included a barrel of musket balls, some 300 spears, guns, and powder; newspapers emphasized that "the spears, it is said, were made by a negro blacksmith on the Eastern shore."[43]

The business activities of New Hampshire's Amos Fortune provide a somewhat unique look at the life of an eighteenth-century free black craftsman. Fortune was 60 years old when he purchased his freedom in 1770 in Massachusetts. After manumission, he purchased the freedom of his first two wives, who died, and then the freedom of his last wife and her daughter. In 1781, at the age of 70, Fortune moved to Jaffrey Center, where he reestablished a successful tannery with an extensive market in both New Hampshire and Massachusetts, while training both black and white youths as apprentices. Fortune was recognized as a community leader and even served as an attorney for various townspeople. His tombstone reads, "Sacred to the memory of Amos Fortune, who was born free in Africa, a slave in America, he purchased liberty, professed Christianity, lived reputable, and died hopefully, Nov. 17, 1801 AE [at the age of] 91."[44]

Food Services and Hair Care Enterprises

Beginning in colonial America, food services provided an important sector in which blacks established business enterprises. Before the end of the eighteenth century, not only did they actively participate in this industry, but their expertise, especially in catering, set the standards in food services until the late nineteenth century. The participation of blacks, both slave and free, in the food service industry began with the marketing and trading activities of slaves not only in agricultural commodities, meat, and fish but also in prepared food. Hawking prepared food as street vendors provided a basis for their entry into the industry. In Philadelphia, black women vendors, many of whom were sole supporters of their families, sold pepper pot soup; and they were "among the many free blacks whose small entrepreneurial roles made them a familiar part of urban street life."[45]

If these street vendors were successful, the profits were often used to rent or purchase a dwelling to house a restaurant or tavern. The most successful blacks in the colonial American food service industries were the caterers, restaurateurs, and innkeepers. Colonial America had a constant infusion of single men, who relied on small restaurants, coffee shops, and caterers for their meals. Also, much of the colonial social life for men of all classes centered around taverns, public houses, and ordinaries.[46] Proprietors who developed a reputation for providing good food and service could make substantial profits.

Also, free black caterers provided the wealthy with sumptuous and elegant meals for their parties and dinners. In New England, the Baroons, Emanuel Manna and wife Mary, both former slaves, were leaders in the field of catering, having opened an establishment in Providence, Rhode Island, in 1736. Start-up capital came from Mary's profitable but illegal whiskey distillery enterprise.[47] The Baroons expanded by opening an oyster and ale house in Providence, which, along with Newport, early on became a summer resort for West Indies planters and their families.[48] In pastry making, the "Dutchess" Quamino of Newport was extolled as "the most celebrated cake baker in Rhode Island." [49] One of the most successful bakers was Cyrus Bustill, born in 1732. During the Revolutionary War, he was employed by the Continental Army in Burlington, New Jersey. When he left the army, Bustill opened a baking shop in Philadelphia, which he ran until he retired in 1791. Bustill was the leader of Philadelphia's black community and in 1803 opened a school in his home for black children.[50]

The most famous African-American in the food service industry in the colonial and Revolutionary War period was Samuel "Black Sam" Fraunces, a West Indian who migrated to New York City in the 1750s. In one of his advertisements in the New York *Post Boy*, 5 February 1761, he announced that he was a "caterer" with experience as an innkeeper in New York since 1755.[51] In 1762, Fraunces purchased the "elegant" DeLancy mansion on the corner of Broad and Pearl Streets for 2,000 pounds. He opened it as a tavern and inn and soon earned the reputation not only as the leading restaurateur of New York but also as having "the finest hostelry in colonial America."

From 1765 to 1773, he operated a vaux-hall. Patterned after its English counterparts, the vaux-hall, a resort and recreation center, was the rage in public entertainment for colonial Americans just before the Revolutionary War. The vaux-hall established by Fraunces set the standards for this type of enterprise; it was known for its lovely gardens, fine liquor, and good entertainment. "Two of his attractions in 1768 were an exhibition of 'elegant waxwork figures,' including Scipio, and a newfangled grotto." Also, the noted Mr. Hulet and Miss Hallam of the American Company presented a series of concerts."[52]

Even before Fraunces sold his vaux-hall in 1773, he was devoting most of his time to the Fraunces Tavern, initially called the Queen's Head. It acquired national fame in 1776 during the American Revolution. In May 1776, John Adams and the Massachusetts delegation lodged there on their way to Philadelphia for the Second Continental Congress. When independence was declared, Fraunces Tavern soon became the stopover for members of the Continental Congress and for officers in the Continental Army. General George Washington and his staff took their meals there.[53] During the Revolutionary War, Fraunces enlisted in the Continental Army, while his wife managed the tavern. He served as a private in Washington's own division until 1782.[54] After the war, he returned to provide food and services to America's new leaders. He kept careful records of these transactions, including the following, which Fraunces submitted to Governor Clinton of New York when he entertained General Washington in 1783.[55]

With this itemized bill, one can begin to appreciate the stress of the war's end on the nation's new leaders, as they began to grapple with the critical problems of governing the United States for the first time under peacetime conditions. When Washington was elected president, he appointed Fraunces as the first White House chef. Until Fraunces's death in 1803, his tavern retained its high reputation as a meeting place for the nation's political and business elite, but "with the understanding that no blacks could eat or stay there."[56] Black exclusion from elite black restaurants was a pattern that was to continue, even after the Civil War.

Fraunces Tavern, 1783
Governor Clinton's Bill, November 25, 1783
His Excellency, Governor Clinton to Samuel Fraunces

	Pounds	Shillings	Pence
To an Entertainment	30	4	6
" 75 Bottles of Madeira at 8/	30	—	—
" 18 " " Claret at 10/	9	—	—
" 16 " " Port at 6/	4	16	—
" 24 " " Spruce at 1/	1	4	—
" 24 " " Port at 3/	3	12	—
" Lights 60/ Tea and Coffee 64/	6	4	—
" Brokage	2	2	—
" Punch	10	10	—
	95	52	6

Source: Spraggins, "History of Negro Business," 5 and "Appendix A-2."

In addition to exclusive food services for the elite throughout the colonial period, there was a demand for barbers, wigmakers, and hairdressers. Colonial white barbers really had no competition until after the end of the Seven Years' War in 1763, when "French wig-makers and hairdressers arrived in the cities, frequently arousing the envy of English perukemakers."[57] The most successful eighteenth-century black in the hair care business was Pierre Toussaint, who, as a twenty-one-year-old slave, was brought to New York by his owners, the Bérard family, French planters from Santo Domingo. After the head of the family, M. Jean Bérard, went back to Santo Domingo to look after his property (he never returned), Toussaint used the money he made as a hairdresser to support Bérard's widow, even after she remarried. After her death, Toussaint purchased his freedom.

Toussaint was described as "the most fashionable coiffeur in the city." His clients were New York's wealthiest families, some of whom included him in their novels, memoirs, and diaries. He was even the subject of a biography, in which Hannah Lee said that "as a hair-dresser for ladies he was unrivalled.... he had all the custom and patronage of the French families . . . [and] many of the distinguished ladies of the city employed him."[58] Toussaint's earnings were substantial. He purchased his sister, his wife, and several boys from slavery, whom he also helped get a start in life as freed men; and he had plans to establish a French and English school for black girls. Toussaint was one of the first African-American philan-thropists, but most of his philanthropy was limited to whites. He provided generously to the Catholic Church and a Catholic orphanage for whites, and he helped underwrite the expenses of white American students to study in Rome for the priesthood. In Catholic Church histories of the nineteenth century, Toussaint is described as "the most conspicu-ously outstanding Negro Catholic in the history of New York" and as "God's Image in Ebony."[59]

Black Business Expansion

There were several additional areas in which blacks in colonial America developed business enterprises. In transportation, they established livery coach and drayage enterprises, but in the northern colonies they were confronted with competition from whites. In South Car-olina, Africans developed a diversity of fishing and boating enterprises. Africans from coastal areas and river plains had distinct advantages in pursuing these enterprises. Their skills in coastal navigation were initially exploited by their owners and then used by the boatmen after they were freed to establish their own enterprises. Africans in colonial America, however, were not limited to domestic waterways in their enterprises. In the sev-enteenth century, Bostian Ken, who had extensive property holdings, was involved in international trade before he "sold his one-third share of the fourteen-ton ship *Hopewell*."[60]

The increasing import-export trade also provided avenues for African skills in the ship-building industry, as well as in the manufacturing of land vehicles, including wagons, drays, and carriages. African skills were also utilized in the manufacturing of containers used for the shipment of agricultural commodities, especially rice and tobacco. Successful free black craftsmen were able to use their profits to purchase property, including slaves; their craft enterprises paid off, therefore, not only because of their skills but also because of their business expertise.

Africans in colonial America, through fortune-telling, conjuring, and divination, also launched the nation's first occult-oriented enterprises. Today, we see a hint of these in the use of black women in psychic enterprises heavily advertised through the media. In a hostile environment, Africans perceived brutal masters, ill health, inadequate diet, substandard living conditions, and separation of family and friends as controlled by the forces of evil. Belief in the supernatural distinguished the daily lives of many slaves, but parallel practices in Western culture—the belief in witches and ghosts, the use of charms for protection and good luck, and so on—made it difficult for whites to suppress African occult practices.

The Salem witch trials of 1692 found both African and white women accused of witchcraft. The power of African conjuring was also seen in colonial New England, where there were cases of bewitched Africans who died slow, lingering "voodoo" deaths.[61] Consequently, colonial whites very early became acquainted with the African occult. Some were susceptible to Africans who seemed to have demonstrated the power to bring good health, fortune, love, and happiness into their private lives, as well as into their business affairs. African diviners and conjurers capitalized on these beliefs, particularly in the use of fortune-telling in establishing psychic enterprises. Other blacks turned to astrology. One account shows that "[a] Maine Negro is said to have made a living as a fortune teller."[62] Invariably, some blacks were brought to court for various offenses related to their activities.

These occult enterprises also included folk healing, including the sale of Native American herbal medicine.[63] Many African women were folk healers and root and herbal specialists, and several were recognized for their healing arts, including "Doctress Phillis" in Barrington, Rhode Island.[64] African expertise in pharmacopoeia was early recognized in the colonies. Cotton Mather, a member of one of New England's leading Puritan families, noted that his "Guramantee [Coramantee] Servant" practiced vaccination. Mather commented that "I have since met with a considerable number of these Africans who all agree in one story. . . . people take a juice of small-pox; and *cutty-skin,* and put in a drop; then by and by a little *sicky-sicky,* then very few little things like small-pox; and no body die of it; and no body have small-pox any more."[65]

With the exception of Dr. James Derham, few blacks in late eighteenth-century America profited from the practice of medicine. Derham was born a slave in 1762 and was owned by a succession of medical doctors. One owner, a Philadelphia doctor, taught Derham to mix medicines and administer simple medical procedures. During the Revolutionary War, he was owned by a British doctor. After the war, Derham was sold to a doctor in Louisiana, where he purchased his freedom and obtained a license to practice medicine. By 1788, as a licensed practicing physician, Derham was making $3,000 annually. He published medical papers and corresponded with Dr. Benjamin Rush, the leading physician in Pennsylvania, if not the nation. On meeting Derham in 1788, Rush wrote, "There is now in this city, a black man by the name of James Derham, a practitioner of physic. . . . I have conversed with him upon most of the acute and epidemic diseases of the country where he lives and was pleased to find him perfectly acquainted with the modern simple mode of practice in those diseases. I expected to have suggested some new medicines to him, but he suggested many more to me."[66]

By the late eighteenth century, a black professional class began to develop in America. Benjamin Banneker was a self-taught mathematician whose skills were used in the surveying of the nation's capital in 1791. Between 1791 and 1796, he published six annual almanacs entitled *Benjamin Banneker's Pennsylvania, Delaware, Maryland and Virginia Almanack and Ephemeris.* Banneker sent a copy of his 1791 almanac to Thomas Jefferson, then secretary of state, to demonstrate the "mental endowments" of African people. Jefferson reluctantly acknowledged the degrading effects of slavery on black intellectual achievement, however, when he wrote that "[n]o body wished more than I do to see such proofs as you exhibit, that nature has given to our black brethren, talents equal to those of other colors of men, and that the appearance of a want of them is owing merely to the degraded condition of their existence, both in Africa & America."[67]

The arts also provided a basis for the development of enterprises by Africans in colonial America. The most famous black musician in the eighteenth century was Occramer Marycoo, later known as Newport Gardner (1746–1826), who achieved recognition as a music teacher, musician, and composer. He was brought from Africa at the age of 14 and sold as a slave in Rhode Island in 1760, where he taught himself to read in English after only a few lessons. He was also given music lessons. Quickly surpassing his teachers, Gardner was allowed by his owners to open a music school, where he taught both white and black students. In 1791 he purchased his freedom and that of most of his family with $2,000 he won in a lottery.

Singing and dancing schools were quite popular in late colonial America, and slaves who had musical ability were highly prized; they were known as "dance musicians." One of the most famous in New York was Frank, who opened his own music studio; and by 1786 " '[a]bout forty scholars' were in attendance." Colonial military companies employed black musicians, as did the American Continental Army during the Revolution. "Zelah of Groton, Massachusetts, a fifer in a Revolutionary regiment, is said to have been a famous musician."[68]

While African artistic expression would not be appreciated in the West until the twentieth century, some eighteenth-century blacks made a living from portrait painting. A Boston newspaper carried the following announcement: "*Negro Artis*. At McLean's Watchmaker, near Towne-Hall, is a Negro man whose extraordinary Genius has been assisted by one of the best masters in London; he takes faces at the lowest Rates. Specimens of his performance may be seen at said Place."[69] One of the most famous eighteenth-century black artists was Scipio Morehead, who painted the portrait of poet Phillis Wheatley that was used in her books. Her poem "A Young African Painter on Seeing His Works" was dedicated to him. Another successful black artist in post-Revolutionary America was Joshua Johnston, a portrait painter in Baltimore from 1796 to 1824 whose subjects were wealthy slaveholders. Stephen Fortune, a black craftsman, "completed the Goddess of Liberty atop the national capitol." Free blacks who stopped to admire his work, however, were subject to arrest, fines, and imprisonment.[70]

Throughout the colonial period, both slaves and free blacks participated in a diversity of occupations, which provided the basis for the development of various business enterprises. The extensiveness and diversity of black participation in the crafts was emphasized in the travel accounts of the German physician Dr. Johann D. Schoef, who visited the United States after the Revolutionary War: "The gentlemen in the country have among their negroes as the Russian nobility among the serfs, the most necessary handicrafts men, cobblers, tailors, carpenters, smiths, and the like whose work they command at the smallest possible price for nothing almost. There is hardly any trade or craft which has not been learned and is not carried on by negroes."[71] African-American participation in the crafts and other urban occupations reflected a generational continuity of African economic activities. The Americanization of Africans, who were confronted with slavery and racism, did not represent an advancement in their economic lives.

In a new nation with an expanding agricultural sector and a growing urban infrastructure, the building and construction trades, which utilized skills in carpentry, bricklaying, masonry, and blacksmithing, provided exceptional opportunities for skilled craftsmen to establish businesses. Manufacturing skills were also in demand for the production of home furnishings and agricultural implements that were necessities for improving the material life of the colonist but were also too expensive to import. Africans in America did continue their occupations as market sellers and hawkers and some became shopkeepers as well. (See table 2.2.)

Black Shopkeepers and Merchants

Free black merchants in urban colonial America, even craftsmen, were generally small shopkeepers, but few black colonial shopkeepers sold large volumes of merchandise or luxury goods. There were, of course, exceptions. Jean Pointe Baptiste DuSable had a virtual monopoly on merchandising activities in the Northwest Territory in the late eighteenth century. He supplied flour, pork, and bread in large quantities to hunters, fur traders, and settlers in the territory. He also manufactured merchandise from his activities as a carpenter and cooper. DuSable was a miller, probably a distiller too, in addition to his activities as a trapper and buyer.

The success of DuSable's trading post, located at what was to later become Chicago, was due to a diversity of business activities and to an absence of competition. Participation in diverse occupations for most colonial black entrepreneurs, however, was the result of not being able to survive in only one area of specialization because of competition and unfavorable market factors. In addition, there were human capital factors that contributed to both success and failure.

The husband of Phillis Wheatley, John Peters, was said to have established several businesses in Boston, including a bakery and a grocery. He even attempted to become a lawyer and physician, but he was said to be a dilettante and an aspiring gentlemen who plowed his profits back into his wardrobe, rather than his business. Described as quite handsome, Peters "wore a wig, carried a cane, and quite acted out *'the gentleman.'* ... *he was a man of talents and information—writing with fluency and propriety, and at one period, reading law. ...*"[72] Doubtless Peters was a man of ability, even if his attempts to succeed as a shopkeeper failed. Yet in colonial America, only a few black merchants and shopkeepers enjoyed any financial success. Samuel Gibson, brought as a slave from the West Indies, secured his freedom and established a successful business as a merchant. He employed the son of his former white master as a clerk in his store and, on his death in 1795 at the age of 34, "left the young man his entire estate."[73]

Still, even when they had no financial problems, black shopkeepers encountered other difficulties caused by racism. In New York, a free black butcher-shop owner and former slave launched a suit in an attempt to recover money and a slave that he had inherited. The businesses of another former slave, William Grimes of Connecticut, were so successful that he was forced out of town by his white competitors. Grimes, after escaping as a fugitive slave from Savannah, had settled in New Haven and established several enterprises that catered to students from colleges in the area, including running a "victualing shop" and delivering furniture to students.

Grimes even set up operations as an informal banker; he said, "I kept money to let, and soon got into full business." In all his enterprises Grimes was quite successful: "In fact, I had such a run of customers that all the shop keepers, that is Huckster shops about the college, and who get their living out of the students fell upon me.... Notwithstanding their efforts, I did a might good business." Grimes's white competitors used race in an attempt to get the backing of the college stewards to support a boycott of his enterprises. When their efforts failed, his competitors brought suit against him, which was successful and finally forced Grimes out of town.[74]

In addition to problems caused by race, most colonial black merchants and shopkeepers encountered difficulties in their attempts to get credit, not just for business expansion, but also from wholesalers. This was especially true for merchants whose businesses required the purchase of dry goods and nonperishable items in order to have a variety of up-to-date merchandise. This was not often a problem for black craftsmen, who worked on commission and who could often get down payments for their work, which would enable them to purchase lumber, leather, fabric, or other materials needed for production.

Invariably, black shopkeepers in colonial America who attained even a modicum of financial success relied on a white customer base. Although the colonial black population was relatively small in the North, it was concentrated primarily in urban areas, which provided a base of black customers that led to the rise of a small group of free black shopkeepers. Yet colonial black shopkeepers always had to compete with white merchants in selling to black customers. In addition, 95 percent of the country's total black population lived in the South; and nearly all of these blacks, both urban and rural, were slaves. Although their funds were limited, slaves either bought goods on a cash basis or made credit purchases, but they shopped primarily at stores owned by whites. Few black shopkeepers then, as now, could sell on credit or secure credit for wholesale purchases of their stock. But at the same time, purchases by slave and free blacks enabled small black shopkeepers to survive.

In colonial America, the major activity of small merchants and shopkeepers was the retailing of manufactured goods (some prefabricated and others specially made), groceries, which generally included nonperishables, dry goods, notions, hardware, yard goods, tobacco, and pharmacopoeia. Slaves purchased such goods by cash, credit, or barter at white shops, which provided a comfortable living for most of the owners. At a white-owned store in eighteenth-century colonial Virginia, slave purchases included "apparel, food, utensils and small tools, spectacles, a dozen buttons, a great deal of cloth, handkerchiefs, a pair of shoes (made on credit for Jack), molasses, sugar, whiskey, brandy, a chamber pot, a screw auger, pewter plates, a pocketknife, and a dozen knives and forks."[75]

In the colonial period, the entrepreneurial activities of free black shopkeepers, with few exceptions, proved the least successful of the business enterprises established by African-Americans, especially when compared to the operations of free black craftsmen, with their holdings in land and slaves. The obstacles encountered by these merchants in promoting their businesses were quite apparent, as evidenced by commentaries made in 1788 by a casual observer, J. P. Brissot de Warville, who was quick to note that "[t]hose Negroes who keep shops live moderately, and never augment their business beyond a certain point. The reason is obvious: the whites ... like not to give them credit to enable them to undertake any extensive commerce nor even give to them the means of a common education by receiving them into their counting houses."[76] Consequently, in colonial America, without access to credit, most free black retail shopkeepers operated marginal businesses that earned comparatively limited profits, a financial pattern of black business activity that would persist, even into the late twentieth century.

Black Business Exclusion

Credit was vital to colonial business, and creditworthiness at all levels was based on the reputation of the customer or prospective debtor and his or her standing and status in the community. This was as true for the large import-export merchants as it was for small urban and rural shopkeepers. In the small mercantile community of colonial America, mutual exchanges of information about the creditworthiness of large merchants extended overseas as a basis for securing credit from English merchants. Informal meetings in coffee-houses and taverns provided the venue for mutual exchanges of information on investments and new commercial opportunities.

In colonial America, the development of successful business enterprises depended as much on commercial family ties and business networks, which provided access to credit, as it did on rugged individualism. Hard work, thrift, and industriousness—the Puritan work ethic—along with Yankee ingenuity and innovativeness, were also vitally important in the development of entrepreneurial initiatives.[77] But in the first two centuries of the developing colonial economy of cash-poor America, access to credit was the critical factor that fueled the growth of the commercial sector. Banks were not organized in the colonies until after 1775, but artisans, shopkeepers, planters, and merchants still needed credit in the promotion of trade.[78]

Invariably, creditors were involved in trade and commerce. Even in rural areas, small shopkeepers, if unable to barter for the exchange of goods, extended credit to their customers. In urban areas, general-store merchants also extended credit to their customers, urban dwellers as well as shopkeepers in rural towns and villages. In turn, these large urban shopkeepers were extended credit by large export-import merchants, who in most instances were also general storekeepers. The inventory of these storekeepers, especially import merchandise available for both wholesale and retail trade, was invariably acquired by credit advanced them by overseas merchants eager for sales in the colonial markets.

The inventory of the large merchants consisted of domestic and foreign goods sold in both wholesale and retail markets. While many merchants operated general stores, their major activity was processing import-export commodities for the domestic or foreign markets. Still, businesses run by large colonial merchants were relatively small-scale enterprises. Even the most successful were generally sole proprietorships or family partnerships, operating from a single location with one or two clerks and a volume of business that did not involve more than four or five transactions a day. Despite what appears as a relatively insignificant volume of trade, substantial fortunes were accumulated by some of the large merchants.[79] This occurred because merchants often owned their own ships or held fractional shares in several or more vessels. Their international trade was handled by the ship's captain or a supercargo, often a family member, or by an overseas agent, all who earned commissions on the sales and purchases of goods for the colonial merchant.

The participation of Americans in the transatlantic slave trade also provides an example of business development through a family consolidation of resources.[80] In Rhode Island, the center of the colonial American transatlantic slave trade, "[t]he family tie was present in most of the partnerships: brothers, father and son, uncle and nephew: through the family unit business skill and capital were pooled."[81] The colonial American overseas merchants, then, represented a close-knit society, consolidating their wealth and trade connections to the exclusion of others through intermarriage within merchant families.[82]

Ultimately, it was the unpaid labor of African slaves working on plantations, that generated the most profitable ventures in colonial America, which contributed immeasurably to establishing the economic foundation of this nation. The large merchants and shippers, along with the prominent planters, those who held extensive acreage and owned over 50 slaves, were the most successful businessmen in colonial America. As unpaid agricultural workers, African-Americans provided commodity production that contributed to the income of their owners, whose wealth also increased with the accrued value of their chattel in slaves.

The leading export crops in colonial America were slave-produced rice and indigo, grown primarily in South Carolina. By the eve of the Revolution, "whites in South Carolina on an individual basis held the largest wealth and earned the highest incomes on the mainland."[83] So when the English Parliament enacted new legislation after 1763 that the colonists deemed restrictive to their economic expansion through trade, they revolted. And while there were some 50 grievances in the Declaration of Independence, the two that had the most support for revolution were those that denounced Great Britain: "For cutting off our trade with all parts of the world" and "For imposing taxes on us without our consent." Yet Thomas Jefferson's first draft of that document, which included a passage indicting England for its participation in the transatlantic slave trade, was rejected until the passage was deleted.

One of the signatories of the final document was the son of William Ellery, head of a leading Rhode Island family whose wealth was derived from the slave trade. Also, George Cabot, ancestor of two United States senators, William Pepperell, and the Brown family of Providence, Rhode Island, became wealthy through their slave trade activities. Indeed, it was the Brown family's substantial contributions to Rhode Island College that led to its being renamed Brown University.[84]

In American business history, scholars praise the genius of the nation's first successful entrepreneurs, as much for their leadership in the exploitation of this nation's resources as for their perspicacious development of international trading markets. Yet the wealth accumulated by the New England slavers, the large urban merchants, and the great planters was derived from the substantial profits earned from both the slave trade and the sale of slaves and slave-produced commodities. Profits earned by merchants and slavers were reinvested in other enterprises, including manufacturing, mining, and especially real estate. And in the absence of hereditary transfers of power and authority, the wealth accumulated by American slave owners, slave merchants, and large merchants enabled them, along with the great planters, to exert a disproportionate influence in colonial American politics to protect their interests.

Without government support, particularly in the legal protection of slavery, which provided a great amount of the wealth of colonial America, entrepreneurial ventures that advanced the economic development of this nation would have been extremely limited. Crown appointments, governorships, custom inspectorates, and other official positions in the colonial government provided a base for white males to accumulate wealth and power. Direct government support that advanced business development in the colonies also included the granting of military contracts, favorable land charters that placed massive tracts of land in the hands of private speculators, and various tax remissions. Consequently, the accumulation of wealth through entrepreneurial endeavors in the private sector was propelled by preferential government support given to white males through various colonial legislative bodies.[85]

This was the commercial world in which the first enterprises were established by African-Americans. They did not have a chance during this period, anymore than they have in the late twentieth century, to achieve business participation rates and generate business profits proportionate to their population. In the colonial American mercantile economy, in which affirmative governmental policies to promote business were based on race and in which subsidized preferential government support was provided for whites, entrepreneurial blacks, with their subordinate status distinguished by both race and class, were severely limited as potential players in the competition for wealth.

Conclusion

From the beginning of the settlement of colonial America, entrepreneurial endeavors and the development of successful business enterprises were conditioned by race and contingent on family networks and commercial relationships with close associates, which provided access to credit and a wide-based consumer market. And from the beginning, blacks in colonial America were locked out from the process by what can only be perceived as preferential treatment for white males by the colonial government's mercantile policies. These preferential policies, which were designed to promote business development, were reserved for and specifically benefited those whites with connections based on their class standing, which gave them access to policy makers who had authority to make those allocations.

Africans in colonial America were limited in access to extensive land grants, and government subsidies and contracts, which were based on government policies that promoted successful entrepreneurial ventures. In colonial America, white opposition to black economic initiatives was institutionalized through law and societal practices, which not only subordinated blacks but also precluded them from a full and unfettered freedom in the pursuit of wealth. Race-based exclusion from credit networks limited the commercial advancement of blacks throughout colonial America, a situation that was quite apparent to even the most casual observer, as evidenced in the commentaries made in 1788 by Brissot de Warville on the inability of blacks to secure credit.

The initial expressions of business activities in marketing and trading by people of African descent in this nation did not have their foundation in colonial America. Most certainly, acculturation to the country's business practices shaped the subsequent development, structure, and form of African-American business activities. Yet neither the propensity for nor the initiative demonstrated by Africans in pursuing business activities in colonial America or their trade and marketing practices can be attributed to any special impetus derived from whites. In the process of transculturation, the business activities of Africans and their Creole descendants in colonial America reflected the persistence of societal values and cultural norms distinctive to the African economic culture in the eighteenth century, when over 95 percent of the Africans that were victims of the transatlantic slave trade were sent to this country.

The entrepreneurial activities of free black merchants, beginning in the colonial era, proved, with few exceptions, the least successful of the enterprises established by African-Americans. Consequently, while African-Americans did participate in the nation's business community at the time, they did so only on the fringes of enterprises in which wealth was created. Still, in the face of the virtually insurmountable obstacles of slavery and institutional racism, a tradition of African-American business activity was established in colonial America that has persisted for almost 400 years.

3

BUSINESS ACTIVITIES OF AFRICAN-AMERICAN SLAVES, 1790–1865

Until he was arrested in October, 1835, as a slave, he went at large and acted as a free man, by keeping an oyster house, and boot-black shop.

—*Bland v. Negro Beverly Dowling*, Maryland, 1837

[The slave] Milly, had . . . accumulated [some money] by selling, for years, with his permission, surplus articles . . . such as fowls, butter, ice-cream, etc., and by manufacturing and selling . . . bed-clothing. . . . Milly stated that she had already several hundred dollars . . . and that she had been collecting some other debts amount[ing] in all to eleven or twelve hundred dollars.

—*Lea v. Brown*, North Carolina, 1860

Alick was a likely mulatto slave of the plaintiff, twenty-five or thirty years old, skilled in the business of attending [managing] a drug store, who had been hired for . . . 1847, to Toland and Curtis, druggists in Columbia. . . .

—*Dr. Sill v. Railroad* Company, South Carolina, 1850

His slaves are sometimes his creditors to large amounts; at the present time he says he owes them about five hundred dollars.

—Frederick Law Olmsted, *The Cotton Kingdom*

Introduction

African-American slaves participated as both "intrapreneurs" and entrepreneurs in all areas of the antebellum southern economy. Slave entrepreneurs, both men and women, were bondsmen who hired their own time from their owners and established business enterprises as sole proprietors. A few formed slave business partnerships. Also, in some enterprises, the more successful slave entrepreneurs hired other slaves as their employees. And there were instances when some even purchased a slave or two for their employees. Slave intrapreneurs, on the other hand, were bondsmen granted decision-making authority in managing the businesses of their owner in both the agricultural and nonagricultural sectors. In managing their owners' businesses, some slave intrapreneurs were given full authority to hire employees and even to negotiate contracts.

While self-hired bondsmen represented only a small percentage of the slave population, slave intrapreneurial activities were much more extensive and must be considered within the context of wealth-holding and business ownership in the South. The leading wealth holders were large plantation owners and businesspeople. Most found it to their economic advantage to use their slaves in managerial positions, as opposed to paying wages to whites for such labor. Slave intrapreneurs had the opportunity to make money, while slave entrepreneurs could generate their own income from the enterprises they established. Still, for the majority of slaves, any opportunity to improve their bleak material lives was enough to give them impetus to develop economic activities. Simply put, slaves found it imperative that they operate in a cash system, which they attempted to develop in all sectors of the antebellum economy.

The economic activities of slaves represented an integral part of their material lives. In addition to their provision-ground activities, slaves also became urban vendors, hawkers, and itinerant peddlers, who could be considered either intrapreneurs or entrepreneurs. There were also slave commercial farmers. In addition, slaves also participated in a flourishing underground economy, , which at times included the independent slave economy, as well as the underground enterprises of maroons, fugitive slaves who lived clandestinely in isolated settlements in the South. All antebellum slaves were not involved in intrapreneurial or entrepreneurial enterprises, but a significant proportion did participate in some kind of independent economic activity at one time or another to earn money.

Slaves had the right to accumulate personal property, with their owners' approval. Sam Williams, a slave ironworker at the Virginia Buffalo Forge, owned valuable personal property—a gold watch. He also held a savings account at a Kentucky bank. As a slave, Sam was limited in his capacity to withdraw his money at will, as indicated in a letter to Sam's bank written by the manager of his plant: "I wish to ask you one question whether Sam Williams can draw his money from the Savings Bank or if he cannot. It is my opinion that he can draw his money if he gives the Directors of the Bank 10 days notice."[1] The letter further states that Sam and Henry Nash, a free black cooper, had a bet, with their watches as stakes, which the writer witnessed.

This chapter argues for a historic view of slave life that includes not only the economic activities of slaves but also the African-American cultural imperatives that gave impetus to those activities. Slaves did operate in a cash nexus and their personal property included not only valuable possessions such as gold watches and bank accounts, but also livestock, horses, and carriages, a reflection of their attempts to improve their material lives. Most important, for self-hired slaves, independent business activities provided opportunities to purchase freedom. For most slaves, self-initiated economic activities were motivated by the need for money to improve their bleak material lives, so that they could purchase even such a simple item as a comb.

Independent economic activities of slaves, however, were illegal, including the businesses established by slave entrepreneurs. Despite this, slaves participated openly in the formal economy, as well as operating enterprises clandestinely in the South's informal economy. The purposes of this chapter, then, are (1) to assess the extensiveness, diversity, and pervasiveness of slave intrapreneurial and entrepreneurial economic activities; and (2) to assess slave laws in force that were constructed to suppress independent slave economic initiatives. Both assessments underscore the extent to which slave economic activities represented an integral part of the business community of the preindustrial South.

Urban and Industrial Slave Intrapreneurship

Slave intrapreneurship, the innovative management of business enterprises that distinguished the economic activities of slaves granted decision-making authority in managing their owner's business enterprises, had existed in all areas of American slave society since the early colonial period. In the seventeenth century, African slaves worked at management levels in various industries and urban businesses throughout the colonies. In New England, slaves captained their owner's sloops at sea. In 1679, the hired slave Mingo managed a warehouse in Boston, while in Deerfield, Massachusetts, a slave managed his owner's store. Also, throughout the colonial era, New England merchants used their slaves as itinerant traders or peddlers. In 1775, the Massachusetts slave Sharper was reported as traveling "on a trading journey to Dartmouth, and the neighboring towns."[2]

That there was a market for slave managers is revealed in newspaper advertisements of the time. Slave intrapreneurs were expected to manage businesses independent of supervision. A 1774 Charleston newspaper article about a fire that started in a soap and candle factory managed by slaves reported that "the management of such Business is generally left to Negroes by Night as well as by Day."[3] A 1785 newspaper advertisement for the sale of a slave carpenter emphasized his management abilities by noting that he was "capable of taking charge of any number of Negro carpenters."[4]Advertisements also provide various examples of how slaves used the relative freedom of their intrapreneurial positions to escape, such as the ad seeking the return of the fugitive slave "Robert . . . a carpenter by trade, who has managed rice and saw mills."[5] The extent to which slave management activities were an integral part of the slave occupational structure is revealed in the cases that came before the antebellum courts (see table 3.1).

TABLE 3.1 Nonagricultural Slave Managers

State	Date	Case and Statement
S.C.	1810	*State v. Anone:* "Polydore, Anone's slave, 'had been long employed in the store. . . . While [the white clerk] was sick, Polydore had the whole management' " (2:312).
N.C.	1827	*Wilkes v. Clark:* "The defendant had a boat commanded by one of his slaves, plying for freight on the river Roanoke, and a quantity of corn was . . . delivered to the slave" (2:52).
S.C.	1846	*Gage v. Mellwain:* "Rogers . . . carried on the blacksmith's business, by his slave, who had entire charge of the workshop. That this man entered on a slate . . . all the work done, . . . a notice was affixed to the door of the workshop . . . that all persons, who had work done there on credit, should be allowed to do so, on conditions that they consent to be charged according to the memorandum made by the negro" (2:402).
S.C.	1850	*Or. Sill v. Railroad Co.:* "Alick was a likely mulatto slave of the plaintiff, twenty-five or thirty years old, skilled in the business of attending a drug store, who had been hired for . . . 1847, to Toland and Curtis, druggist in Columbia" (2:418).
Ark.	1850	*Powell v. State:* " 'that the witness had frequently seen John [Powell's mulatto slave] both serve customers, and receive the pay therefor; that he was frequently alone at the grocery in charge . . . frequently, or generally slept in the grocery . . ., appeared . . . to do anything [he] wanted' " (5:259).
Ga.	1857	*Bailey v. Barnelly:* "his blacksmith . . . was a slave . . . that it was reasonable to rely upon the habits [keeping accounts] even of the blackman, for honesty, to reject them, is to enact that shops kept by negro smiths cannot collect their accounts—a startling proclamation to make the country" (3:59).

Source: Compiled from Helen Tunnicliff Catterall, ed., *Judicial Cases Concerning American Slavery and the Negro,* 5 vols. (Washington, D.C.: The Carnegie Institution of Washington, 1926–1937).

There were instances when slave managers were appointed to supervisory positions over whites. The most notable example of such a late-eighteenth-century slave intrapreneur was Christopher McPherson, who was born a slave in Virginia and freed in 1792. His expertise was as a clerk, accountant, and manager, although, he had only two years of school. McPherson's career as a slave intrapreneur began in 1772, when he was a clerk in his owner's Elk Horn Store in Petersburg. In three years he demonstrated great expertise in management and was made the chief operating officer of his owner's diverse business interests, "supervising his master's ironworks, mills, coal mines, and shipping concerns."[6] In these positions, McPherson supervised numerous white clerks and managers.

Slaves working as managers usually did not supervise white men, but there were enough occasions when this occurred that it seldom generated any undue complaints, even when the slave was given the responsibility of hiring and firing the whites who worked under him. Such a slave was the Mississippi riverboat captain Simon Gray, whose crews numbered from 10 to 20 men and included slaves and whites. While some slaves were hired, most were owned by the Andrew Brown Lumber Company, including Gray, whose responsibility included keeping records on the white crewmen. But he also "paid their expenses, lent them money and sometimes paid their wages."[7]

Apparently the lumber company realized that unless Gray was given this authority, white crew members would attempt to sabotage his work. But one could ask, why hire whites at all? Was it because, as Frederick Law Olmsted said, it was "a matter of form, to comply with the laws requiring the superintendence or presence of a white man among every body of slaves"?[8] Furthermore, why would whites work where they would be supervised by a slave? By the mid-nineteenth century, economic opportunities in the South were becoming increasingly limited for poor unskilled whites, particularly in the acquisition of land. These men were left with only their labor to sell, and it was only as a last resort that they would work as agricultural laborers.[9] Also, with the increased use of corporate slaves in the newly developing industries in the antebellum South, with many being used in management positions, options for landless, unskilled whites were becoming even more limited.

Consequently, poor, unskilled, landless whites were not in any position to protest when their employment opportunities were limited to accepting a job under the supervision of slaves owned by powerful and wealthy whites, whether the job was in agriculture or industry. Nonslave-owning whites might object to the use of slaves in management positions, but they seldom refused to continue to support the institution of slavery, a position that nonetheless limited their economic opportunities. In a racist society, their status as whites, guaranteed by law and social custom, took precedence over their deplorable economic status, despite the fact that the institution of slavery contributed to that condition.

With limited alternatives, then, these whites sought the few available nonagrarian jobs; because of the entrenched forces of slave-owning whites, they lacked the power to force slaves from these jobs. Corporate profits were much greater with the use of slave labor, so poor whites had few alternatives: either work under the supervision of a slave manager, such as Simon Gray, or not work at all. Gray's salary of $20 a month was comparable to that paid slave steamboat stewards, but represented only 20 percent of the salary paid white riverboat captains, who earned a minimum of $100 a month.

In addition, Gray's intrapreneurial responsibilities represented an additional savings of approximately $100 a month for the company that owned him. He was responsible for delivering lumber to riverside plantations and the towns located between New Orleans and Natchez. Besides supervising his white and black crew, Gray was also required to solicit orders for the company's mill and was given the authority to negotiate prices, extend credit, and serve as the company's bill collector. He even did the bookkeeping on occasion. It is also significant that this slave intrapreneur occasionally hired someone else to take over his duties when he was too busy. Given all this, the lumber company saved at least $2,000 a year in salaries, in addition to profiting from the money he made in sales, had white employees been hired to assume Gray's diverse responsibilities.

Slave business managers who also acted as salespeople were not unusual. In North Carolina, Nathan, a 57- year-old slave, handled most of the business affairs of a tannery from 1857 until 1862, which included "week-long business trips to sell leather at markets with a fifty-mile radius of the company." In his sales trips the slave "bargained with buyers over prices, tracked fluctuations in the leather market, knew arithmetic, kept accounts, and, after selling the leather, returned to the tannery with valuable hides and large sums of money."[10]

In addition to their salaries, slave intrapreneurship offered slave managers additional bonuses beyond the relative freedom of mobility. In some instances, slave intrapreneurial activities provided the basis for the development of slave entrepreneurial activities. Often, using the freedom that came from managing their owner's enterprises, slave intrapreneurs made money by surreptitiously selling their skills and services or their owner's goods to customers. In some instances, owners gave their approval to such business activities, as long as the slave managers continued to produce profits for the company.[11]

In Gray's case, however, his relative freedom in conducting the lumber company's business left him under constant suspicion. At times he was charged with appropriating both lumber and money for himself. Several instances of his misconduct were proven. Gray was not relieved of his responsibilities because in a free market system, there is a tendency to separate economic efficiency from other characteristics of the individual.[12] Simply put, he made money for his owner. Moreover, while still working for the company and with its approval, Gray established his own riverboat business hauling lumber, sand, and cordword to the New Orleans market for sale. With his profits, Gray hired a slave as his employee and he also purchased his son's freedom. Gray's intraprenuerial activities illustrate how slaves could use their management expertise to negotiate an improved economic status for themselves. Gray's freedom eventually came in 1863 with the fall of Vicksburg.

The slave Robert Gordon, who managed his owner's Virginia coal yard, is another example of a slave intrapreneur who became a slave entrepreneur. Gordon's skill in managing the coal yard resulted in profits much higher than his owner anticipated. As an incentive payment, the owner allowed Gordon to take the yard slack, which he processed to produce a higher grade of coal. Gordon sold his coal to local manufacturers and blacksmiths, but at prices much lower than that sold by white coal dealers. By 1846, through his entrepreneurial activities Gordon had accumulated $15,000 from sales of this high-grade coal. He purchased his freedom and moved to Cincinnati, where he became a highly successful coal dealer. Stephen Smith, the second richest antebellum black, who established a coal and lumberyard enterprise, also had worked as a slave intrapreneur, managing his owner's Pennsylvania lumberyard before earning enough to purchase his freedom.[13]

Allowing slave intrapreneurs to develop their own enterprises was an incentive used by slave owners to guarantee high performance in the management activities of their slaves. With top slave managers, the value of their expertise even outweighed the potential risk of losing their property value should they escape, which was a constant danger since unencumbered mobility was necessary for many of them to carry out their management duties.

Consequently, there had to be meaningful reciprocity, which, as in the case of Gray and Gordon, meant an opportunity to pursue entrepreneurial activities on their own; if they were not allowed to do so, they would not use their slave management skills to increase the profits of the owner.

In the case of the slave Horace King (1807–1885), who was a covered-bridge builder and contractor, his management expertise plus his superior craft skills underscore the extent to which many slave intrapreneurs acted in the capacity of chief operating officers in their owners' enterprises. While working with his owner, the bridge builder John Godwin, King placed himself in a position whereby he was "more of a junior partner in Godwin's company than a slave. Godwin developed proposals; King supervised construction." King was in effect a civil engineer as well as a bridge designer, and he even had his own slave assistant. King also supervised the building of houses in several Alabama cities for Godwin's construction company. King's expertise in bridge building resulted in his being granted freedom by the legislative actions of both Alabama and Georgia. The wealthy Alabama state senator and plantation slave owner Robert Jemison, who sponsored his manumission, had worked with King on several construction projects through contracts with Godwin. After King was freed, Jemison went into partnership on several projects with the former slave.[14]

The management know-how of slave intrapreneurs was indispensable to their owner, especially in the construction industry. Slave managers mainly supervised other slaves who worked on construction projects. Some even had the authority to negotiate contracts, while handling all responsibilities for completion of a project. Consequently, slave intrapreneurs in the antebellum construction industry represented competition for whites and free blacks. Many antebellum buildings in the South were constructed by slaves under the direction of black construction supervisors.[15] Both superior management skills and craft expertise provided slaves with considerable bargaining power to negotiate for compensation usually not afforded slaves without these skills. In most instances, skilled intrapreneurial slaves were paid cash, which they saved to purchase their freedom.

The Richmond slave Emmanuel Quivers worked as a foreman in the Tredegar Iron Works supervising other slaves. To ensure the continued high productivity and high quality of his work, Quivers and the slaves under his supervision were paid in cash. Within five years, Quivers had purchased himself, his wife, and five children for $750.21.[16] See table 3.2, which provides information on both the value of skilled slaves and the amount paid their owners who hired them out (the information was taken from cases brought before southern courts.) In the 1822 Kentucky *Wright v. Wright* case, for example, a slave blacksmith "worth at least fifteen hundred dollars" was hired out for $360 annually.[17] Had this slave hired his own time, he would have to pay his owner much more than what the owner made by hiring him out.

Yet owners were reluctant to allow their slaves to hire their own time. Instead, capitalizing on their occupational skills and especially their management expertise, owners utilized them in their enterprises as managers or hired them out for their skills or in the capacity of intrapreneurs. Usually slave managers proved so proficient that they became indispensable in the operations of their owner's business (see table 3.1). Slave intrapreneurial expertise provided opportunities for the receipt of pay, and in some cases financial arrangements were made by slave intrapreneurs to purchase their freedom, particularly by those who positioned themselves to hire their own time, which paved the way for the development of their own independent business enterprises.

TABLE 3.2   Cash Values of Slave Occupations, Slave Hires, and Hiring Own Time

State	Date	Case and Statement
Ky.	1822	*Wright v. Wright:* "negro slave . . . 'placed . . . under Benjamin Wright, to learn the trade of a Blacksmith; the slave is worth at least fifteen hundred dollars, and his annual hire, three hundred and sixty dollars' " (1:302).
Ala.	1836	Bank v. Marshall: "In 1836 he sold a negro man (a blacksmith), . . . for . . . twenty-one hundred dollars" (3:150).
Ky.	1844	*Graham v. Taylor:* "The slaves are described as three yellow men between nineteen and twenty years of age, well trained as dining room servants and scientific musicians, in which capacity they had been in the habit, for some years, of playing together on various instruments, at balls and parties, and during the watering seasons. The bill alledges [sic] and several witnesses state, that each of them were worth $1500" (1:425).
Ky.	1855	*McClain v. Esham:* "The slave . . . had been accustomed, without restriction of his owner, to hire himself out to whom and whenever he please. . . . a carpenter, and worth $1,500." The slave had disappeared. "All say that he was obedient and subordinate" (1:196).
N.C.	1855	*Grimes v. Hoyt:* "that the defendant, having received the profits of the labor of Guilford, who is a carpenter, for five years, by which he has realized $250 a year, in the whole, $1200, has permitted . . . Guildford ever since . . . to go at large . . . and only holds him in nominal servitude" (2:196).
S.C.	1856	*O'Neall v. Railroad Co.:* " 'The three slaves were all children of the same mulatto mother by white fathers. The oldest, Andrew [bricklayer and plasterer] . . ., George [a barber]; . . . James [house painter]; . . . All were musicians, young, very likely and smart, and either of them might have been sold for one thousand five hundred dollars. . . . they always lived in houses hired by themselves. The plaintiff O'Neall . . . let the three boys hire their own time, and control their own motions and contract' " (2:448).
S.C.	1856	*Campbell v. Kinlock:* " 'Joe is an excellent bread and cake baker. . . . In 1851 negroes were high; Joe, if sound, would have been worth $1500. . . . negroes employed in [a bakery] . . . are most in the bake-house; let them off on Saturday night. . . . wages of a good cake baker should be about $20 per month. . . . negroes work day and night at this business' " (2:446).
La.	1858	*Marciacq v. Steamer, Captain, and Owners:* "Jacko . . . employed on board the steamboat [as understeward] . . . at $20 per month, . . . paid to himself" (3:660).

Source: Compiled from Helen Tunnicliff Catterall, ed., *Judicial Cases Concerning American Slavery and the Negro,* 5 vols. (Washington, D.C.: The Carnegie Institution of Washington, 1926–1937).

Slave Entrepreneurship

Self-hired slaves who established businesses as sole proprietors and generated substantial profits from their enterprises were slave entrepreneurs. The slave who hired his own time negotiated the terms of his self-employment. Profits earned were used in two ways: his owner was paid for his self-hire, and what remained was retained by the self-hired slave. His money was used for living expenses, for operating and development capital, and for purchasing freedom for himself, family, and friends. In the management of their enterprises, slave entrepreneurs usually kept their own records in much the same way slave intrapreneurs kept records for the businesses they managed for their owners.

Literacy was not a requisite for conducting business in preindustrial America. Some white businessmen, particularly owners of small enterprises, could neither read nor write. Inevitably, however, there were problems for illiterate slave businessmen, who left their bookkeeping to others. The Pennsylvania slave Thomas established a successful cooper business in Lancaster in 1776. Edward Shippen, recorder of the Court of Quarter Sessions and the owner of Thomas's wife, provided him with account books and the use of his law clerk to keep them. Writing to Thomas's owner of this arrangement, Shippen said that "when people were charged for cash & c. [credit] and the Latter seemed always well pleased with the entrys. However, one day as I was walking on my pavement and Thomas was passing by in the Yard pretty near me, I heard him speaking to himself in a grumbling manner, saying that he could never bring [the clerk] to Settle accounts with him."[18]

The slave entrepreneur Free Frank (1777–1854) also could not read or write but handled his own financial affairs, since he could count. Within seven years of starting his saltpeter manufactory, he was able to purchase his wife's freedom in 1817 and then his own in 1819 for a total of $1,600. Free Frank's emergence as a slave entrepreneur provides an interesting case study of the process by which an unskilled slave, using only human capital, was able to manipulate the conditions of his slavery to his own economic advantage.[19] Free Frank was born in South Carolina and lived there until 1795, when his owner moved to the Kentucky frontier. After helping establish his owner's farm homestead, he was hired out as a laborer to new settlers. By 1810, his owner had allowed him to hire his own time with an agreement that he pay a stipulated sum annually.

Usually slaves who hired their own time were skilled in a particular craft and lived in urban areas where a market existed for their goods or services. Free Frank had no particular craft skill other than establishing pioneer farm homesteads. He did have the good fortune, however, of dwelling close to an area where saltpeter, the principal ingredient used in making gunpowder, was produced. During the War of 1812, Free Frank began his mining and manufacturing enterprise, in which he extracted the crude niter from Pulaski County's limestone caves and processed it to make saltpeter.[20]

While Free Frank's enterprise was small, profits were not. Early-nineteenth-century-frontier farm settlements were not self-sufficient, and gunpowder was essential for survival. A market existed for Free Frank's product locally and with the westward moving pioneers. To purchase both his wife's and his own freedom, Free Frank would have to have earned at least $4,000, including the $1,600 he paid for their freedom and the $2,169 that he paid his owner for allowing him to hire his own time. From 1812 until he purchased his freedom in 1819, Free Frank made at least $500 annually from sales.[21] Also, as part of the agreement to hire his own time from his owner, Free Frank had to manage his owner's farm. By 1815, Free Frank was in a position to negotiate a highly unusual written agreement with his owners, who indicated that they would "set at liberty and give freedom to a Negro slave named Frank ... if said Negro gave said Abner McWhorter the sum of five hundred dollars as the price of his freedom.... [and] to do all things concerning the premises in as if we were personally present at the doing of."[22]

The written agreement had been made because Free Frank's previous owner failed to follow through on his promise to manumit him. His new owners, the sons of the decedent, undoubtedly recognized that unless there was some reciprocity, they would lose not only their farm manager but also their slave if Free Frank was left without options for earning money to purchase his family's freedom. Even so, when Free Frank fulfilled his part of the agreement, the owners increased the price of his freedom to $800, which he paid in 1819, after which he was finally manumitted.[23]

Consequently, while a slave, Free Frank had a triple status in the slave occupational hierarchy. In the production and sale of saltpeter, he was a slave entrepreneur. In his capacity as manager of his owner's farm, he was a slave intrapreneur, and in working the owner's farm, he was a field laborer. Yet while Free Frank managed his absentee owner's farm, he also expanded his entrepreneurial activities. He established his own farm, becoming an independent slave commercial farmer, surreptitiously marketing his own produce along with that of his owners.

Invariably, slaves who wanted to become entrepreneurs had to demonstrate to their owners the monetary advantages that would accrue to the owners if the slaves were allowed full independence in pursuing their economic activities. In Virginia, the slave blacksmith Charles White, who was hired out by his owner, used his considerable earning power to negotiate for the right to hire his own time and to establish his own business. In correspondence with his owner, the literate slave wrote: "I would ... be much obliged to you if you would authorize me to open a shop in this county and carry it on ... I am satisfied that I can do well and that my profits will amount to a great deal more than any one would be willing to pay for my hire."[24]

In addition to earning a return on the venture capital to set up his shop and to pay for operating expenses, White's income first had to go to his owner for allowing him to hire his own time and then to pay for his living expenses. He saved the remaining profits to purchase his freedom. It took 15 years before he was able to buy himself from slavery. His blacksmith business was successful, but his white customers were slow to pay, if they paid at all. Legally prevented from making enforceable contracts and also working in the capacity of a slave who hired his own time, which was statutorily illegal, the blacksmith had no standing in court to force compliance of any of his contracts.[25]

Usually, the process by which a slave hired his own time began first with him being hired out by his owner, which is what happened with Free Frank and Charles White, and then moving from the position of a hired slave to that of a slave who hired his own time. Other slaves became entrepreneurs after their owner's death. This is what happened in the case of the slave Anthony Weston, nominally free, who established a millwright business and eventually became one of the wealthiest blacks, slave or free, in South Carolina, leaving an estate of more than $40,000. Weston's wealth was acquired through his activities as a slave entrepreneur and the increased value of his property, both real and chattel. Weston, although a slave, purchased 20 slaves from 1834 to 1845, but in his free wife's name.[26]

Weston's early business activities began before his owner's death. While his owner hired him out from May to November, during the other months Weston was allowed to hire his own time. After his owner's death, he established his own full-time millwright business and conducted himself as though he was free, even paying the free Negro capitation taxes. Weston was promised freedom in 1832, six years after his owner's death, but under the 1820 South Carolina manumission law, only slaves granted specific approval by both houses of the state legislature could be emancipated. Even then, only slaves with specific approval by the state legislature could remain in the state. Unlike Horace King, who had powerful sponsors to secure his freedom and a special legal dispensation to remain in the state, Weston retained his legal status as a slave rather than risk the dissolution of his profitable business had he pursued a course of action that might have resulted in him being forced to leave the state.

The slave Dick Harrington, commonly known as "Free Dick," also passed for a free black. His Alabama owner had allowed him to hire his own time, but when the owner died in about 1850, he made no provisions for Harrington's manumission. Rather, according to a witness in an 1863 court case, Harrington had continued his business activities for 12 years or so, establishing several enterprises whereby he "made his own contracts, and received the money that he earned." Harrington's various economic activities included "ditching for a considerable portion of the time, and [he] made a good deal of money in that way." He was also the proprietor of two shops. In his shoe shop, he "had hands employed under him in making shoes, which he sold to the community at large [and also another] shop ... where he sold candy, cheese, tobacco, etc." The court also noted that

Harrington was a slave owner who had "also purchased ... two negro boys." Finally, the court noted that "Dick, during all the aforesaid period, was generally ... recognized as a free man."[27]

Many of the more enterprising and successful slave entrepreneurs were craftsmen, particularly those in the construction industry. Many of these slave entrepreneurs established their own construction companies, negotiating contracts and hiring other slaves as their employees or apprentices. Slave entrepreneurs in the construction industry succeeded not only because of their expertise, but also because they underbid their white competitors. In the larger towns and cities, slaves who hired their own time were in a much better position to generate income through business activities. Their enterprises differed little from those established by free blacks or whites, for that matter.

The tobacco-merchandising activities of the North Carolina slave Lunsford Lane (b. 1803) were noted in his biography published in 1842. It provides a detailed account of his business operations, which he carried out from his home office in Raleigh. While a slave, Lane had branch offices in several cities that provided outlets for the wholesale and retail distribution of his tobacco. Also Lane mounted a carefully developed marketing and advertising campaign to promote sales of his special brand. He was also strategically circumspect in preventing his owner and other whites from knowing how much money he was making:

> I opened a regular place of business, labelled my tobacco in a conspicuous manner with the name "Edward and Lunsford Lane," and of some of the persons who sold it for me—established agencies for the sale in various parts of the State, one at Fayetteville, one at Salisbury, one at Chapel Hill, and so on—sold my articles from my place of business, and about town, also deposited them in stores on commission, and thus, after paying my mistress for my time ... in the space of some six or eight years ... I had collected the sum of one thousand dollars. During this time I found it politic to go shabbily dressed and to appear to be very poor, but to pay my mistress for my services promptly. I kept my money hid, never venturing to put out a penny, nor to let anybody but my wife know that I was making any.[28]

The practice of slaves hiring their own time was quite extensive in the urban South and provided great flexibility in the use of slave labor in urban enterprises. While self-hired slaves were indispensable to the urban economy of the South, the practice generated tremendous resentment among whites, who denounced it as a great evil, particularly for the freedom it gave slaves from the constant supervision and discipline of their owners. When the 1858 South Carolina Colored Committee, made up of leading white business-people, investigated the self-hired slave practice, it announced its findings with great dissatisfaction: "slaves are permitted to go at large, exercising all the privileges of free persons, making contracts, doing work and in every way being and conducting themselves as if they were not slaves.... whether the slave so working out on his own account, is mechanic or handicraftsman, a stevedore, a laborer, a Porter, a drayman or anything else."[29]

Self-hired slave as proprietors established enterprises in virtually every area of the South's business community (see table 3.3). The largest number of slave business proprietors were craftsmen, followed by slaves who established personal service enterprises such as barbershops and bathhouses. Transportation enterprises in livery, drayage, ferries, and cargo boats were also established. Food services, restaurants, and eating houses, too, provided an avenue for self-hired slaves to establish enterprises, including those who hawked and sold

TABLE 3.3   Slave Business Proprietors

State	Date	Case and Statement
S.C.	1803	*Maverick v. Stokes:* "several witnesses . . . deposed, that they had known the negro . . . at Baltimore, where he had kept a cake and ale house; and also in Wilmington, . . . where he pursued some other business; . . . in both places he appeared to be independent of any master, and conducted himself like a free man. . . . [owner's written certificate] 'Michael has my permission to go about his lawful business' " (2:283).
Md.	1837	*Bland v. Negro Beverly Dowling:* "until he was arrested in October, 1835, as a slave, he went at large, acted as a free man, keeping an oyster house, and boot-black shop" (4:987).
Ky.	1838	*Commonwealth v. Major:* "An old negro man slave, the property of Major, had, with his master's knowledge and permission, and in a house on his land, kept a tippling house" (1:340).
Tenn.	1845	*Jenkins v. Brown:* "John and Tom 'were barbers in the town of Columbia acting for themselves with the permission of their masters. They earned a large sum of money [$2,424.37]' " (2:528).
N.C.	1851	*State v. Nat (a slave):* "This was an indictment against . . . a slave for hiring his own time. Nat . . . was engaged in running a boat on the river, and carrying turpentine, and other articles, to [the town of] Washington and back . . . that he was not subject to the . . . control of any one . . . that he was to give his master eighty dollars a year . . . [that] he and Pritchett [white] were partners in running the boat; that they gave the owner of the boat one-half of what they made, and divided the balance between them" (2:161, 219).
Mo.	1857	*Douglass vs. Ritchies:* "The defendant allowed . . . 'his slave to set up a shoemaker's shop and deal as a free person'; and the plaintiff sold him the goods, 'the price of which he now seeks to recover against the master' " (5:200).
N.C.	1858	*Barker v. Swain:* " 'A negro, called Daniel Jones, employed the plaintiff to sell a buggy and jackass for him. The plaintiff took . . . to South Carolina, and sold then for $450. . . . Some years before . . . McMasters sold Daniel . . . with an understanding . . . that the negro was to have his own time, and the proceeds of his labor, . . . and upon the full payment, . . . to be free; . . . the negro did have his time, and the proceeds of his labor, for a considerable period, and carried on the business of making and selling buggies, . . . while the negro was carrying on his shop.' . . . Held: 'the law makes such dealing with a slave . . . criminal' " (2:223).
Fla.	1874	*Price v. Hicks:* " 'In 1863 . . . [Hicks] was a slave. . . . with the consent of his owner he formed a partnership with . . . Fitts in the business of blacksmithing at Tallahassee, which continued for about a year, . . . Fitts keeping the accounts and collecting the moneys earned. . . . The hire of Hicks from his owner in 1863 was to be paid at $600 per year out of Hicks' share of the earnings. During . . . 1863, there was purchased by the partners . . . two town lots . . . in . . . Tallahassee. . . two mules and one horse were purchased by the firm. . . . A valuable wagon was made by the firm as their property' " (3:108n, 125).

Source: Compiled from Helen Tunnicliff Catterall, ed., *Judicial Cases Concerning American Slavery and the Negro,* 5 vols. (Washington, D.C.: The Carnegie Institution of Washington, 1926–1937).

prepared foods in market stalls or as street vendors. Slaves who were most innovative in the development of their businesses, even in the most traditional enterprises, and who generated large amounts of money were more than businesspeople. They were entrepreneurs.

Plantation Slave Intrapreneurship and Entrepreneurship

Savings in salaries and management expertise were the principal reasons that led white plantation owners to use slave drivers in the capacity of overseers. In his travels through the South in the early 1850s, Frederick Law Olmsted discussed slave drivers, who assumed the management responsibilities of overseers, but without the title. For example, the job title of one slave was watchman, but his responsibilities exceeded those of a plantation overseer. While the slave's diverse duties included complete responsibility for all the plantation stores, allocation of slave rations, and the processing, grading, and packaging of cotton into bales for shipment to market, he was also the plantation engineer who, as Olmsted said, "superintended the mechanics, and made and repaired, as was necessary, all the machinery, including the steam-engine."[30] Olmsted added that the slave owned three horses and a decent house.

Also, just as plantation owners sold the slave's produce, which added to the cash circulated on the plantation, in some instances, plantation slave managers often had slaves to cultivate the land allotted them by their owner; and the slave manager "was usually permitted to sell the produce of his own garden in town for cash. Drivers also went to town to purchase supplies for the master, to do errands, and to transact business for the slaves."[31] Usually drivers were compensated in cash and other benefits, often up to $200 annually. This system was more cost effective for the planter since overseers' salaries usually averaged from 5 to 10 times that amount, from $1,000 to $2,000 a year.[32]

The obvious question then is, why hire whites at all? The law required the presence of a white among slaves, but while plantation owners hired overseers, some of them were required to take advice from the drivers. In those instances, white overseers were retained, not so much for their work, but simply because it was "a matter of form, to comply with the laws requiring the superintendence or presence of a white man among every body of slaves."[33] Moreover, the profits realized by plantation owners were invariably much greater when using drivers as plantation managers. In challenging the myth of the ubiquitous white plantation overseer, Robert Fogel and Stanley Engerman found that "Only 30 percent of plantations with one hundred or more slaves employed white overseers. On smaller plantations the proportion was even lower"[34] (see table 3.4).

Slave drivers as managers were invaluable, performing not only the duties of a white overseer but also field management activities. As Olmsted found, for many plantation owners "the advice of the drivers is commonly taken in nearly all the administration [of plantation commodity production], and frequently they are, *de facto,* the managers."[35] The Arkansas slave Reuben provides an example of a slave driver who demonstrated management expertise. He "took control of his master's farm when it was heavily in debt. By econ-

TABLE 3.4   Plantation and Commercial-Farm Slave Intrapreneurs/Managers

State	Date	Case and Statement
La.	1771	*Chataubaudau v. La Chapelle:* "The first year of his lease he had the promise of a very good crop of indigo but he trusted its manufacture to one of the negroes turned over to him in the lease as an expert in that line, who caused him to lose all his first cut" (3:425).
Va.	1817	*Garnett v. Sam and Phillis:* "Mr. Peck . . . treated Sam more like a white man than a slave; that he said, that Sam was as free as he was, and acted as his Overseer" (1:128).
Tenn.	1848	*Young v. Jones:* "The farm was conducted principally under the direction of a negro man" (2:539).
N.C.	1850	*Armstrong v. Baker:* "sell such of the property as can be best spared and with the proceeds buy a trusty negro fellow, who is skilful in the management of a farm and repairing implements of husbandry" (2:146).
Mo.	1858	*Fath v. Meyer:* "Many farmers own shops entirely under the superintendence of a negro blacksmith" (5:208).
Ky.	1864	*Maupin v. Wools:* "Her old slave Simon managed much of her business on her farm, and, so far, seemed to possess her full confidence, and might exercise some influence" (1:447).

Source: Compiled from Helen Tunnicliff Catterall, ed., *Judicial Cases Concerning American Slavery and the Negro,* 5 vols. (Washington, D.C.: The Carnegie Institution of Washington, 1926–1937).

omy and energy, Reuben in a short while amassed a fortune for the family of approximately one hundred and fifty thousand dollars." Despite his success, Reuben was subsequently demoted because "it aroused the jealousy of the whites, and his mistress had to put a white overseer in 'normal charge' of the plantation."[36]

Literacy, of course, was required for anyone acting as an overseer since that individual was responsible for keeping accounts. The plantation was a business and planters kept business records. In many cases, these records were kept by the slave driver in his capacity as manager. Yet, while the planter's reliance on the intrapreneurial expertise of plantation slaves has been noted in studies of the slave driver, his business management skills have largely been ignored in the emphasis on his physical prowess. As the field supervisor of slave labor, the driver is usually pictured as the "straw boss," the "whipping man," who stood over the slave, while the white overseer handled the management side of the plantation. In this respect, slave drivers were no different than some middle managers who abuse the authority of their positions to maintain production.

The slave driver's management responsibilities, however, did not leave him much time to be driving field slaves with a whip. Only one-third of plantation slaves worked under white overseers. Even when field slaves did, it was the driver's responsibility to collect and analyze information on field production. Consequently, in the plantation South, two-thirds of the slave population was under the direct control of a black manager, the slave driver. In addition to managing the field labor, slave drivers assumed overseer responsibilities. Scheduling production within economies of scale, that is, doing everything to maximize profits, was the driver's highest priority. So while drivers occasionally used the whip to increase production, most of the time they were using their practical and specialized knowledge to manage the plantation.[37]

In addition to plantation slave intrapreneurship, large plantations in particular gave rise to independent slave economic activities, which included the establishment of business enterprises by slaves. The most renowned example was Benjamin Montgomery, who lived on the Davis Bend plantation in Mississippi owned by Joseph Davis, the brother of Jefferson Davis, who served as president of the Confederacy. By 1860 there were 345 slaves on the plantation, considered by some a model of plantation management, efficiency, and social justice. The slaves, for example, even had their own court in which infractions of plantation rules were judged by a jury of their fellow slaves, who also determined punishment. Davis sat as judge.[38]

The intrapreneurial and entrepreneurial activities of Benjamin Montgomery are noteworthy for several reasons. After the Civil War, he was one of the South's richest plantation owners, based on his $300,000 purchase of the Davis Bend plantation.[39] Also, his son, Isaiah, founded the town of Mound Bayou, Mississippi, in 1887, which still exists.[40] While a slave, he was a surveyor, architect, and inventor. Attempts by his owner to patent a boat propeller that Benjamin invented were denied by the United States Patent Office because Montgomery was a slave.

But his greatest economic success while a plantation slave was as a businessman. In 1842 Montgomery set up a store on the Davis plantation and "maintained his own line of credit with New Orleans wholesalers." Montgomery had both slave and white customers, and records show that in one year, the female members of the Davis family ran up a bill for $2,000. Montgomery's success as an entrepreneur in running his own profitable retail business led to increased intrapreneurial responsibilities on the plantation, as Janet Sharpe Hermann reports: "Soon Ben was marketing the fruit crop from the Davis orchards and acting as Davis's agent in purchasing supplies and shipping the huge cotton crop. He sold food and fuel to the steamboat captains who carried freight for the Bend. In time he became the actual business manager for Hurricane and, in the absence of the Jefferson Davis, for Brierfield as well."[41]

Montgomery's entrepreneurial and intrapreneurial success, however, was resented by some whites. In 1856 a steamboat captain wrote a letter to the Postmaster General, objecting to delivering mail to the Davis plantation. The post office was at Montgomery's store, and Montgomery was the postmaster, although an 1810 federal law made it illegal for slaves to handle mail.[42] Presumably, slaves would read incendiary literature and incite a revolt. Montgomery, who had his own modest library, and his wife were literate. Also, until Davis paid a white tutor for his children, their parents provided lessons. Montgomery also paid Davis for his wife's labor so that she could remain home with their five children.

At the age of 10 Isaiah Montgomery was taken to the plantation main house to serve as valet and private secretary for Joseph Davis. At night Isaiah slept on the floor of his master's bedroom to be at his beck and call, and in the daytime worked at writing and filing Davis's social and business correspondence. Benjamin objected, but, as a slave, his control over his family was limited. But with his plantation slave enterprises, he had earned enough to be able to purchase his family's freedom. But he did not. As we shall see, his reasons were based on his reactions to the destructive nature of both slavery and institutional racism.

As slaves, the Montgomery family was subjected to all the horrors of slavery. At any time, the family could have been sold, separately or together. The women could have been sexually abused by whites with impunity. It is doubtful that Davis would have manumitted Montgomery, who proved to be such a valuable slave and who virtually managed the plantation not only as a CEO but also as a chief operating officer. Such a position provided Montgomery with leverage to protect his family from the worst abuses of slavery. What were his alternatives? The effects of institutional racism in America on free blacks were as devastatingly destructive to their survival as was the institution of slavery on black bondsmen.[43] It was not a question of Montgomery liking slavery: in his youth he had even run away. His decision to remain a slave stands as an indictment of the limited opportunities available for free blacks and the constraints on their freedom during this time. To ensure his own family's survival as privileged slaves, Montgomery most likely decided that it was in his best interest to contribute to the continuing success of the Davis plantation.

Yet, interestingly, the intrapreneurial and entrepreneurial economic activities of Montgomery as a slave represented one of the few American examples of slave culture in Africa, where it was not uncommon that "a slave who serves his master well succeeds to his master." Even the court system on the plantation, although instituted by Davis, partially reflected African cultural practices in which the community's preservation is put above the interest of individuals whose actions threaten its well-being. In part, the court parallels the New England Slave Election Day festival, in which slaves elected a "governor," who, with the consent of slave owners, was given authority to make judicial decisions in cases of infractions within the local slave community.

While the "privileged" material life of the Montgomery slave family was highly unusual, if not unique in the annals of American slavery, the intrapreneurial and entrepreneurial activities of Benjamin Montgomery were not. In fact, on large plantations such activities were the rule more than the exception. The Reverend Pierre Landry, a Reconstruction Louisiana state politician and Methodist churchman, while a slave, founded and operated several businesses on an Ascension Parish plantation.[44] In 1854, at the age of 13, Landry was sold to M. S. Bringier, a sugar planter, for $1,665. His first responsibilities were as chief pantryman at the Bringier mansion and superintendent of the yard slaves who worked as groundskeepers.[45]

In the late 1850s, Landry began his business activities and, according to the report in the *Donaldsville Chief,* first "formed a commercial partnership with the Chief Butler, Joseph Burbridge, and they conducted a store on the plantation, dealing in such articles as they were permitted to sell to the other slaves." In expanding their enterprises, the partners started a "[m]oss-press, broom factory and wood yard . . . established in connection with the store." The next enterprise involved the two partners in an "employment recruiting agency." In this venture, they secured plantation slaves for wage-earning jobs in an enterprise described as "plantation ditching by contract . . . the principals dealing with the overseer and subletting contracts to the plantation hands."

Organizing slave labor within a cash system was an efficient way to maintain the Bringier plantation, with 2,000 acres of improved land and 44,000 acres of unimproved land, making it one of the largest in Louisiana. M. S. Bringier owned 386 slaves, and both his real and personal property were valued at $250,000, bringing his total net worth to $500,000. The adjacent L. A. Bringier plantation held 144 slaves, and both plantations were located near that of Louisiana's largest sugar-producing planter, John Burnside, who owned 753 slaves.[46] Despite the apparent abundance of work opportunities and after a prosperous career as plantation slave businessmen, the firm operated by Landry and Burbridge was dissolved by mutual consent in 1863. As he said, Landry moved "on my own request to the engineering and carpenter shops."[47]

As a plantation slave intrapreneur and entrepreneur, Landry, as did Montgomery, demonstrated that there were several ways in which plantation slaves earned money beyond their unpaid agricultural duties. Also, the wages earned by both field slaves and skilled slaves were added to the pool of money that circulated among slaves on the very large plantations, which provided the basis for the independent slave economy that existed throughout the South. In fact, even in the raising of cotton and other cash crops, plantation owners relied on slave initiative. In addition to working their owner's fields, slaves were allocated land for their own cotton cultivation and allowed to sell it on the market. Such a situation occurred to a "slave whose master, a cotton broker, gave him the samples and who, [b]y selling these . . . realized about $800 a year."[48]

On one group of four South Carolina plantations in the 1840s and 1850s, provision-ground cotton production comprised seven percent of the cotton put on the market. The significance of independent slave cotton production, if projected for the South as a whole, "suggests that independent production by slaves played a direct role in making cotton king."[49] Increasingly, owners began buying their slaves' independently produced cotton, with payment not in cash, but in the form of "credit at local merchants." Both actions were taken to limit the commercial activities of the slaves, but such attempts to force credit buying on them were not always successful. While some slaves used up their credit in purchases, even carrying over debts collateralized by future independent production, an even larger number began curtailing their credit purchases. This was a response by the slaves to their owners' attempts to control their financial affairs as well as to their continuing efforts to stifle an expanding independent slave economy. Those efforts were resisted because "the attraction of remaining solvent encouraged most slaves to avoid indebtedness."[50] Still, slaves acquired property (see table 3.5).

Of course, the questions are, to what extent did slave enterprises, such as those developed by Montgomery and Landry, reflect the norm on large plantations? and how extensive were plantation slave intrapreneurial and entrepreneurial activities? With the trans-

TABLE 3.5   Property Acquisition and Disbursement by African-American Slave(s)

State	Date	Case and Statement
Va.	1641	Re: Graweere: " 'John Graweere . . . a negro servant unto William Evans [was permitted by his said master] to keep hogs and make the best benefit thereof to himself provided that the said Evans might have half the increase . . . and the other half reserved for his own benefit [. With money earned] said negro did for his said child purchase its freedom" (1:57, 58).
Va.	1824	*Wicks v. the Commonwealth:* "he [white blacksmith] traded with many of them [slaves] for coal, which they were allowed by their masters to burn and sell" (1:139).
La.	1836	*Rice v. Cade:* "many times, the most correct of our citizens buy a melon, or other trifling article, without the production of . . . permit [from the master] . . . According to . . . law, slaves are entitled to the produce of their labor on Sunday; even the master is bound to remunerate them, if he employes them" (3:512).
Ky.	1837	*Bryant v. Sheely:* "Bryant had bought a horse 'from the slave of Sheely, after Bryant had obtained the written permission of Sheely to trade with said slave. . . . it was proved that slave . . . was trading or dealing for himself, by the allowance of his master' " (1:338).
N.C.	1841	*Wardens v. Cope:* "The plaintiff was a farmer, and had several negroes . . . who were permitted to raise hogs for themselves. The negroes had the hogs in pens . . ., and the plaintiff said that they were the negroes' hogs . . . that the slaves . . . do against the Statute, . . . raise, keep, and mark hogs as their own . . . property" (2:95).
La.	1850	Heirs of Henderson: "Sunday is to be a day of rest . . . except the people [slaves] who may choose to work upon their own piece of ground, or to be paid for their labor by their overseer" (3:575, 605, 647).
N.C.	1850	*Francis v. Welch:* "Love owned a slave, and permitted him to purchase a horse and use it as his own. . . . the said slave sold the horse" (2:146).
Ky.	1851	*King v. Shanks:* "the slave Berry had . . . made some trade and acquired some little money and property. . . . it is highly probable that he had done little services for a compensation to himself, as is frequently the case with slaves" (1:402).
Ala.	1851	*Hurt v. State:* "Hurt convicted . . . for selling a pair of shoes to a slave. . . . Judgment affirmed. . . . Most owners, allow to their slaves reasonable time to make provision for the comfort of themselves and families, and, to that end, permit them to deal with honest white persons, so far as to sell their commodities, or to expend their money in the purchase of necessaries" (3:178).
Tex.	1860	*Sanders v. Devereux:* "in 1857, certain negro slaves, owned . . . by the plaintiff, . . . made crops of cotton, with her consent, on her lands, and with . . . her further consent, that the proceeds . . . should inure to the benefit of said slaves respectively, according to the amount . . . each . . . might produce . . . distinct from the crop made for the plaintiff." Slaves delivered 20,158 pounds of cotton (at $2.00 per hundred pounds) for $403.16 to defendant, who refused to pay. Judgment for defendant on the following grounds: "The right of private property belongs, in this country, exclusively to freemen" (5:309).

Source: Compiled from Helen Tunnicliff Catterall, ed., *Judicial Cases Concerning American Slavery and the Negro,* 5 vols. (Washington, D.C.: The Carnegie Institution of Washington, 1926–1937).

Appalachian expansion of the plantation system to the Lower South, there was a substantial increase in the slave population and a greater concentration of slave ownership. By 1860, of 1,200,000 white households, only 388,000 owned slaves, with only 12 percent owning 20 or more slaves, including 10,000 who owned from 50 to 99 slaves and 3,000 who owned 100 slaves or more.

Mississippi ranked second, after Alabama, in the number of slave owners who held more than 100 slaves. South Carolina ranked first in the number of slave owners who held 300 or more slaves, and Louisiana was second. Also, by 1860, some 160,500 slaves, almost half of that state's slave population, lived in plantation holdings of 50 or more slaves. The largest Louisiana slaveholder owned 940 slaves. In Mississippi the largest slaveholder, who owned five plantations, held some 900 slaves. One planter, with three plantations in Louisiana and three in Mississippi, owned a total of 1,058 slaves. Benjamin Montgomery's owner ranked nineteenth among the leading Mississippi slaveholders.[51] On the combined Bringier plantations, where Landry lived, their total holdings of 520 slaves would rank their owners sixth among Louisiana's largest slaveholders.

What do these figures mean within the context of independent slave economic activity? With 10,000 slaveholders owning from 59 to 99 slaves, an average holding of 75 slaves, about 750,000 slaves lived on plantation units of this size. With an additional 300,000 slaves living on units of 100 slaves or more, by 1860 25 percent of the African-American slave population, a minimum of 1,050,000 slaves, lived on plantation units (although not all were comparable to the Montgomery and Landry plantations). Moreover, on large plantations, only 58 percent of the slaves were field laborers, while some 28 percent were in managerial positions.

Considering the increasing costs of maintaining slave plantations, including rising slave prices, particularly in the newly developing states in the lower South, plantation owners by 1860 were coming more and more to rely on the expertise of slaves such as Montgomery and Landry, a situation that would increase the possibilities of plantation slaves developing intrapreneurial and entrepreneurial activities. Paradoxically, not until the post-Civil Rights era, a century after slavery's end, would African-Americans be employed again as managers in white corporate America.

Slave Women's Business Activities

African-American slave women were at a competitive disadvantage in establishing independent economic activities. Yet, the ethos of a precolonial African commercial culture survived the Atlantic passage, providing the basis for the initiation of independent economic activities by African-American slave women. This ethos resulted in numerous independent economic activities and was passed from one generation of slave women to the next. And each generation was propelled by the desire to earn money to purchase their children's freedom. This desire, then, became the driving force that maintained an African commercial cultural ethos, which has been kept alive by slaves and their descendants from the seventeenth century to the present time in seeking economic opportunities.

From the beginning of the colonial period, the agricultural and domestic skills of African women were exploited for profit by slaveholders. In addition to agricultural skills in farming and food production, slave women were also skilled in household management and food preparation. A colonial South Carolina newspaper advertisement indicates the household skills of a slave woman put up for sale; it was said that she could "milk very well, wash and iron, dress Victuals and do anything that is necessary to be done in the House."[52] African women were also proficient as spinners, carders, weavers, dyers, seamstresses, and quilt makers. They also possessed handicraft skills in basketry and in making brooms, mats, mattresses, and pottery. In health care they were proficient in midwifery and pharmacopoeia.[53]

The most prominent economic activity of slave women, however, was their retail and vending enterprises, which might seem insignificant as profit-making ventures, but which often proved personally and, in a few instances, financially rewarding. The economic success of Aletha Turner, an early-nineteenth-century slave woman in Washington, D.C., enabled her to purchase her own freedom for $1,400, in addition to the money she paid for 22 other slaves over a 25-year period.[54] Turner was a produce vendor who sold fresh vegetables from her stall in the nation's capital. She raised them in her own small garden, and her customers included the most distinguished politicians of that era, including President Thomas Jefferson, who also was a slaveholder. Turner was heir to a tradition of truck farming that began with the economic activities of African plantation slave women first expressed in provision-ground activities.

Food production and marketing provided the initial basis for the development of the independent economic activities of black women in America as market higglers, hawkers, and vendors. As this area of enterprise expanded, some slave women, both urban and rural, acted as commodities brokers of farm produce. They purchased fruits, vegetables, and poultry in rural areas and transported them to urban markets, where they sold them at wholesale prices to slave women vendors.[55] Selling produce enabled African-American slave women not only to participate in the economy but also to pass their valuable market skills from one generation to the next. As a result of their skill, slave women came to dominate the retail produce-distribution sector of the South's economy.

The accounts of travelers are remarkably insightful in detailing the market activities of these women. Anne Royall in her nineteenth-century commentaries said that in South Carolina "[t]he market places are filled with Negro women selling fruits and vegetables." And, of the market women in New Orleans, she noted: "They have control of the markets in New Orleans. . . . These women speak French so fast, it appears to be nonsense, many speak excellent English. These women bring their products to the market very neatly."[56] The occupational participation of urban slave women, then, changed little in the more than two centuries of slavery in America's preindustrial age.

Still, even while participating in those gender-specific economic activities, not all slave women were able to profit from them. The dressmaking skills of the St. Louis slave Elizabeth Keckley (1818–1907) were used to support her owner and his family, while she had to borrow money to pay him for her freedom.[57] Slave dressmakers, however, were paid well for their services. Sally, an Alabama slave dressmaker who hired her own time and rented property to establish a shop, paid $1,200 for herself and her children. Yet Sally found herself in court, unable to prove that she had earned the money for their freedom. Her case records, however, reveal that the court accepted contradictory evidence: "she paid wages for her time, which she had done for several years, previously . . . [and that] Sarah was industrious and a good . . . dressmaker, but there was no evidence that she ever received money for such services." The court made no attempt to reconcile the contradiction in its decision against Sally.[58]

On plantations, where enterprising slave women with dressmaking skills were able to carve out independent economic activities, their initiative was inevitably capitalized on for profit by their owners. Frederick Law Olmsted noted the strategies used by one plantation slave woman, who escaped field work by feigning illness as a subterfuge while she ran her own dressmaking business in the slave community: "I was on a plantation where a woman had been excused from any sort of labour for more than two years, on the supposition that she was dying of phthisis." His accounts of her enterprise not only reveal the extent to which plantation slaves operated in a cash system, but also show their sophisticated medical knowledge:

At last the overseer discovered that she was employed as a milliner and dressmaker by all the other coloured ladies of the vicinity; and upon taking her to the house, it was found that she had acquired a remarkable skill in these vocations. She was hired out the next year to a fashionable dressmaker in town, at handsome wages; and as, after that she did not again 'raise blood,' it was supposed that when she had done so before it had been by artificial means. Such tricks every army and navy surgeon is familiar with."[59]

The enterprising skills of slave women, which went beyond supervising plantation slave nurseries, hospitals, and cloth-making "departments" and serving as "driveresses," were also exploited by plantation owners in various ways. There were instances when slave women acted as intrapreneurs, managing plantation stores, where slaves were allowed to purchase items by cash or on credit up to the value of the goods they produced and sold to the planter, and/or up to the value of extra labor they performed for the owners. Through the plantation store, the money paid slaves by their owners for extra duties was returned to the owner. The significance of the plantation store was that it was managed by a slave woman and it was "[u]sually well-supplied with articles that they [slaves] most want, which was purchased in large quantities, and sold to them at wholesale prices, thus giving them a great advantage in dealing with him [the owner] rather than with the grog shops. . . . A woman has charge of the store, and when there is anything called for that she cannot supply, it is usually ordered, by the next conveyance, of his factors in towns."[60]

African-American slave women also established their own enterprises as independent businesswomen, usually in gender-specific occupations. Their astute business management expertise accounted for the success of their enterprises. Most slave women who established urban enterprises rented property paid for from their earnings as slaves who hired their own time. The North Carolina slave Sally hired her time from her owner and set up a small-town cookshop in a property she had rented. Her profits were used not only to pay her owner, but also to expand her restaurant and to provide for her children while saving to purchase their freedom, which she failed to accomplish because she was sold.[61] Another slave woman named Sally (1790–1849), who was allowed to hire out her own time as a cleaning woman, used her savings to rent a two-story house in the Nashville business district, where she established a laundry and cleaning business and also manufactured soap for sale.[62]

Still, access to property for establishing a shop was not always a requisite for some of the enterprises initiated by slave women. During the California gold rush, slaves brought to that state by their owners, after performing their duties for their owners, used their free time to establish independent economic activities. One slave, Mrs. William Pollock, baked doughnuts at night, which she sold during the day to miners, while her slave husband washed clothes at night to earn money for their freedom.[63] In other instances when slaves lived together as man and wife, they pursued cooperative and independent economic activities, such as the Virginia slave couple who were together for seven or eight years before he escaped to Canada. According to Virginia court records, "he was a slave there; he rented a house in Richmond; he was a painter. The greater portion of his earnings went to his master. His wife earned money by washing, and paid a portion to her mistress."[64]

In the urban South, slave households headed by females were in the majority. Usually, these females used their homes as the base for independent economic activities, but many of their enterprises were pursued outside of their homes. Using their expertise in the health services, slave women established health care enterprises that provided services in their patient's homes. One slave, Jane Minor, established a health service enterprise in Petersburg, Virginia, before she was manumitted in 1825.[65] Ellen "Biddy" Mason, taken as a slave to California in 1849, also hired her own time as a nurse and midwife. From her earnings, Mason purchased her freedom.[66] Consequently, slave women who hired or "stole" their own time could establish enterprises and provide goods or personal services without access to property, working as slave nurses, midwives, and "herb doctors."

The mother of the turn-of-the-century journalist John E. Bruce was also a slave who hired her own time and who established a food-vending business. Initially, she hired herself to work as a tavern cook but left, an option available to self-hired slaves and even some hired slaves. Then, using her skills as a cook, she established her first enterprise at the Marine Corps garrison at Fort Washington, Maryland, which proved extremely profitable because she soon expanded her business. According to her son, "[s]he carried on a little business for herself by selling pies, hot coffee etc. to the marines and exchanging the same for their rations. Her business increased and it became necessary that she should buy a horse and wagon to convey her goods to the fort." In addition to securing rations from the marines, they also gave her presents, as Bruce notes, "in the shape of old clothes, shoes, caps, stockings, etc."[67]

While continuing her catering enterprise, this slave businesswoman then went into merchandising, with a two-fold increase in profits; she ran "a second hand clothing store on a small scale and made quite a respectable living." Bruce indicates, however, that there was opposition from whites because of the success of her enterprises: "the poor whites surrounding us became jealous in a body." They failed in their attempts to force the commander of the fort to order the marines to stop their trade with his mother. Considering the pervasiveness of slave business enterprises, the objections of the whites did not center on the fact that she pursued independent economic activities as a slave who hired her own time. Rather, their objections were in response to the profits she made, a situation that was common when slave enterprises proved successful.

Based on the 1848 Charleston census, 89 out of 3,913 urban slave women, some 2.3 percent, hired their own time and pursued gender-specific occupations as independent business enterprises in their own households. Given that the census information was based on individual dwellings, it is most likely that the slave women listed with specific occupations headed households separate from their owners. Also, since many individual dwellings in preindustrial Charleston combined both the residence and place of business of the head of household, there is little doubt that the urban slave women listed also had established businesses in their homes as well.

Of the 3,913 urban slave women who indicated their occupations, 3,384 women were listed as domestic servants, 378 as unskilled laborers, 45 as superannuated, and 8 as apprentices. Yet, interestingly, only 2 slave women are listed in health services, 12 in food preparation, 18 in food marketing, 24 in sewing, and 33 as laundresses. Certainly, to feed and wash for a population of almost 40,000, there had to be more than 41 market women, including the 5 free black women and the 18 white women listed in this occupational category, which also would be the case for laundresses. Only 45 free black and no white women were listed in this category.[68] It is possible, then, that some slave women counted in the households of their owners and classified in the census as either domestic servants or unskilled laborers, could also have been involved in independent economic activities.

While the data do not reflect the merchandising enterprises or boardinghouses established by urban slave women who hired their own time, its significance is that it underscores gender-specific occupations that slave women transformed into intrapreneurial and entrepreneurial enterprises, such as food shops and laundries, catering, dressmaking, and health care establishments.

Slave women who established business enterprises were those who hired their own time, an activity that was defined under slave laws as a crime against the state. Table 3.6 lists the independent economic activities of slave businesswomen and their owners brought to court for violations of the laws against slaves hiring their own time. In addition, to suppress some of the independent enterprises established by urban slave women, municipal governments passed permit and badge laws.

In the development of their independent economic activities, enterprising slave women had demonstrated that even the most mundane gender-specific activities could prove profitable. Still, as evidenced by the dressmaker Sally, not all slave women who initiated such activities were successful in securing freedom for themselves or their family.

TABLE 3.6   Economic Activities of Slave Women

State	Date	Case and Statement
La.	1777	*Re: Negroes Cezario et al.:* " 'Marguerita . . . answers: that she is . . . a creole and belongs to Mr. Montreuil and that she was hired to herself, giving her master 4 pesos a month as wages, and that she is twenty-three years of age. . . . She pays three pesos a month rent for her room. . . . For food she eats as she can and for clothes she works out by the day' " (3:437).
S.C.	1792	*The Guardian of Sally (a negro) v. Beaty:* "a negro wench slave, the property of the defendant, by working out in town, with permission of her master, had, by her industry, acquired a considerable sum of money, over and above what she had stipulated to pay for her monthly wages, to her master; and having an affection for a negro girl, Sally, she purchased her with this money, which she had been for years accumulating, and gave her her freedom" (2:267n, 275).
Ky.	1831	*Commonwealth v. Gilbert:* "Elizabeth Gilbert was indicted for permitting her female slave 'to go at large, and hire herself out' . . . from the 1st day of June, 1822 to the 8th day of September, 1829" (1:319).
N.C.	1844	*State v. Clariss* (a negro slave): "The defendant . . . unlawfully did hire her own time" (2:109).
Ky.	1847	*Parker v. Commonwealth:* "That mistress of the slave Clarissa was indicted for permitting her slave to go at large and hire herself out. . . . found guilty" (1:380).
Md.	1850	*Anderson v. Garrett:* "Rebecca [slave] came to Baltimore about eighteen years ago, where she has continually resided with her children till within a short period prior to the filing of this petition. That during all this time she was reputed a free woman, and always acted as such, making contracts, renting houses, hiring herself out and receiving her own wages, hiring out her children and receiving pay for their services, and raising and supporting her family by her own industry" (4:112).
La.	1860	*Levy v. Wise et al.:* "The appellants are the sureties of . . . Mary Wise, to whom certain premises ["a house in . . . New Orleans"] were leased by the plaintiff. They urged . . . that [Mary Wise] . . . was a slave . . . and that the contract . . . is null" (3:676).
N.C.	1860	*Lea v. Brown:* " 'his servant, Milly, had . . . accumulated [some money] by selling, for years, with his permission, surplus articles . . . such as fowls, butter, ice-cream, etc., and by manufacturing and selling . . . bed-clothing. . . . Milly stated that she had already several hundred dollars" (2:204, 240, 240n).
N.C.	1864	*State v. Brown:* "That the defendant was the owner of the slave, 65 or 70 years old: that she kept a boarding house for soldiers and other white persons, and was frequently seen in the market and in the stores, buying supplies" (2:252).

Source: Compiled from Helen Tunnicliff Catterall, ed., *Judicial Cases Concerning American Slavery and the Negro*, 5 vols. (Washington, D.C.: The Carnegie Institution of Washington, 1926–1937).

State Laws to Suppress Slave Economic Initiative

Laws suppressing black economic initiative were in force in America from the seventeenth century until the Civil War. An example was the Maryland law under which the 1665 *Calvert v. Wynne et al.* case was decided; the law stipulated that "noe person . . . shall trade, barter, commerce, or game [with slaves without the owner's permission]."[69] Variations of this law were enacted throughout the colonies and remained in force during the entire period of slavery. In this section, the slave laws of South Carolina, North Carolina, and Georgia are presented as examples of legislative attempts by the slave states to suppress black economic initiative.[70] Also, a few city ordinances are given to show the implementation of state laws in urban areas.

These laws provide examples of statutory provisions in the South that prohibited independent slave economic activities. Those laws, concomitant with municipal ordinances regulating slave economic activities, are significant for the insight they provide about the South in its attempts to suppress independent black economic initiative. Of particular interest is the rationale for the statutory enactment of those laws, exemplified by the preface to South Carolina's 1712 slave code. It acknowledged that the colony's economic survival depended wholly on Africans. At the same time, blacks were denounced as wild and barbarous, thus requiring the enactment of special laws to suppress their "inhumanity" to whites:

> WHEREAS, the plantations and estates of this Province cannot be well and sufficiently managed and brought into use, without the labor and service of negroes and other slaves; and for as much as the said negroes and slaves brought unto the people of this Province for that purpose, are of barbarous, wild, savage natures, and such as renders them wholly unqualified to be governed by the laws, customs, and practices of this Province. . . . other constitutions, laws and orders, should in this Province be made and enacted, for the good regulating and ordering of them, as may restrain the disorders, rapines and inhumanity, to which they are naturally prone and inclined. . . .[71]

Yet, the statutes in the South Carolina slave code reveal the extent to which African slaves acted rationally in their own interest, economic and otherwise, as indicated by a 1722 law, which furthers the two purposes of the slave code: suppressing slave resistance and slave economic activity. The law noted that "great inconveniences do arise from negroes and other slaves keeping and breeding of horses, whereby they convey intelligences from one part of the country to another, and carry on their secret plots and contrivances for insurrections and rebellions." To suppress this activity, the statute provided all whites with the authority to seize slave property: "it shall be lawful for any person to seize hogs kept by slaves, and all boats and canoes belonging to any slaves," and "any horse or horses, or any neat cattle."[72] The law was made more specific in 1740; and, although it was a response to the 1739 Stono Rebellion, it revealed the extent to which slaves had usurped the right to claim property. Moreover, the law underscores not only that the slaves' rights of possession were acknowledged by their owners, but also that slaves had escalated their trading activities:

> And whereas, several owners of slaves have permitted them to keep canoes, and to breed and raise horses, neat cattle and hogs, and to traffic and barter in several parts of this

Province, for the particular and peculiar benefit of such slaves . . . it shall and may be lawful for any person or persons whatsoever, to seize and take away from any slave, all such goods, commodities, boats, perriaugers, canoes, horses, mares, neat cattle, sheep or hogs [and deliver them to the justice of peace where they will be sold at public auction].[73]

This law was difficult to enforce. All the owner had to do was to claim that he, not the slave, was the rightful owner of the property. And, in most instances, it was to the owner's benefit to do so. As indicated previously, slaves quickly established that, without some economic benefits for themselves, their labor would be given only reluctantly, which would prove to be economically detrimental to the slave owner. By the nineteenth century, as the court cases in table 3.5 show, the right of slave ownership of property had gained the recognition of the law.

Early on, however, seizing slave property was one way in which the state hoped to suppress slave economic initiative: the purpose being that slaves, once they realized that their property could be confiscated, would lose interest in acquiring anything of value. Even the clothes worn by slaves, if they were of any value, could be stripped off their backs by anyone. Again, the law is useful in revealing how the economic success of slaves affected their ability to acquire clothes of value. Yet, as reports throughout the South reveal, by the nineteenth century, slaves had established the right to wear clothes of whatever value they choose. In 1735, however, this was not the case, as indicated in the South Carolina statute that stipulated:

And whereas, many of the slaves in this Province wear clothes much above the condition of slaves. . . . Be it enacted . . . That no owner or proprietor of any negro slave or other slave whatsoever (except livery men or boys), shall permit or suffer such negro or other slave to have or wear any sort of apparel whatsoever, finer, other, or of greater value, than negro cloth, duffelds, coarse kearsies . . . [etc], and all and every constable and other persons are hereby authorized, impowered and required . . . to seize and take away the same to his and their own use, benefit and behoof. . . .[74]

The economic independence of slaves in hiring their own time and providing for their own livelihood and maintenance through renting property for living or for carrying out a business is also revealed in the early legislation. The same 1735 South Carolina act required "[t]hat if any owner or master of any negro or other slave shall, after the passing of this ACT suffer any negro or other slave to keep, either in their own name, or in the name or under the protection of the said owners or masters, any house or houses of entertainment or trade, shall forfeit the sum of fifty pounds, current money." The act was made more specific in 1740 with the provision that "no slave or slaves shall be permitted to rent or hire any house, room, store or plantations, on his or her own account."[75]

The capacity of slaves to acquire literacy skills that put them in an even greater position to compete successfully with whites is also revealed in another 1740 South Carolina law, which made it illegal for slaves to be taught to read or write. The law not only acknowledged that slaves were reading and writing, but also that they were being employed in capacities that required them to write: "And, whereas, the having of slaves taught to write, or suffering them to be employed in writing, may be attended with great inconvenience. . . . That all and every person and persons whatsoever, who shall hereafter teach, or cause any slave, or slaves to be taught, to write, or shall use or employ any slave as a scribe in any manner of writing whatsoever . . . shall, for every such offence, forfeit the sum of one hundred pounds current money."[76]

Slave laws also reflected the extent to which southern whites feared being poisoned by their slaves. The two statutes in force to suppress such activity, however, acknowledge that slaves worked as medical assistants and that they were recognized as doctors, apparently because of their successful healing powers. As one statute proscribed, "It shall not be lawful for any physician, apothecary or druggist, at anytime hereafter, to employ any slave or slaves in the shops, or places where they keep their medicines or drugs, under pain of forfeiting the sum of twenty pounds." The other statute applied only to the slave and it stipulated that "no negroes or other slaves (commonly called doctors) shall hereafter be suffered or permitted to administer any medicine, or pretended medicine." The punishment stipulated for slave "doctors" was "corporal punishment, not exceeding fifty stripes."[77]

North Carolina laws restricting slave independent economic activities were much the same in that they made it illegal for slaves to engage in the following enterprises: trade with each other for certain articles, including liquor; hire their own time; act as pilot on any waterway; and raise any horses, cattle, hogs, or sheep. Another law stated that "all such belonging to any slave or in any slave's mark, shall be seized and sold by the country wardens."

Laws were also in force to suppress slaves' attempts at self-improvement. It was illegal for slaves to preach in public or to teach other slaves to read, and for free people to teach slaves to read or write, "the use of figures excepted." Also, it was illegal to give or sell books or pamphlets to slaves.[78] Such laws suppressing literacy were as concerned with slaves using this ability to forge tickets and permits for themselves to trade, as they were for slaves writing passes that would enable them to escape.

Moreover, the following articles enumerated in the North Carolina statutes that could not be sold by slaves reveal the extent to which slave merchandising was an important part of commodity distribution in the South: "cotton, tobacco, wheat, rice, oats, corn, rye, pork, bacon, beef, leather, raw hides, iron castings, farming utensils, nails, meal, flour, spirituous liquors or wine, peas, salt fish, flax, flaxseed, hogs, cattle, sheep, wool, lumber, staves, tar, pitch, turpentine, fodder, shingles, hoops, white oak heading, potatoes, mutton, cotton or woolen cloth, yarn, wearing apparel, or gold or silver bullion."

Georgia state statutes also prohibited the purchase or sale of most of these articles. Also, slaves in Georgia had to have a ticket from their owners or hirers authorizing the sale of such items, including the amount for which the merchandise was to be sold. At the same time, the law conceded the difficulty of suppressing independent slave economic activity, but still attempted to control it by requiring that transactions involving the sale or purchase of cotton, tobacco, wheat, rye, oats, corn, rice, or poultry, either sold or purchased by slaves, could not be more than one dollar. This 1816 statute, however, also allowed slaves to sell without restrictions certain items that they manufactured, including "brooms, baskets, foot and bed-mats, shuck collars, and such other thing or things, article or articles, as are known to be manufactured or vended by slaves for their own use only."[79]

The Georgia laws also acknowledged slave ownership of property by noting that "slaves shall not own boats or livestock." Again, seizure and sale of the property was the state's attempt to discourage slave economic initiative, as was the law that made it illegal to teach or employ others to teach slaves to read or write, "or employ any slave as a scribe" or as a typesetter. Also, it was illegal to sell alcohol to slaves, to give slaves information on poisons, or for slaves to hire their own time, as stipulated in the law that denounced slave owners who "permit such slave for a consideration or otherwise to have, hold, and enjoy the privilege of laboring, or otherwise transacting business for, him, her, or themselves, except on their own premises."[80]

Interestingly, an 1837 Georgia state statute stipulated that slaves shall not hire their time or trade for themselves, but acknowledged at the same time that slaves had a monopoly on the merchandising of poultry and eggs: "Nothing herein contained shall prevent any slave or slaves, from selling poultry at any time without a ticket, in the counties of Liberty, McIntosh, Camden, Glynn, and Wayne." The 1837 statute made it illegal to rent houses, rooms, stores, or plantations to slaves.[81] The court made very clear the reasons for this, as seen in a 1772 Georgia case in which the court stated "[t]hat Slaves are permitted to Rent houses in the lands and Invirons . . . of Savannah in said houses meetings of Slaves are very frequent, Spirits and other liquors are sold, and Stolen goods often Concealed."[82]

The criminal justice system in the southern states did little to deter slaves' business initiative or their independent economic activities at any level, whether plantation, urban, industrial, or what took place in the underground economy. Most slave economic activities operated in the open. Unless charges were filed against them, slaves escaped prosecution. If charged and found guilty, owners were subject to fines. Free people, white and black, found guilty of purchasing stolen merchandise from slaves were also fined and sometimes sentenced to jail. There were instances when restitution was made by the slaves to avoid prosecution, such as in the 1852 Alabama *Patton v. Rambo* case. In this instance, a slave, who hired his own time and found employment in a general store, was charged with theft of a considerable amount of merchandise. Ironically, despite his confession of guilt, the slave was not prosecuted, since he produced cash equivalent to the value of goods he admitted stealing. According to the records,

> the slave was allowed by his master . . . to hire his own time, make contracts, etc., and to keep what he made, paying his master hire. . . . [He] was employed by the defendants . . . in their store . . . detected in purloining goods . . . [the] constable examined his house, and found . . . goods belonging to the defendants, and five hundred and eight dollars. . . . the slave had three or four hundred dollars before he entered the defendants' service. . . . the slave confessed . . . that he . . . had frequently stolen from them, and had sent some of their goods to Limestone county . . . he was satisfied he had taken enough to amount to two hundred and fifty dollars, would willingly pay it. . . . The defendants . . . accepted . . . the slave kept the goods.[83]

The case is important beyond that of a slave on record admitting to theft and the leniency accorded him by the victims, the white store owners. First, it demonstrates the existence of a network that slaves established in fencing the stolen merchandise. Second, while the purchasers of the merchandise are never explicitly identified, if they were slaves, then such a transaction would underscore the extent to which slaves operated in a cash system, participated in the economy as consumers, and contributed to the viability of the economy. Third, if the goods were sold to whites, it suggests how inextricably the distribution of goods in the South, in other words, consumer demand and supply, was linked to the combined input of blacks and whites. Moreover, that Rambo's employers were willing to accept a cash payment for the stolen goods, and, indeed, if the goods were sold to slaves, suggest the extent to which the profits of white shopkeepers depended on sales by and to slaves. Finally, the case provides an example of a slave who hired himself out as an employee, but who became an entrepreneur.

Any economic activity pursued by slaves without the permission of their owners or sanctioned by the state was considered illegal and therefore defined as a crime by and against the state. Even slave marketing and trading activities and the business activities undertaken by slaves who hired their own time, including those who established craft and personal services enterprises that operated openly and with the permission of their owners, were considered illegal. Particularly, the extent to which the state attempted to either control or suppress slave marketing and trading practices illuminates the pervasiveness and extensiveness of the independent economic activities developed by African-American slaves. The state defined the activities of slave hawkers, vendors, and peddlers who operated without their owner's permission as crimes in much the same way as it defined as crimes certain economic activities carried out surreptitiously by slaves, for example, the fencing of ill-gotten goods.

The extent of state intervention in the independent economic activities of slaves is reflected, then, not only in the legislation that attempted to control every avenue of business activity developed by slaves to enhance their economic benefit, but also in the myriad court cases in which both slaves and whites were convicted. As table 3.7 shows, whites who purchased illegal goods from slaves were threatened with a jail sentence and fined or sometimes imprisoned. The more successful slave craftsmen, who paid their owners substantial sums for the privilege of being allowed to hire their own time, were at times hauled into court, reflecting concessions made by the state to white craftsmen who competed with them. Yet very seldom were the most successful slaves who initiated economic activities that provided personal services to wealthy and powerful whites convicted; and, not surprisingly, the owners of these slaves and their powerful clients likewise avoided prosecution.

The people usually convicted, both whites and blacks, were, not surprisingly, involved in petty crimes, which included the sales of insignificant items by slaves to poor, powerless whites. Consequently, while laws stipulated punishment for whites who aided and abetted

TABLE 3.7 Slave Underground Economic Activities and White Convictions for Illegal Purchase of Goods from Slaves

State	Date	Case and Statement
Md.	1665	*Calvert v. Wynne et al.:* "noe person . . . shall trade, barter, commerce, or game [with slave]. . . . [Defendant and wife] . . . with Frank Indian and dyvers others of the slaves of Philip Calvert. . . . bartered trade commerced for Ten poultry or Henns" (4:20).
Ga.	1772	*Re: Slaves:* "That Slaves are permitted to Rent houses in the lands and Invirons . . . of Savannah in said houses meetings of Slaves are very frequent, Spirits and other liquors are sold, and Stolen goods often Concealed" (3:6).
S.C.	1802	*State v. May:* "convicted . . . for buying corn from a slave. . . . it appeared that the defendant kept a small retail store in the neighbourhood, and the prosecutor's negro had been seen carrying corn to this store, and delivering it to a clerk, who had care of the store" (2:67, 281).
S.C.	1810	*State v. Thornton:* "The indictment charged the defendant with trading with a negro slave . . . for an iron band . . . of a mill shaft, which had been stolen from the mills of M'Ra and Cantey" (2:174, 293).
D.C.	1816	*U.S. v. Pickering:* "an indictment for dealing with a slave without the consent of his master" (4:169).
S.C.	1810	*State v. Anone:* "Polydore, Anone's slave, 'had been long employed in the store. . . . While the white clerk was sick, Polydore had the whole management.' " Anone wanted white clerk " 'to buy all the corn he could, and if the negroes brought 10,000 bushels to buy it.' " White clerk objected to slaves selling corn without a "ticket" of permission and claimed " 'that the negroes brought so much corn, that they must have stolen it.' " Judge charged that " 'Anone had instructed Polydore to trade with negroes without tickets' " (2:312).

(continued)

TABLE 3.7 Continued

State	Date	Case and Statement
S.C.	1824	*Slack v. Littlefield:* " 'The constable . . . went to the plaintiff's house, and found there about sixty pounds of picked cotton, which defendant claimed as his own.' " Twenty-four pounds of cotton were purchased from a slave, " 'but the permit [for sale] was not produced.' " (2:328).
S.C.	1830	*State v. Taylor:* "The defendants had been convicted of unlawful trading with a slave . . . [and] for receiving goods stolen by a slave" (2:532).
N.C.	1842	*State v. Tomlinson:* "The defendant was indicted and tried for trading with a slave" (2:99).
N.C.	1845	*State v. Cozen:* " 'The indictment charges, that he [a free man of color], . . . did buy of . . . and receive from a certain negro slave . . . one peck of corn,' " (2:114).
Tenn.	1847	*State v. Weaks:* "The defendant was indicted . . . for permitting [in 1844] a slave, his property, to trade in spirituous liquors as if a free person of color" (2:532).
Tenn.	1849	*Morrow v. State:* " 'The indictment . . . charges that the defendant unlawfully did permit . . . Jim, . . . to trade in spirituous liquours, horses, cows, hogs, provisions, and other property, as if a free person of color, . . . to hire his own time' " (2:538n, 541).
Ala.	1851	*Hurt v. State:* "Mr. Hurt was convicted . . . for selling a pair of shoes to a slave. . . . Judgment affirmed. . . . In requiring the articles to be specifically stated, . . . the Legislature designed to suppress . . . a general evil in some parts of the country, growing out of a clandestine traffic between slaves and a particular class of white persons. . . . if a negro may buy all sorts of dry goods . . . he might soon . . . become a pedlar among other negroes and the class of white men, whose conduct led to the passage of the act" (3:178).
Miss.	1852	*State v. Barroum:* "unlawfully did buy . . . from . . . slave named Elleck . . . seventy-five pounds of cotton" (3:330).
N.C.	1853	*State v. Abernathy:* "The defendant was indicted . . . for the offense of buying and receiving from a slave ten pounds of iron" (2:176).
Tex.	1854	*State v. Wupperman:* "indicted under the second Section of the Act . . . which prohibits the buying of any produce of a slave 'without the written consent of his . . . master . . . or overseer' " (5:290).
Ga.	1855	*Ricks v. State:* " 'indictment for buying cotton from a slave, without permission. . . . defendant bought . . . paying . . . in liquor and tobacco. . . . witness heard them also talk of a former transaction of the same kind, and made an arrangement for a future one" (3:40).
Ga.	1855	*Dacy v. State:* "indictment for receiving corn from a slave" (3:42).
Mo.	1857	*State v. Goode:* "Goode was indicted in 1855 for buying five deer skins from a slave belonging to Jones 'without having the master's, owner's, or overseer's permission in writing therefore.' " (5:202).
Ga.	1859	*Carpenter vs. State:* "indicted for receiving from a slave . . . eight hides, value of thirty-four dollars, . . . that he got the hides from a negro about three o'clock in the morning. . . . butchers . . . give . . . [their] negroes permission to sell meat after market hours; and it is usual for them to do so" (3:68, 188).
N.C.	1859	*State v. Carroll:* "The defendant was convicted of trading with a slave, and sentenced . . . to 'one month's imprisonment' " (2:228).
S.C.	1859	*State v. Farr:* " 'shop-keeper . . . convicted of buying "one bushel of" corn from a slave [not having a permit]' " (2:462).
Fla.	1860	*Clem Murray (a Slave) v. State:* "was indicted . . . two counts. . . . in the first it is alleged that [he] did . . . play and bet at a gaming table. . . . In the second, he is charged that he did . . . in a place of which he . . . had the charge . . . Clem's barber shop, permit [a free black] . . . to play for money" (3:121, 177).
Tex.	1860	*Kingston v. State:* "indicted for . . . buying five Shanghai chickens from a slave, . . . of the value of $6 each" (5:310).
Mo.	1864	*State v. Rohlfing:* "The appellant was indicted . . . for dealing with a slave [without owner's written permission], . . . that he had borrowed the money of the negro, and given him his note of it" (5:219).

Source: Compiled from Helen Tunnicliff Catterall, ed., *Judicial Cases Concerning American Slavery and the Negro,* 5 vols. (Washington, D.C.: The Carnegie Institution of Washington, 1926–1937).

slaves in their economic "crimes," the state was more interested in going after those whites who engaged in "criminal" activities with large numbers of slaves, whose independent economic activities, while of limited pecuniary value to their owners, were viewed as a dangerous trend toward greater economic opportunities. This sentiment can be seen in the report of the 1851 Alabama *Hurt v. State* case:

> Mr. Hurt was convicted ... for selling a pair of shoes to a slave.... Judgment affirmed. ... In requiring the articles to be specifically stated, ... the Legislature designed to suppress ... a general evil in some parts of the country, growing out of a clandestine traffic between slaves and a particular class of white persons.... if a negro may buy all sorts of dry goods ... he might soon ... become a pedlar among other negroes and the class of white men, whose conduct led to the passage of the act.[84]

Municipal Ordinances to Suppress Slave Economic Activities

Municipal ordinances were also specific in their attempts to suppress the economic activities of slaves. The following ordinances passed in Charleston, South Carolina, in 1806 were typical of those in force in southern towns and cities until slavery ended. The ordinances made it illegal for slaves to: (1) carry on any mechanical or handicraft trade for their direct personal benefit; (2) put a slave as an apprentice in any mechanical or handicraft trade under the supervision of another slave; and (3) buy, sell, or trade goods unless they had a ticket and then could sell only meat, fruit, and vegetables or, with a ticket, milk, grain, fruit, and other goods from their owners' plantations. It was also illegal to employ slaves in shops without the presence of whites.[85]

In addition to laws that attempted to strip slaves of their property and to suppress independent slave economic initiative, a cap was put on the wages that could be earned by slaves. In New Orleans, day laborers could earn no more than a dollar a day; in Charleston, the maximum daily wage set in 1817 was $ .81, until 1837 when it was raised to a dollar. Doubtless, the state hoped that limiting the amount of money that slaves could make in selling commodities would discourage their economic activity. Moreover, in several cities, particularly in the lower South, laws requiring licenses for slaves to work, which involved the purchase of occupational badges by either a slave owner or a slave who hired his own time, were another method devised by municipalities to suppress slave economic initiative.

With these laws in force, only slaves with badges could be legally hired. In New Orleans, slaves hired by the day wore brass badges to indicate their availability for short-term jobs. Even slaves pursuing occupations that required few, if any, skills were required to have them. Also, badges were required for slave women who were nontraditionally occupied as fisherwomen, porters, and laborers. Badge laws also acted to suppress the traditional economic activities of slave women as domestics, vendors, and hawkers. In Charleston, even the selling of cakes required a badge. Often, success in the sale of eatables provided a basis for the establishment of catering enterprises, food shops, and various types of restaurants.

The badge laws also included punishment for an slave owner or hirer if his slave was caught without a badge while engaging in economic activities. The law usually required that the owner or hirer be fined from $20 to $50, and the punishment for slaves who disobeyed economic initiative suppression laws ranged from 20 to 50 lashings. The badge laws also show the attempts by southern cities to suppress the occupational participation of slave tradesmen and craftsmen.

These and similar measures were a response to the threat posed to white craftsmen by their black counterparts. Black craftsmen had the greatest degree of freedom of any slaves who hired their own time or who were hired out. They were considered "privileged" slaves, described by one South Carolina newspaper in the late 1850s as an "ebony aristocracy."[86] As the ardent proslavery spokesman James H. Hammond noted in emphasizing the threat of slave craftsmen, "Whenever a slave is made a mechanic, he is more than half freed, and soon becomes, as we too well know, and all history attests . . . . the most corrupt and turbulent of his class."[87] Slave craftsmen proved the greatest threat to the slave system. Leaders of the three great slave conspiracies in the nineteenth century were craftsmen: Gabriel Prosser, Denmark Vesey and Nat Turner, a slave carpenter and foreman/manager of a small plantation.[88]

Yet, there has been a failure by scholars in analyzing slave laws to emphasize the extent to which black economic initiative was linked to the suppression of black resistance.[89] State laws attempted to suppress not only assaults on the person and property of whites through arson, poisoning, and/or murder, and revolts but also the sustained competitive threats by slaves to white occupational and economic hegemony. With their emphasis on slave assaults against white people and their property, scholarly studies of antebellum slave laws have limited their analysis primarily to a focus on slave "crimes" and have failed to see that southern slave laws were constructed to suppress independent slave economic activities. Moreover, the punishment for slaves found guilty of hiring their time, while seldom enforced, required that they be sold out of the state. Yet, ironically, extradition was the punishment usually reserved for the most recalcitrant slaves, those suspected of encouraging or participating in criminal assaults against whites and their property.[90]

Moreover, slave participation in the crafts and in industry coalesced a class conflict between white factions: labor against capital, landless whites versus southern white industrialists who "openly advocated the use of slaves in industry in order to guard society from the white working classes."[91] In hiring or owning slave labor, white industrialists not only saved on wages and were protected against strikes, but also were guaranteed a lifetime labor force. Unskilled white laborers, alone, seemed to object to the use of slaves in industry, as opposed to southern white craftsmen, whose only objection was to the use of slave craftsmen. As Robert Starobin said, "White artisans did not object to the use of slaves in all industrial occupations . . . [or even] to abolish slavery altogether, only to exclude Negroes from certain trades and to curtail such pernicious practices as . . . self-hire privileges."[92]

From the beginning of slave employment in nonagricultural occupations in the seventeenth century, especially in the crafts and trades, whites in those occupations objected vehemently to slave competition. Southern white craftsmen not only organized associations to protest against the use of slave craftsmen, they also used violence to suppress their labor activities. In Wilmington, North Carolina, in 1857 white craftsmen burned a building constructed by slaves, with the threat that "all buildings erected by slaves in the future would receive similar treatment."[93]

What, then, are the implications in this assessment of slave economic activities in reviewing these laws? Simply put, laws are enacted basically for two purposes: to discourage behavior deemed destructive to society in the promotion of the general welfare; and to encourage behavior society finds constructive in promoting the general welfare. In antebellum America, the economic independence and financial success of an involuntary and servile workforce threatened to undermine the economic profitability of a white-dominated society. Even more, it threatened to destroy the very foundation and fabric of that society, which was built on white economic supremacy and achieved by the forced labor and economic subordination of people of African descent. Yet, notwithstanding statutory attempts to suppress slave economic initiative, the practice continued, as denounced in an 1859 editorial in the Columbia (South Carolina) *Bulletin*: "Despite the laws of the land forbidding under penalty the hiring of their time by slaves, it is much to be regretted that the pernicious practice still exists."[94]

Conclusion

As stated in its introduction, this chapter argues for the construction of a historic reality inclusive of every facet of slave life. Independent African-American slave economic activities existed and were pervasive throughout the South before the Civil War. Laws in force to suppress black economic activities reflected the extent to which southern whites felt as threatened by slaves as independent economic participants, as much as they feared the threat of slave resistance. The independent economic activities of African-American slaves, then, cannot be dismissed as inconsequential simply because of the limited funds accumulated through those efforts or because few succeeded in achieving freedom through self-purchase. Moreover, the marketing and trading activities of slaves who hired their own time as hawkers, vendors, and peddlers, although viewed as providing a means for the fencing of stolen merchandise and referenced in the codes as slave crimes, illuminate the pervasiveness of independent slave enterprise.

What is also critical to understand, as court cases illustrate, is that the laws that proscribed slave independent economic activities actually underscore the reality that slaves would and did use every opportunity to acquire cash, not only to improve their material life, but also to further their hope of purchasing their freedom. In making money, some slaves were entrepreneurs. The slave coal dealer Robert Gordon emerged from slavery in 1846 with $15,000 in savings, while Anthony Weston accumulated $40,000 as a millwright, amounts far in excess of the average income earned by antebellum whites. More typical of the earnings of self-hired slaves, however, was the annual profit of $500 earned by Free Frank, a slave entrepreneur who demonstrated the ability to make a relatively large amount of money by using commonly available resources. Also, the manufacturing, advertising, marketing, and distribution activities of the self-hired slave tobacconist Lunsford Lane, with his branch offices and sales agents, characterize him as an entrepreneur, rather than as just a business proprietor.

In the face of public policy, which decreed that all income from slave labor was owed to slave owners, and the diversity of repressive laws designed to suppress slave economic initiative, tremendous ingenuity and risk taking were required for any slave to undertake independent economic activities. Innovation, risk taking, the ability to sense the wants of the consumer, even to create demands for a product, and to supply those wants—these entrepreneurial qualities distinguished the business activities of those slaves.

Yet, it is certainly ironic that, since slavery's demise more than a century ago, public policy and objections from the white community have consistently emphasized that black Americans lack a historic tradition of economic initiative and business participation. During the age of slavery, the criticism, paradoxically, was just the opposite, as reflected in two centuries of laws that attempted to suppress slave economic initiative. Luther Porter Jackson, in a critique of an 1852 southern newspaper editorial denouncing slave violations of these laws and their egregious effects on white supremacy, said,

> This editor charged that, in defiance of this code, numerous slaves hired their own time, set up business on their own account, received the profits of their own labor, and, in short, did everything that white men could do. He said that some slaves even owned real estate . . . and furthermore that such property had been bought with money raised by the slave. The writer deplored this situation and warned that if the South intended to retain its peculiar institution, "all such approaches by the blacks to the condition of the whites must be abolished."[95]

4

"THEY ARE CAPITALISTS": ANTEBELLUM FREE BLACK BUSINESS ACTIVITIES

William Goodrich Pennsylvania. [Fancy Goods] "Oct 45. Has a barber shop, Cars on R. R. Deals in Jewels.—Oyster Co. Printer. Toys. June 20 48. A colored man worth 20m [$20,000] close, shrewd, attentive, and safe for contracts. July 49. Shrewd and thrifty, Making money and likely to go on doing so. . . . May 52. Well Off. . . . Honest. . . . [Aug] 1852. Has a great many irons in the fire but seems to be making money, runs a train of cars on the Columbia RR."

Bernard and Albin Soulie, Louisiana. "Merchants & Ex[change] Brokers. May 30 53. Good for $100m [$100,000]. May 20 54. F.M.C. [free men of color]. . . . Are [very] wealthy, estimated w[orth] from 250 to 300m [$250,000. to $300,000]. . . . July 55. They are Capitalists. . . .

Mar 19 57. They are rich, w.$500m. Dg a lar. bus. [doing a large business]."

Stephen Smith, Pennsylvania. Lumber. "Sept 16 53. Smith was formerly a slave to old 'Ben Boude'. . . . Good as the best, worth $100m. July 18 57. King of the Darkies—w[orth] $100m. . . . Apr 1 65. Smith wor[th] $500m."
　　　　　　　　　—R. G. Dun & Company Mercantile Agency Credit Reports

Introduction

The businesses established by antebellum free blacks were capitalist enterprises oriented toward the market and geared to making a profit. The credit reports of the R. G. Dun & Company mercantile agency, a few of which open the chapter, are invaluable for illuminating the fiscal side of African-American business activity prior to the Civil War. While only a few black enterprises were included in the reports, they document that antebellum African-Americans established a diversity of enterprises in the nation's preindustrial economy that paralleled mainstream American business. An industry-by-industry assessment of the business enterprises established by them before the Civil War provides the focus of this chapter.

While antebellum black America's "high-status" occupations, such as barbering, catering, and tailoring, are included for discussion, the chapter also focuses on black businesses beyond those limited to personal service enterprises. Antebellum blacks also established other enterprises as wholesale and retail grocers and dry-goods merchants. They owned transportation enterprises. They participated in the extractive industries and were inven-

TABLE 4.1   Martin Delany's Report on Urban Black Businesses, 1852

Business Enterprise	Location	Proprietor
Merchant clothier	Detroit	Banks, Robert
Pharmaceutical	Pittsburgh	Barett, Owen A.
Employment agency	New York	Bell, Phillip
Construction	Cincinnati	Bell & Knight
Merchant tailor house	Philadelphia	Bowers, John C.
Bedstead manufactory	Cincinnati	Boyd, Henry
Merchant tailor house	New Orleans	Cardovell, Mr.
Hair dresser/money broker	Philadelphia	Cassey, Joseph
Lumber merchant	Penn Yan, N.Y.	Cassey, Joseph C.
Jeweler	New York	Clark, Edward C.
Construction/real estate	Pittsburgh	Collins, Henry
Wood factor/shipping	Charleston	Dereef, Edward
Steamboat owner/shipping	St. Louis	DeSara, David
Resort owner	Newport, R.I.	Downing, George
Restaurateur/caterer	New York	Downing, Thomas
Sail manufactory	Philadelphia	Forten, James
Merchant clothier	Buffalo	Frances, Abner
Merchant clothier	Buffalo	Garrett, James
Merchant/RR cars owner	York, Pa.	Goodrich, William
Daguerreotype gallery	York, Pa.	Goodrich, Glenalvon
Merchant clothier	Boston	Hayden, Lewis
Tanner/currier	Chillocothe, Ohio	Hill, One
Wood factor/shipping	Charleston	Howard, Robert
Employment agency	New York	Hutson, William
Building contractor/glazier	Columbus, Ohio	Jenkins, David
Concert band leader	Philadelphia	Johnson, Frank
Restaurateur/concert hall	Pittsburgh	Julius, John and Edna
Livery stable/hotelier	Chicago	Knight, Henry
Construction/plastering	Cincinnati	Knight & Bell
Steamboat owner	St. Louis	Meechum, [John] Berry
Restaurateur/caterer	Philadelphia	Minton, Henry
Lumber merchant	Penn Yan, N.Y.	Platt, William
Restaurateur/caterer	Philadelphia	Prosser, James, Sr.
Bootmaker	Philadelphia	Riley, William H.
Wholesale grocery/food processing/ship chandlery	New York	Scott, Henry
Lumber and coal merchant	Philadelphia	Smith, Stephen
Merchant tailor	Albany	Topp, William
Wholesale/retail grocer	Cincinnati	Wilcox, Samuel
Millwright manufactory	Charleston	Weston, Anthony
Lumber and coal merchant	Columbia, Pa.	Whipper, William

Source: Compiled from Martin R. Delany, *The Condition, Elevation, Emigration and Destiny of the Colored People of the United States* (Philadelphia, Pa.: 1852), 92–110, 142. The Downings and Goodriches were fathers and sons. Partnerships included Smith and Whipper, and Dereef and Howard.

tors and manufacturers. Antebellum free blacks, moreover, were also informal bankers and investors in internal improvements, municipal and government bonds, and bank stock. They were real estate speculators, brokers, and developers. They were commissioned brokers and owned large slave plantations. Their businesses were located in urban and rural areas throughout the North and South. And, as the new nation expanded westward, free blacks also expanded their business activities by participating in the development of antebellum western frontiers. They were town founders and city fathers. In pursuit of profits, antebellum free blacks established import-export firms as they sought business opportunities in international markets in the Caribbean and West Africa.

The diversity of businesses established by antebellum free blacks prompted Martin Delany, a leading antebellum black intellectual, political activist, newspaper publisher, and businessman, to include a discussion on black businesses in his 1852 book in order "to refute the objections urged against us, that we are not useful members of society. That we are consumers and nonproducers—that we contribute nothing to the general progress of man."[1] See table 4.1 for Delany's list of leading antebellum black businessmen. Moreover, there were efforts made by black organizations, especially the National Negro Convention, to promote business activities. Its membership primarily included businessmen, who were also antebellum America's leading black abolitionists and promoters of rights for free blacks. Its existence is noteworthy, illuminating the long history that the black community has had in organized efforts to improve both its political and economic position in America.

Despite some successes, most antebellum black businesses remained marginal enterprises, earning minimal profits. Black businesspeople were confronted with both legal and societal constraints that restricted their participation in many occupations. Antebellum black entrepreneur John Malvin, who established a business in Great Lakes shipping said, "I found every door was closed against the colored man in a free state, excepting the jails and penitentiaries."[2]

Mutual Aid and Benevolent Societies

With the founding of African secret burial societies in the seventeenth century, religion and the search for capital resources, which motivated the European settlement of America, were also the same forces that prompted the initial independent economic activities of Africans in this country. Within the context of the African religious cosmos, death represented not the finality of existence, but a transition. The death of an African required a ceremonious and opulent funeral and burial to ensure the promise of an honorable and prosperous afterlife. Very early in the history of their enslavement in the colonies, Africans attempted to fulfill those cultural dictates through the establishment of secret burial societies. For some with strong traditional religious beliefs, the hope existed that after death they would return to Africa.[3]

Most slaves, however, were concerned only that they accumulated enough money to provide themselves with a decent funeral, based as much as possible on their African traditions. A slave's ability to accumulate funds for funeral expenses were limited. Mutual cooperation was the only recourse, which resulted in the creation of African burial societies. They were secret. The fear of slave conspiracies by whites limited collective (usually more than three) activity by blacks. Consequently, African slave burial societies, especially in the South, were clandestine operations.[4] In New England, the initiative taken by Africans to organize for the purpose of providing mutual assistance and relief was noted by Puritan leader Cotton Mather, who, in an December 1693 entry in his diary, wrote: "a company of poor Negroes, of their own accord, addressed me, for my Countenance, to a design which they had, of erecting such a meeting for the welfare of their miserable nation that were servants among us."[5]

In 1780, the first free mutual aid society on record, the African Union Society, was established in Newport, Rhode Island, by the black musician and businessman Newport Gardner. While founded for the purpose of providing benefits to widows and children, it also made loans to debt-encumbered members, provided apprenticeships for youths, and encouraged thrift. Its members were advised to use their savings to purchase property and develop real estate; they were counseled that it "will be safest and most beneficial when laid out in lots, houses and small farms."[6]

The most historically significant mutual aid society was Philadelphia's Free African Society, founded in 1787 by the two of the country's most prominent African-American religious leaders, Richard Allen and Absalom Jones. A year's membership was required before benefits were paid to a claimant, but only if financial distress was not due to the claimant's negligence. Widows were paid benefits. Children of deceased members remained "under the care of the society," which paid for their education or apprenticeship training. Fees that went unpaid for three months led to dismissal.[7] The society was dissolved in 1792, with stipulations that the funds accumulated be used to purchase a site for the building of a church. In 1793 two black churches were founded. One was the African Episcopal Church of St. Thomas, initially the African Church of Philadelphia, headed by Absalom Jones. The other was the Methodist Mother Bethel Church, founded by Richard Allen, which in 1816 became the first autonomous black denomination, the African Methodist Episcopal (AME) Church.

While both the Free African Society and the African Union Society were phased out, the foundation was laid in the late eighteenth century for the establishment of subsequent mutual aid societies, which became important institutions in antebellum black economic life.[8] Risk sharing was the most prominent feature of these societies, which provided a cultural base for the founding of black insurance companies.[9] In 1810 the African Insurance Company was established in Philadelphia with a five-man board of directors and "a capital stock of $5,000." Absalom Jones was founder and a director.[10]

Historical assessments of mutual aid societies have limited their analysis to their insurance and social assistance benefits. The extent to which their funds were used to encourage black business development, however, is seldom emphasized. The constitutions of several mutual aid societies stipulated that once a certain amount of money, usually in excess of $200, was accumulated by the organization, members could borrow funds in rotation to be used as venture capital for the establishment of a business, in much the way as members have access to funds in rotating credit associations. The African Benevolent Society of Wilmington, Delaware, and the Brown Fellowship Society, founded in 1790 in Charleston, South Carolina, provided in their by-laws that members could borrow money for business activities.[11] A propensity for saving, then, distinguished both African slaves and free blacks from the beginning of their settlement. The pooling of money deposited by members to pay for funeral and burial expenses provided the foundation for the institutional development of black insurance companies, while the business loan capabilities of mutual aid associations formed the basis for early African-American banking activities.

Banking, Finance, Investment, and Credit

The initial impetus for African-American banking activity began with African slaves in colonial America. With free blacks, the post-Revolutionary War era marked the expansion of both formal and informal banking activities. With the establishment of the nation's first banks, blacks, individually and in groups, placed their money on deposit.[12] The Free African Society deposited its funds in a savings account at the Philadelphia Bank of North America. At its founding in 1830, the National Negro Convention Movement required that "all monies above that sum [$100] shall be deposited in the United States Bank."[13]

Antebellum blacks also invested in bank stock as groups and individuals. By 1815 the New York African Society for Mutual Relief had acquired $500 in bank stock.[14] In South Carolina the 1835 estate of Thomas Inglis, a barber, included $19,303 in stock and bonds at the Mechanics Bank.[15] Julien Lacroix of New Orleans had assets estimated by Dun to be worth $250,000 in 1854, including "stock holdings ... in the Louisiana State Bank"[16] Andrew Marshall owned stock in the Marine and Insurance Bank of the State of Georgia.[17] Samuel Wilcox, a successful Cincinnati black businessman and also a bank stockholder, said, "I have taken stock in banks, so that there may be *one* colored man there to vote. I own a thousand dollars in the Kentucky Trust Company, and am often invited over to meet the Directors."[18]

Through their purchase of bank stock, several antebellum blacks sat as official members on bank boards. Pennsylvanian Stephen Smith, the wealthiest northern antebellum black, sat on the board of the Columbia Bank in the 1830s. It was reported that he "was the largest stock-holder of his day in the Columbia bank; and, according to its rules, would have been president had it not been for his complexion. Being thus barred, he was given the privilege of naming the white man who became president in his stead."[19] Also Robert Purvis was said to be a "member of the largest money corporation in the city of Philadelphia."[20]

In the South special laws and statutes incorporating state banks made it illegal for blacks to purchase bank stock. In New Orleans two free men of color sued the Citizens' Bank of Louisiana in its attempt to expropriate their stock under an 1836 state act that limited purchase of capital stock in the bank to white American citizens. The original bank charter required only that bank stock be purchased by owners of real property. The men, both property owners, purchased their bank stock in 1833: one owned $20,000 or 200 shares; the other, $15,000 or 150 shares. The court upheld their right to own the stock.[21] The American judiciary was always careful that it not infringe on private property rights. Under the principal of law of stare decisis, appropriation of private property could establish a dangerous precedent.[22]

The most extensive banking activity of wealthy antebellum blacks was in the informal sector, where they acted as ex-officio private bankers. While holding savings for fellow blacks, they made loans with interest not only to blacks but also to whites, who did not want their precarious finances a matter of public record. As the National Negro Convention reported, "Many of our people in the cities have money loaned at interest, and which netts [sic] them but 5 per cent."[23] These informal banking activities, however, provided a valuable source of additional capital for investment, invariably in real estate, by antebellum free black businesspeople.

In the South, wealthy barbers and slaveholders also acted in the capacity of private bankers, including William Johnson of Mississippi, the "Barber of Natchez." Johnson recorded his loan transactions in his day book. In 1836 he carried entries for the following amounts on loans repaid: June, $100, $60, $50, $20; November, $300, $50, $1750 ("p[ai]d me through the agricultural Bank Seventeen Hundred and Fifty Dollars"), and $20. In Georgia the Reverend Wilkes Flagg, a former slave and a blacksmith with his own shop, accumulated some $25,000 by 1860, which over the years "he loaned from time to time to reliable whites." In Louisiana large black planters and slaveholders, including Cyprian Ricaud, the Metoyer family, and various New Orleans merchants, also acted in the capacity of private bankers.

Many black informal bankers also discounted bank notes, capitalizing on the numerous state banks that issued their own notes (currency) at disparate rates of exchange. By giving favorable rates in the currency exchange market, many of these bankers became quite wealthy. In this capacity, they were known as "note shavers," men "who would discount notes as banks do now, but presumably at a greater profit."[24] The Philadelphia barber Joseph Cassey, who left an estate of $75,000, was described by Martin Delany as a "money broker [whose] name and paper was good in any house in the city," adding that "there was no banker of moderate capital, of more benefit to the business community than was Joseph Cassey."[25]

Also, the wealthy black entrepreneur Stephen Smith included note shaving as one of his business activities. As Delany said, in addition to his real estate activities, "The principal active business attended by Mr. S. in person, is that of buying good negotiable and other paper." See table 4.2 for various Dun & Company credit reports on Smith and his business partners.

Slave-born John C. Stanley, "Barber Jack" of North Carolina, whose mother was African born and his father white and who was manumitted by the state legislature, both loaned money and discounted notes. With $40,000, he purchased slaves, and it was said that "he made most of his money by discounting notes." In this enterprise Stanley was also a front for whites: "Certain white men of means who did not care to go openly into the business of sharp discounting took him for a partner and furnished the means."[26]

The very wealthy Soulie brothers were private bankers heavily involved in money exchange as money brokers, "[doing] large discount bus [business]," as reported in the Dun mercantile records.[27] The Soulie brothers were also financiers, described by Dun in one entry as "capitalists." Their informal financial activities as "private bankers," with their money exchange and loan activities, greatly enhanced their wealth-generating capacities as entrepreneurs in the formal sector. While Martin Delany failed to provide a name, he said that in New Orleans "[i]n 1839–40, one of the most respectable Brokers and Bankers of the City was a black gentleman."[28] Dun also reported that Julien Lacroix's assets included "accounts receivable," and in 1860 reported that D. R. Macarty (also spelled McCarthy) of New Orleans was a money broker.[29]

It was not only individual blacks that expressed interest in investing and banking. In its efforts to encourage greater financial activity by blacks, the National Negro Convention advocated that blacks not only invest in government securities but also that a black bank should be established. In the 1834 revision of its constitution, Article IV stipulated: "When the Treasury of the convention shall contain a larger sum than five hundred dollars, it shall be invested in United States securities."[30] In 1847 the organization's newly formed Banks and Banking Institutions Committee called for the establishment of a national black bank, explaining that "a Banking Institution originating among the colored people of the U. States [is needed] because they at present contribute to their own degradation by investing capital in the hands of their 'enemies.' "[31]

TABLE 4.2 Dun Mercantile Credit Reports on Smith, Whipper, and Vidal, 1853–1877

Smith, S. Whipper, W. Vidal, U.B. Lumber Lancaster

Sept. 53 Colored men "Smith" w $100,000. Whipper w. $20,000 took in a partner—last name by the name of "Vidal" was a clerk for them. They do their bus on the River. Smith was formerly a slave to old "Ben Boude"

Sept. 56 Good as the best worth $100m

July 57 King of the Darkies w $100m

Mar. 58 Smith lives in Philad. it is said w 100m$

Smith Whipper & Co. Philadelphia Coal & Lumber Broad & Willow

Dec. 55 (Are all colored men) Smith stands at head of the concern and is alone consid'd worth full $100M cr undoubted

Mar. 58 Diss'd [dissolved] this day by mutual consent the bus will be continued by Stephen Smith and Wm B. Vidal under the firm of Smith & Vidal.

Smith & Vidal

Oct. 59 Wealthy, in first rate standing

Mar. 62 Hear of no change. S. owns considerable RE, is reputed well off. V a man of means and property. Good, safe, wealthy.

Apr. 64 Do a large bus. Smith reputed worth 500m$ outside coal and lumber trade

Apr. 65 Diss'd Apr 1, 65 Smith retires wor 500m$ W. B. Vidal continues

W. B. Vidal

Apr. 65 W. B. Vidal continues. He is son-in-law of S. & can have his assistance if required. Is an educated darkey of considerable pride of char. Does a gd cash bus pays cash & is est wor. 30 to 50M very reliable & good.

June 66 A negro with a wealthy father-in-law & has good capabilities of his own is doing well pays & has good credit considered good

July 67 A Negro does a good bus has means pays & is good but the darkies say he sticks them whenever an opportunity presents itself

Oct. 71 Is a colored man allowed small amount of credit

Jan. 73 Good for wants prompt pay

June 74 In good cr with the trade generally think he has property of his own, but may be mistaken, he does a nice business, his wife has probably more than he, she is a niece of Stephen Smith a wealthy colored man, recently deceased We would sell him

June 77 Dead

Wm. Whipper Columbia

July 61 No change

Sept. 62 Has RE and good cr

Jan. 63 Same as before

Dec. 63 A colored gent, RE does a gd. bus. is prompt & sf

June 64 A col'd person dg. well in gd cr

Jan. 65 Wor 30m$ owns ppty in Canada & also in Phil. has good cr here

Mar. 67 Better (21/2.21/2)

Dec. 68 Lives in Philad. Sold his ppy . . . w 45m$

Source: Compiled from R. G. Dun and Company, Pennsylvania, 132:322, 79:31, 121; R. G. Dun and Company Collection, Baker Library, Harvard University Business School, Boston, Mass.

Moreover, by the 1850s southern state legislation became increasingly restrictive in limiting black economic advances. In Maryland an 1853 statute made it illegal not only for blacks to become members of the homestead and building associations that were established to promote savings among the poor, but also for blacks to form comparable savings institutions.[32] In response, at the 1855 National Negro Convention, information was provided to show that blacks had enough money to support their own black bank since they had "Six Hundred Thousand Dollars invested in Savings Banks in and around New York and its vicinity and also similar amounts around other cities."[33]

The informal banking activities of free blacks were essential if they were to have access to credit. In addition to the funds made available for business ventures by the more wealthy mutual aid organizations, antebellum blacks attempted to organize formal rotating credit associations, an informal banking system that provides venture capital on a rotating basis to members who make regular deposits.[34] In 1850 the American League of Colored Laborers, founded in New York for the purpose of encouraging black craftsmen to become independent business owners, proposed a plan to create a fund that would be used to provide venture capital to assist them.[35]

A more ambitious financial plan, however, was proposed at the 1855 National Negro Convention that expanded the idea of a rotating credit association. While the plan never materialized, the proposal envisioned both a business cooperative and an investment bank. Interest earned from profits would provide funds for venture capital. The organizational design was based on "[c]o-partnerships, say from three to five in each business as the parties might prefer to engage; on the principle of divisions of labor and division of profits according to capability—looking to it that their financial man and bookkeeper be looked up to as an index of security." The business plan was both bold and progressive in the profits anticipated; the goal was to "let all the partners in the Union work to make the Capital pay if possible 25 per cent and keep on until the investment becomes a paying one: and thus show the fallaciousness of the 6 per cent idea of Savings Bank investments. A thousand dollars might in a judicious outlay in a lucrative business pay from 25 to 75 per cent."[36]

In addition to their informal banking activities and proposals for establishing savings banks and formal rotating credit associations, antebellum blacks also invested in corporate enterprises, especially in internal improvements, municipal utilities, and insurance company stock. Stephen Smith owned $18,000 worth of stock in the Columbia Railroad and $9,000 worth of stock in the Columbia Bridge Company. William Goodrich had investments in the Lancaster branch of the Baltimore Railroad.[37] Dun reported Julien Lacroix's assets included "stock holdings in two railroads ... and in the Hope Insurance company."[38] Wealthy South Carolina wood merchant R. E. Dereef owned several thousand dollars in six-percent stock of the City of Charleston, in addition to stock in the Charleston Light and Gas Company. Edmond DuPuy held 267 capital shares in the New Orleans City Railroad Company and 73 shares in the New Orleans Insurance Company.

William Johnson, the Natchez barber, owned shares in the Natchez Railroad. In a diary entry for 30 March 1836, he wrote: "To Day I subscribed for 26 Shairs of the Rail Road Stock, I in the First place put my name for One thousand Dollars. But Mr Wm Alister told me if it two much for me that he would take one thousand dollars of it. I then put my name Down for $2000 .... Rail Road Meeting this Evening there were several speeches made by Different Persons."[39] Also, by 1864 wealthy commission broker John Clay owned 19 shares of the New Orleans Gas Light Company and 10 shares in the Bank of Louisiana.[40] There was even an attempt by an African-American to deal on the New York Stock Exchange before the Civil War, but he was refused a seat.[41] Also, just before the Civil War, the Union Bank Society was founded in New Orleans.[42]

Throughout the antebellum period, free blacks attempted to increase their access to capital by seeking loans through commercial banks. In his agribusiness enterprise, Louisiana black planter Jean Baptiste Meullion secured bank loans by mortgaging his property in slaves. In 1833 he got a $5,000 loan from the Union Bank of Louisiana and another one in 1840 for $1,250. The slaves, a woman and her four children valued at $2,580 and a male slave at $1,590, had been purchased by Meullion at an estate sale in 1817 for $4,170.[43] Consequently, while antebellum free blacks lacked political and civil rights, paradoxically, a minuscule number of free blacks had access to bank credit. They were the large black planters and other wealthy real estate holders who had collateral in real and chattel property.

Yet even some of the very wealthy blacks were reported in the Dun reports as poor credit risks. Samuel Moore, listed as a real estate broker in 1853, was reported worth $50,000. An entry in 1868 disclosed the source of his wealth: "some time ago he drew $50m in the lottery." In 1854, while he was described as a "rich color'd man of gd. char & cr," subsequent entries in 1857 and 1858 said, "[n]ot in gd reputation"; "[c]an say nothing in his favor, Is bad repute"; "[n]ot consid'd reliable." In 1866 Moore's worth had been reduced to $10,000; four years later he was worth $75,000, but still reported by Dun as "unreliable & unsafe."[44]

The Lacroix brothers Francois and Julien, despite their wealth, also had a checkered credit history. In 1854 Dun reported Francois as "[v]ery wealthy. owns R.E. all over the City. owns buildings. Cor of Comm & St. Charles—w $200m, also has negroes." Subsequent entries emphasize his extensive real estate holdings: "Dec 12 58. Rich. Gd as gold"; although an 1859 entry said he paid slowly: "Buying a good deal of [property] but does not pay promptly; asks for renewal of his paper at Bank." Dun revised its report, noting,: "wor[th] $300m [$300,000]. Cr. standing & char. no. 1." Again, in May 1861, Dun said he was "Perfectly responsible wealthy stands A.1 among the trade."[45] Julien also had extensive real estate holdings, which Dun reported in 1854: "He is vy wealthy est. w $250m [$250,000]." Yet, his creditworthiness was questioned, as a Dun entry noted: "some of our most reliable Banks and Exchge Houses say No 2.... Bnk Presidt marks No 3." Despite those negative credit ratings, Dun recommended him as safe for credit: "very careful, cautious, indus & fortunate. Owns R.E. to a lar am't."[46]

Plantations and Commission Brokers

In 1850 7.5 percent of the nation's free black population of 439,494 owned real property.[47] The largest black property holders, as a group, were the planters. In 1850 there were 242 free persons of color classified as planters, those who owned more than 20 slaves. The large planters, however, were those who owned 70 to more than 100 slaves, with extensive acreage developed in cotton, sugar, and rice production.[48] Of antebellum America's 21 leading black wealth holders, 5 were large black planters in Louisiana, with wealth in excess of $100,000. All were sugar planters, except the Metoyer family, who grew cotton. The wealthiest Metoyers, Jean Baptiste and Augustin died in 1838 and 1856, respectively. In 1830 the Metoyer family owned 287 slaves.[49] By 1860 the Metoyers had accumulated $750,000 in land and slaves.[50]

The founder of this short-lived antebellum American black dynasty was a former slave, Coincoin, the American-born daughter of two Africans brought to colonial Louisiana in the mid-eighteenth century. Unlike other black women who inherited established plantations, Coincoin built her family's extensive holdings in land, some 12,000 acres, and slaves from a gift of about 80 acres of undeveloped land. Information on Louisiana's five leading

TABLE 4.3   Louisiana's Leading Black Planters and Slaveholders

Name	Value of Real Property ($)	Value of Personal Property ($)	Cash Value Farm ($)	Acres of Land	Numbers of Slaves
1. Dubuclet, A.	200,000	6,400	500,000	1,265	91
2. Ricaud, widow	200,000	1,000	—	4,300	71
son	20,000	500	—	—	81
3. Reggio, A.	70,000	90,000	48,000	2,400	100
4. DeCuir, A.	150,000	1,000	20,500	1,075	112
5. Metoyer, A.	80,000	130,000	80,000	4,100	119

Source: Compiled from Joseph Karl Menn, *The Large Slaveholders of Louisiana, 1860* (New Orleans: Pelican Publishing, 1964), 93–95, 245–46, 299, 312.

black planters in 1860, including the value of their real, personal, and chattel property, the cash value of their farms, and the total number of acres and slaves owned, is provided in table 4.3 (property values listed are assessed at only 72 percent of the real value).[51]

The wealth of the Ricaud family reflected a recent purchase that added to their holdings, with 1,300 of their 4,300 acres improved. Sugar production for 1859–1860 was 627 hogsheads, and they owned $2,000 in livestock. Their 152 slaves lived in 90 slave dwellings.[52] The 1859 Ricaud property acquisition generated national publicity. The *Christian Examiner* reported: A WEALTHY NEGRO FAMILY.—An immense estate in Louisiana, embracing over four thousand acres of land, with two hundred and fifty negroes belonging to the plantation was recently sold for a quarter of a million of dollars. The purchaser was a free negro, who is said to be one of the wealthiest men of the South." A Louisiana newspaper validated the purchase price, noting that, given the alleged numbers of acres and slaves, the selling price would have been "nearer a million and a quarter than a quarter of a million."[53]

Before America's industrial revolution, large slave plantations were the country's most profitable enterprises; and Louisiana's large black planters provided the basis for the development of blacks as commission merchants and cotton and sugar brokers. Knowledge of their activities extended beyond the state. A Cincinnati bank stock investor, who was himself a commission merchant, relayed the following information to a contemporary, who subsequently reported that "Wilcox (in Cincinnati) said that he knew three or four colored cotton-brokers in New Orleans. The census gives nine colored brokers. One of them is the largest broker in New Orleans."[54]

Several of the wealthiest blacks in New Orleans were listed in Dun as commission merchants and exchange brokers who handled the marketing of the cotton and sugar of the large black planters (see table 4.4). There were several kinds of brokers whose major activity consisted of filling orders from northern and overseas buyers. Some represented private investment houses, while others worked directly for cotton-importing houses and manufacturers. J. Soulé is listed specifically as a broker in Dun, with his business described as "agent for parties in France—does a brokerage bus.... estimated wor 50m$." Pierre A. D. Casenave and D. R. McCarthy are listed in Dun, respectively, as "Com" [commission merchant] and "Broker." Casenave is described as having "a choice business" and his enterprise as "an old & Rich house w. at least 100m$." McCarthy is described as "agent for the est of sevl absent parties. Is himself w abt $40m."

TABLE 4.4   Dun on Free Black Brokers/Commission Merchants in New Orleans, 1853–1879

Bernard & Alvin Soulie   Merchts Ex Brokers   84 Beinville

May 53   Good for $100,000

May 54   Free Men of Color, age 45–50. Brothers. Are agents for some large estates. loan money on property. Are very wealthy estimated worth from $250,000 to $300,000. Their credit standing are 1st rate.

July 55   They are Capitalists

Aug. 56   Rich & in good credit, doing large discount business.

Mar. 57   Are rich, worth $500,000. Doing a large business.

Feb. 60   They are colored men of ample means for their bus, are steady, industrious & good businessmen. Stand very high here

Oct. 63   Good

Dec. 65   Same Rate 1 1/2.1

July 68   A. is in France, are wealthy & Retired from active bus

Oct. 69   Are wealthy & retired from business

Sam'l Moore   Broker in RE   19 St. Charles

May 53   Good. w $50m

Aug. 54   About 50 married. A rich colored man of good character & Lives on his income more than does some brokers. Assessed on R.E. $35,700

Feb. 55   Has fair means but they not within his credit reach. Is doing a good business. Has no credit, needs none.

July 55   No change

Aug. 56   Colored man, small means & bus.

July 57   Not in good reputation.

July 58   Not considered reliable

Mar. 59   Can say nothing in his favor. In bad repute.

Feb. 60   Good for 00&

June 66   Stands for worth $5000 to $10,000

June 68   A colored man, it is reported that long time ago he drew $50,000 in the lottery. owns no RE & is no ways reliable

Jan. 69   Has means which he drew in the Lottery, not doing much bus is responsible for what he does

Feb. 69   No change

July 69   Has some money, does very little—asks no Cr.

Mar. 70   Doing well. NO Credit

Oct. 70   Estimated worth $75,000 but regarded unreliable & unsafe.

J. Soulé   Broker   Rampart & Barrack

June 59   Colored, ag'd abt 50. Owns R.E. slaves, & by some is estimated wor 50m$ Is agent. for parties in France—does a brokerage bus Mar'd, sober, hon. & reliable.

J. R. Clay   Gen Broker   52 Royal Street

June 77   In bus a long time. Stands well here does a good bus chiefly in R.E. consid' reliable prompt & energetic has large means w 75m$ owns R.E. w 24m$ & the rest of capl is invested in mortage notes

Mar. 79   died las night

D. R. McCarthy   Broker [Dry Goods]   88 Bourbon St

July 48   Is a col' man does a good bus in good cr is now in NY buying goods consd w $36m is very respt man B&A Soulie are brothers in law of Mc. & are very wealthy, do a com' bus.

Feb. 49   Is a quadroon—gentlemanly & correct—w $15m. Keeps over $20m stk & probably sells $60m w a yr & respected by those who know him.

May 54   He retired from the Dry Goods bs. abt a yr. ago. He is now agent for the est of sevl absent parties. Is himself abt $40m.

Sept. 59   Is a f.p.c, aged abt 50; steady, sober & prud. Is the Acting Agt for numberous parties here [and abroad], collecting rent. Has a desk at the Office at "B & A Soulie" Is wor some 60m$ consid'd An old Broker, engaged in the bus many yrs, is a colored man is the acting agent here for parties in france in attending to their property

(continued)

TABLE 4.4   Continued

D. R. McCarthy   Broker
June 66   All right wor over 40m$

H Pottier   Cotton Broker   164 Common St
June 66	Stands No 1 wor over $10m
Oct. 68	Well off does a good business, buys largely and regarded as good
Feb. 69	Worth over $100,000 and perfectly good.
Oct. 69	In business many years prior to the war is a man of good habits, character & business capacity. Owns R.E. worth $100,000, total worth, $200,000 prospects good Bus requires no capital
Feb. 70	No change, wealthy, perfectly good for what all he does
Oct. 70	Is an old resident, a reliable Broker in high standing does a good business & regarded good for what he does. Means Estimated at about $150,000.
June 72	Will soon retire from business. He is a rich man worth fully over $200,000.
Jan. 73	Is wealthy & perfectly good for what he does.
June 74	One of the oldest and most reliable brokers here. Estimated worth over $200,000.
Jan. 76	Owns large and valuable Real Estate, Does good business & is honest and energetic. Good credit. Worth at least $250,000
Mar. 79	Is mainly a cotton buyer operates on a large scale Is rich & regular. Perfectly good.

Source: Compiled from R. G. Dun and Company, Louisiana, 11:30; 11:2; 11:17; 15:379; 9:97, and 13:83b; 10:526, and 13:83; R. G. Dun and Company Collection, Baker Library, Harvard University Business School. Also see Francois Lacroix, Julien Lacroix, and Colvis and Dumas, listed respectively in Dun as tailor and grocer, and tailors, but who speculated in real estate.

The Dun report on Honore Pottier specifically lists him as a Cotton Broker. The first entry made, however, was after the Civil War in 1866, with a subsequent entry noting, "In bus many yrs prior to the war . . . wor at least 250m$ [$250,000]." The last entry in Dun for Pottier was in 1878: "Is mainly a cotton buyer operates on a large scale." The Soulie brothers, Bernard and Albin, who retired to France after the Civil War, are also listed in Dun as "Merchts Ex Brokers."[55]

The commission merchants, on receiving the sugar or cotton brought from the plantations, usually by steamship, would arrange for storage as they negotiated the sale of the commodities at the best price. Commission merchants made 2.5 percent on each sale. Some also acted as informal brokers for planters, purchasing foodstuffs, hardware, farm equipment, and luxury goods. Also, commission merchants provided banking services for planters, either by loaning money or by providing credit against the sale of future crops, while serving as financial advisors. It was to their advantage to keep the planter solvent and to put him in the most profitable position for the sale of his commodities.[56]

Considering the amount of wealth they accumulated in real and chattel property, antebellum black planters were astute businessmen. For 49-year-old August Dubuclet, the cash value of his plantation in 1860 had increased by $119,400 since 1850. The Donato family in Plaquemines Parish were also large slaveholders. At his death in 1845, Martin Donato left an estate of 89 slaves and $46,000 in cash. In 1860 Thomas Durnford's estate in real property was valued at $50,000, personal property at $65,000, and the cash value of his farm at $30,000. He owned 1,300 acres of land and 75 slaves. From 1835 to 1859, the value of his property increased from $93,750 to $124,938.[57]

Frontier Real Estate Speculation

In the nineteenth century, free black pioneers also established commercial farms on the nation's frontiers, where they purchased public land at very low prices for speculation, development, and resale. In the 1820s, the former slave Free Frank acquired 759 acres in Kentucky in 10 separate transactions under two state land-granting systems.[58] In Illinois in the 1830s, he acquired 800 acres in 9 transactions. Most was public land purchased at $1.25 an acre.[59] Free Frank's commercial farm and land speculation activities in Illinois provided the capital to purchase 13 family members from slavery at a cost of $13,000. In 1850, 600 acres of Free Frank's land were assessed at $7,000.[60]

Free Frank was also a town founder, developer, and proprietor. In 1836 he laid out the town of New Philadelphia in Illinois, on the site of an 80-acre tract of undeveloped public land that he purchased from the federal government for $100. The founding of black towns was a post-Reconstruction phenomenon, so New Philadelphia was the first site specifically platted as a town by an African-American.[61] Free Frank staked out his town in blocks, streets, alleys, and 144 town lots, 60 by 120 feet. He also built roads leading to New Philadelphia, a major stagecoach stop between the Illinois and Mississippi rivers. Free Frank also contracted to build a Free Will Baptist Seminary. By 1850 the occupational distribution of the town's black and white population differed little from that of other frontier towns. New Philadelphia was included on national maps and in business gazetteers.[62]

In the 1840s the National Negro Convention, always probusiness, began to promote commercial farming, noting that "[f]arming ... now has got to be a scientific business." The devastating effect on urban blacks of the depression following the Panic of 1837 precipitated the organization's new economic agenda. When the convention met in 1843, it proposed that blacks invest in commercial farms rather than urban enterprises. Based on the convention's formulations, a profitable farm operation could be established for $300, whereas "that sum in money or in merchandise, commercial, or in most mechanical business, would be a capital insufficient." The report emphasized that "in most of the business operations, with a capital so small, despair would attend at every step."[63]

In actuality, it was not enough for free blacks with $300 just to pack up and go West. Many states, such as Illinois, Ohio, and Indiana, required free blacks on entry to post a security bond from $500 to $1,000. Also, while early black pioneers on the western frontiers could take advantage of purchasing public land for $1.25 an acre, the total cost of establishing a 160-acre commercial farm in Illinois, for example, amounted to about $945: $200 for the land itself; $320 for breaking up the land at $2.00 per acre; $175 for fencing; and $250 for cabins, corncribs, and stables. Also, racial hostility confronting free blacks living on isolated frontier homesteads was not always encouraging to black settlement in the West.

Moreover, once blacks acquired land, maintaining possession was often difficult. As one free black man who emigrated to Canada from Indiana said, "I had a great deal of property there.... it was not safe, for any loafing white might destroy or steal, and unless a white man were by to see it, I could get no redress."[64] Free Frank resorted to a court of arbitration when a white Baptist minister and the town's postmaster attempted to swindle him out of his ownership of half of New Philadelphia's town lots. In the 1850s several western states passed laws that made new black settlement within their borders illegal.

And, with the 1857 Dred Scott decision, attempts were made by the United States General Land Office to deny claims staked out by blacks under the 1841 Preemption Act.[65]

Before the Civil War, then, there were comparatively few blacks on the frontier, but they engaged in a variety of important activities and enterprises as farmers, fur traders, and cowboys.[66] The California frontier accounted for the emergence of antebellum America's largest black real estate holder, San Francisco's William Leidesdorff (1810–1848), who was also the country's wealthiest black prior to the Civil War. Leidesdorff was a speculator in San Francisco town lots and also a builder and developer in that city. After settling in California in 1841, he took out Mexican citizenship and served for nine years as vice consul to Mexico. During the war with Mexico, he was a sutler provisioning the American army. With California's independence, Leidesdorff emerged as a civic leader: he was elected to the San Francisco city council, established its first public school system, and was the city's first treasurer.

Clearly, Leidesdorff was passing as white. Described by contemporaries as dark and "swarthy," only after his death was it irrefutably established that he was of African descent. Yet one Californian who did business with Leidesdorff said, "I believe [he] had a dash of Negro blood in his veins." A San Francisco black woman, also a contemporary, said they both were from St. Croix: "[I] knew his mother, who was a Negress. His father was a Danish sugar planter."[67] Yet another contemporary described Leidesdorff as "of dark complexion with black hair and eyes, he looked more like a Spaniard than a Dane."[68] Some claimed he was Jewish. Doubtless, whites simply refused to accept that such a highly successful entrepreneur, a man of intelligence, initiative, enterprise, with shrewd business acumen, who stood in the forefront of San Francisco's development, was of African descent.

Leidesdorff had numerous additional accomplishments. He built the first hotel in that city, and his entrepreneurial ventures included an import-export business, ship chandlery, shipyard, lumberyard, and trading vessel. In 1844 he brought the first steamboat to San Francisco. He was also an agent for the American Russian Fur Company. Most of Leidesdorff's wealth, however, was in real property. He owned 360 San Francisco city lots. Also, through his Mexican citizenship, he acquired a 35,000-acre land grant, located directly across the American River from Sutter's Mill, where gold was discovered in January 1848. A newspaper article of the time proclaimed: "New Gold Mine—It is stated that a new gold mine has been discovered on the American Fork of the Sacramento, supposed to be on the land of William A. Leidesdorff of this place."[69]

He died in 1848, and his estate was purchased from his mother by Joseph Folsom for $75,000; today, the vast proportion of Leidesdorff's property now makes up Folsom, California. The city was platted on the site of Leidesdorff's Ranchero de los Americanos, which sold for $163,000. Some 309 of Leidesdorff's San Francisco city lots sold for $607,695. When the estate was finally settled in 1856, his property was valued at $1,442,232.[70] Adjusting for inflation and the devaluation of the dollar, his estate today would be valued at $15,000,000.

Urban Real Estate: Speculation and Development

In the North the leading antebellum black holder of urban property was Pennsylvanian Stephen Smith, who speculated extensively in real estate. There was no question of Smith's African racial heritage; he was known as "Black Steve." Smith's reputation as a real estate dealer was in "displaying much wisdom in his purchases," while his success at real estate speculation was attributed to his following the market. As contemporaries said: "He was always present at sales, looking for bargains. Whenever property changed hands at a public sale Stephen Smith was sure to be a bidder." His Philadelphia properties were eventually valued at $50,000.

New Orleans, however, had the country's largest concentration of urban black real estate holders, speculators, and developers. By 1860, the value of their property, primarily that of the free people of color, was estimated at $13 million to $15 million. It was also estimated that free blacks in New Orleans at the time owned $22 million, or one-fifth, of the city's taxable property.[71] Their extensive participation as real estate investors, speculators, and developers and as building tradesmen and architects was significant in the development of New Orleans housing. In the historic area known as Faubourge Tremé, a leading developer was Drausin Macarty. In the late 1840s and the 1850s, he purchased entire blocks beyond Esplanade Avenue and constructed Creole cottages and shotgun houses.[72]

The Dun reports describe Macarty as "steady, sober & prud[ent]" and that he worked out of the office of his brothers-in-law, Bernard and Albin Soulie, as an "[a]cting agt for numerous parties—collecting rents."[73] The Soulie brothers, who moved between Paris and New Orleans, were reported in the Dun records as "agents for some large estates [which] loan money on property."[74] Their real estate brokerage firm was located on North Rampart Street. Another relative, Norbert J. Soulé, is also listed as a broker in Dun. An 1859 entry states that he was "Colored.... Owns R.E. slaves, & by some is estimate wor 50m$. Is agent for parties in France—does a brokerage bus Mard' [married], sober, hon., & reliable." The builder Pierre E. Courcelle also worked for the Soulie brothers.[75]

Julien Colvis and Joseph Dumas, while listed in Dun as "m[erchant] Tailors" and described as "French Quadroons," were reported in 1849 as "w in RE $150m." They were builders and investors in New Orleans real estate from 1830 to 1869.[76] In their father-and-son brokerage firm, Francis and John Raquet Clay did a substantial business as estate executors of wealthy blacks, earning two and one-half percent in commissions. They were also moneylenders on property and "made most of their loans to whites with building interests.... demanded 8 percent annual interest with loans for no less than $500."[77] Samuel Moore is also listed by Dun as a real estate broker: "Samuel Moore, Broker in R.E."[78]

Dun also reported that Francois Lacroix, listed as a "M[erchant] Tailor" in 1854, was "[v]ery wealthy. owns R.E. all over the City. owns buildings. Cor of Comm & St. Charles—w $200m." In 1860 Dun noted that he "[h]as lar means, supp wor $300m."[79] His brother, Julien Lacroix, listed in Dun as "[r]et. Grocer," also had extensive real estate holdings. In 1854, Dun reported that he was "vy wealthy est. w $250m.... Owns R.E. to a lar am't."[80] The Lacroix brothers acquired their property in much the same way as did Stephen Smith: "The brothers appeared, separately, at estate sales, at private auctions, especially at civil sheriffs' sales, where bargains could be had by anyone with the wherewithal to finance a down payment." They then made the down payment and, "like everyone else, gave promissory notes for the balance."[81]

The extent of Julien's property was revealed in 1857 when he sold some of his holdings—more than 75 properties, including unimproved lots as well as rental buildings—to Francois. The latter also acquired property in his capacity as a syndic, including property owned by free black Nelson Fouché, a real estate speculator who was also a builder trained in masonry, architecture, and mathematics. Fouché owned lots in the 1200 block of North Claiborne Avenue and in large sections of the city commons. Although he was a successful builder, Fouché went into bankruptcy in 1853 and again in 1858, when his property was confiscated by Francois, who, as "the syndic of his creditors, sold off [his three-story brick storehouse] and many other investments in New Orleans and St. Tammany Parish."[82]

Free blacks also pooled their money in organizations founded to invest in real estate. The New York African Society for Mutual Relief, founded in 1808, invested in real estate.[83] The founders and members were black businessmen, primarily craftsmen who owned their own enterprises and other black entrepreneurs.[84] The society's first president, William Hamilton, was a house carpenter; its first secretary, Henry Sipkins, was a mechanic; and six members were boot makers, all business owners. George deGrasse and Thomas L. Jennings were real estate dealers, and E. Vincent and E. Davis were dealers in feed. As membership increased, other businessmen joined: Henry Scott, a pickle manufacturer; Thomas Boggot, a soap chandler; and Cato Alexander, an innkeeper. Philip A. Bell, a newspaper editor and publisher, also ran an employment agency, and there were several ministers who owned businesses. Usually, no more than 65 men were members.[85]

By 1815 the society had acquired $500 in bank stock, a building, and a "respectable sum in cash on membership dues that were only $.25 per month."[86] Real estate investments

TABLE 4.5   Benezet Joint-Stock Association Yearly Financial Statements, 1862–1865

January 13, 1862	
Amount of stock sold	$302.00
Assets	
24 shares of stock	$1,200.00
15 ″ forfeited	750.00
6 ″ loans	257.07
	2,207.07
Balance in treasury	78.18
	2,285.25
January 12, 1863	
Assets	
29 shares of stock @ par	$1,450.00
15 ″ forfeited	750.00
6 ″ loans with trust	272.48 3/4
	2,472.48 3/4
January 11, 1864	
Assets	
35 shares of stock @ par	$1,750.00
16 ″ forfeited	800.00
6 ″ loans	234.47
	2,784.47
Amount received during year	489.87
Expended	414.62
Balance in treasury	75.25
January 9, 1865	
Received during year	$477.75
Balance in treasury	6.71
	$484.46
Expended	400.00
Balance in treasury	$84.84*

Source: Compiled from Benezet Joint-Stock Association, record book in Tinsley L. Spraggins, "The History of the Negro in Business Prior to 1860" (M.A. Thesis, Howard University, 1935).

*$84.46

account for the society's financial success. It purchased its first property in 1820 for $1,800. Funds from the sale enabled the society to purchase two additional properties, including a five-story flat, for rental property. In 1852 its annual business report showed $192.75 in membership dues, while rental income amounted to $2,000. In 1860 the society had assets of $15,000 and was the only black organization whose financial success could be attributed to real estate investment.[87] In a similar venture, a Cincinnati real estate and construction firm established in 1840, the Iron Chest, purchased property and constructed buildings, which they rented to whites.[88] Both provide examples of black group activity in real estate speculation and development.

Antebellum free blacks also formed real estate investment companies that made loans to its members. In 1854, 58 blacks formed the Benezet Joint Stock Association of Philadelphia.[89] It accumulated real property valued at $3,000 and personal property at $3,100, but eventually failed because of the loan policy of the association.[90] The company also loaned money to its members, based on the value of the stock held, which averaged about $11 a share; but by 1860 the Association reported: "The Loan feature has been a failure, the cause need not be stated as by this time (it is well understood) there are now over due loans."[91] The association forfeited outstanding loans that it accumulated for more than 11 months. See table 4.5 for the annual financial statements of the association from 1862 to 1865.

In San Francisco blacks founded the first African-American savings and loan association in California, the Saving Fund and Land Association, which in 1859 "purchased land and made small loans to local blacks." Henry Collins, a Pittsburgh land developer who was associated with Martin Delany in the publication of his newspaper, the *Pittsburgh Mystery,* was one of the leaders of the Savings Fund and Land Association. In 1852 Delany indicated that Collins was leaving for California, "where he intends entering extensively in land speculation." The association was only one of the several financial activities in San Francisco with which Collins was involved. In California, he was described as a "capitalist."[92]

Construction and Craft Trades

Throughout antebellum America, black real estate speculators also operated as building contractors and developers. In the North there were few employment opportunities for free black craftsmen, most of whom had to rely on black consumers. William Goodrich, who speculated in real estate in York County, Pennsylvania, owned, according to Dun, "a large amt of R E," including land and a farm in Canada. In 1848 Dun reported his property was valued at $20,000, but in 1856 said, "R E here [the United States] is worth $15m$." Dun indicates that Goodrich was a building contractor, having "[b]uilt one of our finest stores here." Goodrich constructed Centre Hall, a five-story building, at that time, the tallest in the city.[93]

Pittsburgh's Henry Collins, however, not only owned a construction company, which he established with $150, but was also a developer of one of the city's wealthiest residential districts. According to Delany, "there was little else than old trees in that quarter of the city when Mr. Collins began," and he "continued to build, and dispose of handsome dwellings, until a different class of citizens entirely, was attracted to that quarter of the town." About Collins's success as an urban developer, Delany added: "Collins' advice and counsel was solicited by some of the first lawyers, and land speculators, in matters of real estate."

In San Francisco Collins became the largest black real estate owner in the city. Collins had applied a knowledge of real estate investment obtained in Pittsburgh to San Francisco real estate and became one of the wealthiest of the state's black leaders.[94]

In Ohio antebellum blacks participated actively in the construction industry as independent contractors. In Cincinnati John Woodson, a master carpenter, owned a construction company that employed 8 to 10 men.[95] In Steubenville Luke Mulber started in the business by hiring himself out to carpenters for $10 a month in order to learn the trade. Within three years, he established his own business with several employees. Madison Tilley (1809–1887), who moved from Tennessee to Cleveland in 1837, was "an excavating contractor who at times employed as many as 100 men with his 20 wagons and 40 horses."[96] His property was valued at $40,000. In addition, a few antebellum blacks secured municipal contracts. In 1847 David Jenkins "received by contract, the painting, glazing, and papering of some of the public buildings of the State." In 1851 the Cincinnati plastering firm of Knight and Bell posted a $10,000 bond when it was granted a contract for plastering the public buildings of Hamilton County; as Delany said, "they put in their 'sealed proposal' . . . and got the contract."[97]

These men were the exceptions, however. In the North, antiblack prejudice within the ranks of white craftsmen forced most skilled black craftsmen out of the trades. Those who succeeded inevitably established their own construction companies, which were few in number; they succeeded primarily by underbidding their white competitors. Also, some black contractors used whites to front for them. When Henry Boyd, a cabinetmaker from Kentucky, first settled in Cincinnati in 1826, he was unable to secure employment since white craftsmen refused to work with him. After six months working as a stevedore, he found a job as a journeyman house builder. Within a year he quit and formed a construction company in partnership with a white man, who secured the contracts while Boyd did the work. Boyd dissolved the partnership 10 years later, when he established his own furniture factory.[98]

In Philadelphia a contemporary survey of the black male population showed that "less than two thirds of those who have trades follow them," although blacks in Philadelphia participated in the trades at a much higher rate than those in other northern cities.[99] Another source reported that in 1838 there were 26 carpenters and 13 cabinetmakers in Philadelphia, while it was noted in 1859 that there were 49 carpenters and 20 cabinetmakers. In the entire state of Massachusetts in 1860, however, there were only 20 black carpenters, one cabinetmaker, and two chair makers.[100]

In the South, notwithstanding the region's cultural mores that equated manual labor with blacks, whites vehemently opposed black participation, free and slave, in the trades. Nevertheless, by 1860, 80 percent of its 125,000 craftsmen, both black and white, were slaves. White craftsmen were not successful in driving slaves out of the construction industry, but they made it extremely difficult for free blacks to participate in it. In the South the largest number of black craftsmen were carpenters. In 1860 in the seven states of the upper South and Washington D.C., there were 221 carpenters whose property holdings averaged $885. In the eight lower southern states, there were 210 carpenters whose property holdings averaged $1,300.[101]

There always were a few successes. The building contractor James Boon, who was born a free black in 1808, established his construction company in Raleigh, North Carolina, after he ended an apprenticeship when he was 21. From then until the late 1850s, he was involved in all areas of the construction trades: building, remodeling, and repairing. He even worked as a skilled artisan in making furniture, and his subcontracting activities enabled him to stay afloat in the construction industry. Boon employed up to nine people and a bookkeeper, and was involved in the drayage business and rental properties. Also, using his property as collateral to execute deeds of trust enabled Boon to borrow money to underwrite his business expenses, while at the same time assuring his creditors repayment of the debt.[102]

As with blacks in the construction industry, those with furniture-making skills had to establish their own business because of white prejudice. One of the most successful free black furniture makers was Thomas Day of Milton, North Carolina. His manufactory, which employed slaves, in addition to a white journeyman, made beds, chairs, and cabinets. His chifforobes and four-poster beds were especially impressive, done in the Empire style of the time and adorned with an American eagle. In his advertisements Day indicated that he specialized in "[m]ahogony [sic], Walnut and Stained FURNITURE." Day also was a craftsman in housing construction, doing the interior woodwork in building fireplace mantles, stairways, banisters, and intricate ceiling and wall moldings in the homes of wealthy planters. In 1847 Day's bid to build library shelving at the University of North Carolina, while higher than that of the most respected white firm, was accepted by the governor because of his reputation for high-quality workmanship. Day's workshop, residence, and showroom were housed in one building. In 1860 Day held property valued at $4,000.[103]

Inventions and Manufacturing

As the new nation developed, several free black craftsmen invented devices that made important contributions to several industries that furthered the nation's economic advancement. Few of their inventions, however, were patented. And even fewer were able to capitalize on their inventions.

One who did, however, was Philadelphia black businessman and manufacturer James Forten (1766–1842). He invented a device that increased the performance of sailing ships, thus helping to cut the high costs of ocean shipping and aid the nation's fast-growing international trade. Forten manufactured the device in his factory that produced sails and riggings, which he had purchased from the owner of the shop where he had been employed as the foreman. Forten employed a workforce ranging from 25 to 60 men, black and white. In describing his shop, a contemporary said, "Last year I visited a gentleman in Philadelphia who employs a considerable capital in the business of sail making. He invited me to see his establishment, which occupies several lofts."[104]

Until his death, Forten was regarded as the wealthiest black in the North, with a fortune estimated at $300,000, which had dwindled to $67,000 when he died in 1842.[105] New technology in the maritime industries, specifically steam-powered vessels, accounted in part for Forten's financial decline, while the Panic of 1837 prevented him from collecting on outstanding loans. Forten, however, had also used much of his financial resources in support of abolitionist activities and in the development of black churches, schools, and community organizations.[106]

Several free black inventors and manufacturers contributed to rapidly increasing techno-logical innovations in agriculture. Henry Blair of Maryland was granted two patents for his inventions, a corn harvester in 1834 and a cotton planter in 1836.[107] Norbert Rillieux of Louisiana was antebellum America's most noted free black inventor. A machinist and engineer who studied in Paris, Rillieux invented a vacuum pan for refining sugar that revolutionized the sugar-refining process. He secured a patent in 1843 and another one in 1846. Rillieux also invented an improved and practical system for sewage disposal in New Orleans, but the municipal government refused to adopt it.[108]

In South Carolina two antebellum blacks made improvements in agricultural machinery. Charleston's Anthony Weston, who was nominally free and regarded as one of the best millwrights in the South, created innovations in the design of the rice-threshing machine, which resulted in increasing the output of processed rice from 500 to 1,000 bushels a day. Weston was only one of four southern businesspeople mentioned by Martin Delany as having "acquired an independent fortune, by his mechanical ingenuity and skillful workmanship." Four years after he established his shop, Weston, although a slave, purchased 13 slaves valued at $7,675 through his free wife. Six slaves worked in the factory manufacturing and repairing mills. Weston's real estate holdings were valued at $40,075.[109]

William Ellison (1790–1861) of South Carolina, a former slave, was one of the South's largest black manufacturers. Before he purchased his freedom at age 26, Ellison, apprenticed to a cotton-gin maker, learned the design and mechanics of cotton gins as well as bookkeeping skills. After he was freed, Ellison's increasing holdings in land and slaves reflected his success as a manufacturer. In 1840, 14 of Ellison's slaves worked in his factory repairing and manufacturing cotton gins. They used their carpentry skills in making the frame and their blacksmithing skills in forging the metal sawteeth, which separated cotton fiber from the seed. The price of most cotton gins was between $1,200 and $2,000, while a cotton gin made in 1836 that cleaned and pressed cotton bales sold for $600.[110] Some of Ellison's gins sold for $150 and his market extended to Mississippi. In 1849 his shop manufactured and sold 15 machines, and his blacksmith shop, which handled small repairs, grossed $1,500 in 1849. By 1860 his 63 slaves were valued at $53,000, and his 900 acres at $8,300.[111]

In several northern states, including Pennsylvania, New York, and Ohio, free blacks attempted to counter opposition to their participation in the business community as craftsmen by organizing. In 1850 the American League of Colored Laborers was founded in New York to promote black participation in the mechanical arts and commerce. The league proposed an industrial fair to be held in 1859, where the work of black craftsmen would be put on sale, with 70 percent of the revenue going to the exhibitors and 30 percent to the organization. These funds were to be used to assist "colored mechanics" to go into business for themselves as shopkeepers and merchants.[112] Unfortunately, the fair never took place.

Prior to that, however, an exhibition, the first for African-Americans, was held in Philadelphia in 1851 to display their technological innovations and manufacturing contributions to the nation's increasing industrialized economy. The *New York Tribune* provided coverage of the exhibit, called the Colored American Institute for the Promotion of the Mechanic Arts and Science, including a review of "an invention by Roberts for replacing cars on the track when thrown off, which is quite ingenious. There are many creditable things.... For the whole we think the exhibition reflects credit on the colored people."[113] Delany notes that Roberts had invented his car-lifting machine in 1842.[114]

Consequently, by the 1850s there was an increasing emphasis by black leaders on the acquisition of mechanical skills and on encouraging blacks with such skills to establish their own enterprises. As the nation industrialized, some blacks capitalized on the new inventions in establishing enterprises. In New Orleans Thomas Isabelle operated a sewing-machine and hardware store that provided "special types of machines for tailors, shoemakers, and seamstresses . . . while offering to repair and adjust sewing machines at the short-est notice."[115]

Still, most businesses established by antebellum blacks were personal service enterprises, where human capital skills allowed them to compete on a level playing field, especially in tailoring, catering, and barbering. All were high status occupations and also among the most lucrative antebellum black enterprises.

Catering, Restaurants, Hotels, and Taverns

Until the rise of the industrial city and the emergence of high-quality American hotels, with their fine restaurants and food services, few whites could compete with African-Americans in providing catering services for the rich, well-born, and powerful. Each major urban center had its prominent black caterer. Philadelphia, however, was the center of the antebellum black American catering industry. W. E .B. DuBois described the city's black caterers as a guild whose "masters include names which have been household words in the city for fifty years: Bogle, Augustin, Prosser, Dorsey, Jones and Minton."[116]

Philadelphia's black caterers succeeded because they stroked both the palates and the egos of their clients. Their culinary specialties were lobster salad, deviled crabs, chicken croquettes, and their unsurpassed terrapin.[117] While few of Philadelphia's first black cater-ers had any formal education, they were masterful politicians and diplomats, described as "gentlemanly," even "aristocratic," "possessing great wit and charm," "commanding great influence," "dictatorial," but always of "fine business attainments." The services provided were delivered with impeccable manners, taste, and elegance, and as Dubois said, Philadel-phia's black caterers "filled a unique place in a time when social circles were very exclusive and the millionaire and the French [white cordon bleu] cook had not arrived."[118]

Although many of the first black caterers were from the French West Indies, American-born Robert Bogle professionalized the industry in the early nineteenth century and is rec-ognized as "the originator of catering."[119] He provided elegant dinners and banquets in the homes of the wealthy, served by a retinue of uniformed waiters, whose services matched that of the most correct English butlers. Bogle began as a hotel waiter and owned a coffee shop before he became a caterer. It was Haitian-born Peter Augustin, however, who, with his catering business established in 1818, eventually made Philadelphia the cen-ter of American catering. His clients included the city's elite and distinguished foreign luminaries, such as Charles Dickens. Augustin's classic dish, terrapin, sold for $14 to $16 a quart. On returning home from America, many Europeans placed orders for its delivery to Paris and London.[120]

Catering for Philadelphia blacks became a family business, passed from one generation to the next, often with intermarriage among the families. Augustin's son married the daughter of another leading Philadelphia caterer, Eugene Baptiste. Initially a cabinetmaker, Baptiste capitalized on his wife's cooking skills and established their catering enterprise in 1818. The antebellum enterprise had three large kitchens and employed from 40 to 100 people specializing in all areas of food preparation and service.[121] The Augustin-Baptiste catering business continued into the early twentieth century.[122]

By the 1840s a challenging new group of Philadelphia black caterers emerged, the tri-umvirate of Jones, Dorsey, and Minton, who ruled the catering world from 1845–1875. In addition to their catering business, they also owned restaurants, invariably the first step to a catering enterprise. Thomas Dorsey (1810–1875) came to Philadelphia as a fugitive slave, was returned to slavery, but was purchased by friends he had made in Philadelphia.[123] Henry Jones, from Virginia, was in the catering business for 30 years. Like many of the elite Philadelphia caterers, he also provided service to wealthy whites in New Jersey and New York. He died in 1875 and left a considerable estate. Of Henry Minton, the third of these illustrious caterers, Delany said, he "is the proprietor of a fashionable restaurant and resort for business men and gentlemen of the city."[124]

Philadelphia's black caterers sold their dinners or banquets by the plate, with prices as high as $50 per plate. Consequently, these businesses were regarded as highly lucrative enterprises, as shown by an entry in the Dun report regarding one of the sons of Henry Minton. The Dun entry emphasized that the caterer had the financial capacity to back his son's business, which is described as "Gents furnishing": "Oct 2. 60 Colored—Aged abt 23. single son of Henry Minton who keeps a restaurant at 204 South 12th St & who owns cons'd [considerable] city ppty [property], furnishes the capital & set his son up in the business here.... He is backed up by his father in that way is safe for all his bus wants."[125]

The Dun report of New York jeweler Edward V. Clark indicates that catering was a business that involved more than just superb cooking. The presentation of the food was paramount, including the quality of dinner service used, which required considerable capital. In this instance, Clark, described by Delany as "among the most deserving and active business men in New York," combined his jewelry business with that of "public waiter," the term applied to caterers. Dun lists Clark as a "Jeweler," but emphasized that his "principal bus is to loan silver, glass ware etc to the 'upper ten' for dinners & evening parties, at which he is said to be doing well, & keeps a stock of such articles, amounts to about $5m."

According to Dun, Clark established his business in 1849 "with 2 1/2 @ 3m cash." Previously, he worked as a porter for the New York jewelry firm of Platt Brothers. His stock, worth $5,000, had been purchased with money borrowed from Platt Brothers, a loan that he repaid in fewer than 16 months. In 1853 Dun reported: "(besides his Jewelry bus) He is a public waiter & gets up dinners & suppers in which business he is making money. Had on the 1st of January last Silver & plated dining & Tea Sets which he bought w $1500 on which he owes $100." An 1854 Dun entry noted that he was "in a good retail business. Pays well. Makes money & has good credit for all he wants.... He is worth 10m$."[126]

Thomas and George Downing were leaders in the catering field for almost a century in both New York and Rhode Island. Thomas was born a slave in Virginia, as was his wife, who was free when their son, George (1819–1903), was born.[127] After moving to New York in 1812, Thomas opened a restaurant and oyster house in the business district. His customers were leading bankers and merchants, and the establishment quickly gained a fine reputation, even among foreign travelers.

George expanded the family's enterprise in 1844 when he moved to Newport, Rhode Island, to establish his own catering and restaurant business. In Newport George purchased the Sea Girt Hotel, a $30,000 property, doubtless with financial backing by his father, who Delany said, "made three fortunes." The large Sea Girt building had eight large stores on the first floor, with hotel accommodations for the wealthy on the upper floors. An 1848 advertisement indicates the menu and the kinds of catering services George provided:

> Downing of New York, at the solicitation of a number of his *customers* and friends from the *South* has opened a suite of Game and Oyster Supper Rooms on *Cottage Street,* where

he will have on hand New York Oysters, Woodcock, Soft Crabs, Lobster Salid, Green Tur-
tle Soup, Ice Cream, Confectionary, &c.

The ad also indicated that Downing could serve large parties and that ladies would be
provided food service in private: "Some of the above rooms are calculated to support 30
persons. N.B. A Private Ice Cream Saloon for ladies." In addition, Downing provided
delivery service for his delicacies; another advertisement for Downing's enterprise read:
"ICE CREAM, CALVES FOOT JELLY and Charlotte DE RUSE, *sent to cottages by Downing.*"[128]
The Sea Girt building was destroyed by fire at a loss of $30,000. Downing subsequently
rebuilt the business on the same site, which became known as Downing's block.

In the spring of 1850, Downing ran a notice in the Newport newspaper advertising
stores to rent: "George L. Downing is now building three handsome and commodious
Stores, on the Hill, on East Touro street, which will be let as soon as completed, certainly
by the 10th of June. The Stores are admirably located for summer trade, and those who
desire an excellent location, will do well to apply immediately to the builder . . . or George L.
Downing."[129] The first Dun entry on George Downing in March 1865 lists his business
only as "Colored Confectioner," but indicates he is "Good for wants."[130]

While the leading antebellum black caterers and restaurant owners in the North profited
from their enterprises, their southern counterparts were more successful in establishing
restaurants and hotel enterprises. The leading wealthy whites in the South were primarily
slave owners who preferred to be served by their own retinue of domestic slaves and were
often more comfortable with southern food as the mainstay of their diet. A few slave owners, seeking more diverse cooking, sent their male slaves to Paris for training in French cuisine. Some free blacks also went to France to expand their culinary skills.[131] An urban business elite, southern travelers, and wealthy slaveholders constituted a clientele anxious for
fine food and luxurious lodging.

Free blacks in the urban South capitalized on this market by establishing exclusive restaurants, luxury inns, and hotels, but there were also blacks who succeeded as caterers. In
Petersburg, Virginia, free black Jack Mccrae ran a restaurant and a catering business, as did
his one-time partner John Brewer.[132] In South Carolina, Jehu Jones ran an exclusive hotel,
the former Burrows-Hall Inn, which he purchased in 1816 for $13,000 from profits made
in his tailoring enterprise. Wealthy guests of the Jones Inn (later the Jones Hotel) included
the governor of the state. One English traveler praised its clean tablecloths, the silver, and
claret, noting that the usual "salt pork and greasy corn cake" were not served.

Jones's staff consisted of the six slaves he owned, and the property he owned amounted
to $40,000. After his death in 1833, the inn changed hands several times. In 1847, it was
purchased by John and Eliza Lee, a black couple. A newspaper advertisement of the day
announced that the hotel was "to be re-opened . . . that long established and popular
House known as Jone's [sic] Hotel. . . . The subscriber . . . has had long experience in catering. . . . [signed] John Lee Former Proprietor of Lee's House." The Lees owned eight
slaves. Mrs. Lee's brother, William Seymour, who ran a tavern and inn, owned six slaves
who provided the cooking, serving, and maintenance service for the inn, which remained
open until he died in 1862.[133]

In the South the market for food services provided by free blacks was not just limited to
wealthy whites. Both urban slaves and free blacks patronized cookshops, groceries, and
grogshops owned by free blacks. Grogshops served liquor despite southern statutes making it illegal for unlicensed free blacks to sell liquor to slaves and for slaves to purchase any
alcoholic beverage. Often cookshops or confectionery stores were covers for the grogshops

that also provided gambling and prostitution. Often the shops were raided and the owners taken to court. Most hired lawyers for their defense and got off with a fine.

Even when these illegal businesses were closed, they were reopened surreptitiously in new locations, built with hidden passageways and doors so their patrons could escape. Richmond, Virginia, was the location of two such enterprises. Free black Clinton James ran a multipurpose enterprise, a grocery, barroom, snack room, and kitchen on the first floor of a building he owned, which was located behind one of Richmond's exclusive hotels. Enterprising free black Richard Taylor ran the Taylor House, which provided all the services of a hotel, in addition to alcohol, gambling, and prostitution. As profitable and successful operators of these enterprises, James, Taylor, and others like them gained the respect of the black community and often emerged as their leaders.[134]

Northern free blacks were not forbidden to sell liquor. In Cincinnati, in addition to five drinking shops owned by free blacks, the black-owned Dumas Hotel, "had, as did all hotels of that day, its place for 'bucking the tiger,' and in it was the biggest colored Faro game in the country."[135] On the western frontier, the intrepid black explorer James P. Beckwourth (1797–1867), one of the founders of Denver, established a hotel and trading post in 1852 in what is now Beckwourth Valley. Beckwourth was a fugitive slave from St. Louis who in 1815 joined a fur expedition as a scout, hunter, and Indian fighter. The trail he discovered, Beckwourth Pass, became the main route for settlers moving to California during the gold rush.[136]

Around the same time in California, William Leidesdorff opened the first luxury hotel in San Francisco. After the 1848 gold rush, free blacks and former slaves in California provided food services to the great numbers of men whose sole interest was searching for gold. Initially, many blacks worked as cooks in bars, hotels, and mining camps; some who saved their money from the high wages opened restaurants and cookshops. George Washington Dennis, three months after being brought to San Francisco as a slave by New Orleans gamblers, purchased both himself and his mother from slavery for $950. As a slave, he had been a porter, making $250 a month, in addition to any sweepings of gold dust he could gather from beneath the gambling tables. Once freed, George and his mother paid $40 a day for the use of a hotel table on which they served food, from which they earned $225 a day.

Still, the food service industry was precarious and profits inevitably reflected the state of the economy. The Panic of 1857, which hit New York hard, impacted on the catering business of Edward Clark. In 1855, Dun reported that "Bus has ben slack with him the past years & he is not thought to have made much, but is regarded as honest & safe for a moderate credit." The following year, Dun reported that Clark "has made some money know, too, how to take care of it." Dun's last two entries for Clark were in 1857. In June an entry noted that his jewelry business was gone: "Has sold out his regular bus. Is sf for what crdit he will ask for in business of supplying parties." Several months later, Dun reported Clark as "Failed."

In the hierarchy of antebellum food services, Philadelphia's black caterers were an elite group. In the South, blacks were the owners of exclusive restaurants and hotels. The financial success of both groups can be attributed to their wealthy white clientele, whose power provided a protective covering against any disturbances to their pursuit of the luxurious and exclusive services provided by blacks. Yet, food services in all areas of the country provided a viable source of income for free blacks, whether their patrons were white or black, rich or poor. Human capital, skills, and resourcefulness provided the basis for their success, as they would in other industries blacks entered.

Barbershops and Personal Service Enterprises

Blacks in antebellum America dominated the barbering business primarily by owning shops that serviced wealthy whites.[137] In both the North and the South, barbering enterprises that catered to wealthy whites emerged as one of the most prosperous businesses for blacks and placed their owners among the occupationally elite in antebellum black America.[138] For example, it was said that the wealth of blacks in Pittsburgh prior to the Civil War was "[r]epresented by a group of men who ran barbershops, hairdressing saloons [sic] and bathhouses." In the North, the most successful antebellum free black barbers owned exclusive shops, either as separate establishments in the urban white business districts or in exclusive white hotels.

Cleveland barber John Brown ran his shop in the New England Hotel, the largest and most luxurious in the city.[139] John B. Vashon (1792–1855), Pittsburgh's leading black, was originally from Virginia. His contemporaries noted that although he could pass for white, Vashon took pride in his African heritage. Along with his barbershop, Vashon opened the first public city bathhouse west of the Alleghenies in 1820. Luxurious services and continuous renovations, as seen in an 1839 advertisement, account for his success:

CITY BATHS

The subscriber respectfully informs the citizens of Pittsburgh, and strangers visiting here, that his Warm, Cold, Shower Baths for Ladies and Gentlemen . . . having undergone thorough repairs, and being brilliantly illuminated with Gas Lights, are now open for the season, every day, (Sunday excepted), from 6 o'clock, A.M. to 11: o'clock, P.M. The subscriber feels grateful for the patronage so liberally bestowed upon him by the public and will spare no pains to merit a continuance of its favors."[140]

Antebellum black barbers were also leaders in promoting the institutional development of the black community. Vashon was a member of the National Negro Convention; and Lewis Woodson, also a successful Pittsburgh barber and a minister, was one of the founders of Wilberforce University.[141] One of Cincinnati's leading barbers was William W. Watson, who had been a Kentucky slave until his freedom was purchased for $750 by his brother-in-law, a barber who borrowed the money from his wealthy white customers. Within a year, Watson had earned enough to repay the money with interest. He then established his own barbershop and, with profits earned from that enterprise, purchased his mother, brothers, and sisters from slavery. As his business flourished, Watson made substantial contributions to the black community and contributed "largely" to the building of black churches.[142] His wealth was estimated, as one contemporary said, at "some $30,000."

In promoting their St. Louis barbering business, partners Louis Clamorgan and Mr. Iredell enticed prospective patrons with advertisements that described their luxurious shop. An 1845 newspaper ad announced their "Splendid Hair Cutting and Shaving Saloon," with recently installed baths with tubs of "the finest Italian marble, the rooms large, airy and elegantly furnished." By 1860 Clamorgan's brother, Henry, was proprietor of Clamorgan Baths, also known as the Italian Baths. His barbershop and rental property were valued at $10,000, and his personal property at $3,000. Quite often, the barbering business became a family enterprise, passing from one generation to another, including female family members. In Pittsburgh, Lewis Woodson established his family in the barbering business, which he launched in 1834. He was the father of 11 children, including 6 sons who became barbers. Lewis owned five barbershops, three of which were located in downtown hotels.[143]

In the South free black barbers also accumulated wealth, which most of them invested in real and chattel property. The wealthy North Carolina barber John Stanley (who had a white father and an Ibo mother) started as an apprentice and then established his own shop. With his profits, he purchased 64 slaves, including his wife, children, and brother-in-law, who were among the 18 slaves that he freed.[144] Invariably, the staff of most successful antebellum free black barbers in the South included the slaves they owned.[145]

While the financial success of antebellum black barbers is generally well known, only the business records of William Johnson, the "Barber of Natchez," are available to provide insight into how these men were able to accumulate wealth. His diary covers the period from 1835 to 1851, when he was murdered by a white man with whom he was involved in a land-boundary dispute. Johnson owned three barbershops and a bathhouse in Natchez, with plans for establishing another shop in Jackson. He also owned a plantation run by a white overseer that brought him additional profits from the sale of commodities produced by his slaves. In addition, Johnson also owned a general merchandise and notions store, racehorses, and held part interest in the Natchez racecourse.

Johnson's established his first barbershop in Port Gibson, which he sold when he moved to Natchez. He worked initially in another shop until 12 October 1830, when, as he wrote in his cash book, "[Natchez] October 12th 1830. being The first commencement of my work after I had Bought out the interest of Wm. Miller." From that date to 30 October, Johnson made $51.37. In November, he made $110.29. Johnson charged a flat rate of $1.50 to $1.75 a month for shaving (one individual paid $40 for 21 months of shaving), and $.75 for each haircut.[146] Johnson's employment of slave apprentice barbers in his three barbershops increased his profits. Averaging $100 per month from each of his three shops, Johnson's income could approach $3,600 annually. Table 4.6 shows Johnson's cash book. His daily earnings for November 1830 are typical of the money earned by antebellum barbers.

TABLE 4.6   Cash Book Account of Natchez Barber William Johnson, November 1830

Nov. 1	4.50	Nov. 16	5.00
Nov. 2	1.50	Nov. 17	4.25
Nov. 3	2.62 1/2	Nov. 18	3.37
Nov. 4	2.62 1/2	Nov. 19	3.62
Nov. 5	2.00	Nov. 20	0.00
Nov. 6	5.25	Nov. 21	2.00
Nov. 7	1.87	Nov. 22	5.00
Nov. 8	6.37	Nov. 23	3.70
Nov. 9	4.12	Nov. 24	4.37
Nov. 10	3.50	Nov. 25	12.25
Nov. 11	1.62	Nov. 26	2.25
Nov. 12	4.50	Nov. 27	2.25
Nov. 13	4.50	Nov. 28	3.00
Nov. 14	4.75	Nov. 29	3.50
Nov. 15	3.50	Nov. 30	2.50
		Total	$110.29

Source: Compiled from William Johnson, Cash Book, November 1828–September 1834, William T. Johnson and Family Memorial collection, 1793–1837, Special Collections, Hill Memorial Library, Louisiana State University Libraries.

Barbering offered financial advantages for antebellum blacks, and their participation is important in African-American business history for reasons that far outweigh their numbers. By 1850 the numbers of free black barbers in various cities were: 14 in Charleston; 122 in New York (80 blacks, 42 mulattoes); 41 in New Orleans (35 mulattoes, 6 blacks). In Boston there were 26 blacks out of 935 barbers, and in St. Louis, 33 blacks out of 780 barbers. In Philadelphia there were 61 black barbers and hairdressers and 4 barbers and perfumers in 1838; whereas, in 1859, there were 248 black barbers.[147] Antebellum blacks carried the barbering business to California. In 1852 there were 18 black barbers in San Francisco and 23 in Sacramento. San Francisco's William H. Blake owned a general store, but his advertisement in the black paper the *Pacific Appeal* showed that he was "a supplier of cutlery, soaps, oils, perfumeries, and other articles used in the barbering business, at both wholesale and retail prices." Also in the 1850s James Richards Phillips (1836–1902), who settled in San Francisco in 1854, opened a bathhouse and barbershop, Phillips & Company, which employed "ten barbers and had twenty bathtubs."[148]

Invariably, the obsequiousness of black barbers has been emphasized as the basis for their success. Yet deference has always been a requisite in any enterprises that cater to the wealthy, even those providing professional services, regardless of race. In the case of antebellum black barbers, the most important factor that contributed to their financial success was their astute business acumen. The most successful were not reluctant, for example, to invest their profits in providing state-of-the art services in elegant shops for their clients. Specifically, antebellum black barbers, who serviced the rich, stood in the forefront in providing the country's most advanced services in the health and hair care industry before the Civil War.

Tailors and Clothing Stores

Until the Civil War, blacks also dominated the high fashion sector of the tailoring and clothing industry. The success of New Orleans black tailors provided the basis for their substantial wealth, although they also engaged in shrewd real estate investments. Charles Gayarré emphasizes that "[a]s tailors, they were almost exclusively patronized by the elite, so much so that the Legoasters', the Dumas', the Clovis', the Lacroix', acquired individually fortunes of several hundred thousands of dollars."[149] A Dun report describes the firm of Colvis and Dumas as "[Master] Tailors," with the first entry in July 1848 noting, "Do a gd custom bus to order for cash, consid' good. June 49. French quadroons, w in RE $150m Import their own Stk. educated men, knw as fash^ble tailors through the entire South."[150] The Dumas Brothers were described as "dealers in imported weaves, whose tailoring establishment manufactured and sold fancy pants, cashmere waists, silk waists, velvet waists, French shirts, and tailor's furnishing goods."[151] Francois Lacroix was also known as owning "one of the most fash^ble tailoring establish[ments] in the City . . . [who], imports largely from Paris . . . . June 15 60 wor 300m$." His advertisement in the 1853 city directory announced: "Lacroix, Francois, merchant tailor (established 1817) importer of French cloth, fancy casimere, and the best and most extensive assortment of clothing of every description, made in Paris, by the first fashionable tailors, and an elegant variety of gloves, cravats, stocks, etc; [at] 23 St. Charles."[152]

Antebellum black tailors, with their skills and innovative designs, were important in developing the American fashion industry. The leading New Orleans black tailors were in the forefront of innovative designs because they traveled to Paris and brought back the latest fashion trends, to which they added their own stylish modifications. Returning to Paris, they in turn influenced the European fashion industry. One of the leading black tailors in 1850, Mr. Cordovell had been in business for about 25 years and was said by Delany to be the "originator of fashions in the city of New Orleans"; in addition, his fashions were "said to have frequently become the leading fashions of Paris."

Delany emphasized the extent to which Cordovell's designs were copied by American tailors, saying he was informed "by Mr. B., a leading merchant tailor in a populous city, that many of the eastern American 'reports' [of European designs] were nothing more than a copy, in some cases modified, of those of Cordovell." On Cordovell's retirement in Paris, Delany adds, "it is said, that he still invents fashions for the Parisian reporters, which yields him annually a large income." In 1848, the entry from the Dun report on the Cordovell and Lacroix's firm reads: "Creoles, Dg a large perhaps the most fashion'ble bus in the city: long in bus & are rich."[153]

Antebellum black tailors in the North also achieved some success. In Detroit Robert Banks was the city's leading tailor, but discontinued his business after being burned out twice.[154] Chicago tailor John Jones (1826–1879), a leading abolitionist, was worth $10,000 before 1860. He had migrated from North Carolina to Chicago in the 1840s and established his shop in the city's developing business district. In Buffalo, New York, business partners Abner H. Frances and James Garrett started their clothing store with venture capital of $75, and, before their business failed in 1849, earned gross profits of "sixty thousand dollars annually."[155] The Dun reports of the Albany, New York, tailor William H. Topp are important for the information they provide about the reputation and steady profits earned by most antebellum black tailors (see table 4.7).

What is not so generally known is that antebellum blacks also cornered the market in the secondhand-clothing business. In Boston, David Walker ran a successful used-clothing business until his mysterious death shortly after publication of his pamphlet calling for a slave revolt. An 1829 advertisement for his enterprise in *The Rights of All* announced:

> Kept constantly on hand for sale by David Walker, number 42 Brattle St., Boston, a great variety of new and second hand clothing in the neatest manner and on the most reasonable terms.[156]

William Still, who became famous for his publication on the Underground Railroad, also ran a secondhand clothing business, which provided venture capital for his more successful stove-manufacturing enterprise. Philadelphia surveys of antebellum black enterprises and occupations in 1849 and 1856 show that there were 52 blacks dealing in secondhand clothing. Henry Minton recalled their impact on the antebellum clothing industry: "At that time, the Negro controlled that business, the Jew not entering it and displacing the colored man until after the war."[157] In New York it was reported that "secondhand clothing stores were frequently run by Negroes." In San Francisco during their first decade of settlement in the 1850s, blacks established secondhand clothing stores as viable enterprises.

Frederick Douglass's eulogy of the black New York clothier Thomas L. Jennings (1791–1859), who was also an antebellum political activist, mentions his work in the clothing industry: Jennings "entered business on his own account, and invented a method of renovating garments, for which he obtained letters patent from the United States." Douglass added that "[f]or many years, Mr. Jennings conduced a successful business as

TABLE 4.7   Dun on Antebellum Free Black Merchant-Tailor William Topp, 1847–1857

William H. Topp   Mer Tailor   Albany

Apr. 47	Very upright discreet & worthy. partly of col descent but has many friends in the city commercial life, without means he has made money. retains all his customers. Doing a safe & profitable bus. don't think would contract debts rashly, think him entirely gd for modest credit.
Aug. 47	Doing a fine bus & laying up money. safe for reasonable cr
Feb. 49	Does the most fashionable bus in the city tho' a col'd man has the best class of customers tho' not the most numerous is of gd character & habits, doing well believe making money and safe for purchases
Mar. 50	Does a modest bus is estimated worth 3 or 4m$, with small portion RE, frugal char & habits, industrious and in fair credit at home
Sept. 50	A very light negro & good looking, owns a house & lot, quite a fashionable tailor, industrious, attentive, doing a good bus. chiefly for the Upper 10, worth about 3 or 4m$ very good bus.
Aug. 53	Age 40 excellent man, very good merchant, good char about 4m$. has made money, but is not making much now, been in bus a long time & maintained a good reputation, in good credit
Mar. 54	Keeps a fashionable store, stock $5 @ $8m. worth 3m industrious & worthy of cr.
Sept. 54	Very excellent man Owns RE & is worth $5m. Dg a Gd bus & is much respected, very fashionable, considred good
Sept. 55	Is a col man, owns R.E. & is w 5 or 6M$, steady careful & industrious, dg a gd bus is prompt pay
Mar. 56	Is an aristocratic darkey a NO 1 in business line Does a fashionable bus. owns RE.
Sept. 56	Color'd man. Dg a Gd bus' Owns RE & is considred good maintains the honor of his people
Mar. 57	No change. dg a gd bus & mkg money is a very aristocratic darkey
Nov. 57	Is very much out of healthy and it is not tho't he can live long. is supposed to have made money, to be worth some money, good for all he wants, own a home in Green St, w 4 m$
Dec. 57	Dead—he was worth several m$ [thousand dollars] He owns RE—His estate will no doubt pay debts in full

Source: Compiled from R. G. Dun and Company, New York; R. G. Dun and Company Collection, Baker Library, Harvard University Business School.

Clothier."[158] Before Jennings went into the secondhand clothing business, he was a slave in New York and served an apprenticeship under a tailor, then freed under the state's gradual emancipation laws.

Wholesale, Retail, and Commission Merchants

Of the few antebellum free blacks who achieved success as merchants, most of them did so in the wholesale and retail merchandising of foods, dry goods, and fancy goods. The businesses of black shopkeepers, whether successful or not, were invariably located in the black enclaves of urban ghettoes, which also housed the poor of other races and ethnic groups. In Philadelphia in 1859, there were 166 shopkeepers, most of them surviving from day to day. Throughout the South in 1860, Loren Schweninger found only 19 shopkeepers, 25 grocers, and 25 merchants whose profits enabled them to purchase property. The less successful black shopkeepers had a black consumer base, while the successful ones catered primarily to whites with high-quality merchandise. Unless they had capital, establishing a retail grocery or dry-goods store in rural areas usually meant that free blacks and slaves "would go from farm to farm to do business, but in the city they usually had established shops."[159]

In Cincinnati Samuel T. Wilcox, who by 1860 was worth $59,000, built up both a large wholesale market in New York, Boston, and Baltimore and a local retail trade among elite white families. Initially a steamboat steward, Wilcox saved money to provide capital for his enterprise. Explaining why he went into the grocery business, Wilcox said, "I might have bought a farm and lived on my money, but I wished to show, if I could, that colored people could do something besides being barbers.... Many advised me not to try, and said nobody would buy groceries of a colored man."[160]

In describing how he built his retail grocery business and his wholesale pickling and preserving manufactory, Wilcox said, "I build this house and stored, fitted up the cellar for milk and butter, and have a manufactory of pickles. This morning I received five letters on business from the South. In those boxes there is a thousand dollars' worth of goods just packed for Terre Haute."[161] The layout of his local store was a feature that attracted customers: Delany said he had "the most extensive business house of the kind ... the establishment is really beautiful ... having the appearance more of an apothecary store, than a Grocery House."[162]

New York's Henry Scott also built up a very successful wholesale food distribution business. Delany said that "[h]e, like most of the others, had no assistance at the commencement, but by manly determination and perseverance, raised himself to what he is." In developing his business, Scott capitalized on the opportunities available in New York's extensive transportation industry. Delany added that Scott's firm has "for many years been engaged extensively in the pickling business, keeping constantly in warehouse, a very heavy stock of articles in their line. His business is principally confined to supplying vessels with articles and provisions in his line of business, which in this great metropolis is very great." Scott's attention to business and his careful accounting practices so impressed Delany that he said, "There have doubtless been many a purser, who cashed and filed in his office the bill of Henry Scott, without ever dreaming of his being a colored man." The Dun reports contain numerous entries indicating that Scott was black, for example:[163]

Henry Scott & Co.	Ira Lee Jr., Pickles, & c.	217 Water
Dec 17 51.	"S" has been over 20 yrs in the bus. "L" was taken in some time ago: are mulattoes: both very honest men: "S" owns 2 or 3 houses & lots ... is considered worth 8m@ 10m and very responsible.	
Aug 31 53.	Doing good modest business, good for all their contracts.	
Mar 15 54.	Safe for any amount they can buy. Doing a fair retail business making money.	
Jun 26 54.	Are doing well, & in fair credit.	
Mar 17 55.	Doing a limited business; slow paying, but thought ultimately good for what they owe.	
Ag 20 55.	"Henry Scott" alone. [C]ontinues to do a fair business ... reputed worth 12m to 15m. [S]ome find him a little slow but none question his responsibility, his partner "Lee" died about 3 years ago & "Scott" has since done by alone.	

As a group, retail grocers in Louisiana were the most successful. Wealthy real estate holder Julien Lacroix is listed in Dun as, "Ret Grocer. June 54. A. F.M.C. Abt 50.... In bus 20 yrs..... Has a vry extens gro & does a vry gd bus. He is vy wealthy est w $250m.... May 21 59. Has a lar Stock & a handsome Ret Trade, & although slow in his payments has a Cr for all he wants." Lacroix's grocery was located in a Creole storehouse, part of a complex that he built. His business was described as "something of a specialty establishment and carried a large selection of imported wines, liquors, cordials, and olive oils by the case, along with canned fish and syrups, fine soaps, barrels of beer, vinegar, rice and sugar, smoked beef, and cheeses and hundreds of smaller items."[164]

Before D. R. McCarty became a broker, he had quite a successful retail dry-goods business. The first entry made by Dun in 1848 notes that he was "a col'd man, owes R.E. . . . is now in NY buying goods consd w $30m." In 1849, Dun said, "Keeps over $20m stk & prob sells $60m w a yr." Later that year, Dun reported that McCarty had reduced the size of his business before he eventually sold out and that Rillieux & Reggio were "Successors of D. R. McCarty." In 1850 Dun provides their first listing and reports their immediate success: "their business has fine cap. buy largely at Auction & I have the best Authority for saying that you may trust them to their own extent." In 1852 Dun said that they "[h]ave like nearly all the D. G. Men increased their bus & means."

Interestingly, several months later, Dun advised, "Let them alone." Whether they were having difficulty securing credit is not known, but two months after this Dun notes: "they have depend' upon 'A Reggio' the father of R of the firm to aid them but he has been protested. I do not thk it prud to cred them." Two years later, Dun revised its review: "Are hon. & indus & dg a gd sales. amt to abt $40m. Are making money & hv ample cap. . . . Pay with the greatest punctuality & are in excellent cr . . . backed by 'McCarthy' whom they succeeded."[165]

Several Dun reports provide information that show successful antebellum black businessmen provided financial support for their sons, in-laws, or close family friends who went into business. Pennsylvania's William H. Minton, whose business was listed in Dun as "Gents furnishing," had the support of his father: "He is backed up by his father in that way is safe for all his bus wants." Family reputation was important in Dun's credit ratings, as seen in the entries of the sons of two black planters. Of G. Donato, a grocer in Opelousas, Louisiana, Dun said, " 'The Donatos' are very respectable colored people and altho we do not know this one particularly, we think he is a pretty safe trader, prudence and industry being the family characteristics of the 'Donatos'. . . . [H]is father (we believe he is a son of old 'Martin Donato,') was quite wealthy." Concerning the grocery firm of Felix Metoyer and Brothers in Natchitoches, Dun reported, "Successor to Henry & Metoyer do a f m business and perfectly gd for thr Contracts."[166]

In the Isle Brevelle Cane River colony in Natchitoches, from the 1820s on, wealthy black planters, determined to keep their money in their community, operated several kinds of businesses that were "supplemental to the plantation economy, such as merchandising, money lending, milling, ginning and operating a ferry." These enterprises were located in the colony and in New Orleans, sometimes in partnership with each other, other times with whites.[167] Free black Oscar Dubreuil operated a general store, whose customers were primarily the Cane River black planters to whom he sold "dry goods, groceries, medical supplies, cosmetics." Dubreuil's account books for 1856–1858 showed that he did a credit business of $25,000, and that his "largest credit business was in the whiskey line."[168] This situation and others like it show that it was possible for black merchants, with a financially supportive black consumer base, to succeed in business.

In some instances, black merchants were involved in several enterprises. Dubreuil was also a tailor, ran a ferry, a billiards hall, a livery service that included a hearse, and was an undertaker.[169] In Pennsylvania Dun reported that William Goodrich "trades extensively." His mercantile business was described as "Fancy Goods," with an inventory that ranged from jewels to toys. Goodrich was also a printer, owned an oyster company and a construction company, in addition to running railroad cars on the Columbia Railroad. As the Dun entry emphasized, Goodrich had "a great many irons in the fire." He was worth over $20,000.[170]

Undertaking and Cemetery Enterprises

"Funeral services are much esteemed by the Negroes," noted Frederick Law Olmsted in describing a funeral procession in Richmond: "There was a decent hearse, of the usual style, drawn by two horses; six hacking coaches followed it, and six well dressed men, mounted on handsome saddle horses, and riding them well, rode in the rear of them.... Twenty or thirty men and women were also walking together with the procession, on the sidewalk. Among them all was not a white person."[171] From the beginning of their settlement in the American colonies, blacks took the initiative in providing for the burial of their dead. With the founding of black churches, black religious leaders were the primary agents in such activities.

During the Philadelphia's catastrophic yellow-fever epidemic in 1793, Richard Allen and Absalom Jones joined as partners in a nonprofit undertaking business. The mayor had requested their help in burying the dead, the first time an American governmental body formally recognized the existence of black-community leadership. After Allen and Jones submitted their carefully itemized bill, the city was reluctant to pay. Its rationale: blacks should be honored by the opportunity to perform a civic duty.[172]

Several occupational groups provided items and services for funerals. Carpenters, cabinetmakers, and upholsterers made coffins. When Adam Suder of New York City established a cabinetmaking business in 1828, he advertised in the first black newspaper in America, *Freedom Journal:* "Adam Suder, cabinet maker in New York would acquaint his friends and public, that he has opened business at 166 Duane St. where he will thankfully receive and punctually fill all orders taken by him." Suder also indicated that he could make coffins "in the shortest notice."[173] In Philadelphia a third-generation descendant of antebellum black caterer Henry Minton said, "We realize the outgrowth of the undertaking business from the carpentering." In that city two black families of carpenters, the Almonds and the Duteres began to specialize in the undertaking business. Subsequent generations of both families continued this enterprise into the twentieth century.[174] Indeed, at the 1851 Colored American Institute exhibit in Philadelphia, the *New York Tribune* noted that "Dutere, an undertaker, has some fine work in his line."

In another instance of a businessman combining undertaking with another occupation, the prominent Philadelphia black caterer Robert Bogle, before his death in 1837, also ran a funeral business, doubtless an enterprise fostered by economies of scale. The horses and carriages used in the transportation of food and other items in his catering enterprise were also used for the funeral procession and to transport the deceased to cemeteries. Bogle, after all, was a businessman. Undertaking was an enterprise that was not subject to the economic highs and lows of other businesses. While only a few people could afford to eat well, no one got through life without dying. Also, it was not unusual for Bogle to provide both services within a twenty-four hour period: "at one using all the suavity and pleasantness of manner desirable, and at the other evincing a solemnness and dignity that was most impressive."[175]

By the mid-nineteenth century, arterial embalming professionalized the undertaking business in urban America. Undertakers capitalized on new technology in preparing the dead for burial. Rather than laying out a decaying corpse wrapped in a shroud, they prepared the body for viewing, as though the deceased were asleep in his or her best clothes. Embalming became commonplace by the 1850s, and perhaps no undertaker was more successful in this expanding industry than Pierre A. D. Casenave.

In New Orleans, this black entrepreneur cornered the market in providing funeral services for the wealthy whites of the city and those blacks who could afford his services. Casenave, the son of a cabinetmaker and himself a cabinetmaker by trade, claimed he had perfected a secret embalming process, which provided perpetual preservation of the deceased. His undertaking business was only one of Casenave's successful enterprises, with his wealth coming primarily from his business as a commission broker. In his first entry in Dun in 1853, Casenave is listed as "Com[mission Merchant]." In June 1861, a Dun entry described him as having "[a]n old and rich house w at least 100m$.[176] By professionalizing his services, Casenave developed an enterprise that included "a hearse, four carriages, and a cab," which earned him the reputation as being "the grandest undertaker of funeral splendor in New Orleans."[177]

Extractive-Industry Enterprises

In antebellum America, free blacks developed profitable enterprises in several extractive industries: lumber, fishing, and mining. In the early nineteenth century, the black merchant shipper Paul Cuffe held part ownership in a New England saltworks.[178] The slave Free Frank purchased his own and his wife's freedom from the profits he made from his saltpeter manufactory in Pulaski County, Kentucky during the War of 1812. Free Frank mined crude niter from limestone caves and then processed it into saltpeter, the main ingredient in the production of gunpowder. After his manumission, he expanded his operations by opening a branch of this enterprise in Danville, Kentucky.[179]

In both the North and South, blacks participated in the lumber industry. As the demand for building materials and firewood increased in America's expanding preindustrial urban areas, logging and sawing attracted black participation and provided opportunities for auxiliary enterprises, including those for cutting shingles and barrel staves for the cooperage business.[180] Blacks also established enterprises in turpentine extraction and distillation. Eastern North Carolina, with its extensive pine forests, provided the basis for entrepreneurial ventures in this enterprise for more than 100 free blacks.[181]

Blacks who owned lumberyards also profited from the tremendous expansion of construction in antebellum cities. In San Francisco William Leidesdorff placed the following advertisement: "LUMBER—William Alexander Leidesdorff has made arrangements to supply this town with LUMBER, persons wishing any kind of lumber can have their orders executed by leaving them at the Store . . . San Francisco, May 29, 1847."[182] The leading antebellum black lumber merchant, Stephen Smith, shipped "two million two hundred and fifty thousand feet of lumber" from Philadelphia to Baltimore in one year."[183] This was a major undertaking, which, as Martin Delany said, required employing "a large number of persons" in addition to "purchasing many rafts at a time." In western New York state, the leading lumber merchants were Joseph Cassey, who had been Smith's bookkeeper, and

William Platt. Black lumber merchants employed fugitive slaves, who found refuge in isolated areas cutting trees and processing lumber.

In the South free black lumber and wood dealers owned slaves as their employees; as Delany said, "In this business a very heavy capital is invested." The South Carolina wood dealer Robert Howard used slaves to transport wood from 1841 to 1865, as did R. H. Harney, William Rollins, and the Dereef brothers, Richard and Joseph. In describing the business operations and markets of the Dereefs and Howard, Delany emphasized that they were "very extensive Wood-Factors, keeping a large number of men employed, a regular Clerk and Bookkeeper, supplying the citizens, steamers, vessels and factories of Charleston with fuel."[184] The wood market was apparently quite large: over 50 percent of Charleston's free black businesspeople were wood dealers.

Still, it was possible to have a smaller-scale wood business without the use of slave labor. North Carolina's Lunsford Lane combined a firewood business in Raleigh with his tobacco shop; he said, "I entered into a considerable business in firewood, which I purchased by the acre standing, cut it, hauled it into the city and deposited it in a yard, and sold it out as advantageously as I could." Owning two horses and several drays and wagons enabled Lane to deliver firewood to his customers.[185]

Blacks were also involved in gold mining, initially in North Carolina and Georgia in the 1830s, then in California in the 1850s. While free blacks joined the California gold rush, some of the early miners in that state had been slaves who purchased their freedom with the gold they mined. Free black miners worked claims in various places in California, including one where they were so numerous the place was known as Negro Bar. In addition to mining as individuals, blacks in California also pooled their resources and organized mining companies. In Brown's Valley, a group of blacks discovered gold and organized The Sweet Vengeance Mine Company. Another group of black forty-niners also struck it rich in Brown's Valley and organized The Rare, Ripe Gold and Silver Mining Company, incorporating it in 1868 with a capital stock of 1,200 shares at $10 per share, with offices in Maryville. Also, one of California's leading mining engineers and metallurgists was a black man, slave-born Moses Rodgers, who came to California in 1849 from Missouri. He also owned several mines, as did William Robins in Nevada County and Henry Milies in Calaveras County.[186]

In addition, the first quartz mill in California was established by Robert Anthony, who came to California as a slave in 1849. Within two years he purchased his freedom with money earned from mining. In establishing his mine, Anthony used both water and horse power, which allowed him to mine below the earth's surface. The wealth earned by California's blacks was tremendous . In less than five years of settlement in California, it was reported that "[t]he colored people of Nevada county possess property to the amount of $3,000,000 in mining claims, water, ditch stock, and some real estate."[187]

There were antebellum free blacks on both the Atlantic and Pacific coasts and those living near inland waterways who owned businesses in the fishing industry. Paul Cuffe briefly turning to cod fishing before he launched his international-trade enterprise. Profits from a successful whaling expedition off the coast of Newfoundland with his crew of 10 blacks enabled him to expand his international fleet.[188] Indeed, Cuffe's career at sea began in 1775 on a whaling ship in the Gulf of Mexico and the Caribbean. In Georgia free black fisherman Anthony Odingsells used slaves in his fishing enterprise, and a Charleston free black fisherman owned two slaves.

In Petersburg, Virginia, free blacks virtually monopolized the river-fishing industry on the Appomattox River. In the early nineteenth century, Richmond free black Joseph Dailey owned a five-acre fishery. Also, while oystering required large capital investments, in the Chesapeake Bay area a few blacks operated oyster enterprises.[189] In California in the 1850s, while a large number of free black men worked in the fishing industry, only one black was reported to have owned a fishing sloop.[190] Blacks in the extractive industries were also involved in transportation enterprises. Stephen Smith owned rafts, and the Dereef brothers and Robert Howard were "proprietors of several vessels trading on the coast."[191]

Transportation Enterprises

Until the rise of the railroads, water transportation was the principal means of moving passengers and heavy cargo, first along the Atlantic coast, then on inland waterways, rivers, and lakes. Antebellum blacks developed enterprises involving water and land transportation that carried both cargo and passengers. The largest shipping company developed by a black in the early nineteenth century was founded and owned by the New England merchant shipper Paul Cuffe (1759–1817). He launched his enterprise when he was 20 with a small open schooner that he built. By 1806 Cuffe owned a small fleet: a 12- and an 18-ton ship; a 69-ton vessel, the *Ranger;* and a 109-ton brig, the *Traveller*, which he also built and co-owned. Cuffe also held three-quarter interest in the 268-ton ship, the *Alpha*.[192] In Virginia prior to 1810, free black Christopher McPherson held investment interests in a cargo ship.[193]

Antebellum free blacks also pooled their resources to organize ship companies. In New Bedford, Massachusetts, a black ship company was organized in 1837, and in Cincinnati blacks founded a cooperative steamboat company to capitalize on the Ohio and Mississippi River trade.[194] On the Great Lakes, Cleveland's John Malvin (1795–1880) was owner of a small shipping fleet, which included a canal boat, the *Auburn,* and a lake boat, the *Grampus,* used for transporting "limestone from Kelley's Island to Cleveland in order to supply the budding iron industry." Malvin initially worked as a cook on a lake vessel and as a sawmill engineer before obtaining a master sailing license.[195]

The South's extensive inland waterways also provided an opportunity for the development of boat transportation, an area of enterprise in which free blacks had the edge over slaves. Although slaves had established a monopoly in the boating trades beginning in the seventeenth century, by the nineteenth century, few slave owners were eager to allow their slaves to work as boatmen because of the increased chance of escape. Some free black boatmen who owned slaves, however, employed them in their river-shipping enterprises. Between 1840 and 1860, Virginia boatman Richard Parsons owned nine slaves, and Washington Logan owned at times one or two.[196]

Before the family of Liberia's first president, Joseph Jenkins Roberts (1809–1876), emigrated to that country, they owned and operated boats on the James and Appomattox Rivers.[197] Richard Jarrett ran a boat from Petersburg to Norfolk. In Petersburg free black John Updike owned 200 feet of property on the Appomattox, using his own wharf as a base for his trading vessels. He also traded on the James River between Petersburg and Norfolk. From 1824 to 1862, Updike owned four sloops and schooners, which at times were used for collateral in securing loans: the *Jolly Sailor,* the *Two Brothers*, the *Jannett,* and the *William and Mary*. Three of his vessels were built in Virginia and one in New Bedford, Massachusetts.[198]

Urban land transportation enterprises established by blacks included conveyances that carried both passengers and freight. In Richmond, until 1810, free black Christopher McPherson owned a prosperous carriage and drayage business, which included both hauling freight and providing carriages for hire.[199] By 1810 Charleston's Joseph Morton owned four drays or carts, four horses, and two slaves who "hauled all sorts of items and merchandise through the city." In Charleston, however, only 3 of 22 black draymen owned slaves.[200] In several cities the largest livery stables were owned by blacks who rented saddle horses and carriages, including Henry Knight in Chicago, Robert Clark in Petersburg, Albert Brook in Richmond, and William Wormley in Washington.[201] Richmond's James Robinson was quite successful in his dray enterprise: by 1860 he owned 10 horses and a large number of wagons.

Some of the blacks who owned carriages and hacks kept their horses in stables owned by other blacks, such as did Petersburg carriage driver Richard Kennard, who used advertisements to promote his enterprise: "Hacks for hire. If you want a very fine carriage, horse, and driver, send your orders to Richard Kennard, at Mr. Reuben Ragland's stable on Lombard St. Remember the name Richard."[202]

In the South both large livery owners and draymen owned slaves that they employed in their enterprises. Indeed, as Luther Porter Jackson emphasized, "the free Negro draymen and teamsters employed slaves on a scale comparable to the blacksmiths." With few exceptions, most livery owners had been slaves themselves and, once free, they either purchased or employed hired slaves to groom horses, clean stables, and drive conveyances.

In Virginia, Edmund Kean, a former slave who bought his freedom in 1849, owned 3 slaves by 1851 whom he employed in his livery business. By 1860 he owned 10 slaves. In Charleston, Isaac Matthews owned a livery stable that employed 5 slaves. In Virginia's Prince Edward County, Booker Jackson gave up his profitable shoemaking business to establish a livery stable. By 1859, in addition to three vehicles and four horses, he owned two slaves; one year later he "owned three slaves, four vehicles, and five horses." In Petersburg former slave Robert Clark, who purchased his freedom with money earned while working as a hotel waiter, immediately opened a livery stable. Before 1860 he owned both real and personal property valued at $9,000 and had "continually on hand for hire, horses, buggies and carriages, open or closed."[203]

In the antebellum transportation industry, technological innovations and developments, particularly the railroad, signaled the onset of industrial America. At least two black entrepreneurs, Stephen Smith and William Goodrich, capitalized on this new mode of transportation by establishing their own railroad enterprises. This is what Martin Delany had to say about Goodrich's endeavor: "Mr. William Goodrich of York, Pennsylvania, has considerable interest in the branch of the Baltimore Railroad, from Lancaster. In 1849, he had a warehouse in York and owned ten first-rate merchandise cars of the road, doing a fine business." This assessment was corroborated by Dun, which indicated that as early as 1845 Goodrich had "cars on R.R." An 1852 entry was more specific, stating that Goodrich "[r]uns a train of cars on the Columbia RR." Also, Delany said that by 1850 Smith's firm ran "twenty-two of the finest merchantmen cars on the railway from Philadelphia to Baltimore."

In addition to being businesspeople who wanted to reap a profit from their operations, black owners of transportation enterprises engaged in activities that assisted the entire antebellum black community. For example, in the North blacks used their transport enterprises to assist fugitive slaves in fleeing the South. For Stephen Smith, William Goodrich, and others, then, the Underground Railroad was a reality. Goodrich lived in York County, which was adjacent to Lancaster County, where Smith lived, and both bordered the slave state of Maryland. The two assisted fleeing slaves by hiding them in a false end of a boxcar. As Smith's partner, William Whipper said, "Some went to Pittsburgh by boat, others 'in our cars' to Philadelphia." Cato Johnson, who had a teamster business that hauled cars over the Susquehanna River bridge, also carried fugitives hidden in his wagons.[204] Black undertakers also participated in the Underground Railroad, but in a unique way: "A common practice among Philadelphia's black undertakers was to hide fugitive slaves in caskets in their funeral parlors until it was safe to transport the fugitives out of the city."[205]

Black owners of transportation enterprises also provided a means for free blacks to leave America. A black Charleston businessman and slave owner named Mr. Creighton (possibly Samuel) purchased a schooner in order to sail to Liberia in 1821. He offered his slaves their freedom on the condition that they accompany him, but only one of them accepted his offer.[206]

International Enterprises

Before the Civil War, blacks participated in international trade as merchant shippers and owners of import-export trading companies. Initially, Sierra Leone and Haiti attracted the attention of black businessmen interested in either investing or participating in international trade. But by the 1820s, Liberia emerged as the focus of antebellum trading enterprises. In the early nineteenth century, the international trading activities of Paul Cuffe carried him to the West Indies, England, Sweden, and Russia before he made his initial voyage to Sierra Leone in 1811. There he formed a trading and mercantile company, the Friendly Society of Sierra Leone, in partnership with African-born John Kizell, a repatriated former South Carolina slave. Kizell had fought with the British in the Revolutionary War and left with them after their defeat, finally settling in Sierra Leone.

Despite his success as a shipper, Cuffe engaged in emigrationist activities that have historical significance. In 1815 he embarked for Sierra Leone with a group of African-Americans, 18 adults and 20 children. Once Liberia was established for the colonization of former African-Americans, however, black shippers made it the focal point of their international trading ventures in West Africa. The first African-Americans emigrated to Liberia in 1820, including the Reverend Daniel Coker from Baltimore. After emigrating, he became a coastal trader on Sherbro Island, off the coast of Sierra Leone, even captaining one of several vessels that he eventually owned in his shipping enterprise.[207]

In Baltimore, several trading companies were formed to establish trade relations with Liberia. In 1829 Hezekiah Grice of Baltimore promoted the formation of a black mercantile company to trade with Liberia, indicating that "there are fifteen or twenty coloured persons here who will adventure $100 each and that several others up the Susquehanna in Philad. and N. York and at Liberia will become stockholders to a similar amount; and that he believes that several societies that exist among the blacks in this city will invest a portion of their funds in such an enterprise."[208] Maryland granted the company, the Chesapeake and Liberia Trading Company, a charter of incorporation in 1845, referring to it as that "nigger company."[209] By then it was reported by a free black in Baltimore that "several of that city's fraternal organizations desired to invest in the Liberian Trade."[210]

Free blacks in Virginia also took a special interest in establishing trade with Liberia and viewed investment in Africa as similar to the model established during the English colonization of America. Several African-American trading companies were founded by blacks from that state, including the largest antebellum black shipping and trading enterprise, Roberts, Colson, and Company.[211] This import-export company was founded by two blacks from Petersburg, Virginia, in 1829. While Roberts went to Liberia, the prosperous barber William Nelson Colson remained in Petersburg, where he purchased merchandise, primarily "clothing and fancy goods," that was manufactured in that city, New York, and Philadelphia, and that was shipped to the company's trading house in Liberia.

In Liberia Roberts purchased products for export. An 1833 shipment included "forty-seven tons of camwood, eight puncheons of palm oil, eighty-eight small ivories and seven large ivories." The items were purchased by the Philadelphia Grant and Stone store, which netted the company $3,389.80.[212] Colson died in 1835 on his first business trip to Liberia, but the firm continued under the direction of Nathan H. Elebeck, the brother of Colson's widow. Roberts's commercial success in Liberia, enhanced by his acquisition of town lots and farmland, including a coffee farm, enhanced his prestige and political standing. After an appointment as governor, Roberts was elected Liberia's first president in 1847, serving two terms. He also served as Liberia's diplomatic representative in Europe and America.[213]

There were also African-American firms based solely in Liberia. The trading firm of Colston Waring (1793–1834) and Francis Taylor, established in Monrovia in the mid-1820s, was successful from its inception in selling "firearms, ale, and rum imported from Liverpool." In 1830 the firm had sales in the amount of $70,000.[214] For capital, Waring, once a Baptist minister, used $1,000 from the sale of his Petersburg property before leaving for Liberia in 1823. Taylor was already based in Liberia when Waring arrived, initially as a missionary for the African Baptist Missionary Society of Petersburg. When it failed to provide support for his Liberian ministry, Waring established a trading company.[215]

The businesses established by African-Americans in Liberia, both rural and urban, were similar to those in America. Unlike them, however, food and personal service enterprises in Liberia were the least successful. Some skilled blacks emigrated to Liberia. In 1854 Colonel Montgomery Bell of Nashville, Tennessee, liberated 50 of his slaves and paid their passage to Liberia. All of the men were ironworkers and, as William McLain of the American Colonization Society noted, "they thoroughly understand the business, and have among them miners, colliers, moulders, and are fully competent to build a furnace for making iron, and carrying it on themselves."[216]

Commercial farmers were also successful. Several large plantations were established in Liberia by expatriate African-American sugar planters, who, with their own steam-powered mills, processed sugarcane for both local and export markets.[217] By the late 1850s a thriving commercial trade in palm oil, rice, camwood, and animal skins was in progress, with European and American ships docking in Liberia and several settlers having "amassed considerable wealth by this means."[218] Some black emigrants had acquired their wealth in America before emigrating to Liberia. The Bladen County, North Carolina, merchant Louis Sheridan, who had a successful dry-goods and general-merchandise store, who could purchase stock on credit up to $12,000, and who had property valued at nearly $20,000, left for Liberia in 1837.[219]

Several African-Americans, who attempted to establish trade with Haiti and to develop businesses in that country, eventually went to Liberia. In 1819 Baltimore blacks organized the Maryland Haytian Company to charter ships for emigration to Haiti. George McGill, a Baltimore businessman who ran an oyster cellar and a messenger service and who had purchased himself and several family members from slavery, was the leader of this enterprise. Before it could get started, however, McGill made several unfavorable comments about Haitian economic development, and Haitian government support did not materialize. McGill later emigrated to Liberia, as did his daughter and her husband, John Russwurm, one of the founders of the first black American newspaper, *Freedom's Journal,* in 1827. McGill's sons, including Samuel, a physician, also emigrated and became successful merchant traders. They owned a fleet of vessels, including their Baltimore-built schooner, the *Moses Sheppard of Monrovia*. By 1859, one McGill brother was the agent for Lloyds of London in Liberia, and another was worth $30,000.[220]

The probusiness National Negro Convention also promoted international trade. At its 1847 conference, a letter from the Jamaica Hamic Trade Association in Kingston proposing trade with African-Americans emphasized the Pan-African basis of the proposal: "By the mysterious providence of God, we find that captivity has dispersed our race far and wide." Trade with whites was not excluded, but a "favored nation" status was offered to African-Americans on the basis that "[I]n this island our people constitute emphatically the market, and in America abound those commodities which are in greatest demand amongst us." The Jamaica group proposed that economic advancement of diaspora Africans should proceed on the Jewish model: "Commerce ever has been the great means by which the Jews, her ancient people, have been able to preserve their national existence. . . . if we would acquire any very great influence for good, we must join the march of Commerce."[221]

Interest in emigration by African-Americans escalated in the decade before the Civil War. Some wealthy Louisiana black planters emigrated to Haiti and established plantations. Louisiana planter Omar Chevalier emigrated to Mexico, where he established a shipping business but died soon afterward. Former North Carolina slave Julius Melbourne inherited an estate of $20,000 from his former slave owner, "who raised him as a gentleman" from the age of five. He increased his net worth to $50,000, then emigrated to England where he set up his son in a London mercantile business for $20,000. Early on, Louisiana free people of color, particularly those involved in real estate, had acquired extensive international properties. The Soulies, Dumases, McCarty's, and Lacroix "had business offices and homes in France as well as New Orleans."[222]

In 1858 several hundred blacks left San Francisco and emigrated to Vancouver Island to seek their fortunes in the gold strike in British Columbia. When San Francisco businessman Mifflin W. Gibbs left, he took with him a large stock of miner's outfits, flour, bacon, blankets, shovels, and picks and was said to have established in Vancouver "the first general store to compete with the flourishing and extremely wealthy Hudson's Bay Company."[223] Blacks on the West Coast also expressed interest in establishing trade relations with Asian countries, including Japan and China. Former New Yorker Peter K. Cole (1831–1900), who settled in San Francisco and worked there as a bookkeeper, was one of the city's leading black intellectuals. During the Civil War, he traveled to Japan, Egypt, and Palestine. On his return to the United States in 1865, he gave a series of lectures, the most popular entitled "Hints in Regard to Commencing Commercial Trade with Japan," in which he advocated "the purchase of a commercial vessel by local blacks for trade with the Orient."[224]

White Attacks against Black Business

Attempts by antebellum free blacks to establish businesses and promote their survival and success required a shrewd and calculating tenacity. Whites used both legal and extralegal means to prevent blacks from participating in businesses as well as to drive successful free blacks out of business. The initial trading activities of Paul Cuffe were limited to the New England coast, since his ventures to southern ports were seldom successful. Either his ships or his cargo were lost to pirates. Also, southern white authorities refused to allow him to dock at most ports. Cuffe persisted, but he failed to make a profit from his early ventures. On one voyage he made a $1,000 profit from the sale of 3,000 bushels of corn. By 1810 Cuffe turned to international trade. When he died in 1817, he left an estate estimated at $20,000. In addition to the wharf and warehouses that he built, profits from his trading activities in both international and national markets enabled him to acquire $3,500 in property, farmland, houses, and a partnership in a saltworks.[225]

In contrast, after his manumission Free Frank was forced to take on a white partner, the slave owner of his children, in his saltpeter enterprise. When Free Frank attempted to buy his son, the slaveholder demanded that the manumission could be secured only if Free Frank gave up his ownership of the saltpeter manufactory, which he did. The successful black Virginia commercial farmer Jacob Sampson, who operated a profitable tavern, was also forced out of his business, which was located across from the county courthouse. In 1844 Goochland County revoked his license, some nine years before the state legislature made it illegal for free blacks to sell alcohol.[226]

The 1830s marked the beginning of white repression of blacks in food services and related industries. In Kentucky an 1833 Louisville ordinance made it illegal for free blacks to obtain a license to sell liquor. Then in 1839 Louisville made it illegal for any black, slave or free, to "keep a confectionary or victualling house or cellar, or a fruit store or cellar, or sell fruits or melons out of any store, house, or on any street or any other place." Washington D.C. had enacted a similar ordinance in 1836 that made it illegal not only for blacks to sell alcoholic beverages but also for "any free negro or mulatto, or . . . any person acting for any negro or mulatto . . . [to keep] any tavern, ordinary, shop, porter cellar, refectory, or eating house of any kind, for profit or gain."[227]

The transportation of merchandise in cities provided the black owners of a cart or a dray the opportunity for self-employment, and for slaves hiring their own time, an opportunity for freedom. Livery and dray businesses were profitable enterprises for free blacks, and literacy was not a requisite for entry. Rather, physical prowess, energy, and hustle were the requirements for success. Through hard work, conscientious and enterprising carters and draymen could provide a decent means of living for themselves and their family. Yet, blacks were virtually driven out of this occupation. In New York, one mayor said that public policy demanded the exclusion of blacks from this enterprise for their own protection.[228] In Virginia, the Richmond city council passed an ordinance in 1810 that not only prohibited free black draymen from obtaining a license but also made it illegal for blacks to ride in hired carriages unless they were slaves whose masters hired or rode in the carriage with them.

Urban transportation enterprises established by free blacks encountered not only violent competition from their white counterparts but also sabotage from their white employees. In California, George Washington Dennis used profits from his restaurant enterprise and real estate investments to establish the first livery stable in San Francisco. One of his largest contracts was with the British government for purchasing and breaking 500 cavalry horses, which he then "shipped them to the British government." Yet Dennis left the livery business after an Irish employee poisoned 90 of his horses. The man was found guilty and sentenced to 14 years in prison.[229] In Nashville, free black wagoner Jim Dungey "got into a fight with a white man in his employ."[230]

Martin Delany notes that two St. Louis blacks, David Desara and Barry Meachum, who owned steamships on the Mississippi River, lost their business. Both were skilled riverboat pilots who made a great deal of money from the river trade. Both, however, left the management of their enterprises to whites and ended up bankrupt. Meachum had sent one of his sons to Oberlin College to study business management, but Delany notes that he lost his "two fine steamers plying on the Mississippi" before the young man completed his courses.[231] There were also instances of free black merchants who lost their businesses because of dishonest white clerks who kept their account books, such as a free black in Easton, Maryland. In 1819, he lost "a shop in which he sold fruits, whiskey and sporting goods. He employed white clerks who robbed him of his money that he was forced out of business."[232]

Another case involved Solomon Humphries of Macon, Georgia, who had established a general store after purchasing his freedom. With a line of credit reaching $10,000, he purchased wholesale goods from white merchants in Savannah, Charleston, and New York, as illustrated in a newspaper advertisements in 1832: "Just received from New York and Charleston, a large and handsome assortment of dry goods, groceries, hardware and cutlery, crockery, hats, shoes, bridles, saddles, linseed and lamp oil, iron, window glass, putty, salt, blacksmith's tools, etc." Humphries, described as "modest, retiring, and all too trusting of his white friends," was forced out of business: "his white clerks speculated with funds in their keeping to such an extent that Humphries lost most of his property before his death."[233]

One of the most successful antebellum black manufacturers, Cincinnati's Henry Boyd, who invented a corded bedstead and built an enterprise from his invention, was forced out of business because of racism. Delany said that he "is the patentee, or holds the right of the Patent Bedsteads" and that his market extended beyond Ohio: "He fills orders from all parts of the West and South, his orders from the South being very heavy." After Boyd established his manufacturing plant in the building he constructed in 1836, his business grew and the plant expanded to four buildings. For 23 years, Boyd employed from 20 to 50 black and white workmen, including immigrants. In 1850, it was reported that, "His own return of taxable property was $26,000."[234] Moreover, Boyd was said to have "used the most approved machinery and paid excellent wages."

And yet his business was burned out three times because of the success of the enterprise. After the 1859 fire, Boyd, without insurance, finally closed his business. Delany noted that prior to that, "There are hundreds who deal with Mr. Boyd at a distance, who do not know that he is a colored man."[235] R. G. Dun & Company however, did not provide an entry on Boyd until he was on his way out of business, noting that while Boyd's product was good, the black manufacturer was not a good businessman. Also, the Dun entry emphasized, incredibly, that he was sabotaged by his own employees.[236] Doubtless, only deep-seated racial antipathy could have driven Boyd's white employees to jeopardize their obviously much needed income to destroy a black man's business and reputation.

Hy [Henry] Boyd Patent Bedstead Factory   8th Broadway

Apl 13 57. Sold out a yr ago under great embar'—not yet clear of debts numerous judgt on record, unsatisfied—has some ability does gd work & gets high prices but is loose & inaccurate in bus. gives cr too generally, not a g'd financier & being a color'd man has to submit to unusual exactions on the part of his *white employees* [emphasis by Dun] —is hardly a safe customer— his wife has property.

Yet, was it racism alone that contributed to Boyd's business failure? Poor management practices, as the Dun report shows, cannot be discounted. Perhaps Boyd was a better inventor than he was a manager. Or did he simply become so overwhelmed in his constant confrontation with racial prejudice that his business techniques—the easy credit, the reluctance to fire recalcitrant white employees, for example—were an attempt to deflect racism in a hostile urban environment? As a partial answer to that question, it should be noted that, at the time of the 1857 Dun report, Boyd had been a successful businessman for over 30 years, 10 years with his construction firm and 20 years with his bedstead manufactory, before he was forced out of business. After that, he continued as a cabinetmaker for another 10 years. Finally, in 1870 Boyd gave up that business and became a city employee.

While Boyd's enterprise was burned down three times to drive him out of business, even greater violence was used to drive the successful lumber merchant Stephen Smith out of business and out of town. In Columbia, Pennsylvania, his success as a real estate speculator generated white enmity and led to a race riot in 1834, an attempt to frighten Smith and other blacks to leave town and sell their property below market value. When this did not work, the following letter was sent Smith in 1835:

> S. Smith:—You have again assembled yourself amongst the white people to bid up property, as you have been in the habit of doing for a number of years back. You must know that your presence is not agreeable, and the less you appear in the assembly of the whites the better it will be for your black hide, as there are a great many in this place that would think your absence from it a benefit, as you are considered an injury to the real value of property in Columbia. You have [sic] better take the hint."[237]

While Smith did leave Columbia, he did not sell either his extensive real estate holdings or his profitable lumber business. He moved to Philadelphia, where he escalated his real estate activities and became even more successful, emerging as the country's wealthiest African-American prior to the Civil War.

There were instances, then, when whites were not always successful in their attempts to force a black entrepreneur out of business. Robert Gordon, the Cincinnati coal dealer, was able to fight off aggressive white business tactics with "large amounts of capital at his disposal."[238] In their attempts to drive Gordon out of business, the city's white coal dealers lowered their prices. In response, Gordon made no attempt to sell his coal at a lower price. Instead, he stockpiled his own coal and, to fill current orders, purchased coal from his competitors, using blacks who could pass for white to buy it. When winter came and the rivers froze, preventing new coal supplies from reaching the city, Gordon was able to take control of its coal market by selling his coal at prices higher than was ever seen in the city. Gordon won the "coal war." In addition, his shrewd tactics, rather than generating additional white hostility, earned him the respect of the white coal dealers. And he remained in business. By 1879, it had expanded considerably, and Gordon's wealth was estimated at more than $200,000. He employed both bookkeepers and laborers. He had his own coal wagons, built his own docks, and purchased coal by the barge.[239]

These incidents underscore the racial conflict that existed when blacks moved into competitive areas of white enterprise, a situation that seemed more volatile in the antebellum North, with its aggressive spirit of industrialization. In the South, by contrast, black businesspeople who had the backing of powerful whites could find some success. A review of the petitions of blacks requesting to remain in Virginia, a response to the 1805 law that required all slaves freed after that date to leave the state, show that most were skilled craftsmen, coopers, blacksmiths, hack and dray drivers, even a miller and a confectioner. Whites who supported their petitions gave various reasons for doing so. The petition on behalf of a cooper, for example, said that he was a "[u]seful person to the merchants and grocers of Richmond." The reason given for a confectioner was that he was "a source of great convenience and utility to our citizens."[240]

While the most successful black enterprises, those with an elite white customer base, were usually protected by their powerful clients, this was not always the case, especially when black businessmen failed to "keep their place." In Washington, D.C., Beverly Snow, who ran a hotel famous for its food services, was driven out of business in the riot of 1835 (often called the Snow Riot). It presumably was the result of Snow's alleged derogatory remarks about the wives of white mechanics. Also William Wormley's business, the largest livery stable in the city, which rented saddle horses and carriages, was destroyed in the riot.[241]

Antebellum black businessmen, then, who lost the goodwill of whites would be subject to acts of violence. In Raleigh, North Carolina, Lunsford Lane, who manufactured pipe tobacco that he packaged and sold for $.15, was tarred and feathered by a mob after he had returned from New York to purchase his family from slavery. Only the intercession of the governor, who smoked his tobacco, saved him from death.[242] Even the wealthiest blacks recognized how much their continued success depended on white goodwill in antebellum America's two worlds of race.

In one instance, when the wealthy Louisiana black sugar planter Thomas Durnford was traveling on a Mississippi steamboat with several white planters, he sat at a separate table for dinner. When asked by two of his traveling companions to join them, Durnford, worth over $100,000, which placed him near the top of antebellum America's wealthiest blacks, replied: " I am very grateful for your kindness, gentlemen . . . and I would cheerfully accept your invitation, but my presence at your table, if acceptable to you, might displease others; therefore permit me to remain where I am." [243]

The potential for black business success by antebellum free blacks is seen in the discussion of their economic activities at a convention held by white slaveholders in Baltimore in 1859, where free blacks were denounced for becoming formidable competitors in the white working population.[244] In addition, the 1850 census reported that "[I]n the city of New York the colored people have invested in business carried on by themselves the sum of $75,500, in Brooklyn $76,000."[245] In 1855, the National Negro Convention presented the following information on the value of urban black businesses by region: in the Midwest states of Ohio, Illinois, and Michigan, $1,500,000; in the New England states of Massachusetts, Maine, Rhode Island, $2,000,000; and in New York and Pennsylvania, $3,000,000. In California by 1850, blacks who had migrated to that state had, within two years, established businesses valued at $200,000. They also had claims in gold mines valued at $300,000.[246]

Conclusion

Despite their lack of political or civil rights, antebellum blacks lived in an age of "expectant capitalism." Money making was pervasive, and antebellum blacks were not immune to the attraction of business or the profits that could be earned by establishing a business enterprise. Moreover, as Milton Friedman explains in his discussion of the free enterprise system in *Capitalism and Freedom:* "History suggests only that capitalism is a necessary condition for political freedom," since many nations can be identified that have "economic arrangements that are fundamentally capitalist and political arrangements that are not free."[247] The existence of black entrepreneurship, both slave and free, provides an example of an economic arrangement in this nation's antebellum free enterprise system that was fundamentally capitalistic, but within which some of the capitalists, the African-Americans, were not fundamentally free.[248]

Still, within the context of American law, race mattered a great deal in determining not only the legal and economic status of African-Americans but also their societal status. That there were economic successes can be attributed to the remarkable business ability of antebellum black entrepreneurs to capitalize on the free-market system, particularly in its protection of private property and its market-driven incentives for the production of profit. The most successful antebellum black businesspeople must be considered entrepreneurs within the context of what Joseph Schumpeter calls the tradition of the "creative capitalist." As he emphasizes, entrepreneurial motivation for the creative capitalist extends beyond the desire for the accumulation of profits—rather, it is also motivated by noneconomic forces: "the will to conquer, the impulse to fight, to prove oneself superior to others, to succeed for the sake, not of the fruits of success but of success itself."[249]

Paradoxically, the structure of antebellum America's free enterprise business community provided the only arena in the nation's slave society in which African-Americans, denigrated as inferior, incompetent, and "cursed with an inherent ineptitude," could achieve some success. In the face of limited employment opportunities, most antebellum free blacks who developed business enterprises were motivated by a simple goal: sheer economic necessity and survival. Only three percent of antebellum free blacks were business proprietors, a figure that has remained constant into the late twentieth century. Yet, before the Civil War, black businesspeople contended with severe racially based societal constraints, iniquitous public policies, and legal impediments—in addition to the institution of slavery. The pursuit of business by free blacks at that time nonetheless represented the persistence of a tradition established by Africans beginning in colonial America. Yet this pursuit also represented a tradition of enterprise that survived their enslavement.

5

ANTEBELLUM FREE BLACK
WOMEN ENTERPRISES

"Daughters of Africa, awake! arise! Distinguish yourselves" Do you ask, what can we do? Unite and build a store of your own. Fill one side with dry-goods and the other with groceries. Do you ask, where is the money? We have spent more than enough for nonsense to do what building we should want. We have never had an opportunity of displaying our talents; therefore the world thinks we know nothing.
—Maria W. Stewart, 21 September 1832

Introduction

Free black women in antebellum America established a diversity of business enterprises. As with black men, domestic and personal-service occupations provided the foundation for the entry of most of these women into the American business community. Yet antebellum free black women, too, owned plantations and were actively involved in managing these capital-extensive, labor-intensive agribusinesses. They also owned commercial farms and developed truck garden enterprises. In addition, they were merchants, real estate developers, and speculators. A few were engaged in finance as bank stockholders, informal bankers, and investors in internal improvements. Yet, in the antebellum urban South, the most successful black businesswomen, like their male counterparts, were slaveholders who employed their slaves in their businesses or hired them out as an enterprise. Free black businesswomen, some who themselves were former slaves, trained their slaves to be hairdressers, seamstresses, and specialty cooks. Also, many antebellum free black women in both the North and South who owned real property established boardinghouse enterprises. In the South, those who owned slaves employed them as their domestic staff.

At all levels of economic activity, antebellum free black women were extremely hard working. They were also business minded and proficient in the development and management of their enterprises. This chapter focuses on the following broad areas of business activities in which antebellum free black women participated: banking, finance, and investment; plantations and agribusiness; catering, restaurants, and inns; dressmaking and fashion design; hairdressing; health care; boardinghouses; slave ownership; and merchant and retail shops. Yet while antebellum free black women developed a diversity of businesses, the majority were self-employed as laundresses. A review of the diversity of enterprises established by them introduces this chapter. It provides a basis to expand on the reality of the antebellum free black woman, who actively sought her own economic liberation, as opposed to those prevailing stereotyped images, such as that of a mammy, imposed on her in a racist and sexist slave society.

A Diversity of Enterprises

Before the Civil War, there were few areas of enterprise developed by free black men in which free black women did not participate. Even in the international-business arena, there were black women who established enterprises. New England-born Mary Gardner Prince (1799–c.1856), who accompanied her husband to Russia, established a garment-making business in St. Petersburg. She lived in Russia from 1824 to 1833 and learned Russian in "six months so as to be able to attend to my business." One of her enterprises was running a boardinghouse for children. At the same time, she responded to a demand from the Russian nobility for children's clothes: "The baby linen making and children's garments were in great demand. I started a business in these articles." The Russian empress encouraged her in developing this enterprise, according to Prince, by purchasing baby clothes that Nancy said were "handsomely wrought in French and English styles." Apparently, Nancy also made women's clothes for she said the empress also purchased "of me garments for herself." The business was a success; Nancy indicated that to fill the orders she took on both "a journeywoman and apprentices."[1]

The transportation business also engaged free black women, as did the extractive industries. In Petersburg, Virginia, Lurany Butler, who by 1817 owned and managed a cargo-hauling business, eventually employed a hired slave as her enterprise expanded. The free black woman Jane Cook was in the river transportation business with her slave husband, owning "two lighters," flat-bottomed boats that were challengingly named "the *Democrat* and the *Experiment*." Four years after the Kentucky slave-born Clara Brown purchased her freedom at the age of 55, she moved West and settled in Central City, Colorado. Using the money she made from the cookshop and laundry business she established—$10,000 in seven years—Brown invested in Colorado gold mines by staking prospectors for a half interest in their claims. With profits from this venture, Brown purchased not only the freedom of her husband, two sons, and a daughter but also that of 30 other relatives and friends before the start of the Civil War. She also subsidized two wagon trains of free blacks to Colorado from Fort Leavenworth, Kansas.[2]

If necessary, antebellum free black women could swing an ax or an anvil, make a chair or a pair of shoes. The wife of Frederick Douglass, said her daughter, "sustained her little family by binding shoes [and]. . . . It was mother's custom to put aside the earning from a certain number of shoes she had bound as her donation to the A.S. [antislavery] cause"[3] Black women could also pilot a ferry or drive a stagecoach and even be thrown off one because of their race: "In 1861, Mary Randolph found herself evicted from a Denver-bound stage because she was black. She spent the night on the Kansas plains snapping her umbrella open and shut to scare off the coyotes."[4]

While most of the enterprises developed by antebellum free black women were in urban areas, they also participated in agribusiness as owners of plantations, commercial farms, and truck gardens. By 1860 Virginia's Sally Scott, who owned an orchard, had also established a vineyard and produced in that year "130 gallons of wine."[5] Expanding their provision-ground enterprises as truck farmers, antebellum free black women produced vegetables and fruit and raised poultry for sale both to wholesale markets and as retail vendors, hawkers, and peddlers. The wives of antebellum black commercial farmers also established enterprises in the production of goods for sale both in local country stores and in urban markets.

The business activities of slave-born Lucy McWorter (1771–1870), whose freedom was purchased in 1817 by her slave entrepreneur husband, Free Frank, included both farm production and domestic manufacturing. Lucy lived on both the Kentucky and Illinois frontiers, where her husband, who purchased his freedom in 1819, established commercial farms. McWorter's domestic manufacturing activities included cloth making (spinning, weaving, and knitting) and candle and soap making. Food processing included making cheese and butter and canning fruits and vegetables. She collected and processed honey, wax, and medicinal herbs; and she also raised poultry. McWorter was like a lot of other frontier women, for whom it was not uncommon to "raise three or four hundred fowls, besides geese, ducks and turkeys, in a season."[6]

In antebellum America, black women often worked as business partners with their husbands, and so they were prepared to take over the enterprise if their spouses died. Henrietta S. Duterte (d.1903) of Philadelphia was the wife of an undertaker who died in 1858. When she took over the enterprise, she was "the first practicing female mortician in the United States, if not in the world." And she was also a highly successful and capable businesswoman. Yet, as with many blacks who established businesses in antebellum America, her enterprise was not recorded in the Dun mercantile credit records until after the Civil War. It was almost 20 years after she took over ownership and management from her husband that a credit report was entered for her in Dun; and there was only one entry, with no indication that she was black:

Henriett S. Duterte   Undertaker   632 Lombard St.
Oct 26 77.   A middle aged widow in business many years. Succeeded her husband & has a very fair business. Is active & attentive, Stands fairly & is reg[ular] & a fair risk for mod[est] lines has Est wor[th] 3 to 4m$.[7]

Even before Duterte's entry into the world of undertaking, one antebellum free black woman had capitalized on the funeral trade in another way. An 1838 survey of black occupations listed a black woman with the occupation of "shroud maker." The survey, published by the Pennsylvania Abolition Society, tabulated and analyzed the occupations of free black heads of household in Philadelphia, distinguishing those in which women and men participated. Table 5.1 lists the various occupations in which antebellum free black women participated in developing self-employed business enterprises. However, since only one occupation is listed for each person, the survey fails to reveal that some black women participated in a diversity of enterprises.

Elleanor Eldridge (1785–1865) of Rhode Island provides a most remarkable example of how black women transformed a variety of gender-based domestic and manufacturing activities into profit-making enterprises. Her self-employed activities included several listed in table 5.1: does her own work; is a dealer and nurse; sews rugs; is engaged in "service"; and is a whitewasher. Moreover, several of the occupations in which she participated, including one of her most lucrative, soap manufacturing, a business she established in partnership with her sister, was not listed. She was also a mattress maker and for 20 years was

TABLE 5.1   Self-Employment Occupations of Philadelphia's Free Black Women, 1838

Biscuit makers	3*	Nurses	12
Boardinghouses	13	Oakum pickers	29
Cake bakers	4	Pastry cooks	2
Cooks	103*	Plain sewers	16
Days work	581	Quilters	2
Dealers	5*	Seamstresses	67
Do their own work	171	Service providers	309
Dressmakers (mantua makers)	150	Carpet/rugs sewer	1
Eating houses	9	Shopkeepers	30
Hairdressers and barbers	61*	Shroud maker	1
Hair workers	3	Spooler	1
Hucksters	55*	Tailoresses	13
Ironer	1	Various employments	23
Midwives	3	Washers	1071
Milliners	7	Whitewashers	74
Music teacher	1		

Source: Compiled from "Penna. Abolition Society of Analysis of Census Facts Collected by Bacon and Gardner," 1838, The Historical Society of Pennsylvania, Philadelphia. There are 140 different occupations listed for 4,817 people. Also see *Register of Trades of the Colored People in the City of Philadelphia and Districts* (Philadelphia: Merrihew and Gunn, 1838), where 57 different occupations for 656 people, primarily business owners, are listed.

*Indicates both male and female occupational participation.

in business with another sister in "white-washing, papering, and painting," occupations usually limited to men.

Moreover, while boardinghouse keepers are listed in the survey, there is nothing to indicate that free black women in Philadelphia were property owners. In Rhode Island, however, Eldridge earned enough through various pursuits to buy property. She began working at the age of 10 for $.25 a week as a domestic and, by the age of 14, had acquired phenomenal cloth-making skills that included not only all kinds of spinning but also "plain, double and ornamental weaving. This double weaving, i.e. carpets, old-fashioned coverlets, damask, and bedticking, is said to be a very difficult process." Three years after she began working for herself, she purchased a lot and built a house that she rented for $40 a year. When she was 46, Eldridge purchased another lot for $100 and built a house for $1,700, later contracting for two additions, one for herself, while renting the rest of the dwelling for $150 annually. In addition, when her biography was published, she went on regional lecture tours to promote her book.[8]

Occupational patterns for antebellum free black women in other northern cities were consistent with those in Philadelphia. In New York, an 1855 state census listed the following occupations of free black women: 5 bakers; 17 boardinghouse keepers; 179 dressmakers and seamstresses; 437 laundresses; 17 nurses; and 9 prostitutes. Nine men and women were listed as working in restaurants and catering enterprises. While 101 blacks were listed as hairdressers or barbers, most were men. In 1860 in Cleveland, the occupations listed for black women were: 5 dressmakers; 5 seamstresses; 1 tailor; 1 grocery owner; 3 boardinghouse keepers; 3 housekeepers; 15 domestics; 27 laundresses; 1 nurse; and 2 farmers.[9]

Antebellum free black female occupations in the South differed little from those in the North. In Richmond County, Georgia, in 1819, the following occupations listed for free black women were: sewing, 29; washing, 26; spinning and weaving, 11; sewers and washers, 11; baker, 1; and midwife, 1. In Petersburg, Virginia, in 1860 free black self-employed

TABLE 5.2   Self-Employment Occupations of Charleston's Slave and Free Black Women, 1848

Occupations	Slave Women	Free Black Women
Dressmaking		
Mantua makers	4	128
Seamstresses	20	68
Tailors	0	6
Sales/shops		
Fruiterers	1	1
Hucksters	11	0
Market dealers	6	4
Health services		
Nurses	2	10
Food shops		
Confectioners	0	2
Cooks	11	0
Pastry cooks	1	16
Housing		
Hotel keepers	0	1
Housekeepers	0	4
Domestic		
Laundresses	33	45

Source: Compiled from J. L. Dawson and H. W. De Saussure, eds., *Census of the City of Charleston, South Carolina for the Year 1848* (Charleston, 1849), 34–35, in Ulrich B. Phillips, *American Negro Slavery* (New York: D. Appleton and Company, 1918; Baton Rouge: Louisiana State University Press, 1987), 403.

women were occupied as: fishmongers, 4; fruit sellers, 2; seamstresses, 10; cookshop employees, 2; midwives, 2; and washerwomen, 38. In addition, there were free black women planters, commercial farmers, and nurses.[10]

The occupations of most self-employed free black women differed little from those of their sisters in slavery (see table 5.2). The occupations listed were among those that free black women transformed into self-sustaining enterprises. It is certainly true, as Ira Berlin said, that, "Like poor white women, most free Negro women worked as cooks, laundresses, house-keepers and peddlers."[11] Yet, for some free antebellum black women, participation in these occupations provided a base for developing business enterprises.

Only when antebellum free black women acquired minimal wealth and property through their business activities did white America realize that they had built an economic structure founded on occupations involving menial labor. The response of whites to the enterprise of antebellum free black women was the legal suppression of their economic activities. In St. Louis and Louisville, even the most mundane activities, such as peddling fruits and vegetables, were made illegal, as was the establishment by free blacks of eating houses, cookshops, and restaurants in Washington, D.C.[12] Despite various legal prohibitions and social constraints, black women persisted in developing business enterprises.

Banking, Finance, and Investment Enterprises

While many antebellum free black businesswomen invested their profits in buying the freedom of family and friends, a small number, mostly wealthy slaveholders, were hard-and-fast capitalists. Economic security was a priority with them, and wealthy free black women relished their lofty financial status, perhaps none more than the wealthy St. Louis widow Mrs. Pelagie Rutgers, reportedly worth $500,000 left by her white husband. One account describes her as "a member of the Catholic church, but is not noted for her piety; she worships the almighty dollar more than Almighty God."[13] Most other wealthy free black women, however, were as serious and systematic in improving their economic standing through the accumulation of wealth as their black male counterparts who increased their holdings through financial investments.

In antebellum America, there were also free black women who invested in internal improvements and bank stock. Suzanne Belazaire Meullion, the daughter of black planter Jean Baptiste Meullion, held stock in the New Orleans, Opelousas and Great Western Railroad Company.[14] Antebellum free black women also held bank stock. Until 1836 Marie Louise Panis in New Orleans owned 490 shares of stock in the Citizens' Bank of Louisiana worth $49,000. Their value is seen in the collateral put up for the bank by the purchasers of her shares, who noted they "[h]ad acquired from Marie Louise Panis, a free woman of color, 490 shares of capital stock in the Citizens' Bank." As a guarantee, they mortgaged a Plaquemines Parish sugar plantation that included the planter's mansion, sugar mill, warehouses, kitchens, slave cabins, infirmary, tools, carts, and livestock, as well as 70 slaves.[15] In 1860, the South Carolina free black woman rice planter Margaret Mitchell Harris auctioned her 44 slaves for $25,300 and "invested the proceeds from the auction in stocks and bonds."[16]

Antebellum black women also acted in the capacity of private bankers and investors in businesses, either their own or the enterprises of family members and friends. The 1839 estate inventory of Dominique Metoyer showed that she loaned money at 10-percent interest, having $3,270.65 in nine outstanding loans due her at the time of her death.[17] A former South Carolina slave, Dye Waring, made a loan of $1,600 in 1838 to a white lawyer, Abraham Moise, who promised repayment in "two equal annual payments and interest of seven percent per annum." As security, he put up a Charleston town lot that measured 60 by 180 feet. Moise paid the loan in full in 1844.[18] The sister of Paul Cuffe, Freelove Slocum (1765–1834), who established a school in New York, invested in her brother's international shipping enterprise and also established a small merchandising establishment for the sale of goods that Cuffe brought back from his trading ventures.[19]

The country's wealthiest antebellum black businesswoman was New Orleans merchant Madame Eulalie "CeCee" d'Mandeville Macarty. She also acted as a private banker. In her business activities, Madame Macarty had "unlimited credit [and had] increased her income by discounting notes."[20] By 1830, with her ownership of 32 slaves, she was the largest black slaveholder in New Orleans.[21] Madame Macarty also invested her money in expanding the mercantile enterprise she had established in selling "fancy goods" imported primarily from France. Innovative marketing, sales, and distribution operations distinguished Madam Macarty's mercantile activities. Rather than limiting sales to New Orleans, this intrepid entrepreneur used her slaves to make up a formidable sales force, with assigned territories in various parishes outside New Orleans. Madam Macarty owned a depot in Plaquemines Parish that provided a base for the sale of her goods north to Attakaps.[22]

By the 1840s, Madame Macarty, through her diverse business activities, including the discounting of bank notes and her informal banking and loan activities, was worth more than $155,000. She had also been involved in a relationship with white businessman Eugene Macarty for 49 years. After he died, his white collateral heirs attempted to seize her property through a lawsuit, charging that she acquired it with Mccarty's financial help and it was thus legally theirs. Madame Macarty, however, had the supporting testimony of leading New Orleans businessmen. In its decision, the court confirmed that the fortune she had accumulated over 50 years was based entirely on her own efforts. Moreover, the court acknowledged that the capital for the development of her mercantile business and for her activities in discounting bank notes was derived from both her property and the $12,000 inherited from her family. The court enjoined the plaintiffs from "disturbing her in the enjoyment of the fruits of the labor and thrift of a long life." As the court said, Madame Macarty was *"une femme extremement laborieuse et econome."*[23]

Plantations and Agribusinesses

Many antebellum black females who owned land acquired it from an ancestor, usually a slave woman who either inherited it or was given it by her slave owner, who usually was also the father of her children. These black female landowners were usually part of a group known as free people of color. They were invariably light-skinned, but reflected their mixed-racial heritage by being often tinted with the bronze coloring of their Spanish, French, Indian, and African forebears. They were the octoroons, quadroons, and mulattoes of the African-American population. The matriarch who established the Metoyer plantation and slaveholding dynasty, Marie Thereze, Coincoin (1742–1816?), however, provides an exception to the model of how this class acquired property and wealth.[24] Coincoin's matriarchy differed from that of other black women planters who, invariably as slave mistresses, had inherited land and slaves from their owners. Coincoin alone established the basis of her family's wealth in land and slaves.

Coincoin was the daughter of African-born parents brought to America as slaves.[25] She became the mother of 4 children by black men, then had 10 by her slave owner, Claude Metoyer. In 1786, when she was 44 years old, Metoyer ended his relationship with Coincoin. Most of her children were still enslaved. So that she would not become destitute, he gave her 86 acres of undeveloped land.

By sheer determination, tremendous energy, willpower, and a formidable business acumen—doubtless an expression of both a transfer of African cultural attitudes and her acculturation of colonial French business practices, Coincoin eventually acquired over 1,000 arpents (about 1,200 acres) of land and 16 slaves before she died. Including those of her sons, the family holdings by 1816 amounted to about "11,000 and 12,000 acres of land and at least ninety-nine slaves."[26] The money that she paid for all her land and slaves came solely from her entrepreneurial efforts in the enterprises she developed.

Coincoin had never worked in the fields. For 20 years, she had virtually lived as Metoyer's "wife" and domestic servant. But after the relationship ended, she took to the fields to plant tobacco in order to support herself and her children and to earn money to purchase their freedom. By 1792, she was shipping rolls of tobacco to the New Orleans market on her own barges. In another enterprise, she shipped 300 bear hides and two barrels of bear grease to New Orleans. She also planted indigo and, with her knowledge of medicinal herbs and roots, engaged in "the manufacture of medicine."

In addition, she expanded her land holdings by petitioning for land grants from the Spanish government. On the land acquired from Metoyer, she expanded her enterprises to include livestock raising and commercial farming. In 1807, she acquired her third tract of land and purchased a plantation. She was 65 years old, a plantation owner and a slave owner; and her children were free. The children by Metoyer began to purchase land and, as a family, they became the South's largest antebellum black slaveholders. Her first mulatto son, Nicolas Augustin (1768–1856), who expanded his mother's holdings, also established the patriarchal base of the family.

There were some people who insisted that "white blood" alone accounted for the wealth generated by free people of color in their business activities. The sheer absurdity of this contention requires no debate. If a white heritage provides the basis for acquiring wealth, how then does one explain the limited earnings and low socioeconomic status of many "full-blooded whites"? How, too, does one explain the entrepreneurial abilities of Coincoin, who laid the foundation for the Metoyer family wealth? She was African, with not one drop of white blood in her veins.[27]

Coincoin was, first and foremost, an entrepreneur, as was Metoyer. While her children by black men did not achieve the success of her children by Metoyer, neither did the children by his white wife achieve the success of his black children by Coincoin. The historical debate continues. Why did more antebellum light-skinned free blacks achieve greater business success than dark-skinned blacks? In Louisiana, inherited wealth by children of large white planters and wealthy merchants and their slave women, both mulattoes and blacks, gave free people of color a head start in acquiring capital for business development. The "protection" of powerful white relatives and friends and the network of business connections derived from those relationships were added advantages that enhanced the success of the enterprises developed by free people of color. The courts, too, were often supportive of protecting their property rights.

The initial economic foundation of their business success, however, was the social and cultural climate in which they first developed their enterprises in the late eighteenth century under the three-tiered (black, white, mulatto) Latin American–based caste system. The racial climate under the French and Spanish was decidedly less hostile in the acceptance of black business activities than it was in the English colonies.[28] Racial demographics in Louisiana in the colonial period under the French were a factor whereby black/mulatto business activities were not discouraged. The existence of a black majority in an agriculturally based slave economy, coupled with the absence of white merchants who could provide urban-based goods and services, as they did in the English Colonies, left a vacuum in the economy for the provision of these goods and services.

In Louisiana, the free mulatto population, with otherwise limited employment options, filled that vacuum by establishing businesses that provided urban-based goods and services. Their intrusions into the economy can be understood within the context of "emergency conversion," whereby necessity erodes traditional values. Consequently, over time, free people of color became businesspeople, entrenching themselves in urban-based occupations in which they provided goods and services to whites.[29]

By the nineteenth century, family origin also remained a significant factor in determining the degree of wealth held by free people of color, as well as the extent and kind of their participation in the antebellum business community. Black women continued to inherit land from slaveholders, either from their lovers or white fathers. Unlike Coincoin, who established her own plantation enterprise, most black women who inherited property were given established plantations. In Virginia in 1832, Priscilla Ivey inherited a 1,304-acre plantation from her former slave owner, which she ran until her death in 1856. In 1852, former slave Frankey Miles inherited an 1,100-acre plantation. Her two slave-born children inherited 600 and 670 acres.[30]

With subsequent generations of the black-planter class, there were antebellum free black women who acquired or inherited plantations from their black fathers, husbands, or broth-

TABLE 5.3   Account of Cotton Sales of Mlle. Belazaire Meuillon,
April–May 1861

Date of Sale	Bales of Cotton	Price Paid
March 9	14	$679.00
March 13	27	$1,370.06
March 13	14	$630.89
April 13	15	$707.42
April 19	15	$758.68
Total	85	$4,146.05

Source: Compiled from documents dated March 9, March 13, April 13,
and April 19, 1861, folder number 4, Meuillon Family Papers,
1776–1906 (Parish of Landry), Special Collections, Hill Memorial
Library, Louisiana State University.

ers. These free women of color managed the agribusinesses they owned; one was Mademoiselle Suzanne Belazaire Meullion, who inherited the family plantation from her father.[31] In contrast to her brothers, she was regarded as an expert manager: "well-educated and business-like and appears to have dwarfed her less efficient brothers, Cheval and Antoine Donato."[32] Table 5.3 presents information on the sale of Suzanne's cotton to the brokerage firm of J. W. Burbridge in March and April of 1861 for $4,146.05, minus brokerage and shipping costs. On April 19, from a sale of $758.68, Suzanne's net profits were $707, after deductions of $51.26 were made for the following: freight, $12.75; cartage, labor, weighing, and storage, $7.50; river insurance, $8.25; fire insurance, $3.79; and commission fees of 2.5 percent, $18.97.[33]

Catering, Restaurants, and Inns

The antebellum food service industry provided the basis for black women to establish enterprises that included food stalls, cookshops, bakeries, confectioneries, restaurants, and catering enterprises. Many free black women who participated in this industry were initially food vendors who prepared their food at home or at their stalls for sale to a busy urban population. In a small Louisiana town, one free black woman supported her five mulatto children by selling coffee and cakes at her market stall. Another was an ice-cream peddler who supported her husband. Free black Anne Winchler supported six children by selling milk. By 1860 she had acquired $600 in property.[34] Some black women were able to establish small eating establishments. In Columbia, Pennsylvania, while Stephen Smith was building his lumber business, his wife, Harriet Lee, "kept an oyster and refreshment house."[35] In 1808, Rachel Lyon of Philadelphia established a restaurant at the Walnut Street Theater that opened that year; she "continued it until she retired with a splendid competence in 1850."[36]

While the antebellum catering industry has been regarded as being run by free black men, free black women were also actively and profitably involved. In the bakery business, one of the most profitable enterprises established by an antebellum black woman was that of Kathy Ferguson (c.1774–1854) in New York City; she was recognized, as Frederick Douglass said, as a "celebrated" cake baker. Her specialty was wedding cakes, and her reputation for excellence was such that she did not have to advertise. Ferguson combined her cake-baking with a catering enterprise for wealthy whites. She also specialized in the cleaning and care of fine linens, lace, and silk. It was also known that Ferguson "gave away all she earned beyond that needed for her own support." A slave until she was 16, she established a Sunday school in 1793 in New York; and she used her home, over the years, to care for more than 40 homeless or destitute children, half of whom were white.[37]

In Newton, Massachusetts, free-born Nancy Lenox Remond (1788–1867) established an enterprise as a fancy cake maker, which she continued after her marriage to John Remond, a successful black merchant in Salem. Four of her daughters went into business, including Susan Remond (1814–?), who expanded her mother's enterprise as a pastry cook and confectioner. Susan established a bakery in her home, in addition to a small restaurant where she served only the elite; it was said that she "controlled the trade of Salem in culinary productions."[38] In Cincinnati, Kate Jones established a successful catering business and was acknowledged as "par excellence in this art." When she retired, another caterer was said to have "purchased her wonderful collection of china, linen and silver, much of which could not be duplicated in America."[39]

In Plymouth, North Carolina, Mary A. Lee established a profitable bakery and by 1860 had acquired property worth $2,750.[40] In the South, black women in the catering business generally used their profits to purchase slaves as their employees. One of the most successful was the former Charleston slave Sally Seymour, who was manumitted in 1794. Of unmixed African descent, she began cooking to support her mulatto children. Within seven years, she purchased her first slave, a woman, for $400; and in 1814, she purchased a male slave for $800, whom she employed as a cook in her catering business until her death in 1824. By then, she had acquired two other slaves to work in her pastry shop, which had expanded into a catering business. Seymour's closest competitor in the 1820s was Camillia Johnson, whose five female slaves worked as both cooks and servers. By the 1830s in South Carolina, there were eight free black women caterers who owned a total of 34 slaves. The number of black caterers, men and women, began to decline in the 1840s, as did the number of slaves owned by this group.[41]

The most successful black women in the field combined food service with the operation of inns and taverns. In Charleston, after his death in 1833, Jehu Jones left the ownership and management of his elite Jones Inn to his stepdaughter Ann Deas, who continued to maintain its high standards. The five female slaves she owned worked as domestics and cooks. Deas also trained cooks, whom she sold for high prices on the basis that they had obtained their culinary skills at the Jones Inn. Black women also ran inns in partnership with their husbands. In 1847 the Jones Inn was taken over by John and Eliza Lee, former owners of Lee's Boarding House. Eliza, whose mother was Sally Seymour, capitalized on her mother's outstanding reputation as a cook. While running her boardinghouse, Eliza also trained slaves who served as apprentice cooks before they were sold by their owners. When the Lees took over the Jones Inn, their eight slaves were used as hotel staff.[42]

Black women also owned and operated taverns and inns, some legally and some illegally. In the South it was illegal for anyone to sell liquor to slaves and, in some cities, it was illegal for free blacks to sell liquor. The inns and taverns operated by the more successful free black women did not cater to slaves or even free blacks. In Louisiana, before it became illegal for free blacks to sell liquor, black women owned taverns. In 1819 five women of color paid $1,000 for permits to operate "taverns, cafes, [and] billiards [halls]" that entitled them to sell liquor.[43]

Dressmaking and Fashion Design Enterprises

The dressmaking enterprises of antebellum free black women, as did the tailoring enterprises of their male counterparts, contributed significantly to the development of the American clothing industry. While sewing was a domestic art acquired by most antebellum women, black as well as white, dressmaking and mantua-making enterprises required more skills than those usually possessed by seamstresses. Dressmaking was also highly competitive since it was an occupation in which both black and white women participated.

A steady and generous income could be earned by highly competent dressmakers, a condition that was especially important for genteel free black women—for example, those whose financial circumstances were reduced by widowhood or unmarried daughters of deceased fathers who had supported them. Also, propertied black women became dressmakers. Catherine Stanley, who inherited $4,000 in property from her father, the wealthy North Carolina barber and slaveholder John Stanley, established a dressmaking enterprise in New Bern that catered to the city's elite, rich white women.[44] Also AME Bishop Richard Allen's daughter, Sarah Eddy, combined dressmaking with a millinery enterprise.[45] Grace Bustill Douglass (1782–1842), the daughter of Philadelphia's prominent baker Cyrus Bustill, "operated a millinery store from her Arch Street home."[46]

Even wives whose husbands pursued middle-class occupations established dressmaking enterprises to supplement the family income. The wife of Martin Delany, Catherine, was a seamstress and dressmaker. Also, some women established clothing enterprises as adjuncts to the garment businesses of their husbands or other male family members. In the 1838 survey of the occupations of free black women in Philadelphia (table 5.1), Henrietta Bowers was listed as a "tailoress." She was the wife of one of the Bowers brothers, John and Thomas, who were regarded as two of Philadelphia's leading tailors.[47] The dressmaking business was also profitable and regarded as a prestigious occupation for antebellum free black women, particularly in the South. Carter G. Woodson includes mantua makers, along with fashionable tailors and shoemakers, as having "a consideration in the community far more than that enjoyed by any of the colored population in the Northern cities."[48]

One of the reasons that dressmaking was profitable was that it was highly specialized, as revealed in an 1859 survey of black occupations in Philadelphia in which 13 separate occupations, most associated with dressmaking, were listed (see table 5.4). Dressmaking was profitable also because it catered to wealthy clients, the only ones who could afford quality garments made by professional specialists. In addition, the highest paid entrepreneurs in the garment business were those who employed various specialized journeymen or assistants. Some enterprises also combined dressmaking with other clothes-manufacturing trades. In Brooklyn, three free black women established a firm that was advertised as engaged in "Fashionable Dressmaking, Shirt-making, Embroidering, and Quilting."

In 1860, Philadelphia had the largest number of antebellum free black dressmakers and specialists in the women's garment trades. New York in 1855, with a black population of 11,840 people, had 179 black dressmakers and seamstresses, a relatively small number. An informal census for Cincinnati in 1852 listed "twenty dress-makers and shirt-makers, fifty or sixty seamstresses." Most dressmaking enterprises were sole proprietorships, and the most successful owners were able to purchase property. The 1852 Richmond, Virginia, city directory showed that 12 percent of the free black women listed were seamstresses and noted that, "among women, the seamstress ranked high as an owner of property." In 1860,

TABLE 5.4 Dressmaking Trades of Free Black Women,
Philadelphia, 1859

Dressmakers	566
Dress- and shirtmakers and milliners	2
Dress- and shirtmakers and pastry cook	1
Embroiderers	9
Embroiderers and dressmakers	3
Embroiderer and milliner	1
Embroiderers and shirtmakers	2
Embroiderers and tailoresses	2
Embroiderers and dress- and shirtmakers	4
Milliners	4
Milliners and dressmakers	45
Tailoresses and dressmakers	23
Tailoresses, shirt- and dressmakers, and embroiderers	2
Total	664

Source: Compiled from Benjamin C. Bacon, *Statistics of the Colored People of Philadelphia* (Philadelphia: T. Ellwood, 1859), 13–14.

Richmond's most successful seamstresses and their property holdings were: Virginia Cunningham, property valued at $3,452; Elizabeth Beatty, $2,315; Mary J. Sullivan, $1,644; Mary Hope, $1,630; and Rhoda King, $1,255.[49]

Free black women succeeded in this highly competitive business not simply because they were expert seamstresses and dressmakers, but primarily because of the creative fashion design they brought to this enterprise. In New Orleans, many of the seamstresses were free women of color, especially the quadroons, who established dressmaking enterprises when their plaçage relationship ended. (Plaçage relationships were contractual monogamous sexual relationships between free women of color and wealthy white men.) As dressmakers, they demonstrated exceptional taste and fashion, bringing to their enterprises a sense of design and a Parisian flair: "They were not deficient in taste, and some of them rose almost to the importance of modistes, and shaped the dresses of the *elegantes* of the white race."

These women were also expert shirt makers, specialists in Irish linen. Customers paid $60 for a bolt of cloth, out of which eight shirts could be made at a cost of $2.50 each, earning the dressmaker $40 in clear profit. One of the reasons for the generous profits was that the seamstresses employed by the dressmaker were unpaid slaves.[50] While their slaves were also accomplished seamstresses and "a source of revenue to their mistresses," a contemporary observer, Charles Gayarre, noted that the quadroons themselves were "exceeding[ly] expert at all kinds of needle work." The most successful free black woman in the antebellum clothing industry, although known as a dressmaker, was primarily a designer. Former slave Elizabeth Keckley (1818–1907), who was Mrs. Abraham Lincoln's dressmaker, owned perhaps the largest dressmaking enterprise in antebellum America, specializing in custom-made outfits and employing 20 seamstresses in her Washington, D.C., establishment.[51]

Often dressmaking was combined with millinery enterprises. The more successful hatmakers, however, were those who could devote their full effort to the millinery business. One of the most successful was Grace Douglas of Philadelphia, of whom it was said, "made bonnets for the elite belles of her day and they were sold from five to fifty dollars"; the success of her business required her to hire two or three apprentices.[52] Also, Sarah Johnson, who did "plain sewing," advertised her hat-cleaning and sizing business, which she operated out of her home, in *Freedom's Journal,* announcing that she specialized in "bleaching, pressing, and refitting Leghorn and straw hats in the best manner."[53] Dressmaking continued as an important enterprise for free black women, but many of the skills were lost by subsequent generations, as other employment opportunities opened for them in the North. In 1860, two New York ads ran that were specifically for free black women. One announced an opportunity to learn vest making and to operate Singer sewing machines, while the other offered jobs that included training in the use of sewing machines.[54]

Health Service Enterprises

Health care services provided another area of enterprise and profitability for antebellum free black women, who were employed as nurses, cuppers, leechers, "herbal doctresses," and midwives. There were also free black women engaging in more specialized health-related enterprises. In the 1820s, free black Amelia Gallé of Petersburg, Virginia, used the beneficial effects of hydrotherapy in promoting the bathhouse she inherited from her former slave owner and the father of her child.[55] Although bathhouses were run by men who provided separate facilities for women, Gallé had managed the bathhouse for years before she became the owner-proprietor and was "the first black businesswoman in Petersburg to exploit the full possibilities of newspaper advertising." Gallé was a master of persuasion with ads that were as effective as those of her twentieth-century counterparts.

Gallé launched her advertising campaign with what today we would call a soft sell, a two-line newspaper ad in the early spring: "She has the pleasure of tendering to her patrons . . . her most grateful thanks. . . ." The hard sell came in the heat of the summer. The ad emphasized that Gallé would provide baths at a minimal price in order to share the health benefits of her baths with her patrons and to help them watch their budget. Moreover, bathing at her establishment, she claimed, would diminish, if not eliminate, all of the ills brought on by the summer heat, such as heat rash and the need for lotion; for those who failed to bathe frequently, her ad noted the availability and low cost of bathing at her establishment.

HEALTH

Purchased Cheap

> In Consequence of *Small Change* being scare, and wishing to contribute toward the health of the ladies and gentlemen, the subscriber has the pleasure to inform her patrons and the public, that she has reduced the price of her baths to 25 CENTS for a single one. She will make no comments on the necessity of Bathing in warm weather:—suffice it to say, that with Mr. Rambaut's FAMILY MEDICINES, and some Cold or Warm BATHS, the health of her friends will keep at a proper degree of the thermometer, without the aid of Calomel or any other mineral Medicines.[56]

In their capacity as nurses, antebellum black women provided home health care as an enterprise. In the 1853 New Orleans city directory, the occupation of Tabitha Alexander was listed as "furnished room and nurse." In Petersburg, Virginia, Jane Minor, a nurse, was manumitted from slavery in 1824 for her skill and commitment to the health of her patients and for her " 'most unexampled patience and attention in watching over the sick beds of several individuals of this town' in the preceding year." Some 19 slaves were purchased and manumitted by Minor, but it appears that she acted as an agent for whites who wanted to manumit their slaves without public attention. Also, some slaves gave her money to purchase their freedom. One slave woman purchased by Minor, Phebe Jackson, who had no doubt served as her apprentice, when freed, went on to establish her own health care enterprise as a cupper and leecher (engaged in drawing blood). She kept a careful record of her business in her account book, which showed the number of visits made and the charges for her services: "a dollar for cupping, half again as much for leeching, and children bled for half price."[57]

Antebellum free black nurses were able to secure above-average pay for their services. The 1855 New York census listed 17 free black women nurses. In Louisiana, the nursing services of free women of color proved extremely profitable during periods of epidemics: "when yellow fever broke out their services were sought by both White and Black patients. Their usual fees amounted to about $10 a day but many served for nothing during times of epidemics."[58] Many had come from Santo Domingo, in what is now the Dominican Republic, and were considered specialists in the treatment of yellow fever, one of the reasons being that blacks were thought to be immune to yellow fever.

Antebellum free black women were also skilled midwives. Often half of their patients were white, not only because of the respect accorded their skills but also because their fees were less than that charged by medical doctors, who were called in when there were complications with a delivery. Marie Suzanne of the Metoyer family was a practitioner of midwifery, as was her grandniece, Sidalise Sarpy Dupre, both of whom, it was said, "regularly assisted with deliveries on the Isle." Marie did not have to work, but she did so because it was a tradition of the female descendants of Coincoin. In 1838, when she died, her estate was valued at $62,600.[59] Still, the more successful nurses were able to earn a better-than-average income. In North Carolina, John Hope Franklin said, "Free Negro women also secured considerable employment as midwives and nurses."

Antebellum free black women were also employed in the practice of herbal or botanical medicine. Sara Green, who advertised her services in the New York newspaper *The Rights of All* as an "Indian Doctress," announced that she was able to cure the following "piles, dysentery, smallpox, wounds, and bruises . . . oppression of the lungs . . . in-grown toenails and rabies, or [as she said the] bite of a mad dog."[60] For those who found no relief for their physical, emotional, or psychological ailments through traditional medical practices, prescription drugs, homeopathy, and hydrotherapy, some resorted to psychic healing through conjurers, faith healers, and voodoo practitioners.

The most successful antebellum free black in this enterprise was the New Orleans "Voodoo Queen" Madame Marie Laveau (c. 1790–1881), initially a hairdresser. Because she practiced with and was succeeded by her daughter, some people thought that they were one and the same and that she had found the secret to eternal life, which enhanced their confidence in her healing enterprise. The treatments prescribed by Laveau required the purchase of her amulets, charms, and magic healing potions. Her "patients" were not limited to blacks, slave and free. Wealthy whites purchased her potions and amulets and also participated in Laveau's prescribed healing exercises, which were strenuous cardiovascular "feverish dances," but reported in the newspapers as sex orgies. One account of Laveau's well-attended sessions said, "Blacks and whites were circling around promiscuously, writhing in muscular contractions, panting, raving and frothing at the mouth. But the most degrading and infamous feature of this scene was the presence of a very large number of ladies (?) moving in the highest walks of society, rich and hitherto supposed respectable, that were caught in the dragnet."[61]

In New Orleans, Laveau succeeded as a psychic healer by utilizing traditional African healing practices combined with Catholic rituals, as well as by her shrewd understanding of the emotional stresses that precipitate many physical illnesses. Laveau was known for her ability to provide remedies for people under stress, suffering under slavery, or merely for those who wanted improvement in their love and financial lives. Laveau was the last resort for many people, but she had a demonstrated record of success.[62]

As a businesswoman, Laveau, simply put, was an innovator. She was also in the forefront of modern medicine's increasing emphasis on nontraditional medicine and health care. Laveau also prescribed visual imaging as a form of cure, bonding as a basis for getting in touch with others, sex therapy, and the use of herbs to restore health. Doubtless her potions were more effective than the placebos prescribed in many of today's medical treatments.

Black women were also faith healers. The free woman of color Betsy Toledano, who described herself as a voodoo priestess, when arrested, defended her right to practice voodoo "on the grounds of the constitutional guarantee of freedom of religion." The court's decision was that she was free to practice her religion, but that the attendance of slaves at her religious services was in violation of the law. She was fined and her case dismissed.[63] In the antebellum health care industry, given the state of medical knowledge and care, women, although labeled herb doctors and voodoo practitioners, often performed as competently as men who were accorded the title of physician.[64]

Hair Care Enterprises

The participation of free black women in the antebellum hair care business has been overlooked in the emphasis placed on black men as barbers. From the late eighteenth century until the 1820s, black men, especially emigres from the French West Indies, were even hairdressers to wealthy white women. For black men, their occupation as hairdressers-barbers slowly gave way in the antebellum era to their dominance as barbers for wealthy white men. An analysis of the occupations of black males in the hair care business in Boston in 1850 shows 26 barbers and 20 hairdressers. In Charleston in 1850, there were 17 male barbers and 6 hairdressers. In St. Louis in 1850, there were 33 male barbers, but no hairdressers. In the three decades or so before the Civil War, considering the climate of racism and the persistent image of unrestrained black male sexuality, it does not appear that there would be too many free black men serving as hairdressers for white women.

However, only one antebellum black female hairdresser is known to have left an account of her experiences in the trade. Eliza Potter, a black hairdresser to wealthy women, wrote a book about her experiences with the privileged classes, primarily a litany of the inane activities and idiosyncrasies of her wealthy, white female clients; the book, incidentally, was published anonymously. Potter worked as a hairdresser in Cincinnati in 1850 and in 1856–1861, and in Louisiana in the interim years. Besides "doing hair" in New Orleans, she also practiced her trade, traveling throughout the state from one plantation to another, while also training slaves as hairdressers.[65]

New Orleans quadroons were also known for training their female slaves as hairdressers, who were then hired out to provide these services in the homes of white women. It was a lucrative business. Most wealthy women had their hair dressed daily as part of their toilette. As Potter said, reviewing her experiences, "I know gentlemen and ladies who would not put on a suit of clothes without the servants say[ing] it is suitable, but if the same servants chance to offend them, they will sell them to go as far as [railroad] cars and boats will carry them."[66]

New Orleans was the center of the hair care industry for white women in antebellum America. The effects of sun, heat, and humidity offered new challenges in the treatment and style of their hair. Cincinnati's Sarah Walker Fossett, wife of Peter Fossett, a caterer, was born in Charleston in 1826 and was sent as a young girl to New Orleans to learn the hairdressing trade. There, she "studied under a French specialist the care and treatment of the scalp and hair. The manufacture of hair goods and the dressing of same was also mastered." When she left New Orleans, she went to Cincinnati with a prominent white family who introduced her to an elite segment of the trade: "Through their influence she secured entry in its exclusive group and had no superior in her profession."[67]

Increasingly, however, and in greater numbers, antebellum free black women began to capitalize on the hair care business. As they moved into the industry, their customer was the white consumer, since most antebellum free black women barely had money to eat or pay their rent. Professional hair care was not very high on their agenda. Virginia Vashon, the daughter of Pittsburgh's first black barber, John Vashon, married Jacob Proctor, who owned a barbershop in downtown Pittsburgh. Virginia Proctor established a wig business, Virginia Proctor's Hair Shop, on the second floor of her husband's establishment.[68] It serviced both white men and women.

The three Remond sisters, Cecilia Remond Bacock (?–1912), Maritcha (1816–1895), and Caroline Remond Putnam (1826–1908), established their hairdressing enterprise, the Ladies Hair Work Salon, in Salem, Massachusetts. They also opened a wig factory, which became the largest enterprise of its kind in the state. In addition, they manufactured a tonic for hair loss, which they marketed as Mrs. Putnam's Medicated Hair Tonic. While some of their sales were local, most of their business was done through their mail-order service that covered several states in New England.[69] Their market was primarily made up of white women, who saved the hair from their combs and brushes, which they took in to be made into hairpieces.

Yet, for many black women with inadequate nutrition and under the severe stress of being black in white America, hair loss was also a problem, especially in urban areas. Their hair and scalp problems were treated by botanical healers and herb doctors, who enhanced their profits from sales of herbal remedies they concocted and recommended for hair treatment. Although professional hairdressing was limited to white women, most black women used some form of hair and scalp preparations. The prevailing hairstyle for both black and white women of the time, regardless of texture, featured a center part with hair combed and brushed down to each side and, if possible, pulled back in some sort of bun or elaborate curls. Hair pomades were used by many black women with tightly curled hair to keep the hair in place and "slicked down" as it was brushed down from the center part of the head.

Hair and scalp ointments were made largely from herbs and medicinal plants, often with a perfumed base, which many black women mixed together for their own use. Primarily, these were rural women, with greater access to medicinal herbs. Some even prepared hair salves, tonics, and ointments as part of their domestic-manufacturing activities, since an urban market existed for these hair preparations among both white and black women. The domestic manufacturing of hair preparations and tonics for black women survived the transatlantic passage from West Africa, where palm oil was used as a base for hair preparation and in cosmetics.[70] African-American women continued the tradition of using oils from indigenous plants and animal fats in the United States as a base in the manufacturing of hair preparations, adding various mixtures of processed herbs and pressed dried flowers for fragrance.

Antebellum black women, however, made use of both domestically manufactured and commercial products. And there were free black women who dressed the hair of other black women. The more successful free black women hairdressers advertised their services. Most used their homes as a place of business, often combining hairdressing with sales of notions, trinkets, and accessories for women.

Boardinghouse Enterprises and Property Ownership

About five percent of antebellum free black women in business operated boardinghouses, which were advertised in the antebellum black press of the day. In New York, Gracy Jones in 1828 advertised that she would give board and lodging to all "genteel persons of color." A month later, Eliza Johnson, recognizing the competition, advertised that she not only provided lodging and boarding but also oysters and "a quantity of the best Refreshments."[71] In an 1861 advertisement, Mary Johnson indicated that the boardinghouse she ran in New York City charged weekly rates of $2.50 for women and $3.00 for men, with nightly rates at $.75. In many ways, the antebellum boardinghouse enterprises established by free black women, especially those run by quadroons in New Orleans, were predecessor of today's popular bed-and-breakfast enterprises.

The management style and appointments of these boardinghouses enabled free women of color to charge high prices. In describing these enterprises, Charles Gayarré said, "the female quadroons may be said to have monopolized the renting, at high prices, of furnished rooms to the whites of the male sex."[72] Many of these boardinghouses had been purchased as residences for these free women of color by white men as part of the plaçage system, which involved a negotiated and consensual sexual relationship, in which payment to the woman as a mistress was made before the couple became sexually involved. The negotiations also included provisions for any children that would result. Usually both parties were young and the men were single. Once he married a white spouse, the relationship ended, and the free woman of color transformed her home into a boardinghouse to supplement her income: "The average wealth of this group, amounting to over $1000 each, testified to both their good reputation and their prosperity."[73]

Eliza Potter emphasized the extensive ownership of boardinghouses by free women of color when she said, "it is a common thing to have these furnished rooms, and in no mean street either." Her description of one black woman boardinghouse keeper, a former slave, is indicative of how some of these women obtained their property: "The colored lady who kept the house I have mentioned, was very beautiful and very wealthy; she owned a great deal of property and many slaves, and kept two houses more like some of the elegant mansions of the nobility, than anything else. She inherited this property by her husband and master[;] he emancipated her."[74] The personal characteristics that made the black women boardinghouse keepers in New Orleans so successful were affability, kindness, and an anxiousness to please, which even extended to caring for sick boarders, who would be nursed by the older quadroons, assisted by the younger ones.

Apparently, stealing was a problem in some boardinghouses but not in those run by the quadroons. Gayarré said, "As to their honesty it was proverbial, and seldom was anything purloined from the sick or dead." Moreover, he emphasized in describing the boarding-houses run by the quadroons that "Those furnished rooms were models of Dutch cleanli-ness—large post bedsteads with immaculate mattresses, sheets and mosquito bars as white as snow—no dust visible any where, everything for comfort, and the toilette at its proper place and in the best order—in the morning the nicest cup of hot coffee, in the evening, at the foot of the bed for ablution the never failing tub of fresh water, over which was spread a sweet smelling towel."[75]

In 1860, there were 359 free black women property holders in Louisiana, with more than 80 percent living in New Orleans. Even if all of them had obtained their property as a result of the placage system's negotiated consensual sex enterprise with white men, which was not always the case, their limited property holdings illuminate the full extent of the sexual exploitation of black women. Simply put, the few placage relationships, over time, could not have produced the mulatto population of the United States. Moreover, free women of color had a history of property ownership in Louisiana during both the Span-ish and French colonial periods, when, it was said, "Women, through good management of their property and inheritances, often held the balance of power along the [Bayou] road. Many were shrewd business-women who actively bought, sold, and subdivided huge tracts."[76] Their heritage of property ownership, management, and development continued in antebellum America: "Julia Street in New Orleans was named for a free woman of color named 'Julia,' and who owned large real estate holdings on that street."[77]

The wealth allegedly accumulated by Mary Ellen "Mammy" Pleasant, (c. 1814–1904), the most recognized antebellum free black boardinghouse keeper, has engendered a great deal of speculation. In San Francisco, she established an elite boardinghouse, patronized by wealthy white men, where she employed three domestic servants. By 1870 she owned real property worth $15,000 and personal property worth $15,000. But Pleasant's boarding-house was the least of her entrepreneurial activities. She established one of San Francisco's most elegant restaurants, an informal employment agency, and a chain of laundries, in addition to her activities as a financial investor, advisor, and informal banker.[78] She was also said to be one of the investors in the Atheneum Saloon, which operated on the first floor of the Atheneum Institute built by blacks in 1853. The second floor was used for intellectual, cultural, and political activities by San Francisco's blacks.[79] As one contempo-rary said, "She handled more money during pioneer days in California than any other col-ored person."[80]

Yet because of racism and sexism, Pleasant's financial acumen, wealth, and influence have been attributed to what some say was her "real" profession, that of a high-class prostitute and madam. Pleasant's life did spawn speculation as to "whether this strange woman was a witch or a great financier."[81] What else could explain how a free black woman could gen-erate the wealth she did? In the 1884 *Sharon v. Sharon* case, which received national atten-tion and in which Pleasant testified, the court acknowledged her entrepreneurial genius. Others ascribed her business abilities to her practice of voodoo. Pleasant was known to be the financial advisor to Thomas Bell, a wealthy white boarder. It was claimed she advised him to purchase land on which oil was found: "that she went into a trance and saw the future of the oil land wealth and induced Bell to buy." The claim is without merit because oil had been found on three sides of the tract purchased by Bell, who was also not known for relying on the occult in making his business decisions.[82]

Pleasant's whole life has sparked historical speculation. In one instance, she claimed to have been born in Philadelphia, but a contemporary said Pleasant admitted being born a slave on a Georgia cotton plantation, where she picked cotton and was a house slave. Somehow, she got to Boston with assistance from a planter, who purchased her from slavery for $600, having recognized, she claimed, her "bright mentality," while she was in the fields picking cotton. In Boston, the story goes, she married a wealthy black, Alexander Smith, said to be Cuban and a supporter of the antislavery cause. On his death, she inherited $50,000, which she brought with her to San Francisco in 1849: "with $50,000 in gold from the sale of Cuban bonds from her first husband's estate ... she loaned out money at 10 per cent per month and accumulated a fortune."[83]

Pleasant has also achieved historic notoriety from her claims that she provided $40,000 to support John Brown's raid on Harper's Ferry. When Brown was captured, there was a note in his pocket that said, "The axe is laid at the root of the tree. When the first blow is struck, there will be more money to help." The note was signed "W. E. P." Pleasant said she deliberately made the *M* to look like a *W*.[84] Since everything about Pleasant seems bigger than life, the speculation about the truthfulness of this claim tends toward the negative.[85] Pleasant's diverse business activities did bring her in contact with prominent, wealthy white men in California; it was also said that "[I]n 1849 she migrated to San Francisco where she opened a boardinghouse and immediately began to issue loans at high interest rates and speculate in real estate property."[86] Pleasant accumulated wealth and used it as capital to finance her other enterprises.

Through her various successful business ventures, Pleasant became well acquainted with San Francisco's leading political and financial figures, all of whom, it was said, "frequently sought her advice." Moreover, it seems highly unlikely that one of her boarders, California's future governor, Newton Booth, would conduct his campaign from a brothel or even the boardinghouse owned by an ex-madam. Mary Ellen was separated from John James Pleasant, who also lived in California and was the father of her daughter. Whatever the source of her wealth, in California she used it in the fight against racism.[87]

Black Women Real Property Owners

Black women who established boardinghouses were of course property owners. By 1860, however, less than 2,000 free black women in the South owned property. There were even fewer black female property owners in the small towns and large cities of the 22 northern states, the West, and the nation's territories, a condition that underscores the depressed economic status of the majority of antebellum free black women. In 14 major American cities in 1850, out of a total of 48,888 free black females, only 438 owned property.

This level of property ownership represents an incredibly dismal picture of the appalling economic circumstances of both free black women and free black men. Washing, sewing, and cooking were virtually the only socially approved occupations for antebellum free black women. That they were able to pursue these activities without repression explains why the more industrious washerwomen and seamstresses were among the largest occupational groups of free black women to secure property. In Virginia in the 1850s, washerwomen "were acquiring homes as well as the relatively well-to-do." In Shreveport, laundress Catherine Davis by 1860 had an estimated worth of $5,000 in property.[88]

Washerwomen represented the largest occupational group of black women—80 percent of them were laundresses and domestics—but they were also employed in the group's lowest paid occupation.

By 1860, slightly more than half of the black women property owners in the South, about 980, were washerwomen, seamstresses, and hairdressers. Some 95 percent of black women who worked participated in one or more of these occupations. The other half (about 937) of the antebellum free black women property holders in the South were self-employed, which indicates the significance of business enterprise as a basis of economic advancement for these women. A seamstress could establish a business in a rented room, including her own home. Also, other than needles, thread, and scissors (and before the advent of the home sewing machine), the tools of the seamstress' trade were not very costly. In North Carolina in 1860, there were 175 free black women seamstresses and 244 spinners. There was also a dressmaking shop and a bakery shop owned by two black women, who held property valued, respectively, at $4,000 and $2,750, which suggest these women were business owners, rather than being employed.[89]

Black Women Slaveholders

Antebellum black women acquired slaves by purchase, inheritance, or both; and antebellum free black women planters and slaveholders were as systematic in the management of their slaves as they were in their capital-extensive agribusinesses as money-making enterprises. Doubtless, with production and profit dependent on large numbers of unwilling and unpaid workers, black women planters recognized that sentiment was a luxury they could ill afford. True, the Metoyer matriarch Coincoin was noted for her Christian piety and took as much interest in providing for the religious instruction of her slaves as she did for that of her own children. As a devout Catholic, she saw that her slaves received the sacraments, that slave children born on her plantation were baptized, and that slaves were buried in consecrated grounds. As Gary Mills said, Coincoin "always treated her slaves with gentleness.... [and] reportedly administered no corporal punishment; misbehavior on her plantation was corrected with imprisonment in the 'jail' which she had erected for that purpose on her property."[90]

Yet, Coincoin's piety, devoutness, and gentleness did not extend to freeing her fellow blacks from slavery. And, most certainly, the Metoyer slaves did not share in the wealth they produced for her family. But could plantations be profitable without slave labor? Yes! One free black female planter employed 22 free persons of color on her plantation.[91] The existence of a jail on Coincoin's plantation, then, suggests that the Metoyer did not own loyal and faithful slaves happy to work for nothing.

Aside from the female planters, the largest group of female property holders in the South, both real and chattel, were those in the garment-making industry. In antebellum Charleston, free blacks who worked as tailors, shoemakers, dressmakers, and seamstresses were "the largest group of colored slave masters." In several instances, some free dressmakers had been slaves. Within six years after becoming free, Philada Turner had earned enough money from her seamstress enterprise to purchase a slave woman as an assistant and also her daughter's freedom in 1810 for $500. Fifteen years later, she sold the slave for $300. Usually, the work of a seamstress was among the least arduous of female occupations, but in 1839 black seamstress Sarah Johnson advertised for the return of her runaway female slave. By 1850, of the 16 free black dressmakers in Charleston, 13 owned slaves, most of whom were acquired after they had been in business several years. Profits from the dressmaking enterprise of free mulatto Caroline Lubet enabled her to buy three slaves from 1847 to 1850. Two of the slaves cost $924. Lubet had the services of her dressmaking assistants until 1865.[92]

Eliza Potter, the peripatetic black hairdresser to wealthy women, did not refrain from recounting their atrocious treatment of their slaves. Potter attacked women slaveholders, both white and black, especially those who had escaped the poverty of their birth. One extremely cruel white slave mistress, she wrote, was poisoned three times by her slaves. Of a dark-skinned black woman raised in genteel poverty in Cincinnati, Potter wrote, "She is now a slaveholder in the city of New Orleans; the most tyrannical, overbearing, cruel task-mistress that ever existed; so you can see color makes no difference. . . . It is a well known fact, those who are black themselves as the ace of spades will, if they can, get mulattoes for slaves, and then the first word is 'my nigger.' "[93]

In another account of the treatment of slaves by free black women slaveholders, Anne Royall in her travel commentaries expressed her thorough indignation at the treatment she received at a Louisiana bayou inn operated by a black women she described as a "mulattress," who was very "insolent." Although the woman also owned several taverns, Royall did not describe her abilities as a businesswoman, but emphasized that she was "a great tyrant" in the harsh treatment of her slaves. Then, in an unusual spirit of pettiness, Royall emphasized that the innkeeper drank and was involved in a disreputable relationship with an Irishman, who, she said, "made love to her and it was returned, and they lived together as man and wife. She was the ugliest wench I ever saw, and if possible he was uglier, so they were well matched."[94]

Black slaveholders in the planter and business classes, including the women, could make no claim to be benign oppressors. In the economic exploitation of their slaves, they were no different than white slaveholders. They bought and sold slaves, regardless of family connections or color. Indeed, some were exceptionally cruel, such as a female slaveholding member of the Metoyer family, who, it was said, was "mean" to her slaves. Her behavior seems to have met reproach only from a post–Civil War descendant who said, "The good Lord got even with Tante; her mansion was burned during the Civil War, her second husband ran through her money, and she was forced to live the rest of her days, bedridden, in one of her slave cabins."[95] In addition, some free black female slaveholders were as bitter as whites that the Civil War had wiped out their property in slaves. In one instance after the Civil War, a former female slaveholder rejected an offer of marriage from a black Union soldier because "[s]he regarded him as responsible for losing her slaves."[96]

Merchants and Shopkeepers

The leading black woman merchandiser in antebellum America was Madame Macarty, but she was a property owner in addition to having $12,000 in capital and slaves before she established her trade in "fancy goods." Most antebellum free black women, however, progressed to shopkeepers from their initial activities as door-to-door vegetable and fruit vendors: "Some sold ginger cakes, watermelons, and fruits in the neighboring towns, or on Saturdays and 'big' days at the crossroad stores and post offices."[97] Whenever possible, most attempted to set up stalls in the city markets for the sale of their goods, an initial step to independent enterprise that could lead to establishing a business. In such coastal towns as Petersburg, Virginia, "men fished in the river while their wives maintained stalls in the city market for the sale of fish."[98] As New York food vendors, free black women sold hot corn and baked pears. Censuses and directories of the time were not always accurate in recording the numbers of black women merchants. In reviewing the New York City directory for 1810, which listed only one black woman, Shane White found, however, that "black women were very prominent as sellers of produce in New York markets and streets."[99] The 1819 Charleston city directory shows that seven of the nine leading black grocers, fruit dealers, and confectioners were women. The 1840 Cincinnati business directory lists Miss G. Butler as a fruit dealer. The New Orleans city directory lists two free women of color as grocers and one each in dairy sales and oysters sales. As Robert Reinders said, "Negroes retained a hold as market sellers, but free Negro peddlers were replaced by whites."[100]

In Virginia, Elizabeth "Madame Betsy" Allergue of Petersburg was a shopkeeper who established a store in 1801. In 1809, she added a partner, a white merchant, who in the paper of partnership said, "I declare that the partnership which I had entered into with Elizabeth Alergues [sic] was joint and equal both as to capital and profit." When she died in 1824, she owned property and six slaves. In Alexandria, Mary Savoy owned a grocery store that was said to be almost as successful as the confectionery shop owned by Randle Evans, who was worth $1,000.[101] In Philadelphia, Sarah Hawkins owned and managed a dry-goods store, where "she sold goods and ready made dresses."[102]

For both free black men and women, merchandising required capital and credit, which few antebellum blacks had, a condition that limited their participation in the business community as shopkeepers. The widow of Henry Minton, the leading Philadelphia caterer, established her enterprise during the Civil War with access to credit despite carrying a relatively small inventory. Here is the R. G. Dun mercantile credit reports on her enterprise that was made after the Civil War.

Mrs. Regina Minton   Fancy Goods   416 Girard Ave

Feb 28 66.   A widow lady in bus. some 2 or 3 yrs. has a good stand[ing] & had made money, has been advertising to sell out to quit bus.

July 19 70.   Out of bus.[103]

Many antebellum free black women gained business experience in running dry-goods establishments and shops by working as clerks for their husbands, brothers, or fathers. Their employment as shopkeepers was particularly noticeable in New Orleans because of the number and concentration of black-owned businesses in that city; as Martin Delany noted, "In many stores on Chartier, Camp, and other business streets, there may always be seen colored men and women, as salesmen, and saleswomen, behind the counter."[104] In Cleveland, Hezekiah Parker, the owner of a grocery and dry-goods store, was employed as a steward on a Mississippi riverboat, left the management of the store to his wife, described by black abolitionist William Wells Brown as having " 'goaheadativeness' to a far greater extent than most women. She would be a fortune to any businessman."[105]

A single woman could establish a business since she was not limited under the law of *femme couverture,* which required that all property owned by women be listed in their husband's name. Consequently, a married woman could not establish a business of her own unless she had legal authorization from her husband, as was the case with Catherine Sasportas, the wife of black businessman Sherry Sasportas. A 1817 deed granted her the legal right to establish a business as a "sole and seperate [sic] trader and dealer... as [if] she were a feme sole." The document was also specific in that her profits would remain solely her own. Most important, for her husband, the document absolved him from liability for any debts she might incur.[106]

In New York, black women merchants owned confectionery and fruit stores in addition to secondhand clothing shops.[107] In 1841, the black press recognized the short-lived, New York–based Female Trading Association, "a cooperative grocery store in New York with 100 female members." An advertisement lists the items the store sold: grits, rice, beans, pork, soap, starch, candles, brooms, and brushes. In an editorial, the *Colored American* said, "We believe this is the first successful organized effort of this kind among the colored people of this city and we cannot in too decided terms express our admiration."[108] In 1833, the National Negro Convention gave a vote of confidence to and urged support of free black businesswoman Lydia White who owned a produce store: "All who feel an interest in promoting the cause of universal freedom, is [sic] cheerfully recommended to her store, No 42 Fourth-Street, in the city of Philadelphia." By 1838, White had moved her business, according to an advertisement she placed in the first black monthly magazine, the *National Reformer:* "Lydia White's Requited Labor Grocery and Dry Goods Store, No 219 N. 2d Street, Philadelphia."[109]

Around this time, the free produce movement emerged, with its origins in the National Negro Convention, which recommended that black businesspeople should only sell, and black consumers should only buy, products that had been neither produced nor derived from slave labor. Those who complied purchased imported clothes made from cotton and imported food such as sugar and tobacco.[110] One of the movement's leading proponents was Frances Ellen Watkins Harper, who wore free labor clothes. In an 1854 letter, she wrote that "I spoke on Free Produce, and now by the way I believe in that kind of Abolition. Oh, how can we pamper our appetites upon luxuries drawn from reluctant fingers. Oh, could slavery exist long if it did not sit on a commercial throne?"[111] The free produce movement continued up to the Civil War.

Conclusion

In antebellum America, only a few free black women acquired substantial wealth as businesswomen, but the resolute few who worked for themselves achieved greater earnings than those who worked for others. Yet, with the exception of the wealthy antebellum merchant and financier Madame CeCe Macarty, black female planters as a group had the highest earnings, followed by their urban slaveholding sisters in the South, who established enterprises in the traditional areas of food service, dressmaking, and boardinghouse. In a society that was not only racist and sexist but also one decidedly hostile in its oppression and exploitation of black women, the economic achievement of black women, both slave and free, through the business enterprises that they established, is remarkable. These women, by capitalizing on the most menial occupations, transformed them into profit-making enterprises to provide for their own survival and that of their children, a situation that represents, perhaps, the one true success story of antebellum America.

6

BLACK BUSINESS FROM 1865 TO 1900

We would like to see more [black businesses] started on a larger scale. If single individuals are not able to conduct such, let several unite their means. Must we sit and
pray and hope for better times when the white man will see our need and give us better wages? Certainly not. Let us put our shoulders to the wheel; imitate our white
brother instead of abjectly depending upon him: establish and carry on every specie
of industrial enterprise for ourselves, employing and paying fair wages to our people.
—*Richmond Virginia Star,* 18 November 1882

Introduction

The history of African-American business after the Civil War is marked neither by a beginning of independent enterprise nor by an attenuation of business activity. Rather, there was
a continuation and expansion of entrepreneurship within the tradition of self-help activities that had distinguished black economic endeavors from the beginning of settlement in
this nation. The post–Civil War era, however, marked the demise of the antebellum giants
of black business, such as the lumber merchant Stephen Smith, who by 1865 was worth
$500,000. Consequently, while there was attrition in certain areas of antebellum black
enterprise, there was also the development and expansion of new black businesses, with
concomitant increases in wealth among some late-nineteenth-century black entrepreneurs.
The most successful was the New Orleans commission broker and real estate speculator
Thomas Lafon. Before the Civil War, he was worth $10,000; at his death in 1894, he left
an estate of $500,000.

While southern whites continued to resent and resist independent black economic initiative and activity, they had no alternative but to rely on blacks, who constituted one-third
of the South's population, to provide the essential goods and services needed for the reconstruction and redevelopment of the region. The Civil War devastated the South, and reconstruction required the restoration of a whole economic infrastructure. Credit, brokerage,
and transportation services were needed to facilitate the marketing of agricultural commodities, which were of foremost importance in the restoration of the South's economy.
The end of slavery also required new and distinctive distribution mechanisms to provide
food, clothing, and shelter to the urban and rural South. In the antebellum South, many
of the urban provisioning and development services had been provided by slave and free
blacks. Also, the need for new construction facilities and services was paramount. Accord-

ing to an 1865 census of occupations in the South, there were only 20,000 skilled white craftsmen and tradesmen, compared to 100,000 skilled blacks, most of whom were former slaves.[1]

While not all black artisans or mechanics, particularly in the construction trades, became business owners, the same initiative displayed by antebellum blacks in developing independent enterprises came into play after the Civil War. With few options available, the white postwar South could do little in its attempts to suppress the development of independent black economic activities. After the Civil War, then, there was a continuation of black business activity, with many black businesspeople reestablishing their antebellum enterprises. Moreover, the diversity of enterprises developed by blacks in the post–Civil War South underscores their innovative responses to the limited capital available to them in their legal transformation from slavery to freedom. Black cooperative-financed enterprises expanded beyond mutual benefit societies into four areas: manufacturing, real estate, banking, and insurance. In the late nineteenth century, while most attempts to establish manufacturing enterprises failed, cooperative financing through building and loan associations proved more successful.

Ironically, there was as much, if not more, diversity in black business activity in the new black towns founded in post–Reconstruction America than among urban blacks in both the North and South. The development of business activities in these black towns also demonstrate another example of black economic resistance not only to the intensity of economic oppression and political repression but also to white terrorism and violence. For the masses of blacks in the New South, however, sharecropping, crop lien, and tenant-farming systems pushed most into a state of debt peonage and tied them to the land almost as effectively as they had been under slavery.[2] Yet, as Carter G. Woodson said, denouncing assessments that depicted freedmen after the Civil War as lazy and shiftless, "The progressive, thrifty and industrious group was neglected, and views have been given only of the indolent ne'er-do-wells...."[3]

Black Businesses and Black Codes

The continuity of postwar black-business activity could be seen even during the Civil War. Before and during Union occupation, blacks, slave and free, as much as possible, persisted in attempting to maintain a livelihood. In New Bern, North Carolina, a survey of black occupations and income was taken in 1864 by the Union army's Superintendent of Negro Affairs. About 305 blacks responded, providing information on their gross income, which totaled $151,562; this included 24 blacks who reported incomes of more than $1,000. The highest income was $3,150 reported by a turpentine farmer, while the average annual incomes reported for the following occupation were: grocers, $678; barbers, $675; carpenters, $510; blacksmiths, $468; turpentine farmers, $446; coopers, $418; and masons, $402.[4] Table 6.1 lists the top incomes of blacks in each occupation.

In the immediate post–Civil War period, blacks in the urban South confronted Black Codes formulated to restrict their participation in occupations that could lead to independent enterprises. The codes were particularly harsh in Mississippi and South Carolina, where blacks outnumbered whites, and in Louisiana where blacks constituted almost 50 percent of the state's population. The South Carolina Black Code stipulated that unless blacks had licenses, they could not participate in any craft or, for that matter, "any other

TABLE 6.1   Civil War Black Businesses and Incomes,
Newberne, N.C., 1864

Turpentine farmer	$3,150
Dry goods and groceries	1,200
Carpenter and grocer	3,000
Lumber	1,200
Carpenter and grocer	2,400
Cotton farmer	1,100
Grocer	1,500
Carter	1,000
Grocer and baker	1,500
Cooper and tar maker	1,000
Grocery and eating house	1,500
Shoemaker	1,000
Staves/wood/shingles	1,500
Turpentine	1,000
Turpentine	1,500
Undertaker	1,000
Turpentine	1,300

Source: Report of Captain Horace James, Superintendent of Negro
Affairs in North Carolina, *Freedmen's Record* September 1865, 142, in
The National Freedman, 1 April 1865, 90–91.

trade, employment or business" other than farming or as a servant, either "on his own account and for his own benefit or in partnership with a white person or as an aid or servant of any person." Before a license could be purchased, however, a prospective black businessperson had to show evidence of good character, which could be provided only by whites. Prospective shopkeepers and peddlers had to pay $100 for a license, while artisans were required to pay $10. Operating without a license resulted in a $200 fine, with half of the money going to the informer.

In South Carolina, blacks could not own distilleries or places of business where liquor was sold. If found in violation of the code, they were subject to fines, corporal punishment, and hard labor. Alabama, too, did not grant licenses to blacks to sell liquor, with equally punitive measures for violations. Similar codes were in effect in Mississippi, in addition to a law that prohibited blacks from renting or leasing urban property. The 1865 Black Code in that state, moreover, stipulated that blacks must present written evidence that they had a lawful home and were employed, a requirement that they had to fulfill once a year. Also, any black employed by a municipality was required to have a license. In Mississippi and most other southern states, there were also restrictions on black possession of firearms and ammunition. Violators were punished by standing at a pillory for one hour or by whipping with not more than 39 lashes. Municipalities also enacted ordinances to strengthen the state Black Codes. In Opelousa, Louisiana, the only freedmen who could live in town were those who continued to work for their former masters.[5]

Although the Reconstruction involved more than restoring agricultural productivity, this was the sector of the economy in which the South moved quickly and effectively to control black labor. A few blacks acquired land through federal homestead laws, but land reform, confiscation, and redistribution to the freedmen generally remained an elusive dream. There were a few private attempts to deal with the situation, such as that by the New Orleans Freedmen's Aid Association, organized in February 1865 by wealthy New Orleans black businessmen in an attempt to offset the failure of the federal government to initiate any viable land policy that would provide the freedmen with economic independence. They rented plantations for the freedmen to work under the crop lien system and even advocated confiscation of property owned by former Confederates. The Confederates, however, reclaimed their property after the war and, with Louisiana's Black Codes making it illegal for blacks to rent or buy land, the freedmen's efforts became moot.[6]

With minimal opposition from the federal government and through labor contracts enforced by the federal government, freedmen farm laborers were exploited by the unrepentant white South. Even some former antebellum black planters, who reestablished their plantations in the post–Civil War South, made use of these labor contracts to assure themselves of a steady labor supply. By the late 1860s, the family of William Johnson, the "Barber of Natchez," had recovered from the setbacks of the war and began to expand their plantation activities. Immediately after the war, however, the oldest Johnson son and now head of the family, B. Byron Johnson, had to pay three dollars to secure a license to operate the barbershop in Natchez. Moreover, notwithstanding that he served in the Mississippi Federal Colored Militia, Byron, as a large property owner, had to sign an amnesty oath in 1865.[7] Also, in compliance with the Black Codes, his mother had to pay six dollars to hire two servants, as required by the Office Provost Marshall of Freedmen.[8]

By 1869 the Johnson family, in addition to owning the Magnolia Plantation, had leased two additional plantations, Carthage and Black Lake, all worked by freedmen "labor squads" under contract. In an unsuccessful attempt to "protect" the freedmen from labor exploitation, the federal government required planters to negotiate sharecropping contracts with them. The labor contract made by Byron Johnson and his mother was standard for black agricultural laborers in the postwar South and required: (1) "a certain portion" of the land would be worked by the freedmen, for which they would receive "one half of the Crops cultivated" during the one year period; (2) that the Johnsons would "furnish the mules, plows, and implements to be used in the cultivation of said crops.... also to pay one half of the Expenses incurred in carrying on said Carthage Plantation ... one half of the mule feed included"; (3) that for the privilege of sharecropping, the freedmen laborers would "furnish their own rations, paying for same and one half of the mule feed.... Also to pay one half of the expenses on said Carthage Plantation."[9]

For the sharecroppers, the labor contracts might have seemed fair, but there were other requirements that were decidedly exploitative and required them to work under conditions that differed little from those of slavery. Foremost, the freedmen were to perform "respectful, faithful and obedient labor." Failure to do so meant that they would "forfeit all His or Her" one-half interest in the crop, which would be retained by the Johnsons. Moreover, if, during the year, a worker became "Lazy, Insolent, or disobedient, or refused to do full duty," he could be dismissed by "two thirds vote of the [freedmen] labor squad." In addition, the freedmen forfeited any monetary compensation for work previously performed up to the date of dismissal by the labor squad. As to work conditions, the labor contract required that freedmen would "faithfully perform six days labor in the week, commencing each morning at day light, and working until dark. Allowing one hour at dinner in winter and two in summer." Also, freedmen were required to pay a dollar a day for "lost work," regardless of the reason and under any conditions, including pregnancy and ill health.[10]

As southern states were readmitted to the Union, the South was left alone to control black agricultural labor through the sharecropping, crop lien, tenant-farming, and convict-leasing systems. Moreover, white violence and terrorism escalated, as legal and extralegal means were used to force the economic subordination of African-Americans throughout the late nineteenth century. Yet, while the Civil War devastated the South and demoralized much of the white population, blacks persisted in the development of independent economic activities. Consequently, as in antebellum America, despite the Black Codes and other suppressive measures, African-Americans from 1865 to 1900 capitalized on the South's need for their independent economic activities. Yet they remained financially subordinate to whites.

The Dun Agency and Louisiana Black Business

After the Civil War, the R. G. Dun mercantile agency increased its credit-reporting activities on black businesspeople. The reports illustrate the different impacts the Civil War had on antebellum black businessmen and white businessmen.[11] The reports document the declining fortunes and even cessation of the enterprises of several leading antebellum black businessmen in the postwar era.[12] For example, Dun reported that Francois Lacroix, a real estate speculator and investor and merchant tailor, was worth $200,000 in 1854 and $300,000 in 1860. Dun's last listing for him in 1866 reported him out of active business.[13] Dun reported that his brother, Julien, also a highly successful real estate investor, speculator, and grocer, was worth $250,000 in 1854, but in 1864 noted that he was "said to be worth near" $50,000. Julien died in 1868, owning a small grocery store, with the total value of his estate worth $128,842.[14] The Lacroix brothers died intestate, and so did not succeed in passing on their vast properties to their heirs. The sons of Julien Lacroix succeeded him in the grocery business but failed at it, as reported by Dun: "February 27, 1871. Succeeded their father are colored men doing a good business—make money are close, prudent, attentive, very prompt & wor about 7m$." "June 72. Busted up, out of bus."[15]

Pierre Casenave and his sons also experienced downward economic mobility before going out of business. Pierre Casenave acquired his antebellum wealth primarily through his business as a broker and commission merchant; he also ran an undertaking business. The father was reported by Dun to be worth $100,000 in 1864. In June 1866, Dun notes, "All right worth over" $40,000. In the last entry before his death in 1869, Dun reported, "Broke. very honest & honorable man. keeps a small store in Attakapas."[16] (See table 6.2.) Casenave's sons did fairly well for several years in the undertaking business, but one got involved in politics and eventually the business failed.[17] The Dun reports, then, are also instructive about the impact of political activities on the finances of post–Civil War black businessmen.

In the case of Francis Dumas, however, Dun reported financial losses caused by uncollected debts resulting from monetary loans to other blacks, as indicated in an 1871 entry: "recently met with some losses by having advanced money to planters of his own color." Dun noted, however, that Dumas was "backed by his father who is worth a 1/2 million $." Dun's first entry was in July 1860, with one entry made during the Civil War in May 1861: "Import most of their gds." The next entry, for May 1866, noted that, in addition to their father furnishing them with capital worth between $30,000 and $50,000, "They keep a good Stock but do not possess business qualifications of a high order, still are highly respectable men of their class." In December 1866, Dun noted: "Have a Splendid stk of gds. & have done a fair bus," but with a credit rating of "2 1/2–2 1/2." In November 1869, they sold out at auction: "quit the business."[18]

TABLE 6.2   Dun on Casenave Family, Commission Merchant and Undertakers, 1853–1882

Pierre A. D. Casenave   Com. Merchant   89 Custom Ho St 124 Canal St

Feb. 53	A pet of "Judah Touro" & was for many yrs his confidential clk: is wealthy & owns R. E. v hon & may be crd for any amt wh he may contract.
May 54	Creole about 30 & single. of gd char. & standing & stead indus habs. Was formerly Clk to the late "Judah Touro" who left him a legacy of $10m & appointed him one of his executors. He is w $25m above all liabs. Owns his dwelling house—.Does vy respect'l bus. His cr is undoubtd here & he is consid perfectly gd for all contracts
Sept. 54	Some of our most reliable Banks & Exchange Houses say No. 2. An extra cautious Bank President marks No. 2 to 3.
July 55	Perfectly Sound & Safe.
July 56	Very safe. No. 1.
Mar. 57	Has between $30,000 and $40,000, is highly honorable, has a choice business. Credit very good.
Sept. 59	Some years in the business. Married, age about 43. Steady habits & good character. Is a man of ample means for the amount of business does a fair business & is in good Credit.
June 61	Stands well, credit good
June 64	An old & rich house w. at least 100m$
Dec. 65	Rate 2 1/2
Jan. 69	Broke, very honest & honorable. keeps a small store in Attakapas
July 69	Dead

G. Casenave & Bros   New Orleans   Undertakers
St. F. Casenave, P. Casenave, Jr. F. Casenave

Sept. 66	Succeeded the father "P. Casenave" are quadroons—Creole, more properly now called "colored persons" All highly intelligent smart, active bus men. doing a leading bus in their line also a large livery bus. own the RE they occupy. Credit good. worth $25 – 30m$ (c 1–2)
Nov. 68	Owns R.E. worth 20m$ also has Stock horses and carriages worth 25 to 30m$ (Reports G. C.)
Nov. 69	No change well off owns R.E., carriages, Horses, worth 25 to 50m$
Sept. 70	Is attentive to business owns property pays well & regarded good est worth 30m$
Feb. 72	Makes money & pays well in excellent credit and standing.
Mar. 75	Has been many years in the bus is a highly respected colored man has lately been appointed Recorder of births Marriages & Death an office said to be worth 4 or 5m$ a year. owns the stables he occupies which has been assessed as high as 10m$ but now worth 6m$ also carriages horses. Wor about 4m$ his property is not clear & as far as one can learn has always pd well & estimated to be worth 8m$ (previous rating too high).
Jan. 76	Suit vs him for $189.42 will probably be paid in a few days. His business very dull & he is cautious—asking payment in advance for those he does not know—his credit will not be affected by the suit as he is well known and consdired good.
July 77	Business is dull. . . . parties here advise cash transactions
Dec. 77	Sued 15th by James Cunningham co. of Rochester, N Y for $194.36 on two notes past due with 7% interest from May 19/77 until pd.
June 79	Cannot recom'd for other than cash.
Dec. 79	No change. Is honest & pay his legitimate expenses, but is mixed up in political matters & there are several suits against him.
June 80	Doing little business. Made himself very unpopular—think the major portion of his means by being mixed up in politics. Not thought desirable in a credit way.
Mar. 82	Judgment was lately rendered vs him . . . & to satisfy same, sheriff will sell establishment.
Apr. 82	Many years in this business & being a respectable colored man accumulated means which he afterward lost by being mixed up in political matters. Now has nothing visible in his name. Was seized several times by parties & advertised to be sold out but manages to arrange everything with parties to who he became indebted. His business is very dull & has no credit.

Source: Compiled from R. G. Dun and Company, Louisiana, 10:497; and 13:141; R. G. Dun and Company Collection, Baker Library, Harvard University, Business School. Also, David C. Rankin, "The Origins of Black Leadership in New Orleans during Reconstruction" *Journal of Southern History* 40, no. 3 (August 1974): 423 n. 17, lists St. Felix Casenave, born in 1835, as a New Orleans black political leader.

In November 1871, Dun provided its first separate listing of A. P. Dumas as a "Broker," also noting that he was an "Agent for the La State Lottery." Dun's last entry, two years later, said, "[o]ut of bus. is collecter of state taxes."[19] In June 1872, there is a separate listing for F. [Francis] E. Dumas, with Dun noting that a previous estimate of his worth, $8,000 to $10,000, was too low, that in money, capital, and real estate, he was worth about $30,000 to $40,000. The last Dun entry for Dumas was in January 1880, indicating he had just returned from France, was not in business, but "Lives on the rental of his ppty [property]." Francis E. Dumas was one of the wealthiest blacks in the state, a plantation holder who enlisted his slaves in the Louisiana Native Guards. General Benjamin Butler said Dumas was "a man who would be worth a quarter of a million dollars in reasonably good times. He speaks three languages besides his own, reckoning French and English as his own. . . . He has more capability as a Major than I had as Major General." In 1868, Dumas came within two votes of being nominated for governor of Louisiana.[20]

While several Louisiana politicians achieved great wealth from their astute business activities and political connections during Reconstruction, a Dun entry for a small South Carolina black businessman who was also a state legislator describes him as "worth nothing." It is not clear whether the description was about his activities as a businessman or a politician. Incidentally, the concern of some whites, that post–Civil War blacks were going into politics, is revealed in a Dun entry of a black Mississippi restaurant owner. (See table 6.3.)

TABLE 6.3   Dun on Small Black Businessmen and State Politics, 1870–1880

Henry Riley (Col'd)   Branchville [S.C.]   GS [General Store]

Dec. 70	Sell for cash
June 71	should not ask [for] credit, away from home
Dec. 71	No change
June 73	In bus about 2 years and dg a small bus. tho making a good support & said to be honest & reliable for his color & will pay small though has no business knowledge & consid. in debt. Owns no RE & has cap in bus about 3c$ [is] a member of the Legislature—would not recommend him
Mar. 74	Worth nothing doing a very small bus Scarcely making a living Sell him for cash.
July 74	Worth 00$ sell for cash
Aug. 75	No change
Feb. 76	Greatest caution
Feb. 77	Has little or nothing. Caution advised
June 78	Sold out.

Henry Riley Col'd   Branchville   Gro

Aug. 79	Standing not very good. Small negro trade—stock of 3c$ no other means. not recommended for credit.
Feb. 80	Doing a very small bus only & what he owns is mortgaged. Credit not advised.

Johnson (Colored   Flueyville [sic]   Restaurant

Apr. 73	Works hard, but has 00$ and is irresponsible has small stock on hand, but will eventually become a Senator or something else.
Aug. 73	Has been closed for sometime, intends to open this Fall if he can get the mean, his character & habits are tolerably good, don't think has capacity enough to carry on business.

Source: Compiled from R. G. Dun and Company, South Carolina, 12:92, 156; Mississippi, 3:8; R. G. Dun and Company Collection, Baker Library, Harvard University Business School.

Black Planters and Rural Merchants

After the Civil War, most of the large antebellum black planters lost not only their great wealth in slaves but most of their land as well. A new black-planter class emerged, however, including former slaves, whose land was worked by other former slaves as sharecroppers, tenant farmers, and/or independently hired farm laborers.[21] The largest post–Civil War black planter was the antebellum slave intrapreneur and entrepreneur Benjamin Montgomery, who was described as "all-black, not a mulatto." In 1866, Montgomery purchased two plantations, Briarfield and Hurricane, about 4,000 acres, for $300,000. Briarfield had been owned by the former Confederate president, Jefferson Davis, and Hurricane by his brother, Joseph, who had been Montgomery's slave owner. The terms stipulated an annual interest payment of $18,000 for 10 years, after which the full payment was due.

Dun reports indicate the early success of the plantation enterprise and of the dry-goods stores Montgomery established. In the first Dun entry for the Montgomerys in 1868, Dun reported, "They are negroes, but negroes of unusual intelligence & extraordinary bus. qualifications."[22] Other members of the Montgomery family participated in the business as planters and merchants. Benjamin's wife, Mary, comanaged Briarfield, while the business office was headed by their son, Isaiah. Their daughter, Virginia, worked as one of the bookkeepers and posted accounts in various ledgers: a gin book, a mill book, account books for the blacksmith and wheelwright shops and drayage hauling, an invoice book, bill of lading books, a receipts book, and bale lists for cotton purchased as commission merchants and for cotton sold. In addition, she posted the quarterly reports, tenant accounts, inventories, and audits, and she also prepared the annual fiscal reports.

By 1872, the Montgomery credit rating was "A No 1," and in 1873 their net worth was estimated by Dun to be $230,000. As Janet Sharp Hermann said, "Since only about 7 percent of southern merchants in this period received ratings of $50,000 or above, the Montgomerys were among the wealthiest merchant-planters in the South."[23] They lost their plantations, however, as a result of a series of disasters, including depressed economic conditions brought on by the Panic of 1873, natural disasters and reduced crop yields, low cotton prices, a suit by Jefferson Davis for return of the plantations, and, finally, the death of Benjamin Montgomery in 1877. During the time the Montgomerys held the plantations, they had paid $130,000 to $140,000 in interest. The Ursino plantation, which Benjamin had purchased in 1871 for $75,000, and its encumbrances of $30,000 were also lost.[24] By 1886, the Montgomerys were virtually bankrupt. In 1881, the Davis lands were sold at auction for $75,288.

The Montgomery stores, established on the plantations and in Vicksburg, Mississippi, reflected the rise of planter merchants, as they capitalized on the new purchasing power of the freedmen, especially profiting from credit sales and high interest rates. The Hurricane plantation store was especially profitable. About 1,600 laborers worked there as sharecroppers, many of whom were the Montgomerys' former fellow slaves. Daily sales at the store averaged $165, or $50,000 to $60,000 per year. At the time the average annual volume of sales for merchants was $4,000 to $5,000, while merchants with sales of more than $10,000 were considered quite successful.[25] Dun reports show how white merchants tried to capitalize on the purchasing power of the freedmen. Not all were successful, as one entry on a white planter who established a grocery store on his plantation shows: "June 73. In bus abt 1 yr, a very sm. affair his store is on his plantation & his trade is principally with

TABLE 6.4   Dun on Small Black Planters and Merchants, 1875–1880

David Hair (col'd)   Fort Motte   Planter & Gro

Mar. 75	Established 6 months. Good character & credit in very feeble health, small business but appears to be getting along well in small way & making a little money. Owns R.E., estimated worth 3 to 4m$ Considered good for small amounts.
July 75	No change
Feb. 76	Claims to be white. before and during the war was regarded as colored returns R.E. $810, Personal Property, is under homestead and undesirable
June 76	Clever Honest good man, Stands fairly & Regarded good for small amounts, means limited
July 77	Regarded good for a small credit. Estimated worth $1500 to $2000
July 78	Personal Property $550. Real Estate $740. Good character, making a living limited credit though sure.
Jan. 79	Has become a very slow pay, attributed to his bad health and poor success in business. Has some little means but not advisable for credit.
Aug. 79	Estimated worth $1.00 to $1200, small bus. Fair standing very limited credit advisable
Feb. 80	Farmer, owns some property & pays cash for what he buys.

Henry Thomas (col'd)   Mr. Vances Ferry [S.C.]   Planter & GS

Mar. 75	Established 5 years. Age 40 married of good character. Steady & industrious habits. doing small safe business & making a little $ Owns R.E. & is Estimated Worth $1,000 to $1,500. Good for small amount.
Feb. 76	In Charleston County.
June 76	No means. No credit
Feb. 77	Small concern. Stands fair, means limited but good for limited amount, but caution advisable
Jan. 78	Means very limited, requires little credit. Best sell for cash.
Jul. 78	No means or responsibility.

Source: Compiled from R. G. Dun and Company, South Carolina, 12:12, 137; R. G. Dun and Company Collection, Baker Library, Harvard University Business School.

negroes. is a man of gd char. no experience as a [merchant]. The last entry, for March 1874, notes that he was "doing a fair bus."[26] (Table 6.4 lists the Dun reports for a few small black planters.)

At the same time, blacks also sold seed cotton to some white country storekeepers. In one entry, Dun reported: "Jan'y 78. Jew. Not in fair standing Principally engaged in liquor trade. Buys seed cotton from Negroes & he is very unfavorably regarded by the trade Consid' tricky & unreliable. Caution advised."[27] Dun also reported on the grocery and dry-goods business of the Chamber brothers. The first entry was for July 1875, the last for July 1878. In the January 1878 entry, Dun reported: "Only fair char. Do little or no bus. Are sort of professional gamblers, playing poker most of the time. also buy seed cotton from Negroes. Are vy unfavorably regarded."[28]

Dun on Post–Civil War Small Black Businesses

One of the reasons the Dun mercantile credit records are important is that they document the continuity of black business activity from the antebellum period through Reconstruction in several areas: shoemaking; blacksmithing; clothing, grocery, and dry-goods stores; and tobacco manufacturing. (See tables 6.5 and 6.6.) By the late nineteenth century, while craft enterprises had declined as a major area of profit for black businessmen, there were continuous attempts made by them to move into retail sales, primarily as grocers and in

TABLE 6.5   Dun on Reconstruction Small Black Businessmen, 1866–1882

Jean Bonseigneur (colored)   Shoemaker/Boots and Shoes
May 66   Indifferent in character and habits. Slow Credit bad. Has some means owns some RE a small retailer and good for all he will do.
Sept. 69   About 60 years old. Been in business 25 years does a small retail business owns several town lots and other property is very well off. Estimated to be worth from 15 to 20m$ is very good and responsible.
Aug. 73   Says that business is declining daily and that he done but little of late. Still regarded good a worthy citizen.
June 76   Dead succeeded by M. Bonseigneur his son whose mother owns property he also has property of his own from his father but to what amount cannot be ascertained.

M. Bonseigneur
July 77   Young man owns some property and does a odd little business. Stands in fair credit. Keeps a few hundred dollars stock. regarded good for small credit.
Nov. 82   Young man. Succeeded his father who died and left some R. E. in this city. Morris B has some little mean is bus about four hundred dollars stock. Makes most of it and gets expenses. Mother is said to assist him. Has so far paid small purchases promptly. Is well regarded good.

Jno. Waler (colored)   Branchville   Shoemaker & Grocery
June 73   In bus about 1 year. said to be a negro with fair bus, though no bus capability—worth not more than 3 @ 4c$ capable doing vry little in the Grocery though makes a support in repairing and making shoes his old occupation—would recommend him
Apr. 74   Worth nothing never will be is a man of little or no char. would not recommend him
Feb. 75   Going out of bus. soon
Mar. 75   Insolvent and about used up
Aug. 75   Changed his place of business and has given judgment more than carries all his stock in store and has given a mortgage
Feb. 76   Sued and judgments
June 76   Broke & sold out by Sheriff Judgment
Feb. 77   Has no credit or means—Small concern—Just makes a scant living
Jan. 78   Now shoemaking no credit
July 78   Out of business.

Paul Wyse (col'd)   Lexington [S.C.]   Blacksmith
July 73   Doing very little though apparently an indus. man. Own a small piece of R.E. abt 5c$ though trade, decline to recommend him & advise caution
Jan. 74   Hard case,
June 74   No property Lives in Columbia.

F. Dickson (Col'd)   Orangeburg   Fruit Fish & c
Mar. 75   Very small affair only recently established worth 1c 2$ Don't think he will do.
July 75   Character very fair very small business, capital about 2c$ is making a support Not desirable for credit
June 76   Honest—R.E. 1m$ Fair risk for a small amount Doing well honest & reliable—Fair risk for a small amount
Feb. 77   Doing well honest & reliable est wor 10c12$ [$1,000–$1,200] in good credit.

Chas thorn (Col'd)   Orangeburgh [S.C.]   Gro & Conf't
June 71   In bus 8 mos. Owns sml R.E. & at $150 or so in bus gd honest 'Nigger' and think wor of a sml cr.
Dec. 71   Business greatly increase, he has lately bought a valuable lot in town worth $1500 . . . paid half cash for the same
June 72   Character honest business capacity good tha & he [is] honest worth in RE & money about 1m$
June 73   In bus several years—are doing well & mak'g a good living—said to be honest & indus & looked upon as good for small amounts—est w. 3M$ including RE
Mar. 74   Stands well for a negro. are making a good living, means small say from 5 to 6c met his obligations with a fair degree of promptness—is considered a fair risk for small amounts

(continued)

159

TABLE 6.5   *(Continued)*

July 74	No change
Jan. 75	Burned out yesterday—Loss est 1m$ No insurance—Has resumed business & is doing well in a small way. Owns R.E. & is E/W [Easily Worth] 1m5c$ [$1,500] Considered good for small amounts (Previous rating too low)
July 75	Stands well as to character, making a little money Pays local bills promptly and for small amounts considered good No change as to means
Feb. 76	Good for small amount on short time
June 76	Steady and attentive, but small bus and very profitable
Feb. 77	Small affair dg limited business char good steady & industrial good for a limited amount
Jan. 78	Fair char. small bus not wor over 2c3c$ okay responsibility
July 78	Stock 5c$ P.P [Personal Property] 1c$ R.E. 15c$ but mortgaged for value Small business—standing only fair not considered very safe—cautious credit advised
Jan. 79	Worth 1m to 15c$ and R.E. Thought fair for a limited credit.

Chas Thorn (col'd)   Orangeburgh [S.C.]   Gro & Confec

Aug. 79	Small negro trade very fair standing Est'd wor 11m to 12C & very limited credit if any advisable
Feb. 80	Out of business & credit not good.

E. F. Cleckley (Col'd)   Near Fort Motte   General Store

Mar. 75	Age 27 Runs the business for his father "Rufus C. Cleckly" has a stock of about 1m$. No business experience, doing by little & not likely to succeed.
July 75	Stands fair as to character. Has very little means small bus won't do to trust [him]
Sept. 75	Rufus Cleckley was in business before the War but failed. I don't think he has settled with his creditors yet. Since the war . . . has been sort of an agent for W. W. Smith (white) of Charleston who has been advancing pretty heavy through Cleckly, he is living with his colored children, his eldest boy E. F. Cleckly carried on bus here on a small scale but his father is the actual head of concern, has never been married & is about 45 years.
Feb. 76	Unreliable & tricky
June 76	Cash advised
Feb. 77	Out of business.

Compiled from R. G. Dun and Company, Louisiana, 9:149, 286; South Carolina; 12:117; 11:164; 12:123; 12:104, 105; 12:136; R. G. Dun and Company Collection, Baker Library, Harvard University Business School.

dry goods. Most encountered limited success compared to the number of whites who suc-ceeded as merchants. Yet, there were some blacks who did succeed as merchants.

Moreover, even when black businesspeople were favorably regarded for their character, inadequate venture and operating capital were factors contributing to their failure. Also, black merchants encountered a lack of consumer confidence: their business abilities were doubted by both races.[29] Dun entries on several black grocers in Reconstruction South Carolina document the limited capital available to black merchants in order for them to carry on a viable enterprise, as well as show the extent to which their efforts often were held in contempt by whites. A Dun entry for the black merchant Charles Thorn, however, shows that the possibility existed for a black merchant to overcome negative stereotypes. As Thorn succeeded in his grocery and confectionery enterprises, he went from being described in Dun as a "Nigger" to a "negro."[30] (See table 6.5.)

Still, for merchants in the New South, the disposable income of their consumer base was extremely limited; in 1869 and 1876, for example, the annual income of black farm labor-ers in South Carolina was only $60.[31] Yet, the southern black population was over five mil-lion people, representing a purchasing power of at least $300 million.

The new purchasing power of the much-expanded black consumer market was recog-nized by whites as early as 1868. As a white Mississippian noted at that time, "The

TABLE 6.6   Dun on Reconstruction Black Tobacco Manufacturers

George Alces   New Orleans   Cigar Manufactory

Aug. 69	Has been successfully Engaged in the Bus. for many years, is about 35 years of age Married of good character & habits Very Energetic and Enterprising prompt in his payments conducts his business with prudence has a capital in Business of 50m$ & owns R.E. in this city worth 20m$ clear
Mar. 70	Doing a good bus.—Estimated worth 45 @ 50m$—regarded good.
Aug. 70	Doing a good bus. has means & regarded safe & reliable
Mar. 71	Doing a large increasing business. perfectly good credit
Sept. 71	Making money and in excellent Standing and credit
Apr. 72	Has made money & is now worth in capital in business & unincumbered R.E. fully 125 to 150m$
Jan. 73	Does a large bus. owns some valuable R.E. pays promptly and perfectly good.
July 73	No change to note still going on as usual stnding & credit high worth fully in Cap in bus. and R.E. say over 100m$
Jan. 74	Mortgaged . . . two properties . . . to secure the Sum of 11m$ for which he gave 4 promissory notes two for 3m$ each and the other 2 for 25c$ [$2,500] each. All payable one year after date at the Union National Bank. Said notes bearing 8% interest per annum.
June 74	Good character habits & business capacity. Regarded as Entirely safe.
Apr. 75	Sold out.

L. [Lucien] Mansino   New Orleans   Cigar Manufacturer

Mar. 72	A married man, about 60, of good character. habits and capable, sober and industrious, doing a good business, stands well, honest, safe and reliable and in good credit for his wants, is worth in R.E. and capital 18 to 20m$
July 73	Still at his old place—doing well stands well considered honest & entitled to credit for wants— carries a pretty fair stock, owns one or two properties and is generally estimated worth 10 @ 12m$ and in good standing and credit.
July 76	Regarded as a good & careful bus man, doing a small but safe business & has good credit
July 77	No change does a good business, very safe for wants—estimated worth 10m$ or over
Mar. 79	Still continues to do a nice safe business. Is regular, a good honest man & making some money although for sometime past business has been very dull in this line. He owns some R.E. & is estimated worth in all about 12m$ Locally regarded good for contracts.

Source: Compiled from R. G. Dun and Company, Louisiana, 16:475; 15:85; R. G. Dun and Company Collection, Baker Library, Harvard University Business School. This was the last Dun entry for Mansion, who was the uncle of Georges Alces. See David Rankin, "The Origin to Black Leadership in New Orleans during Reconstruction" (*Journal of Southern History* 40, no. 3 [1974]), 438, where Mansion is listed as one of New Orleans's black Reconstruction politicians. John W. Blassingame, *Black New Orleans, 1860–1880* (Chicago: University of Chicago Press, 1973), 137, describes Mansion as a "wealthy cigar-maker" and "a minor poet." Also, Loren Schweninger, *Black Property Owners in the South, 1790–1915* (Urbana: University of Illinois Press, 1990), 300, includes Mansion in a listing of blacks worth over $100,000. See R. G. Dun, La. vol. 15, p. 84, for another entry on Mansion dated March 18, 1872, which notes: "He is wor in R.E. & cap'l in bus. 8 to 10m$," whereas the new or revised entry on March 28 said: "w. in R.E. & cap. 18 to 20m$."

negroes, since they have become producers on their own account, keep a large amount of money in circulation in the country, and consume on a much larger scale than formerly, which makes the business of supplying them as lucrative, if not more so, than planting or renting."[32] In the retail service sector then, the postwar black consumer market brought fledging black businesses into competition with white enterprises.

Still, the income earned by those small black businessmen who succeeded offered a greater degree of self-sufficiency than the starvation wages that marked the economic lives of the great majority of blacks in post–Civil War America. Dun entries on New Orleans shoemaker Jean Bonseigneur begin 7 February 1853, and with his death in January 1876. Before the Civil War, he employed "3 or 4 hands," his credit was "good," and he was described as a "steady industrious man of good character" and "correct and prompt in his dealings." The first entry after the war suggests a thoroughly discouraged man, described by Dun in 1866 as "indifferent in character and habits," who continued a business that went into a slow decline. After his death, the enterprise was taken over by his son, who did moderately well.[33] (See table 6.5.)

Black participation in the secondhand sales business, a profitable area developed by blacks in antebellum America, also saw a decline, as evidenced by Robert Adger, Jr. (1837–1910). His father was described by Henry Minton as "[o]ne of the most prominent business men of the last portion of the antebellum period." In 1850 he operated the largest secondhand furniture store in Philadelphia and owned four buildings to hold his inventory. After the Civil War, he relocated to the first floor of Liberty Hall, a building purchased by a consortium of 10 leading antebellum black businessmen, including William Still, William Whipper, and Stephen Smith, who put up a total of $23,000. This joint enterprise marked the beginning of cooperative real estate business ventures by blacks in the post–Civil War period. In Dun's first listing of the son in 1876, however, the enterprise was described as mediocre:[34]

Robert Adger	Ho Fng [House Furnishing]	Philadelphia
Dec 76	A middle age man, has been in bus here sometime. Is an attentive & indust & does a fair bus, but is not known to the trade for cr. Keeps a small stock in a not very attractive store & his responsibility is said to be limited to cash transactions would be best, though by some is given a small cr.	
Oct 82	Keeps a sm stock & does a sm bus. sold mostly for cash & those terms are recorded. Not thought to have much means, but can't est	
Jul 88	On 9th inst. a judgment bond was entered on him. This is merely a bond of indemnity to secure faithful performance of the duties of a clerk in the Office of Receiver of Taxes. It will not affect him in any way	

The son remained in the business until 1888, spending the last 20 years of his life as a post office administrator. By 1912, as Roger Lane said, "Liberty Hall which had housed several other black businesses had "gone over to Jewish store storekeepers 'on the edge of the ghetto.'" The secondhand-furniture business established in 1874 by Henry Harding, a former Nashville hotel owner and real estate investor, remained a successful enterprise until his death in 1888. A similar business was one of the first enterprises established by Warren C. Coleman of the Coleman Manufacturing Company. He started in 1876 by selling clothes and scrap iron in Concord, North Carolina. The profits he earned provided venture capital for Coleman's subsequent enterprises. At the turn of the century, his wealth was estimated at $100,000.[35]

There were some opportunities for success for the black merchant. As early as 1866, the Atlanta grocery store owned by James Tate proved successful, eventually providing him with the base to accumulate $60,000 in property. Still, by 1880 in South Carolina, there were only 49 stores owned by blacks, including the Columbia grocery store of William Taylor, who, it was said, "had such a large trade in his grocery at Columbia that he had to call in the police on Saturdays to handle the crowds." Perhaps the most successful grocer and dry-goods merchant was Samuel Harris, whose Williamsburg, Virginia, store was established during Reconstruction. By the late nineteenth century, he was "doing business of more than $50,000 a year. [Also he had] his own vessel for shipping goods." In Baynesville, Virginia, William Hamilton Johnson, a grocer, acquired property in walnut forests, shipping walnut logs to Germany, before his business failed in 1896. Within a few years, he reestablished his enterprise, which included several schooners and an expansion of his mercantile activities in Maryland.[36]

Post–Reconstruction Black Agribusinesses

In the post–Reconstruction rural South, the most successful blacks were commercial farmers, whose agribusinesses ranged from cotton and sugar production to the large sheep- and cattle-ranching operation of Henry Black in Pecos County, Texas. Still, only 11 blacks in the South succeeded in the agribusiness sector to the extent that they acquired wealth exceeding more than $100,000. Three were from Louisiana: Newton Smith, a cotton planter; J. F. Henderson, a farmer and wood merchant; and M. S. Alexander, a sugar planter who produced from 600,000 to 700,000 pounds of sugar a year, grossing over $30,000 annually. In Macon County, Alabama, the Reid Brothers, Frank and Dow, by the 1890s, owned and leased some 2,185 acres, having expanded the farm activities and land holdings of their father. Their farm included a cotton gin, blacksmith shop, and gristmill, and they also owned a country store. Their holdings were worked by tenant farmers. Frank Reid was worth from $20,000 to $50,000.

In Davidson County, Tennessee, the former slave Reverend H. W. Key began commercial farming in 1865 with leased land. In 1879 he purchased his first 75 acres. By 1900 Key owned 360 acres valued at $25,000, worked by seven tenant-farming families. At the turn of the century, Albany, Georgia, farmer Deal Jackson, with 2,000 acres of land planted in cotton, employed 40 tenant-farming families to work his land. Black farmers also extended their agribusiness activities to include brokerage. Reverend I. M. Powers was a North Carolina strawberry farmer, as well as a broker for white berry farmers and an agent for several commission houses in the North.[37]

Black commercial farmers in the North also expanded their farm activities. In Indiana, Albert Carter's hay farm outside of Indianapolis used a steam baler to compress from 25 to 40 tons of hay daily. In addition to shipments to Indianapolis, the family's interstate market extended from Chicago to Louisville, New York City, Philadelphia, and Baltimore. By 1870 the former slave John Walker, who purchased his freedom in Virginia and eventually that of his family by following his wife's owner to Missouri, was reportedly worth $40,000 and the wealthiest corn farmer in Hadley Township, Pike County, Illinois

In Kansas, Junius G. Groves (b. 1859), known as The Negro Potato King, was one of the most successful post–Reconstruction commercial farmers. He was born in slavery in Kentucky and in 1879 joined the black exodus to Kansas. Eventually, he acquired 500 acres in an area where prices had increased from $125 to $250 an acre. He also owned and operated a general-merchandise store and established several orchards containing 7,000 apple trees, 1,800 peach trees, 700 pear trees, 250 cherry trees, as well as apricot orchards and grape vineyards. His estimated worth was from $40,000 to $80,000. In one year, he produced 721,500 bushels of potatoes. Groves was also a broker, both buying and shipping potatoes purchased from other growers. As Booker. T. Washington noted, "he has a private railroad trace which leads from his shipping station to the main line of the Union Pacific Railroad."[38]

There were other blacks in the post–Reconstruction period whose extensive business activities required the building of railroad lines. William Still expanded his antebellum coal yard by moving to a larger site and laying "the necessary railroad tracks" to provide easy access to the coal shipped to him. A South Carolina sawmill enterprise, J. J. Sulton and Sons, also had its own line. The mill was started in 1825 by a white slave owner, who left it to his black son, Dennis, who began expansion of the business in 1873. In 1876 he turned the sawmill over to his son, J. J. Sulton, who took his two sons into partnership. In 1903 they moved the mill to Orangeburg, South Carolina, where, with the expansion of their business, they built "a private railroad siding, upon which the cars enter their yards." Early on, the lumber business had proved profitable for the East Saginaw, Michigan, lumber merchant and real estate dealer W. Q. Atwood. In 1880, he was worth $100,000.[39]

Freedmen's Savings Bank and True Reformers Bank

Even before the Civil War, blacks accumulated capital and attempts were made by them to establish a national black savings bank. During the war, two kinds of banks were established for blacks in the South by the Union army of occupation. In 1864 the Free Labor Bank was established in New Orleans by General N. P. Banks. Deposits were accepted from not only his several thousand black troops but also free people of color and freedmen plantation laborers. One group, the "Rost Host Colony, deposited $21,605.83 in the Free Labor Bank."[40] In 1864, Military Savings Banks were established at Beaufort, South Carolina, and Norfolk, Virginia, primarily for black soldiers; but deposits were also accepted from free blacks. Established in August, the Beaufort bank had $65,000 in deposits from blacks by December; by April 1865, there was more than $200,000 in unclaimed deposits.[41]

The National Freedmen's Savings and Trust Company, popularly known as the Freedman's Savings Bank, was established 3 March 1865, when it was incorporated by a congressional act. By December 1865, deposits by blacks amounted to $210,126. Branches were established in 35 cities, including the one in Washington, D.C., which opened in August 1865. The New York City branch was the bank's central office from 1865 to 1869; in 1870, the Washington branch became its headquarters.[42]

Contrary to what some blacks thought, the Freedmen's Bank was not a government institution. It was a privately held financial institution, owned and managed by whites. The congressional bill establishing the Freedmen's Bureau, which was a governmental agency, was signed by President Lincoln the same day he signed the Freedmen's Bank bill of incorporation.[43] Moreover, the bank's passbook reinforced its image as a governmental institution. On its cover was a collage containing the pictures of Lincoln, General Grant, General Howard, and the United States flag draped over a public building. Printed on the cover was the statement "The government of the United States has made this bank perfectly safe."[44]

The Freedmen's Bank remained in existence for nine years, failing in 1874 because of mismanagement by the whites who controlled it. While few blacks were employed by the bank during the first years of operation, a few were eventually hired as tellers, clerks, and bookkeepers. Even then, they constituted only a small proportion of the total number of Freedmen Bank employees. After 1870 black businessmen and community leaders were brought in as token members of advisory councils, but management positions remained filled with whites. Moreover, deposits from branch banks were sent to the Washington bank, primarily for investment. Section V of the Act of Incorporation specifically indicated that deposits were to be reinvested in "stocks, bonds, treasury notes and other securities of the United States." Consequently, black savings were seldom available for loans to blacks for reinvestment in the black community. The only advantage to black depositors was the interest received on their savings, initially 1 percent. Also, when investment profits exceeded 10 percent of deposits over liabilities, the "surplus" would be divided among the depositors "in such manner as the board of trustees shall direct."

Events beginning in 1870 eventually resulted in the failure of the Freedmen's Bank. An amendment to its charter allowed the bank's finance investment committee, which set bank operational policies, to invest one-half of the bank's funds "in bonds and notes secured by mortgage on real estate." Also, branch banks could use "available funds" to invest in real estate in their own communities. Only a limited amount of these funds, however, was made available to blacks. Instead, white managers, both at the branches and especially at the central bank in Washington, used black deposits as their private funds, borrowing, but seldom paying back in full, loans that they took out. In some cases, they even canceled their loans or dumped questionable securities on the bank, either as collateral or as payment. In Washington, William S. Huntington, who sat on the bank's finance committee, just dropped in one day and picked up a $3,000 loan that he never repaid. Also, by 1871, most of the white bank officers were "connected with some outside interest that borrowed from the bank."[45]

While the New York office had been conservatively managed by whites who viewed their position and responsibility as a "philanthropic venture," the finance committee of the Washington central office was headed by men such as Henry D. Cooke, president of the First National Bank. He was also a cousin of Jay Cooke, who on one occasion borrowed $500,000 at five percent interest from the Freedmen's Bank. At the time, depositors were paid six percent interest on their savings and, as one black bank clerk said, "when the cash balanced, all of us went out to celebrate the event."[46] While the Washington Freedmen's Bank had a black cashier, "Daddy" Wilson, he was a figurehead, used by the white financial committee to endorse their questionable banking practices.

In 1873 Jay Cooke's company failed, followed by Henry Cooke's First National Bank, which resulted in a run on the Freedmen's Bank by black depositors. Attempts made by the trustees to restore confidence failed. In March 1874, Frederick Douglass was appointed president of the Freedmen's Bank. He quickly pumped $10,000 of his funds into the bank before reading the January 1874 national bank examiner's report, which stated that the bank was operating at a deficit of $217,886. By then, the bank had virtually ceased functioning. In June 1874, at the insistence of the Controller of Currency, the Freedmen's Bank was closed, owing 62,131 depositors $2,939,925. During its existence, $57,000,000 had been deposited by blacks. Two congressional committees were established to determine reasons for the bank's failure.[47] But despite concrete evidence of widespread fraud and embezzlement, only a few people were ever prosecuted. By 1900, nearly 56 percent— $1,638,259—of the amount on deposit when the bank failed in 1874 was repaid.

In retrospect, both W. E. B. DuBois and Booker. T. Washington claimed that the failure of the Freedmen's bank was psychologically damaging to blacks. However, black economist Abram Harris said, "If the setback to the Negro's economic progress had been as profound as described by these leaders, it is hardly likely that the Negro would be found organizing banks of his own in less than fifteen years after the failure of the Freedmen's banks."[48]

In the wake of the failure of the Freedmen's Bank, blacks formed two kinds of banks: private banks and fraternal order savings banks. In March 1888, the Grand United Order of True Reformers Bank of Richmond, Virginia, was the first black bank chartered, although it did not begin operations until April 1889. The slave-born Reverend William Washington Browne (1849–1897), who founded the fraternal Order of the True Reformers in 1881, was also founder and president of the True Reformers Bank. Under his management, the bank was referred to as the Gibraltar of Negro Business.[49]

The True Reformers Bank had been established by the order to provide a depository for the insurance premiums collected by the organization. In addition to the bank and insurance company, the True Reformers also developed several areas of cooperative enterprise. Real estate activities were foremost in their financial operations. They owned a $45,000 office building, a hotel, and additional business and housing properties in 10 Virginia cities and in Washington D.C., Baltimore, Louisville, and Cincinnati. The order also established the 634-acre Westham Farm that included 130 lots for town development, all of which, the order said in 1902, had been sold. The settlement was named Brownsville. The True Reformers also established a newspaper and printing house, a chain of department stores, and a home for the elderly, which was run by the insurance department of the order. (See table 6.7 for a summary of the bank's finances in the early 1900s.)

The True Reformers Bank, however, failed in 1910. According to Abram Harris, the bank's financial interests were subordinated to that of the order, primarily due to "the Order's attempt to finance itself and its subsidiary corporations through the bank with apparently no intention of liquidating the loans at maturity." As subsidiaries to the parent company of the True Reformers, each section operated cooperatively, while remaining independent from the others, with separate management divisions and independent financial responsibilities. The department stores, newspaper, printing enterprise, and hotel and real estate operations were operated under the Reformers Mercantile and Industrial Association, the chief borrower. In addition to the bank's highly undiversified portfolio, there was also mismanagement and corruption by the bank officers, including the cashier and bookkeeper[50]

Although the True Reformers Bank failed, it had made substantial contributions to the development and advancement of the black community. As Booker T. Washington said in reviewing the early history of the real estate operations of black fraternal orders, "Some of these organizations have started commercial enterprises. Others have loaned their funds to members to aid them in lifting mortgages from their farms in order to replace them by others at a lower rate of interest. At other times they have loaned money to their members to enable them to build houses."[51] The financial support provided by the True Reformers Bank to the black community can be contrasted to that supplied by the Freedmen's Bank. The latter operated with a multimillion-dollar capital base obtained from deposits by blacks, but its banking policies precluded it from providing even minimal financial support for black business development. Rather, its funds were allocated to provide personal and business loans to whites, as opposed to the financial investment made in the black community by the True Reformers Bank.

The $500,000 loan made to Jay Cooke by the Freedmen's Bank could have provided significant venture and development capital for black businesses; at the time, most black businesses were established with venture capital of less than a thousand dollars. After the Civil War, several attempts by blacks to establish tobacco manufactories failed due to a lack of capital. In 1865 three former slaves in Richmond, Virginia, attempted unsuccessfully to secure a loan from the Freedmen's Bank to establish a tobacco manufactory after being displaced as tobacco workers. Before the Civil War, the tobacco industry had primarily employed blacks, and several black tobacco manufacturers enjoyed some financial success (see table 6.6). In the absence of any banking institution that would underwrite loans for

TABLE 6.7   Bank of the G.U.O. of True Reformers (Established 1889)

Total Receipts of True Reformers' Bank

1890	$ 9,811	28		1892	$ 79,052	79		1894	$162,433	32
1891	55,937	70		1893	108,205	98		1905	807,995	17

The Report, August 2, 1902

From the Finance Department	$ 135,737	45
From the Real Estate Department	21,014	00
From the Regalia Department	7,636	58
From the Reformer Department	7,427	32
From the Supply Department	21,254	13
From the Record Department	44,131	37
From the Old Folks' Home	8,127	44
From the Richmond Mercantile Store	57,237	92
From The Washington Mercantile Store	11,982	50
From the Manchester Mercantile Store	14,946	75
From the Portsmouth Mercantile Store	12,872	49
From the Roanoke Mercantile Store	5,577	24
From Fountains	47,659	35
From Rose Buds	5,666	71
From individuals	259,653	74
From societies	62,228	78
From loans	18,391	14
From collections	1,409	44
From exchanges	665	50
From clubs	14,686	67
From Hotel Reformer	4,793	39
Total	$ 796,099	91
Cash balance forwarded from the last report	103,229	96
Total receipts, including balance forwarded	$ 899,329	87
Total disbursements by depositors, discounts, mortgages, etc.	820,740	53
Cash balance to date	$ 78,589	34
Amount of cash handled at last report	6,996,349	38
Amount of business done this year	1,616,840	44
Total amount of business done to date	$8,613,189	82
Average monthly business done	134,736	70
Number of letters received this year	11,831	
Number of letters sent out	8,979	
Number of letters and packages referred to other Departments	2,066	
Number of depositors at the last report	10,631	
Number of new depositors this year	744	
Total number of depositors	11,375	

(continued)

TABLE 6.7   Continued

Statement, April 6, 1906

Resources			Liabilities		
Loans and discounts	$ 463,564	21	Capital stock paid in	$ 100,000	00
Stocks, bonds and mortgages	5,000	00	Surplus fund	86,972	00
Furniture and fixtures	2,500	00	Undivided profits, less amount		
Checks and other cash items	2,555	32	paid for interest, expenses		
Due from State Bank and pri-			and taxes	27,807	30
vate bankers	12,811	24	Time certificates of deposits	224,083	21
Specie, nickels, cents	7,150	63	Individual deposits subject to		
Paper currency	47,866	00	check	102,584	89
Total	$ 541,447	40	Total	$541,447	40

The bank has paid in dividends to the stockholders $160,350 to date.

Report, 1907

Receipts					
			Balance from last year	$ 78,216	76
Grand Fountain	$ 392,762	78	Receipts for year	1,008,996	40
Fountains	31,284	76			
Rose Buds	2,524	54	Total	$ 1,087,213	16
Individuals	382,978	06	Disbursements	1,000,811	83
Societies	135,799	73			
Loans	51,172	52	Cash Bal. at last report	$ 86,401	33
Interest	1,617	37			
Collections	1,593	91	Capital stock paid in	100,000	00
Supplies	16	69	New depositors	1,803	00
Exchange	67	84	Amount paid in dividends	18,884	00
Richmond Division	6	75			
Clubs	9,171	45	Amount cash handled		
			at last report	14,923,240	76
			Business done this year	2,009,808	22
Total	$1,008,996	40	Total	$16,933,048	98

Source: W. E. B. DuBois, *Economic Co-Operation among Negro Americans* (Atlanta: Atlanta University Press, 1907), 139 – 140.

business development, blacks founded cooperative financial organizations to raise capital, but it was always inadequate. In 1869 a joint-stock company was organized by Richmond blacks to underwrite the financing for the establishment of a cigar manufactory, but failed to secure enough capital.[52]

In Washington, D.C., a cooperative effort made through the formation of a joint-stock company to establish a tobacco and cigar manufactory was successful. It opened in 1869, but eventually failed due to a lack of development capital. Consequently, the founding of black banks would grow out of this need for mobilizing capital to provide for business development. The financial activities of the True Reformers Bank thus provides a counterpoint to the failure of the Freedmen's Bank to use black bank deposits as a capital base for underwriting the economic development of the black community. With few black businesspeople having the necessary collateral to secure loans from white banks, black banks were established. By 1934, a total of 134 black banks were founded, in addition to credit unions, building and loan associations, and industrial loan societies.[53] Few, however, survived. While black banks adopted a conservative lending policy, at least mortgage loans were made to blacks and even to some black businesses.

Cooperative Manufacturing Enterprises

In the late nineteenth century, in the absence of financial institutions to underwrite venture capital loans, financial cooperatives were founded. Their appeal for funds was based on the premise that the manufacturing enterprises they formed would provide employment for blacks. One of the most successful was the Chesapeake Marine Railroad and Dry Dock Company, organized by blacks in Baltimore in 1865. As stated in its 1868 charter of incorporation, the company was established for the purpose of "conducting the business of building ships and other sea going vessels, the hauling of such vessels out of the water and rebuilding, repairing and refitting them for sea voyages."[54] The company was capitalized at $40,000, with 8,000 shares put on the market at $5 each. The initial $10,000 was raised by a consortium of black businessman led by Isaac Meyers, a union organizer.

During the company's existence, John Henry Smith, its cashier, was directly involved in the finances behind the negotiations for the acquisition of the shipyard and in its management as chief operating officer. By 1870 the company employed from 200 to 300 men, with a weekly payroll of $10 to $17.50 and a $2,000 annual ground rent. During its first two years of operations, the shipyard was awarded government contracts, which it subsequently lost. In the early 1870s, there was a slump in the shipbuilding industry, which led to depressed prices. Despite this and even though the skilled black caulkers refused to take lower wages, the company was able to pay a dividend in its sixth year of operation. Public confidence among blacks in the company, however, was lost when it was found in 1879 that the contract for the purchase of the shipyard was in actuality only an 18-year lease. The company failed when the shipyard's owners refused to renew the lease.

Several other manufacturing companies in the post–Civil War South also failed. One of those was the Southern Stone Holloware and Foundry Company, incorporated in 1897 in Chattanooga, Tennessee, with a capital stock of $5,000 that sold at $25 per share. Purchase of its stock was limited "only to colored people, either for cash or upon monthly payments." The company started on a small scale manufacturing fire grates, stoves, boiler grate bars, and refrigerator cups. It also provided a repair service. Despite the company's ownership of land, buildings, machinery, and patterns, and with little debt, it folded in 1901. While shares amounting to $1,466 had been sold, the lack of operating capital limited production. The company's short-term success, however, encouraged the establishment of two new foundries in Chattanooga in 1900. One was capitalized at $25,000, but it also failed.[55]

Several attempts by blacks in the New South to establish cotton mills and provide jobs for blacks were also unsuccessful, including the Afro-American Cotton Mill Company in Anniston, Alabama. In Nashville, J. C. Napier and S. W. Crosthwaite headed a group of black political and business leaders to establish the Colored Citizens Cotton and Manufacturing Company in 1882, but it failed, as did the efforts made by a group of blacks in Augusta, Georgia, to establish a cotton mill in 1878.[56]

Perhaps the most ambitious manufacturing enterprise established in the late nineteenth century was the Coleman Manufacturing Company, a textile mill incorporated in 1897 in Concord, North Carolina. Construction of the mill was completed the same year, with plans for the purchase of machinery that would provide employment for about 300 black operators. The mill opened in 1901 in a plant that covered 100 acres of land. The factory was a three-story brick building with "two boilers of 100 horsepower each and the modern equipment of looms, spindles and other necessary machinery. Several tenement cottages were erected and rented to the employees, who were paid about one-half as much as the same workers in Massachusetts."

The company was established by slave-born Warren Clay Coleman (1849–1904), an entrepreneur whose numerous enterprises were representative of the multibusiness activities of black businessmen in the New South. He pursued opportunities for accumulating individual wealth, as well as establishing economic activities to provide employment to blacks. Coleman's initial business had included the sale of secondhand clothing and scrap iron, after which he achieved success through real estate speculation and property acquisitions in Concord, with venture capital acquired through peddling and trading groceries and dry goods and through farming. In 1881 he opened a downtown general-merchandise store in Concord, while continuing his real estate activities in buying and renting property, all of which gave him considerable standing in the community. By 1895, with his mercantile business and property holdings, Coleman was considered one of the richest blacks in the South. His plans to establish a cotton mill were influenced by the success of Concord's whites in the textile industry, including the Cannon family.

When Coleman's mill opened in 1901, the industry was in a depressed state. Even the Cannon company laid off workers. Despite the bad conditions, however, from the beginning, securing adequate venture and development capital was the major problem that accounted for the mill's eventual failure. The mill was capitalized at $100,000, with shares purchased by the Duke family, in addition to a loan from one of the family members. However, blacks, including Booker T. Washington, were slow in responding to Coleman's appeal for financial support. Coleman did get financial help from Richard Fitzgerald, one of Durham's wealthy blacks, whose brickyard enterprise was extremely successful. Fitzgerald had contracts with the state of North Carolina for public buildings and with the Duke family and the American Tobacco Company. Fitzgerald was also the largest employer of blacks, about 50 to 110, in the South. His real estate activities were also profitable.

With Fitzgerald's success as a businessman, Coleman named him president of his company, while he became secretary-treasurer. Yet, the Coleman Manufacturing Company was forced to close in 1904 when the Duke financial backer foreclosed on the property to secure recovery of his $20,000 loan. A year earlier, Coleman had been forced to resign from his position to stop foreclosure. Attempts were made to keep the mill going by a consortium of blacks, but they were eventually forced to sell to the Cannon Mills.

Several factors, then, can account for failure of Coleman's mill, factors that apply equally well to other black manufacturing enterprises. The most important was that access to credit from financial institutions to secure both venture and development capital was virtually nonexistent. Consequently, factories established by blacks in the late nineteenth century were invariably undercapitalized. In addition, in their financial prospectus offering stock options, black businesses generally did not include operating expenses and did not make financial provisions for the deterioration of fixed capital. Although it was charged that the owners of the Baltimore shipyard mentioned earlier speculated with the profits, the reality was that only limited capital was available for repairs and the renovations needed to accommodate the new steel-bottomed ships.[57] A lack of operating capital, then, limited the company's ability to respond to new technological developments. In addition, John Henry Smith, the chief operating officer, failed to inform the board of directors that they were lessees, not owners, of the shipyard. His failure was ultimately a reflection of the racist attitudes of whites, who remained reluctant to support black enterprises. Smith said that his strategy to lease the shipyard was based on the assumption that, once blacks demonstrated to whites that they could successfully run a shipyard, "there would be a greater willingness to sell land to a black owned and operated company."[58] Negotiating racism had to be factored in any business plan developed by blacks.

Another major factor that helps explain the failure of nineteenth-century black manufacturing enterprises was the inexperience of the management in operating them. Management of the shipyard rested in the hands of a 12-man board of directors, elected annually. Their capabilities as businessmen were unquestioned. All were successful. All were literate, with the exception of the wealthiest board member, Joseph Thomas, who was company treasurer, but whose estate was worth $150,000.[59] The board, however, had limited knowledge of the industry, which perhaps accounts for the charges against them of gross mismanagement of the shipyard's financial affairs.

In both instances, then, there was a loss of confidence on the part of blacks to continue to support these enterprises. Warren Coleman, while a successful merchant and astute real estate speculator, lacked not only experience in managing an industrial enterprise but also expertise in textile manufacturing and knowledge of the industry; the same is true for the successful bricklayer and entrepreneur Richard Fitzgerald, who was president of the company. Unlike the shipyard, however, which had experienced and skilled workers, Coleman employed blacks who were inexperienced because of their exclusion from employment in southern textile mills; and the mill did not remain open long enough for the development of those skills, which might have made a difference in the success of the company.[60] Even so, despite capital limitations and inexperienced management, both the shipyard and textile mill began operations at a time when both industries were operating in a depressed market.

Consequently, in the age of the greatest expansion of American railroads, oil, steel, textiles, meatpacking, electronics, and the beginning of massive international financial investment, African-Americans entered the twentieth century without one manufacturing enterprise of any significance. Unlike preindustrial antebellum America, when black enterprise paralleled mainstream American business, blacks were completely excluded from the post–Civil War rise of industrial America. For the masses of blacks, their main source of buying a piece of America through financial investment was in the acquisition of property.

Cooperative Real Estate and Fraternal Building and Loan Associations

While rural blacks in the post–Civil War period attempted to acquire farm property, urban blacks were intent on acquiring homes. Throughout the urban South, blacks organized building and loan associations that enabled them to purchase homes. As early as August 1865, freedmen in Kinston, North Carolina, formed a joint-stock association to pool their resources for either building or purchasing homes. There were several building and loan associations in Baltimore that accumulated from $12,000 to $15,000 in shares scheduled for maturity in seven years. Two other building societies were organized in that city in

1881 and in 1886; they issued stock with a par value of $125 per share, with issues limited to 1,000 shares. Another Baltimore building and loan association founded in 1868 had 100 members whose investments "facilitated the purchase of forty or fifty houses."

In Nashville several building and loan associations were organized, including the Southwestern Real Estate Company of Nashville in 1872, the Bilbo Avenue Building and Real Estate Loan Association in 1888, and a branch of the American Building and Loan Association in 1889.[61] In Augusta, Georgia, the Workingmen's Loan and Building Association was organized in 1889. In Atlanta the Georgia Real Estate, Loan and Trust Company was founded by blacks in 1890. Within four years, it owned $25,000 in property in that city. In Washington, D.C., the Odd Fellows' Hall Association was incorporated in 1889, with stock selling at $10.00 per share. The Masonic Hall Building Association was founded in 1893. In Philadelphia, the Burean Building and Loan Association was founded and incorporated in 1888.

By 1898, the Hampton Conference reported that there were 17 building and loan associations in Pennsylvania, New York, Maryland, the District of Columbia, Virginia, Georgia, Florida, and Arkansas. In Virginia, according to Booker T. Washington, "Perhaps the most numerous and popular form of cooperative business in which our people have engaged is that of the building and loan associations." He added that half of the homes owned by blacks in Virginia were built with funds acquired from black building and loan associations. Additional ones would increase in both number and capital in the first decades of the twentieth century, particularly in large cities in the North, a response to the escalation of black migration to that section of the country.[62]

Black Town Business Enterprises

During the period following the Reconstruction to World War I, more than 100 black towns were founded. The founding of all-black towns had one major purpose— the achievement of economic self-determination. It should be noted, however, that the "All-Negro community was in no way a retreat from American standards and values, and certainly not an anachronistic revival of Africanisms, but rather an attempt to develop fully and to exploit thoroughly the American culture."[63] The first town founded by an African-American was New Philadelphia, Illinois, established in 1836 by the former slave Free Frank. New Philadelphia, however, was virtually abandoned by 1884, having been bypassed by the railroad when it came through Pike County in 1869. The town remained primarily an agricultural settlement for blacks until the 1940s. By then, Pike County blacks had moved to Chicago, St. Louis, Kansas City, Oklahoma, and Denver.

Black towns are defined as those in which the population was 95 percent black, but this definition excludes the entrepreneurial activities of black town founders and proprietors, who profited from the sale of town lots. Before the Civil War, New Philadelphia's townspeople were both white and black. From 1865 until the town was phased out, the population was all black, with its population increased by former slave migrants from Missouri. Brooklyn, Illinois, initially a town founded by whites, also became all black in the post-Reconstruction period. The town had a black population when it was established by whites in 1837, and it was not until the 1880s, when blacks gained political control, that whites began a gradual but almost complete departure from the town.[64]

Several of the most important post-Reconstruction black towns were founded by whites for the specific purpose of selling town lots to blacks. Nicodemus, Kansas, established in 1879, Langston, Oklahoma, in 1891, and Boley, Oklahoma, in 1904, were all founded by white speculators. Overall, more than 60 black towns and settlements were founded after 1879. By 1910, there were 30 black towns and 13 settlements in existence. Many survived to the 1950s.[65] The settlement of all-black towns in post-Reconstruction America reflected the response of blacks to the intolerable conditions of life in the New South, described by Nell Painter as a "young hell."[66] Violence was very much a part of the post–Civil War South, as whites organized terrorist groups such as the Ku Klux Klan and Knights of the White Camellia to force blacks into a state of subordination approximating slavery.

In 1889, Oklahoma's Indian Territory, which originally had been ceded to Native Americans, was opened to settlement, with 10,000 blacks among the first to arrive that year. Despite their comparatively small numbers, African-Americans hoped that Oklahoma would become an all-black state. In 1889, the first black town, Lincoln City, was founded. It soon had a population of 300. Boley, located on the Fort Smith and Western Railroad, along with Langston, were the two most important all-black towns in Oklahoma. Both were established by whites. Two years after Boley was founded in 1903, blacks had established stores selling dry goods, groceries, hardware, millinery, shoes and drugs, in addition to restaurants, real estate offices, a $6,000 gin, a shingle mill, two sawmills, and a hotel.[67] By 1910, Boley's black population numbered 3,000.

Langston's white founder hired a black agent, Edward P. McCabe, to promote the sale of town lots to blacks. McCabe had worked as an agent in promoting the town of Nicodemus, Kansas, and was also one of the founders of the Oklahoma Immigration Association in 1889. He also founded Liberty and several other black towns in Oklahoma during the period of territorial government. Although he never lived in Langston, McCabe promoted Oklahoma as a place for settlement through the newspaper he founded in 1890, the *Langston City Herald*. In one advertisement, he announced, "Langston City is the Negro's refuge from lynching, burning at the stake, and other lawlessness and turns the Negro's sorrow into happiness."[68]

The businesses established in Langston provide an example of the economic viability of black towns founded at the turn of the century. In its first year, Langston had a population of 600, with six retail groceries, one wholesale grocery, two liquor stores, two blacksmith shops, a feed store, and two barbershops, with a total value of $85,000. By October 1892, there were 25 black businesses, and an attempt was made to bring a railroad to the city. In 1892, the Langston Board of Trade was organized. Through its efforts, additional businesses were established, including two meat markets, a second feed store, two brickyards, two boot and shoe stores, a harness and saddle shop, and a gristmill. There were several manufacturing enterprises: a cooperative yeast-powder factory, a soap factory, and a broom factory. The town also had three restaurants, an opera house, three saloons, and a billiard hall. In addition, a two-story bank and two more hotels were opened. Telephone service was established in 1895. With the establishment in 1897 of the Colored Agriculture and Normal University of Oklahoma, renamed Langston University, the future of the town was assured; although, by 1910, its population was only 339.[69]

The most publicized all-black town established in the late nineteenth century was Mound Bayou, Mississippi. It was founded in 1887 by Isaiah Montgomery, son of Benjamin T. Montgomery, who purchased 840 acres from the Louisiana, New Orleans, and

Texas Railroad, on which he subsequently platted Mound Bayou. Before a town could be established, the settlers had to clear the land and drain the swamps. The first businesses were a mercantile store and, to capitalize on land-clearing activities and provide a cash crop, a sawmill was built in partnership by a Montgomery cousin, Benjamin Green, and Martha Montgomery, Isaiah's wife. The town grew slowly, but by 1898, with 183 blacks, Mound Bayou was incorporated as a village, and as a town in 1912. Its success was due to its location in Bolivar County, which was half-way between Vicksburg and Memphis and, more importantly, Mississippi's most fertile and largest cotton-producing county.

By 1907, while only 500 people lived in Mound Bayou, there were some 4,000 blacks in the outlying areas. Beginning in 1887, the railroad had sold 40-acre tracts at $7 an acre, with $1 down and the balance to be paid in five equal installments of $55.80. The county's rural population was serviced by about 44 businesses, including groceries, dry-goods stores, three blacksmith and wagon repair shops, a photographer, harness maker, three restaurants, several boardinghouses, and barbershops, which did a total annual business of $600,000. In addition to the sawmill, there were three cotton gins. There were no liquor stores because Bolivar County was dry. By 1912, Mound Bayou had a telephone exchange, waterworks, and an electric-power station. The Bank of Mound Bayou was established in 1904 with Charles Banks as president. Along with Thornton Montgomery, Banks established the Mound Bayou Loan and Investment Company. It bought up all the mortgages held by the railroad, which had threatened a mass foreclosure on the land purchased from it by blacks.

The opportunity for blacks for self-determination in order to achieve unrestricted economic development, which had prompted the founding and settlement of black towns, proved impossible. Economically, blacks were never fully isolated from whites. Moreover, in the South, especially in those areas with a preponderance of blacks, violence by whites in their efforts to limit the Fifteenth Amendment's protection of black voting rights continued.

However, in 1890, Mound Bayou's town founder, Isaiah Montgomery, as the only black member of the Mississippi Constitutional Convention, supported disfranchisement of most of the state's 123,000 black voters, thus giving whites an edge of 40,000 votes. While Montgomery encountered virulent national recrimination from blacks, he subsequently found support from Booker T. Washington, whose philosophy of challenging southern-white racism proceeded from the assumption that there could be a trade-off of black votes for white noninterference in black economic progress. As Washington gained power and prominence after his 1895 Atlanta "Compromise" speech, he actively promoted and supported Mound Bayou's economic development.[70]

The period of black town founding ended by 1920. Most black towns had been established as central place market towns where merchants, craftsmen, and professionals provided products and services to farmers who settled the agricultural hinterlands. Initially, they provided a sufficient population base to support the businesses established by the townspeople. In addition, it did not hurt business that the townspeople and farmers often were relatives. Yet, with the exception of Mound Bayou, few black towns, especially in the Great Plains, achieved the critical mass necessary to survive.[71] By the turn of the century, many black towns experienced a decline.

In the South, several factors contributed to their decline. Cotton production was curtailed by boll weevil infestations. The increasing mechanization and diversification of farming drove black farm laborers from the land. When World War I curtailed European migration, "pull" factors, especially the opportunities afforded by industrial jobs in the North, proved greater than "push" factors, including the heightened violence in driving blacks out of the South after 1910.

As result, many people in southern black towns left during the period known as the Great Migration that occurred around World War I. In the short period in which they prospered, however, they provided an attractive social, political, and economic alternative to racial subordination in the New South's agricultural-based economy. Still, given the reality of the interdependence of a national economy, the late-nineteenth-century decline of traditional market towns nationally, and an expanding industrial infrastructure developing in an increasingly hostile and racially segregated America, few black towns had the economic viability to survive.

Yet, ironically, there was as much diversity of black businesses in large all-black towns as in some urban black-business districts in the South. In 1911, the Boley, Oklahoma, business district had 1 bank, 2 insurance agencies, 5 hotels, 4 department stores, 7 restaurants, 3 drugstores, a jewelry store, a funeral parlor, and 2 photographers. The town's population was 4,000, but it also had 4 cotton gins, 2 livery stables, a lumberyard, and an ice plant. In Muskogee, Oklahoma, in 1914, where "the business life of the Negro centers on South Second street," there were 3 black banks, 12 real estate dealers, and the T. J. Elliot Department store, considered the largest and finest black-owned store in the country. It employed 25 salespeople. There were dry-goods stores, a manufacturing company, 6 building and 3 concrete contractors, 12 shoe stores, 12 barbershops, 10 groceries, 4 drugstores, 10 restaurants, 2 ice-cream parlors, 10 coal dealers, 1 movie theater, a bottling works, 2 confectioneries, 1 dairy, and 1 undertaker. While there was a harness shop and 8 blacksmith shops, Muskogee also had 4 "cab lines."[72]

Urban Black Businesses

Black businesses in many urban areas were not as diverse or numerous as those in many small all-black towns. Blacks in Savannah, Georgia, for example, had established two banks in 1913 and several industrial insurance companies. But a survey of the black business community that year showed only "a first class millinery store, an up to date gents furnishings and dry goods store, a well stocked drug store, several large and well filled confectionery stores and scores of small businesses." The survey emphasized the absence of a first-class shoe and furniture store and noted, "Our people use coal and wood and plenty of it. Why cannot there be established among us several up to date coal and wood businesses by our people?"[73] While blacks in Dallas, Texas, in 1912 had the Penny Savings Bank, the only retail businesses of which they could boast were "Scott's Grocery store, Lew's Dry good company, Hopper's drug store, Williamson's drug store, Auto Cafe, Palm Barber Shop, Stone's Cafe and Gilmore & Baltimore News Agency."[74] Moreover, while Dallas's black population numbered some 23,000, only 784 owned property, valued at $1.5 million.[75]

In Kansas City, Missouri, in 1914, it was reported that there was "Two hundred thousand dollars invested here by colored men and women in business enterprises and $5,500,000 of realty in the possession of the race." Unlike the Dallas survey, the Kansas City report was enthusiastic in its assessment of black-business activity, emphasizing that "[e]ven the women here have become affected, or inoculated, with business, and quite a number of them are engaged actively in business, conducting such establishments as bakeries, cafes, dressmaking, millinery and floral shops."[76]

Moreover, while there was greater diversity of businesses in black towns at the turn of the century than in black urban America, in some instances there had been even more diverse and viable black businesses in antebellum urban America than in the late nineteenth century. Cincinnati, Ohio, provides an example of the impact not only of the Civil War on black businesses activity but also of the three controlling forces that shaped America's post–Civil War economic development. Industrialization, immigration, and white urbanization all affected the course and development of black-business activity in the closing decades of the nineteenth century.

Prior to the Civil War, blacks operated businesses in the mainstream of preindustrial America. In post–Civil War urban America, however, the three controlling forces marked the diminished role that black-urban businesses began to play not only in Cincinnati but also in other cities, where "[t]he success stories of the 40s and 50s would not be duplicated twenty years later, in large part because of changes within the city itself." By 1880 the wealthiest black businessmen in Cincinnati were those who had established their enterprises prior to the Civil War, including Robert Gordon, a coal dealer; Thomas Colson, pickle and catsup manufacturer; Robert Harlan, racehorse entrepreneur; photographers J. Pressley and Thomas Ball; and caterer Peter Fosset. In antebellum America, steamboats provided steady employment and incomes for blacks, which often paved the way for their acquisition of property.

Yet even by 1860, the manufacturing industry, as opposed to river transportation, was the major economic force in Cincinnati; but these newly developing industries seldom hired blacks. At the same time, jobs previously held by blacks as stewards and dockhands were usurped by both native-born whites and new immigrants. Because blacks were increasingly relegated to low-paying, unskilled occupations, their low wages limited their ability to accumulate capital for establishing wealth-generating enterprises, which ultimately forced black enterprises to the periphery of mainstream business activity. Consequently, while the number of Cincinnati blacks in business increased from 52 in 1850 to 102 in 1880, the number of business owners remained constant. The other blacks listed as being in business were employees who worked, for example, as clerks or barkeepers. Moreover, most of the business owners in Cincinnati in 1880 were saloon keepers or self-employed, primarily in the informal economy as hucksters and peddlers.[77]

Chicago also provides an example of black business activity in the late nineteenth century. In 1885, a directory of black professionals and black-owned businesses in the city listed about 200 enterprises. The leading black business was the barbershop, followed by sample rooms, a combination liquor store and saloon. The great majority of blacks in business owned small personal-service enterprises that catered to the growing concentration of blacks on both the South and West Sides of the city. They operated coal yards, lumberyards, restaurants, and secondhand-furniture and clothing stores. Even after the Civil War, the few black businesspeople who accumulated wealth remained in the service trade, while also speculating in real estate. The slave-born barber James Thomas, through his real estate speculation and holdings in St. Louis, by 1879 had a total wealth "estimated at $400,000, making him one of the richest Negroes in the United States."[78]

Caterers and Hotel Owners

Prior to the Civil War, blacks maintained a virtual monopoly on the catering business. But their leadership in this industry declined in the closing decades of the nineteenth century in the face of competition from the new exclusive restaurants and luxury hotels established by whites in industrialized urban America. The elegant dining rooms and ballrooms and European cuisine and services provided by the white hotels reflected the taste of the rising group of white nouveau riche industrialists. Before the Civil War, few whites had used— or, more specifically, could afford—the services of elite black caterers; and those who could afford them died before end of the century. In 1871, the Washington, D.C., Wormley Hotel was established by wealthy black caterer James Wormley (1819–1884), who was worth $87,000. It attracted leading national politicians and foreign dignitaries, and its facilities and service set the standard for the new post–Civil War luxury hotels. The five-story Wormley had an elevator, rooms and apartments with telephones, an elegant first-floor dining room, basement bar, and barbershop. When Wormley died, leaving an estate of over $100,000, the hotel continued operations under his son James's management until 1893, when it was sold. The new owner continued under the Wormley name until 1897. James and Wormley's other son, William, were businessmen in their own right, each with extensive real estate holdings. By 1915, each was worth over $100,000.[79] As hotel owners and caterers, the Wormley family was one of the exceptions in the decline of blacks providing food and hotel services to elite whites. Increasingly in the closing decades of the nineteenth century, elite black caterers were no longer a status symbol for wealthy whites, especially in the face of America's new racist standards and mores.

After the Civil War, while the services of black caterers were still in demand and in the face of competition from whites, attempts were made to professionalize their services through organizations. In New York City, the Corporation of Caterers was founded by 12 black caterers, who incorporated in 1869. Their main objective was to "consolidate the business interests of its members." They also sought to control the quality and efficiency of services by preventing the participation of "irresponsible men attempting to cater at weddings, balls, parties, and some hotels on special occasion." Five of the incorporators owned imported silver, china, and other caterers' service valued from $1,000 to $4,000. Membership in the organization increased rapidly, and by 1872 the group had reorganized as the Waiters' Beneficial Association, which had more than 100 members. With a new emphasis on mutual insurance benefits, which provided for sickness and burial expenses, the original purpose of the organization "was side-tracked," including new standards set by the organization.[80]

In Philadelphia, which had been the center of the catering industry before the Civil War, two black catering organizations were founded. Both reflected the move toward cooperative enterprise among blacks in the late nineteenth century. The Philadelphia Caterers Association was founded in 1866, and in 1894 the Caterers Manufacturing and Supply Company was established. It served as a wholesale enterprise, which purchased and then rented tables, chairs, linens, glasses, silver, and china to Philadelphia's black caterers. It was founded by Peter Dutrieuille (1838–1916), who had married into the Augustine and Baptiste catering families, antebellum leaders in Philadelphia catering. Dutrieuille had established his own catering enterprise in 1873, and it remained in the family until 1974. The Augustine-Baptiste firm also continued operations into the early twentieth century. In 1910 their business was worth $60,000.[81]

After the Civil War, several of Philadelphia's leading black catering families continued running successful enterprises, including Thomas Dorsey, who died in 1876, and Henry Minton, who died in 1884. Also it was reported that Levi Cromwell along with P. J. Augustine in 1879 were worth $50,000. While a few blacks in the catering business, such as the wealthy Bostonian Joseph Lee, who invented a bread-making machine, continued to serve the white elite, they were a decided minority.[82] The Dun reports on the

TABLE 6.8   Dun Report on Newport Black Caterer George T. Downing, 1865–1878

G. T. Downing [Newport] Colored Confectioner	
Mar. 65	Good for wants
May 65	Good
Apr. 68	Doing a fair business and in fair credit
Sept. 68	Owns Real Estate. It is mortgaged, is slow moderate credit
May 69	Doing good business. Is slow as can be & credit very limited.
Nov. 69	Doing a fair business, not worth much. Is slow pay & credit poor.
Aug. 70	May be worth 3 or $4000 is very slow pay, in very poor credit and shouldn't be trusted [be] extremely cautious. This is the celebrated colored caterer in Washington, D.C.
July 71	Owes everybody here who will let him, pays with the greatest of difficulty is believed to be worth 00
Jan. 73	No change
Aug. 74	Slow and not in general credit.
Aug. 75	Has R.E. is taxed [for] $30,500, mortgaged $18,000. Is believed to owe heavily & to be worth [?] & his credit is very unsatisfactory here.
Sept. 75	Mortgaged Building flat on Bellevue Avenue to Savings Bank
Apr. 76	Not in good credit here, lately given up his Restaurant at Washington. Credit locally is very poor
Nov. 76	Considerable Real Estate here & must have an equity of $10,000 at least. generally slow pay but think responsible & could be made to pay
Aug. 77	Means largely in Real Estate which is pretty small mortgaged. May have a surplus of $8,000 to $10,000 Very Slow Pay
May 78	continues very slow and has about all he can do to meet his obligations doubtful what is worth— not very safe for credit.

Source: Compiled from R. G. Dun and Company, Rhode Island, 3:62; R. G. Dun and Company Collection, Baker Library, Harvard University Business School.

successful antebellum black caterer George Downing also provide some insight into the decline of some blacks in this industry. As the reports show, Downing's Newport catering business experienced a downturn after the Civil War (see table 6.8).

In 1866, Downing went to Washington, D.C., where he "took charge of the Capitol cafe" for 13 years, making political connections with men such as Charles Sumner. On returning to Rhode Island, Downing continued his activities in the "equal rights" movement, in which, it was said, he demonstrated an interest either "in person or by letter at every meeting of importance in the East for half a century past." Downing, moreover, turned down political appointments such as a Captain's commission in the Rhode Island State Militia and the Collector of the port of Newport. His attitude was: "that he would be obliged to sacrifice some of his labor for his people by holding such an official position."[83]

Even with the decline of black caterers, a new group of blacks entered the industry. One of the most successful was Chicagoan Charles H. Smiley (1851–?), who provided a full range of services for any event he catered. For weddings, he furnished not only the cake, floral arrangements, and church decorations but also male and female security people to safeguard the wedding gifts. By the turn of the century, Smiley's catering enterprise was so extensive he owned 16 horses to pull his delivery wagons and was said to be the largest employer of blacks in Chicago. Among the new Chicago black businessmen at the time, Smiley was one of the few whose clientele was white.

This was also the case with two East Coast blacks who entered the catering business in the closing decades of the nineteenth century. In Westchester County, New York, Charleston-born Francis J. Moultrie (1842–?) established a successful catering business, which by the 1890s was grossing $25,000 annually. He operated his extensive business with 10 wagons.

In Germantown, Pennsylvania, the caterer John S. Trower (b. 1849) established a restaurant that he opened near a local train station in 1870. His business was an immediate success. When he expanded it into a catering enterprise, Trower's first and largest customer was the Cramps Ship Building Company, which he began servicing in 1889. As his business expanded, Trower purchased a $75,000 three-story building. The business offices, dining room, delivery department, and ice-cream plant were on the first floor. A reception room and dining hall that seated 150, along with a kitchen, were on the second floor, with a laundry and storerooms on the third floor, and additional storage rooms and a china closet in the basement. Trower's trade extended beyond Philadelphia to cities in the South and West.[84]

With their business success, some of the leading caterers in the early twentieth century were also involved in establishing financial institutions. John Trower was president of the Cherry Building and Loan Society and treasurer of the Reliable Mutual Aid and Improvement Company. Francis Moultrie was president of the Yonkers Investment Company. These men represented the last successes of blacks in an industry that, since the eighteenth century, had enabled them to secure a more-than-comfortable living. Perhaps, the Augustine-Baptistes and Dutrieuilles succeeded into the twentieth century because, with their French heritage in the West Indies and Bordeaux, where the father of the latter family was born, they were able to respond to the changing tastes of the new white elite in industrial America. But these situations were rare. Most black caterers after the Civil War continued to serve the standard American fare of meat and potatoes, but the new white elite preferred haute cuisine.

By the late nineteenth century in Philadelphia, there were fewer than 10 blacks in catering who made at least $3,000 to $5,000 from their business. While changing food tastes and racial attitudes contributed to the declining numbers of blacks in catering, there were also new licensing laws enacted to regulate the industry. Beginning in the late 1880s several states, including Pennsylvania, required the posting of a $2,000 bond to secure a liquor license, with annual license fees ranging from $500 to $900. Few blacks entering the catering business for the first time could afford the license, much less the bond. For the few who could, the law required that liquor could be sold only in a business that was permanently located. Black caterers, consequently, were precluded from serving wine and liquor with their haute cuisine meals, which probably accounted more for the declining patronage of their white clientele than changing racial attitudes.

By the turn of the century, the black catering business was in a decline, with most caterers limiting their services to small dinner parties and other social occasions for the white middle class. In some instances, black caterers developed food services for a specific clientele on a daily basis. In Cincinnati, Ed J. Berry, one of the city's leading black caterers, continued to serve food at receptions of all kinds, but in the summer expanded his business to provide food services for the large summer resorts in the area. While profits by no means compared to those earned by antebellum black caterers, such enterprises, even at the turn of the century, provided a means of self-employment. In New York, W. E. Gross, one of the founders of the Public Waiters Association in 1869, was still in business in 1911, but his clientele was "mainly among the Colored people." The association had folded in 1905, with only 33 members; by contrast, in 1870, there had been almost 500 black public waiters who worked in the catering business.[85]

After the Civil War, blacks with an interest in food services went into the hotel business, some attempting to maintain a white clientele, as had their antebellum predecessors. By the turn of the century, however, blacks in the hotel business, as those in catering, relied on a virtually all-black trade. The demand for black-hotel services had expanded, a response both to the increased mobility of blacks and to the discrimination they experienced in attempts to stay in white hotels. In Cincinnati, several hotels were founded by blacks in the late 1890s: the Sumner House, the "Bee," and the Douglass Hotel. By the 1920s, there were only two hotels in the city that catered to blacks, and both were owned by whites. In New York, the Marshall Hotel was one of the more successful hotels owned by blacks. In Washington, D.C., in 1877, the Nail brothers, John Bennett (1853–1942) and Edward (? –1899), established the Shakespeare House, which they sold in 1887. They also owned a hotel in New York. In 1893 they reopened the Shakespeare House in a new building purchased for $50,000. With improvements, it was worth $75,000 by 1905. John Nail, along with his son, John (Jack) E. (1883–1947) remained leaders in Harlem real estate until the 1940s.

In the South, the Commercial Hotel established by J. L. Thomas in Union Springs, Alabama, in the early twentieth century was successful, but Thomas sold out shortly after it opened. As Washington said, with his usual understatement, "The times proved unfavorable, however, for a Negro to run a hotel for whites, and Mr. Thomas soon decided that it would be wise for him to sell out. He did so with good profit." The Thomas family had owned a successful restaurant and grocery, with annual sales of $40,000, before going into the hotel business. The Berry Hotel, established in Athens, Ohio, by E. C. Berry in 1893, was successful. Berry had owned a restaurant before establishing his hotel, which had fifty rooms with baths and an elevator; it grossed $35,000 annually. Most of his clientele was white, but it was said that Berry "never refused to serve colored men at his hotel—indeed, he says he would rather lose his customers than to be guilty of that sort of disloyalty." Berry retired before 1910, but until his death was considered by blacks as a leading business-man.[86]

Conclusion

In post–Civil War America, the free-enterprise system failed the nation's blacks. Yet, without any economic assistance and despite white resistance to their business activities, African-Americans contributed significantly to rebuilding the South's postwar economy, while continuing their challenge to make free enterprise work for them. However, they did not receive the economic assistance necessary to level the racial playing field in order to profitably participate in the industrialization of this nation. In post–Civil War America, a billion-dollar reconstruction and development program was needed for African-Americans, the kind provided by the United States a century later in the rebuilding of the economies of the war-devastated nations of its former enemies in Europe and Japan.

Freedmen had hoped only for "forty acres and a mule." For the 90 percent of the black population who were slaves in 1860, farm ownership, even at a virtually self-subsistence level, could have provided the foundation for black economic independence and expansion of black business activities. Indeed, many blacks came out of slavery with property accumulated as a result of their pre–Civil War independent economic activities. Many lawsuits brought before freedmen courts by former slaves involved the Union army confiscation of property accumulated by blacks under slavery, as well as unpaid wages. Still, despite the efforts of blacks not only to resist attempts to control their labor but also to acquire and maintain property ownership, the post–Civil War period in the South was

TABLE 6.9   Black Economic Progress, 1863–1913

	1863	1873	1883	1893	1903	1913
Homes	9,000	50,000	128,000	210,000	390,000	555,000
Farms	20,000	175,000	380,000	550,000	775,000	937,000
Businesses	2,000	4,000	10,000	17,000	25,000	40,00
Wealth(000)	$20,000	$50,000	$75,000	$150,000	$300,000	$700,000

Source: Monroe N. Work, *Negro Year Book: An Annual Encyclopedia of the Negro, 1914–1915* (Tuskegee, Ala.: Negro Year Book Publishing Company, 1915), 1–4.

marked by economic transition, as it attempted to reformulate the place of blacks as a subordinate people.

In spite of legal and extralegal means made in the South to suppress black economic initiative, these efforts were not always completely successful. However, the reality that must be considered, as Carter Woodson suggests, is that "[t]he number [of blacks] found in business for years after the emancipation, therefore, did not far exceed the number thus engaged before the Civil War."[87] In point of fact, black-business ownership after the Civil War did not approach pre–Civil War figures until after Reconstruction. The number of businesses owned by blacks in 1865 was calculated at about 2,000. This figure, however, is not inclusive of the enterprises established by slave entrepreneurs. Still, despite racist attempts to suppress black economic initiative, within 50 years of freedom, African-Americans showed substantial economic progress. (See table 6.9.)

By 1910, a people, virtually landless before the Civil War, owned 20,000,000 acres, 31,000 square miles, of land: "an area almost equal to that of Vermont, New Hampshire, Rhode Island, Massachusetts, and Connecticut."[88] Moreover, in the closing decades of the nineteenth century, the foundation was laid for the emergence of a new group of successful black capitalists. As this chapter emphasizes, while the Civil War released blacks from slavery and, in many ways, provided a venue for greater business participation, racial constraints in the nation's business community persisted into the twentieth century. While racial constraints became even more repressive with the rise of Jim Crow, there was, however, an expansion of independent black-business activities.

7

THE GOLDEN AGE OF BLACK BUSINESS, 1900–1930

We are living among the so-called Anglo-Saxons and dealing with them. They are a conquering people who turn their conquests into their pockets.... Living among such people, is it not obvious that we cannot escape its most powerful motive and survive? ... To say the least, the policy of avoiding entrance in the world's business would be suicide to the Negro.... As a matter of account, we ought to note that as good a showing as we made, that showing is but as pebbles on the shore of business enterprise.

—John Hope, 1898

Introduction

By 1900 American business was fueled by industrialization, particularly by the massive production of coal, iron, oil, and steel. Giant monopolies, forged in the wars of cutthroat corporate takeovers by the nation's captains of industry, controlled America's productive wealth.[1] But where were black entrepreneurs? As the nation charged ahead and became the world's financial giant, African-Americans were locked out of the gargantuan supply of capital flowing from investment banks, foreign interests, and massive government subsidies. Black business remained on the periphery, a shadow economy, its profits eclipsed by the financial giants of the age. In 1900 the total wealth of black America, $700 million, amounted to less than that of the nation's first billion-dollar corporation, United States Steel, organized in 1901.

During America's greatest industrial and business expansion, there were few black manufacturing enterprises that reflected industrial America. The freedom granted blacks after slavery, however, had not included access to America's wealth-generating resources. While black inventors made significant contributions to the advancement of the nation's industries, the most ambitious manufacturing establishments undertaken by blacks included a few enterprises manufacturing cotton, oil, textiles, dolls, and furniture. In the early twentieth century, however, blacks early laid the foundation for the development of the largest and fastest growing industry in which they were involved—the hair care and beauty aids business.

In African-American business history, the period from 1900 to 1930 marked the first of three waves in the rise of black corporate America. This was the golden age of black business, which saw the emergence of leading black capitalists who achieved millionaire status and established million-dollar enterprises. Their wealth reflected their success within a black economy, which developed in response to the nation's rise of two worlds of race. But while black business activity expanded from 1900 to 1930, most black businesses established during this period, with the exception of banks, insurance companies, and the hair care industry, did not survive the Great Depression.

Although Herman Perry (1873–1928) was one of the most successful black entrepreneurs in the golden age of black business and was involved in the major areas of black business expansion, he died bankrupt, disgraced, and in virtual obscurity. At the height of his business success, Perry was the subject of an article in a 1924 issue of *Forbes*. In commenting on his diverse enterprises in banking, insurance, construction, and real estate, the author said: "For, let it be remembered, Herman Perry is the directing genius of a $30,000,000 enterprise, earns $75,000 annually, is insured for $1,000,000 and is said to be worth $8,000,000."[2] While the title of the article was "The Largest Negro Commercial Enterprise in the World," the subtitle announced that Perry was the "Commercial Booker [T.] Washington." Along with William E. B. DuBois, Washington, the founder of Tuskegee Institute, and Marcus Garvey were the leading ideologues of black economic thought in the first wave of black corporate America. They were also symbols of the age of black business expansion through cooperative efforts.

Washington and DuBois on Black Business

Before 1915 the leading black economic nationalists were William E. B. DuBois (1868–1963) and Booker T. Washington (1856–1915). While their philosophies differed on education, civil rights, and black political participation, both were resolute in their insistence that business was crucial for the survival of the race. In 1895, when Washington made his infamous Atlanta Compromise speech, he warned African-Americans that "agitation of questions of social equality is the extremist folly"; but, at the same time, he said, "No race that has anything to contribute to the markets of the world is long in any degree ostracized."[3] Three years later, at the 1898 Fourth Atlanta Conference, the theme of which was the "Negro in Business," DuBois also stressed the importance of black business as a springboard for racial toleration: "We must cooperate or we are lost. Ten million people who join in intelligent self-help can never be long ignored or mistreated."

The 1898 conference, convened by DuBois, proceeded from the premise that the cooperative support of black business was imperative. DuBois said that "The mass of the Negroes must learn to patronize business enterprises conducted by their own race, even at some disadvantage." That blacks were being forced into a separate economy was foremost in the minds of the conferees. Several themes that pervaded the conference addressed the challenges confronting black businesses within the rise of industrial America. As DuBois cautioned, "The character of commercial life is slowly but significantly changing. The large industry, the department store and the trust are making it daily more difficult for the small capitalist with slender resources."[4] The black small-business community, unorganized in effort and goals, then, was even more vulnerable than labor in attempting to survive the formidable competition in American business and industry.

In meeting the challenges of the new business climate in industrial America, DuBois voiced the strategies needed by blacks in the resolutions he drafted at the 1898 conference.

They were presented by Professor John Hope, then president of Atlanta Baptist College, who also supported the promotion of black business; he said, that "the growth of a class of merchants among us would be a far-sighted measure of self-defense, and would make for wealth and mutual cooperation." The strategies proposed by DuBois called for: (1) a college education for black businesspeople; (2) black businesspeople to encourage customer loyalty by being courteous and honest and by using careful business methods; (3) blacks to patronize black business, even to their disadvantage; (4) black churches, schools, and newspapers to promote black business; and (5) blacks to engage in personal savings. Finally, to encourage the development of a national black consensus in support of black business, DuBois proposed "The organization in every town and hamlet where colored people dwell, of Negro Business Men's Leagues, and the gradual federation from these of state and national organizations."[5]

Two years after the conference, Booker T. Washington organized the National Negro Business League (NNBL) at a meeting held in Boston. It was attended by 300 blacks from 34 states, professional people as well as businesspeople. The purpose of the league, as Washington said, was to encourage more blacks to go into business. Both men and women were eligible to join on the payment of a two-dollar annual fee. With Washington as president (until his death), the NNBL grew. By 1905, there were about 320 chapters, and by 1907 it had 3,000 members. By 1915, membership was estimated from 5,000 to 40,000 people, with over 600 chapters in 34 states and the Gold Coast of West Africa.[6]

Washington's philosophy of promoting black business and the activities of the NNBL, as well as his politics of political accommodation, were influential in the black international community of the time.[7] In South Africa a letter to the editor of the black newspaper *Ilanga Lase Natal* in 1903 explained that the NNLB was "an association composed of negro men and women who are engaged in nearly every line of business in which white men engage, blacksmiths, hotel-keepers, chemists, bankers etc." The letter ended with the comment that if Washington were to address blacks in Natal, he would say "It is much wiser for us to emphasize opportunities than grievances."[8] Even after his death in 1915, Washington's philosophy continued to have an impact in South Africa. In 1920 an editorial in the black newspaper *Umteleli wa Bantu* called for a "Trade School for Natives"; the editorial further stated, however, that, unlike Washington, South African blacks did not want philanthropy, but rather they were "anxious to relieve the white man of his burden." In a spirit much like Washington's but doubtless in anticipation of a different outcome, the article said South African blacks would "welcome a policy of segregation which will permit of our national development."[9]

Moreover, Washington's position that industrial education would be the salvation of blacks was embraced by others in addition to businesspeople. Even blacks who denounced his politics, that they accept the temporary loss of voting and civil rights, agreed when he said, "Our knowledge must be harnessed to the things of real life."[10] DuBois's educational program for leadership training of the Talented Tenth—the talented and college educated blacks—did not preclude preparation for business participation either. Rather, his program of business education was important not only for its emphasis on business ethics but also for its training in manhood: "If we make money the object of man-training, we shall develop moneymakers but not necessarily men; if we make technical skill the object of education, we may possess artisans but not, in nature, men. Men we shall have only as we make manhood the object of the work of the schools—intelligence, broad sympathy, knowledge of the world that was and is, and of the relation of the men to it—this is the curriculum of the Higher Education which must underline true life."[11]

In an increasingly oppressive racial climate that discouraged challenging expressions of black manhood, the social and economic reality for many blacks, given their impecunious state, as Washington said, was that "the opportunity to earn a dollar in a factory just now is worth infinitely more than the opportunity to spend a dollar in an opera." Consequently, while Washington's reactionary public political stance and his emphasis on industrial education had its opponents, he won the admiration of many blacks. In addition, he was the one black man whom white America listened to, a black man whom whites sought out for advice. Also, he exploited his success with them. While Washington stood as a symbol of racial accommodation, he also generated financial support from white philanthropists not only for black education but also for black businesses.

White America, moreover, had appointed him as their voice for black America. In a nation of two worlds of race, Washington became the African-American's ambassador without a portfolio, as he advised the Roosevelt and Taft administrations on "Negro affairs." In explaining Washington's success as a leader, W. D. Allison, a black certified public accountant, secretary of the Chicago Business League, and editor of the *Commercial Journal* said, "Dr. Washington's intellect was so powerful that he could control his emotions and adapt himself to his environment."[12] Consequently, while Washington was far from being the perfect symbol of DuBois's black manhood, he was the only black of his time who approached the model of the successful white American—appeasing the masses while profiting from their acquiescence to a social, political, and economic system that exploited them.

In Washington, then, blacks demonstrated that they could produce a model of white success; he was a flawed symbol of black manhood, but a superb capitalist who attained the standards of success and power established by white America. He achieved this status mainly by his establishment of the Tuskegee Institute, a multimillion-dollar enterprise. DuBois himself admitted that Washington had "intuitively grasped the spirit of the age" with his emphasis on "triumphant commercialism."[13]

Perhaps this was why Washington's, rather than DuBois's, picture graced the homes of black America. In 1908 the journalist Ray Stannard Baker said, "As I have been traveling over this country, South and North, studying Negro communities, I have found the mark of him everywhere. . . . Wherever I found a prosperous business place, a good home, there I was also to find Booker T. Washington's picture over the fireplace or a little framed motto expressing his gospel of work and service." But Baker recognized and emphasized that "Many highly educated Negroes, especially in the North dislike him and oppose him, but he has brought new hope and given new courage to the masses of his race. He has given them a working plan of life."[14] Certainly, with the founding of the NNBL it was Washington, not DuBois, who put his indelible stamp on the promotion of black business during the first half of the golden age of black business. Yet Washington's influence was not limited to businesspeople because the individuals attending NNBL league conventions represented a "diversity of interests."[15]

In the early part of this century, several national business organizations were founded in conjunction with the NNBL. The National Bankers Association, the National Association of Negro Insurance Companies, the National Association of Funeral Directors, and the National Association of Real Estate Dealers met each year with the NNBL, and their members were affiliated with the parent organization. Also, the National Bar Association, the National Press Association, the Colored Undertakers and Embalmers Association, the National Negro Retail Merchant's Association, and the National Negro Tailor's Association were organized during this period, each to promote the specific interests of the group.

During the 1920s additional black business associations were founded. The National Design Model and Dressmakers' Association, "which intends to do something to help the dressmakers," was founded in New York in 1920. In 1921 the National Beauty Culturists League was founded. The National Builders Association was founded in 1923 and the Independent National Funeral Directors Association in 1924. In 1926 the Federal Automobile Association was founded in Washington, D.C., and in 1929 the Nashville-based National Motors Assurance Association was established; both were formed to provide services comparable to those of the American Automobile Association.[16]

In addition, various local and state business organizations were organized. At the 1901 NNBL convention in Chicago, Mrs. Alberta Moore Smith noted in a speech that "The first and oldest women's business club in this country is the Chicago Club," of whom she was the president.[17] New York City had several black business groups. The Colored Liquor Dealer's Association was founded in 1912. Its membership included blacks who owned saloons and hotels, and its purpose was "to improve the tone of their business," and encourage cooperation to bring about better conditions. The New York Colored Business Men's Association, formed in 1915, was a response to "the peculiar problems which have to be faced by the colored businessman in New York city." Their main concern was to develop plans by which "the patronage of the race could be attracted to race merchants to a larger degree than obtained at that time."[18]

In Nashville, a Negro Boosters organization and a Women's Business League were created. One project of the Negro Board of Trade of Nashville was the purchase of 100 vacant lots throughout the city for cultivating Irish potatoes. The lots were to be turned over to senior citizens, with the Board of Trade providing seeds and plowing. In Atlanta, the Boosters' Club, organized in 1915 by Atlanta Mutual Insurance Association executive Truman K. Gibson, was founded "to encourage Negroes to trade with one another; to buy groceries, take out insurance, buy medicine, and employ Negro professional men in every case where it can be done without inconvenience or inefficiency."[19]

Throughout the period of the NNBL's expansion and the proliferation of black business and professional associations in the first wave of black corporate America, Washington and DuBois continued to promote the issue that a separate economy was being forced on blacks. Both agreed that business expansion was critical to black economic survival. DuBois went further and emphasized that cooperative efforts were needed by blacks in developing business enterprises. In outlining the principles of the Niagara Movement, which was an attempt to challenge Washington's accomodationist political position, he stressed in 1905 that, since denial of equal opportunities to blacks in the economy tends "to crush ... small business enterprise," blacks must push for "business cooperation."[20] In a 1907 Atlanta study, DuBois reviewed the historic tradition of black economic cooperation. In that same year, he also announced that he was a "Socialist of the Path," but maintained that he believed neither in the entire abolition of private property nor "that government can carry on private business as well as private concerns." Yet, while DuBois promoted black business in the spirit of capitalism, he also emphasized that the extreme poverty of blacks required them to ally themselves with labor as opposed to capital.[21]

At the 1909 National Negro Conference, which preceded formation of the National Association for the Advancement of Colored People (NAACP), DuBois again emphasized the need "to build firmly the strong foundations of a racial economy."[22] With the 1910 founding of the NAACP, DuBois, as editor of its journal, *Crisis*, began to publish information on black business activity. Throughout his editorship that ended in 1934, he published various articles on his theories concerning black business development through cooperatives.[23]

According to DuBois, cooperative enterprises should also include economic programs that provide insurance benefits as well as financial assistance, such as low-interest loans. A 1918 meeting held by DuBois to encourage interest in cooperatives led to the founding of the Memphis, Tennessee, Citizen's Cooperative Stores in 1919.[24] During the 1930s DuBois became even more insistent that blacks must establish cooperatives and support black business. In his 1940 autobiography he presented his economic program for black America, the "Co-operative Commonwealth." As he explained, blacks in America involved in the development of business must face the reality that "in the first place we have already got a partially separate economy in the United States."[25] Perhaps in no other area was a separate black economy reflected more glaringly than in the development of black banks and insurance companies.

Black Banks and Insurance Companies

The economic thought of both DuBois and Washington coalesced in the founding of black banks and insurance companies at the turn of the century. Both men, who viewed the business activities of blacks taking place within a separate economy, believed that cooperative efforts were essential for the expansion of black economic life. As a result, several black insurance companies and banks founded on this principle were established in the late nineteenth century. Invariably, some of the founders, including fraternal organizations such as the True Reformers, were involved in establishing both kinds of financial institutions for the deposit of insurance funds collected from their members.[26]

American racism forced blacks to take this "economic detour."[27] Indeed, the establishment of the first black bank during this period, the Capital Savings Bank in Washington, D.C., in 1888, was in part a response to a comment made in the United States Senate that "with all their boasted progress, the colored race had not a single bank official to its credit."[28] From 1888 to 1934, some 134 black banks were founded. The Mechanics Savings Bank in Richmond, Virginia, established in 1902, was one of the country's largest black banks until it closed in 1922. Founded by John Mitchell Jr., who became its president, it was a depository for the funds of the Knights of Pythias.[29] This kind of symbiotic financial relationship resulted in fraternal organizations establishing both insurance companies and banks. Subsequently, there were black insurance companies that also founded banks.[30]

The first black insurance company established during this period, the Southern Aid Society, based in Richmond, Virginia, was founded in 1893 by B. L. Jordan, who had worked with True Reformer founder W. W. Brown.[31] In part, the creation of the company was a response to a meeting of 2,000 blacks in 1884 representing about 40 organizations. Their intent was to develop insurance programs that increased health and death benefits for blacks. With the exception of Metropolitan Life, white insurance companies were reluctant to provide coverage to blacks. The exclusionary policies of these companies were reflected in an 1896 publication that warned, "Because of social diseases, living conditions, and other undesirable circumstances, companies would be unwise to insure Negroes."[32] In addition, when blacks began to organize companies that provided industrial insurance, in which premiums are paid in small weekly installments, whites attempted to drive them out of business, using their influence with state legislatures.[33]

Initially, with few laws regulating insurance companies, the number of black companies had increased by the turn of the century. Virginia, which earlier in the century had the largest number of black mutual aid burial societies, also had the largest number of black insurance companies. The state's insurance laws, passed in 1903, required a $200 license fee, one percent of an insurance company's gross receipts, and a $10,000 deposit for a company to stay in business. The laws were supposedly designed to protect policyholders, but as DuBois said, black companies "noticed that southern legislatures only began to awaken to this need of protection when Negro societies began driving the whites out of business."[34]

The Independent Order of St. Luke, founded in 1867 by former slave Mary Prout to provide health and death benefits to its members, was one of the most successful black insurance companies of its day. By 1907 its 650 branch offices were located in 14 states. Beginning in 1903, its funds were deposited in its bank established under the leadership of one of its members, Maggie Lena Walker (1867–1934), a black woman who was America's first woman bank president.[35] Walker, a member of the Order of St. Luke since 1883, was elected its executive secretary in 1899. In 1901 she organized an insurance department, having had experience working for the Women's Union, a women's insurance company. In 1903 she organized the St. Luke Penny Savings Bank: its purpose was to serve as a depository for the order's funds. With Walker as president, the other bank officers, three vice presidents, the cashier, and the assistant cashier were men. In 1910, with the failure of the True Reformer Bank, the St. Luke bank emerged as the most powerful black financial institution in Richmond. In 1920, complying with a Virginia law that required the separation of banks from their fraternal orders, the bank was reorganized as the Saint Luke's Bank and Trust Company. In 1929 it merged with two other black banks to become the Consolidated Bank and Trust Company, with Walker as chairman of the board until her death.[36]

In addition to establishing the bank, Walker, as had the True Reformers, managed and established other enterprises. The Order of St. Luke owned and operated a department store, the St. Luke Emporium, from 1905 to 1910; published a newspaper, the *St. Luke Herald*; and was involved in real estate, all of which provided employment for black women. Moreover, Walker encouraged black women to go into business. Speaking at the twenty-first NNBL convention, which met in Philadelphia in 1920, Walker urged black women to go into business: "Never have these opportunities been greater than they are today. . . . The passage of the Women's Suffrage Act will be a tremendous help and we will soon be making the men hustle to keep their jobs."[37]

While Walker's contribution to black banking is well known, during that same period Mary McLeod Bethune (1875–1955) was also involved in black insurance companies in Florida. She was both a stockholder in and a director of the Afro-American Life Insurance Company in Jacksonville, Florida, first organized as the Afro-American Industrial Benefit Association in 1901 by seven black men. Bethune was also one of the founders and, for a number of years, a director of the Central Life Insurance Company of Tampa, Florida.[38] In Mississippi, Minnie Cox (1869–1933) and her wealthy husband, Wayne Cox, founded the Delta Penny Savings Bank and the Mississippi Life Insurance Company, which she served as secretary and treasurer. Wayne Cox's wealth was derived from real estate speculation. After purchasing thousands of acres of land at $.25 to a $1 an acre, he sold part of his holdings for $50 to $75 an acre.

At the turn of the century, Minnie's appointment as post mistress of Indianola, Mississippi, became a national cause celebre. In 1902 whites in the town petitioned President Theodore Roosevelt for her removal. He initially refused, suspending the town's postal service, but acquiesced in 1904. After her husband's death, Cox headed the insurance company, appointing Dr. Joseph Edison Walker (1880–1958) as president in 1917. The company's success intensified the town's racial animosity, forcing Mississippi Life to relocate to Memphis in 1923. Dissension within the company forced Cox to increase her shares, which enabled her to dismiss Walker and appoint her son-in-law as president. The company was then bought by black financier Herman Perry, an effort that failed and eventually led to the downfall of his financial empire.[39]

In 1908 Herman Perry founded the Standard Life Insurance Company of Georgia, after working for several white insurance companies in New York.[40] In 1913 Standard Life became the first black old-line legal reserve company to write only ordinary business and the third to qualify as a legal reserve. Mississippi Life was the first, followed by North Carolina Mutual Life. Standard Life operated in 11 states and Washington, D.C. Its $150,000 building and office equipment worth $100,000 were the pride of black America. By 1924 the company and its affiliates employed about 2,500 people.[41] Perry also founded the Mechanics Savings Bank in Augusta, Georgia, and in 1921 the Citizens Trust Company in Atlanta, which was capitalized at $250,000. A full-service commercial bank, it provided both demand and savings accounts, farm and business loans, administration of estate services, and a women's department.

In addition to his financial institutions, Perry was also involved in managing his other enterprises, including the Service Engineering and Construction Company, Service Farm Bureau, Service Foundation, Inc., Service Fuel Corporation, Service Holding Company, Service Laundry, Service Pharmacy, and Service Printing. His Service Realty built nearly the entire west side of Atlanta, with his Sunset Hills Development Company that covered "200 blocks with twenty-four residences to the block, with an average value of $4,500 per residence for a total value of $21,600,000." Service Engineering was the contractor. The Service Company, organized in 1917, was the holding company for all of Perry's subsidiaries. It held $8,498,217 in assets, including $2 million worth of real estate, 300 acres in Atlanta, and 1,000 acres of farmland. In addition, Service Construction owned seven four-ton trucks, eight boxcar loads of building materials, and one million feet of lumber. In 1924 it held $448,576 in contracts, plus a $212,000 contract from Atlanta to build a public school.[42]

In 1925, when Perry's Standard Life failed, it took with it Mississippi Life, which Perry had bought. It seems Perry used Mississippi Life's assets to meet his financial obligations. Also, most of Standard's money was invested in Perry's subsidiary enterprises and the consensus was that "the cause of Standard's failure lay in this diversion of its funds."[43] Some blacks, however, saw Perry's failure as a conspiracy by whites to destroy him, while others indicted him for the loss of black America's symbol of business success. Appeals were made to white philanthropists. Julius Rosenwald and John D. Rockefeller agreed to underwrite $400,000 to salvage Standard, but only if Perry stepped down from heading the company. He refused, and his financial empire collapsed, one of the first black conglomerates in the first wave of black American corporations.

The black-owned National Benefit Life Insurance Company, founded in 1898 by Samuel Wilson Rutherford, however, increased its capital stock to reinsure Perry's Standard Life. In taking over Standard's remaining assets, National Standard increased its total insurance in force to $75 million on more than 300,000 policyholders, which made it the largest enterprise ever owned and controlled by blacks. Its employees, office staff, agents, and medical examiners numbered over 2,000. However, National Benefit became overextended and failed several years later.[44] Meanwhile, Perry's attempt to start over in St. Louis and Kansas City failed, and he died soon after. Some suspected suicide.

Perry was recognized as an eccentric financial genius, able to conceptualize one business plan after another, but was said to be "impatient of routine, prone to shun the drudgery of details." His only interest was in making money, some said to the point of fanaticism. He did not own a car, his friends had to make him buy a decent suit of clothes, and it was only in 1924 that he purchased a home reflecting his status.[45] In the initial organization and development of his enterprises, Perry did not lack diligent persistence, as some claimed. In managing them, however, he lacked the traits that contributed to the success of other black financiers during this time, including John Merrick, Charles Spaulding, and Alonzo Herndon, who founded insurance companies and banks that survived.

What was to become the nation's largest black insurance company, North Carolina Mutual Life Insurance Company, was founded in 1899 by the slave-born John Merrick (1859–1919), who had built a real estate fortune from his barbershop enterprises. In its first year, the company almost failed. Merrick and Dr. A.M. Moore, joined by Robert Fitzgerald, the wealthy owner of a successful Durham brickyard, then hired Moore's relative, Charles Clinton Spaulding (1874–1952), as the company's full-time general manager. He became the driving force behind the growth and expansion of North Carolina Mutual from 1900 until he died. Under Spaulding, the company expanded to other states and extended coverage beyond industrial sickness, accidents, and burial benefits to become a full-line insurance company.[46] In 1995, North Carolina Mutual was ranked first among black insurance companies in assets and insurance in force. Atlanta Life Insurance ranked second.[47]

Atlanta Life was founded by Alonzo Franklin Herndon (1858–1927), who was described by his contemporaries as the "Greatest Negro Financier."[48] Atlanta Life developed from a mutual aid association founded by two black ministers in 1904 to provide sickness and burial benefits. Premiums were $.05 to $.25 a week. In 1905, unable to raise money in response to a newly passed Georgia law requiring mutual aid associations to deposit $5,000 with the state to protect policyholders, the ministers sold Herndon their association for $160. He then put up the $5,000 deposit and renamed his company Atlanta Mutual, which eventually became Atlanta Life. At the same time, Herndon purchased two other black benefit associations, also unable to put up the required deposit. Most of the companies he purchased in the early years of Atlanta Mutual's growth were small assessment companies. Before Herndon's death, Atlanta Mutual expanded into several other states by buying out 15 other black insurance companies.[49]

Born a slave with only a year of formal education, Herndon first worked as a farm laborer. He then moved to Atlanta in 1882, opening his first shop in 1886. From 1887 to 1896, he operated a shop in one of Atlanta's finest hotels until it burned down. He then opened two shops and in 1902 established his opulently furnished Peachtree shop, which, like his others, served only whites.[50] At one time, his three shops employed 75 blacks. Herndon invested extensively in real estate, which on his death was valued at $324,107 and included both residential and commercial properties. In 1927 he was worth more than $500,000.[51]

Often black insurance companies preceded the founding of black banks. The Mechanics and Farmers Bank of Durham and Raleigh was established by the founders and officers of North Carolina Mutual Life Insurance Company. The Nickel Savings Bank was the depository of the funds of the People's Insurance Company, which Rev. Evans Payne founded. Black banks during this period were established by blacks of all professions and educational backgrounds. The Citizens Saving Bank and Trust Company of Nashville was founded in 1904 by the black Baptist minister Richard Boyd, who also built the National Baptist Publishing Company into a multimillion dollar enterprise before 1915.[52] In Washington, D.C., John R. Hawkins, who was financial secretary for the AME Church, was also president of the Prudential Bank.

The Industrial Savings Bank in that city was founded by John W. Lewis, a laborer with no formal education who was reported to be "truly remarkable for his ability to organize men and money [and] a natural talent of high degree for commercial and high financial developments." Lewis was the bank's president. The other founders were also laborers.[53] The Alabama Penny Savings Bank in Birmingham was founded in 1890 by B. H. Hudson, a successful grocer, and W. R. Pettiford, a Baptist minister, who was also the bank president. He established three branch banks in Montgomery, Selma, and Anniston. By 1907, Alabama Penny had 10,000 depositors and "more than 1,000 of them have purchased and own their own homes."[54]

Yet, as black financial institutions grew, the black press reported various attempts by whites to gain entry to "big black businesses." A newspaper headline in 1913 announced: "White Promoters in the South Scheming to Get Controlling Interest in Various Concerns." In Birmingham, black financial institutions were targeted for takeover by whites, with one newspaper noting, "It becomes apparent as the Negroes in Birmingham begin to make and save money that it is the intent of white men to use as much of this money as possible in enterprises to be owned and controlled by them." The strategy used by whites was to establish a financial institution, with blacks as front men to give the impression that it was owned by blacks. In one case, a white insurance company, with capital stock of $500,000, was being organized in Birmingham for just such a purpose: "It is an open secret that a group of leading white men are seeking a controlling interest in one of the leading colored banks. They intend to let Negroes control the bank outwardly, but to be controlled inwardly by this group of white financiers. It would be most unfortunate if our Negro banking institutions should pass into the hands of white men."[55]

By 1912 there were 64 black banks in the country. All but three were located in the South, including five in Oklahoma's all-black towns; two were in Illinois, the Enterprise and Binga banks, and the third was the Philadelphia-based People's Savings Bank. Eventually, most of the black banks founded before 1930 failed, even the larger ones. The Solvent Savings Bank and Trust Company, founded in Memphis in 1906 by real estate millionaire Robert Church, with authorized capital of $100,000, failed. In 1920, with 20,000 black depositors, it was the first black bank to have one million dollars in deposits, but about 80 percent of its loans were commercial. Most were unsecured and for a term longer than three months. Farm loans tied up 20 percent of the bank's working capital. Also, bank officers borrowed large sums to finance their other enterprises, a situation that contributed to Solvent's failure.[56]

In the 1920s Chicago's Binga State Bank and the Douglass National Bank became the largest banks organized by blacks before 1932. Before they failed in the early 1930s, they had combined resources of $4 million and controlled 36 percent of the country's total black bank resources. At that time there were 21 black banks holding combined resources of $11 million.[57] The Binga Bank, the nation's first privately owned black bank, was established in Chicago in 1908 by Jesse Binga (1865–1950). Born in Detroit, he came to Chicago in 1893 after spending eight years in the West working as a barber, eventually owning his own shop, and then as a porter for the Southern Pacific railroad. As he made his way back east, Binga was involved in land investments in Utah. In Chicago he worked briefly as a fruit peddler and coal dealer. Within five years, he was involved in real estate, the source of the capital used to establish his bank.

In 1920 Illinois declared private banks illegal. Binga secured a state charter of incorporation but continued to run the institution as a private bank until it collapsed in 1930. His real estate activities were closely tied to the bank's failure. Binga borrowed from white banks, using mortgages held by his bank on black real estate as security. But in the late 1920s, with Chicago's housing market in a slump, the downtown banks were unwilling to accept his mortgages, which tied up $800,000 of Binga's resources. Also, Binga had set up the Binga Safe Deposit Company, using its securities in shares as assets for his bank. The shares, which constituted the largest single block of the bank's securities, were worthless, as were other holdings listed as assets, leading to an impairment of the bank's capital stock and a shortage of $500,000 in the bank's actual assets over liabilities. Also, when the bank went into receivership, there were 686 outstanding loans, of which only 40 percent were secured. In addition, among the 651 personal loans were those Binga made to himself under other people's names. As a result, he was arrested and charged with fraudulent banking practices.[58]

The Douglass National Bank in Chicago, founded in 1922 by black entrepreneur Anthony Overton (1865–1946) also failed, but not because of any fraudulent banking practices (although there were some "indiscretions").[59] Overton, born in Louisiana, earned a law degree in 1888 from the University of Kansas. He practiced law and served briefly as a judge before venturing into the cosmetic business, the source of his wealth. Overton moved to Chicago in 1911 and expanded his business activities. His real estate operations there were centered around his Great Northern Realty Company. In 1924, Overton founded the Victory Life Insurance Company, which by 1925 had expanded to eight states.[60] He began with three employees and in two years had 308 people employed in the home and branch offices, while showing an increase in insurance in force from $680,000 to $2.25 million. In 1927, Victory became the first black insurance company to operate in New York State.

In the early 1930s, however, Overton's insurance company went into receivership. Its loss was tied to the 1932 failure of his Douglass Bank, despite its $2 million in resources, the largest amount held by any black bank in the country. As with most black banks that failed, Douglass bank had an insufficient diversification of investments. Also his Victory Life Insurance funds were entangled with the bank's funds. In addition, the bank carried a large amount of real estate loans, over half secured by collateral that could not be easily liquidated, since they had been made to churches and fraternal societies.[61] The bank sustained heavy losses by carrying these uncollected loans or writing them off.

Another 15 percent of the loans were secured by stocks and bonds, many of which were of inestimable worth and mainly issued by Overton's Bee Building Corporation and his Victory Life Insurance Company. These loans were not carried as assets, but the bank's funds were too closely tied up in them. Despite the loss of his bank and insurance company, Overton remained in comfortable circumstances the rest of his live. His cosmetic company survived, along with his newspaper, the *Chicago Bee*, which ran from 1925 to 1945. His magazine, the *Half-Century,* first published in 1916, failed in 1925. In contrast, Jesse Binga was seventy years old in 1935 when he was found guilty of embezzling $22,000 and sentenced to the Joliet State Penitentiary for 10 years. He served 3 years before he was released in response to a petition drive led by blacks in Chicago, the Inter-Church Council of Chicago, and the efforts of the renowned lawyer Clarence Darrow. Once freed, Binga was put in the custody of a Catholic priest and began a new life as a church janitor.

The Binga and Douglass banks, however, were not the only Chicago banks that failed in the early years of the Great Depression. In 1929 alone, about 70 banks failed in the city. Recognizing that Overton had not engaged in fraudulent practices as a banker, the Reconstruction Finance Corporation (RFC) attempted to rescue the Douglass Bank but could not salvage it from bankruptcy. By 1934, at the height of the depression, out of 134 black banks founded in the country since 1888, both private and those operated with state or national charters, only 12 still existed.[62] By World War II there were only 6 black banks remaining, including 4 founded at the turn of the century: the First Tuskegee Bank, founded in 1894; Maggie Walker's Consolidated Bank and Trust, 1903; Spaulding's Mechanics and Farmers Bank, 1908; and Herman Perry's Citizens Trust, 1921. In 1996, all four were still in existence.

Transportation and Leisure Enterprises

In response to racial discrimination and exclusion, the actions of blacks have ranged from individual endeavors to mass demonstrations and legal challenges in the courts, in addition to economic initiatives in the establishment of business enterprises providing services to African-Americans. In the latter part of the nineteenth century, segregation in transportation and places of public accommodation was sanctioned by the federal government. The Supreme Court declared the 1875 Civil Rights Act unconstitutional in 1883, but this did not preclude blacks from challenging the increasing number of municipal and state segregation laws. Still, when the Supreme Court rendered its infamous 1896 decision in the *Plessy v. Ferguson* railroad discrimination case, it confirmed the "separate but unequal" segregation practices that existed in all areas of public life in both the North and South.[63]

The transportation, leisure, and entertainment enterprises developed by blacks at the turn of the century were also direct responses to the era's climate of racial separation and exclusion. Blacks built parks, recreation centers, and resorts. In virtually every American city with a black population of sufficient size and enterprise, there was increased construction of black hotels, theaters, and other buildings that provided public space for black civic and cultural activities. These buildings were often constructed by fraternal organizations or similar financial enterprises. Black banks, insurance companies, and real estate loan associations were not only symbols of the increased financial holdings of blacks but also an expression of defiance to white attempts to impose a separate and subordinate status on America's citizens of African descent.

In establishing these enterprises in the early twentieth century, blacks proceeded individually, in partnership, through corporate and cooperative financing, and, in the development of a black streetcar line, through floating a municipal bond issue. At least five efforts were made by southern blacks to develop their own municipal and intercity transportation facilities. In 1883 a consortium of blacks headed by Rev. Joseph Pierce began to build a railroad from Wilmington, North Carolina, to a seacoast resort at Wrightsville Sound. Unfortunately, after the construction crew graded roads, built bridges, and laid the cross ties for nine miles, the supervisor of the project died, bringing it to an end. Several years later whites secured a charter and completed construction.[64]

The black entrepreneur Wiley Jones, however, built a streetcar line in Pine Bluff, Arkansas, that was successful. Jones was the owner of a 55-acre forest preserve, known as

Wiley Jones Park, where he built an amusement park and fairground for the city's blacks. Most of them lacked transportation to get there, which prompted Jones in 1894 to build his own streetcar line and purchase trolleys. Jones, who was born in slavery, was a saloon keeper, liquor wholesaler, and livestock dealer. He also held extensive real estate in Chicago, St. Louis, San Francisco, Texas, and Oklahoma, in addition to properties in several counties in Arkansas. His holdings at one time were valued at $200,000.[65]

In Memphis wealthy real estate holder Robert Church, in response to legislation that denied blacks access to public parks, also built a park for blacks. Built in 1899, Church's Park was located on his Beale Street property. He landscaped the grounds and also built a 2,000-seat auditorium, which became a cultural, recreational, entertainment, and civic center for Memphis blacks and the site of conventions held by black organizations. Church's initial financial success came from his saloon in Memphis, an enterprise he began after the Civil War; in addition he owned a hotel and restaurant. His wealth also derived from his extensive real estate holdings, many of which were located in the city's red-light district, acquired at rock-bottom prices during the Memphis yellow fever epidemic of 1878–1879.[66]

In the early twentieth century, blacks in both Jacksonville and Nashville established municipal transportation lines in response to legislation that discriminated against blacks. In Jacksonville an initiative was begun as a response to a 1901 municipal ordinance that gave streetcar conductors police power to arrest any black who did not obey their orders regarding where to sit and when to give up their seats to whites. Jacksonville blacks boycotted the system. Leaders of the black community met at the St. Paul AME Church and initiated plans to start their own trolley company. Surprisingly, the city council responded favorably to their demands. First, the council approved the petition for a franchise to establish the North Jacksonville Street Railway, Town and Improvement Company to build the trolley line. Five days after service began, the city provided blacks access to a city park by taking down the sign, "Niggers and Dogs Not Allowed."

In financing construction of the line, a municipal bond capitalized at $150,000 was issued. Whites held the principal of the bond issue, which left "$100,000 of the shares in the hands of the colored men." Construction of the streetcar line was completed in 1901, although at a financial loss. Before construction, the black railway company was forced by the bondholders to accept a bid $20,000 higher than the lowest bid. The service was profitable but not enough to pay off the bond within the allotted time. In the first quarter of operations, after expenditures of $1,555, net profits amounted to $3,318.05. Even had the company sustained similar profits throughout its operation, it would still have fallen short by about $57,000, in addition to the interest needed to pay off the $150,000 bond. In 1908, after seven years in operation but unable to meet the deadline for full payment, the company went broke; the white bondholders foreclosed and took control.[67]

Blacks in Tennessee also responded to a discriminatory transportation law by establishing their own municipal transportation system. The state legislature passed a law in 1905 that required all municipal transportation services to be segregated. Nashville's black community leaders, headed by the local NNBL branch, launched an immediate boycott of the services in June. Black businessmen, including the Reverend Richard Boyd, head of the National Baptist Publishing Company and also president of the NNBL branch, along with James Napier, organized the Union Transportation Company and raised $20,000 by stock subscription. By October five steam-driven "auto buses" had been purchased that provided service to blacks on Nashville's main streets. These were soon replaced by "fourteen electric buses" that had the power to climb the city's hilly streets. Each bus carried 20 passengers.

The boycott lasted until July 1906. The enterprise failed in part because of attacks on it by the city government. After the Nashville Railway and Light Company "broke its promise to provide power," the black company immediately established its own power plant by setting up a dynamo in the basement of Boyd's publishing company. Special municipal taxes levied on the buses, however, added to the company's operating expenses. Also, with the black population dispersed throughout the city, the bus company, already undercapitalized, could not provide convenient service for the entire black community.[68]

In response to segregated railroad transportation, blacks attempted to build several of their own lines. In Arkansas in 1914, a consortium floated stock for the financing of a railroad: "A company of colored men are building an interurban road between Washington and Columbus Arkansas. According to information the road is well underway and it will be but a short time before the cars will be running.... the enterprise calls for considerable financial skill and ingenuity. In event of success the road will be the first one in the country to be completely managed by colored people .... Shares of stock are on the market."[69] In Oklahoma, a black railroad construction company was owned by E. E. McDaniels, who in 1907 was said to be worth $50,000, and T. E. Currie. Their company also worked as subcontractors for white railroad companies.[70]

Segregation laws actually proved profitable in two ways to black business partners George W. Browne and Walter Langley, who owned a summer resort in Maryland. In 1901 the state passed legislation requiring segregated transportation, which made it difficult "for colored organizations to charter excursion boats owned by whites until late in the fall." Browne and Langley purchased the steamer *Starlight*, valued at $30,000, that could "carry over 1,200 passengers." In 1911 alone, the partners claimed that their steamer carried "nearly 110,000 passengers during the excursion season ... and their receipts exceeded $21,000." Their steamship was the only one that provided blacks with transportation to their resort area during the summer, and their resort was the only one open to blacks.[71]

White resorts, even in the North, excluded blacks. In 1912 the Royal Union Improvement Company, founded by W. P. Dabney, advertised opportunities for urban blacks to experience country life: "The Company will also operate a Country Club, C.C.C.C., Colored Citizens Country Club," which was located outside of Cincinatti.[72] Idlewilde, Michigan, a resort area for elite blacks in the Middle West, was made famous by Chicago's Dr. Daniel Hale Williams, a black physician who performed the world's first open-heart surgery, when he built a vacation cottage and then a hotel on the island.[73] The Lincoln Hills Development Company, founded in 1922 by a group of black investors, established Winks Panorama, a Colorado mountain resort for blacks. In 1925 Winks Hamlet, who organized the investors, built a lodge for blacks, operating it until 1965.[74]

What the masses of urban blacks needed most, however, was rapid and dependable city transportation to get to work. The sector of the industry in which blacks succeeded in providing transportation for other blacks in both northern and southern cities was in taxicab enterprises. Within seven years after Henry Ford put his Model T on the road in 1908, blacks opened numerous taxicab companies. In 1915 the AME journal, the *Christian Recorder*, published an article entitled "The Jitney Car, An Opportunity for Negro Business Men," which provided information about the industry: "The so-called jitney automobile is spreading rapidly all over the country and seems destined to continue to spread until it becomes one of the most profitable businesses in the century. Jitney cars are automobiles which have a regular line, doing their traffic largely in streets having no street cars, and giving a ride for a 'jitney' or a five cent piece." The article then proceeded to explain why blacks needed to capitalize on this developing industry, emphasizing that the field was new and the amount of capital was small—"one secondhand car will do to start with, and that can be gotten for a small sum." Racism in public transportation was emphasized: "Jitney cars, like sight-seeing cars, will discriminate against Negroes, there being cars marked 'white' and others marked 'colored' in the South. The Negro business man can run the 'colored' car as well as the white man. Now is the time for the Negro business man to come in 'on the ground floor' in the jitney 'bus business.' "[75]

In New York William H. Peters and Samuel Hamilton started both a taxicab and car-rental company in 1916, beginning with "two Packard automobiles, for rental business and one taxi cab." By 1930 it was reported that "Their business is said to represent a half million dollars investment. The firm has 250 special built taxi cabs and a working force of more than 750 persons."[76]

Blacks also capitalized on the new automobile industry by establishing car-repair shops, gas stations, as well as car dealerships. Homer Roberts, one of the first black car dealers, established the Roberts Automobile Company in Kansas City, Missouri, in 1919 by selling cars "from the curb." In 1921 he opened a showroom, featuring different makes of new cars each week. One year later Roberts's tremendous success won him an award from the area's automobile distributor" for the greatest number of retail sales." That same year he built a new $65,000, 14,000-square-foot showroom, service center, and body shop. He had 45 black employees and sold all makes of cars. His customers were black, and 75 percent of the cars bought by blacks in the Kansas City area were sold by Roberts.[77]

While the automobile was important for improving urban transportation for blacks, it both enabled blacks to travel without being subjected to the humiliating experiences of segregated, second-class railroad cars and contributed to the opening of black motels and resorts. Blacks also developed urban recreational and leisure facilities in response to Jim Crow segregation and exclusion. In Knoxville, Tennessee, a group of young black businessmen, headed by Professor William Brooks, manager of the black baseball team, the Knoxville Giants, purchased a park in that city in 1920, explaining, "Knoxville will have a park that its colored citizens and their friends may visit and enjoy all of the amusements that are afforded by any other modern parks and in connection a baseball field will have its place." Brooks was the secretary of the newly organized Colored Southern League, founded in Atlanta in 1920.[78] Despite restricted civil and political rights and limited financial resources, blacks individually and cooperatively capitalized on racism to build an economic infrastructure that in some areas paralleled that of white America.

Real Estate and Construction Enterprises

From 1900 to 1930 black real estate and construction companies were instrumental in building homes, churches, office buildings, hotels, theaters, and auditoriums for blacks, in addition to developing subdivisions and housing tracts. Often, financing came from black building and loan associations. One of the most successful, the Metropolitan Mercantile and Realty Company, was incorporated in 1900 and was capitalized at $100,000. Two years later it authorized an additional issue of $400,000 in capital stock and increased its par value from $5 to $10 per share. In the first three years, annual dividends of 7 percent were paid, while the company also "placed upon the market a $50,000 bond issue of six percent, gold coupon ten year bonds." Metropolitan's stockholders were located not only all over the country but also in the West Indies and the Philippines. At one point the company had to fight off an attempted takeover by whites.[79]

The company's main investment was in real estate, primarily homes for stockholders, with the company advancing 80 percent of the purchase price. Stockholders repaid the loan as rent at six-percent interest. The company, using black contractors, built homes, churches, and office buildings for fraternal groups. Metropolitan also advanced funds for home purchases throughout the Midwest and South. It employed over 300 white-collar workers, both men and women, as cashiers, merchants, salespeople, agents, commissioned representatives, bookkeepers, stenographers, typists, and messengers. In 1904 Metropolitan founded a bank in Savannah, Georgia, established a store in Plainfield, New Jersey, and also operated an industrial assessment benefit association.

The construction industry proved to be a lucrative one for many blacks. The Windham Brothers Construction Company, founded in Birmingham in 1895 by Thomas C. Windham, who was joined three years later by his brother, Benjamin L., was very successful. In 1903 the company had $50,000 in contracts, increasing to $300,000 by 1914. Employing over 100 men throughout the year, it constructed some of the most important commercial buildings in Birmingham's black community, as well as houses and churches. The company also constructed buildings in the city's white business section and in 1910 a $100,000 apartment building for whites. By 1913 Windham Brothers had construction projects "carried on from the Mason and Dixon line to the Gulf of Mexico." The company remained in business until 1966, with offices in Chicago, Detroit, Indianapolis, and Nashville.[80]

In Jacksonville, Florida, contractor and builder J. H. Blodgett started his business in 1894 with $1.10 after being arrested as a tramp because he was wearing a straw hat in the winter. Between 1902 and 1914, Blodgett built over 230 houses, all as rental property.[81] In 1920 in Baltimore, Albert Johnson, at one time a whitewasher, founded a construction company that eventually employed 35 to 40 men, with a "payroll amounting to more than $1,000 per week."[82] By 1914 his contracts were worth $300,000. By the 1920s large black contractors were working on multimillion-dollar projects. Also, a few construction companies were founded by architects and engineers. The Isaiah T. Hatton and Company designed and supervised construction of the Virginia Beneficial Insurance Company building in Norfolk, as well as 18 churches, 32 apartment houses, 2 public schools, 73 homes, 2 banks, and 3 office buildings.[83]

In the 1920s engineer and contractor Frederick Massiah did the reinforced-concrete work for the $10 million, 10-story Walnut Plaza apartment building in Philadelphia, which required 700 tons of steel. He also constructed the only elliptical concrete dome in America at that time, which was part of the Church of the Ascension. In New York the Irving Fireproof Centering Company, founded by Samuel A. Irving, outbid several hundred other contractors to do the foundation work for the Hospital Center of New York, including the Presbyterian and Columbia Medical Schools and Sloan Hospital. Black engineer Archie Alexander built the $2.5 million central-heating plant for the University of Iowa.[84]

There were also consortiums of black investors that developed real estate projects. The Washington D.C. Whitelaw Hotel, "the first luxury hotel for African Americans" in that city, was built in 1919 at a cost of $158,000. John Whitelaw Lewis, a black businessman, financed it by organizing a building association, the Whitelaw Apartment House Corporation, that sold stock to investors.[85] There were, of course, individual successes in real estate. In Brockton, Massachusetts, Walt Terry, a former janitor, factory worker, and Pullman porter, owned 46 properties "aggregating $500,000" by 1910.[86] In 1919 he moved to New York and expanded his successful real estate operations. In Morrisville, Pennsylvania, John W. Lewis Jr., a black contractor and real estate dealer, was said to have "practically built up the town," surpassing other builders in the county, both black and white, as well as being the largest black builder in the state.[87]

In the North during the early twentieth century, urban black Realtors were important in securing housing for blacks; but their real estate activities, unlike those in the urban South, were limited primarily to the acquisition of rental property for management and sale rather than in acquiring land for housing development. Some northern urban Realtors, such as Chicago's Jesse Binga, acquired slum property at rock-bottom prices, renovated it, and then rented it at high rates to the increasing numbers of black migrants to the city. Binga was also involved in "block busting," the practice of purchasing property in a transitional white neighborhood and selling it to blacks. When the first black purchaser moved in, whites in the neighborhood would usually panic and quickly sell their houses, invariably at prices below market value. The properties then were sold to blacks at prices above market value.

Also, Binga purchased single-family dwellings and apartment buildings that he divided into smaller units and kitchenettes, a practice that doubled both the occupancy of a building and the rent he collected. Black Realtors seldom worked in collusion with white Realtors because, in their efforts to purchase property in "better" areas, they were subjected to the same redlining practices that faced individual blacks. The activities of northern black Realtors in expanding the housing market for urban blacks, however, led both directly and indirectly to the development of the physical and institutional black ghetto. As the *New York Age* reported in 1912, "Large Amount of Property in New York and Vicinity Being Handled by Negroes—Many Are Doing Well."[88]

New York's pioneer black Realtor was Phillip A. Payton Jr. (1876–1917), "the father of Harlem," who was also the most successful black real estate speculator in the early twentieth century. His first venture in getting apartments to rent to blacks was in 1902, which, according to Payton, "Came as a result of a dispute between two landlords in West 134th street. To 'get even' one of them turned his house over to me to fill with colored tenants. I was successful in renting and managing this house and after a time I was able to induce other land-lords to make the change." Through advertising, Payton aggressively promoted himself as a specialist in securing black tenants for Harlem property that had been initially developed for white middle-class renters. Because they refused to pay the high rent, much of the property remained vacant. With black migration increasing to New York, there was a market for decent housing. Blacks were willing to pay the exorbitant rents and many could afford to do so by taking in roomers.

In 1904 Payton founded the Afro-American Realty Company, capitalized at $500,000, with 50,000 shares offered at $10. The primary investors were his 10-man board of directors, who purchased 500 shares each. Payton's search for investors led him to appeal to Booker T. Washington, who did not invest. However, Washington's personal secretary, Emmett Scott, did and sat on the board as his point man, providing him with a base for expanding his influence in New York and eventually the entire East Coast, the stronghold of his rival, W. E. B. DuBois.[89] While Payton played politics with Washington, participating in the NNBL's convention in New York in 1905, Payton's interest was in securing investment support to expand the Harlem housing market for blacks. This meant maintaining majority control in the company he founded, as opposed to subordinating his interest to Washington, whose power and access to white philanthropy in part came from his advocacy of black submission to whites.

A letter sent by President Theodore Roosevelt to the NNBL's New York convention is indicative of the message whites wanted conveyed to blacks. In his opening comments the president said: "I wish all success to the National Negro Business League. Your organization is absolutely out of politics; and in stimulating activity among your people and working to increase their efficiency in the industrial world is also doing far-reaching work."[90] The NNBL was not about stimulating the efficiency of blacks as industrial workers, and Payton was a Realtor in the world of business and finance. His company's success in one year was spectacular.

In 1904 Afro-American Realty opened with $100,000 in capital. It acquired 4 five-story apartment buildings while managing 10 additional buildings. Its property holdings expanded to 20 buildings in 1905: 6 were owned by the company and 14 were leased, earning annual rents of $66,000. In total, the company controlled property with a market value of $690,000. Payton also continued his own private real estate business, owning, as he said, "from time to time nine five-story flats and five private houses, or in other words, I have had title to $250,000 worth of New York Realty."[91] Within four years, however, the company folded. The 1907 recession in part contributed to its failure. Tenant unemployment led to nonpayment of rent, and job scarcity limited the company's ability to attract new tenants.

Consequently, the Afro-American Realty Company failed to meet its mortgage payments. All but one member of the board of directors resigned, and Payton was subsequently sued by his investors for suspect business practices, including fraud. He was charged with inflating the value of the company's holdings, falsely claiming ownership in property that was held under short-term lease by the company, failing to promote the sale of stock that would have provided additional capital, and charging exorbitant rents.[92] With only Payton and Fred R. Moore, secretary-treasurer, remaining as board members, the Afro-American Realty Company was dissolved in 1908.

Two of Payton's salesmen, Henry C. Parker and John Nail, who became one of the leading black Realtors in New York, formed their own company, Nail & Parker. In 1909 Nail negotiated the sale of the black St. Phillips Protestant Episcopal Church for $140,000 and of its cemetery two years later for $450,000. In 1912 the church purchased 10 new Harlem apartment buildings for $650,000, the largest real estate deal made by blacks in New York up to that time.[93] Harlem's black churches were the area's largest property owners because of their early investments in real estate, which were handled by black Realtors.[94] In some instances, when blacks purchased rental property in Harlem, white tenants were asked by black Realtors, including Payton, to vacate their apartments immediately. Even St. Phillips Church asked white tenants to vacate the apartment buildings it bought in 1912. As black Realtors expanded their holdings beyond Harlem, the practice continued. In one highly publicized incident in 1920, it was reported that "White tenants must make room for colored folk in apartment houses in Bedford Section of Brooklyn controlled by Negroes."[95]

Despite the failure of Afro-American Realty, Payton continued his real estate activities with modest success until 1917, when he acquired six large modern apartment buildings in Harlem. They were only four years old, valued at $1.5 million and "recently owned by a Mexican syndicate, of which the late General Huerta, former dictator of Mexico, was head."[96] Payton died shortly after the purchase. In 1918 the Payton Apartments Corporation, with capital of $250,000, was organized by Thomas J. Calloway, offering stock at $20 per share through the black-owned E. C. Brown Company of Philadelphia.[97] After World War I, the demand for black housing increased and black Realtors literally advanced block by block in securing Harlem property for blacks. In one instance it was reported that "The north side of West 135th street, between Seventh and Eighth avenues is now almost entirely in the ownership of colored investors." Eight of the buildings, which were worth an average of $25,000 each, were owned by Fitzherbert Howell, who immigrated to New York from Trinidad in 1903. By 1919 his office handled transactions of "$1,000,000 in property values."[98]

Extractive Industry Enterprises

At the thirteenth annual convention of the National Negro Business League in Chicago, Booker T. Washington said in his keynote address that "If the white man can secure wealth and happiness by owning and operating a coal mine, brick yard, or lime kiln, why can not more Negroes do the same thing.... Activity in all these directions finds no races or color line."[99] By 1912, when those comments were made, African-Americans had a long tradition of participating in the extractive industries. While most were mine workers, blacks had established mining companies even before the Civil War. Similar efforts continued into the early twentieth century. These were small-scale ventures, however, with few financial successes. In California Moses Rodgers, who had been involved in several gold-mining companies, was the first person in that state to successfully drill for natural gas. As with most black mining ventures, "Inadequate financial backing, however, prohibited him from attaining much monetary success."[100]

There were also several attempts to establish black coal-mining companies at the turn of the century. The Birmingham Grate Coal Mining Company, with a capital stock of $10,000, began mining operations in 1898 with The Reverend Thomas W. Walker as president. It leased a mine 18 miles from Birmingham, with a black as the mining supervisor. In its initial operations, 25 to 30 tons of coal were mined a day, which was soon increased to 125 tons. The goal was 250 tons daily, a figure established by contracts negotiated with white companies. The company continued its operations into the early twentieth century.[101]

Invariably, when blacks owned land rich in mineral resources, the development of it was undertaken by whites. In Oklahoma blacks owned oil land, but their earnings were derived primarily from leasing it. Few invested in or established drilling enterprises or refineries. Most of the Oklahoma oil land owned by blacks was located in the state's Indian Territory. Before the government opened Oklahoma to settlement, it allocated 160 acres of desolate land to Native Americans and blacks. Blacks who had been slaves to the Native Americans were known as Creek freedmen or "native Negroes."

Perhaps, the state's wealthiest black was Sarah Proctor. In 1913 she leased her land to a white man who discovered oil on it; one account reported that "Miss Sarah Proctor's two oil wells are increasing in output, and today one is yielding 1,800 barrels a day and the other 2,000 barrels a day." The article noted her income as "$457 every day of her life ... $14,250 a month, or $171,000 a year. Beginning January 1, 1914, nine more wells will go into operation, and her already enormous wealth will then literally leap high into the millions."[102] By the 1920s there were several black oil enterprises in operation, including the

Black Panther Oil Company, the first black-owned petroleum firm in Oklahoma, and The Ardmore Lubricating Oil Company, "a Negro Oil Company" established by 1920.[103]

Black Inventions and Manufacturing Enterprises

In the late nineteenth century, blacks were active in securing patents on their inventions in all areas of industry. Had they been able to capitalize on their inventions, American blacks would have been able to make significant gains in the manufacturing sector of the economy. Jan E. Matzeliger (1852–1889), who invented the shoe-lasting machine, was unable to generate funds for establishing a factory to use his invention, which attached soles to the upper body of shoes. His patent was sold to Sydney W. Winslow, a white man who established the United States Shoe Machinery Company. By 1922 U.S. Shoe had gobbled up 40 smaller shoe factories. It operated with a capital stock of more than $20 million. Within 20 years after Winslow purchased Matzeliger's patent, his company's sales rose from $220,000 to $2.42 million.[104]

Among the 1,000 blacks who had secured patents by the turn of the century, several were distinguished by their prolific output (see table 7.1).[105] In 1872 Elijah McCoy (1843–1929) patented the first of his many lubricating devices for machines, trains, and ships. Before his death McCoy held almost 60 patents. Some he assigned to other companies, including the one for his hydrostatic oil lubricator, which he assigned in 1883 to the Hodges Company of Detroit. McCoy's interest was research. Assigning his patents provided him with the capital to establish his own company, the Elijah McCoy Manufacturing Company of Detroit. However, he ended up as a minor shareholder, earning only limited profits from his patents.[106]

Lewis Latimer (1848–1928) was an inventor who secured his first patent in 1874. He also worked on the drawings for Alexander Graham Bell's patent applications for the telephone in 1876. In addition, since 1871 Latimer was employed by the patent-law firm that handled Bell's patents. In 1880 a competitor of Thomas A. Edison, who had patented the incandescent bulb in 1879, hired Latimer, who, along with a colleague, made improvements on the bulb. But they assigned their 1882 patent on the "Manufacture of Carbons for Electric Lamps" to the firm they worked for, the United States Electric Lighting Company of New York.[107] From 1880 to 1882, Latimer headed both the team that established U.S. Electric's factories for the production of bulb filaments and the team that installed the electric-light systems for New York City, Philadelphia, and London. In 1884 Edison's company hired Latimer away from U.S. Electric. At General Electric, the company that Edison formed by buying out other electric companies, Latimer worked as chief draftsman and engineer.[108]

While Latimer's inventive genius was lost in building the nation's electrification infrastructure, the most prolific black inventor during this period was Granville T. Woods (1856–1910), who received his first patent in 1874. While Woods's inventions in transportation and communication were numerous, General Electric, Westinghouse, and the Bell company reaped enormous financial success from them, since he assigned many of his patents to these companies. Wood's 1884 patent for a telephone transmitter was sold to Bell, while he assigned his patent for an electric railway system to the American Engineering Company of New York.[109] Unlike McCoy, however, Woods's assigned many of his patents for electrical devices to his own factory, the Woods Electrical Company, which he

TABLE 7.1   Selected Inventions of Black Inventors McCoy, Latimer, and Woods, 1872–1903

Elijah McCoy (1843–1929)

McCoy patented the first automatic lubricator, followed by over 50 patents for lubricators, including the following:

Date	Invention	Patent	Inventor
2 July 1872	Lubricator for steam engines	129,843	McCoy, E.
6 Aug. 1872	Lubricator for steam engines	130,305	McCoy, E.
20 Jan. 1874	Steam lubricator	146,697	McCoy, E.
1 Feb. 1876	Steam cylinder lubricator	173,032	McCoy, E.
4 July 1876	Steam cylinder lubricator	179,585	McCoy, E.
15 Nov. 1898	Oil cup	614,307	McCoy, E.
27 June 1899	Lubricator	627,623	McCoy, E.

Lewis Latimer (1848–1928)

Date	Invention	Patent	Inventor
10 Feb. 1874	Railway car water closets	147,363	Latimer & Brown
13 Sept. 1881	Electric lamp	247,097	Latimer & Nichols
21 Mar. 1882	Globe support/electric lamps	255,212	Latimer & Tregoning
17 June 1882	Manufacturing carbons	252,386	Latimer, L.

Granville T. Woods (1856–1910)

Date	Invention	Patent	Inventor
2 Dec. 1884	Telephone transmitter	308,176	Woods, G.
7 Apr. 1887	Device for message transmissions	315,368	Woods, G.
3 June 1887	Steam boiler furnace	299,894	Woods, G.
7 June 1887	Relay instrument	364,619	Woods, G.
5 July 1887	Polarized relay	366,192	Woods, G.
16 Aug. 1887	Electromechanical brake	368,265	Woods, G.
11 Oct. 1887	Telephone system and device	371,241	Woods, G.
18 Oct. 1887	Electromagnetic brake device	371,655	Woods, G.
15 Nov. 1887	Railway telegraphy	373,383	Woods, G.
29 Nov. 1887	Induction telegraph system	373,915	Woods, G.
29 May 1888	Overhead conducting system for electric railway	383,844	Woods, G.
26 June 1888	Electromotive railway system	385,034	Woods, G.
17 July 1888	Tunnel construction for electric railway	386,282	Woods, G.
14 Aug. 1888	Galvinic battery	387,839	Woods, G.
18 Aug. 1888	Railway telegraph	388,803	Woods, G.
1 Jan. 1889	Automatic safety cutout for electric circuits	395,533	Woods, G.
10 Nov. 1891	Electric railway system	463,020	Woods, G.
21 Nov. 1893	Electric railway conduit	509,065	Woods, G.
13 Oct. 1896	System of electrical distribution	569,443	Woods, G.
19 Dec. 1899	Amusement apparatus	639,692	Woods, G.
29 Jan. 1901	Electric railway	667,110	Woods, G.
9 July 1901	Electric railway system	678,086	Woods, G.
19 Nov. 1901	Electric railway	687,098	Woods, G.
10 June 1902	Automatic air brake	701,981	Woods, G.
3 Sept. 1902	Regulating/controlling electrical translating device	681,786	Woods, G.
26 May 1903	Electric railway	729,481	Woods, G.
13 June 1903	Electric railway system	718,183	Woods, G.

Source: Compiled from Burt McKinley Jr., *Black Inventors of America* (Portland, Ore., National Book Company, 1969), 141–48.

established in Cincinnati in the early 1880s and in which he held 100 percent ownership. Still, before he died, Woods spent his last years in litigation, using virtually all of his profits fighting off white companies that wanted to gain control of his patents.[110]

Consequently, while blacks generated a variety of new inventions for industrial America, their race and limited finances precluded them from capitalizing on their patents. Simply put, black inventors lacked capital for the development, manufacturing, and marketing of their inventions. At the turn of the century, new inventions in electricity and transportation, in a situation that is similar to what is happening today in computer technology, were quickly superseded and rendered obsolete by a constant stream of even newer inventions. In an age of the rapid consolidation of America's new industries, black inventors and manufacturers had little chance of competing with their white counterparts. The grandson of the slave entrepreneur Free Frank, John E. McWorter, held several patents for an aircraft similar to the helicopter. In his 1911 patent application, McWorter said, "Another object of the invention is to provide an aeroplane which is so constructed that it can rise directly from the ground through the action of propellers with a vertical lift." In 1921, however, McWorter assigned his 1918 patent to the Autoplane Company of St. Louis, Missouri.[111] Also, Garrett A. Morgan received little profit from his invention, patented in 1923, of a traffic signal that benefited America in the new automobile age.[112]

In the burgeoning automobile industry during this time, Patterson, Sons and Company in Ohio was the only car-manufacturing company founded and owned by blacks. In 1916 it introduced its first car, the Patterson-Greenfield at the Ohio State Colored Fair, where one buyer was said to have "at once canceled his order for a Dodge, when he saw this car and put in his order for one."[113] The company was established as the C. R. Patterson and Sons Carriage Company in Greenfield Ohio, in 1865 by slave-born Charles Patterson (1833–1910). By 1900 the company was manufacturing 28 different models of buggies, school wagons, surreys, and hearses. Its most popular model was the doctor's buggy. With almost 50 employees, the company produced about 500 horse-drawn wagons and buggies annually, with yearly earnings of $75,000. When Charles died, his son, Frederick Douglass Patterson (1871–1932), took over. He designed and manufactured the company's two automobile models: a roadster and a four-door touring car, both priced at $850.

By 1919 Patterson, however, had manufactured and sold only 30 cars. In the absence of manufacturing facilities for mass production, he could not compete with the Detroit automakers. After 1920 the company turned to manufacturing truck bodies and bodies for Ohio school buses and the Cincinnati municipal transportation system. Also it had a contract with the Ford Motor Company. Despite these small successes, the company closed in 1938.[114] Its rise and fall reflected what happened to the enterprises of many other black inventors and manufacturers. They contributed to the expansion of the nation's new industries, but few became rich from either their inventions or their manufacturing enterprises.

The limited profits earned by blacks, whose inventive genius helped lay the foundation for much of the technological infrastructure that propelled America's industrialization, again demonstrates the failure of the free enterprise system to work for them. When black inventors sold their patents to the nation's major industries, their earnings were minuscule compared to those of the giant companies that capitalized on and profited from the black inventions. In the early twentieth century rise of black corporate America attempts made by blacks to make inroads into the new airplane, oil, telephone, and even movie and record industries to develop large manufacturing enterprises failed. A few blacks whose inventions stood on the periphery of industrial America were able to establish small manufacturing companies.[115] But most of them, such as Alice H. Parker of New Jersey, who took out a patent in 1918 for a gas "heating-furnace," were never able to capitalize on their early inventions.[116]

Three of the most ambitious manufacturing ventures undertaken by blacks in the early twentieth century were the Mound Bayou cottonseed oil mill, the Ocala Mills, and the Berry & Ross doll and clothes manufactory. The Mound Bayou Mill was considered one of the largest manufacturing enterprises ever undertaken by blacks. The project was launched in 1907 by Charles Banks (1873–1923), who conveyed his original plans for a textile manufacturing plant to Booker T. Washington in 1902, emphasizing that vertical integration would prove extremely profitable. Banks then sought the support of the Mississippi state branch of the NNBL, which endorsed the project but only for pressing cotton seed oil. In its prospectus, the company noted this fact and also indicated that the "Oil Mills have earned profits ranging from 15 to 40 per cent during the past year." In 1907 the Mound Bayou Mill was incorporated in Mississippi and capitalized at $100,000, with stock selling at $1a share. Its 1907 prospectus announced that

> This enterprise is planned to specially appeal to the working classes and industrial masses of Negroes generally, and for this reason particularly, the shares have been fixed at one dollar each, so as to facilitate the profitable investment of a portion of their weekly and monthly earnings in the establishment and operation of a great plant and to participate in the manufacture of a valuable commodity in which the race figures so conspicuously as producers and consumers.[117]

Shares in the mill were put on the market in 1908. By 1910 sufficient capital had been raised to begin construction of the mill. Yet, while Banks, along with Isaiah Montgomery, who was president of the company, made a national appeal to blacks, stock sales moved slowly. For example, William Johnson's daughter, who carefully conserved the family's wealth that her slave-owning father had accumulated before the Civil War, purchased only 30 shares in June 1908.[118] Banks turned to Booker T. Washington, who recommended him to several northern white philanthropists who invested in the mill. By 1912 Banks raised $100,000 to pay for the mill, its machinery, and equipment. He also secured $50,000 in bonds for working capital.

Construction was completed in 1912. The contractor and builder was Thomas W. Cook, a successful black architect who had his own construction company. He designed the plant and supervised construction. The factory was brick, 250 ft. × 60 ft., with a two-and-a-half-story seed shed measuring 350 ft. × 90 ft. The mill had the capacity to crush 40 tons of cottonseed in 24 hours, but it was designed so that its capacity could be doubled, with room left for two additional cotton-seed oil presses. At the time of completion it was reported that Mound Bayou "easily markets each season $50,000 worth of raw, or bulk cotton seed, and when passed through the plant will practically double in value."[119]

In November 1912 a formal ceremony was held to celebrate completion of the mill. Booker T. Washington, the featured speaker, indicated that the mill was the most ambitious commercial and manufacturing enterprise undertaken by blacks, emphasizing that "Money invested in this plant will not only bring in steady returns in the way of dividends, it will result in affording employment for a large number of the educated men and women of our race."[120] While they needed employment, it would seem that the training and talents of educated blacks could be put to better use than as mill hands. The ceremony, however, provided Washington another opportunity to reinforce to white America the critical importance of institutions such as the Tuskegee Institute, with educational programs based on the philosophy that blacks should be trained to work in industrial America.

Julius Rosenwald of Sears, Roebuck, and Company was one of the investors in the Mound Bayou Mill, as was a white Memphis mill owner, B. B. Harvey, who leased the mill and began operations under his management in the spring of 1913. Without providing any accountability to the investors, Harvey was suspected of siphoning off Mound Bayou profits to run his own mill. Knowledge of the mill's financial difficulties led Procter and Gamble to offer to buy it, with plans to operate it as one of its subsidiaries. Charles Banks refused the offer and the mill closed with no dividends ever paid the investors.[121] In 1920 the mill reopened after having paid Rosenwald, who "settled on a 50 per cent basis, the proposition having come voluntarily from him," according to Banks. After the mill reopened, he reported that it was "running night and day, employing about fifty persons." As before, it was leased out and again it failed.[122]

The second largest black manufacturing company established in this period was the Ocala Mills; unlike the Mound Bayou Mill, information about the Ocala Mills has remained obscure. Located in Ocala, Florida, it manufactured women's knitted underwear. During its short existence, unlike the Mound Bayou Mill, Ocala Mills paid substantial dividends, which perhaps accounted for its failure. The mill was established in 1914 by the Metropolitan Realty and Investment Company. The company had previously established the Metropolitan Savings Bank and the St. George's Hotel. Metropolitan Realty was incorporated in 1908 with capital of $25,000. Almost from its founding, investors earned large profits, with the company paying "dividends regularly since 1910, some years paying semi-annual profits." Dividends paid in 1910 were 10 percent; in 1911, 12 percent; in 1912, 20 percent; in 1913, 24 percent; in 1914, 12 percent; and in 1915, 18 percent. The company projected that for 1916, "the dividend would not fall lower than 18 per cent."[123]

The president of Metropolitan Realty, George Giles, a wealthy real estate dealer, was also president of the mill. With the creation of Ocala Mills, Metropolitan Realty increased its capital stock to $75,000. The first issue of $25,000 of the additional stock was taken by the stockholders, and the second issue was offered to the general public. The mill began operations in 1914 with 25 employees. By 1915 the company was turning out 60-dozen garments a day and employing 45 women. From the profits it made, the company built a new $28,000, three-story brick factory in 1915. At the beginning of 1916 the mill had $30,000 worth of orders booked and estimated that $100,000 worth of business would be done that year. Moreover, with the demand so great, a company representative said "that the firm will only take orders during a part of the season, to avoid overselling."

It is evident that 1916 was a highly successful year for Ocala Mills. By August some 108 girls from Ocala and surrounding towns worked at the mill, including some whose families were stockholders. The large number of employees represented the mill's tremendous growth from the time it was founded with no employees that had any textile-manufacturing experience. A northern textile expert was hired to train four young women, one of whom became the mill supervisor and instructor of new employees. The original goal for a full operating workforce was 150 women.[124] Also, in 1916 it was reported that the New York firm of Clift & Goodrich had been selected as the agent to handle the entire output of Ocala Mills and that it had "foreign representatives in Amsterdam and Rotterdam, Holland, Antwerp, Belgium and Copenhagen." Also, the company reported that "The National Park Bank of New York City is the New York fiscal representative of the company."[125]

The brief history of Ocala Mills offers an interesting parallel to the early-nineteenth-century New England textile mills, which employed factory girls who contributed so much to the growth of the industry in antebellum America. The exceptionally high dividends that Ocala Mills paid also has historical significance. Doubtless, the owners wanted to be on record to counter prevailing stereotypes that blacks who invested in black manufacturing enterprises were never paid any dividends. In addition, profits were also reinvested in mill improvement and expansion. Finally, the professionalization of the mill's financial policies and its marketing initiative, including international sales, reflected the increasing maturity of black manufacturers in their business activities before World War I.

The third major manufacturing company established by blacks in this period was Berry & Ross Incorporated, which, like Ocala Mills, experienced tremendous success in the first years of operation. The company, founded in 1918, also has historic significance because it was one of the few black manufacturing companies founded by black women. One was Evelyn Berry, the company treasurer and designer of "Berry's Famous Brown Skin Dolls," and the other was Victoria Ross, CEO and secretary. In its first ad campaigns, however, the company indicated that inquiries should be addressed to "Messrs Berry & Ross." On the other hand, a newspaper article at the time indicated they were black women and also provided a picture of Evelyn Berry.[126]

The rapid but short-lived success of Berry & Ross can be attributed not only to the demand for their dolls but also to the aggressive advertising campaign launched by the two women, in addition to their ability to secure operational capital to expand their enterprise. The dolls were described as "not of the ordinary burlesque type, as seen heretofore in the various toy shops of the country, but are of such a design of which any Race man or woman may well be proud."[127] A 1919 advertisement noted that at its incorporation the company had been capitalized at $10,000, and for only 30 days it would "OFFER 800 Shares of Stock at $10.00 each, to 12,000,000 Americans." The advertisement added that the offer was "A GILT EDGED RACIAL PROPOSITION WITH A CONCRETE FOUNDATION. Buy a share for your boy and girl and help make their future secure. Dividends paid annually as the net proceeds from time to time will warrant."[128]

Confidence in their product and an appeal to race loyalty were the basis of the company's highly successful advertising campaigns. In another ad announcing the sale of stock, Berry & Ross indicated that additional manufacturing space was needed to fill all of the orders for their dolls, which came in all sizes and styles, with prices ranging from $.25 to $15. Whites also purchased their dolls, and the company noted that "some of the foremost department stores in New York City, Boston, Philadelphia and many of the southern and western cities have made it imperative that the company enlarge its quarters in order to supply the demand." The company also emphasized that meeting this heavy demand would require "the employment of a larger number of women and girls."

Berry & Ross appealed especially to parents of black children, as in the following ad: "What Evelyn Berry and Victoria Ross, the founders of the Berry & Ross corporation, have accomplished, your child can and will, if you but grasp the opportunity of teaching it the real value of Negro industry to the race."[129] In 1920 the company expanded its product line to include manufacturing clothes for people as well as dolls, as indicated in the following ad, which also announced investment opportunities in the company:

NEGRO CLOTHING FACTORY. BUY DIRECT FROM US AND SAVE MONEY.
Ladies' Suits and Coats, Silk Shirtwaists, Children's Dresses, Bungalon Aprons, Middy
Blouses, Men's Shirts and Overalls

COLORED DOLLS
Stock on sale, $10 per share. Pays 6% every 3 months
Guaranteed
$50 buys 5 shares, $10 down and $5 monthly
$100 buys 10 shares, $20 down and $10 monthly
BERRY & ROSS Inc.
Factory: 36–38 W. 135th St., N.Y.C.[130]

Six months later, another ad indicated that the company had moved to larger quarters to meet product demand: "The Berry and Ross Manufacturing Company, Incorporated, manufacturers of women's and children's dresses and the well-known Berry's Famous Brown Skin Dolls, 36–38 West 135th street, have bought the two properties, 48 and 50 West 135th Street for manufacturing purposes." At the time the company employed 30 women and had a weekly output of over 2,000 women's and children's dresses.[131] Six months later, in August 1920, Berry & Ross made plans to expand the enterprise to Norfolk, Virginia. A subscription drive to sell $9,000 in stock opened at the city's Second Calvary Baptist Church, where the company put on a display of the various dolls and clothes it manufactured.[132] Blacks purchased stock in the company, and in December 1920 Berry & Ross bought the three-story Church Street Building, with plans to open a "full-line department store in January." It was reported that the new store "forms another link in the chain of stores which this company is establishing."[133]

The Berry & Ross company faded into oblivion, as did most early-twentieth-century black manufacturing companies throughout the country. Most were incorporated and capitalized with the sale of stock, but there were also efforts by black individuals in establishing small manufacturing enterprises. Blacks established factories that produced textiles, clothing, carpets, mattresses, pottery, toys, and furniture, in addition to those for processing food, including ice cream, candy, and sausages. There were also black factories that made embalming fluids and tooth paste. Some, such as H. L. Saunders, who manufactured white jackets for personal service workers, were successful. In Los Angeles the Hefflin Manufacturing Company, which made both furniture and toys, "was valued at $200,000." A Palmyra, New York, factory, owned by a black corporation, employed 50 people and manufactured enameled signs for both wholesale and retail sales. In Brooklyn, the Welmon & Carr Company, founded by Matthew A. Welmon, manufactured gas engines.[134]

Yet black manufacturing activities during this period have been ignored, considered by some to add little to the reconstruction of black business history. But because these enterprises failed does not provide a basis for obviating their existence in the historical record. They have historical significance because they underscore the continuity of black business activity and emphasize the presence of black business initiative, no matter the outcome of these endeavors. The failures of black enterprises, then, call for a fuller examination of the extent to which racism in America continued to limit black economic advancement during the early emergence of black corporate America.

In the early twentieth century, most black manufacturing companies were locked in a spiraling circle of failure. While the entrepreneurial zeal and capacity to create these enterprises was evident, undercapitalization was the major factor that prevented blacks from being able to compete with white manufacturers: "large scale production, well organized methods of distribution, superior advertising techniques, supersalesmanship, and ability to secure capital easily and on reasonable terms made it impossible for these Negro companies to carry on their business successfully."[135] Some black enterprises in the first wave of black corporate America, however, enjoyed great success, and no more so than those in the health and beauty aids industry.

The Hair Care and Beauty Aids Industry

Black participation in the black hair care business had developed before the Civil War and continued into the late nineteenth century. But distribution was limited for the most part to local markets. An exception was the East India Toilet Goods Company, formed in 1889 by Sidney Lyons and his wife, Mary, in Guthrie, Oklahoma. In 1909 they moved to Oklahoma City, where Sidney sold his toiletries, primarily a hair grower, door-to-door from a horse and buggy. The business prospered. In 1926 the Lyons built a manufacturing plant and expanded their product line to include face powder, perfume, and bleach. Lyons products were sold both nationally and internationally.[136]

The four most successful people in the black hair care and beauty aids business in the early twentieth century, however, were Annie Minerva Turnbo-Malone, Madame C. J. Walker, Anthony Overton, and Sarah Washington. All produced hair preparation products and cosmetics for blacks. They introduced the mass-marketing techniques of products by African-Americans on a national and international scale. Only Madame Walker, who revolutionized the black hair business with her straightening comb, however, remains an icon for blacks in this industry. While Walker, Overton, and Turnbo-Malone achieved millionaire status, there is reason to believe that Turnbo-Malone was America's first self-made female millionaire, black or white. Historically, that honor had been accorded to Walker, whose most formidable competitor was Turnbo-Malone.

In 1900 Annie Minerva Turnbo-Malone (1869–1957) began manufacturing hair care products in the all-black Illinois town of Lovejoy, where she had studied chemistry in high school. The success of her product, the "Wonderful Hair Grower," encouraged Turnbo-Malone to move to St. Louis in 1902 where she, along with her agents, started door-to-door sales. In promoting her product, Turnbo-Malone also gave customers personal hair and scalp treatments. After the 1904 St. Louis World's Fair, where Turnbo-Malone advertised her product with great success, she expanded her market. She traveled through the South, demonstrating her product and treatments, and training new sales agents. In 1906, in response to the number of imitators who tried to cash in on her success, Turnbo-Malone copyrighted her product name as Poro. She then expanded her product line, established franchised beauty schools, and hired additional sales agents for increased distribution.

Responding to the tremendous growth of her company and the demand for training in black hair care, Turnbo-Malone constructed the Poro College building, completed in 1918 at a cost of $350,000. The equipment alone was worth more than $150,000. Around this time Malone had 240 employees and 68,000 agents.[137] In the early 1920s, a $175,000, 20,000-square-foot addition was made to the building; it was fireproof, connected by tunnels and bridges, and contained "mechanical carriers that bring Poro products from the laboratories to the shipping tables." Turnbo-Malone had one of the largest mail-order shipping businesses in St. Louis; the "shipping room [was] a branch post office under Government supervision. Here parcels are packed and weighed, insured and mailed—over 1,000 parcels handled by 41 employees." In addition, the building contained a dining room that was open to the public and served meals to Poro employees at prices below cost, and hotel accommodations for blacks visiting the city.[138]

In 1922 Turnbo-Malone introduced a new product line for black skin care, which, along with her hair products, was sold internationally. Her agents traveled to the West Indies, South America, Africa, and the Philippines. While making sales calls, they also recruited new agents, which brought her employee force up to 75,000. Employee efficiency, high sales, and purchasing property for home ownership were rewarded with gold jewelry and diamond rings. In 1927 Poro College, however, went into receivership as the result of the money Turnbo-Malone was required to pay her former husband of thirteen years in a divorce settlement.[139]

In 1930 Turnbo-Malone moved to Chicago, where she purchased an entire city block and opened a new Poro College. Her financial affairs continued to go downhill, however. In 1937 her Chicago college went into receivership, and she also lost most of her St. Louis property to pay for the settlement in a lawsuit by a former employee. He worked only six weeks as Turnbo-Malone's general manager, but claimed she failed to give him one-third of her profits, as agreed on when he was hired. Also, beginning in 1933, the federal government charged Turnbo-Malone with failure to pay delinquent excise taxes. Left virtually penniless, she was 82 years old in 1951 when the government seized the last of her property.[140]

Madame C. J. Walker (1867–1919), whose enterprise also earned her a million dollars, still had her wealth intact when she died in 1919, leaving generous endowments to the black community.[141] She was born Sarah Breedlove and began her career manufacturing hair preparation products and selling them door-to-door in St. Louis in 1905. The ingredients, she said, came to her in a dream. Others, however, have alleged that her inspiration was really industrial espionage because, before launching her own business, Walker had worked for Turnbo-Malone as a sales agent. But it was her improvement on the hair-straightening comb, combined with her hair preparations, which became known as "The Walker System," that provided the foundation for her great financial success. Her second husband, Charles Walker, a newspaperman whom she married in 1906, upgraded her advertising and promotional efforts, including the suggestion for the name she eventually assumed, Madame C. J. Walker.[142]

In 1908 Walker moved to Pittsburgh to be closer to her national market. Eventually, her mail-order market included Africa, the West Indies, Cuba, and Panama. Her daughter, A'Lelia McWilliams, by her first husband, acted as manager of the Pittsburgh office. There Walker established Lelia College, which provided training in the Walker System, which was also taught through the school's correspondence course. In 1910 Walker moved her business to Indianapolis, where she set up a factory, college, and research laboratories. The Walker Manufacturing Company was incorporated in 1911, with Walker as the sole stockholder. With some 500 agents, monthly gross sales grew from $400 to $100,000. In 1916 she moved to New York, where she built a million-dollar mansion. By then, the company had more than 75 different hair and skin preparations and cosmetic products. Walker also used incentives to encourage higher sales by her agents. In 1917, having organized the Madame C. J. Walker Hair Culturist Union of America, she established its first national convention. Malone, by the way, also held similar conventions.[143]

After her death in 1919, the Walker Manufacturing Company continued to grow, making new advances in black hair care. Marjorie Stewart Joyner, who had begun working with Walker in 1916 as national principal of the Walker School, invented a permanent waving machine in 1928 whose patent she assigned to the Walker Company.[144] The Madame C. J. Walker Building in Indianapolis was constructed in 1927. It housed the national office of the Walker Beauty College, the manufacturing plant, and a pharmacy, along with a theater, restaurant, and ballroom. Soon after, the company was hit hard by the depression. Its peak annual earnings were $595,000 in 1920; in 1931 earnings had dropped to $130,000, and in 1933 to $48,000.[145]

Anthony Overton (1865–1946) enjoyed success in the health and beauty aids industry that came from manufacturing cosmetics for black women, especially his "High-Brown" face powder. With venture capital of $1,960, Overton first began manufacturing baking powder in 1898, founding the Overton Hygienic Manufacturing Company in Kansas City, Missouri. He turned to producing face powder when he discovered the tremendous demand for it from black women, a result of white cosmetic companies completely ignoring the market. In 1911 Overton moved the company to Chicago, where it produced a line of 52 products, with sales of $117,000. In 1915 the company was capitalized at $286,000 and expanded to 62 different products. The *Chicago Defender* reported that the Overton Company was "a well established house [that] makes baking powder, starch, extracts, proprietary medicines and toilet articles.... He now has agent networks throughout the country. He does a mail order business.... Mr. Overton manufactures all his goods [which] are copyrighted [High Brown] as many others having tried to imitate."[146]

By 1920 Overton was the country's leading producer of cosmetics for black women, with international sales and distribution extending not only to West Africa and the West Indies but also to Egypt, India, the Philippines, and Japan. In 1923 the Overton Hygienic Building was built and housed Overton's diverse business enterprises. His cosmetic company was located on the third floor. His Victory life Insurance Company and the Douglass National Bank were on the first floor, along with offices for his two publications, the *Half-Century* and the *Chicago Bee,* the latter a national black newspaper with an all-black female staff. In 1927 Dun & Bradstreet assessed Overton's manufacturing company as a million-dollar enterprise. It was manufacturing over 250 products, including those for other companies.[147]

While Sarah Spencer Washington was a contemporary of Walker, Malone, and Overton, she began her company in 1913 and did not establish her New Jersey-based Apex News and Hair Company until 1920. Washington also developed a system of black hair care products, which were sold door-to-door. Apex product sales grew throughout the 1920s and into the 1930s. By 1937 Washington had built her own laboratories and manufacturing plant. She produced a line of about 75 hair and beauty aids products. At one time, 35,000 agents worked for Apex, which remained a leader in hair products for blacks until the 1960s.

In the early twentieth century, the successes of these manufacturers encouraged more blacks to go into the hair care and beauty aids business. With venture capital of five dollars, Dr. Julia P. H. Coleman in 1911 established the Hair Care-Vim Chemical Company in Washington, D.C. and also the Hair-Vim Vogue and School. In 1919 Coleman expanded and opened a branch of her company in New York.[148] In Chicago Madame Mada Brice developed and manufactured Always Young Cream, Afro-American Scalp, Queen Creams, and Pure Greaseless Cream, which had national sales. By 1913 she owned land in Tennessee, Oklahoma, and Chicago.[149]

The Chicago-based Kashmir Chemical Company, founded by Claude Barnett, who also established the American Negro Press Association, manufactured both skin and hair preparations under the brand name, Nile Queen. The Kashmir Company was advertised as the "Home of Exquisite Toilet Necessities."[150] In 1920 the Rose Chemical Company in Savannah, Georgia, which manufactured cosmetics and beauty aids, was organized by a group of black men in that city. Traveling sales agents sold the company's products: a soap, peroxide cream, hair dressing, rouge, perfume, cleansing cream, face powder, and a comb.[151]

Even though nearly all of the customers for black hair care and beauty products were women, some of the companies were founded and headed by men, a situation that increased when the industry grew tremendously in the 1960s.

The women owners of the early companies, Malone, Walker, and Washington, were pioneers in providing new avenues of employment for black women, whose occupational choices in the early twentieth century were limited. In the professions, black women were primarily teachers, social workers, and nurses. Also, they found white-collar employment in black businesses, most notably banks and insurance companies. For the masses of black women, however, domestic service occupations were their only options. Training in hair care opened new avenues for employment. In 1907, New York's Madame C. E. Crawford established a school that prepared black women to work as maids on Pullman cars because they "must know how to manicure and dress hair." By 1915 graduates of her school had obtained positions as maids.[152] The black hair care and beauty aid industry in the early twentieth century, then, led to expanded job options for black women not only in sales but also in the establishment of beauty shops, which proliferated and became a prominent feature of black business districts.

World War I and Black Business

African-American businesspeople viewed the economic implications of World War I in much the same way as did white businesspeople—that there would be a greater opportunity to make profits. Black businesspeople supported the war effort and encouraged other blacks to do the same. They also attempted to capitalize on the increase in black purchasing power by intensifying their efforts to encourage blacks to support black businesses. In 1918, when the NNBL met in Atlantic City, New Jersey, for its Nineteenth Annual Conference, the keynote address given by Dr. R. R. Moton, principal of Tuskegee Institute, was entitled "What the Negroes of the United States Are Doing in Helping to Win the War." In his speech Moton proposed that the NNBL "take the imitative in creating and developing commercial opportunities within the race, and in this way, take advantage of the newer and more favorable conditions occasioned by the World War."[153]

Before America entered the war in 1917, black businesspeople were asked by other blacks to give their projections on the impact of the war on their enterprises. It was reported that W. Fred Trotman, the only black broker on Wall Street and reputedly "a conservative and unostentatious business Man," said "the European wars and other remote causes have developed a condition in the financial world which gives to the careful investor opportunities which have not been seen since the close of the Civil War." In 1914 Trotman was reported as being "for 11 years an investment broker in the heart of the Wall Street financial district and at present the only successful broker of his race there."[154]

The *Tulsa Star* interviewed T. J. Elliott, owner of the largest black department store in the country and reported his projections on how the war would affect clothing prices: "He sees nothing in the near future but higher prices for all woolen and leather goods ... [because] the demand of the warring European nations to clothe the soldiers engaged has drained the world's supply of wool and leather. He predicts no more marked down sales of clothing and points to ladies' shoes made entirely of cloth except the tips and soles."[155]

The war also had an impact on black banking activities. From 1916 to 1917, several black banks were founded: two each in Georgia and Virginia, and one each in Philadelphia, Chicago, New Orleans, Columbia, South Carolina, and Charleston, West Virginia. During the war, however, only one black bank was selected as a depository for government funds; the Virginia Mutual Savings Bank in Portsmouth was chosen because of its spectacular sale of Liberty Bonds in three drives, with the last one involving 1,925 blacks purchasing $102,000 worth of bonds. Black bank deposits also increased. From May to November 1918, when the war ended, deposits in the Wage Earners Savings Bank increased from $443,559 to $596,081. In 1918 Wage Earners was the only black bank "invited by the J. Pierpont Morgan Banking House to participate in the Half Billion dollar English and French War Loan."[156]

Black inventors also attempted to contribute to the nation's war effort, hoping not only to sell their patents but also to establish factories for production of their inventions. The black inventor Garrett A. Morgan, whose gas "breathing" mask was adopted by the army, first attempted to generate capital from the black community for manufacturing the mask. Even after fire departments throughout Ohio contracted to buy Morgan's mask, it was reported that "Day after day, week after week, and month after month Mr. Morgan vainly endeavored to convince the colored people of Cleveland as to the possibilities of organizing a company to manufacture his instrument. Finally he was compelled to present his proposition to the white people of the above-named city, who seized the golden opportunity, organized the National Safety Device Company, and now own the controlling stock in the same."[157] The company then hired Morgan as general manager. During the war, his "national safety helmet," as it was called, was "used by the United States and the Allies to combat poisonous gases and as a safety device on submarines."[158]

With America's entry in the war, leading black businesspeople encouraged black patriotism. They also emphasized that blacks must continue to protest the undemocratic racial practices that existed in a nation fighting a war "to make the world safe for democracy." When Madame C. J. Walker spoke at the first national convention of her sales agents in Philadelphia in September 1917, it was reported that she "advised her people to remain loyal to their homes, their country and flag, stating that, 'after all, this is the greatest country under the sun,' but, said the Madame, 'We must not let our love of country, our patriotic loyalty cause us to abate one whit in our protest against wrong and injustice; we should protest until the American sense of justice is so aroused that such affairs as the East St. Louis riot be forever impossible.' "[159]

The war also had an impact on black advertising campaigns, with one advertisement combining a bit of race-baiting with an appeal to black consumer loyalty. An advertisement placed in the Chicago *Defender* by the Berry & Ross Doll Company made the following sales pitch: "An Appeal to 12,000,000 Americans: Your Race Is On Trial: Upon you depends the verdict. In 1914 American concerns placed with German manufacturers in Germany contracts for $6,000,000 worth of toys. The war made it impossible for Germans in Germany to DELIVER German products to Americans in America." The ad then proceeded to offer stock options in the company.[160]

After the war, several black businesses announced that payment for the purchase of shares in their companies could be made with Liberty Bonds. The Progressive Manufacturing Company in Chapel Hill, North Carolina, incorporated with "$50,000 Authorized Capital," advertised that it was selling stock at $25 per share, with "Liberty Bonds accepted."[161] The Berry & Ross Doll Company also offered several payment plans for purchase of its stock, including its "Liberty loan easy payment plan," which allowed the purchaser to make a small down payment, with the balance to be paid in 90 days. It would also "accept Liberty Bonds of the first, second, third, fourth and fifth issue at their present market value as payment on any amount of shares purchased."

The war effort increased the incomes and broadened the shopping patterns of many black Americans. Indeed, the post–World War I era saw the first formal recognition by white corporate America of the importance of the black consumer dollar, as indicated in an article published in a 1919 issue of *New York Women's Wear*, a trade paper published in New York. The article called attention to the necessity for white retailers to recognize the new purchasing power of black consumers, using St. Louis as an example:

> The trade of Negroes in St. Louis at the present time is worth while, merchants say. The Negro is valued as a buying unit in department stores for his trade as a rule is on a cash basis. Not so long ago, the Negro population was not particularly considered as a buying unit. What it bought was really very cheap, or it did not buy at all. But that time has gone by, and today, because of the great increase in the wages of the laborer, the Negro's trade must be taken into consideration. This especially applies where there is a large colored population, as there is in St. Louis, where there are probably 60,000 Negroes. Under present labor conditions the wage earner is bringing big money into the home and where there is money for the Negro, there will be clothes. The number of Negroes you see now in the shops is noticeable. A few years ago, they would never have entered. Furthermore, they do not buy cheap things, but the best and latest models."[162]

Yet, the purchasing power of the black consumer during the war had also led to price gouging by merchants in the black community. New York's black business leaders, led by George Harris, organized the North Harlem Board of Trade to develop means to suppress those practices. The initiative for the board "took form during the period of the war, when wholesale profiteering by unscrupulous merchants in the respective colored sections of the country was rampant." The membership was to include about 300 black merchants in North Harlem, and a plan was made to establish a "magistrate's court . . . for the handling of cases of the race."[163]

Black Business Districts and White Competition

Migration and statutory and institutional racism contributed to the development of black business districts in American cities during this time. And the most significant event was the Great Migration of World War I, when blacks from the South moved to large industrial centers in the North.[164] In the South, migration also took place from rural areas to emerging industrial centers of that region. In both northern and southern urban centers, increased black populations were concentrated in segregated residential areas, which encouraged the development of black business districts. Increasingly in the South, black business districts would be anchored by black financial institutions, banks, insurance companies, building and loan associations, and national offices of black fraternal organizations. In Durham, North Carolina, John Sibley Butler noted that Parish Street, where these enterprises were located, was known as "the *Negro Wall Street*."[165]

The same description was also applied to the black business district in Tulsa, Oklahoma, but more as a testimony to the variety of its black enterprises than to the large number of black financial institutions. The district's success, however, was short-lived. In 1921 a race riot broke out—a white response to black economic success. The black business district was devastated, attacked not only by mobs of armed whites on the ground but also by bombs dropped from the air to complete the destruction. The riot ended after the National Guard was called out. Some 6,000 blacks were marched into detention camps, allowed to leave only when their badges were signed by their white employers for them to return to work. Other blacks fled Tulsa, some aided by the NAACP, which organized a relief and refugee fund to assist them. By 1923 Tulsa's Greenwood black business district began its recovery, which came mostly in the form of personal service enterprises, distinctive to most black business districts, whether in the North or South.[166]

In the early twentieth century, as racism intensified in the South and black business districts developed, blacks continued to patronize white businesses where they could legally do so. This occurred despite the feeling among blacks that the service provided in black businesses was comparable to, or even better than, that of white businesses. In Atlanta a millinery shop owned by two young black women advertised in 1914 that it made dresses "from the latest patterns from Paris and New York." The local black newspaper contrasted it with white shops as "a place where Negro women can buy hats, try then on, have their dresses fitted and be treated like ladies." In addition, the paper noted that, "There are establishments up to town where many of our educated Negro women buy their hats and their suits and the white people will not let them try the hats on. They buy them without fitting them." But in the black-owned shop, black women could expect "every courtesy and every consideration that a fashionable lady would desire."[167]

In the North tremendous black population increases accounted for the development of both the physical and institutional ghetto that locked blacks into distinct and separate sections of these cities.[168] Black business districts in those cities, as in the South, developed on major streets in the center of the black population. In Chicago these districts were geographically separated from the central business district, often by light industrial areas. Chicago's South Side black business district developed quickly from 1910 to 1920. Yet in New York, as late as 1912, while there was increasing residential segregation in Harlem, a few "traditional" black businesses continued to serve whites, even as they increasingly began to rely on black customers.[169]

The new black businesses that were established appealed for black support on the basis of race loyalty. In New York the O. K. Towel Supply Company, which owned the Trogan Laundry Company, opened in 1914 to provide service to the "forty colored shops in Harlem alone." Their ad emphasized that "these two businesses are owned by a colored firm and will guarantee that the service of the supply will in every way measure up to that of any other in the city."[170] In 1915 a Harlem tailor, who sold suits on the installment plan, also appealed to race loyalty: "We are the only colored concern that has opened a tailoring business catering to negroes only. We don't ask for white trade for we feel that we have enough good, loyal Colored men in our city to support a first-class business.... This is strictly a Negro enterprise. We make you a high class tailored suit and let you wear it and pay just one dollar ($1.00) per week. You don't have to go and get a white man to go your security. It is a Negro transaction all the way through."[171]

As black businesses increased in black business districts, there were various innovative enterprises developed, including the Banks Fried Chicken and Restaurant Company that opened in 1913. Thomas Banks started his business from a pushcart. By 1919 he had established four restaurants. In attempting to expand into them a Bank's Fried Chicken chain, he incorporated and offered a stock option. The company was capitalized at $100,000. Banks retained a 51 percent interest, with the balance put on the market at $10 per share, but it was "alleged that he was able to dispose of only a small amount, probably from $2,500 to $3,000." In 1920 the Banks Fried Chicken and Restaurant Company was put in receivership. Prohibition accounted for its failure because many "of its patrons were among the class who also patronized the saloons." When Prohibition closed the taverns, it also closed Banks's restaurant. As a former company official said, "the bulk of the fried chicken business was done between the hours of 11 P.M. and 2 A.M."[172] Bank's efforts to establish a chain of fried chicken enterprises, then, predated that of the highly successful Kentucky Fried Chicken chain, which now has an international market.

With the increasing urbanization of blacks in American racial ghettoes, black business activity became more dependent on the development of a separate black economy. Yet in many cities in both the North and South, enterprises owned by native whites and immigrants, Europeans and Asians, were located in black business districts and represented a group economy based on the consumer purchases of blacks. Consequently, while black businesses relied primarily on a black consumer market, they did not exist in a wholly separate economy. White businesses captured most of the black consumer dollars that came primarily from wages paid by whites. Ironically, the surplus value of the labor of twentieth-century black wage earners was returned to whites in much the same way that the surplus value of the slaves' labor was absorbed by their master. The black purchasing dollar in black business districts, then, circulated back into the white community.

Particularly in retail sales, black merchants as a group could not compete with whites, either in the variety or quantity of merchandise. In addition, the quality of merchandise offered in black business districts by both black and white merchants was almost always decidedly inferior. But white merchants, with a much larger operating capital, could afford both to purchase and to sell their goods on credit. This was perhaps the single most attractive feature to the cash-poor black consumer. However, interest rates on credit sales to blacks for goods, already with high markup prices, also increased profits for white merchants. The lack of access to credit defeated black merchants. Few could obtain credit from wholesalers, which would have enabled them to increase the quantity and quality of goods sold. Without credit, high overhead costs invariably limited the inventory of black retailers to the most basic items. And with limited merchandise turnover and slow sales, few could afford to sell their goods on credit.

Moreover, while black consumers might use the complaint that they were subjected to rude and unprofessional treatment from black business owners as their rationale for shopping in white stores, often they received the same treatment from white salespeople, who treated them with even more disdain and contempt. Doubtless, the behavior of white salespeople reflected a deep resentment that they were dependent on a group of people whom they considered inferior but who, at the same time, provided them with a livelihood.

There were other inequities that existed between black merchants and their white counterparts in black business districts. A survey done in 1916 by a black newspaper, *New York Age,* provided information that compared the number of blacks employed by black businesspeople with those employed by whites who operated businesses in Harlem. It found that, on 135th Street from Fifth to Seventh Avenues, there were 117 businesses that employed a total of 365 people. Blacks owned 65 of the businesses and employed "190 colored men, forty-three colored women and three white men. The white proprietors employ ninety-seven white men, nineteen white women, ten colored men and three colored women." The occupations of the 10 black men who worked for whites were listed as: a presser in a tailor shop, a helper in a real estate office, and porters in a saloon, tailor shop, grocery, furniture store, drugstore, and three wine shops. The 3 black women worked as laundresses. The white men employed by blacks worked in a real estate office, tailor shop, and drugstore.

The newspaper also reported on the ethnicity of new immigrants who owned businesses in Harlem; they included Italians, Greeks, Jews, French, Russians, Germans, and Chinese; among them were 10 tailors, 2 general contractors, 2 plumbers, and 1 painter and decorator. In addition, there were 3 furniture dealers, and the same number of clothing dealers, launderers, wine shop proprietors, grocers, and shoemakers. There were 2 cigar and stationery stores, 4 lunchrooms, a real estate office, fish market, drugstore, print shop, plumber, butcher, saloon, and shoe store, in addition to jewelers, pawnbrokers, and dry cleaners.[173] Virtually all of the consumers in Harlem were black. Also, the paper estimated that whites made more profits than blacks: "Investigation shows that the Negro merchant is receiving but a small proportion of the trade. The highest estimate places that proportion at about thirty-five per cent, while many place it as low as fifteen per cent.... It is a safe and conservative statement when the proportion is given at about twenty to twenty-five per cent."

The survey confirmed that blacks had a monopoly in two business sectors in Harlem, including barbering, since "men of other races do not conduct barber shops which cater to race trade." The other was in real estate: "Another business in which the colored business man enjoys predominance ... or properly speaking, the renting agency." The survey also showed that, with the exception of one black man who had just purchased a home in a rural area (previously, he lived in the building where he conducted his business), all of the black businessmen lived in Harlem. However, "Every white proprietor, except the five previously referred to, lives outside of the district." And it was emphasized that many white business owners "take no active interest in the business.... The employer's part of the work is to draw his profits from the trade given him by the Negroes of the district which trade is handled by his employees."[174]

The black press denounced blacks for failing to trade with their own people, emphasizing that money spent at white stores left the community. One commentator reported his reactions to the practice: "After observing the large Negro population in Harlem, the visitor invariably wants to know why, in the majority of instances, colored people reside in the flats and the white people occupy the stores beneath for business purposes." The press also reported how blacks were condemned by other ethnic groups for failure to patronize black businesses. In the *A.M.E. Review* the editor, Rev. R. C. Ransom, published a conversation with a "Hebrew friend" who said, "Why do your people keep themselves down? Why don't they rise up like other people and grasp their opportunities? There are thousands of Negroes in Harlem who spend hundreds of thousands of dollars a year, yet they give it all to the white people." Ransom's response was, "we had been an agricultural people." The Hebrew gentleman replied that "You have had fifty years. I would think you would be equal at least to the Syrian, the Greek and Italian immigrant."[175] But Rev. Ransom did not respond that these immigrants were white, which gave them an advantage in racist white America.

Even in the South, concern was expressed at the inroads made in the black business community by immigrants. In 1920 the *Norfolk Journal and Guide* made a survey of the 12-block black business district in that Virginia city, which contained a total of 102 businesses. The survey noted that some of the businesses were "owned and operated by whites, Greeks, Jews, Chinese, and Japanese but patronized wholly by our group."[176] In a strongly worded editorial in 1917, the *New York Age* admonished blacks for their failure to patronize black business, claiming that black businesses in the South succeeded because black consumers lacked options to shop elsewhere. Then, it compared the business successes of Jews and Italians with those of blacks:

> How do you imagine that the Italians have so many banks in this city? How do the Jews manage to invade and eventually dominate every field of commercial activity in this great Metropolis? It is primarily due to the fact their own people make the sacrifice of not only distance, but very frequently lack of equal returns that has enabled the Jew to become the power in the modern world he has become; that has enabled the Italian, whose illiteracy is greater than that of the black man when he comes to this country, whose poverty in a strange land is many fold greater than that of the colored citizen, to be breaking into every line of industry and commerce.... Let us then patronize the colored men in business, even though for the time being we do so at some sacrifice. We are helping not only him, but ourselves, our children and our children's children.[177]

Cooperative Finance and Investment

Throughout this period blacks continued in attempts to advance their economic position in business through cooperative efforts. In 1912 one of the most interesting proposals to encourage black group investments was made by a U. S. Army unit, the black 9th Cavalry stationed at Fort D. A. Russell. Through Squadron Sergeant Major Milton T. Dean, an appeal was made to blacks to develop and support black businesses: "We must awaken from that fear of venture and lack of push to enter new fields, such powerful factors in the material advancement of other people. Can you not come to us, can you not attempt, at least, the gathering in of the thousands of dollars which now flow into the pockets of the white man?" The unit also announced that it wanted to play a prominent part in bringing about a stronger black identity and that it could quickly have "$110,000 available for investment" in legitimate businesses; the unit also proposed establishing "a department store to consist of a banking system ... such a store to be opened in one of the cities where a large population of Negroes is found."[178]

In analyzing the plan, the *New York Age* reported that funds could be made available from the 9th Cavalry, as well as from the 10th Cavalry and the 25th Infantry, all of which were stationed in the United States. Using figures compiled from troop and regimental records, the newspaper found that the three units would have $38,120.25 per month and $457,443 annually available for investment. In American business and military history, surely this is the first instance where servicemen proposed to use their pay as venture capital to finance cooperative business ventures for the economic advancement of a civilian population.

There were also attempts to encourage cooperative group investment by using traditional capitalistic methods. In the post–World War I era, even with limited incomes, blacks were as much caught up in the stock-buying frenzy that gripped the nation as were whites. In 1921 an attempt was made to establish a stock exchange in Harlem for trading in securities of corporations owned and managed by blacks. The name proposed was the Harlem Stock Exchange, with plans for "issuance of $100,000 stock in the corporation managing the exchange—$25,000 common and $75,000, 8 per cent participating preferred. The par value of common and preferred will be $5 a share." The planners also indicated that there were "more than 100 corporations in New York owned by and selling securities to negroes. Banks, real estate companies, moving picture companies and other businesses."[179]

The desire to profit from stock investments was not limited to blacks in the nation's financial center. The Philadelphia Bresford Corporation advertised the sale of "Federal, Municipal, Railroad and Utility bonds in denominations of $100, $500 and $1,000." Also, in Detroit in October 1926, "A national stock exchange devoted to the sale of Negro securities was opened."[180] These proposed ventures, however, were all short-lived, their demise as much the result of a lack of investment support as the 1929 stock market crash.

Because there was tremendous interest by blacks in corporate investment and cooperative financing at the time, stock fraud was inevitable. The most extensive scheme involving black Americans was carried out by Thrift Race of the World, a wholly owned black corporation that claimed to have 158,000 members in its investment group. In 1919 the board chairman, H. E. Bryant, announced that he planned to purchase the successful black-owned Central Overall Company. He also claimed to have purchased 52 acres of land in a section of northeast Washington, D.C., for $500,000 for the development of an industrial park. The company announced: "in the coming years a manufacturing plant to cost in the neighborhood of a million dollars will be built.... capitalized at $100,000,000, and will first float its stock among its members and then the general public."[181] A year later the *Philadelphia North American* ran a searing headline, "Much-Titled Negro in Clutches of Law." While Bryant had developed several different companies that he felt would appeal to blacks and had been successful in selling thousands of dollars worth of stock, the paper reported, "So far, the only thing given to investors had been the engraved stock certificates."[182]

International Business

The early twentieth century also found blacks continuing their interest in international business, particularly in developing trade ties with blacks in Africa and the West Indies. In Chicago the J. H. Zedricks & Co., a mail-order house, was established in 1905 by John H. Zedricks, who developed an international market through advertising. In the first year he sent out "3,000 four-page circulars, with an additional 10,000 letters going to all parts of the world." In 1907 he paid a $2,500 fee for incorporation of his manufacturing enterprise and mailed out a 25-page printed catalogue. During the first two years of his business, Zedricks shipped small orders throughout the United States, Liberia, Panama, Haiti, and Cuba.[183] In 1913 the African Union Company was incorporated in New York, founded, as it said, "to handle African products on a large scale and to aid in the development of Africa generally." The corporation leased land containing mahogany trees and other varieties and palm-oil plantations in West Africa, developing extensive markets for their exports. With the onset of World War I, however, the company went bankrupt.[184]

After the war several import-export companies were founded by black Americans. The New York–based Thomas and Thomas Company was incorporated in 1919. It imported cocoa, spices, and fruits from the West Indies and exported American products to those islands. The company was also an "agent for the steamship companies that sail from New York to the West Indies."[185] In Newport News, Virginia, the Paris Import and Export Corporation was incorporated in 1920, capitalized at $200,000. It exported American products and imported mahogany, palm oil, coca, cocoa beans, animal skins, and hides. One of its first consignments was for "636 bags of cocoa ordered from Coomasie, which has now reached as far as Lagon, [sic] West Africa."[186]

Also, after World War I several attempts were made by blacks to establish steamship companies. The Inter-Colonial Steam Ship Company was founded in New York. In promoting interest in its venture, the company sent its agent, Hattie S. Cofield, to various cities in the Tidewater region in 1919 to generate investment capital, which she did. In 1920 the company purchased its first steamship, which it named the *Inter-Colonial*, "from the United States Shipping Board at a cost of $16,720.33, appraised to be worth $100,000." By 1922 the company had assets of $130,000. The African Steamship and Sawmill Company, founded in 1920, was capitalized at $1 million. Both companies failed.[187]

The most ambitious attempt made by blacks to establish an oceangoing steamship line was undertaken by Marcus Garvey with the founding of his Black Star Steamship Line in 1919, which was part of his Universal Negro Improvement Association (UNIA), a business development program. The purpose was to develop trade relations among blacks in America, the West Indies, Central America, and Africa, "thereby building up an independent economy of business, industry, and commerce, and to transport our people ... on business and pleasure."[188] The corporation was capitalized at $500,000, with stock sold at $5 a share. In 1920 the steamship line was recapitalized at $10 million. Three ships were purchased, none actually seaworthy. Still, when the Black Star Line's first ship, the *S. S. Yarmouth*, was launched in October 1919, there was a tremendous celebration. The following day, 5,000 blacks attended a UNIA rally, where it was reported that "Those in the audience bought $115,000 worth of stock."[189]

The Black Star Line was not limited to transporting goods in the international market. It also provided passenger service between New York and various foreign ports, including Hamilton, Bermuda, for $75; Port-au-Prince, Haiti, $90; Colon, Panama, $100. In December 1920 the Black Star Line announced that a group of black businessmen would embark on a 35-day trade mission to the West Indies and Central America on the *S. S. Antonio Maceo*. The group was said to include "Negro bankers, Bishops, Heads of Corporations, and other Business and Professional men of the Race." Their itinerary included Bermuda, Cuba, Jamaica, Panama, and Costa Rica.[190]

Garvey's nationwide sale of stock in the Black Star Line through the mail ultimately resulted in his downfall. In 1922 the federal government indicted him for using the mail to defraud the public; the specific charge was selling stock in a company, that was in financial trouble. At supplementary proceedings held in the Supreme Court of Bronx County, New York, in April 1922, Garvey testified under oath that several financial institutions held the mortgages on Black Star steamships; that only $900,000 of the $10 million in capital stock was sold; that the shipping line was not operating at that time; that it had no money in the bank; that it had never paid any dividends; and that its present indebtedness was $200,000.[191]

Marcus Garvey and the UNIA

Marcus Garvey (1887–1940) was born in Jamaica, where he established the Universal Negro Improvement Association in 1914, the year he began correspondence with

TABLE 7.2   Universal Negro Improvement Association Financial Report—
Year Ending July 31, 1922

Receipts	General Funds
Balance in Bank Aug. 1st, 1921	$10,913.67
Membership Fees	3,662.03
Sales of supplies to Branches	10,328.59
Death Tax	28,723.39
20% dues from Branches	14,722.59
Convention Funds	10,484.21
Sale of Almanacs and Pictures, etc	3,522.75
Assessment Tax	20,543.17
Fees for Charters	5,192.05
Contributions (voluntary)	34,165.25
Loans (Schedule)	6,987.50
Refunds	592.52
Redeposit checks	3,247.18
Exchange checks	580.71
General Check (Schedule)	10,254.49
	$163,920.01
Construction Loan Notes	23,713.53
	$187,633.54

Disbursements	
Light and Heat	$ 870.06
Telephone, telegraphy and cables	2,553.23
Postage and expressage	4,512.30
Minor repairs	351.98
Furniture and Fixtures	1,368.85
Salaries of officers	42,394.56
Salaries of employees	39,929.90
Salaries of men in Liberia	2,678.50
Travelling Expenses	8,735.72
Printing	11,263.88
Stationery and Office Supplies	2,141.22
Loans	1,668.00
Death Benefits	4,439.64
Real estate and Mortgages	25,384.75
Pay't to B.S.L. lease 54-56	3,000.00
Advance to B.S.L. a/c/lease	3,668.98
Pay't to N.Y. Local a/c purchase N.World	1,300.00
General	17,192.38
	$175,129.63
Construction Notes Rec'd	10,962.68
Interest on same	828.85
	$186,921.16
Receipts	$187,633.54
Disbursements	186,921.16
Balance	$712.38

(continued)

TABLE 7.2   Continued

Resources

Cash, in various Funds	$ 20,881.24
Furniture and fixtures	6,335.35
Machinery	23,963.42
Real Estate	18,400.00
Stock in Black Star Line & Factories, Inc.	37,460.00
Good Will in Negro world	60,000.00
Accts. Receivable, principally from Branches	93,707.93
Notes Receivable	13,628.94
Inventory	4,222.55
Leases and Deposits	7,118.98
Total	$285,718.31

Liabilities

Notes Payable	$184,187.47
Mortgages Payable	5,500.44
Loans and Accounts Payable	37,000.48
Salaries and Death Claims	34,141.99
Total	$260,870.38

Source: W. E. B. DuBois, "U.N.I.A.," *Crisis* (1923), 121–22.

Booker T. Washington, whom Garvey greatly admired. Washington, however, viewed Garvey's program as merely an extension of his National Negro Business League.[192] In 1916 Garvey came to the United States. After he visited 38 states to assess the condition of black America, he concluded that black leadership was opportunistic, devoid of any viable programs for the advancement of the race, and distinguished only by the extent of its "treachery and treason." Garvey settled in Harlem, which became the center of the UNIA. By 1920 it had become the largest organization of blacks ever established in America. Garvey's black nationalistic appeal, "One God, One Aim, One Destiny," called for race pride. His bombastic denunciations of white racism as well as his economic programs also won him great admiration from blacks not only in America but throughout the black world.[193]

In 1919, as part of the UNIA's black economic development program, Garvey established the Negro Factories Corporation, capitalized at $1 million, which offered 200,000 shares of common stock at $5 a share. Its purpose, as Garvey said, was "to build and operate factories in the big industrial centres of the United States, Central America, the West Indies, and Africa to manufacture every marketable commodity." The corporation established a factory to make uniforms for UNIA members and another one to make black dolls. Several restaurants and groceries, a steam laundry, and a printing plant were other UNIA enterprises. Garvey's most successful venture was as editor and publisher of the *Negro World,* a weekly newspaper with a circulation of 200,000 that sold for $.05 in this country and $.10 overseas.

In addition to the Black Star Steamship Line, the UNIA's business operations also generated controversy. In 1922 W. E. B. DuBois published an account of the finances of the UNIA from a financial report submitted to the *Crisis* by the UNIA (see table 7.2). Based on an analysis of this and other reports, DuBois challenged the number of members the UNIA reported it had. While Garvey claimed two to four million UNIA members in 1921, DuBois, based on dues paid into the UNIA, estimated it had 15,262 members, or a maximum of from "ten to twenty thousand active members."[194] DuBois's estimate may be low, however, because in the mid-1920s, when Garvey was in prison, there were more than 700 branches of the UNIA in 38 states, along with 200 international branches, most of them in the West Indies and in Central and South America.

Economic Ideologues

In retrospect, Garvey's program for the economic uplift of blacks differed little from those proposed by Washington and DuBois. In the first wave of black corporate America, these three ideologues of early-twentieth-century black economic thought promoted cooperative business as the only salvation for African-Americans. While Washington encouraged black business activity and founded the Tuskegee Institute, and DuBois formulated plans for cooperative enterprises, only Garvey followed through in establishing a business conglomerate that included the masses.[195] Yet, given the racial climate at the time, the three could only proceed on the assumption that blacks would never get a chance to gain entry as equals to American big business. Consequently, all three men promoted the development of black business within the context of a separate and independent group economy that would parallel mainstream American enterprise. Yet, shrewd and successful political leadership, bombastic demagoguery, and intellectual achievement do not always translate into business expertise or make for long-lasting business success, any more than business expertise provides the basis for effective political leadership.

Rather, black business success in the initial rise of black corporate America was found in men like the Durham triumvirate of Charles Clinton Spaulding, A. M. Moore, and John Merrick of North Carolina Mutual Life Insurance, businessmen who founded enterprises that succeeded. They, too, were "race men." Spaulding, North Carolina Mutual's president, began his business career as manager of a cooperative grocery. With his real estate operations, Merrick built houses for Durham's black industrial workers. With the hospital he founded in 1901, Dr. Moore was regarded as a humanitarian as well as a businessman. Also, while building North Carolina Mutual, the three spearheaded the development of the Mechanics and Framers Bank and a textile mill.

After Moore's and Merrick's deaths in the early 1920s, Spaulding founded the Bankers Fire Insurance Company, a savings and loan association, and the Mortgage Company of Durham. In 1924 he established the National Negro Finance Corporation (NNFC) in Durham, with authorized capital of $1 million. Its purpose, which foreshadowed the federal government's Small Business Administration program, was to loan money to blacks to establish legitimate businesses and to strengthen enterprises already in existence. The program failed, but it had the support of R. R. Moton, president of the NNBL, who was appointed president of the NNFC. By 1930 Spaulding, at the helm of the "world's largest black business," possessed the power and recognition that Booker T. Washington had enjoyed a generation earlier. Spaulding's achievements in race relations, the allocation of public funds, the political arena, and in black higher education were result of his effective and successful management of capital.[196]

While the three ideologues of early-twentieth-century black economic thought advocated that the black economy must be independent of white capital, their economic activities often undermined this position. Washington's power resulted from the largesse of white philanthropists. And although DuBois attempted personal business ventures, he was not successful. While black capital poured into Garvey's business organizations, white financial institutions held mortgages on UNIA properties. Moreover, there were criticisms of Garvey's Back to

Africa program by black intellectuals at the time, such as DuBois, who emphasized that "Africa belongs to the Africans. They have not the slightest intention of giving it up to foreigners, white or black." In 1922 the black historian Carter G. Woodson said that while Garvey's Back to Africa program was impractical, "the emigration of a few Negro captains of industry to that land of undeveloped resources will mean much more to the Negro than the distant protest of those who from afar decry the white man's exploitation."[197]

In his promotion of pan-Africanism, DuBois also saw African-American economic support important to African development.[198] Yet it was Washington who, by giving advice to Presidents Roosevelt and Taft, had an impact on the economy of an African state during that time. The ultimate outcome of his influence on America's Liberian policy was not favorable to Liberia, resulting in the economic hegemony of the Firestone Rubber Company in the 1920s.[199] DuBois's Pan-African contribution to African decolonization would not see results until the mid-twentieth century. During the depression of the 1930s, however, he became even more insistent that African-Americans must establish cooperatives and support black business. In his 1940 autobiography, DuBois presented his economic program for black America that he called the "Cooperative Commonwealth." As he explained, the reality that must be faced by black Americans in the development of business was that, "we have already got a partially separate economy in the United States."[200]

As black business districts developed in American cities and towns in the twentieth century, the traditionally predominant black enterprises—tailors, barbershops, millinery and dressmaking shops, saloons, billiard halls, and mortuaries—increased in numbers, as did black restaurants, lunch counters, and other dining places. A 1928 NNBL survey of 2,757 black businesses in 33 cities found that 19 percent were groceries; 14 percent were barbershops; 11.3 percent were cleaning, pressing, and tailoring establishments; 11 percent were restaurants; and drugstores and auto repair shops each constituted 6 percent.[201] Still the number of black enterprises increased from 1890 to 1940 (see table 7.3).

TABLE 7.3   Blacks in Business, Owners and Employees, 1890–1940

Type of Enterprise	1890	1900	1910	1920	1930	1940
Agents/Salesmen	2,288	4,904	9,054	8,293	25,534	24,571
Barbers/Hairdressers	17,480	19,942	22,534	31,352	34,263	28,229
Bankers/Brokers/Clerks	114	82	241	142	267	907
Hotel Keepers	420	481	973	1,020	1,064	1,000
Journalists	134	210	220	251	367	376
Photographers	190	247	404	608	545	122
Restaurant Keepers	2,157	3,993	6,369	7,511	10,543	11,263
Retail Merchants	6,646	9,095	13,924	23,526	28,213	17,422
Saloon Keepers	932	890	1,663	96	—	100
Undertakers	231	453	953	1,558	2,946	3,415
Wholesale Merchants	535	148	257	67	130	70
Grand Total	31,127	40,445	56,592	74,424	103,872	87,475

Source: U. S. Bureau of the Census, *Negro Population in the United States, 1790–1915*, 526–527; U. S. Bureau of the Census, 1920, vol. 4: *Population—Occupations;* U. S. Bureau of the Census, *Negroes in the United States, 1920–1932*, 310–327; U. S. Bureau of the Census, 1940, vol. 3 *Population*—Labor Force, part 1: U. S. Summary, p 88–90, and Census of Business, vol. 3: Service Establishments, 1939; in Vishnu V. Oak, *The Negro's Adventure in General Business* (Yellow Springs, Ohio: Antioch Press: 1949; Wesport, Conn.: Negro Universities Press, 1970), 48, 192–193. Also, "The 1940 census reports show that they [blacks] owned 720,000 homes, operated 680,000 farms, conducted 57,000 retail stores and service establishments doing a total business of over $108,000,000, and accumulated a wealth of $3,000,000,000" (Oak, 32).

Conclusion

The extent and diversity of African-American cooperative efforts in the emergence of black corporate America in the early twentieth century represent a lost page in the African-American experience. Even the new financial institutions that were established at the time represented merely the expansion and professionalization of the early mutual benefit and fraternal societies that had originated a century ago. The most distinctive advance in cooperative black-business activity from 1900 to 1930 was the expansion of corporate entities and cooperative efforts made through the sale of stock in order to secure capital for the establishment and expansion of business enterprises in manufacturing, transportation, and real estate. Insurance companies, banks, building and loan associations, and real estate and construction companies were the only enterprises that put large sums of money in the hands of blacks.

Still, despite limited capital, the efforts made by blacks in the early twentieth century to promote business development through cooperative finances represented their continuing pursuit to capitalize on America's partially free enterprise system. Most black businesses founded in the first three decades of the twentieth century were personal service enterprises, and there were continual inroads made by blacks into international trade. While the economic activities of blacks in the new century loom insignificant within the broad scope of the American economy, black business was not a myth.[202] In many ways, then, this period can be considered the golden age of black business activity, especially because of the diversity of manufacturing enterprises established, including the successful hair care products industry, as well as because of the proliferation of the two major kinds of financial institutions, banks and insurance companies. These enterprises have historical significance in exemplifying the first wave rise of black corporate America.

8

FROM THE DEPRESSION TO CIVIL RIGHTS
IN BLACK BUSINESS

Where There Is No Jim Crow!

Nobody ever heard of anybody being barred from investing in one of our great companies like General Motors, Procter and Gamble, International Telephone and Telegraph, Standard Oil and United States Steel because of skin color, hair texture or features. In short, there are no laws or customs stopping Negroes from becoming capitalists and enjoying some of the profits of ownership in America's giant corporations.

—editorial in the *Pittsburgh Courier*, 30 April 1955

Introduction

Black American business, after almost three decades of expansion, was hard hit by the Great Depression. Throughout the 1930s the high unemployment rate of blacks, already with low incomes, had a devastating impact on black business, which depended almost entirely on black consumers. By 1935 about 25 percent of blacks were on relief. In Norfolk, Virginia, the relief rate was 81.3 percent. In the nation's 15 cities with the largest black populations, the effect of growing black unemployment on black businesses from 1929 to 1935 can be seen in declining retail sales (see table 8.1). New York City was an exception to this trend, with only 11.2 percent of employable blacks on relief and an increase of almost $500,000 in black retail sales from 1929 to 1935. But in Atlanta, where 65.7 percent of blacks were on relief, there was a decline in black retail sales from over $1,151,850 in 1929 to $694,000 in 1935. The rate of decline in retail sales in other cities also underscores the extent to which black unemployment during the depression resulted in a drastic reduction in income for black store owners.

In addition, while the number of black retail businesses declined by only 10 percent, from 24,969 stores in 1929 to 22,756 in 1935, aggregate retail sales fell by more than half, from $98.6 million in 1929 to $47.96 million in 1935. Ironically and sadly, this decline marks probably the first time in the history of the country that blacks achieved some semblance of economic equality with whites: from 1932 to 1935, the total volume of all retail

TABLE 8.1   Black Retail Stores and Sales in 15 Cities, 1929 and 1935

City	Black Population 1930	Number of Retail Stores 1929	1935	Total Value of Sales ($) 1929	1935
New York	327,706	391	960	3,322,000	3,805,000
Chicago	233,903	815	724	4,826,897	2,735,000
Philadelphia	219,599	787	729	1,630,000	3,150,000
Washington	132,068	244	279	1,495,854	1,593,000
Detroit	120,066	358	504	2,951,471	1,128,000
Baltimore	142,106	282	383	1,062,946	893,000
Atlanta	90,075	391	297	1,151,850	694,000
New Orleans	129,632	771	289	2,300,374	574,000
Memphis	96,500	379	324	1,552,583	566,000
Houston	63,337	259	252	1,343,588	565,000
Cleveland	71,899	215	184	1,156,859	550,000
St. Louis	93,580	310	250	1,457,427	521,000
Richmond	52,988	189	170	657,961	314,000
Birmingham	99,077	200	132	601,916	193,000
Pittsburgh	54,983	150	81	830,013	147,000

Source: Florence Murray, ed., *The Negro Handbook, 1946–1947* (New York: A. A. Wyn, 1947), 321.

sales in the United States also declined by half, $49.25 billion to $25.75 billion.[1] However, while national aggregate retail sales from 1929 to 1939 declined by 13 percent, the decline in black retail sales was 28 percent. Also, in 1939 black retail sales amounted only to less than two-tenths of 1 percent of the national total.[2] In twentieth-century America, whether the economy was in a period of depression or prosperity, only a small percentage of black dollars was spent at black-owned businesses.

Double-Duty Dollar Campaigns

Historically, white businesses have always captured a large proportion of the black-consumer dollar. In Chicago the purchasing power of the city's blacks in 1935 was $81 million, which was $32 million more than aggregate receipts of all black businesses in the country. Yet, while $11 million was spent on groceries, only 5 percent, about $550,000, was spent at black-owned food stores.[3] In 1939 total food purchases nationwide by blacks in black grocery stores amounted to $24 million. With a black population of 12,808,073 in 1939, this was equivalent to each black person in the country spending only $2 of his or her annual food purchase dollars in black grocery stores.[4] In Chicago, a survey of stores owned in that city's black business district in 1938 showed that "three-fourths of the merchants in Bronzeville were Jewish," and *"While Negro enterprises constituted almost half of all the businesses in Negro neighborhoods, they received less than a tenth of all the money spent by Negroes within these areas"* [Drake and Cayton's italics].[5] (See table 8.2.)

In response to the limited profits made by black businesses, aggressive "Don't Buy Where You Can't Work" campaigns, primarily in major northern cities, were launched by blacks. This strategy, withdrawing patronage from nonblack-owned businesses, however, represented a continuation of the efforts made by blacks since Reconstruction to capture

TABLE 8.2   Business Ownership by Race—Chicago's (47th Street) Black Business District, 1938

Type of Business	Black	White	Total	Type of Business	Black	White	Total
Food Stores	*3*	*45*	*46*	*Prepared Food*	*8*	*13*	*21*
Bakeries	0	1	1	Chili parlors	1	1	2
Candy shops	0	1	1	Ice cream parlors	0	4	4
Fish markets	0	3	3	Lunch rooms	3	4	7
Food marts	0	1	1	Restaurants	3	4	7
Grocery and Markets	2	38	40	Chicken shacks	1	0	1
Poultry houses	1	1	2				
				Drugstores	*0*	*9*	*9*
Business Services	*4*	*15*	*19*				
Currency exchanges	0	2	2	*Other Retail Stores*	*7*	*19*	*26*
Insurance companies	1	1	2	Cigar stores	0	1	1
Real-estate companies	0	7	7	Florist shops	0	1	1
Savings and loan companies	1	3	4	Jewelry stores	0	1	1
Telegraph offices	0	1	1	Liquor stores	1	8	9
Plumbing companies	0	1	1	Taverns	5	6	11
Sign painters	2	0	2	Paint stores	0	1	1
				Window shade companies	0	1	1
Automotive Services	*1*	*3*	*4*	Cosmetic products	1	0	1
Tire and battery stores	0	2	2				
Filling stations	0	1	1	*Personal Service*	*42*	*37*	*78*
Garages	1	0	1	Cleaners and pressers	5	8	13
				Furriers	0	2	2
General Merchandise Stores	*1*	*16*	*17*	Laundries	1	8	9
Credit clothing stores	0	4	4	Photograph studios	2	2	4
Dry-goods stores	0	9	9	Storage	0	2	1
Five and ten cent stores	1	2	3	Tailor shops	5	9	14
Notion stores	0	1	1	Shoe repair	1	6	7
				Barber shops	12	0	12
Clothing Stores	*8*	*49*	*57*	Beauty parlors	11	0	11
Dress shops	3	13	16	Funeral systems	4	0	4
Lingerie shops	1	6	7	Old gold and silver salvage	1	0	1
Men's dry goods and furnishings	1	9	10				
Millinery shops	1	8	9	*Bookies*	*1*	*1*	*2*
Shoe stores	2	11	13				
Men's and women's furnishings	0	2	2	*Repair Service*	*2*	*7*	*9*
				Leather bindings	0	1	1
Furniture and Household Stores	*0*	*15*	*15*	Radio service	2	6	8
Sewing machine agents	0	1	1				
Furniture stores	0	14	14	*Miscellaneous*	*6*	*2*	*8*
				Herbs and incense shops	1	1	2
				Pool rooms	5	1	6
Hardware Stores	*0*	*4*	*4*	Totals	83	237	320

Source: Compiled from St. Clair Drake and Horace Cayton, *Black Metropolis: A Study of Negro Life in a Northern City,* rev. and enl. ed. (Chicago: University of Chicago, 1993), 450–51. Businesses surveyed were located on Chicago's south side, a mile-long strip from State Street to Cottage Grove on East 47th Street.

the black consumer dollar. In the 1930s these campaigns were fervently encouraged by black religious leaders because, historically, "To the Negro community, a business is more than a mere enterprise to make profit for the owner. From the standpoints of both the customer and the owner it becomes a symbol of racial progress, for better or for worse. And the preacher is expected to encourage his flock to trade with Negroes."[6]

The focus of this movement was the *double-duty dollar.* Throughout the depression and into World War II, the double-duty dollar doctrine gained nationwide momentum in black churches, the black press, and black organizations.[7] Blacks were told to spend their dollars at black businesses, a practice that, as the volume of business increased, would lead to higher profits that could be converted into salaries paid to new black employees. Based on the success that white retailers enjoyed in black business districts, the assumption was that black purchasing dollars could also support black businesses, while providing increased employment to blacks. The first Don't Buy Where You Can't Work, campaign started in Chicago in the early 1930s. As white stores with black patronage began to hire blacks, the campaign spread to other cities, including New York, Washington, D.C., Baltimore, and St. Louis.[8]

The 1930s double-duty dollar concept prompted several basic protest methods used by blacks in their Don't Buy Where You Can't Work campaigns: (1) organized boycotts, as in Chicago; (2) trade pact agreements in New York; and (3) block-by-block picketing in St. Louis, an approach that was used in the protest campaigns in other northern cities.[9] Some campaigns called for white businesses located in black communities to fire white workers and replace them with blacks. Despite the rioting against white businesses that broke out in New York City in 1935, this demand was subsequently rejected by the Harlem Coordinating Committee for Employment. It was founded in 1937 with a platform specifically stating that jobs for blacks "must be accomplished without the victimization of white for black workers."[10] The committee's jobs campaign agenda, which demanded that blacks be hired only when white workers were promoted or resigned, was adopted in Newark, Philadelphia, Boston, and Washington D.C., where the Negro Ministers Alliance, founded in 1935, spearheaded the local movement.[11]

While aggressive Don't Buy Where You Can't Work group boycotts took place in the North, they were virtually nonexistent in the South. The cumulative effects of individual boycotts, however, often proved as effective as organized boycotts in securing courteous treatment as well as jobs for blacks in white stores. In Atlanta in 1935, after white grocery clerks in a grocery beat up a black man accused of stealing a pound of sugar, individual blacks boycotted the store. It eventually went out of business. Increased black patronage at other white stores did result, for the first time, in black employment at those stores.[12]

Black boycotts of white businesses during the depression, however, remained controversial in the black community. Some blacks disagreed with the demand that white businesses should fire whites and hire blacks. The fear was that white businesses with black employees but only a few black customers might fire those employees. There was also the fear of white retaliation. As explained by black conservative George Schuyler, "the boycott is too dangerous a weapon to be used in the campaign for jobs, especially by a minority as weak as the Negro American."[13] Yet the federal injunction sought by white Harlem merchants to suppress black boycotts of white businesses as restraint of trade was found unconstitutional by the Supreme Court in 1938.[14]

The Don't Buy Where You Can't Work campaigns did lead to an increase in blacks employed in white businesses but were less effective in helping black businesses. By 1938 urban black businesses, especially in the North, were beginning a slow recovery, but most of those enterprises remained concentrated in the service sector.[15] Chicago provides an example (see table 8.2). Before, during, and after the Great Depression, black businesses across the country received only a fraction of the black consumer dollar. In 1939 aggregate retail sales for black businesses reached $71.5 million; but this was $27.1 million less than 1929 sales of $98.6 million, although about $21 million more than 1935 sales of $49 mil-

TABLE 8.3 Black Retail and Service Establishments, 1929, 1935, and 1939

Year	Number of Retail Stores	Sales ($)	Active Owners	Number of Employees	Payroll ($)
1929	24,969	98,602,000	27,405	12,036	8,047,000
1935	22,756	47,968,000	23,036	12,036	4,874,000
1939	29,827	71,466,000	29,116	13,778	5,386,000

Year	Number of Service Enterprises	Sales ($)	Active Owners	Number of Employees	Payroll ($)
1935	22,172	25,281,000	22,868	13,975	5,710,000
1939	27,368	36,653,000	28,582	14,180	6,241,000

Sources: On retail stores see United States Bureau of the Census, *Negroes in the United States, 1820–1932* (Washington, D.C.: Government Printing Office, 1935), 494–529. Also see special mimeographed bulletin number 2075, "Retail Trade: Negro Proprietorships—United States, 1939," 29 August 1941. On service enterprises see Vishnu V. Oak, *The Negro's Adventure in General Business* (Yellow Springs, Ohio: Antioch Press, 1947; Westport, Conn.: Negro Universities Press, 1970), 74.

lion. Also, from 1935 to 1939, while there was a 14.5 percent increase in black employees in black retail stores, from 12,036 to 13,778, their salaries in 1939 were 33.1 percent less than in 1929 (see tables 8.3 and 8.4).

In 1940 the country's black population was 12,808,073, but black business owners and their employees numbered only 87,475, less than 1.5 percent of the number of workers in the black labor force. Even when World War II provided jobs and increased earnings, few blacks were in any economic position to establish viable businesses; although, for some,

TABLE 8.4 Black Business Owners, Retail/Trade/Service Enterprises, 1939

Type of Business	Number of Businesses	Annual Income ($)	Employees Full/Part Time	Payroll ($)
Eating/drinking	12,610	26,527,000	8,385	3,042,000
Barber/beauty shops	11,293	12,963,000	7,540	3,290,000
Food/general stores	11,270	24,697,000	2,223	779,000
Shoe repair/shine	6,115	4,258,000	1,008	347,000
Cleaning/repairing	3,343	4,759,000	1,525	653,000
Auto repairs/service	1,950	2,868,000	774	413,000
Other repairs/service	1,590	1,340,000	220	103,000
Funeral parlors	1,501	7,691,000	1,914	935,000
Filling stations	1,268	6,917,000	798	463,000
Custom services	698	1,021,000	606	184,000
Drugstores	548	4,470,000	846	418,000
Apparel stores	333	779,00	137	68,000
Business services	299	530,000	157	84,000
Other retail stores	3,798	8,076,000	1,389	616,000
Miscellaneous services	579	1,223,000	436	232,000
Total	57,195	108,119,000	27,958	11,627,000

Source: Vishnu V. Oak, *The Negro's Adventure in General Business* (Yellow Springs, Ohio: Antioch Press, 1949; Westport, Conn.: Negro Universities Press, 1970) 76.

cooperatives appeared to provide a solution that would tie black businesses and black consumers into profitable reciprocal alliances.

Black Cooperatives

The cooperative movement among blacks in the twentieth century was especially strong in retail enterprises, such as grocery, drug, shoe, and department stores. Sometimes, several hundred people constituted the membership of a cooperative association, but as few as 50 people could pool their funds to establish one. In 1907 W. E. B. DuBois compiled a partial list of three kinds of cooperatives that were in existence: producer, wholesale, and consumer co-ops.[16] Blacks found it particularly difficult, however, to organize effective and long-lasting cooperative ventures. This can be seen in one attempt made by a black cotton farmer in the late 1920s to buy all of the cotton produced by neighboring black farmers with the hope of securing a higher price; but the results were that "whites in the town were incensed; told him that what he did was 'white peoples' business' and gave him the choice of returning the cotton to the Negroes from whom he purchased it or leaving town."[17]

After World War I, the black church was the center of some of the efforts to organize cooperatives. In 1919 the pastor of the Metropolitan AME Zion Church in St. Louis, the Reverend B. G. Shaw, organized the Cooperative Liberty Company. It was capitalized at $50,000 with shares sold at $10 each for the building of the first of a string of cooperative stores to be owned and operated by blacks in Missouri. Most of the cooperative's members belonged to the church, with no member allowed to purchase more than $100 worth of stock. Merchandise was sold at prices just above cost and profits were used to pay dividends. Eventually, Rev. Shaw hoped to establish a bank with a $250,000 capital.[18] In 1920, with $15,000 subscribed, the cooperative's first venture, a grocery and meat market, was opened, with plans to open a shoe and dry-goods store; although the initial proposal was for a cooperative department store.[19]

In Chicago a cooperative organized by black alderman Robert Jackson at the Bethel Church in 1919 established two grocery/meat market co-ops within six months in Chicago's black business district. Store No. 1, as it was called, located on East 35th Street, was established in November 1919. The mortgage was quickly paid and the store was said to be a "howling success." Store No. 2, on East 31st Street, was opened in May of the following year. The cooperative had more than 300 members who purchased shares at $5 each. Each share gave the holder an interest in all stores that were opened. The first 1,000 shares were sold in full and a second 1,000 shares were put on sale in May 1920. The strategy was to increase the number of shares sold, which would then lead to increased patronage, more profits, more stores, and more jobs.[20]

When interest was high, cooperatives were established in literally a matter of weeks. In Lexington, Kentucky, a group of 100 black men formed a cooperative. After collecting $2,000 in subscriptions, they opened a grocery store and meat market employing three clerks and a woman bookkeeper.[21] In another instance, black insurance agents in Savannah, Georgia, organized a cooperative that was capitalized at $100,000. They opened a department store that carried dry goods, groceries, and men and women's ready-to-wear apparel, which was said to compare with that in the city's best white department stores; they also had excellent delivery service. The agents accumulated the capital when "going from door to door to sell insurance [they] also sold stock in their company."[22]

The most ambitious cooperative in the country up to this time was the Colored Merchants' Association (CMA), a voluntary chain of black groceries founded in 1928 by A. C. Brown in Montgomery, Alabama. Its purpose was to reduce the operating costs of black retail merchants through cooperative buying.[23] Under the leadership of Albon Holsey, NNBL secretary, the CMA became a national organization that encouraged black grocers to unite in a chain of stores. CMA stores were organized in Montgomery, Birmingham, and Winston-Salem, North Carolina. From May to July 1929, 35 black stores had become CMA members. Eventually CMA stores were opened in most of the major American cities. In the South, CMA stores were established in Dallas, Atlanta, Richmond, Norfolk, Nashville, Louisville, Jackson, Mississippi, and Tulsa, Oklahoma. In the North, there were CMA stores in New York, Brooklyn, Philadelphia, Detroit, Chicago, and Omaha.[24] In October 1929 the CMA established its national headquarters in New York City, along with its first Harlem store.

The CMA required each retail member to purchase one share of CMA stock for $10 and pay a weekly fee of $2 for services provided by CMA. Through its headquarters, the CMA provided training in modern sales techniques and merchandise promotion for its members. In turn, member stores were required to remodel or rearrange their merchandise and displays according to CMA standards with the help of CMA representatives. Other services included market analysis, collective advertising, sales suggestions, collection and credit plans, inventory and bookkeeping systems, and 250 biweekly handbills bearing the retailer's name, address, and telephone number. CMA members were also required to use a uniform system of accounting.[25] In addition, while members used the CMA label, they retained ownership of their stores.[26]

Despite the depression, there were 23 member stores and 2 model stores in Harlem in 1931. With CMA assistance one of the model stores increased its business in one week from $450 to $1,200. One of the reasons for such success was that the association purchased, at quantity discounts, merchandise from wholesalers through competitive bidding. Then, by operating on a cash basis in buying wholesale, CMA was able to secure even larger discounts. Also by 1931, with the increase in CMA store purchases, wholesale grocery houses began to hire black salespeople. In October 1932 CMA opened a warehouse for the purpose of selling CMA brand-label canned goods, coffee, and detergents. Indeed, with the move to sell CMA brand labels, it was reported that in Fort Wayne, Indiana, "Marjorie Wickliffe of Indiana is making plans for a factory. Two hundred and fifty-three CMA stores will buy her mayonnaise made by Wickliffe Manufacturing Company."[27]

By 1933 the depression eventually had an impact on CMA stores. In Harlem, "Three CMA stores owned and operated by C. Benjamin Curley were sold at public auction Tuesday noon. Lack of operating capital was given as the main reason for the failure."[28] Other CMA members withdrew from the cooperative, while few new stores joined. As Albon Holsey, a CMA official, explained, many prospective CMA retailers were in debt to wholesalers, and "some of the wholesalers were racketeering in character. In many instances, the threat of foreclosure was used to prevent them from joining CMA." Also he emphasized that there was a lack of cooperation among CMA members: "efforts to educate black retailers failed. Members refused to attend meetings."

Moreover, the professionalism of CMA management was subject to question, with some members claiming that "white men owned CMA," with Holsey as a front man. Even more, Holsey said that the CMA began to lose the confidence of the black consumer. Some CMA merchants undersold other CMA merchants, he said, "thus causing the Harlem public to feel that we 'didn't know what we were doing.' "[29] In 1936 the warehouse was liquidated. The black economist Abram Harris, assessing the failure of CMA, said members "always found it difficult to sell C.M.A. brands. The Negro, like the white consumer, is habituated to the popular brands carried by the chains."[30]

Despite the CMA failure, from the depression through World War II, blacks continued to organize cooperatives. There were four major kinds of cooperatives organized by blacks: producer, including farm and manufacturing co-ops: wholesale; consumer; and credit union co-ops.[31] Each co-op member paid a minimum fee to join. The combined financial resources were used as venture capital to establish a cooperative business owned by members who share in the profits. The black Florida Farmers' Cooperative Association, a producer co-op founded in 1918, had branches in 10 counties by 1923. In 1941 there were branches in 38 counties, after it expanded with the wholesale distribution of a brand-name syrup, Flocane. It was the only black co-op product handled by Eastern Cooperative Wholesale, Inc., which sold to consumer co-op stores from Maine to Florida.[32]

One of the most progressive black cooperatives was the Columbia, North Carolina, Tyrrell Credit Union, a producer, wholesale, consumer, and credit union cooperative founded in 1938 with $360. By 1946 it had made loans worth $129,000. Membership during that period grew from 22 to 492.[33] The Tyrrell Credit Union funded several cooperative enterprises, including a 588-acre demonstration farm that provided training in modern poultry and dairy methods. A sawmill financed by the co-op produced lumber for both building new homes and restoring the homes of its members. The co-op also underwrote a loan for the purchase of two acres in Columbia's black community for the purpose of establishing retail and service cooperative stores. There were also plans to establish a co-op canning factory, refrigeration plant, storage depot for farm crops, and a hotel and playground.[34]

During the 1930s and 1940s, cooperatives were also established by black colleges. The Community Consumers Cooperative, founded at Georgia State College in 1934, was one of the oldest and the largest. By 1943 it had 700 members from among students, faculty, and the community. Co-op profits were used to construct the Wilcox Gymnasium building and a student union. During the war, members cultivated Victory Gardens and established the Victory Poultry Production Enterprises. In 1943 the $20,061 it made in profits resulted in a five percent dividend paid to its members.[35] Also, during the depression and war years, the People's Cooperative supermarket was in operation at the Tuskegee Institute.

The most common types of cooperatives in the black community were consumer and credit union cooperatives. In consumer co-ops, profits were distributed in two ways: through "patronage refunds," which were based on the amount spent on merchandise purchased from the co-op; and through interest earned on the amount invested. Members also saved on consumer purchases, since goods were sold at the lowest retail prices. An added benefit was that co-op members were assured of the quality of the goods.

Still, some co-ops were successful, others were not. Chicago provides two examples of co-ops that flourished, then fell disbanded. On the city's near South Side, the People's Consumer Cooperative was founded during the depression. Its members were primarily civil service workers who lived in the Rosenwald, a privately owned apartment complex. The co-op grew slowly, but business picked up after World War II, when weekly profits increased from $2,000 in 1945 to $4,676 in 1946.[36] The Altgeld Gardens co-op, located in a public-housing project on Chicago's far South Side, was even more successful in its retail sales, but it had other problems. Shares in the co-op sold for $15, but by 1946 only 300 of the 1,300 families in Altgeld were members. Even with weekly sales of $9,000, the co-op was $13,000 in debt to its wholesaler, the Central States Cooperative, which eventually required that the co-op hire an experienced manager in order to secure future credit.[37] Before 1950, both co-ops were out of business.

The cooperative movement in black America, nonetheless, made great strides throughout the 1930s to the mid-1940s, especially in the number of cooperative credit unions founded by black churches. Members of credit union cooperatives received interest on each share purchased and were entitled to loans without collateral. The Harlem Consumers Cooperative, founded in 1938, encouraged the establishment of church cooperative credit unions, including those of the Abyssinian Baptist Church and the Mt. Olive Baptist Church, both founded in the early 1940s. A credit union co-op associated with a black church in Detroit had 3,000 members.[38]

Interracial cooperatives were also founded, invariably by churches or religious organizations. One of the most successful was the Cooperative Consumers of New Haven, Inc., founded in 1935 with 17 members. One of its leaders was the Reverend R. Foster of the Varick AME Zion Church. By 1943 it had 800 members and operated a supermarket grossing $200,000 annually in sales. Its 479-member Federal Credit Union made loans of $129,727.[39] In Washington, D.C,. the interracial Consumers Cooperative Association (CCA) developed from the Colored Ministers Alliance Emergency Committee of 1935; its store opened in 1938, but operated at a loss until 1944. In Los Angeles the Victory Cooperative supermarket was founded by the black Reverend Clayton D. Russell of the People's Independent Church in 1942. Whites, including other ministers and a university professor provided advice. In its first year, with 17 employees, the co-op grossed $173,000 and had $26,000 in profits.[40]

Black cooperative enterprises were encouraged not only by the comparatively radical DuBois but also by the conservative George Schuyler.[41] One of the reasons for their support was that blacks could combine their capital to form often profitable cooperative ventures that provided alternatives to white stores, which often had high prices and poor-quality merchandise. In 1944 the median volume of business for black corporations was $22,500, and for cooperatives, $12,500; but the figure for partnerships was $3,961, and for sole proprietorships, $3,049.[42] In comparative capital accumulation ventures, the most successful black group enterprises were banks and insurance companies. Yet in 1942, there were only 6 black banks nationwide; whereas, there were 136 black credit unions established in 27 states and Washington, D.C. By 1945 there were 11 black banks, but only 65 black credit unions, as the increasingly urbanized black population deposited their savings in white banks.[43]

Nationally, however, there was a post–World War II decline in co-op ventures and membership.[44] While cooperatives provided economic advantages to their members, blacks, as loyal Americans, were determined to be part of the capitalistic free-enterprise system, pursuing individual avenues to wealth, even when it was to their disadvantage. And so cooperative enterprises, which provided benefits to the poor, were viewed by some blacks as socialist.[45] Paradoxically, cooperative purchases of stock in corporations, which benefited only the rich few, were encouraged. The decline in black participation in consumer and credit union cooperatives during this time stands in contrast to the period between the world wars, when there had been greater economic cohesion among blacks on the periphery of the nation's economy. Black America, however, never developed into what DuBois envisioned as a "co-operative commonwealth."[46] Yet the highly successful Harlem-based Divine Peace Mission Movement, founded during the depression on the principles of communal capitalism, added a new dimension to cooperative ventures.

Divine Peace Mission Movement Cooperatives

The Divine Peace Mission Movement Cooperatives provide an example of the first successful application of mass cooperative principles by a black religious-based organization in developing a chain of successful business enterprises. At its height during the depression, some claimed the movement had a million members. The Peace Mission was loosely organized, however, and it appears the number of hard-core converts, "angels," as they were called, seldom exceeded 4,000. Their leader, Father Divine, who was born George Baker in 1880, claimed more than 20,000 members; this number included whites, who constituted 10 percent of the movement and a few of whom were very wealthy. Most of Father Divine's followers, however, were poor black women.

Initially, Father Divine ran an employment service to provide jobs in domestic services for his poor members, who were required to turn over their salaries to him. His primary economic goal, however, was to organize his angels into groups, establish businesses, and turn over the profits to him. Acting on Father Divine's principle of communal capitalist cooperatives, his angels, who also included men, provided the economic base for the Divine Peace Mission Movement Cooperatives. Under his direction they established profit-making enterprises: restaurants, laundries, dry cleaners, clothing stores, groceries, and supermarkets. The angels also founded construction companies and painting and decorating firms. Angels also established coal businesses, farm cooperatives and even an "industrial village" at High Falls, New York.[47]

The Divine Peace Mission Movement Cooperatives succeeded during the depression by undercutting competition, primarily by providing high-quality goods and services at low prices. Also Father Divine imposed rigid rules of economic cooperation that proved successful: "While followers gave all their money and all their services to the establishment of communalism, they were to take out no profits from their investments but only enough money to supply them with barest necessities."[48] Surely, Father Divine was a capitalist. He used profits from these enterprises to support the organization he headed. Through his ownership of hotels and apartments, he provided housing for the homeless. Indeed, he was said to be Harlem's leading landlord. He also provided food for the hungry—during the 1930s, 2,500 free meals a day. He also gave jobs to the unemployed and even provided alcohol counseling. All of Father Divine's social welfare efforts attracted national attention.

His wealth, although derived from profit-making enterprises and the contributions of wealthy whites, was a source of controversy. Moreover, despite his philanthropic works and self-help enterprises, Father Divine was attacked for the rigid discipline he imposed on his converts, which included celibacy. Also, his insistence that his followers accept him as God generated controversy, hostility, scandal, lawsuits, and attacks from both the black and white press, especially from the Hearst newspaper chain. And while Father Divine denounced racism, he incensed the black press by blaming blacks for their impoverishment. With such views, perhaps he should be recognized as an early black conservative. Also, he could be considered a proponent of Afrocentrism for his opinion that the impoverishment of blacks was a result of internalizing the negativity associated with being black. His solution was that people of African descent should deny that they were black, at least within the negative context of the term as it used by whites. Such a denial would thus break the negative image that whites associated with the idea of "blackness."

Through his preachings, Father Divine was doubtless among the first blacks to introduce "New Thought" economic principles to the black masses.[49] These teachings held that blacks could use their mental capacities and positive thinking to achieve wealth, principles that had significant appeal not only to impoverished blacks but also to some whites. Today, the core of his message, which is reflected by conservative black thinkers who also blame blacks for their low economic status, has won considerable approbation, even from conservative whites. Simply put, Father Divine commanded his converts to work hard and prosper: "My mind is that everyone of you should be practical, profitable . . . and produce more and earn more." Indeed, the words of one church hymn were, "If you say you love Him [Father Divine], Get a Job and Go to Work."[50] Conversion to Father Divine's movement required that his angels avoid welfare, which, he said, "is unevangelical, contrary to this Christ teaching."[51]

By 1942, with improved economic conditions, interest in the Divine Peace Mission Movement declined along with a drop in membership and few new converts. While the movement was often called a "chain-store religion," Father Divine's promotion of business ranks him among the more successful of that special genre of "Think and Grow Rich" motivational speakers. Despite the decline, he should be remembered not only for his encouragement of black business participation but also for the direction and financial backing he provided the business enterprises established by his angels. His financial success, exemplified chiefly by his home in Hyde Park, New York, close to that of Franklin D. Roosevelt's, only enhanced the credibility of his promoting the benefits of positive thinking as the first step to securing wealth (and some people thought he even owned his own plane).[52] And his legacy has survived. Even as late as 1953, the Divine Peace Mission Movement Cooperatives owned several hundred businesses in major urban centers, from Harlem to Los Angeles; and the movement continues to own property in the late 1990s.

Policy Enterprises—The Numbers Racket

The illegal enterprises of blacks, especially policy or the numbers game, in which comparatively large numbers of blacks were profitably employed, could be considered a form of cooperative venture. Policy could be profitable in several ways. Once the money was pooled by playing the numbers, as with the lottery, policy enterprises paid off more profitably than cooperatives, especially for the "bank" operators who ran the wheel that gave the winning numbers. Other employees were well paid, including the numbers runners, people who took the numbers, collected the money, and made the payoffs; people skilled in law and accounting were also involved in the operation. Players also had a chance of succeeding against the odds. Usually 40 percent of the daily "investors" won, occasionally taking a profit of as much as 600 percent on a penny's investment. While a wheel was used in Chicago for determining payoff numbers, which some players accused of being fixed, in Harlem winning numbers were always the last three digits of the daily Federal Reserve Clearing House report published in the newspapers.[53]

African-Americans started playing the numbers game in the late nineteenth century. In Chicago, although it was declared illegal in 1905, the game continued under black control until the 1920s. Then, white gangsters, expanding on their illegal bootlegging operations, attempted control when they saw the game's enormous profitability. In Harlem after the repeal of Prohibition in the 1930's the gangster Dutch Schultz practically eliminated the black policy bankers. Using armed force and organization, Schultz forced blacks out as independent operators. With few exceptions, those who remained stayed as salaried employees in an operation that generated $20 million annually.[54]

In Chicago, blacks managed to hold onto the numbers games much longer. Even so, whites managed to gain a foothold. In 1931 a group of 15 men, including 12 blacks, formed a syndicate to control the numbers game. This included paying off an estimated $40,000 a week to the forces of law and order—judges, the police, aldermen, and other politicians, for protection from legal harassment.[55]

The most successful black policy operators in Chicago during this time were the three Jones brothers, educated sons of an highly respected minister. As did most black policy kings, they established legitimate businesses from their profits, which provided additional employment for blacks. In 1937 they opened the Jones Brothers Ben Franklin Store, the city's "only colored variety store," in the heart of the black business district on 47th Street. While only a "medium-sized" variety store, with an "outlay of $100,000," it was the first large black-owned retail business in the district.[56] Thousands attended the opening, including world heavyweight champion Joe Louis and Bill "Bojangles" Robinson, who won fame as Shirley Temple's tap-dancing partner. In addition, the Jones Boys, as they were also called, owned a modern food store and in 1939 expanded their real estate operations by constructing the Ultra Moderne Small Apartments on the second floor of their 47th Street building.[57]

The Jones Boys amassed millions of dollars from their policy operations before white gangsters succeeded in taking over in the early 1940s; one brother was killed and the others fled to Mexico after one brother was released from jail after "taking the rap" for the family's collective income tax evasion activities. Like most black policy operators, the Jones Boys were armed, but they did not have the firepower that backed white gangsters then or black gangs today who are often armed with AK-47s, Uzis, and MAC-10 submachine guns. Among blacks, policy was "clean," an activity that was illegal but not prone to excessive violence.[58]

In the 1930s and 1940s, black policy kings were regarded as heroes in the black community not only for their ability to generate wealth but also for their substantial philanthropic contributions to black institutions and organizations, as well as their political connections, often used to secure patronage jobs for blacks.[59] If policy operations were compared to legitimate business enterprises, policy would have ranked as one of the country's largest black businesses in terms of management size, numbers of employees, and profits. In 1938 there were 483 policy stations in Chicago that employed 5,000 people, "with a weekly payroll of $25,885 and an annual gross of at least $18,000,000."[60] The average weekly take of these policy stations was $6,000, with the owners netting about $3,000 each (see table 8.5). Legitimate businessmen who allowed policy stations to be set up in their shops earned 25 percent of the gross profits generated at the stations.[61]

While Chicago policy operations alone generated $18 million in 1938, the country's leading black enterprises, eating and drinking establishments— which ranked first in the number of nationwide enterprises, 12,610, and employed the largest number of people, 8,385, in 1939—generated an aggregate *national* income of only $26.5 million (see table 8.4). Yet despite the profits made and employment provided, policy is viewed in American business history as an inconsequential cottage industry, limited in operations and profits as part of the informal economy of the black community.[62] The term *informal economy* was probably developed in a Third World context, applied to those sectors of the urban economy that do not appear in national statistics of Third World governments. As the definition of informal economy developed, it was used in reference to: "Ways of making a living

TABLE 8.5   *The Chicago Syndicate** "Employees and Estimated Wages in Policy Racket for One Week: 1938," and "Financial Analysis of Three Policy Companies for One Week: 1938"

Number of policy stations	483	
Median number of employees per station	3.5	
Median wage per employee	$9.00	
Total wages paid		$15,214.50
Number of pick-up men	189	
Median wage	$33.00	
Total wages paid		$3,597.00
Number of checkers/clerks	125	
Median wage	$25.00	
Total wages paid		3,125.00
Number of doormen, floormen, janitors, stampers, and others	118	
Median wage	$15.00	
Total wages paid		1,770.00
Commissions to walking writers	$2,075	2,178.75
Grand Total of Wages Paid Weekly		$25,885.25

Interstate Company

Income		Expenditures	
Approximate weekly "take"	$6,000.00	Weekly salary of Checkers	$265.00
Approximate expenditures	3,085.00	Pick-up men	170.00
Approximate weekly net income of owner	2,915.00	Rent (owns building)	—
		Political payoff**	250.00
		Hits, 40% of take	$2,400.00
			$3,085.00

East 7 West Company

Income		Expenditures	
Approximate weekly "take"	$7,200.00	Weekly salary of Checkers	$240.00
Approximate expenditures	3,797.00	Pick-up men	135.00
Approximate weekly net income of owner	3,403.00	Manager, 10%	372.00
		Political payoff	250.00
		Hits, 40% of take	$2,800.00
			$3,797.00

Monte Carlo Company

Income		Expenditures	
Approximate weekly "take"	$6,000.00	Weekly salary of Checkers	$230.00
Approximate expenditures	3,250.00	Pick-up men	310.00
Approximate weekly net income of owner	2,750.00	Rent (owns building)	60.00
(Two owners, each receive)	1,375.00	Political payoff	250.00
		Hits, 40% of take	$2,400.00
			$3,250.000

Source: St. Clair Drake and Horace Cayton, *Black Metropolis: A Study of Negro Life in a Northern City*, rev. and enl. ed. (Chicago: University of Chicago, 1993), 479–80.

*The Syndicate was established in 1931. The policy racket or "numbers game" was "organized as a cartel with a syndicate of fifteen men (including twelve Negroes) in control of the game."

**Political payoff in 1938 was estimated at $30,000–$40,000 weekly.

outside the formal wage economy, either as an alternative to it, or as a means of supplementing income earned within it."[63]

Within this context, the numbers racket provides an American model of an industry that operated in the American informal economy. Yet what is especially significant in twentieth-century black business history is the extent to which informal, often illegal, business activities, including policy, provided venture capital for the establishment of many legitimate black enterprises. Some notable black entrepreneurs built legitimate businesses on profits made from enterprises considered less than respectable and often illegal. Robert Church used the profits from the gambling activities in his Beale Street saloons as venture capital for the million-dollar real estate empire he established in the late nineteenth century.

In Chicago increased capital for the bank established by Jesse Binga in 1908 was said to have come from his wife's $200,000 inheritance from her father, John "Mushmouth" Johnson, who had been the gambling kingpin on Chicago's South Side.[64] Indeed, in the first half of the twentieth century, policy money also funded the establishment of various legitimate enterprises in the black community. And in the 1930s and early 1940s, it was said that, "About twenty per cent of the largest Negro business enterprises, and those most conscious of the value of public goodwill, are owned by policy people."[65] Without these funds the picture of black business in the first half of the twentieth century would be even more dismal than the historical record shows.

Access to black policy dollars provided black communities with a privately funded, informal cash subsidy, which was used as venture capital in the promotion and support of black business; this reality must be factored in when analyzing black business activity in this period.[66] Within this context, black business history becomes a record of economic strategies devised by black Americans to establish themselves, either through a formal or informal enterprise, in the profitable game of American capitalism. By the 1940s then, one cannot ignore how the economic recovery of blacks from the depression proceeded as much from their own efforts as from state and federal relief programs, in addition to their participation in World War II on both the battlefront and the home front.[67]

World War II and the National Negro Business League

During World War II, promoting the recovery and expansion of black business, along with capturing the black consumer market, were major goals of the National Negro Business League (NNBL).[68] At its 1940 conference, which met in Detroit at the invitation of the Booker T. Washington Trade Association, the NNBL's theme was "Present Trends and Opportunities for Negroes in Business," with seminar topics such as "What Improved Business Techniques Are Needed in Negro Business Today?" In addition to businesspeople, blacks who worked with various federal agencies, the FCA, the WPA, and the Census Bureau, including Emmer Martin Lancaster, advisor on Negro affairs for the Department of Commerce, also attended the conference. Consequently, the government's position, which centered more on how blacks should respond to the war than on the recovery of black business, was subtly represented and promoted in the proceedings.

Aubrey Williams of the National Youth Administration emphasized that while business training was important as a basis for the improvement of black businesspeople, education for young people must teach them "to think accurately and most of all in these trying times, to distinguish between truth and propaganda. They must not be led astray by false prophets who have them believe the democratic ideal is not a workable one." His theme was reflected in the greetings to the NNBL by President Roosevelt. In the preface to his remarks on where blacks should stand during the war, he first acknowledged "The principles laid down by your illustrious founder and first president, Booker T. Washington, and carried on through the efforts of your league to advance the economic progress of the country." Then Roosevelt cautioned the NNBL that its position on the war should reflect national policy: "Particularly in this period of discord and suffering abroad we in America should stand together to preserve the principles of freedom and tolerance that are the American way in life."[69]

Until America entered the war in 1941 the NNBL found it difficult to reconcile the nation's emphasis on preserving freedom and democracy for Europeans with the persistent racism and intolerance confronting blacks at home. At its January 1941 conference, NNBL president Dr. Joseph Edison Walker (1880–1958) invoked the religious foundation of African-American culture to frame the organization's stand on the war, even suggesting that blacks take the position of Christian pacifists: "our greatest strength lies in our spiritual character and nothing should be done by our government to undermine this great inheritance." Yet Walker also encouraged blacks to support America's war policy: "our government is pledging its resources and skill to help the democratic countries which are engaged in this struggle. At times our patriotism and loyalty are put to severe test; however, we shall not allow prejudice nor discrimination to deter us from the path of duty followed by our forefathers—'America First.'"[70]

Once America entered World War II, the NNBL threw its full support behind the war effort. The theme of the 1942 NNBL Conference held in Chicago was "Gearing Negro Business to A War-Time Economy." Among the topics explored were "The Impact of the War on Small Business Enterprises," "Gearing Local Business Groups for the War Effort," and "After the War: What in Education?" In his keynote address, Dr. F. D. Patterson, president of Tuskegee Institute, emphasized that black America must be allowed full participation in the war effort, saying "that racial morale cannot be preserved with less than full participation in all branches of industry and the fighting forces." At the same time, he urged black businesspeople to capitalize on the wartime earnings of black consumers by providing "the commodities and personal services required by the new buying power of colored people in dense areas."

Also at the three-day 1942 conference, the National Negro Housewives League, a group that promoted and supported black businesses, met in conjunction with the NNBL, which it had done annually since its founding in 1932. One of its annual projects was the sponsoring of a scrapbook contest for school children on the theme "The Negro Economic Progress." At its 1942 meeting, however, the principal speaker was Dr. Mae McCarroll of the Planned Parenthood Federation of America. Her topic, described by one newspaper as a somewhat "unusual subject," at least for a business conference, emphasized "the importance of placing technical information on parenthood in the hands of those in lower economic levels." This view found support from Fannie B. Peck of Detroit, national president of the housewives league who, in her speech, "The Colored Woman in the War Emergency," reviewed the black woman's advancement in businesses. She also urged "Negro women to assume their rightful places in the newer responsibilities facing all womankind." These women no doubt were promoting delayed motherhood as a patriotic gesture, which would allow more women to be available to work in defense plants or even serve in the armed services.[71]

The attempts of black women during World War II to contribute to business-related areas of the war effort were not always successful, especially their attempts to participate in white women's business organizations. In 1943, New York City's Mid-Town Business and Professional Women's Club, founded in 1942, sued the state organization, the New York State Federation of Business and Professional Women's Clubs, charging that it was denied affiliation because it had two black members: Anna Arnold Hedgeman, regional director for race relations of the Office of Civilian Defense, and Marguerite Roach, a war plant stenographer. In its defense the state organization said the Mid-Town Club was never a member and had no grounds to sue, and that the national charter granted them "was just a clerical error." The state organization also denied that it was racist, noting "We have no bias against Negroes. We had a Negro member in 1919 and we have one now."[72]

The NNBL had included women in its activities since before 1915. At the 1943 conference a committee appointed by NNBL president Walker to study the field of manufacturing among Negroes, "with a view to encouraging the establishment of more such enterprises," included several black businesswomen, the most notable being Sarah Spencer Washington, founder of the Apex Beauty System. Also Dr. Charlotte Hawkins Brown, founder and president of the Palmer Memorial Institute, gave the principal address, entitled "Courtesy, An Asset in Business."[73] The 1943 NNBL Conference was also significant in that Walker reversed his earlier position on the role of the black church in the war effort: "We have arrived at the point where we should build smoke-stacks as well as church steeples."[74]

While the NNBL promoted black business advancement, at the same time it was denounced for the conservative position taken on racial inequities faced by blacks on the home front. Indeed, a resolution proposing that the NNBL protest "against the continuance of the mob law in the south which denies justice to the Negro even in these days of war for the preservation of democracy" was ruled out of order by President Walker. Despite vehement objections to the arbitrary ruling from Professors Walter Chivers of Morehouse College and V. V. Oaks of Wilberforce College, Walker emphasized that the NNBL's main purpose was economic advancement.[75] But in response to the nationwide race riots that erupted in 1943, Walker said "a race riot can, 'in one bloody night, undo a trade balance which required a decade to build.' "[76]

A "trade balance" involving black Americans! Just what was the NNBL president talking about? Doubtless, his statement was a response to government reports concerning the black consumer market, discussed by black leaders as early as 1940. At a meeting that year of the Hampton University Association of New York, its president emphasized the spending power of blacks in the South's 17 largest cities, explaining that "blacks consumed $2,000,000,000 worth of goods annually, two and one-half times greater than our exports to Great Britain, France, Germany, Poland and Finland, which in 1938 totaled $800,000,000." He explained that America had sustained an enormous financial loss by keeping blacks in a subordinate economic position: "within our own borders lies one of the greatest markets still undeveloped. This consumer outlet, represented by our Negro population, would expand in enormous proportion with the advancement of their living standards."[77]

In 1942 David Sullivan, said to be the "leading authority of colored business," reported that the gross income of blacks was $7 billion. He also noted that blacks spent 42 percent of this on consumer goods and services, an amount that "exceeded nearly two and one half times the total American exports to South America."[78] Interestingly, in 1942 the New York State Chamber of Commerce elected C. C. Spaulding, former president of the NNBL and president of North Carolina Mutual Life, to its membership. He said that this membership provided a black person with an opportunity to sit in meetings with "the giants of

American commerce [as they] discuss problems of the economic welfare of our country."[79] Doubtless, "the giants of American commerce" viewed Spaulding's membership more as a link to black consumers than as an opportunity to develop plans for a joint effort of black and white American business to fight the war.

Consequently, while the NNBL promoted black support of the war, it was as concerned as the New York Chamber of Commerce in developing the means by which the war could be used to advance business, specifically black business, even if that meant downplaying black opposition to white racism. Walker explained in his 1943 presidential address that the NNBL must "assume leadership in a program to build factories, to manufacture some of the necessities of life and thereby consolidate the gains and experience acquired in the war emergency." The NNBL viewed the war as opening new avenues of business advancement for blacks as well as providing employment for them. As he said, the war effort could provide thousands of blacks with the opportunity to learn valuable skills in fields such as welding and aeronautical mechanics: "How may we consolidate these industrial gains and use this experience to further the progress of the Negroes." Walker also proposed that at the war's end blacks should cash in their war bonds and use them as venture capital to build factories to manufacture basic consumer goods for blacks.[80]

Blacks were large purchasers of Liberty Bonds, and during the war the NNBL and other black organizations and financial institutions promoted the purchase of war bonds and stamps for two purposes: to support the war effort and to provide savings to be used after the war for the development and expansion of black business. Saving stamps and bonds went on public sale in May 1941.

By 1944 black insurance companies "held upwards of $18,000,000 worth of war bonds and seven Negro banks have around $6,000,000 invested." Black businesspeople also used their influence to promote the sale of war bonds. By 1944 black Philadelphia entrepreneur R. R. Wright, then 88 years old, had "sold $2,500,000" worth of government bonds. In 1944, with the money raised by the sale of war bonds to blacks, the Negro Chamber of Commerce of Shreveport, Louisiana, along with Office of Civilian Defense block leaders, underwrote the "purchase of a fighter plane to be named the "Negro Chamber of Commerce of Shreveport," which cost around $75,000.[81] Yet while black Americans and the NNBL threw their support behind the war effort, the federal government was limited in its reciprocity, especially in areas that could promote the advancement of black business.

Black Business Defense Contracts

While the war effort produced a tremendous upswing in the nation's economy, black business profits increased but were minimal compared to that earned by white American business. In Birmingham a two-day joint conference on black business, designated as a "wartime clinic," was held in 1943. It was sponsored by the NNBL, the Negro Division of the U.S. Department of Commerce, and the Birmingham Negro Business League. One of black America's leading entrepreneurs, A. G. Gaston, was president of the latter organization and vice president of the NNBL. Black and white government officials participated, presenting the papers entitled "How Small Businesses May Turn Their Productions to the War," "The Procurement of Government Supplies," and "Financing Negro War Production Enterprises."[82]

Statistics on black business activity during World War II, however, fail to reveal attempts made by black manufacturers to secure federal defense contracts. All of the studies of black economic activities during World War II have emphasized the access by blacks to industrial employment as a result of Executive Order 8802, effective 25 June 1941. It was the response of President Roosevelt to labor leader A. Philip Randolph, who threatened to lead a march on Washington unless the government mandated that companies with defense contracts hire blacks.[83] But Executive Order 8802 made no provision for providing defense contracts to black manufacturers.[84]

Consequently, while black business activity did increase during the war, only a few black manufacturers, most of them discussed later in this section, secured defense contracts. Even after the war, blacks claimed that "When colored small businessmen tried to get some of the wartime contracts floating around the Capital, they were given the brush-off." Also, it appeared that blacks in the federal government failed to provide any assistance. In one instance, a group of black owners of small, independent machine shops and industrial plants in Harlem sent George Harris, a leading businessman in the city, to Washington to lobby for defense contracts for blacks. He failed, with one reason being that the " 'black cabinet' steered clear of Harris and gave him no help, declaring this was not in their line."[85]

Even as the nation prepared for war, the federal government was not receptive to black businesses bidding on defense contracts. In 1940 the black-owned Glover Institute of Technical Design and Garment Making located in Los Angeles "entered bids for the making of army and CCC uniforms." The company was said to be "the first Negro firm in the West to seek a governmental contract in open bidding under the National Defense Industries set-up." It had 13 machines of all types that could manufacture uniforms, overcoats, caps, and jackets. The company's first bid, however, was rejected. The lowest bid proposed contracts worth a minimum of $100,000.[86]

The American Enterprises Association of Toledo, Ohio, which was organized in 1940 to secure a government contract, put in a low bid for the manufacture of 5,000 army overcoats. The bid was rejected "because the factory was not then ready." The company reapplied in 1941 but was notified by the Defense Contract Service two weeks before the bid that "it could not bid on army clothing contracts because of 'considerable unemployment' within the industry." A month later the government rescinded its order and invited the company to bid on 35,000 wool overcoats. But while the company was the low bidder— "68 cents lower [per unit] than the next lowest bidder" —it did not get the contract.

This sort of racial discrimination by the government was so blatant that Michigan Congressman Albert J. Engel took up the cause of the American Enterprises Association. He emphasized the extent to which it could provide employment to some of the 17,000 blacks in Toledo who found it difficult to get jobs outside of either the NYA or WPA. He noted too that a company spokesman said that had they been given the contract, "it could have commenced production within thirty days and employed up to 500 of Toledo's unemployed Negroes." In 1942, Engel launched an attack on the government for the racial discrimination that it allowed to exist in defense industries. He noted that many Toledo industries with defense contracts refused to hire blacks, although there were "9,000 white women employed in Toledo factories, many making defense materials."

As Engel said, while black manufacturers were discriminated against in securing defense contracts, at the same time "the government is letting, or will let, contracts for over 56,300,000 items of clothing which cannot possibly be made by the groups within the industry itself." Engel also denounced the duplicitous acts of the federal government in inviting blacks to bid for defense contracts that had little chance to be awarded. Of the Toledo company he said, "this group who have been encouraged by the government for over a year, followed instructions, mortgaged their homes, spent money, took up collections in churches—nickels, dimes, and quarters—to pay the expenses of representatives here, are unable to obtain a contract for one overcoat or able to earn $1 in the defense industry."[87]

Throughout the war the American Enterprises Association continued to submit bids. Finally, four years after its first bid, the company was awarded a government contract in March 1944 for the manufacture of 16,000 garments, becoming, "one of the few Negro-owned and operated war plants [that] produces military garments under United States army and lend-lease contracts." Five months later, the company got another government contract for 30,000 garments. The company president, Olander J. Smith, a Northwestern University Law School graduate, employed all races. Of his production record, Smith said "Since March the United States Quartermaster Inspection Division has not rejected a single garment of the association. They have given us a perfect production record."[88]

Of the few black manufacturers to get a government defense contract, one of the more successful was the Pacific Parachute Company. Organized in Los Angeles in 1942 with $3,000 in investment capital and a factory with only "nine sewing machines on one floor," its president, 29-year-old Howard "Skippy" Smith, was said to be the "youngest war manufacturer in the county." His first 16 employees, mostly women, had been trained to operate sewing machines on an NYA project. The Pacific Parachute Company succeeded initially in securing a defense contract because its founding began with a subcontract from a company with a defense contract.[89] By 1945 the company had grown into a $500,000 concern, with 200 employees of all races. Within a year, however, both the Pacific Parachute Company and the American Enterprises Association were out of business: "the two better known manufacturing industries that did enter the field failed after making strong efforts."[90]

Moreover, in just seven years after the war the two companies apparently had been all but forgotten, as evidenced by a statement in a black newspaper in 1952: "Only one Negro has been widely publicized for receiving a contract from the Federal Government." He was George J. Washington, at that time a 49-year-old Chicago shirt manufacturer who, during the war, was "reportedly the only Negro shirt manufacturer in the United States." His company reported that it "made more than a million shirts for the armed forces under a military contract."[91] Washington started his company in the late 1930s, and by 1954 he was the nation's only black shirt manufacturer. His Washington Shirt Manufacturing Company earned net profits of $750,000, had a payroll of over $85,000, and had annual sales of over two million shirts. Before, during, and after the war, Washington's trademark Dunbar shirts (after black poet Paul Laurence Dunbar) were sold in many of the country's leading department stores.[92]

It appears that black businesses with an established pre–World War II record of successful operations were those few that secured government contracts. Aside from shirt manufacturing, most were in construction, especially those that submitted bids for building military installations. Architect Paul R. Williams was one of the most successful black businessmen in securing government defense contracts. He was associate architect for a $12 million United States Navy base on the West Coast, in addition to two naval air bases. As chief architect, he also designed 1,000 homes in Los Angeles, 400 in Nevada, and 300 at Fort Huachuca, Arizona.[93] The Nashville-based, black-owned McKissick Brothers Construction Company, founded in 1909, won a $4 million defense contract in 1941 to build a 2,000-acre airfield and air base at Tuskegee Institute for the training of the black 99th Pursuit Squadron. In constructing the four mile-long runways, the company employed 1,900 workers, including about 450 black carpenters in addition to black electricians, plumbers, and masons.[94]

The less well-known New York-based Phenix Color and Chemical Company, founded in 1922 by Jamaican-born Dr. Thomas M. Williams, who earned his doctorate in chemistry from McGill University, also expanded its business during the war, as it began "to work for the United States Government and its allies in doing research work in the testing of high octane gases, color pigments, paints for camouflage and various biological stains." Before World War II Williams's company had supplied gasoline bleaches and dyes and did research for the nation's largest industrial firms and oil refineries, including Ford, Standard Oil, Shell, Socony Vacuum, and units of the Servel Oil Company and the Globe Oil Company.[95]

Also during World War II the federal government, through the War Food Administration (WFA), negotiated a lease with the black-owned Kerford Quarry Stone Mining Company in Atchison, Kansas. The 1944 lease was for use of the company's limestone caves by the federal government for the storage of foodstuffs, in addition to experimental wool and cotton. With blast refrigeration, the cave could be cooled from its normal 50 degrees to 30 degrees, consequently converting the cavern's storage capacity of 1.4 million square feet to the equivalent of 3,500 refrigerator freight cars. With conversion, the Kerford caves would increase by "one tenth ... the total refrigeration space now available to the government." Construction of a storage plant equal in size to the caves, according to WFA officials, would cost $15 million.[96]

The initiative for the lease was led by Claude Barnett of the Associated Negro Press (ANP), but his initial efforts to interest the Department of War to lease or buy the caves for storage of ammunition failed. Barnett then appealed to the secretary of agriculture, for whom he was the black adviser. Impressed with the caves' storage potential, the secretary recommended purchase, but a lease was eventually negotiated. The government spent $2 million to put the caves in shape, but the project was abandoned in August 1945; although in 1950 a proposal was put before the Senate to purchase the caves.[97]

This lease is relevant to black business history because when it was negotiated it was "one of the largest transactions negotiated by the government with a Negro business concern since the beginning of the war." Also, the Kerford Quarry Stone Mining Company was "one of the largest single businesses owned and operated by Negroes in the United States." In the mining of nonmetallic limestone, the company was classified as a heavy industry. It employed both blacks and whites and had "as many as 300 men on their payroll."

The lease negotiated by the black-owned Kerford Company and even the company itself provide another example of black business activity that has been lost to the historical record. Any analysis of African-American business that relies on statistics, quite accurately, chart a very dismal picture of black enterprises. These statistics, however, do not reveal the dynamism and pervasiveness of black business endeavors. This limitation results in erroneous assessments that make it appear that black businesses were limited to only seven types of basic retail and service enterprises. Reliance on statistics alone, then, fails to show the historic persistence of blacks in their many attempts to establish enterprises in areas besides the retail and service industries.

World War II Black Businesses

In 1943 a survey made by NNBL president J. E. Walker showed that "a high percentage of Negro retail enterprises are surviving the impact of the war, with those in many areas showing substantial increases."[98] A year later, the most comprehensive study of black business was made by Joseph Pierce, who confirmed Walker's conclusions. Pierce's survey was conducted among 3,866 businesses that, with the exception of Cincinnati, were located in 11 cities in former slave states (see tables 8.6 and 8.7). Pierce's survey found that there was a 74 percent increase in black business sales from 1941 to 1944, that 7 percent showed a decline, and 19 percent showed no change.[99] The three categories of general businesses established by Pierce included 99 different kinds of establishments. Retail enterprises constituted 42.5 percent, service enterprises, 48 percent, and miscellaneous enterprises, 9.5 percent. The leading enterprises in annual dollar volume were barber and beauty shops, which made up 25 percent of the total, followed by cleaning and pressing operations, confectioneries, groceries, drugstores, and filling stations.[100] Only hair shops and funeral parlors did not compete with comparable white businesses.[101]

Black undertakers represented the only business group in which the percentage of blacks in that industry was equal to the percentage of blacks in the American population. There were approximately 3,000 black undertakers, constituting one-tenth of all American undertakers.[102] Also this group, "with a median annual volume of $8,240.50," had the largest volume of business in the service enterprises, while the most numerous, barber, beauty, and cleaning shops, "reported median volumes of $2,350, $2,025, and $2,774.50 respectively." The sales of groceries and eating enterprises—$4,199.50 and $3,274.50, respectively—constituted 75 percent of the total retail sales, while liquor stores showed a median annual volume of business of $12,499.50 and bars, $9,299.50. In the miscellaneous category, life insurance branch offices and casket factories showed "median annual volumes of over $25,000."[103]

War rationing had an adverse impact on black America's most profitable service business, mortuary enterprises. In 1944 the Office of Defense Transportation ordered a "drastic reduction in the amount of gasoline allotted to funeral homes ... for the second quarter of this year." All funeral homes were affected, but the impact on black establishments was greater than on white-owned ones. In Alabama the Montgomery Funeral Directors Association, an organization of five black funeral homes, announced a cutback in services. Since most blacks did not own cars, black funeral homes provided transportation to insurance companies to help them file claims, to county offices to file death certificates, and to

TABLE 8.6   Black Businesses and Annual Median Sales Volume in 12 Cities, 1944

City	Number of Businesses	Median Annual Volumes of Business			
		Retail ($)	Service ($)	Miscellaneous ($)	All ($)
Atlanta	843	3,864.79	3,399.50	3,782.11	3,834.80
Baltimore	124	15,832.83	9,599.50	20,624.50	13,803.85
Cincinnati	185	2,383.72	2,310.14	4,999.50	2,377.72
Durham	170	3,447.78	3,749.50	3,905.75	3,377.72
Houston	282	2,556.32	2,155.17	6,240.50	2,377.72
Memphis	506	2,732.06	1,905.74	4,687.00	2,283.33
Nashville	162	1,776.32	1,466.35	6,666.17	1,715.43
New Orleans	252	2,133.62	1,709.18	7,499.50	1,902.52
Richmond	241	3,666.17	1,958.76	5,312.00	2,308.47
Savannah	203	2,392.24	2,726.77	7,499.50	2,783.59
St. Louis	244	4,909.22	3,046.48	16,666.17	4,016.17
Washington	694	9,999.50	3,693.94	5,535.21	4,448.02
All cities	3,866	3,579.05	2,496.66	7,245.26	3,260.01

Source: Joseph Pierce, *Negro Business and Business Education* (New York: Harper and Brothers, 1947), 72.

TABLE 8.7   Percentage Sales to Blacks at Black- and White-
Owned Stores, 1944

Types of Goods or Services Purchased	Percent of Sales to Black Consumers	
	Black Stores	White Stores
Groceries	27.9	72.1
Drugstores	41.1	58.9
Men's clothing	0.9	99.1
Women's clothing	1.1	98.9
Children's clothing	1.0	99.0
Men's shoes	0.6	99.4
Women's shoes	0.3	99.7
Children's shoes	1.0	99.0
Furniture	2.9	97.1
Hardware	4.3	95.7
Household supplies	15.9	84.1
Flowers	47.0	53.0
Car repairs	41.8	58.2
Gas, oil, etc.	54.8	45.2
Shoe repairs	75.0	25.0
Cleaning/pressing	74.4	25.6
Tailoring	80.3	19.7
All types	27.6	72.4

Source: Joseph Pierce, Negro Business and Business Education (New York:
Harper and Brothers, 1947), 52.

train and bus stations and rural areas to pick up family members. In announcing the changes the association said, "We have a war to win and sacrifice must be made."[104]

While black funeral-home owners made sacrifices, the mortuary business remained one of the most profitable for blacks, since the wakes of most blacks were conducted by black morticians. In 1939 there were 3,000 black funeral directors and 1,258 funeral homes. The number of blacks who died from 1936 to 1939 was estimated to be around 182,000. With average funeral costs in 1941 of about $100, black funeral-home owners grossed in the neighborhood of $18.2 million. Also, blacks spent approximately $6.4 million annually on caskets, embalming fluids, and accessories.[105]

In the 12 cities studied by Pierce, there were only 19 manufacturers: 1 each that made flowers, cabinets, food, chemicals, and hair preparations; there were 5 casket manufacturers and 8 cosmetic manufacturers.[106] Service and retail enterprises, then, dominated the black business picture in 1944, underscoring the continued difficulties faced by blacks in establishing viable manufacturing enterprises. Moreover, during World War II white businesses continued to capture the black-consumer dollar (see table 8.7). Also, while some blacks were forced out of business during the war because they were too successful, there was an overall growth in the black economy during this time. Urban population shifts during World War II also encouraged black business expansion. In New York, as whites moved out of one Bronx neighborhood, many businesses closed, but "among the newcomers [was] a large proportion of enterprising Negroes."[107] Also, as black employment increased in heavy defense industries located on the edge of major cities, the move of blacks to the suburbs encouraged the development and expansion of black businesses in those areas.

In the Detroit suburbs of River Rouge and Ecorse, where there were 15,000 blacks in a total population of almost 34,000, a thriving black business community developed that replicated urban black business districts. In those suburbs about 12 to 15 grocery stores, 2 shoe repair shops, 4 beauty shops, 2 restaurants, 2 hotels that also served food, 4 cleaning and pressing shops, 1 furniture upholstery shop, 1 drugstore, 6 beer taverns, and several service stations were established. There was also a black hospital owned by a black doctor and staffed by black nurses and a dietitian.[108]

The war also contributed to the development and expansion of black businesses in the territories of Hawaii and Alaska. In 1944 the Smith Harlem Dispensary was the largest black business on the island of Oahu. In addition to several black restaurants and a retail clothing store, the black-owned El Morocco Club employed 21 of the 50 people who worked in black businesses in Hawaii.[109] In Alaska the largest number of blacks in business were women who opened boardinghouses. In 1929 Alabama-born Zulu Swanson moved to Alaska from Oregon, where she had worked as a domestic before opening a cleaning establishment. With profits from the sale of that business, Swanson settled in Anchorage and bought a 9-room boardinghouse, which she expanded to 23 rooms. She said that by establishing boardinghouses in response to the construction boom of World War II, "almost overnight, our patient and far-seeing women became financially independent."[110]

Black GIs and Business

Over 1.2 million African-Americans served in the military during World War II, many of whom for the first time had a disposal income. With few places to spend their pay and with fewer consumer goods available to purchase, most of them sent the money to their dependents or saved it.[111] The finance departments of the military provided lectures on how the servicemen could use their savings after the war. In the Pacific, First Lieutenant Dunbar McLaurin served as a war bonds officer in the finance department of General MacArthur's staff: "His mission was touring the Pacific giving lectures to Negro troops on saving their funds and in this effort he was accredited with having sold over $2,000,000 worth of bonds."[112] In 1940, McLaurin, at the age of 21, had been the youngest person to earn a Ph.D. from the University of Illinois. His field was economics.

Black servicemen expressed a tremendous interest in establishing businesses after the war, as indicated in a study made in 1945 that found that "Experience or no experience, Negro GIs want to go into business for themselves in postwar America."[113] The study showed that 12 percent of them, 144,000 men, had plans for owning a business after the war, with "some 84,000 having definite plans, while the plans of the remaining 60,000 men are still tentative." Most of the businesses planned were small, one-man retail or service enterprises requiring a low capital investment. By comparison, the business plans of white servicemen were less concentrated in the retail and service fields and focused more on much larger business opportunities.

The study noted, however, that only one-eighth of black GIs with definite business plans had experience in operating the business that they planned to open; although one-half of the group had experience working in that type of business. By comparison, slightly more than one-fifth of the white GIs were self-employed before the war. Also, 10 percent of black World War II veterans, some 120,000 individuals, were planning on becoming farm owners, including the 102,000 planning to return to the South.

Several factors account for the post–World War II interest in establishing businesses by black GIs. The existence of an African-American business culture and tradition made them responsive to the information provided by the government on establishing businesses. Historically, blacks have established businesses simply because of their failure to find employment. A decade of high black unemployment rates during the depression and the limited possibilities that awaited blacks in a postwar economy, which would have to absorb millions of demobilized soldiers, were important factors that made black GIs receptive to establishing a business after the war. Undoubtedly, the most important factor was that the war provided more than a million black men for the first time with savings that could be used as venture capital, thus underscoring the degree to which limited access to capital has served as a major obstacle to black business development.

In 1943 the minimum capital required to establish a retail business, according to Dun & Bradstreet, was $2,500, which was needed "to equip a store with merchandise and fixtures, and to have sufficient cash left over, for fourteen typical retail lines in an average-sized community." Yet the median initial capital outlay expended by blacks to establish a retail store in 1943 was $549.50.[114] With their savings and higher incomes, black veterans as a group were in a much better position to establish competitive enterprises. In 1948, surveys showed that the average income of World War II black veterans in the 25–34 age group was $1,772, compared to $1,488 for nonveterans in the same age group. Overall, black incomes were low. In 1950, 50.4 percent of blacks had incomes of less than $1,499, while only 1.3 percent had incomes from $4,500 to $4,999; 2.5 percent from $5,000 to $5,999; 1.6 percent from $6,000 to $9,999; and less than .3 percent had incomes of $10,000 or more.[115]

For some black World War II veterans, their military training, especially in technical fields, gave them an advantage in securing higher paying jobs in industry. In addition, their savings provided them with the capital to establish businesses, especially in areas that would expand in the newly developing postwar economy, such as the aviation industry. Several flying schools had been founded by blacks in the 1930s; in one instance, black businessman R. R. Wright offered a scholarship to encourage blacks in aviation, explaining that "The country is calling for 20,000 aviators each year, there is no reason why our young men should not qualify and try and become army pilots."[116]

It was not until World War II that the first serious attempt was made by blacks to establish a commercial airline. The Washington-based Union Airlines was founded in 1943 by William H. Hawkins, who became president and general manager. In October 1943 he filed an application with the Civil Aeronautics Board for a certificate of public convenience and necessity in order for Union Airlines to begin charter operations. Its first purchase was a five-passenger WACO 285 H.P. Jacob, christened the *Mary Bethune*.[117] Hawkins founded the airlines in anticipation of the postwar availability of black pilots, especially, he said, black veterans of the 99th Pursuit Squadron and 332nd Fighter Group; the enterprise eventually fizzled out. Also, after the war, several black veterans of the 332nd, 477th, and the Air Transport command in Chicago formed a consortium "dedicated to the establishment of a Negro owned and operated commercial airline .... [to provide jobs and] lick some of the problems of discrimination."[118]

International Business

Throughout the depression and into the post–World War II era, blacks persisted in their attempts to develop international enterprises. In the 1930s R. R. Wright established an import firm that specialized in importing Haitian coffee. In 1939 the controversial *Pitts-burgh Courier* columnist George Schuyler, using Wright as a model to encourage more black participation in international trade, noted: "There must be many things that the Haitians import which a Negro-owned company could supply. Soap, perfume, and cotton clothes come immediately to mind. We already have the cosmetic factories (Walker, Poro, Apex, etc) to supply the first two."[119] With few exceptions, international trade in consumer goods was curtailed during World War II, but black interest revived after 1945.

There were some international business activities, however, in which blacks participated during World War II. The successful architect Paul Williams designed a large air terminal, a ten-story hotel, and several private residences in various countries in South America.[120] The Phenix Color Chemical Company, both before and during the war, also did a "tremendous business," in Central and South America, supplying "practically every government of our Latin American neighbors with large orders of various chemicals for public health work." Brazil, Mexico, and Cuba were known to be "three of the company's largest purchasers of these supplies."[121]

African-Americans also established businesses in foreign countries during World War II. Mississippi-born James Samuel Lynch Fykes Jr. continued to operate his business on the island of Malta, where he had established Chez Jim, a restaurant, bar, and grill that specialized in Mediterranean-American food. Malta was a British possession, and during World War II Fykes's business survived "the full might of Nazi and Fascist dive-bomber raids."[122] In 1943 the Jones brothers, Chicago policy operators who fled the United States for Mexico, opened two dress shops, Jacqmar I and Jacqmar II, in downtown Mexico City. By 1951 the stores were doing extremely well. The largest was also a factory, with 15 employees, including a designer and artist. It manufactured the shop's specialty, hand-painted skirts for women's beachware.[123]

The most extensive overseas business operations undertaken by an African-American after the war were those established by Dunbar McLaurin. After his successful stint as an army lieutenant selling war bonds to black GIs in the South Pacific, McLaurin remained in the Philippines, where he established a business in Manila selling surplus army vehicles. After that, he established a firm that sold spare parts and reconditioned trucks and jeeps that he purchased from the United States. McLaurin's initial business operations were so successful that he was said to have "a gross intake running well into seven figures within six or seven months."

By 1947 McLaurin Enterprises included six different businesses: "a gold mine, sugar plantation, a taxicab company, a rattan factory, an army-surplus vehicle company and an Oriental Picture exchange which produces native Tagalog films." At the time, his company employed 78 people, including 3 black servicemen, 33 shop repairmen, 18 security guards, 4 office clerks, 2 business managers, and 8 maintenance foremen. In 1948 McLaurin opened his Far Eastern Trade Association, with offices in Shanghai and Hong Kong. By 1950 this import-export business had offices in both Manila and New York City.[124] At that time his Manila workforce force included 400 Filipinos with a weekly payroll of $22,000.[125]

America's leading black engineer at the time, Archie Alexander, also participated in international business activities. A 1912 engineering graduate of the University of Iowa, he established his first company in 1914 and was in partnership with whites in two subsequent companies. In 1950 he established the American Caribbean Company, which did work in Venezuela and Puerto Rico and also negotiated with the Haitian government to build a hydroelectric power plant, along with flood control, irrigation, and drainage systems. Alexander's other million-dollar engineering projects included the construction of municipal power and sewer plants, bridges, and highways, in addition to railroad relocation work.[126]

While the West Indies and South America were primary targets for the international business activities of blacks, the emerging independence of African states, beginning with Ghana in 1957, opened new avenues for African-American business interests. The black-owned Simmons Royalty Company specialized in brokering and negotiating oil leases with Liberia, Ghana, Nigeria, and the Ivory Coast for America's "huge multinationals like Phillips Petroleum, Texaco, and Signal." The firm was headed by Jake Simmons Jr., whose interest in Liberia's mineral wealth began in 1952. Simmons's usual brokerage fee was two percent of the value of the mineral lease rights obtained for those companies. In addition, he retained an override percentage of the oil drilled and "sold portions of his override for sums ranging from a few thousand dollars to nearly $100,000."[127] Leases brokered by Simmons resulted in billions of dollars worth of oil drilled in these countries. In the newly emerging African states, Simmons's company represented the transformation of black-American businesses from operations engaging in minor international business transactions to ones dealing in multimillion-dollar investments.

Food, Beverage, and Bottling Enterprises

At the present time, black enterprises in the food, beverage, and bottling industry have grown into a multimillion dollar businesses. Blacks were involved in the beverage and bottling industries as early as the depression, but these businesses were small in market distribution and profits. During World War II, the Henry Armstrong Beer Distributing Company in Kansas City, named after the famous triple-crown champion boxer, was established. Earl W. Beck was the owner, and his associate was Al Jordan, the 1941 Golden Gloves heavyweight champion. The company was small but had a truck, warehouse, and handling equipment that ensured deliveries to about 50 stores in the black business community.[128] In 1955 a black-owned brewery was established in Philadelphia with the claim that "There is no instance, here-to-fore, on records wherein a Negro has attempted the brewery business at the brewery and bottling level." When company president John Randolph Smith, who was blind, introduced his Colony House Premium Beer, he said, "fifty metropolitan cities in the United States had already been selected as prospective distribution areas."[129]

The heavyweight-boxing champion Joe Louis was involved in several bottling and beverage companies. In the mid-1940s the Joe Louis Punch Company was established, which guaranteed Louis $50,000 a year for five years for the use of his name. The company had bottling plants in New York, Washington, D.C., and Baltimore, but went into receivership in 1948. Declining sales, compounded by Louis's poor showing against Jersey Joe Walcott, hastened the company's folding.[130] Still, Louis was the leading black sports figure in the 1950s. In 1952 he endorsed the white-owned Joe Louis Distilling Company, a subsidiary of Kentucky's National Distillers, of whose board he was a member. This venture provided him with $100,000 in the first year of the agreement. In his promotional tours, Louis said, " I have planned and worked to bring you a product that experts assure me is the finest sour mash four-year-old Kentucky Straight Bourbon available any where." Aware of the impact of his endorsement on the public, he cautioned children and athletes not to drink: "Any alcoholic beverage, no matter what its name is not for children." Louis also said that "Liquor and participation in sports don't mix." Yet, for the average adult who drank in moderation, Louis's pitch was, "I promise you many hours of top enjoyment with JOE LOUIS KENTUCKY STRAIGHT BOURBON, because you can't buy a better whiskey in this world."[131]

While the endorsement of national name-brand products by superstar black athletes today is commonplace, usually their only contract responsibility is to make commercials. In the 1940s and '50s, however, black sports stars whose names were associated with white companies had to work for those companies by going on sales trips to promote the products, even if, as in the case of Joe Louis, they owned a small share in the corporation. In 1954 Joe Louis, in partnership with black Chicago businessman Jesse Thornton, established the Joe Louis Milk Company as a subsidiary of Thornton Enterprises. In announcing the partnership, Thornton said that, "unlike his many other business adventures, Louis is president of the company and active enough to discount rumors that the Joe Louis Milk Company, Inc. is his business in name only."[132] Thornton was secretary-treasurer, and the plant and executive offices were located on Chicago's South Side.

While the Joe Louis Milk Company was the only black-owned and operated dairy company in the nation, it encountered difficulty in securing distribution of its products in national retail chains.[133] In Chicago, Walgreen Drugs operated 20 stores in black communities but refused to sell Joe Louis milk. In 1955 black community groups threatened Walgreen with boycotts, "picket lines, leaflets and street corner meetings." Walgreen remained obstinate in its refusal to buy Louis's milk, asserting that consideration would not be given to brands preferred by blacks. They responded that Walgreen had "a moral obligation to the Negro people not only to hire them but also to buy from Negro merchants whenever possible." Black consumer loyalty, they maintained, could no longer be bought with the "measly $10,000" that Walgreen gave the black YMCA or the "little business it gave to Negro manufacturers of hair straightening greases and cosmetics."[134]

Eventually, all of the Joe Louis brand-name companies failed. Products carrying his name, while sold in heavily populated black communities, were unable to maintain black customer loyalty. Even his Brown Bomber Baking Company failed. Established in 1939, by 1941 it was reported as the "largest Negro-owned and operated commercial bakery in the country." It had 24 trucks, 92 employees, and a distribution base of 1,200 grocery stores and about 900 restaurants in New York and New Jersey. A new plant was built in the Bronx. Company benefits included life insurance with black-owned Victory Mutual Life, and "Brown Bomber employees operate their own union in a law-abiding manner."[135] It appears, however, that the Joe Louis name sustained sales more than the quality of his products did: all of the Joe Louis brands failed as his prominence as a sports figure faded. But superstar status was important! Jersey Joe Wolcott and Floyd Patterson also endorsed products, but only as long as they were heavyweight champions.

While Louis's products failed to sustain sales, several black food-processing companies in competitive markets kept their customer loyalty. The Minnie Lee Pie Company, established in 1937 by Minnie Lee Fellings, was selling 3,000 pies daily in 1939. Her three delivery trucks served 225 stores and restaurants in Chicago.[136] In Birmingham, Alabama, Gertrude Alexander, a candy manufacturer, had 400 wholesale customers.[137] These were companies whose products were identified with quality, such as Parker House Sausage and Baldwin Ice Cream.[138] Also, New Orleans food manufacturer George McDemmod sold his potato chips and bacon rinds to 1,400 dealers in nine states and several South American cities. With plants in Chicago, Detroit, and Buffalo, his 1950 annual gross receipts amounted to over $100,000.[139]

Ultimately, the success of black food manufacturers and the Joe Louis-brand products confirm marketing assessments made of black consumers as early as World War I: that blacks are especially inclined to purchase not only leading brand-name products but also high-quality products. In black communities during this time, Baldwin Ice Cream and Parker House Sausage were recognized as high-quality brand-name products. In 1954 financial analyst Sylvia Porter, assessing black consumer patterns in one of her nationally syndicated columns, said, "because of his basic hatred of any suggestion of inferiority, the Negro buyer often is a better customer for a quality product than for an inexpensive one."[140] Understanding the psychology of black consumers' product preferences and buying patterns, as well as acknowledging their emphasis on product quality, then, is as important for black companies as it is for white companies. This necessity perhaps explains the reasons behind the successes and failures of black food-processing companies established during the depression and World War II.

Segregation and Black Transportation Enterprises

In the first six months of 1941 Cleveland black businessman Alonzo Wright, who owned a chain of eight gas stations, "grossed approximately $600,000."[141] This is just one example of how American racism and segregation in enterprises associated with motor-vehicle transportation encouraged the development of profitable black businesses in the industry, particularly in the taxicab industry. In Texas, Hobart T. Taylor Sr. invested family money from the sale of farm property to start a cab company in 1931, which expanded during World War II. By the 1970s the company was worth $5 million. Real estate speculation in urban and rural property added to Taylor's wealth.

World War II resulted in increased profits for black jitney businesses, especially those in large urban centers in the North and South. Chicago was the center of the black jitney industry. From World War II until the 1960s, the city's jitneys were extremely profitable, despite the "taxi wars" on the South Side, where drivers competed with each other for paying customers. During the war passenger complaints increased as jitney drivers refused to travel beyond the two major streets, Michigan Avenue and South Parkway (now King Drive), claiming that "they had to conserve their rubber because of war economy."[142] In Durham, North Carolina, however, eight black taxi companies requested a permit to consolidate because the government mandated that "each cab is allowed only five gallons of gas a day now."[143]

With continued segregation in public transportation continuing after World War II, the number of black taxi firms increased. Many companies were started by black veterans, who in turn provided jobs for other veterans. Seattle's first black taxicab company was founded in 1946 with 22 employees, including "a blind veteran of the Merchant Marine" hired as "chief dispatcher."[144] Increasingly, white taxi companies in both the North and South objected to blacks entering the business. In Orlando, Florida, in September 1946 the mayor, city manager, police chief, and the white cab-company owner opposed the petition of two black veterans seeking a permit to operate a "Negro taxi service." Almost 50 percent of the taxi passengers in Orlando were black. The owner of the white company, who had a monopoly, protested that a black company would reduce his business by 50 percent. He also stated that plans were underway for improving his taxi service to blacks.[145]

The South had ambivalent responses to blacks who applied for permits to operate taxi companies. In 1947 the editor of the *Black Dispatch* in Oklahoma City got a call from a city councilman who said, "Tell the people on your side of town that the way is now open down at the city hall for them to apply for a taxi cab permit." Blacks had operated cabs as independents in the city until an ordinance was passed requiring liability bonds. In addition, the service provided to blacks by white companies was poor. The councilman, to affirm the extent of his commitment, said, "I told a white man today who said he was going to ask for a permit to handle this business that I would oppose him."[146]

White cab companies in northern cities also profited from their monopoly of the taxi business and, as in the South, used local governmental agencies and policies to maintain their lock on the business. In 1947 Pittsburgh's black-owned Owl Cab Company, with 15 cabs (10 more were soon purchased), was finally granted a permit to operate but with routes limited to only two city wards. In 1948 the company inaugurated a policy of hiring white drivers, with the claim that more would be hired as soon as "its quota was raised to seventy-five cabs." The Pennsylvania Public Utility Commission, however, had limited the company to a maximum of 25 cabs. While the commission had also restricted Owl's area of operations, the white-owned companies, Yellow Cab and Peoples Cab, had franchises that allowed them to operate countywide. Unable to compete and $86,000 in debt, Owl Cab was put in receivership by the Court of Common Pleas, which ordered the sale of its remaining 19 cabs. By 1959, Owl was out of business.[147]

Black taxi companies, however, also profited from segregation, which gave them a monopoly in providing service to blacks. By 1948, Louisville blacks had carried on a two-year war against black cab companies that were overcharging them. There were seven black cab companies in the city with a total of 122 taxis. Those without meters developed their own fare rates using a zone system, which was openly abused. The practice continued despite a 20-year city ordinance that required that all cabs be equipped with meters. Finally, in response to black protests, Louisville's police captain set a deadline for the guilty companies. Most complied and installed the $200 meters; but for those who had not met the deadline, the captain said he was "tolerant because I didn't want to see any of them forced out of business."[148]

Other black cab companies were successful. In Chicago by 1958, Herman Roberts, a black World War II veteran, emerged as a successful South Side businessman, having begun his cab company in 1946. In the early 1950s, Roberts had a fleet of 36 radio-dispatched cabs and 125 drivers and mechanics who were employed in his own garage.[149] In Savannah, three years after it was founded in 1952, black-owned Milton's Cab Company was the largest in the city. Its owner, World War II veteran Milton Hall, started the company with one car. By 1954, he had 27 radio-dispatched cabs, employed 50 drivers, 5 dispatchers, 2 mechanics, and a superintendent; and he had gross earnings of more than $10,000 a month.[150]

One of the most successful black transportation enterprises that developed in response to segregation was the Safe Bus Company, incorporated in Winston Salem, North Carolina. It was founded in 1926 by Ralph Morgan, his brother, and the owners of 12 other black jitney companies as a result of Duke Power Company's refusal to extend its trolley lines into the rapidly growing black sections of the city. To avoid the unprofitable cutthroat competition that had plagued them in the years after Duke Power's decision, the companies merged into one enterprise. It was capitalized at $100,000 but only had $22,000 in assets, although the 14 companies owned a total of about 35 buses. Their first "jitney" busses were trucks with straight seats. The business was an immediate success, with the white City Bus Company failing in its attempt to buy it out. By 1940 the company, "with 54 Diamond T, Reo Dodge, Yellow Coach, and Twin Coach busses, serviced 11,000 black passengers a day," with 21 hours of service provided daily.

In 1941 Safe Bus bought out Camel City Cabs, and by 1943 the company, with 48 busses and 20 cabs employed 123 drivers and an office staff of three full-time secretaries.[151] In 1958 the company began operating on "a non-segregating seating basis." By then Safe Bus had a $200,000, 55-vehicle fleet of both diesel and gas-powered busses, with service provided on special routes of up to 75 miles in the surrounding area of Winston-New Salem. The company serviced 3,000,000 passengers annually, had 89 full-time employees, and had an annual payroll of more than $225,000. It was headed by Delphine W. Morgan, the widow of one of the founders. As a result of the company's financial success, which perhaps was even more of a factor than the 1956 decision that declared segregation on Montgomery city buses unconstitutional, "The white-owned City Bus line long since took note of the desegregated ways of the 32 year old Safe Bus and followed suit."[152]

In Disputanta, Virginia, segregated transportation led to the development of a $100,000 business from a $10 investment. With the building of a new highway in 1937, Mr. and Mrs. Matthew Jackson relocated their home adjacent to it, using one room as a grocery that sold provisions to black motorists and that served as a waiting area for black bus customers. In 1939 Jackson wrote the Greyhound company, informing it that 80 percent of its passengers were black; he said that "I got tired of seeing my people standing outside in the cold and in the rain." Two years later, Greyhound responded. Within one day after the visit of a company representative, Greyhound gave Jackson a license to operate its ticket agency for the city. Throughout the 1940s the business expanded, as much a response to black bus passengers as to providing services for blacks who lived in the area and black motorists. The Jacksons built a two-room restaurant with a seating capacity of 70, state-approved rest rooms with hot and cold running water, an auto-accessory store, garage, poolroom, theater, and dance hall.[153]

Desegregation and the Demise of the Black Hotel Industry

Beginning in the late 1940s, the black hotel industry enjoyed a boom period that lasted for about 10 years. By the late 1950s it experienced a rapid decline as blacks increasingly took advantage of their newly acquired access to public accommodations.[154] During World War II, separate public accommodations were still sanctioned by the federal government, which, at the same time, indirectly provided assistance to the black hotel industry. In 1941, for example, the United States Travel Bureau, Department of the Interior, published a pamphlet, *Negro Hotels and Guest Houses*. In its 1943 survey, the bureau reported that there were 529 black hotels nationwide: New York had the largest number, 54; Virginia, 32; New Jersey and Pennsylvania, 26 each, including 14 in Philadelphia; Texas, 24, Ohio, 23; and, Illinois, 17, all in Chicago.[155]

Immediately after the war, the American hotel business for both blacks and whites was in a general slump, with a 25 percent drop in business due to strikes, the loss of wartime industrial jobs, and the demobilization of the armed forces. In 1946 the president of the National Negro Hotel and Restaurant Association, Love B. Woods, owner of Harlem's

Woodside and Mariette Hotels, summarized the results of his survey of black hotels in Harlem and other larger cities: "the majority of hostelries are doing in the main a weekend trade. Throughout the week at least one fourth of their rooms remain empty." Woods indicated, however, that business was returning to a prewar status, with every indication that the black hotel business was not only recovering from a slump but also expanding.[156]

In the early 1950s there was little indication that discrimination and segregation would ever end in the industry. Throughout the decade blacks expanded their activities in the hotel industry. Many established black hotels that they renovated and expanded. In San Francisco, Fannie and Major McCoy, who already owned the San Francisco Manor Plaza Hotel, purchased a black-owned hotel in what was said to be the "fifth largest realty deal [made by blacks] in the past year.[157] In Akron, Ohio, Mr. and Mrs. G. Matthews, who had opened their hotel in 1920 with 11 rooms, had by 1955 expanded to 60 rooms, with both a beauty shop and barbershop. The hotel's logo was "A Business With A Soul."[158]

Throughout the 1950s, the openings of new black hotels and motels, which were located in black business districts and on major highways, were celebrated with great fanfare and attended by leading black and white civic and community leaders.[159] The most widely known new black motel at the time was the $300,000 A. G. Gaston Motel in downtown Birmingham. Built and owned by a leading black entrepreneur in 1954, it was labeled "the finest hostelry for Negro Americans in the nation." Gaston said that its opening "means that many persons passing through our city now will have a fine place to stay. I have long regretted there was no top-flight hotel or resting place for Negro visitors in our city and I was determined to make our new motel one that would attract Negro tourists."[160]

As in the early twentieth century, the black hotel business was not limited to providing overnight accommodations. There was a continual demand for luxury resorts. Within 12 years after Sally Walker invested $2,500 in a two-building farm, she had developed it into a 300-acre Catskill Mountain resort worth $400,000. By 1954 she was welcoming both national and international guests. Walker's promotion of her resort extended to "the West Indies Islands, South America, Canada, Johannesburg, West Africa"; and it was noted that "it is not rare to see in her mail requests for reservations from vacationists in Europe." In addition to a lodge, semiprivate bungalows, and the Paradise Farm Annex, which was a 41-room hotel purchased by Walker in 1954, there were three dining rooms, two dance halls, a casino, a beach house, a ten-acre lake for swimming, fishing, and rowing, tennis and basketball courts, softball fields, and plans for an eighteen-hole miniature golf course and 475-foot driving range.[161]

By the early 1950s, whites began to recognize the profitability of the black consumer market in the motel and hotel industry. White investors were, however, usually interested only in providing modest motel accommodations for black motorists. In 1954 two whites in Humboldt, Tennessee, built the nine-unit Booker T. Washington Motel for $20,000; they advertised it as "a rest haven for Negro highway travelers between Chicago, Atlanta, Nashville and other points in the deep South." Even before it opened, the white owners were making plans for additional units, a restaurant, and recreation center.[162]

The 1954 Brown decision made little impact on the increasing numbers of white investors interested in constructing black hotels and motels. The decision ended the federal government's support of the principle of separate but equal established in the 1896 *Plessy v. Ferguson* decision. The Brown decision, that segregated education for black children and white children was inherently unequal, unleashed a social and political revolution that did not end in 1964 with the passage of the Civil Rights Act. Although racial attitudes

255

changed in American business toward the consumer and there was an expansion of the black middle class, overall income disparities between whites and blacks remained virtually constant. And black business receipts, while they increased by the end of the twentieth century, would account for less than two percent of all American business receipts, despite the expansion of black business activities. In American economic life, separate but unequal would continue after 1954.

As one white investor said in 1955, "The shortage of good hotel accommodations for Negro travelers from coast-to-coast is proving a new frontier for investors wanting to enter this business." This assessment was made by one of Texas's biggest white hotel owners, Peter Lane, who in 1955 announced plans to secure a $2 million loan from Wall Street investors to build a chain of hotels and motels for blacks in Texas, Louisiana, New Mexico, and Oklahoma. He indicated that many black guests at his recently opened $250,000, 40-room Dallas hotel had complained of "having driven 400 miles during the day because they couldn't find decent accommodations." During this time, white investors made overtures to black community leaders for support of their hotel ventures. Announcing his proposal to build a new $400,000 black hotel with a gas station, restaurant, and drive-in theater, Lane said he was planning to form a syndicate of black business and professional people to participate in his venture.[163]

White investors no doubt realized that building hotels for blacks put them in a highly competitive position with black-owned hotels and motels. Without black support, whites felt that their ventures might fail. Certainly, the actions of Lane and other white investors interested in building luxury hotels for blacks demonstrated their awareness of the sophistication as well as the political influence of black leaders.

However, it was extremely difficult for leaders of the black community, who routinely implored blacks to support black businesses, to explain why they would advocate patronizing white businesses when comparable black businesses existed. Obviously, for both black leaders and white investors, resolution required that they be given a piece of the action. Blacks were financially compensated in several ways. As whites entered the black hotel business, then, their usual pattern was to secure the endorsement not only of black civic leaders and the black elite but also of big-name black entertainers and sports figures who were paid for the use of their name. Executive management positions were also offered to them. In 1955 nationally known black bandleader and composer Noble Sissle was hired as executive vice president of Lucky Lakes Estates, a million-dollar white resort planned for blacks in the Catskills.[164]

In 1957 in Miami, two whites made plans for the building of a "Swank Negro Hotel for Virginia Key." They were Robert E. Kizer, who owned public utility plants in New York and Pennsylvania, and Frank Teller, said to be an international banker. They proposed building a $4 million, 300-room hotel located on 10 acres of oceanfront property, "comparable in luxury to the new white hotels in the area." They said that their board of directors would include "Cab Calloway and Lena Horne and many prominent Miamians."[165] Blacks who sat on the board of directors were also compensated financially for their name as well as their time.

In the mid-1950s, neither blacks nor whites interested in investing in all-black hotels envisioned the epoch-making changes in segregation laws that would take place in only a few years. When a proposal made by two white investors in 1955 for building "a $1,500,000 Negro hotel" on Virginia Key was presented before the Miami city council, it was referred to the city engineers, who were instructed "to advise them where land would be exclusively for Negroes." The investors were so confident that segregation would remain the American way of life that in their proposal, "they asked for a 99 year lease" of city property for their all-black hotel.[166]

Investing in black hotels by whites in the 1950s was motivated more by a desire for profits than by a political climate moving toward desegregation. Indeed, some whites came up with the idea that money could even be made in integrated hotels. In Carthage, Missouri, a white businessman who owned the White Tourist Court Motel, announced in 1953 that blacks were welcome. The motel was located on Route 66, which at the time was the main highway between Oklahoma City and St. Louis. The owner said that "This is an All-American establishment and I want Negro tourists to know that this is one motel where they won't be refused. . . . I want them to know that if there is space available, they will be accommodated here."[167] Even black motel owners began to seek white patronage. In 1955, when the 23-unit Franklin Hotel opened in Salisbury, Maryland, by black World War II veteran Melvin C. Hutt, it was reported that "One of the first steps toward integration in Maryland was the opening of the new, modern Franklin Hotel."[168]

As major white investors were moving into the black hotel industry, it was also becoming increasingly evident to them that integrated accommodations could prove profitable. One of the first groups of investors to tap this market constructed the $3 million Las Vegas Moulin Rouge hotel and casino, located on 50 acres near the city's black residential section. It opened in April 1955, and its establishment as an interracial hotel was national news and highly controversial. As one report emphasized, the hotel challenged the forces of segregation represented by powerful and wealthy men from Texas, Oklahoma, Arkansas, and Mississippi "who established the custom of Jim Crow . . . with those 'oil' bankrolls. . . . Until this week they had things their own way. Their money told the men who run the fabulous places along the strip . . . like the Dunes, The Flamingo, The Sands, The New Frontier . . . that they didn't want to associate with Negroes, unless Negroes served them."[169]

The Moulin Rouge, however, was not only the first Las Vegas establishment to hire blacks as croupiers, roulette operators, and card dealers, but also the first where blacks could gamble legally.[170] Moreover, the staff was integrated and managed by Sonny Boswell, former star of the Harlem Globetrotters.[171] Joe Louis held a 2 percent interest and was also employed as the hotel's official host. Yet six months later, in November 1955, the Moulin Rouge, once said to have "brightened this fabulous desert spa like an atomic entertainment bomb," closed. Mismanagement and a surplus of employees were cited as reasons, but some claimed that there was "a certain amount of pressure from operators on the Strip, who were losing some early morning trade because of the late shows at the Rouge."[172]

As whites made inroads into the black hotel industry, efforts were made by blacks to maintain a significant presence. In 1953 black hotel owners and managers in New York organized the National Hotel Association. William H. Brown, manager of the Hotel Theresa, the nation's largest black hotel, and chairman of the organizing committee, stated that the purpose of the group was to upgrade services provided by black hotels, motels, tourist courts, and guest houses. Excluded from white trade associations, the organization also saw itself providing a service in the collection and dissemination of "vital information concerning trends, statistics, and latest techniques of the hotel industry."[173]

In many ways the decline of Detroit's black hotels signaled the beginning of the end of the black hotel industry. Despite attempts at remodeling—the $500,000 black Garfield hotel in 1955 underwent renovations at a cost of $100,000—the city's black hotels were losing guests. In the late 1950s Detroit's black hotel owners, as those in other large urban centers, launched a campaign against blacks for not patronizing their hotels. In 1959 owners of the city's five leading black hotels met with the Booker T. Washington Trade Association for the purpose of finding an answer to the competition from white hotels, which were " threatening to put them out of business."[174]

In addition, large black organizations, particularly sororities and fraternities, some with more than 100,000 members, were denounced for their failure to support the city's black hotels. From 1956 to 1958 several black conventions were held in Detroit's large white hotels by Alpha Kappa Alpha and Delta Sigma Theta sororities, the Kappa Alpha Psi fraternity, the National Association of Colored Women's Clubs, and the national organizations of black real estate brokers and pharmacists. In only one instance did members of these organizations stay at the city's black hotels. When Kappa Alpha Psi held its convention, "only seven reservations at Negro hotels had been received."

Black hotels, unfortunately, could provide neither the space nor the accommodations needed for conferences held by the large black organizations; also black hotel owners said, "Many Negroes are using integration as an excuse to pass up their hotels."[175] Despite the fact that black-owned hotels in Detroit could claim only a combined total of 681 rooms and suites representing an investment of over $1.7 million in up-to-date accommodations, they were losing money. By 1960 the patronage of blacks at major hotels, at least in the North, was common and accepted, a situation that marked the end of blacks as emerging players in the hotel industry.

The last hurrah for the black hotel industry occurred when the Hotel Theresa, long a Harlem landmark, achieved both national and international notoriety by hosting Fidel Castro in 1960 after his much publicized departure from the Hotel Shelburn. In Harlem, Castro's historic visit was given even more attention when it was reported that one of his visitors at the Hotel Theresa was Malcolm X, described then as "one of Harlem's leading apostles of black supremacy, he claims membership in something called the Cult of Islam, he denounces 'white devils' and promises their early extinction. He is a thundering headache to responsible leaders of New York's Negro community." The final comment on Malcolm X's visit was, "No one who knows the Cuban's sure instinct for trouble could be surprised that Malcolm was received at Hotel Theresa."[176]

By 1960 the black hotel industry, which had sustained the black business community since the late eighteenth century, was rapidly becoming history. Black-owned motels in racially segregated urban communities would continue operations, but they relied primarily on local trade, rather than travelers.[177] The decimation of the black hotel industry, then, presaged what would be the impact of the Civil Rights movement on black business after 1964. In 1959, an op-ed commentary entitled "Dangerous Symptom" noted in response to the black Detroit hotel owner's plight: "The colored businessman is in a vicious cycle. He cannot compete on equal terms with the white man because he lacks capital and he lacks capital because his own race does not patronize him; therefore he cannot compete."[178]

Securities Investment Enterprises

Paradoxically, in the one area in American business in which there was no discrimination by law, few blacks had the incentive to participate, and the even smaller number who were so inclined lacked the financial capacity to do so. Throughout a good portion of the twentieth century, but particularly after World War II, there was a growing recognition by some white American financial analysts that black Americans represented an untapped potential market for investments in stocks, bonds, and other securities. As financial analyst Sylvia Porter said in 1954, "The Negro market for securities investment alone is calculated at above $1,000,000,000."[179] Even before white America recognized the availability of capital in the black community, there were black securities investors tapping this market from the 1920s on. Yet, interestingly, from the 1930s to the 1960s, as each black investment company was established, it was announced in the news media as being the first.

In 1932 the R. T. Bess Company, founded by Robert T. Bess in 1923, was announced as "the only colored stockbrokers in Wall Street." The company was located on Broadway until 1930, when it moved to Wall Street. Bess said that during the depression, while "his company had seen suicides in the 'Street' resulting from business reverses, because of the Wall Street crash. . . . his company had been able to weather the storm by 'sticking at the wheel.' " Bess had 9 whites and 6 blacks working in his office. In 1932 he promoted the interests of the Standard Television and Electric Company, manufacturers of television receivers and transmitters, which he said "offered an opportunity to colored people to reap millions of dollars in profit."[180]

The Bess Company was not the only black securities firm operating in the 1930s. During the height of the depression, the Evanita Holding Company, located at 240 Broadway and headed by John J. Gundles, was also announced as the only black securities firm operating on Wall Street. In 1935 Evanita paid a 5 percent dividend to its investors from its earnings that year. In comparison, Standard Oil of California, New York, and New Jersey had declared a dividend of less than 3 percent, R. H. Macy, 2 percent, General Motors, 2.5 percent, while American Telephone, Chase National Bank, and Consolidated Gas paid less than 5 percent.[181]

Beginning in the late 1940s the number of blacks employed in investment firms increased. In 1949 Lawrence Lewis was reported as the first black to sell stocks and bonds on Wall Street. He was registered by his employer, Abraham and Company, members of the New York Stock Exchange, New York Curb Exchange, and Chicago Board of Trade and Commodities Exchange. A World War II veteran, Lawrence worked previously at a San Francisco brokerage firm, where he advanced from a messenger to clearinghouse cashier, but left when his company would not register him to trade. Lawrence said he got his new job because brokers are aware "they can reach an untapped market," and he noted that he would "emphasize the Negro field." He promoted sales by a nationwide circulation of information to black professionals and major black institutions, explaining that gilt-edged securities were a better risk than real estate investment. Abraham and Company also opened an office in Harlem's Hotel Theresa, since it was known that moneyed blacks who visited New York stayed there.[182]

In the 1950s several black investment firms were founded. Norman L. McGhee, president of the Cleveland-based McGhee & Company Investment Securities, established his company in 1952. McGhee, licensed as a broker-dealer, was said to be the first black to establish an investment firm authorized to deal in general securities. By the mid-1950s he had established offices in North Carolina, South Carolina, Michigan, and Illinois. When McGhee opened his Chicago office in 1956, it was announced that his was "the first investment firm headed by a Negro licensed as a broker-dealer and authorized to deal in general securities." His Detroit office was located in the American Title Building, and in Chicago the company was located on the South Side.[183] By 1958 McGhee had sold about $5 million worth of stock to several hundred blacks. He anticipated that sales would increase to that figure annually within the next five years; even then, he said "that would barely prick the surface of the potential among the Negro people in the United States.[184]

In 1955, when Philip M. Jenkins established his investment firm, Special Markets, Inc., he was also characterized as the first black to head his own brokerage firm in the Wall Street area. Jenkins's investment strategy was to tap the ethnic market in the United States and foreign countries; he said that "with the recent economic stirrings in Asia and Africa there are definite advantages in introducing a Negro brokerage house at this time."[185] Jenkins also noted that he would provide investment forums for black churches and lodges. While he employed whites, the firm's black officers said they had "assured themselves of control by a voting-trust agreement."[186]

Even in the South, white investment firms recognized the potential market among blacks. While black investors in stocks and bonds date to the antebellum era, those that invested in the 1950s were regarded as the first blacks ever to do so. In Montgomery, Alabama, at this time, it was said that "For the first time in history, Southern Negroes are buying stocks." In 1954, as the manager of the Montgomery branch of Merrill, Lynch, Pierce, Fenner & Beanne also noted, "the most interesting fact of the Montgomery market is Negroes are becoming stock buyers.... Ten years ago, that was unheard of. There were no Negro buyers of stock down here." Less than 10 percent of people in Montgomery played the market, with less than 1 percent having investments of significance. Included in the 9 percent were "Tuskegee Institute personnel." The Merrill, Lynch representative said that they "began to buy stock, then other Negroes, and today it is pretty general for Negroes to open accounts. It is a sign they have surplus money to invest and of a new prosperity."[187]

This comment was made one year before the Montgomery bus boycott led by Dr. Martin Luther King began, which marked the beginning of the Civil Rights movement. Also in 1954 Sylvia Porter in her syndicated column noted: "It was only a short while ago that even the college-educated Negro often had to settle for a job as a waiter or red cap. It's only in our generation that the Negro has reached economic maturity and the market has come of age."[188] In 1950, with the announcement that the black consumer market had a potential worth of a billion dollars, white America began to take notice of a new financial market that could be tapped. Capitalizing on this interest, black publisher John H. Johnson produced a film, *The Secret of Selling the Negro,* that was released in June 1950 at a private showing in Milwaukee. Commenting on the film, Porter said:

> In bits and pieces, a great new and exciting pattern is being drawn in America—the pattern of the vast, vital and booming Negro market with billions to spend on every type of quality product and service.... The total income of America's 15,000,000 Negroes has quadrupled since the start of World War II.... The average income of our Negro citizens has soared even faster than the average income of our Whites. Since 1939, the Negroes' average income has climbed four times against a rise of less than three times in the income of Whites. As a whole, it's estimated the Negro market now reaches $15,000,000,000 a year.

Yet while white America was marveling over the $15 billion black consumer market and how it could get more of the black consumer dollar, the noted black sociologist E. Franklin Frazier claimed that, to the contrary, "the figure was closer to $5 billion." Furthermore, in his ongoing examination of the black business myth, he emphasized that "from the standpoint of providing employment for Negroes, Negro businesses provide employment for less than one-half of one percent of all employed Negroes."[189] In another critique the president of Fort Valley State College said, "American Negroes are basically consumers.... We spend that much every year, but little of it finds its way back into Negro businesses."[190] A Jackson, Mississippi, newspaper editorial emphasized that while the black press called for blacks to use their "spending power against white people in the forms of boycotts of one kind or another," the money paid to black businesspeople and professionals by the black masses are from salaries paid by whites.[191]

Moreover, during the early Civil Rights movement, blacks were in a depressed economic state as a result of the 1957–1958 national recession. In March 1958, while the white male unemployment rate was 8 percent, over 15 percent of black male workers were unemployed, which matched the unemployment rate for whites at the height of the Great Depression, when massive reform programs were put into effect to provide them relief. Yet when the economy recovered by November 1958, 11.4 percent of black males remained unemployed, compared to only 4.8 percent of white male workers.[192] In addition, in the late 1950s, there were no government programs put into effect to remedy the unemployment situation of blacks, as the government had for whites during the New Deal.

Most thinking black leaders, including investment specialist Norman McGhee, were realists in recognizing the limited economic position of blacks; and he joined the Urban League in challenging government reports that emphasized black economic progress. Reports from the U.S. census for 1950 to 1958 showed that there was 45 percent increase in the average black family income, from $1,869 to $2,711; the average white family income, however, increased 54 percent, from $3,445 to $5,300. The disparity between black and white family incomes had widened from 54 percent in 1950 to 51 percent in 1958. Consequently, while blacks had $18 billion in purchasing power that year, the black population remained, as McGhee said, a "non-participating consumer," since the reality is "that whenever money is spent, it follows that someone has profited from it." This situation shows why he emphasized that it was time for blacks to profit by investing in the "part-ownership of the agencies of production and distribution."[193]

More than any other black of his time, McGhee made a pronounced effort to encourage black investment activity in the private sector. Through his weekly column in the *Pittsburgh Courier*, "Using Your Money," he launched a one-man crusade to encourage black investment. In one column he emphasized the importance of removing not only "mental barriers" that blacks had against investment but also racial barriers. He used, as an example, the case of a black woman who was advised by one of his salesmen to buy stock in the bank in which she was a depositor. Before investing, however, the woman checked with her bank and was told it "had none of the shares for sale." McGhee added that nothing his salesman said could convince her that "shares of this bank's stock were for sale in the open market, and not the bank's office." He said that such mental barriers are so powerful that the typical black believes stock market investing "is a field too mysterious and dangerous for him to enter, let alone seek to benefit from it."[194]

In another column McGhee mentioned that when a national black sorority came to him to invest its scholarship fund of $50,000, it did not want to pay his commission of $1,200. Rather than use him as a broker or even take his advice, the sorority invested elsewhere in securities that, in less than two years had increased to only $60,000; but the stock he recommended "increased to almost $100,000."[195] In 1957 Allen University in South Carolina became the first black college to place funds for investment with a black brokerage company when it placed more than $20,000 with McGhee's firm. The investment was in selected common stocks and mutual funds shares, and the college based its choice on the "Evidence of the widespread acknowledgment in financial circles of the increased standing of McGhee & Company as an investment brokerage firm, the first in the nation headed by a Negro."[196]

In his columns McGhee recommended that blacks invest in companies whose products they purchased. For example, McGhee showed that if the country's 17 million blacks (based on 1960 population figures) purchased a minimum of two pairs of shoes annually, shoe companies would take in about $200 million. He then listed various shoe companies that represented a billion dollar industry and indicated that by investing in them, blacks would share in the profits.[197] Another plan proposed by McGhee was taken from the wartime policy of meatless days. By not eating meat for one day a week, he said, blacks could save money and at the end of the year purchase stock in companies such as Armour, Cudahy, Swift, Wilson, and International Packers. He indicated that their stock could be purchased for as little as $10 a share: "At the end of 10 years, there will have been amassed in the hands of the Negro in America something over one hundred million shares of stock in the principal meat-producing and packing companies of America. . . . placing themselves in position to demand new areas of employment in this industry."[198]

Several black investment companies were founded in the 1960s. When the H. L. Wright and Company, Inc., located at 99 Wall Street and headed by Tuskegee graduate Harry L. Wright, began business as brokers, dealers, and underwriters in July 1960, it was once again announced that it was the "first colored owned brokerage firm to be located on Wall Street." The firm was chartered by New York State and registered by the Securities and Exchange Commission, with Wright given approval as a broker-dealer to engage in a general investment business. The firm was also a member of the National Association of Securities Dealers. Wright, then forty-four years old, had been involved in investment activities for only six years before starting his firm.

In tapping the African-American market, Wright said the firm's operations "will be directed toward the development of a substantial wholesale bond business with insurance companies and other institutions owned and operated by Negroes, and will also engage in the retailing of select issues and the underwriting of securities." Wright indicated that in its underwriting activities, his firm, which also employed whites, would tap an international market, specifically that it would "devote the major portion of its efforts in spearheading private American investments in underdeveloped countries, especially newly independent African Nations."[199]

The potential of blacks in the investment world was seen, for example, in 1960 when the black-owned investment brokerage firm Patterson and Company, headed by senior partner John T. Patterson, participated in a national multimillion-dollar stock underwriting deal. The stock issue was for the Capital Life Insurance and Growth Stock Fund.[200] Patterson and Company also took initiatives to attract black investors. In 1959 it hired Harry Belafonte's ex-wife, Marguerite, to direct its investor information department. A year before, she had served as cochair of the Freedom Fund Committee of the NAACP and helped raise over a million dollars. In her new position Belafonte said, "I have seen that in our country, business and finance go hand in glove with first class citizenship. There is an immense educational job to be done in this area."[201]

Conclusion

This chapter opened with an excerpt from a 1955 newspaper editorial entitled "Where There Is No Jim Crow!" The editorial went on to say that "The Dream of all colored Americans has been to find a place where there is no color prejudice or discrimination, where they can be equal of others and get the same consideration." In 1955 this was still a dream as much it would be at the end of the twentieth century. While it was as true then as it is now that the only equal opportunity available for blacks in white America is investment in corporate America, income inequalities leave most blacks living from paycheck to paycheck. Equality in investment opportunities requires racial income parity.

Blacks as capitalists? Is this the other side of African-American history? In January 1960 McGhee announced an investment program for black America, indicating that the new decade would see the "emergence of the Negro to full citizenship status." In his first column for that year McGhee called for black leaders to develop an economic program that would include asking each black family to invest in stocks. The potential aggregate amount raised would amount to $500 million and would enable blacks to "acquire sizable holdings of common stock in such companies as: General Motors, Westinghouse Electrical, Sears Roebuck, Standard Oil."[202] He added, that with voting stock in those corporations, blacks could use their dollar power to force changes in discriminatory employment practices.

By 1960 the Civil Rights movement had taken priority and black leadership called for blacks to secure equal access to public accommodations and full civil and voting rights. While the period from the depression to the 1960s was one in which blacks survived economic catastrophes and major wars, and when there was an escalation of black protest, there was a persistent hope that business development and investment activities were essential for the economic advancement of black America. Yet the philosophical perspective shared by some blacks is that white America remains a home for capitalist exploiters of the poor, regardless of race. While troubling to black Americans, this perspective has not deterred most from their support of capitalism or their drive to be capitalists, whether in the formal or informal economy.

Black business statistics, moreover, provide compelling evidence in support of E. Franklin Frazier's "myth of Negro business," that in its failure to capture the black consumer dollar, black business lacks the capacity to sustain a separate black economy. Black business remains locked in an historic economic stranglehold. White businesses operate with a virtually monopolistic advantage enabled by a government-supported financial system that limits access to capital necessary for black businesses to be competitive in attracting the black consumer dollar. Within this context, Frazier's myth of black business serves to heighten a historical reality—the forces that drive American capitalism have never allowed blacks in this nation full economic freedom to compete with an equal footing on the playing field of free enterprise.

9

THE FEDERAL GOVERNMENT
AND BLACK BUSINESS:
THE 1960S TO THE 1990S

We conclude that maximum utilization of the tremendous capability of the American free enterprise system is a crucial element in any program for improving conditions in both our urban centers and our rural poverty areas, which have brought us to the present crisis.

—Advisory Panel on Private Enterprise,
National Advisory Commission on Civil Disorders,
29 January 1968

At its worst, "black capitalism" is a dangerous, divisive delusion—offered as a panacea by extremists, both black and white, some businessmen who see a chance for profit and a few well-intentioned, but misguided, liberals. Attempts to build separate economic enclaves with substantial federal tax subsidies within specific geographically limited ghetto areas is apartheid, anti-democratic nonsense.

—George Meany, AFL-CIO, 1969

We ... do not view our nation's history as one that is so racially benign, or our present circumstance as one so liberated from invidious discrimination that remedial measures to overcome the anticompetitive effects of ethnic prejudice are rendered unnecessary.

—United States Commission on Minority Business Development, 1992

We call on the government to stop undoing hard won gains such as affirmative action ... to adopt an economic bill of rights including a plan to rebuild the wasting cities.

— Mission Statement of the Million Man March, 1995

Introduction

In the wake of the Civil Rights movement, black power demands led to federal government support of black capitalism. Through the Small Business Administration (SBA) and

Department of Commerce minority business programs, the federal government, for the first time, provided direct support of black American business.[1] The amount of money received was comparatively limited, never approximating what was secured by white American business in subsidies, grants, loans, loan guarantees, procurements, and tax breaks. Yet in less than a decade, some white Americans began to demand a retrenchment. Some of them, along with their allies of color, claimed that federal assistance allocated black business during the Johnson and Nixon years, primarily grants, guaranteed loans, set-asides, and procurement contracts, amounted to preferential treatment.[2] Through a glass darkly, those critics refused to see, much less acknowledge, that in the post–Civil Rights era most of the financial support by the federal government continued to go to white American businesses.

This chapter provides a historical assessment of federal government policies that impacted black business. It includes a review of the origin of the SBA, civil rights legislation and black capitalism initiatives. A brief assessment of the views of black leaders, including Dr. Martin Luther King, on American capitalism and black capitalism is also provided. In addition, the business competition faced by blacks from the nation's new immigrants in the post–Civil Rights period is considered. The chapter then compares black mayoral politics and its positive impact on black business with federal government policies, including Supreme Court decisions, that sanctioned the dismantling of federal affirmative action initiatives for minority business in the 1990s. The responses of black Americans who oppose affirmative action as preferential treatment in violation of the Fourteenth Amendment's Equal Protection Clause are also addressed. The chapter begins with a brief overview of federal assistance to black business in 1990, an assessment that challenges assertions of preferential treatment for blacks and black businesses. Is there a thesis to this chapter? Yes, and it is that the federal government owes a great deal to black America.

Preferential Treatment for Whom?

The SBA defines a small business as a firm having fewer than 500 employees. Based on 1987 figures, only 10,000 of the 17 million businesses in the United States had more than 500 employees. Accordingly, the federal government classified "approximately 99 percent of all firms in the country" as small. Consequently, 99 percent of all American businesses, not just black businesses, in the post–Civil Rights period were "theoretically eligible to participate in the small business set-aside program."[3] Yet, of the 17 million businesses in America, only 1.2 million were minority firms, including 424,200 black businesses (see table 9.1). And as late as in 1995 only 15 black businesses had more than 500 employees.

In addition, while only 1 percent of American firms are considered "other than small" businesses, government figures show that this 1 percent "captures approximately 80 percent of the federal prime contract dollar." The remaining 20 percent, nondisadvantaged small businesses, secured 16 to 17 percent of the federal prime contract dollar, leaving minority, namely small disadvantaged businesses, with from 3.2 to 3.7 percent of the federal prime contract dollar (see table 9.2).[4] In America after the Civil Rights movement, then, white businesses continued to be advantaged by preferential treatment in federal government assistance.

TABLE 9.1   Minority-Owned Firms and Business Receipts, 1987

Minority	Number of Firms	Percent all U.S. Firms	Total Receipts ($)	Receipts per Firm ($)	Percent of all U.S. Receipts
Black	424,165	3.1	19,763,000,000	46,593	1.0
Hispanic	422,373	3.1	24,732,000,000	58,555	1.2
Asian*	355,331	2.6	33,124,000,000	93,222	1.7
American Indians**	21,380	.2	911,000,000	42,610	0.05
Total****	1,213,750	9.0	77,840,000,000***		3.95

Total Number All U.S. Firms	13,695,480	
Total All U.S. Receipts	$1,994,808,000,000	
Average Gross Receipts ($)		
Total All (U.S.)	$145,654	
Total Minority	64,132	
Total White Men	189,000	

Source: United States Commission on Minority Business Development (Washington, D.C.: Government Printing Office, 1992), 3, 4, and 5.

*Includes Pacific Islanders.

**Includes Eskimos and Aleuts.

***$78,530,000,000

****Details do not add to totals. Firms owned equally by two or more minorities are included in data for each group but counted only once at total levels.

The amount of federal assistance represented by prime contract and subcontract dollars allotted to disadvantaged businesses can scarcely be considered preferential treatment. Yet opponents of federal assistance to black businesses claim that they are the recipients of preferential treatment, despite the limited dollar amounts they receive and the large percentage of federal prime contract and subcontract dollars secured by the "other than small" businesses compared to that secured by minority disadvantaged businesses.

Dinesh D'Souza is one critic who denounces the amount of money allocated to small disadvantaged businesses, specifically federal assistance to black business; he says, "In

TABLE 9.2   Fiscal year 1990 Distribution of Federal Contract Dollars

Fiscal year 1990 Distribution of Federal Prime Contract Dollars

	Prime Contract Dollars (Millions $)	Percent (%)
Nondisadvantaged small business	29,314.3	16.48
Small disadvantaged business	6,658.1	3.74
Other than small business	141,868.3	79.77
Total	177,840.7	99.99

Fiscal Year 1990 Distribution of Federal Subcontract Dollars

Nondisadvantaged small business	24,809.6	36.04
Small disadvantaged business	2,447.6	3.56
Other than small business	41,589.4	60.41
Total	68,846.6	100.01

Source: United States Commission on Minority Business Development, *Historically Underutilized Businesses (HUBs): Final Report* (Washington, D.C.: United States Government Printing Office, 1992), 29, 31.

1990, the total value of federal set-asides exceeded $8.5 billion." This critic, however fails to mention in his indictment that the total value for *all* government set-asides amounted to $246,687.3 billion. Yet he emphasizes that in the allocation of federal assistance to American businesses "minority businesspeople are scarcely disadvantaged."

Minority businesses make up 9 percent of all American businesses but have gross business receipts that total only 3.9 percent of the total for all American businesses. Minorities, however, constitute 22 percent of the nation's population. Black Americans, 12.2 percent of the population, have gross business receipts of only 1 percent of the American total. Consequently, D'Souza disingenuously obscures the reality that 80 percent of all federal prime contract dollars are allocated to only 1 percent of all American businesses. Moreover, this fervid critic of affirmative action, who also denies the existence of racism in America, claims that federal assistance to minority businesspeople, especially blacks, is really "America's racial ransom" obtained unethically from American tax dollars by greedy, well-heeled black businesspeople.[5]

It cannot be emphasized, however, that black businesspeople are not greedy enough if all they could get from the federal government was a portion of the $8 billion that, out of $246 billion, was disbursed to all minority businesses. Indeed, if there were an equitable distribution of federal funds to American businesses, African-Americans alone, constituting 12 percent of the population, should have been allocated $29.52 billion, rather than only a share of the $8 billion given to all minorities.

In the post–Civil Rights era, considering the comparatively limited economic advances of black business, the ultimate reality is that federal assistance to black business by no means represented a policy of preferential treatment for black businesses, much less an equitable distribution of federal funds, which is called for by the Fourteenth Amendment's equal protection guideline. Specifically, equal protection would have required that black business receive $29.52 billion in assistance. Had the federal government exceeded that amount in its allocation of federal assistance to black business, then the claim of preferential treatment would have validity.

The Small Business Administration in the 1950s

Preferential treatment for white businesses has been the established norm in America. The government's prior failure to provide support for small white businesses, other than ad hoc programs and agencies created during times of national crisis, led to the founding of the Small Business Administration in 1953, during the first year of the Eisenhower Administration. In formulating policy to promote small businesses, the SBA drew on both New Deal and World War II legislation.[6] Founded as a temporary agency, the SBA was essentially an outgrowth of the Reconstruction Finance Corporation (RFC), which was empowered to make loans to businesses until it was abolished in 1953.[7] From 1934 to 1946, the RFC made 35,000 loans in the amount of $3.3 billion. Just about all of these went to big business, as evidenced by the fact that "11,000 loans of $5,000 or less composed 1 percent of those loans by value."[8] The purpose of the SBA was fourfold: (1) aid, counsel, assist, and protect, insofar as is possible, the interests of small business concerns in order to preserve free competitive enterprise; (2) ensure that a fair proportion of the total purchases and contracts or subcontracts for property and services for the government ... be placed with small business enterprises; (3) ensure that a fair proportion of the total sales of government property be made to such enterprises; and (4) maintain and strengthen the overall economy of the nation.[9]

When these objectives for the federal support of small businesses were made in 1953, no one complained. It was understood that small white businesses were the target for federal support. Yet when these same objectives were applied to minority businesses some 16 years later, beginning in 1969 with President Nixon's black capitalism initiatives, charges were made that federal assistance to minorities was preferential treatment. These belated moves to include black business, however, were a tacit acknowledgment by the federal government that the SBA did not have the interests of small black businesses in mind. The SBA's initiatives after 1969 were merely attempts to provide equal protection under the law, as required by the Fourteenth Amendment.

Moreover, after 1954, there were black businesses that made attempts to capitalize on the federal government's programs to aid small businesses. In 1954 the National Hotel Association (organized in November 1953) took the position that "Negro hotel owners should use SBA to secure loans for needed remodeling, new construction and refurbishing their outmoded buildings."[10] Congress had strengthened the SBA, giving it authority to make construction loans to hotels, motels, and other types of small business enterprises. Despite the 1954 Brown decision, the SBA did finance business projects that tapped segregated markets. In 1957 the $100,000 Dogan Motor Court constructed in Knoxville, Tennessee, for blacks only, was built with SBA funds.[11]

In 1958 the SBA was made a permanent federal agency. Its mandate remained the same as in 1953: to provide for both loan assistance and the procurement of federal contracts to small businesses. In addition to the SBA, the Small Business Investment Company (SBIC) Act was passed in 1958. Its purpose was to encourage the establishment of small business investment firms, which would provide long-term, equity-type financing for small businesses. In support of this program, the federal government would buy up to $150,000 in debentures in each corporation granted a license and charter. The main criteria for application approval was "management ability and integrity." With few blacks involved in investment banking in the 1950s, the SBIC appeared to offer only limited advantages in promoting black enterprise.

Moreover, the competition for funds was intense. When the program was announced, some 9,000 companies and individuals immediately wrote the SBA "expressing interest in forming corporations." One of the first businesses to apply under this act was the Small Business Development Corporation, based in Washington, D.C. Although white real estate broker John P. Murchison organized the group, 9 of its 13 promoters and stockholders were black. The group was established as an investment company, with plans to start business with an initial capitalization of $300,000, while also selling additional stock worth $1 million. In its 1958 application the company stated its purpose was to help solve the primary problems of financing of black businesses: "For years, we have observed the frustrations of an appreciable number of minority group businessmen whose firms have failed, or have not reached attainable goals, due principally to lack of long-term financial assistance, proper business procedures and the utilization of adequate sales and public relations techniques and practices."[12]

In the 1950s there was no specific SBA legislation indicating that the agency intended to focus on small black businesses as a target for government assistance. There is no reason to believe, then, that Murchison, a white person, included blacks in his investment group as a means of providing an opportunity for him to capitalize on government financing. It was not until the federal government specifically earmarked funds for the purpose of promoting minority business that whites recognized the advantages that could be obtained by involving blacks in their application for governmental funding of small businesses. Indeed, a major complaint from the late 1960s on was that some black businesses, which had secured federal minority business funds, were fronting for enterprises owned and often managed by whites.[13]

The War on Poverty and Black Capitalism

By 1960 the federal government, reluctantly and in the face of the intensification of the Civil Rights movement, acted to provide support for advancing the political and civil rights of black Americans. During the second Eisenhower Administration in 1957 civil rights legislation was passed, the first since 1875, which had been found unconstitutional in 1883. In 1960 a second civil rights act was passed. Both acts were largely confined to protecting black voting rights. The initiative for the Civil Rights Act of 1964 was made by President Kennedy, who initially was only a little less reluctant than his Republican predecessor in promoting civil rights for blacks. Before long, however, Kennedy acted decisively in expanding his New Frontier agenda. While attempting to push the civil rights bill through Congress, Kennedy used his executive privilege to end employment discrimination.[14] His executive orders on fair employment were enacted into law as Title VI and Title VII of the 1964 Civil Rights Act, passed seven months after his assassination.

While the 1964 Civil Rights Act did not address specifically the issue of black business, Title VI, Federally Assisted Programs, stipulated that "Every Federal agency which provides financial assistance through grants, loans or contracts is required to eliminate discrimination on the grounds of race, color or national origin in these programs."[15] As a federal agency, the SBA was bound by the nondiscrimation provision. In response, it began to target blacks for financial assistance in developing businesses.

Also, in 1964 President Lyndon Johnson's Economic Opportunity Act established the Office of Economic Opportunity (OEO). It assisted black businesses through its Economic Opportunity Loan (EOL) Program. Its specific charge was to provide loans and technical assistance to poor inner-city residents for establishing businesses.[16] Unlike SBA loans to nonminority small business, EOL loans were targeted for blacks who applied to establish small, marginal, high-risk, mom-and-pop enterprises. Even then, the program proved inadequate. The criteria for those who received EOL loans virtually guaranteed failure. Loans were denied individuals with high personal income or savings and those with technical expertise in business management who could or had demonstrated a capacity to succeed in business.

The EOL program, as part of Johnson's War on Poverty agenda, went into effect in 1965 but within a year, with so many loan defaults, Congress gave full control of EOL to the SBA. Until 1968 virtually all SBA loans to assist blacks in starting a business were EOL loans. Even under the SBA, the default rate of EOL loans was high, although loans were made to people with business experience. In the final analysis, limited venture capital can account in part for the failures of minority businesses funded under EOL.[17] Moreover, the dollar amounts of SBA loans made in 1967–1968 were decidedly in favor of whites; table 9.3 shows the differences among average loan amounts for whites and various minority groups: whites, $37,001; blacks, $13,449; Puerto Ricans, $12,886; and Hispanics, $2,373. The total amount in EOL loans made to whites was $652,379,002 compared to $21,761,390 to blacks. Had there been true preferential treatment in the allot-

TABLE 9.3   SBA Loans by Race and Ethnicity, 1 July 1967–1 July 1968

Race/Ethnicity	Total Amount Loans ($)	Number	Average Amount Loans ($)
White	652,379,022	17,631	37,001
Black	21,761,390	1,618	13,449
Hispanic	15,715,211	6,621	2,373
"Oriental"	3,281,515	101	32,490
American Indian	1,490,980	48	31,062
Puerto Rican	953,570	74	12,886

Source: Small Business Administration

ment of these funds, blacks would have received three times more in loans than they actually did. The SBA minority loan rate had improved somewhat by 1991 (see table 9.4).

The major thrust of Johnson's War on Poverty program, however, was not the promotion of black business, but rather increasing black employment through the 1964 Equal Employment Opportunity Commission (EEOC), which also proved ineffective. Though the EEOC lacked specific enforcement provisions, the major national civil rights organizations and local black community-based organizations capitalized on Johnson's war on poverty to promote the economic empowerment of black communities in creating their own programs.

In 1962 the Southern Christian Leadership Conference (SCLC), headed by Dr. Martin Luther King, founded Operation Breadbasket to put "bread, money and income in the baskets of black and poor people." The impetus for this movement developed from a black community organization in Philadelphia, the Selective Patronage Program, founded in 1960 by the Reverend Leon Sullivan and 400 other black ministers. A revival of the 1930s Don't Buy Where You Can't Work campaigns, the Selective Patronage Program succeeded in obtaining about 2,000 skilled jobs for blacks by 1962, a result of its boycotts of major

TABLE 9.4   SBA Loans to Minority/Nonminority Businesses by Major Industries, FY1991

Industries	Loan Amount ($)	Number of Loans	Average Size of Loan ($)
Construction			
Minority	15,636,598	82	190,690
Nonminority	194,150,918	938	206,984
Services			
Minority	239,920,484	741	323,779
Nonminority	1,013,272,015	4,490	225,673
Manufacturing			
Minority	71,944,802	231	311,449
Nonminority	718,757,496	2,481	289,705
Retail			
Minority	171,611,110	750	228,815
Nonminority	852,139,812	4,548	187,366

Source: United States Commission on Minority Business Development (Washington, D.C.: Government Printing Office, 1992), 25.

businesses in that city. It was the success of Sullivan's program that prompted King to launch SCLC's Operation Breadbasket in Atlanta.[18]

In 1966 the SCLC, expanding the Civil Rights movement northward, established a branch of Operation Breadbasket in Chicago, headed by the Reverend Jesse Jackson. In 1967 he was appointed national director with a twofold economic agenda: to increase black employment and promote the expansion of black business. Targeting bread, dairy, soft-drink companies and supermarket chains, Operation Breadbasket secured employment for thousands of blacks. Jackson also succeeded in negotiating contracts with white retailers to provide more shelf space to stock products, primarily food, hair preparations, and beauty aids, manufactured by blacks. In addition, white businesses were encouraged to use black service enterprises for such jobs as garbage removal and extermination and to contract with black construction companies; also, white companies doing business in black communities were urged to deposit moneys made from the black community in black banks.[19]

Black Power and Black Capitalism

After Harlem erupted in riots and civil disorders in 1964, followed by Watts in 1965, and Chicago in 1966, national civil rights organizations bolstered their programs for increasing black community development, which included promoting black business. The central issue for black America after the Civil Rights Acts of 1964 and 1965, was economic empowerment, which emerged as the agenda of the black revolution of the 1960s. In June 1966, some two months before the Chicago riot, Stokely Carmichael, head of the Student Non-Violent Coordinating Committee (SNCC), called for a "black power" movement, which soon included a black economic nationalist program, "black capitalism." Carmichael's agenda for black capitalism was based on a communal economic effort: "We want to see the cooperative concept applied in business and banking."[20] As black power gained momentum and black economic nationalism propelled the agendas of national civil rights groups and community-based organizations, the demand for black capitalism escalated into an ideology whereby it

> constituted a movement by blacks to gain control over the business development of their own communities. At the same time they reached out into the encompassing marketplace for new entrepreneurial resources. Directing business growth in the black community was considered the first step toward achieving a powerful black economic presence in the larger American economy. Essentially, Black capitalism called for a new kind of social and economic contract among racial groups in America— one based on mutual self-interest rather than integration.[21]

In the 1960's the Nation of Islam, under the leadership of the Honorable Elijah Muhammad, provided black America with one of the most successful expressions of cooperative black capitalism. In its business development activities, the Nation of Islam also aided many highly disaffected blacks to become contributing members of their community. Many of its male members were recruited in prison, including Malcolm X. Yet, through its ethnically based religious and economic solidarity programs, the Nation of Islam built a $80-million business empire, with its own corporate jet to facilitate business negotiations. Each mosque served as an economic unit, raising money for national enterprises, while members assisted each other in the development, promotion, and consumer support of their small business enterprises.[22] The black communal capitalist program of the Nation of Islam followed in the tradition of Marcus Garvey's UNIA and the Father Divine Peace Mission Movement, reflecting the continuity of early-twentieth-century self-help economic initiatives promoted by Booker T. Washington and W. E. B. DuBois.[23]

The black capitalism agenda and success of the Nation of Islam, however, were ignored by white America. The virulent denouncement of white racism by the Nation's leaders and its demands for a separate black America alienated not only white America but also the established leadership of black America. Ironically, however, the Nation's business development program, based on Elijah Muhammad's five-point Economic Blueprint for the Black Man, stated: "Observe the operations of the White Man. He is successful. He makes no excuse for his failure." As Earl Ofari said in an assessment of the Nation's emphasis on developing profit-making enterprises, "it does not seek to over-turn, but instead to copy" American capitalism.[24] The Nation of Islam was not alone in its ideological incongruity: denouncing white American capitalism while at the same time demanding black capitalism.

As the black revolution advanced from the promotion of civil rights to demands for black power, a reversal of nationalist positions by black leaders took place in constructing programs for the economic development of black America. Paradoxically, blacks who had taken a prointegration position in the Civil Rights movement became advocates of separatism in response to black power nationalist agendas and then emerged as proponents of black capitalism. But their goals for black capitalism, ironically, included demands for federal assistance and support from white corporate America. Emerging militant black nationalists, such as Floyd McKissick, of the Congress of Racial Equality (CORE), and Nathan Wright, chairman of the 1967 Newark Black Power Conference, initially viewed any programs to promote black capitalism as antithetical to the black experience. Also, they denounced black businesspeople for assuming a role that they said was analogous to that "played by bourgeois-nationalist political elites in an underdeveloped country undergoing a transformation from colonialism to neocolonialism."[25]

When it was headed by Floyd McKissick from 1966 to 1968, CORE underscored the changing economic focus of the black revolution in the 1960s. When he assumed its chairmanship in 1966, McKissick said, "Black People in the United States live in a state of *de facto* nationhood." In order to build a strong and separate black economy, McKissick called for the formation of either a separate territory for blacks in the United States or a black nation of city-states dispersed throughout the country. Then, only two years later, McKissick, a lawyer and Morehouse College graduate, emerged as one of the strongest proponents of black capitalism when he established Floyd B. McKissick Enterprises, Inc., in 1968, a venture-capital investment firm. Its purpose was to underwrite black entrepreneurship through an alliance with white corporate America, a program also endorsed by Nathan Wright, who advocated that blacks should "seek executive positions in corporations . . . and high management positions in banks, stores, investment houses, legal firms, civic and government agencies and factories."[26]

Martin Luther King and Black Capitalism

During the black revolution in the 1960s, scathing attacks against racial inequities in American capitalism were most prevalent in the speeches of Malcolm X and in the militant revolutionary polemics of the Black Panthers, founded in 1966. Their virulent denouncements of American racism and capitalism paralleled the more reasoned pronouncements on civil rights made by Dr. Martin Luther King Jr., at least until 1967. King's strongly anti-capitalistic pronouncements made then, however, were viewed with interest, particularly because they were seen by some as his response to black power initiatives. After 1965, the demands of black power adherents had eclipsed the agenda of the mainstream Civil Rights movement. With the primary goals of the Civil Rights movement achieved by the Civil Rights Acts of 1964 and 1965, black power, with its agendas for promoting black capitalism, challenged King's ideological leadership of black America.

In 1967 King and the SCLC refocused their efforts on a new aspect of civil rights—the plight of the poor. In his book *Where Do We Go from Here?* he insistently raised the issue of why there were 40 million poor people in the United States: "You begin to question the capitalist economy. . . . We must honestly admit that capitalism has often left a gulf between superfluous wealth and abject poverty. . . . The profit-motive, when it is the sole basis of an economic system, encourages a cut-throat competition and selfish ambition."[27] Whether or not his attacks on American capitalism were a part of King's strategy to challenge the emergence of black capitalism as the prevailing ideology and goal of black America is unclear. But King's denunciation of American capitalism, paradoxically, was closely tied to his emphasis that black business could play only a limited role in contributing to the economic empowerment of black America. He noted that

> The economic highway to power has few entry lanes for Negroes. Nothing so vividly reveals the crushing impact of discrimination and the heritage of exclusion as the limited dimensions of Negro business in the most powerful economy in the world. America's industrial production is half of the world's total, and within it the production of Negro business is so small that it can scarcely be measured on any definite scale.

King's assessments of the zero-sum role of black business also applied to the limitations of black businesspeople. Rather than viewing them as agents of black economic empowerment, King thought that their focus should be limited to serving as a source of inspiration for the black community and as "a resource for the development of programs and planning," as opposed to actively participating in business. King also denounced American capitalism and the futility of utilizing black businesses as the base for black economic empowerment, and assailed the uselessness of black businessmen for anything beyond serving as icons of resourcefulness. King then advocated that black Americans proceed cautiously in attacking the inequities of American capitalism, explaining that "There exist two other areas, however, where Negroes can exert substantial influence on the broader economy. As employees and consumers Negro numbers and their strategic disposition endow them with a certain bargaining strength."

Consequently, just as blacks had knocked down the walls of segregation and disfranchisement by demonstrations of nonviolence, King advocated that blacks should focus their energies on breaking down the walls of institutional racism in the American labor market. Rather than pushing for the expansion of black business, it appears that King preferred that blacks march to the doors of white corporate America and demand employment. And who was better prepared to lead the protest in bringing equal employment to black America than the masterful pilot of civil rights? As an example of success in challenging white corporate America's employment practices, King was able to point to the accomplishments made in Chicago by Operation Breadbasket, under the leadership of Jesse Jackson.

The incongruity in King's thinking, then, is that while he denounced American capitalism and disparaged the role of black capitalism as a basis for the economic growth of black America, he encouraged blacks to integrate themselves in the capitalist system. King reasoned that by seeking employment in capitalist enterprises and by using either strategic consumption or the boycott of capitalist-produced goods as leverage, blacks could secure economic equality, just as they had secured civil rights.

What are we to think? In King's expanded economic ideology, capitalism was the basis of structural violence in American life. Perhaps his new economic ideas explain the basis of his anti-Vietnam War stance and his newly developed poor people's campaign. By 1967 King's stand against America's involvement in Vietnam and his new civil rights agenda had coalesced into an attack on the failure of President Johnson's War on Poverty specifically, and American capitalism more generally, to improve the economic condition of blacks, as it had done for that of whites. King's new agenda ultimately hastened his removal to the periphery of mainstream American social reform by the liberal white establishment that had supported his civil rights agenda.[28] By 1968 King's moment of leadership was passing. Yet no historical assessment can ever detract from the contributions he made in his leadership of the Civil Rights movement, which provided the foundation not only for the constitutional desegregation of America but also for federal assistance programs for blacks and minorities.

Still, King's program for black economic empowerment—that blacks seek employment in white America, as opposed to developing black business—placed his theories in direct contradiction to black power ideologies that focused on black capitalism. Moreover, King's disparaging commentaries on the limits of black capitalism as a basis for empowering blacks also moved him, paradoxically, to both the right and left of mainstream black economic nationalism in the late 1960s. Before 1967, even revolutionary black nationalists such as Malcolm X and the Black Panthers proposed economic agendas that included black capitalism as the basis of black economic empowerment. Doubtless, Malcolm X's economic philosophy was shaped by his membership in the Nation of Islam, with its black capitalistic economic program that had succeeded without any government financing. As Malcolm X said in 1964, just one month after having broken from the Nation of Islam, "Our economic philosophy is that we should gain economic control over the economy of our own community, the businesses and other things which create employment so that we can provide jobs for our own people instead of having to picket and boycott and beg someone else for a job."[29]

While the Black Panthers advocated a militant political agenda that frightened white America, their economic program in the war against poverty was hardly revolutionary. Indeed, the social services provided by the Panthers, free breakfasts, free health clinics, and educational head-start programs, not only fell within the long tradition of black self-help activities but also filled a gap in Johnson's war on poverty. Moreover, the Panthers' economic program for empowering the black community foreshadowed Nixon's black capitalism initiatives: that the federal government in cooperation with white corporate America had an obligation both to provide jobs for blacks and to assist blacks in their development of businesses that could also provide new avenues of employment for other blacks. The Panthers sounded a similar note about black capitalism in their political platform: "We believe that if the white American business men will not give full employment, then the means of production should be taken from the business men and placed in the community so that the people of the community can organize and employ all of its people and give a high standard of living."[30]

The idea that white America give up its institutional exploitation of blacks was also advocated by James Forman, at one time a SNCC executive secretary and briefly a member of the Black Panthers. In 1968 at the National Black Economic Development Conference (NBEDC), convened by the Interreligious Foundation for Community Organization, Forman assumed leadership of a militant wing of black participants. He presented a manifesto denouncing racism and capitalism in America as the basis of black impoverishment and demanded $500 million in reparations from white Christian and Jewish religious organizations, saying they "are part and parcel of the system of capitalism."[31] White America was outraged but a few religious organizations acknowledged that "The church has been an all too willing accomplice in the subtle and unsubtle shades of racism."[32]

The philosophical basis of the manifesto rests on the federal government's affirmative action programs, which provides remedies for blacks who have been historically discriminated against. One church organization noted that *"This generation of blacks continues to pay the price of earlier generations' slavery and subjugation; this generation of whites continues to enjoy the profits of racial exploitation"* (author's italics).[33] In response to the manifesto, several white religious organizations and institutions did step up their giving in support of projects for black community development. In New York the Union Theological Seminary invested $500,000 in black businesses in Harlem, with a commitment to raise $1 million.[34]

White American business also saw philanthropic activities as their contribution to black economic empowerment. In 1968 Whitney Young, director of the National Urban League, "called for the creation of more black capitalists"; however, he opposed the idea of an independent black economy. Support for the Urban League's proposal to provide assistance to black businesspeople in 87 cities came in the form of $5 million in seed money from the Ford, Field, Carnegie, and Rockefeller Foundations.[35] As the Vietnam War began to take precedence over black dissidence and civil disorders in American cities, President Johnson made a last-ditch effort to salvage his War on Poverty, which he had hoped would provide the basis for the economic salvation of the black community.

Since the public sector had failed in developing programs to vitalize inner-city ghettos, however, it was Johnson's hope that the giants of American business could succeed. In 1968 he established the National Alliance of Businessmen with Henry Ford II as chairman. Individual cities also established coalitions between the white corporate community and black community groups as a basis to provide access to grants and loans, jobs for the unemployed, and technical assistance to black businesspeople seeking federal funds but who were unsuccessful in negotiating the bureaucratic paper quagmire. Several major American corporations began establishing factories in the inner cities as part of the private sector's contribution to the War on Poverty. Yet by 1987, of the 15 inner-city factories built by major corporations in the mid-1960s, 9 had either been sold or closed.[36] However, the efforts of white corporate America to empower the black community would subsequently be institutionalized in Richard Nixon's promotion of black capitalism.

Black Capitalism and the SBA

Richard Nixon's promotion of black capitalism began during his 1968 presidential campaign, as in a speech made in April of that year: "By providing technical assistance and loan guarantees, by opening new capital sources, we can help Negroes to start new businesses in the ghetto and to expand existing ones."[37] Nixon's black capitalism agenda, however, was modeled after the proposal made by Senator Robert Kennedy in 1968 for minority business development in which he recommended that loan assistance with long-term credit guarantees be administered by the secretary of commerce and coordinated with the SBA and Department of Labor, with short-term credit provided from treasury, tax, and loan accounts. Also, Kennedy had proposed a technical assistance program that included management training and information on obtaining capital.[38]

The Republican framework for black capitalism, as it would develop, can also be found in a proposal presented to Congress in 1968 by Senator Kennedy entitled "A Business Development Program for Our Poverty Areas." In Brooklyn, Kennedy had participated in organizing community economic development programs in the Bedford-Stuyvesant area. While the programs were controlled by community people, there was input and support from business and government agencies, such as the Community Development Corporation, which promoted the development of local black-owned businesses. As Senator Kennedy said, "It is essential that indigenous resident participation be coupled with economic development programs."[39]

With the riots and civil disorders of the late 1960s, the federal government's interest in stabilizing black communities, then, was based on the agenda of black capitalism, with its focus on black-business development. Certainly, it was cost-effective to provide support to black businesspeople, who constituted less than two percent of the total black population. With the SBA 7(a) program, the federal government provided guarantees against defaults on bank loans made to minority businesses, and in 1966 the Minority Enterprise Small Business Investment Company (MESBIC), the SBA's venture capital program, was established.

More importantly, in 1969 the Minority Small Business/Capital Ownership Development Program, generally referred to as the SBA 8(a) program or the federal government set-aside program, was enacted by Congress. The legislation, drafted by black congressman Parren Mitchell, became the cornerstone of the federal government's minority business policy initiatives. The SBA 8(a) set-aside program guaranteed that a certain percentage of government contracts would go to minority businesses.[40] Legislation was also enacted to increase the number of small disadvantaged businesses (SDBs) participating in the Superconducting/Super Collider (SCC) Project and the NASA Space Station Program.

During the Carter Administration, Congress passed Public Law 95–907 in 1978 that, according to *Black Enterprise* magazine, was "one of the biggest leaps forward ever by government in the field of minority business development." The law required companies bidding for prime contracts with the government to submit a plan that would include subcontracting to minority firms. Also, each federal agency was to establish an Office of Small and Disadvantaged Business Utilization with the mandate, found in Title IV of the 1964 Civil Rights Act, that all government agencies seek the fullest possible use of minority businesses in the agency's purchase of goods and services. As a result, minority-owned businesses were positioned to secure a larger share of federal procurement contracts.[41]

Yet, the monetary assistance provided by the federal government in promoting black business in the 25-year period from Johnson's War on Poverty programs amounted to merely a fraction of the $175 billion in prime defense contracts awarded white American businesses from 1940 to 1944. Still, charges of reverse discrimination marked the challenges made during the post–Civil Rights period to federal government programs that provided assistance to minority businesses. Indeed, those challenges had as much to do with removing minorities from competition with white businesses as they did with returning to the preferential treatment programs that had benefited white American businesses in the pre–Civil Rights era.

A major purpose of the SBA was to be the primary source of assistance for small businesses in order to gain access to capital for business development from the private sector. While minority ventures funded from the private sector do better than those funded by the SBA in regard to profitability, debt, and liquidity, the SBA since its inception has been the financial source for a greater number of black businesses. In dollar volume the 7(a) minority-guaranteed bank loan program emerged as the largest SBA financial assistance program to black businesspeople. By 1984 minority businesses received an estimated $9.5 billion in contracts, grants, and loans from federal agencies. By 1990 the SBA 8(a) set-aside program accounted for "over 40 percent of all procurement dollars received by small minority firms. In fiscal year 1990, this amounted to $3.8 billion.[42]

The Department of Commerce and Black Business

After World War II, while the Office of Small Business (later the Small Business Administration) was set up to take over some of the RFC's programs for small businesses, some of its responsibilities were delegated to the Department of Commerce, which continued to offer funding and other forms of assistance to a few small firms. In 1969 President Nixon, expanding his effort to promote black capitalism, established by Executive Order 11458, 5 March 1969, the Office of Minority Business Enterprise (OMBE) as part of the Department of Commerce. Its purpose was to prescribe arrangements for developing and coordinating national programs for minority business enterprise." The secretary of commerce was invested with four major responsibilities in administering the program: (1) to implement federal policy in support of the minority business enterprise program; (2) to provide technical and management assistance to disadvantaged businesses; (3) to assist in demonstration projects; and (4) to coordinate the participation of all federal departments and agencies in an increased minority enterprise effort.

Subsequently, the OMBE was renamed the Minority Business Development Agency (MBDA), which has five regional offices that provide technical advice and financial assistance, including both venture and development capital, to minority entrepreneurs. Also, the MBDA, in conjunction with the International Trade Administration, promotes international trade opportunities for minority businesses. In 1971 Executive Order 11652 included the following definition of a minority business enterprise in order to help determine businesses that would be eligible for the program: "A business enterprise that is owned or controlled by one or more socially or economically disadvantaged persons. Such disadvantage may arise from cultural, racial, chronic economic circumstances or background of other similar cause. Such persons include, but are not limited to, Negroes, Puerto Ricans, Spanish-speaking Americans, American Indians, Eskimos, and Aleuts."

In 1972 the Department of Commerce initiated the Survey of Minority-Owned Business Enterprises (SMOBE) to provide comprehensive information on minority businesses, which until that time was virtually nonexistent. Also, the Department of Commerce established the Minority Enterprise Development Advisory Council (MEDAC) in 1989, which proved as ineffective as the MBDA, reflecting the Reagan Administration's efforts to dismantle this agency.[43] In 1992 the United States Commission on Minority Business Development, appointed by President Bush in 1989, gave its final report on the MBDA and the MEDAC. Its mandate was to "review and conduct an assessment of the operations of all Federal programs intended to promote and foster the development of minority owned businesses to ascertain whether the purposes and objectives of such program(s) are being realized.[44] The commission, chaired by Joshua Smith, found the MBDA to "lack sufficient resources and to have been previously mismanaged." Given that both agencies were created by executive orders and could be dismantled by them, the commission recommended the statutory creation of the Administration for the Development of Historically Underutilized Businesses, which would absorb the responsibilities of both the MBDA and much of those then relegated to the SBA.

In 1993 Ronald Harmon Brown (1941–1996) was appointed secretary of commerce by President Clinton. He was the first African-American to hold that position.[45] Before his untimely death in a plane crash in the Balkans on a trade mission to Croatia, Brown had used his position to influence both domestic and international economic policies. He participated in negotiating the North American Free Trade Agreement (NAFTA) and also the General Agreement on Tariff and Trade (GATT), both of which, however, found little support from the black business community or the Black Congressional Caucus.[46] Yet while Brown's agenda included promoting an expansion of international trade with Latin American, African, and Asian nations, he also put teeth in the MBDA, which was seen as lacking funding, leadership, and focus, a result of the Reagan and Bush Administrations.

As secretary of commerce, however, Brown had four priorities: to strengthen the department's minority business programs; to develop new jobs; to strengthen the Advanced Technology Program in assisting businesses in both the high-tech and environmental industries; and to promote U.S. exports. Consequently, during his three years as secretary, Brown encouraged federal agencies to intensify their efforts in procuring contracts with minority businesses. He also extended his efforts to encourage private-sector businesses, particularly the *Fortune* 500 and 1000 companies, to increase their procurement contracts with black businesses.

At the same time, Brown's 15 trade missions to five continents and some 25 countries, including China and India, increased American exports by 26 percent, resulting in a "record $80 billion worth of announced business contracts for U.S. made goods and services." On his trade missions Brown was accompanied by delegations of American business leaders, both black and white, representing 200 American businesses. Indeed, about 100 minority business owners accompanied Brown on his trade missions to Mexico and South America. Brown's goal, however, was not only to make but also to close international business deals. On a 1994 trade mission to Brazil, Brown closed a $1.4 billion dollar contract for Raytheon to build a satellite system for Brazil. As secretary of commerce, Brown ushered in a "new era of commercial diplomacy." Moreover, he turned what many perceived to be a low-level executive department into a high-powered agency.[47] In 1994, under Brown's direction, the Department of Commerce's International Trade Administration (ITA) created the Memorandum of Understanding Program with the MBDA that provides "import/export counseling, financing and matchmaking with more experienced firms." Also 15 export assistance centers were established. [48]

Secretary Brown conducted four trade missions to South Africa that influenced its business relations with the United States. An important additional element in shaping America's business policy in South Africa and also in bringing down its apartheid regime was the effort of the Reverend Leon Sullivan, a black Philadelphia minister, in establishing a code of conduct for American corporations operating in South Africa. First proposed in 1977, the code included promoting racial equality in employment practices, providing nonsegregated eating and rest facilities, and increasing the numbers of blacks and other minorities in management and supervisory positions. The Sullivan's Code of Corporate Conduct also called for establishing job training programs, providing housing, funding community education programs, and awarding scholarships to children of black employees. American corporations who agreed to follow the code were regarded as signatories and their compliance was monitored and publicly reported.[49]

Ironically, the code's requirements for American businesses in South Africa often exceeded those that applied to black employees of white corporations in the United States. Indeed, the code asked white corporate America to do more for South African blacks than what African-American leaders in the 1960s had demanded from white corporate America. American corporations pumped millions of dollars into their South African subsidiaries, launched numerous development programs, and contributed to South Africa's Small Business Development Corporation in order to provide training programs in entrepreneurship for black South Africans. At the same time, antiapartheid sentiment in the United States was escalating. Demands were being made for full divestment of American corporations in South Africa, with pressure coming from Rev. Jesse Jackson and TransAfrica, an organization founded in 1977 by Randall Robinson that pushed for sanctions and divestment.

In 1986 Congress overrode President Reagan's veto by passing the Comprehensive Anti-Apartheid Act, pushed by Congressman Charles Rangel, which imposed 18 different sanctions on American businesses in South Africa. The law banned new loans and investments to South Africa unless they were made to black-owned businesses. The act also authorized Congress to expend $40 million for the education of South African blacks in entrepreneurship, social services, and labor. Increasingly, American firms divested their South African holdings, including Revlon, whose South African subsidiary made black hair care products. Presumably, the ultimate insult to the apartheid regime in South Africa by the American government was the appointment in 1986 of Edward Perkins, the nation's first black ambassador to that country.

In 1987 Rev. Sullivan, in the face of increasing pressure from African-American leaders and antiapartheid groups in the United States, disassociated himself from the code, announcing it had failed. He called for a mass exodus of American corporations from South Africa, along with the imposition of broad economic sanctions. By 1987, 162 companies had left South Africa, but an equal number remained. Bishop Desmond Tutu, the 1984 Nobel Peace Prize recipient, also denounced the code, explaining: "Our rejection of the code is on the basis that it does not aim at changing structures. The Sullivan Principles are designed to be ameliorative. We do not want apartheid to be made more comfortable. We want it dismantled."[50]

By the 1990s, in the shaping of America's international economic policies, three blacks had been appointed to cabinet-level positions during the Clinton Administration. In addition to Brown, Michael Espy was appointed secretary of agriculture, and Hazel O'Leary, secretary of energy. In their cabinet positions, all three made important international trade missions to promote American business. Indeed, O'Leary was the first secretary in the Department of Energy's 25-year history to embark on trade missions. These missions, which included leaders of America's energy industries, generated billions of dollars of business for these industries. In 1996, however, O'Leary was brought before a congressional committee and charged with excessive travel expenditures. In addition, Michael Espy resigned his position. It is interesting to note that at the close of the twentieth century,

America's international trade is being shaped by black Americans. Their contributions cannot be ignored in the history of African-American business or by American business in general.

Minorities, Business Competition, and Conflict

With the present new global economy, American businesses have entered a new phase of competition. Foreign multinationals, which have established their subsidiaries in the United States, now compete in the domestic economy with American businesses. Similarly, African-American businesses have increasingly been competing with enterprises established by the nation's new immigrants. Often, they have the advantage of an ethnic solidarity that connects them with countries of their origin. In the United States, black American businesspeople historically have faced competition from each new wave of immigrants, particularly those from Europe.

In the large industrial cities of America, especially from the early twentieth century on, whites have controlled a majority of the businesses in emerging black business districts.[51] Asians, primarily Chinese, have also owned enterprises in black business districts. And in the urban centers of the Northeast, West Indians have established businesses that compete with African-Americans. Indeed, in New York in the 1920s, West Indians, who constituted 25 percent of the city's black population, owned half of the black businesses in Harlem.[52]

The 1965 Immigration Act brought a new wave of immigrants to America, primarily from Latin America, Asia, and the Middle East. In their recent settlement in the United States, a substantial number established profitable enterprises in black business districts. Since then, large amounts of black consumer dollars have contributed to the economic empowerment of successive waves of America's new immigrant groups. In black business districts, the most successful have been the Cubans and Koreans, due in part to their high educational attainments.[53]

A large number of Koreans have immigrated to this country for the specific purpose of establishing a business. One of the reasons for their success is that they have been able to bring substantial sums of money with them to finance the enterprise. In 1981 the Korean government set a limit on the amount of money citizens could take with them when emigrating: $3,000 for each adult and $1,000 for each child under 14. In 1984 the limit was increased to $20,000 for each adult, and in 1986 it was increased to $50,000 for the family head and $10,000 for each family member. Nevertheless, some Koreans "smuggled in huge amounts of illegal money into the United States and invested it in their business."[54]

Such access to capital has been the most important factor in the business success of many new immigrant groups. Particularly for Asians, West Indians, and eastern European Jews, cultural survival mechanisms, self-help organizations, and rotating-credit associations have enabled these immigrant groups to generate venture capital for business development. Among the Chinese the rotating-credit association is known as *hui,* among the Japanese it is the *ko, tanomoshi,* or *mujin,* and among Koreans it is the *kye.* The common West Indian name is *susu,* derived from *esusu,* the Nigerian rotating-credit institution. Among eastern European Jews, the groups were known as "family circles" and "cousin clubs."

The financial feature common to all these groups is that each member contributes the same amount of money each month, with each member having access to the total fund on a rotating basis.[55] In the Korean *kye*, when the pot is substantial, "members bid for the pool by stating the amount of interest they will pay to get first crack at the money." With large amounts such as $100,000, interest might run to 15 percent, which is taken out in advance. The *kye* has also been institutionalized at some Korean banks, where individuals who enter the bank's $10,000, 12-month *kye* saving plan, are eligible for an advance of the full amount after four months of saving.[56]

In comparative studies of minority businesses, sociologists and economists have charted the economic success of these immigrant groups, primarily to compare it with the status of black American businesses. Several theories have been offered to explain the business success of immigrants, including immigrant assimilation, the existence of middlemen minorities, ethnic enclaves, dual-labor markets and, more recently, the Asian-American economic model .[57] On the basis of these studies, which compare the economic success of various immigrant ethnic groups, especially West Indians, with African Americans, the most conservative analysis concludes that race is not a variable in determining economic advancement in America.[58] Rather, social class is regarded as the major factor in economic success, a conclusion that underscores the phenomenon known as the "declining significance of race."[59]

The fact that social class has been identified as the predominant factor in business success should not be surprising, because most immigrants, particularly Asians and Cubans, who succeed in businesses include a high proportion of educated, skilled professionals. At the same time, these and other studies also show that the economic success rate of the post-Civil Rights generation of black professionals, who are highly educated, compares favorably with that of their white American counterparts. Yet these studies base their conclusions on family income, which, if examined in further detail, would reveal that race still operates as a variable in determining economic success. Unlike those of the white middle class, family incomes of the increasing number of black middle-class households reflect primarily the combined incomes of a husband and wife, many of whom have jobs that pay from $28,000 to $32,000. Consequently, if family incomes are adjusted by number of workers in the household, white households rank first in income, then Asians, with blacks trailing far behind.[60]

On the other hand, based on the achievements of Asian immigrants in America, one could argue, in a perverse way, for the significance of race in their economic success. An examination of various comparative measures of achievement, including educational-test scores, income, business participation rates, and gross business receipts, shows that immigrant Asians, as a race, appear to outstrip not only all other minorities but also whites. Because of the ethnic diversity of Asians, however, it should be recognized that their economic progress is advancing at different rates of speed.

Yet, why offer African-Americans the Asian-immigrant model of business success?[61] After all, African-Americans are not immigrants. Neither are Native Americans, native Alaskans, nor many Hispanics, but these groups also rank near the bottom in studies of business success that use such criteria as income and business participation rates (see table 9.5). There must be common variables across cultures that account for disparities in minority achievement, perhaps variables comparable to those found in Japanese culture and history. Compare the limited business achievement of Japanese-born Koreans in Japan with that of Korean-Americans in the United States; also, Korean-American business success is greater than that of Japanese-Americans.[62] Why have Koreans born in Japan failed to apply the Asian-American model of business success to improve their socioeconomic posi-

TABLE 9.5   White- and Minority-Owned Firms per 1,000 Population, 1982 and 1987

Minority	1982	1987
White	61.9	67.1
Blacks	11.3	14.6
Hispanics	14.3	20.9
Mexican	13.7	18.8
Puerto Rican	6.3	10.9
Cuban	41.4	62.9
Other Hispanic	14.2	22.9
Asian	43.2	57.0
Asian Indian	51.3	75.7
Chinese	49.1	63.4
Japanese	59.3	66.1
Korean	68.0	102.4
Vietnamese	14.6	49.6
Filipino	25.5	32.8
Hawaiian	16.6	21.5
American Indian	8.8	11.8
Aleut	58.5	54.0
Eskimo	36.8	44.4
Native American	7.4	10.3

Source: Compiled from *American Demographics* (January 1992):34, from Bureau of the Census, 1982 and 1987 Economic Censuses and Population Censuses.

tion in that country? Are racism and ethnocentrism the common variables that cross cultures, whereby historical forces and societal constraints coalesce as agents that limit opportunities for the economic success of native minorities?[63]

Moreover, why do we find the business success rates of highly educated African-Americans lagging behind those of others with comparable educations? Even more, why do a disproportionately larger number of blacks in white corporate America reach the glass ceiling? Why indeed do we have the rage of the highly successful, well-paid, and privileged blacks, who lambast the extent to which racism persists?[64] The white backlash in post–Civil Rights America cannot be ignored. Along with the relatively limited economic gains made by black Americans, white backlash certainly contradicts theories that argue for the declining significance of race in America.

The 1995 bombing of the federal building in Oklahoma City and the rise of white paramilitary terrorist groups are examples of efforts to defy a federal government that dared to provide federal assistance to minorities and blacks. The intensification of white racism in American colleges and universities also challenges assertions of the declining significance of race.[65] Moreover, one need only also consider the escalation of virulent white racism reflected in the increasing retrenchment of affirmative action programs and events such as the 1992 Rodney King incident and the bombing of black churches in the South in the mid-1990s. Within the context of increased white hostility against blacks and the business advancement of new immigrants, it becomes very difficult to accept as a reality the declining significance of race in America.[66]

Indeed, it becomes extremely difficult to explain the efforts of some white Americans in both the public and private sectors to strip blacks of their comparatively limited economic gains made in the post–civil rights era as only an expression of class differences. Few examples can be found in late-twentieth-century America of whites who object to the wealth of other white Americans. Even the white violence against Asians, who respond in kind with antagonism towards blacks, suggests the ascendancy, rather than the decline, of racism in America at the end of the twentieth century.[67]

Paradoxically, the parallels between the Civil Rights and post–Civil Rights periods with Reconstruction and the post–Reconstruction periods are too great for race to be dismissed. In the late twentieth century, race and racism are the prevailing factors that militate against black economic advancement, especially in business. Even the increasing anti-immigration sentiments that exist in segments of both white American and black American communities in the 1990s parallel those in America in the 1890s. One would hope, however, that present-day black Americans do not have to replicate the ultimatum made by Booker T. Washington in his 1895 Atlanta address in response to America's late-nineteenth-century wave of immigrants when he said:

> To those of the white race who look to the incoming of those of foreign birth and strange tongue and habits for the prosperity of the South, were I permitted I would repeat what I say to my own race, "Cast down your bucket where your are." Cast it down among the eight millions of Negroes whose habits you know ... we shall contribute one third to the business and industrial prosperity of the South, or we shall prove a veritable body of death, stagnating, depressing, retarding every effort to advance the body politic.[68]

As Washington said, America will have no internal peace until there has been a grant of full economic rights and opportunities to black America. The death, destruction, and devastation of the riots and civil disorders in the 1960s bear out Washington's counsel, as have the riots in the 1980s and 1990s. In the late twentieth century, destructive conflagrations—black responses to white America's institutional racism—continue to mark the economic wars of dispossession. At the most basic level is the question of who should control the black consumer dollar in black communities. The business districts in black communities in the 1990s, as in the 1960s, remain the battlefield. The targets, however, have expanded to include immigrant businesses.

In Miami, where increasing Cuban business success generated resentment among blacks, there were four race riots in the 1980s. By the late 1980s, Hispanics made up over 65 percent of Miami's population, compared to the 17 percent African-American population. A major source of animosity from blacks was the federal refugee resettlement fund that provided Cuban immigrants, who fled Cuba after the 1959 revolution, with economic help that financed their business development.[69] In addition, while remaining on the periphery of the struggle for civil rights, Cubans, as minorities, were also eligible for the same business loans and grants as blacks. Indeed, they were often deemed more eligible. After the disastrous 1989 riot, a black newspaper columnist said, "The reality of Miami today and in the foreseeable future is, that the Cubans are the new masters in Miami. They should not be surprised when those who feel they have nothing to lose rise up against the new rulers."[70]

The 1992 Los Angeles riot in the wake of the jury acquittal of four white policemen charged with the beating of Rodney King was particularly devastating, requiring 10,072 National Guard troops to restore order. The riot expressed more than disgust with institutional racism. The loss of $800 million, caused when some 1,600 businesses in the riot-torn area were severely damaged, was not just limited to white-owned businesses. In both cities, black businesses were also destroyed. In Los Angeles, however, "A large proportion were Korean-owned, as rioters vented years of frustration and anger against a group that many blacks said was exploiting their poverty." The rioters expressed a sense of displacement, hopelessness, and dispossession in the face of the American economic system, feelings that transcended race and ethnicity. Of the 7,066 people arrested, 3,517 were Hispanics, 2,564 were black, and 843 were white.[71]

The riots of the 1990s, as did the riots in the 1960s, also marked the decline of black businesses in black business districts. In many ways, the decline was facilitated by civil rights legislation, not only in public accommodations and housing, which drew middle-class blacks out of the urban ghettos, but also in the gains made by them in education and employment.[72] In the 1960s, there was a slow recovery of black business, especially in the service sector. Since then, blacks have faced competition from new ethnic enterprises established by immigrants that fill a market niche in depressed black communities. Despite the riots of the 1990s, most ethnic business owners plan to reopen their enterprises in black business districts. Others plan to consolidate their resources to open even larger businesses because of the high profits they generate in black business districts.[73]

Immigrant minorities who have established enterprises in black business districts are resented by blacks, as much for their economic success as for their prejudices and lack of respect shown the black consumer whose purchases fill their pockets. And black consumers are very aware of the crucial role they play in the success of ethnic businesses, such as in Chicago where "the fate of Korean businesses depends on the economic condition of local black residents."[74] In turn, ethnic merchants contribute very little to the economic empowerment of the black communities in which they do business. Moreover, many black Americans consider it a personal affront that many new immigrants, especially Asians, Hispanics, and Middle Easterners, have been able to capitalize on the gains made for them by black Americans in the Civil Rights movement. Yet, often new immigrants view black Americans with disdain.

America's new immigrants, most of whom are people of color, should never forget that their economic opportunities would have been extremely limited had they immigrated to the United States in the days of racial segregation, economic discrimination, and social exclusion of people of color. The road to the economic success of America's new immigrants was paved by blacks who marched the streets and highways of the South for equal opportunity and affirmative action, resulting in the civil rights and black capitalism legislation enacted in the 1960s. Indeed, without such gains achieved through Supreme Court decisions and the Civil Rights movement, to what extent would colored immigrants from Latin America and Asia have achieved their growing economic success?

Until the 1960s, preferential treatment in all sectors of American life was given to whites. As people of color, they should understand that as long as black Americans are subjected to discrimination based on race, color, and previous historical position, as opposed to class, they too will continue to encounter discrimination. Yet, having gained from the contributions of blacks and from their efforts to be assimilated by white America, many of the nation's immigrants and some of their American-born descendants have internalized white America's racial prejudices.[75]

Many immigrant groups, however, consider themselves white, including 51 percent of the Hispanic population, particularly Cubans, as indicated in the 1990 federal census. Moreover, in both Miami and Los Angeles, the general feeling held by African-Americans is not only that many of the nation's new immigrants have internalized racial prejudices and stereotypes but also that some of them have even embraced the political party that seeks to limit minority economic advancement. Prior to the 1996 presidential election,

Asian and Hispanic immigrant groups were strong supporters of the Republican Party, whose policies since Lincoln and the radical Republicans of Reconstruction, have seldom benefited black America.

In the wake of the Republican Party's anti-immigration position in 1996, America's new immigrants protected their interests by turning their backs on the party in the general elections. Now, where will white America find itself, a declining majority, in the twenty-first century, with the emergence of a new group of immigrants whose ancestral homes are not in Europe? In a global community erupting in racial and ethnic conflict in which America as a nation has shared, where is the declining significance of race?

Black Mayors, Set-Asides, and Enterprise Zones

The election of black mayors, a result of the 1965 Voting Rights Act, also reflected the crisis of race in America at midcentury. The rapid suburbanization of white America as a result of its flight from the nation's cities and the increasing voting power of blacks coalesced in new political power for black America. In the 1970s and 1980s, all of America's largest cities elected black mayors, with their number increasing from 48 to 314 during this time. They were elected in cities that had a majority of black residents and cities in which the majority was white.[76]

On taking office, however, black mayors found they were left with a diminishing tax base. Many white businesses had relocated to the suburbs. Also, with the nation moving from a smokestack economy to a high-tech one, there was a subsequent transfer of American industries either to the suburbs or abroad. This trend to cut labor costs contributed to increasing black urban unemployment. Also a legacy of the Reagan Administration between 1982 and 1989 was the 64 percent cutback in federal funds for cities: "from $33.7 billion to $12.1 billion."[77] Consequently, black mayors had to work within tight budget constraints as they found themselves less able to generate municipal growth in municipal employment, as had their white predecessors.

Still, a high priority of black mayors was to use as much of their political clout as possible to ensure that blacks would not be pushed aside in securing access to federal government set-asides. Also, using their appointment powers, black mayors pushed for equity in awarding procurement contracts to minorities. By securing municipal contracts for minority firms, black mayors encouraged the expansion of black-owned businesses. In the 1980s there were advances in black business in cities with black mayors. The cities that showed the greatest growth in black businesses were Atlanta, Los Angeles, Detroit, and Chicago.[78]

There were four major industries that benefited from set-asides and procurement contracts in cities with black mayors: construction companies, manufacturing firms, wholesale enterprises, and skill-intensive service businesses. Yet, these represent only a small percentage of black businesses compared to the great number of traditional service and small-scale retail enterprises. And so federal affirmative action funds were as limited to black businesses in the post–Civil Rights period as social security benefits had been during the New Deal; social security did not cover blacks in agricultural and domestic work, the two areas in which 80 percent of blacks were employed in the 1930s.

However, the growth of black construction companies underscores the importance of federal mandates as a major factor in black business growth in the post–Civil Rights period. The Atlanta-based H. J. Russell & Company, the largest black construction and development company in the nation, was founded in 1959 by Herman J. Russell. Since *Black Enterprise* magazine's list of the 100 top black companies first appeared in 1973, Russell & Company has been ranked among its leaders. In 1976 the company had sales of $21 million and a staff of 300. In 1995 it ranked fourth on the list, with sales of $172.8 million and a staff of 1,197. The most important factor that contributed to the expansion of Russell and other black construction companies from the 1970s to the 1980s was the influence of black mayors, who also encouraged joint-venture projects with white construction firms.

Prior to the election of Maynard Jackson, who served two terms as mayor of Atlanta from 1974 to 1982, black contractors and construction companies were allotted token contracts. In 1973 Atlanta's black construction firms received only $41,758 out of $33 million in city contracts. In 1981, however, they were allocated $19.2 million out of $56 million in city contracts. What did Maynard Jackson and later Andrew Young, who was mayor from 1982 to1988, do to level the playing field? Jackson, for one, pushed for a series of MBE/EEO municipal ordinances that led to the allocation of 25 percent of Atlanta's set-aside programs for minorities, including one in which blacks landed a proportionate share of contracts and subcontracts in the city's $700 million airport expansion program. Young expanded and revised the city's set-aside programs so that 35 percent of them were reserved for minorities.[79] While the Russell company was a multimillion-dollar enterprise before set-asides, government contracts were important in enabling the company to expand.

There was advancement by some blacks in business and the professions in the post–Civil Rights period, but the amount of federal assistance provided black business was insufficient for the development of enterprises that could have created a diversity of jobs in black communities. The multibillion-dollar Federal Empowerment Zones and Enterprise Communities Program, pushed by Congressman Charles Rangel, marks another attempt by the federal government to encourage business development in poverty areas. Doubtless, Rangel's program was a factor that forced the Clinton Administration to reexamine the economic potential of inner-city communities through the development of enterprise zones, which were then recast as empowerment zones.

By the 1990s, then, the federal government was moving the base of black economic empowerment programs from the nonprofit-sector community programs developed in the 1960s to the private sector. Federal support in the amount of $100 million would be granted to each selected urban zone, and businesses in these zones would be eligible for tax incentives and depreciation write-offs. Whether the kinds of businesses that can provide employment will be attracted to the inner city and contribute to the revitalization of black communities, however, was viewed with caution in the early 1990s by black economic policy analysts.[80]

The Croson Decision, Before and After

In 1989 the Supreme Court's decision in the *Richmond v. Croson* case challenged the constitutionality of minority business set-aside programs at the state and local levels, which was covered under the Fourteenth Amendment's Equal Protection Clause. The impact was the greatest on large black businesses, particularly in construction and manufacturing, since these were the industries that had benefited most from set-asides. In the Croson decision, the Supreme Court struck down as unconstitutional a Richmond, Virginia, ordinance that required 30 percent of each construction contract to be awarded to a minority business. It ruled that cities must first show a pattern of discrimination before instituting a minority set-aside program.[81] Before the decision, black mayors were positioned to ensure that blacks would not be overlooked in securing access to federal set-asides. With the Croson decision, Atlanta's municipal set-aside program was suspended.

A study undertaken by Andrew Brimmer, one of the nation's leading economists and the first black member of the board of governors of the Federal Reserve Bank, revealed, however, that discrimination still existed in the city's construction industry. Brimmer found that 92.7 percent of the total revenue received by black-owned construction firms came from the public sector, where contracts for blacks averaged $180,000, compared to $15,000 for private-sector contracts. With white contractors, 80 percent of their total revenue was from the private sector, primarily all from multimillion-dollar contracts. Also, all of the white-owned firms had bonding capacity (including 16 percent of white firms that had unlimited bonding capacity), compared to only 32 percent of minority firms, whose bonding capacity was some 80 percent less than that of whites. Consequently, based on the Brimmer report, these disparities provided "justification to reinstitute some type of minority business program."[82]

Nationally, the impact of the Croson decision could be as catastrophic for Minority Business Enterprises (MBEs) as the 1896 Plessy decision had been for black America. After Croson, individual states and their political subdivisions took immediate steps to "dismantle their race and gender conscious MBE programs." In response, the Minority Business Enterprise Legal Defense and Education Fund (MBELDEF) assumed leadership in combating governmental retrenchment in MBE programs, as the NAACP had done in dismantling legislation supporting racial segregation and discrimination. Immediately after the Croson decision, the MBELDEF began to track responses to the decision and found several patterns of discrimination in the retrenchment of federal set-asides. The organization found that governmental agencies at the state, county, and municipal levels had instituted cutbacks on set-asides to minority business and reduced the percentage of minority set-asides or completely terminated their programs.

For example, Colorado abolished its program, while Denver reduced its MBE program goals. Oregon terminated its MBE goals, but replaced them with a "good faith effort" and a "race-neutral 'Emergent Small Business Program' targeted to economically depressed areas." In Indiana, the city of South Bend suspended its MBE programs, pending study. In Ohio, Dayton and Columbus reduced their MBE goals. The New York and New Jersey Port Authority removed its mandatory goals, but all other initiatives remained operational. In llinois, the Greater Chicago Water Reclamation District suspended its numerical goals.

It appeared that Florida and California were the two states that responded most aggressively to the Croson decision. The MBELDEF report showed that of the 65 political subdivisions holding MBE hearings, 40 percent were in states with a large Hispanic population: 10 were in California, 10 in Florida, 3 in Texas and 1 in Arizona. Florida provides another example of the immediate impact of the Croson case. In Tampa, MBE participation rates of 22 percent in 1988 dropped to 5.2 percent in the three months following the decision. More specifically, the number of contracts awarded black-owned companies fell 99 percent, that of Hispanic-owned companies 50 percent. In Hillsborough County, MBE awards dropped 99 percent.[83]

In St. Petersburg, a $150,000 study was commissioned by the city to determine whether sufficient discrimination existed to require that a percentage of city business go to minority-owned firms. The study found that in 1989, when the city's purchasing department spent $32.5 million on goods and services, less than 0.6 percent, $179,316, went to minority-owned firms. Of the $64 million that the city spent on construction projects, $8.5 million, or 13.3 percent, went to minority firms.[84] The strategies developed by both the public and private sector in St. Petersburg to discourage and evade allocating municipal contracts and subcontracts to minority business enterprises have been as ingeniously contrived and cleverly executed as the legal and extralegal means used to disfranchise and segregate blacks both before and after the 1896 Plessy decision.

The minority set-aside program was suspended in St. Petersburg in December 1989, with the deputy city manager for public works claiming that "minority business owners have never told him they were dissatisfied with the minority business program," and that "St. Petersburg's program is considered one of the most progressive in the state." An African-American subcontractor for steel construction in the city emphasized, however, that the money set aside for minority businesses in construction was "normally only 5 percent to 10 percent of a project, that there is little profit after going through the bidding process, securing the bonding and insurance and performing the work."

Another tactic used to discourage minority subcontractors entailed reducing the amount of money paid them or refusing to pay them at all, often holding back money by claiming poor workmanship. The minority subcontractor then had the choice of accepting the lower payment or incurring the costs of a time-consuming lawsuit. Also, delayed payments meant subcontractors could go bankrupt. Moreover, black subcontractors often were not notified of upcoming bid opportunities, while small emerging minority firms were excluded from bidding because the city's bond and insurance requirements were so high. Finally, the good-ol'-boys network was in full operation. According to the Hispanic owner of a printing company who was rejected for loans by three banks despite a high bond rating and no bad debts "she has seen those who get business from the city 'wining and dining the decision-makers on their boats.' "

The consultant firm conducting the study of St. Petersburg also found that the city " 'has a history of discriminatory legislation and operational practices' that discourage black entrepreneurship." Municipal officials, however, said the report would be studied by a special committee before being submitted to the city council for a decision on whether the city's MBE set-aside program would be reinstated. Yet, as Timothy Bates emphasized in his assessment of local government responses to the Croson decision, "while minority business programs may continue to enjoy broad-based political support, judicial support for many of these programs is problematic."[85]

By the mid-1990s, then, there was a repositioning of black corporate America not only in construction but also in manufacturing, as blacks in these industries attempted to maintain gains made under federal affirmative action legislation and executive policies. At the time, many of Detroit's largest black manufacturing companies began to supply parts to the auto industry, a response by the black manufacturers to the impact of federal affirmative initiatives. But can they maintain the gains they made in the pre-Croson era?

Trumark is a Michigan-based metal products company that makes auto underbody parts for Ford, its largest customer. It also makes chassis parts for Chrysler, but a Chrysler spokesman noted in 1993 that "things are grimmer for smaller minority-owned suppliers squeezed by the Big Three's focus on cost-containment." Also, "smaller suppliers are being forced to seek subcontracting work."[86] Trumark, founded in 1985, had sales of $20.5 million in 1988, $53 million in 1993, and $60 million in 1994; but in 1995 sales had dropped to $50.4 million. Because of pressure from larger competitors, there is increasing interest among black auto suppliers to merge, which would provide a base for them to establish a more solid footing in the industry.

In 1994 two companies that considered merger were the Bing Group, a steel-processing and metal-stamping manufacturer that makes steel structures for car exteriors, and Regal Plastics Company, a plastic-injection-molding manufacturer that makes custom parts for car interiors. In *Black Enterprise's* top 100 black companies (BE 100s) for 1995, the Bing Group, founded by CEO David Bing in 1980, was ranked 13th, while Regal Plastics, founded in 1985 by CEO Dr. William F. Pickard, was listed 53rd. A merger of companies such as the Bing Group, with sales of $101 million and a staff of 450, with Regal Plastics, which had sales of $35 million and a staff of 350, could lead to as much as $300 million in sales within three to five years. Merging would enable the two companies to "build automobile seating frames, consoles and instrumental panels."[87] Mergers contemplated by black auto parts manufacturers are responses not only to the Croson decision but also to the impact of the Japanese auto industry on the American car industry. In the 1960s Japanese car manufacturers began moving away from buying automobile parts to full systems. In 1989 the American auto industry followed suit.

Federal affirmative action initiatives resulting in 8(a) procurement contracts were also an important factor that encouraged the entry of blacks in the defense industry. However, in addition to the *Croson* decision, the end of the Cold War also had a negative impact on black manufacturers to secure defense contracts. The cutbacks in federal defense spending that occurred after 1990 were the main reasons for this adverse effect. One black defense firm affected was the New Jersey–based H. F. Henderson Industries, Inc., founded in 1954, which manufactures defense electronics. In 1989, it ranked 37th on the *Black Enterprise* 100 list, with $22.9 million in sales and with "70 percent of its 1989 revenues from military contracts." Henderson's international contracts accounted for 25 percent of its sales, with 5 percent from the American private sector. In 1987 Henderson was awarded a $125 million defense contract that was to end in 1996—an average of about $13.8 million annually for nine years—to manufacture spare parts for an artillery computer system. The company's sales were $25.65 million in 1993 and $31.55 million in 1994; but in 1995 Henderson was ranked 80th with sales of $24.6 million. At the end of 1996 Henderson's sales were less than $20.5 million and the company was no longer listed on the *BE* 100s.[88]

The relevant issue for the government is that for African-American businesses to achieve gross receipts commensurate with the proportion of blacks in the population requires equal access to the kinds of federal assistance that have historically been provided the white American business sector. The various alphabet agencies created in the late twentieth century by the federal government to aid black business fell far short of the kind of affirmative assistance previously extended to whites. An effective historical parallel can be found in the government's legislation in the early part of this century to break the monopolistic hold that big business had over unprotected small businesses. In breaking the trusts, the government, while it did not level the playing field, at least provided small business an opportunity for economic survival.

Trust-busting legislation was affirmative action that benefited small white American business. It was also preferential treatment, but in the sense that what the government did for small white businesses was merely to extend to them the three *s*'s of government affirmative action: subsidization, support, and supervision, which had been the basis of growth for America's large businesses. Throughout this century, then, the government has aided small white businesses, through such efforts as New Deal legislation and World War II legislation. Also, the 1950 Cellar-Kefauver Act enabled the Department of Justice to use market share as evidence in cases of restraint of trade, a piece of legislation that benefited small business. Indeed, it would appear that this act could be made applicable to contravene the Croson decision.[89]

Government, Black Business, and Black Economic Thought

In the post–Civil Rights period, then, the federal government failed black American business. Black American business failed not only in achieving parity with white American business but also did not achieve the levels of success enjoyed by other minority businesses. Yet, despite the limited federal assistance to black business, black voices have been added to the illiberal calls of white America not only for a retrenchment of federal support to black businesses but also for a dismantling of those programs. The views proffered by the black intelligentsia and economic analysts on government assistance to black business, however, run along a continuum from the radical left to the reactionary right. Some denounce capitalism as being destructive to blacks, while others advocate that socialism could lead to black economic empowerment.[90]

Those on the right are the black conservatives, libertarians, as some prefer to call themselves, most of whom even deny that race is a significant factor in causing black impoverishment. Affirmative action programs are denounced by them as preferential treatment, unconstitutional under the Fourteenth Amendment and even destructive to the advancement of black America. Yet their arguments seem to give little consideration to the economics of discrimination. Rather, their emphasis, when denouncing affirmative action programs enacted in the 1960s and 1970s to remedy past racial discrimination, is that these programs have demeaned blacks, placing them in a position where others assume that race, rather than competency, accounts for *their* employment.[91] Particularly galling to the sensibilities and sensitivities of these advantaged blacks, whose high income and elevated social status were achieved through affirmative action, is not the social and economic devastation of black communities, but the fact that, despite their high-profile positions, they are stigmatized and viewed as incompetent by whites. William J. Wilson admits that "the life chances of individual blacks have more to do with their economic class position than with their day-to-day encounters with whites."[92] It is these day-to-day encounters that privileged blacks find so demeaning.

In their ivory towers, primarily in the academic world of elite white institutions, these blacks seek acceptance from white America, while they remain remote from black America.[93] Yet it becomes difficult to deny their reasoned assessments of why federal civil rights programs failed, even if these assessments miss the point in recognizing the reality of the disastrous consequences of the failure of federal affirmative assistance to blacks. As Thomas Sowell said in explaining the failure of civil rights affirmative action programs, "The creation of rights is politically attractive. It is often a very low cost way to 'do something' about a social 'problem.' Unlike other measures which may entail large expenditures of tax money and thus provoke voter anger, the creation of rights may cost the government little more than paper and ink. What these rights cost the recipients of the society at large is a larger question."[94]

Certainly, the "costs" of civil rights to America have been high. Whites have become increasingly demoralized because they resent the loss of their monopolistic right to the benefits of preferential treatment. That demoralization has led to an increase in violent expressions of racism, with its destructive tentacles that now reach across the nation. As to the cost of the demoralization for the few successful blacks, it is but a small price to pay for the limited benefits that have trickled down to the masses, particularly those who found employment, as a result of affirmative action.

Unemployed and underemployed blacks, however, would welcome a chance to pay the costs of demoralization, if being viewed as incompetent were the price to pay for merely getting a job that paid a living wage. Doubtless, few of them would regard any effective federal affirmative action program as demeaning to the "content of their character."[95] The alternative, being unemployed and underpaid, is more destructive and demoralizing than being regarded as incompetent. The ultimate reality, however, is that affirmative action is not responsible for blacks in high-profile positions being regarded as incompetent. Blacks were regarded as incompetent before affirmative action. The only difference is that affirmative action has placed blacks in new venues where they are labeled as incompetent, in white academia and white corporate America for example. Simply put, the persistence of racism, not federal affirmative action, is the single most important factor that accounts for the present-day white stigmatization of blacks as incompetent.

Consider the four centuries of preferential treatment and affirmative action that propelled white American businesses and ensured nearly full employment for whites. Has anyone ever heard assertions made against white Americans, who accept government preferential treatment in the economic sphere and even demand more, that they are incompetent? In the post–Civil Rights period, the meager sharing of governmental resources with citizens who are not white is the basis for the demoralization of white America. The reality, which cannot be ignored, is that black economic advancement continues to be hindered by racism.[96]

America's conservative ideologues of color, moreover, have not achieved the right to speak for minority businesspeople, including America's new wave of immigrants, anymore than they have achieved the right to speak for the nation's highly competent, well-educated black businesspeople. Their educational credentials in many instances match or exceed those of America's conservatives, whether white or black. Then, too, why should only minority businesspeople, but not their white counterparts, be denounced for accepting federal assistance? What is the inherent logic in the conservative position that on the one hand argues for excluding black businesses from federal assistance, but on the other is silent on issues of federal assistance to white American business?

Is it the same logic that explains why minorities who oppose affirmative action in areas in which they are advantaged favor it in areas in which they are disadvantaged? Clarence Page, the Pulitzer Prize-winning syndicated columnist for the *Chicago Tribune,* relates the comment made to him by a proaffirmative action Chinese-American in San Francisco: "We have many Chinese business leaders who flatly oppose affirmative action in academia, but are very much in favor of it when they are trying to get city contracts."[97] Moreover, wealthy immigrants, as Terry Eastland claims, are quite willing to use their minority status to secure minority loans, as did the Fanjul family, worth $500 million. While retaining their Cuban citizenship, they have received minority business loans, as has the Asian-Indian Vijay Patel.[98] Eastland notes, however, that, as immigrants, they and others like them never experienced historic discrimination in America, which is the ultimate basis of federal affirmative action.

Yet, while immigrants also take advantage of federal assistance, the consensus among libertarian/conservative intellectuals, black and white, is that only blacks do not need any federal affirmative assistance to place themselves successfully in the mainstream of American economic life.[99] Particularly, conservatives argue that affirmative action is preferential treatment, which they view as a violation of the Fourteenth Amendment. That logic is not only untenable it is positively absurd! Considering the limited federal funds provided to black businesses, what in actuality is unconstitutional, as viewed from either a strict or loose interpretation of the Fourteenth Amendment's equal protection mandate, is the failure of the federal government to provide support to black business in the form of billions of dollars—equal to the funds that were given out as loans and subsidies to bail out Chrysler and to remedy the economic disaster left by failed savings and loan associations.

Throughout the post–Civil Rights period, white American business has gobbled up the lion's share of federal assistance to business. Even small white American businesses profited more than black businesses from the federal government's affirmative action legislation enacted to encourage the development of black and minority businesses. Yet in December 1995, as the Republican Congress was moving to eliminate the SBA 8(a) program, the chairperson of the House Small Businesss Committee, Republican Jan Meyers, called for a moratorium on all 8(a) sole-source contracts, claiming that "The 8(a) program is corporate welfare in the worse sense of the term."[100]

Indeed, corporate welfare does exist but only for the 1 percent of the nation's businesses, America's giant corporations. The fact is, however, that minorities, who constitute some 22 percent of the nation's population, have received only 3 percent of the "corporate welfare" financial assistance provided the nation's business by the federal government. The concept of corporate welfare, however, could be applied more appropriately to the top 1 percent of white American businesses, the recipients of almost 97 percent of all federal prime contract dollars allocated to American business.

Moreover, even during the period of federal assistance to minority businesses, over 90 percent of the venture capital for black businesses from the 1970s on was generated by blacks themselves. As a survey published in the *Wall Street Journal* in 1993 showed, the federal government played only a limited role in providing assistance to the development of black businesses: "On average, 83 percent of the financing for black-owned businesses overall was found to come from personal savings. Lending institutions had provided only 6 percent—the same proportion supplied by friends and relatives."[101] Among the top 100 black businesses in 1995, 58 percent launched their company with less than $50,000. Over 60 percent secured venture capital from loans and 50 percent got capital from banks.

The biggest boost to black business from the federal government came in the 1970s, mainly in the form of programs based on the Civil Rights Act of 1964 and subsequent programs developed under Nixon's black capitalism agenda. But the limited financial assistance extended to black business could scarcely be called corporate welfare. Still, for some black businesses, the meager assistance of the federal government was important. Also, black political participation, resulting from the Civil Rights movement, helped blacks in competing for federal contract dollars.

Certainly, the "rugged individualism" of America's black entrepreneurs remains important. Indeed, the history of black American business development from slavery to the post–Civil Rights period provides a model for black business development without government financial assistance. The self-sufficient development of black business, including slave entrepreneurial enterprises, has a long history in America. Even start-up capital for the most successful black businesses was obtained not from the government, but from personal savings, relatives, and friends. Moreover, without the initiative, risk-taking, innovativeness, and development of new markets that distinguished blacks in their efforts to develop business enterprises from the seventeenth century on, there would be no history of black business in America.

Yet in the late twentieth century, with high-technology enterprises pacing America's economic growth, the importance of government-based assistance cannot be underestimated if black business is ever to be competitive in mainstream American business life. Retrenchment in affirmative action policies not only in business but also in employment and social services can only be viewed as destructive to the economic advancement of black America. In America, business creates wealth. If black America is to ever achieve economic parity with white America, it will not be by relying solely on employment in white America nor will it be achieved, as Malcolm X said, by "having to picket and boycott and beg someone else for a job."

Moreover, government figures on black business, which are based on federal census returns, do not give the full picture, as studies undertaken by black economists Thomas D. Boston of the Georgia Institute of Technology and Margaret C. Simms of the Washington-based Joint Center for Political and Economic Studies have found. The failure of the U.S. census is that it limits its data analysis to individual tax returns of single proprietorships, partnerships, and Subchapter S corporations. Most of the larger black businesses, however, are Subchapter C corporations and are therefore excluded. Also, ownership by race is difficult to determine, using the corporate tax filings required of Subchapter C corporations. In their research, Simms and Boston found that "roughly 60 percent of the corporations are Subchapter C." In *Business Enterprise*'s list of the top 100 black businesses, 7.8 percent of them were sole proprietorships, 3.4 percent partnerships, 30.2 percent Subchapter S corporations, and 58.6 percent Nonsubchapter S Corporations.[102]

Conclusion

By the late twentieth century, it seemed that the federal government and its neoconservative opponents of affirmative action could relate to capitalism in any color but black. Still, despite inequitable federal affirmative action dollar allocations, the civil rights legislation of the 1960s and the federal government's black capitalism initiatives of the 1970s marked the first time in American history that federal government assistance was provided black business. However, President Nixon's financial program to promote black capitalism fell far short of the capitalization that black business needed to achieve parity with white business.

In addition, subsequent Republican administrations destroyed the gains that black business had achieved as a result of federal assistance. From the Reagan Administration onward, as Republicans pushed for budget cuts in social welfare programs, there was also escalating opposition to affirmative action programs to aid minorities in business by placing limitations on loan development and procurement programs.[103] Also, under the Reagan Administration, attempts were made to dismantle the Department of Commerce's Minority Business Development Agency, which provided consultant services, technical assistance, and loans to minority businesses. While President Bush was no special ally of black business, it was thought that his friendship with and support from Republican black multimillionaire and entrepreneur Joshua I. Smith would prove beneficial to minority businesses by reinvigorating the MBDA.

Yet, even with the imminent elimination of the SBA's 8(a) program, even with the Croson decision, which requires affirmative action programs to meet stricter standards in securing government set-asides, and even with congressional efforts, namely the Dole-Canady bill, to end affirmative action in the nation, black business in the late twentieth century has survived, even with some successes.[104] Still, by the mid-1990s, according to assessments made by *Black Enterprise* magazines's board of economists, "the future of affirmative action looks bleak. No matter who gets elected, African-Americans should plan now for reductions in affirmative action for business programs, both at the federal and state levels.... the mood for now in the business, global and competitive worlds is that support systems are probably going to be eroded at both state and federal levels."[105]

If black business is to have a history beyond the twentieth century and to achieve competitive growth, it will require federal assistance, as much as the railroads did in nineteenth-century America and the aerospace and semiconductor industries in the twentieth century. Simply put, after two centuries of supporting white American business and after reaping the economic benefits of black slave labor until 1865, the government owes a great deal to black American business. Indeed, the position of black business relative to white business has changed little from before the Civil War to after the Civil Rights era, both in participation rates and gross business receipts.

In the post–Civil Rights period, then, the federal government has failed American black business. And preferential treatment, the government's traditional remedy for acts of discrimination, is not the answer to the question of how will the government improve black American business. A better answer is that black American business should be provided federal support equal to that provided white American business. As the 1992 United States Commission on Minority Business Development emphasized,

> There appears to be no reason in logic why 99 percent of the businesses in the country are forced to squabble over 20 percent of the Federal purchase dollar, when a select 1 percent continue to capture their 80 percent market share largely undisturbed.[106]

10

THE RISE OF BLACK CORPORATE AMERICA, 1945–1995

Suffice it to say that Negro business is the last frontier for Negroes to exploit in this nation.

—*Houston Informer*

The power in this country is money.

—Arthur George Gaston,
Black Enterprise's "Entrepreneur of the Century"

The road to the future ... depends on ethnic entrepreneurs doing their own thing instead of depending on external banks and financiers who will, out of necessity, force them to do their thing.

—John H. Johnson,
Johnson Publishing Company

Introduction

The founding of million-dollar enterprises distinguished the first wave of black corporate America in the early twentieth century. Financial institutions, insurance companies, and banks, along with black hair care products and cosmetics manufacturers, were the most prominent enterprises. The second wave of black corporate America in the mid-twentieth century, however, was distinguished by the founding of multimillion-dollar enterprises. The leading African-American entrepreneurs were S. B. Fuller, Arthur G. Gaston, John H. Johnson, and Berry Gordy, all of whom established a diversity of business institutions. With the exception of Gordy, all established enterprises before 1945. Except for Fuller, the expansion of the enterprises founded by this group continued into the late twentieth century, during the third wave of black corporate America.

In the 1940s and 1950s, Fuller, however, was the most prominent black businessman of his day. He pioneered the acquisition by blacks of businesses in white corporate America, developing a market for his products that crossed over to the white consumer. But Gordy's Motown Records represented the first instance of the crossover of a black company's products into the mainstream American consumer market. Both developments would distinguish black business expansion in the third emergence of black corporate America in the post–Civil Rights period. Until the 1960s, however, black business produced goods and services primarily for a black consumer market.

In the post–Civil Rights period, only two areas of enterprise remained that produced consumer goods exclusively for blacks: health and beauty aids and publishing. From the 1960s to the 1990s, the leaders in the personal care products industry who developed multimillion-dollar enterprises were George Johnson, who founded Johnson Products, and Edward G. Gardner, who founded Soft Sheen Products, Inc. Black financial institutions also expanded to include black investment banks, which marked the expansion of black finance capitalism. For the first time, blacks handled billions of dollars in bank deposits, insurance premiums, stocks, and bonds. Also, during this third wave of black corporate America numerous black enterprises in the entertainment industry flourished. In the 1970s and 1980s blacks moved into television, notably Robert Johnson's Black Entertainment Television, which was founded in 1979.

This chapter begins with a discussion of the business activities of the "big four" of mid-twentieth-century black American business. It then reviews the major types of black business enterprises as they emerged in the second and third expansions of black corporate America: hair care products and cosmetic manufacturers; entertainment enterprises, including recording, radio, television, and film companies; and financial institutions. Hip-hop enterprises that developed during this period are also reviewed.

The distinguishing feature in the history of black participation in the industries reviewed in this chapter is that their origins can be found in the black experience. Moreover, in the second wave of black corporate America, the mortuary business, insurance companies, and the beauty products industry were virtually the only kinds of black enterprises that generated millions of dollars in business receipts. Their consumer base was limited primarily to black America. In the third stage of the development of black corporate America, however, the expansion of these industries reflected their movement into the mainstream American economy, including competition with white corporations for the black consumer market.

Fuller, Gaston, Johnson, and Gordy

The business activities of America's leading black entrepreneur in the mid-twentieth century, S. B. Fuller (1905–1988), set the stage for the black business expansion that would distinguish the post–Civil Rights era generation of black entrepreneurs. Fuller's distinguishing characteristic as a black entrepreneur was his acquisition of other businesses in white corporate America. They were built on the foundation of his Chicago-based flagship company, Fuller Products, America's largest black business from the mid-1940s to the early 1960s. Yet, because of black protests taking center stage during the Civil Rights movement, Fuller's pioneering business activities have been nearly forgotten as part of the black historical experience and American business history.[1]

Before telemarketing and cable TV shopping networks, the door-to-door peddler was the chief means by which products were brought directly into American homes. This was the marketing device used by Fuller to build a multimillion-dollar business from the sales of the personal care and household products that he manufactured. When S. B. Fuller launched his door-to-door sales operation in 1932, it was more than a response to the economies of scale needed by black manufacturers to survive the depression. The strategy was crucial to the success of Fuller's enterprise. And for the black consumer, it provided an alternative sales mechanism to white retail stores, which often refused to provide shelf space for the products of black manufacturers.

Fuller started his business by buying soap wholesale and selling it door-to-door to the heavily concentrated black population on Chicago's South Side. Even during the depression, he made a profit. In 1939, Fuller purchased a factory where he manufactured a line of 30 household cleaning and personal care products, hair products, and cosmetics. Then, with World War II bringing jobs and money to black Americans, Fuller Products mushroomed. In 1947 he purchased a white cosmetic company, Boyer International Laboratories, which had been his supplier. At times, it had even refused to let Fuller purchase on credit. Boyer manufactured personal care products for a southern white consumer market. With this acquisition, Fuller expanded his line of products to 300 different items and by 1960 had an annual gross of $10 million. He employed 5,000 salespeople, with about 600 employees on direct payroll. Fuller salespeople, men and women, white and black, worked out of approximately 85 branches that he established in 35 states.[2]

Fuller also acquired investment interest in two additional white companies, J. C. McBrady and Patricia Stevens Cosmetics. Using Fuller as a model for black business expansion, John H. Johnson said, "the road to the *Fortune* 500 is paved with the deeds of ethnic entrepreneurs who exploited an ethnic advantage . . . and moved on to major ventures in the general market."[3] Fuller had begun diversifying in the 1950s, establishing what today would look very much like a conglomerate. He moved into publishing, purchasing a major share in the nation's leading black newspaper, the *Pittsburgh Courier.* In the 1930s, its circulation had surpassed that of the *Chicago Defender,* once America's premier black newspaper. Fuller also bought a franchise, which was named the Fuller Philco Home Appliance Center. Then, in Donald Trump-like fashion, he proceed to acquire major real estate holdings, including a $3 million New York real estate trust, Chicago's Regal Theater, and the South Center Department Store, a white business that anchored the 47th Street black business district. He also established the Fuller Guaranty Corporation.[4] With Chicago the meat-packing center of America, Fuller's acquisitions also included a large-scale cattle ranch and commercial farms.

In the mid-twentieth century, access to white corporate America and a white consumer market, however, was difficult for black entrepreneurs. Throughout the 1960s Fuller lived a businessman's nightmare from hell. When some southern white salespeople attending a Fuller convention in Chicago for the first time discovered the company owner and CEO was black, they quit, reducing his staff by almost 50 percent.[5] Further investigation by the White Citizens' Council found that Fuller owned the Boyer company, which manufactured the popular Jean Nadal and H. A. Hair Arranger products, sold primarily to southern whites, who made up 60 percent of Fuller's market. A boycott launched by southern whites against Nadal products proved totally successful.[6] It resulted in the failure of Fuller's attempted sale of Boyer. Then, a $500,000 loan for his department store, collateralized on the promised equity-leveraged sale of Boyer for $1 million, left Fuller in debt, because the prospective buyer, a white-owned liquor company, reneged on the deal.

Forced into bankruptcy, Fuller sold his real estate, cattle ranch, and newspaper. Then, attempting to generate capital, he sold shares in Fuller Products. There was every confidence he would succeed. Investors bought shares in amounts ranging from $100 to the $100,000 purchased by a black church. It was not long before the Securities and Exchange

Commission was informed. In 1964, Fuller was found guilty of the illegal interstate sale of unregistered notes, but placed on five-year probation, with orders to pay back $1.6 million. His financial situation continued to deteriorate. Although welfare recipients were not allowed to be extended credit for retail purchases, Fuller provided his customers who were on welfare installment buying privileges of up to $100 for $30 down in cash. Local social services agencies ordered Fuller's welfare customers to stop paying their accounts, which left him with $1 million in unpaid charges.

Unable to pay his creditors even ten cents on the dollar, Fuller saw his department store seized, while some 2,000 creditors, including many of his former salespeople, filed a class action suit against him.

Subsequently, the Fuller Products Company was reorganized under federal bankruptcy laws and by 1972 had sales of $300,000, a far cry from the $10 million in annual sales a decade earlier. In 1975 a benefit was held by prominent black Chicago businessmen, who raised $120,000 to help Fuller rebuild his business empire.

These business leaders surely must have been ambivalent about hosting the event. Early in their careers, Fuller had helped many of them by providing loans for venture capital; and they were eager to repay his generosities. However, like others in the black community, they were incensed by Fuller's denunciation of blacks as lacking initiative and discipline and by public statements that described black people as "a mess."[7] Even more outrageous, Fuller blamed blacks for the downfall of his company, while it was clear that white boycotts of his products was the precipitant factor. Still, Fuller believed firmly that black businesses could operate in the mainstream of the American business community. In this, Fuller was right. The multimillion-dollar conglomerate that he built in the 1950s had resulted in part from developing a consumer market in white America.

Fuller, however, was ahead of his time and, sadly, only by a decade. Yet, he was representative of generations of black entrepreneurs who established businesses in the age of segregation and tangible racial discrimination. Then, black enterprises were allowed to survive as long as they maintained good relations with whites. Fuller simply refused to concede the racial reality of pre–Civil Rights America: that white goodwill was inextricably tied to black subordination. Even during the height of southern white resistance in the early 1960s, Fuller refused to acknowledge that racist whites, violently opposed to black participation in electoral politics, were as equally resistant to black participation in mainstream American business. Doubtless, Fuller could not concede that, in an era when whites were fighting to deny blacks equal access to public accommodations, they would also object to working for a member of a race that they had relegated to a subordinate social and economic position.

White resistance to the Civil Rights movement, ultimately, was a die-hard effort by whites to maintain the subordinate status of blacks. Yet, during that time, Arthur G. Gaston (1890–1995) also encountered criticism from Birmingham blacks, especially for denouncing the participation of black children in protest demonstrations. Despite what was viewed as his accommodationist position, Gaston was able to sustain his business interests during the height of white resistance to black civil rights protest. He was able to do so primarily because he was a respected race mediator and financial leader, especially since he had built a business conglomerate based on serving the black community. Moreover, Gaston demonstrated his commitment to the black community and to the Civil Rights movement in several ways.

When white banks in Tuskegee, Alabama, attempted economic pressure to force an end to black boycotts and protest, Gaston's Citizen's Federal Savings Bank loaned money to those blacks whose mortgages were being foreclosed. Also, while denounced publicly by the black community as an Uncle Tom, Gaston made a motel that he owned and his house available to SCLC members for accommodations and strategy planning. The motel and his house were bombed during this time. Gaston also donated money to civil rights organizations and "put up the bail for King when King's 'Letter from a Birmingham Jail' was penned."[8]

Gaston's idol was Booker T. Washington, whose behind-the-scenes fight against segregation was undoubtedly his model during the civil rights struggle in Birmingham. Ultimately, Gaston benefited from the Civil Rights movement. After the 1960s, his bank served as a depositor for the city of Birmingham, its county government, and the state of Alabama. Gaston, moreover, strengthened his financial position in the white business community at this time, when his Vulcan Realty and Investment Corporation, established in 1952, purchased downtown Birmingham property for the redevelopment and construction of new office buildings, which were to be built by his A. G. Gaston Construction Company. While the Gaston Motel did not survive much past this period, the radio stations he purchased, one featuring gospel music and the other a rhythm-and-blues FM station, sustained their audiences.

Gaston's ownership of financial institutions, construction and property development enterprises, media ventures, and even a 2 percent interest in a racetrack track paralleled mainstream American business activity. The development of his business empire, however, differed radically from the mainstream because many of his ventures helped blacks who were suffering under the weight of segregation. The Booker T. Washington Insurance Company, which he developed from the funeral home and burial society founded in the 1920s, had provided the capital base for Gaston's subsequent business ventures. In 1939 Gaston established the Booker T. Washington Business College, hiring its graduates, as did other Birmingham black businesses. He also built the A. G. Gaston Home for Senior Citizens and several black housing subdivisions in addition to apartment complexes. Even the Citizen's Federal Savings Bank, established in 1957, was founded to provide mortgages to blacks turned down by white banks.

By the 1990s, Gaston's personal wealth was over $40 million. Then in 1987 in an unprecedented move for a black business of enormous size, Gaston sold his insurance company (in the 1980s it had expanded through acquisition of two other black insurance companies) to his 400 employees for $3.5 million. The company had $34 million in assets and $725 million of insurance in force and was the holding company for all of Gaston's enterprises except his bank. In 1992, three years before his death, *Black Enterprise* honored Gaston as the "Black Entrepreneur of the Century." Citizens Federal and the Booker T. Washington Insurance Company continued into the late twentieth century, ranked as leading financial institutions in *Black Enterprise*.

Also, in 1995 Atlanta-based Thatcher Engineering, ranked 19th on *Black Enterprise*'s top 100 companies for that year with $76.8 million in sales, formed a general partnership with Gaston Construction, reflecting the direction of black corporate America toward mergers and acquisitions in the twenty-first century. The intent of the merger was to provide greater financial leverage and increased manpower; it also marked the cautious beginning of black firms moving toward the vertical integration of capital resources, a practice particularly critical for black construction companies with a limited bonding capacity.[9]

The second wave of black corporate America from midcentury on was also represented by the diversity of the enterprises founded, owned, and personally managed by John H. Johnson (1917–), the first black listed on the *Forbes* 400. He launched his empire with the founding of the Johnson Publishing Company in Chicago in 1942. Then, from his flagship publication, *Ebony,* founded in 1945, Johnson expanded into the manufacturing of hair products, including Duke and Raveen. His Beauty Star Cosmetics Company, a subsidiary of Johnson's publishing operation, was his first nonpublishing venture, which Johnson started as a mail-order firm in 1946. It was reorganized as Supreme Beauty Products in 1960. In 1973 Johnson moved into radio with the purchase of an AM and an FM station, WJPC and WLNR, respectively. His real estate acquisitions included both downtown Chicago commercial property and the third-largest apartment complex, Lawless Gardens, on the South Side. Fashion Fair Cosmetics was founded in 1973. In 1974, with majority share ownership, Johnson also became chairman of Supreme Liberty Life Insurance Company.[10] He was also one of 16 black investors in the company that wired Chicago for cable television.

Johnson, a man who has dined at the White House with seven presidents, who has traveled as special ambassador to Africa, and who serves on the boards of leading corporations and universities, including the Harvard Business School, was, as were Gaston and Fuller, born in poverty. For two years after he and his mother moved to Chicago from Arkansas in 1933, the family lived on welfare in order for Johnson to get a high school education. Johnson graduated from all-black DuSable High School in 1936. With a scholarship, he attended the University of Chicago on a part-time basis for two years, while working part-time at the Supreme Liberty Life Insurance Company. Johnson's business education began there under the mentorship of leading black entrepreneurs, Harry H. Pace and Earl B. Dickinson, whose lessons provided him with what Johnson has emphasized as the basic foundation of his business success. The formula Johnson learned was: ration your time; remain focused; size up situations to determine if they advance your interests; and ignore people or situations that have little or no bearing on your goals.

As Johnson advanced in his training, he learned a more specific lesson from Pace: that friendship and business do not mix. As Pace counseled, "If you want to succeed in business you've got to learn how to work with people that you don't like. And you've got to learn how to compromise. After you compromise, you have to forget the past and go on to the future. For in business, you have no permanent enemies or permanent friends— only permanent interests."[11] A student of Napoleon Hill's *Think and Grow Rich,* Dale Carnegie's *How to Win Friends and Influence People,* and Booker T. Washington's *Up From Slavery,* as well as other books on blacks who had "succeeded against the odds," Johnson said that what guided his business career was his philosophy of "other-focusing." A businessperson, Johnson said, must study people and find out what they want; he emphasized that "you've got to study people and make it to *their* self-interest to advance *your* self-interest."[12]

Within seven years of starting his publishing company, J. H. Johnson was a millionaire. In addition to *Ebony,* he launched *Jet* in 1951, a weekly pocket-sized publication. Yet Johnson's management style, doubtless shaped by his business philosophy, has been subjected to criticism by former employees and to some quiet grumbling by a few present employees. Johnson, however, describes himself as a "hand-on, hands-in, hands-wrapped-around manager." And, he notes, he uses "both hands." Yet Johnson claims that he delegates freely. His wife, Eunice, is secretary-treasurer of Johnson Publications and director of Ebony Fashion Fair. Since the late 1980s, his daughter, Linda Johnson Rice, has been president and chief operating officer of Johnson Publishing. Still, from his position as chairman and CEO, Johnson admits that "I check, double-check, and triple-check." More to the point, he explains, "I'm a details man." Johnson meets with executives of selected divisions at status conferences two or three times a day because he needs to "delegate freely and check on the task every day." He has learned "a rule that what produces a stunning success on Monday, will wreak havoc if applied rigidly on Tuesday."[13]

Johnson's achievement was based mainly on his flagship publication, *Ebony*. It, however, has been subject to criticism that its content is fluff, while it ignores critical issues important to blacks. Yet the circulation of *Negro Digest*, which launched Johnson Publishing in 1942, with its provocative articles that challenged American racism, dropped drastically with the publication of *Ebony*. Even when reissued as *Negro World*, its circulation was limited, as was that of *Ebony Jr,* a magazine for black children. Johnson's *Ebony Man*, first published in 1985, however, survives. But while Johnson said, "I don't want to climb any more mountains—I just want to stay on top of the one I'm on," his business expansion continues.[14] In 1995 he launched *Ebony South Africa*.

To Johnson, staying on top has meant diversifying his business interests, propping up those that are successful and dropping those that are not. Work is Johnson's life, he said—no hobbies, no sports, no games, only a steady diet of "trying to succeed."[15] And Johnson has succeeded. Johnson Publishing, a wholly owned family conglomerate, is the second-largest black business in the nation and the largest black-oriented consumer corporation in America, with $316.2 million in sales in both national and international markets and a staff of 2,600 in 1995.

Motown Records, founded by Berry Gordy in 1959, however, was the most successful black enterprise in the nation between 1973 and 1983. Sales exceeded $50 million annually in the 1970s, and by 1983, Motown had sales of over $100 million. In building Motown, Gordy applied a Johnson-like discipline not only on himself but also on his recording artists. Unlike Johnson, however, Gordy took his management style, in many ways, from the pages of the Ford Motor Company's manual for workers, where Gordy was once employed on the assembly line. Motown was built on the high-quality performances and style of his recording artists. As he managed their careers and groomed them for success, Gordy used the concept of them being part of "the Motown family" as a motivational strategy.

Taking advantage of his self-constructed image as the family's paternalistic and benign father, Gordy assumed control of the careers of his artists. Once family loyalty was instilled in his ambitious and eager young artists, Gordy used his fatherlike regimentation and authority to mold them into superstars. He used the Ford Motor premise that "production could be efficiently organized and automated for the highest quality." At the same time, Gordy "[p]rovided a series of attractive rewards and incentives for hard work, and he instilled at the firm an almost unbearable atmosphere of competition."[16]

The "Gordy-Ford" management style worked. Motown was a success. Even though it eventually lost market position and profitability, Motown Records symbolized a distinct era in twentieth-century American business history. Its distinct treatment of rhythm and blues became known as the Motown sound. It was based on the African musical heritage of black America. It had a polyrhythmic, driving beat derived from a complex melding of gospel, blues, jazz, and the bebop sounds of the '40s and '50s, as well as from the rhythm and blues and soul music of the '60s. As black music changed in the '70s from soul to pop to rap, then to gangsta rap and hip-hop in the '80s Gordy began losing $1 million a month. He sold the company in 1987 for $61 million to a group of investors who, three years later, sold Motown for $325 million.

Motown was black America's first multimillion-dollar, multimedia entertainment empire. Gordy's success with the Motown sound led to his development of Motown Industries, which included Motown Records, with its eight record labels, Motown Productions, Multi-Media Management Corporation, and the Jobete Music Company, the music publishing arm of the company. Also, in the early 1970s, Gordy produced several films. By 1973, he had resigned as president of Motown Records, which was being managed primarily by whites. In 1984 Gordy turned the company's distribution rights over to MCA, which purchased Motown in 1988. Gordy retained ownership of Motown Industries, the holding company for his other subsidiaries, including Jobete, which owned the Motown catalogue of hits and was worth nearly $15 million. In 1986 *Forbes* estimated Gordy's wealth at more than $180 million. By 1992, however, the Gordy Co. (the name of his company after he sold Motown) was removed from *Black Enterprise*'s list of the top 100 black-owned businesses, since its ownership was no longer 51 percent black.

The sale of Motown Records, for black America, represented more than a business decision; it was a symbolic loss, a transfer of an institution important in the economic advancement of black America. Moreover, Motown Records had significance in American history beyond its place as the nation's first black business with sales of more than $100 million. The Motown sound symbolically reflected a point in the nation's history when whites and blacks met at a confluence in American culture and then diverged again into two worlds of race.

In the pre–Civil Rights era, black corporate America operated in a dual economy. The business activities and character of the nation's leading black entrepreneurs, who had built businesses from the ground up in the second wave of black corporate America, were shaped by constraints brought on by America's blatant racial discrimination. With the exception of Motown, these were businesses founded to supply goods and services specifically directed at the black consumer, a market that had been ignored by white corporate America.

Hair Care Products Manufacturers

By the late twentieth century, the one area of business specifically directed to a black consumer market, health and beauty aids—the bedrock industry of black America in the first decades of the twentieth century—had sales of $239 million, which was only 1.8 percent of the total sales of *Black Enterprise*'s top 100 companies.[17] The period from 1930 to 1960, however, saw a relatively limited amount of activity in the industry. The pioneering giants in the early twentieth century, Annie Turnbo-Malone, Madame C. J. Walker, Anthony Overton, and Sarah Spencer Washington, all of whom became millionaires by manufacturing black hair care products and cosmetics, were dead. Washington, who founded the New Jersey–based Apex News and Hair Company, Apex Laboratories, and Apex Publishing Company, was the last of that generation. She died in 1953.

A shrewd businesswoman, described as the "Genius with the Midas Touch," Washington was known as a woman with "tremendous energy, a determined will, and an extraordinary memory." She made all of her purchases in cash, including her manufacturing supplies, which she purchased in carload lots. She also purchased her business property in cash, including a $40,000 warehouse, $25,000 auditorium, $20,000 laboratory, $50,000 rest and tourist retreat, the $18,000 Ellen Memorial Center for Girls, a $21,000 drugstore in a building with six apartments, and the Brigantine Hotel, bought for $100,000 and sold for $150,000. Her home was constructed for $85,000 and she held $75,000 in U.S. Savings Bonds. Banned from Atlantic City's golf courses, Washington converted her farm into a nine-hole golf course and country club. As she said, "This is a predomenantly [*sic*] white country, but I can be black and successful."[18]

Overton and Turnbo-Malone located their companies in Chicago, which marked the city's emergence as the nation's capital of black hair care and cosmetics manufacturing. S. B. Fuller and Charles Murray continued in their footsteps when they established their own companies in the Windy City during the second wave of black corporate America, as did John H. Johnson, with his Supreme Beauty Products. In the third wave rise of black corporate America, the city's leadership in the black hair industry was solidified with the emergence of the new giants in the industry, George Johnson, Edward Gardner, and Jory Luster, who established Johnson Products, Soft Sheen Products, and Luster Products, respectively.

During the second period of black corporate growth, one of the country's most successful hair product companies was the Murray Cosmetic Company, founded in 1926 in Chicago by Charles D. Murray Sr. and his wife, Lilli. Its success was due to Murray's Hair Pomade for black men, but the company also manufactured a scalp and pressing oil for women. During World War II, the product was in such demand that "Negro GIs stationed around the globe often wrote home for a can of Murray's." In fact, the Army considered Murray's, "so vital to the morale of the troops during WWII that scarce and vital materials were allocated to the [company] for production of Murray's Hair Pomade."[19]

Even before the war, the company had an international market, with distribution in Hawaii, France, England, Germany, the Far East, Middle East, and South Africa. Murray's products were synonymous with black men's hair care, but the company also made products for women. By the 1950s Murray had expanded with the building of a new plant in Chicago's southeastern industrial district.[20] But Murray had lots of competition. By World War II, Chicago alone had about 15 hair product manufacturers, including the E. F. Young Jr. Cosmetic Company, which made Young's Hair Pomade. By 1948 its Chicago plant was producing 3,600 cans of cosmetics and beauty preparations every hour, while purchasing its cans by the millions and chemicals by the carload. The company had 5,760 agents throughout the United States.[21]

Still, while blacks made valiant attempts to maintain control of the black hair care business, whites from the 1930s on escalated their efforts to gain a foothold in the industry. In 1939 there was even concern that, with the new Federal Food, Drug, and Cosmetic Act, some black manufacturers might go out of business. The act prohibited interstate shipments of adulterated and misbranded cosmetics. While there were no reports of black companies charged with this practice, the white-owned, Memphis-based Lucky Heart Laboratories, which manufactured personal care products for blacks, pleaded guilty to "falsely and fraudulently representing goods to purchasers."[22]

Nonetheless, white manufacturers of black hair care products were becoming strong competitors. Although black-owned Apex had the leading market share, 25.9 percent, in the mid-1940s, Poro, manufactured by Turnbo-Malone, had only a 2.1 percent share, while the entire Walker Company had only a 1.1 percent share (see table 10.1).[23] Assuming that the others, some 57 brands with a 15.9 percent share, were black-manufactured products, blacks would have had a 45 percent market share. If not, the share for black-manufactured hair products would have been only 29.1 percent. The Walker Company had been hit hard by the depression. Its peak annual earnings in 1920 were $595,000, but by 1931 they had dropped to $130,000, and by 1933, to $48,000. While the Walker Colleges continued in operation, hair preparation sales declined. In 1985 the company was sold.[24]

Apex was the largest black beauty products company on the East Coast, and its products had national distribution; and, at their peak, the training programs in the Apex schools

TABLE 10.1   Brands Purchased by Blacks for Hair, 1945

Brand Name	Purchasers Number	Percent	Brand Name	Purchasers Number	Percent
Apex	11,808	25.9	Fearonce	703	1.6
Vaseline	7,128	15.6	Olive Pomade	633	1.4
Dixie Peach	2,311	5.1	Alice's Pomade	660	1.4
Olivo	2,052	4.5	Mme Walkers	587	1.3
Wingate	2,002	4.4	Watkins	516	1.1
Blue Seal Vaseline	1,853	4.1	Henry's	514	1.1
Formula X	1,690	3.7	Nature Way	448	1.0
Adolphs	1,273	2.8	Vegie Hair Tonic	445	1.0
Indian Sage	1,158	2.5	Black & White	383	.8
Poro (Malone)	949	2.1	Brilliantine	380	.8
Snow White	890	2.0	Any brand	384	.8
Vel's	823	1.8	Others (57 brands)	7,256	15.9

Source: Compiled from Research Company of America, *The New Philadelphia Story: A Report on the Characteristics of the Philadelphia Negro Market . . . Its Buying Habits and Brand Preferences* (Baltimore: The Afro-American Company, 1946). In addition to Apex, Mme Walkers and Watkins were black manufacturers.

provided "employment to 40,000 agents."[25] The black hair care business was a major source of self-employment for black women, many of whom owned small two- to four-chair shops. At the 1946 black National Beauty Culture League convention, leaders in the industry reported that black beauty shop operators did $400 million in business during the war and that it was imperative that they maintain control; their concern was that "serious efforts are being made by white manufacturers to usurp the field through alleged colored companies."[26]

Black professional hair care was also big business in post–World War II America, and one of the most successful was Rose Morgan, whose Harlem-based Rose Meta House of Beauty employed 100 beauticians.[27] Morgan, along with Olivia Clarke, started their business in 1944. Within three years they were serving 69,000 customers annually. Successes such as Morgan's were major reasons that industry leaders at a 1949 Washington conference of black beauticians expressed concern that whites were pushing their way into the lucrative beauty shop business:

> The old line beauticians were losing a long-waged battle to keep the $450,000,000 beauty business in tan hands. Fifteen years ago the veterans such as Cordelia Greene Johnson and Majorie Joyner, saw the handwriting on the wall and turned towards trying to hold the line. The move at that time was for non-colored promoters to buy up beauty shops and rent out booths. From a wedge of this sort they have moved into the actual operating end. This year's convention saw two-thirds of the demonstrators white, or merely having colored to front for them. From hair-styling to permanent straightening and cold waving, the new innovations were chiefly being taken out of our hands. Young operators say their customers demand the newest and point to tendency of the established in the field to stick to methods that were old 25 years ago. Big laboratories and constant experiment cost money, say the others. Whatever the blame, the fact remains that a highly profitable field is surely and not so slowly being taken out of our hands.[28]

After World War II, black hair product manufacturers escalated their research-and-development efforts. In 1948 the Chicago-based Mary Ann Morgan Company, a cosmetics manufacturer, introduced Morganoil, a hair preparation developed by Dr. V. A. Gant, a chemist, toxicologist, and University of Illinois professor, who had "spent 15 years perfecting the formula." The company was located in the city's South Side black business district on 47th and Cottage Grove.[29] In 1954 even Apex introduced a "new greaseless pressing compound in liquid form" called Liquid Press. It was tested at Apex schools, with the company emphasizing that it "performs a hair pressing job without greasiness" and "leaves the hair soft, straight, and shimmering."[30] In 1955 the Walker Company introduced Satin Tress, promoted as a "moisture repellent, non-oily hair conditioning process that retards the tendency of hair to 'go back.' "[31]

The competition among white companies in their attempts to gain a 100 percent market share of black hair care product sales escalated in the 1950s and 1960s. And it was vicious. In 1960 a $4,218,000 lawsuit was made against white-owned Helene Curtis Industries by Summit Laboratories in Indianapolis. While Summit was also a white-owned company, its two vice presidents, chief chemist, general manager, and the coinventors of its highly publicized Hair-Strate Permanent product were black. The suit, filed in the United States District Court in Chicago, charged Helene Curtis with "trying illegally to copy the new 'Hair-Strate Permanent' which a Negro Chemist worked 18 years to develop." Summit also charged Curtis with "unfair trade practices, copyright infringements and unfair competition." It was accused not only of stealing the product but also of "plagiarizing Summit's packaging and sales promotion techniques and its precisely worded technical instructions to [black] beauticians."

Summit claimed that since 1958 it had invested substantial sums in the testing, retesting, manufacturing, and marketing of its Hair-Strate product, in addition to the "training of 6000 beauticians in the use of their product, which was sold both in the United States and abroad." In its suit Summit stated that Curtis's employees " 'attended product demonstrations by plaintiff' and on such occasions 'solicited confidential information (concerning plaintiff's products) from plaintiff's employees.' " Pending the trial, Summit asked the court to enjoin Curtis from production of its product and use of its advertising plans, which it claimed Curtis had plagiarized.[32]

The ultimate goal for black hair care manufacturers was a product that would both straighten the hair of black women without pressing and prevent it from going back to its natural curl, even while wet. With the rallying cry of "I'm Black and I'm Proud" in the black-power movement in the 1960s, there was a decline in interest in the straightening of black hair. The focus on "Black Is Beautiful" included wearing one's hair in a "natural." This proved a boon to George Johnson's Ultra Sheen products in the 1960s.

While the interest in products that chemically straightened black hair diminished, an all-black Cleveland company, which had introduced the hair weave in the 1960s, was reportedly doing a million-dollar business in a market that extended from New York to Los Angeles. The process was invented in 1950 and patented in 1952 by a Malvern, Ohio, black housewife, Christina Jenkins. Her husband, president of the company, said that it was so successful that it was "up there with Fuller Products."[33]

In addition to hair weaves, the market for wigs for black women persisted throughout the Civil Rights period, but the manufacturers were white. In 1973 Naomi Sims, the first black superstar model, founded her wig company and introduced the Naomi Sims Collection. In the first year alone, sales reached $5 million. Sims developed and patented a fiber that approximated black-hair textures. While other wig companies followed, the Sims line was sold in some 2,000 stores in the United States, Canada, the West Indies, Great Britain, and Africa by the 1980s. Sims, however, encountered criticism from ultraradical blacks, who claimed that she was exploiting the desire of black women to have straightened hair in order to look like white women. The criticism came despite the fact that other black manufacturers had achieved success in providing products and processes that straightened black hair.[34]

The most successful black hair care manufacturer since the four pioneers in the early twentieth century was George H. Johnson, who founded Johnson Products in 1954, after having worked 10 years for Fuller Products. Johnson's first success was with his Ultra Wave and Ultra Sheen hair relaxers. In addition, Johnson capitalized on the Afro hairstyle popular in the 1960s, which required careful grooming to retain its natural luster and sheen, with his Afro-Sheen product line. By 1964 it had national distribution, with sales to mass retailers and chain stores. The company took off—throughout the 1960s, Johnson Products had 80 percent of the market in black hair products.

In 1970 Johnson Products became the first black-owned firm to be listed on the AMEX, the American Stock Exchange. His entry into hair care product manufacturing marked the third wave of black corporate America in this industry. By the mid-1970s sales had reached nearly $40 million. Despite the company's sponsorship of "Soul Train," the black counterpart of Dick Clark's "American Bandstand" teen dance program, it began losing market share to Edward Gardner's Soft Sheen Products. The company was established in 1964, but it was not until 1979, when Gardner introduced a line of products that revolutionized black hair care, that the company took off with astounding success. The basic product was Care Free Curl, a relaxer that straightened black hair. Sales soared, since several different products were needed to keep the hair straight and to maintain the style known as the Jheri curl. Moreover, the product required professional application, initially at a cost of $80 to $100, which increased the profitability of black beauticians tremendously. Depending on the shop, a regular shampoo, press, and curl cost between $10 and $15.[35]

The product, however, was not greaseless, a point made most hilariously in a scene in the film *Coming to America*, to which all black Americans could relate, even if they did not use the product. Johnson's Ultra Sheen could not compete with Gardner's Care-Free Curl. Moreover, Johnson had not acted fast enough in introducing new products to challenge Soft Sheen's market dominance. In 1976 Johnson Products ranked 3rd on *Black Enterprise*'s top 100 companies, with sales of $43.5 million, just below Johnson Publications, with sales of $47.5 million and Motown Industries, which ranked 1st with sales of $50 million. Twelve years later in 1988, however, Gardner's Soft Sheen Products ranked 6th on the list, with $85.4 million in sales and a line of 150 products, while Johnson Products ranked 17th, with sales of $33 million. Although Johnson's business decisions accounted for some of the losses, the federal government also accelerated the company's sales decline.

From 1976 to 1979, the Federal Trade Commission singled out Johnson in its efforts to force manufacturers that used lye in their hair-straightening products to indicate on their labels that the ingredient posed health and safety hazards. Johnson spent a year fighting the FTC's discriminatory policy that allowed other companies to continue marketing their products containing lye without the warning. After a year, the FTC required the other companies to add the warning to their labels, although in less strongly worded language. Finally, after two years, Johnson Products was cleared to use the same mildly worded warning that the FTC had allowed the other manufacturers to use.

During that time, however, Johnson lost market share, as other companies, especially Revlon, launched aggressive marketing campaigns that emphasized their products' safety. By 1980, Johnson's market share had dropped from 60 percent to 40 percent. In addition to white competitors, Gardner's Soft Sheen and other leading black hair care product manufacturers also gained market share. Moreover, Gardner continued to profit from the business it did in black hair salons, which accounted for 40 percent of sales. Moreover, Soft Sheen had 35 percent of the total salon trade in black hair care products.

In seeking new sources of growth, Johnson agreed to manufacture products for an enterprise entitled POWER (People Organized and Working for Economic Rebirth), which was backed by the Reverend Louis Farrakhan, who "had received a $5 million interest-free loan from [Libyan President Muammar] Qaddafi to develop black economic enterprises in the United States."[36] Opposition to his proposed participation in POWER was so great that Johnson withdrew, protesting at the same time that his involvement by no means should have been construed as support for "Farrakhan, who has openly expressed anti-Semitic and antiwhite sentiments."[37] Johnson's sales, however, continued to decline. This had a demoralizing effect on his employees, which, according to Johnson, further exacerbated problems in the company. Nevertheless, his acknowledged mismanagement of product distribution, marketing, and development, in addition to the FTC attack, added to the decline in sales.

By the late 1980s, Johnson's bitterness paralleled that of Fuller's, especially when Johnson's nonethnic product line, which had been put on store shelves with his ethnic products, did not take off. Also, Johnson felt that, since his company had been the leader in the revitalization of the black hair care industry, black consumers owed him some product loyalty. In 1989, as part of his divorce settlement, the company stock George owned was transferred to his wife, Joan, who then held about 60 percent of the total shares. After their son, Eric, stepped in as president, the company showed an increase in sales; but he soon left. In 1993 Joan sold Johnson Products to the white-owned IVAX Corporation, manufacturers of the black-cosmetic and skin care line Flori Roberts.

During the decline of Johnson Products that began in the early 1980s and faced with the increasing threat from white-owned black hair care manufacturers, Gardner strengthened his Soft Sheen's industry leadership by reorganizing and streamlining its management and by diversifying its product line. His Bottlewerks, a subsidiary established in 1983 that made bottles for Soft Sheen, as well as for Avon, Proctor & Gamble, and Kraft, showed a profit, grossing $10 million in 1988. Also, in the late 1980s, Soft Sheen became a multinational with its foreign subsidiaries, Soft Sheen International and Soft Sheen West Indies. At the same time, Garner began a program of hiring young blacks with MBAs as he shifted Soft Sheen's corporate culture from one of entrepreneurial leadership to professional management.[38]

In the subsequent development and management of many of these black-owned enterprises, the founder's family played an important role. For example, all of Edward Gardner's four children, who had degrees in law, business, engineering, and chemistry, were actively involved in the business, including research and development. With the growth of these companies, however, even expert family management cannot always provide the competitive edge necessary to survive as black-owned businesses. Family rivalry is often a big problem, which some say accounted for Eric Johnson's resignation as Johnson Products president and CEO, although industry analysts said that he was improving the company's profit picture.[39] Gardner's son, Gary, resigned as Soft Sheen's president as the company revamped its corporate culture.

The appearance of giant corporations in the late nineteenth century, as Alfred D. Chandler found, marked the emergence of managerial capitalism, which resulted in many of these businesses shifting from a management that was family operated to one controlled by professional managers.[40] In black-owned businesses, this phenomenon was taking place almost a century later; it was first exemplified by Berry Gordy when he turned his Motown Records over to professional managers who, for the most part, were white. Increasingly, capital-intensive black enterprises will have to move from family-controlled organizations to professionally managed ones.

However, it is not always the absence of entrepreneurial drive in the second generation of black business founders that necessitates professional management. Rather, these companies need such managers because they require a different set of skills from those of the entrepreneurs who founded them. In 1996, however, Edward Gardner's daughter, Terri, who had been president of Soft Sheen's in-house advertising agency and a senior manager, was appointed president and CEO after her brother resigned about two years later. Her father, the company's founder, remained chairman.

Before this turn of events, however, Gardner had considered the sale of Soft Sheen. The Jheri curl look was out by the mid-1980s and profits were in a decline. Ranked 11th in the *Black Enterprise* top 100 for 1994, with sales of $97.2 million, Soft Sheen in 1995 ranked 15th, with sales of $92.8 million. Gardner also faced competition from four other *BE* 100 companies, Luster Products, Pro-Line, Bronner Brothers, and Dudley Products, whose total sales in 1995 were $145.6 million. Along with Soft Sheen, their combined sales of $243.6 million, however, were dwarfed by one of the giants in the industry. In 1990 the Chicago-based Helene Curtis Industries had sales of $893 million.[41] In the post–Civil Rights period, white companies with aggressive marketing campaigns, especially Alberto-Culver, Revlon, and Helene Curtis had gained not only a large market share of black hair care products but also retained their edge in the black cosmetic and skin care industry.[42] Doubtless, they are confident that they can maintain control of these industries. Yet it is extremely unlikely that after almost a century of participation in the health and beauty aids industry African-American firms are going to yield to their assaults.

The Black Cosmetic and Skin Care Industry

As with African-American hair care manufacturers, blacks in the cosmetics and skin care industry also faced challenges from white competitors. The Overton-Hygienic Company, whose success was due to its famous High Brown Face Powder, was still in business at midcentury, but black women relied principally on skin care products and cosmetics manufactured by white companies.[43] Yet few white companies made special advertising appeals to them, despite their tremendous consumer power; a 1947 market survey showed that black women "spend nearly $300,000,000 a year on cosmetics, with most of it going for brands prepared for white skins."[44] Moreover, a 1945 survey of skin care products purchased by black women in Philadelphia shows clearly that white manufacturers dominated the black skin care market (see table 10.2).

Of the 33,659 black women surveyed, 52 percent regularly used commercial beauty preparations for their complexion, but the leading black-owned company, Apex, had only a 3.6 percent market share. The leading products purchased from white companies were Ponds, Lady Esther, Woodbury, Noxzema, Coty, Jergens, and Max Factor, which accounted for 75 percent of skin care products purchased by black women in 1945. What the numbers show, significantly, is that the majority of black women were more interested

TABLE 10.2   Brands Purchased by Blacks for Skin Care, 1945

Brand	Total	
	Number	*Percent*
Ponds	11,866	35.2
Lady Esther	4,032	12.0
Woodury	3,467	10.3
Noxzema	1,666	5.0
Coty	1,529	4.6
Apex	1,220	3.6
Avon	1,152	3.4
Watkins	1,038	3.1
Black & White	828	2.5
Jergens	646	1.9
Max Factor	637	1.9
Park & Tilford	520	1.5
Others (65 brands)	8,078	24.0

Source: Compiled from Research Company of America, *The New Philadelphia Story: A Report on the Characteristics of the Philadelphia Negro Market . . . Its Buying Habits and Brand Preferences* (Baltimore: The Afro-American Company, 1946).

in enhancing the beauty of their skin than lightening their skin color. The leading skin lightener, Black & White, had only a 2.5 percent market share. The black cosmetics and skin care industry was pioneered by Anthony Overton. Annie Turnbo-Malone and Madame C. J. Walker also produced a line of skin care products. But in their product labeling and marketing, those companies resolutely denied that their products lightened the skin. The market niche for these products, limited as it was, was filled by white manufacturers, who blatantly advertised their products as skin *whiteners*.

A potentially lucrative market existed for skin care products and cosmetics specifically for black women. Around 1950, John H. Johnson's Beauty Star Cosmetics products were available through the mail-order firm he started in 1946. That same year Rose Meta, a division of the Rose Meta House of Beauty, introduced a full line of cosmetics, lipsticks, rouges/blushes, and creams specially developed for women of color. Significantly, these were sold in Grant's Department Store, a first for a black cosmetic company that advertised its products as "made exclusively to glorify women with color."[45] In 1949 the Chicago-based Morganoil company, which also manufactured black hair products, introduced a line of cosmetics for black women, emphasizing that its products were "created to bring forth the beauty and charm of all the varied complexions—distinct in that they are economically priced, but superior in quality."[46]

Also, the Chicago-based Marguerita Ward Cosmetics Company, founded in 1922, resumed manufacturing after World War II. Unlike Murray's hair products for men, the War Department did not find cosmetics for black women important enough to the war effort to ensure the availability of their ingredients; the founder of the company that bore her name indicated that, "During the war I was unable to get the ingredients necessary to produce the quality of cosmetics which I have always manufactured and I was unwilling to produce an inferior product."[47] In 1959 Lena Horne established the Lena Horne Cosmetic Company, with the home office in Oakland, California. Within a year, seven district offices were established, including one in Atlanta. Horne said in her promotions that "We plan to enhance and glorify the natural beauty of Negro women."[48] Launched on the eve of the Civil Rights movement when the slogan was to become "Black Is Beautiful," cosmetics promoted by the light-skinned Horne would undoubtedly have had only limited appeal.

However, the biggest company that emerged in the black cosmetics industry and the most successful in bringing cosmetics for black women into the mainstream market was Fashion Fair Cosmetics. When *Ebony* publisher John H. Johnson launched Fashion Fair Cosmetics in 1973, "Black Is Beautiful" was commonplace and black women conceded that natural beauty could be enhanced by cosmetics. Yet it was five years before the venture made a profit. Indeed, Johnson lost $1 million in each of these years before the line took off. Johnson's strategy was to promote and sell his products to upscale markets rather than to mass-distribution outlets. The strategy paid off! By 1987 Fashion Fair was the largest black cosmetics line in the world and ranked in the top 10 cosmetics lines sold in department stores. It succeeded because it filled a market niche that existed for cosmetics made specifically for the varied complexion shades of black women.

Moreover, just as white cosmetic companies had ignored the special market need for black women's cosmetics, they had also disregarded the special problems of black skin care. In addition to Fashion Fair, this market niche was also exploited by Naomi Sims, who introduced her line of skin care products for black women in 1985. These also sold in the nation's large department stores, and sales reached $5 million by 1988. The black consumer dollar for cosmetics and skin care products in the 1980s and 1990s was spent in the same types of outlets as it was in 1945: 41.3 percent of the black dollars at independent drugstores; 18.1 percent at five-and-dime or variety stores; 17.1 percent at department stores; and 16.7 percent at chain drugstores. While both chain and independent drugstores today remain important in the sale of cosmetics, discount retail giants such as Wal-Mart, Kmart, and Target, having supplanted the five-and-dime stores, now dominate the market. Department store sales, primarily of upscale cosmetics, however, have maintained their former level.

It was for the mass black-consumer market, however, that Carol Jackson Mouyiaris founded her skin product manufacturing company. In 1993 she introduced her Black Opal Skin Care Collection consisting of seven products. By 1995 industry statistics showed that "Black Opal now has a 33% share [dollar volume for the mass market] of the ethnic skin care segment, up from 7 percent in 1994." Yet industry analysts believe that Black Opal can neither sustain its market share nor its expansion, claiming that the company "is growing too big, too fast ... averaging 1,000% per year." In 1995 Jackson Mouyiaris introduced the Black Opal Color Cosmetics line and also the Black Opal for Men skin care line, which was launched with "a near $2 million ad campaign starring Minnesota Vikings quarterback Warren Moon."[49]

Mouyiaris, who used her savings to start the company, put as much energy in studying market demographics as she did in developing her product, which competes with not only Fashion Fair but also Clinique, Oil of Olay, Prescriptive, and the French-based Clarins. Perhaps she learned her lessons in marketing from Charles Revson, who had great success in marketing his Revlon products, and also from Wal-Mart's founder, Sam Walton. The mass market for cosmetics for black women is much larger than the upscale market, which is understandable because 50 percent of the African-American population have incomes of less than $25,000. Yet these women still want quality products, symbolized by slick advertising and attractive packaging, which are as important in attracting black consumers as attracting whites.

An aggressive and slick ad campaign, products whose cost is a relatively low $5.95 to $11.95, and distribution in "over 10,000 chain drug stores and discount variety stores" accounted for the booming sales of Black Opal in the mid-1990s. While the black skin care and cosmetic market is highly competitive, black companies in the industry are still growing with the introduction of new lines. This is notwithstanding a comment made in 1986 by a high-ranking Revlon executive who said that "In the next couple of years, the black-owned businesses will disappear. They'll all be sold to the white companies."[50] And one transaction bears out his prediction. In 1993 Johnson Products was sold to the IVAX Corporation, which manufactures the Flori Roberts black cosmetic and skin care line. The former owner, Joan B. Johnson, announced that her sale to a company with an international distribution network "will help us increase both sales and profits." She also said that "another advantage is that we'll now manufacture and distribute IVAX's Flori Robert's cosmetic line."

Was Johnson implying that an increase in profits made by IVAX from the sale of products manufactured by its Johnson Products subsidiary to blacks would benefit the African-America community? The issue here is, to whom do blacks owe consumer loyalty: black-owned companies or white owned-companies that produce products for blacks? With white companies escalating their appeal to blacks, the issue is broad and complex. As president of the IVAX subsidiary, Joan Johnson differs very little from other blacks in white corporate America who hold executive positions in the black-oriented skin care and cosmetics divisions of companies such as Revlon, Avon, Maybelline, and Cover Girl.

Ironically, as the market grows increasingly competitive, leading black companies now boldly market skin lightener products. Johnson's Fashion Fair line includes Vantex, with ads that emphasize "Watch your blemishes fade away," but the product label clearly states it is a "Skin Bleaching Creme." In response to medical advancements in skin care since the 1970s, Vantex also includes sunscreen capabilities. The term that today's manufacturers use for skin lighteners, presumably to avoid offending sensibilities, is *fade cream*. It is used not only by the long-standing leader in the skin lightener industry, the E. T. Brown Drug Company, manufacturers of Palmer's Skin Fade Cream, but also by Black Opal with its Advanced Dual Complex Fade Gel.

Yet the market for skin lighteners is not confined to women of African descent. Other women of color in Asia and the Middle East and Europeans with Mediterranean ancestry also use the product. In the mid-1990s the internationally acclaimed supermodel Iman, a Somalian, introduced a line of cosmetics for women of color, Africans, Asians, Hispanics, and Native Americans. Industry analysts say these groups "make up 30% of U.S. Cosmetic buyers." Iman and a partner hold a 51 percent interest in her company[51] IVAX is the manufacturer.

Even though Fashion Fair, with its 10 percent share, will remain the sales leader in the upscale cosmetics market for black women, it faces increasing competition not only from white companies but also from the new black-owned cosmetic and skin care manufacturers that make products for both markets. For example, in the early 1990s, John H. Johnson introduced his Ebone' Cosmetics line for sale to this combined mass market. Consequently, at the end of the twentieth century, blacks still have a choice of skin care products and cosmetics manufactured by blacks. But a Revlon official cautioned in 1986 that "when you produce what the consumer wants, loyalties disappear."[52]

Black Financial Institutions

Does this fundamental principle of the free-enterprise system—that customer loyalty disappears in the face of stiff competition—also apply to black financial institutions? Between 1880 and 1910 blacks founded hundreds of fraternal insurance organizations. The emergence of black insurance companies, however, began in the early twentieth century. The leaders were Alonzo Herndon of Atlanta Life, C. C. Spaulding of North Carolina Mutual, and Harry C. Pace of Supreme Liberty. Still, by 1927, when the 32 largest black insurance companies held 85 percent of the market—some $316 million worth of policies in force—in that same year, a single white-owned company had written $900 million worth of insurance for blacks. The black insurance industry, however, survived the depression and subsequent rough times, with some companies, such as Supreme, even continuing to make loans to black property owners when white banks and Realtors were routinely turning down black applicants.[53] This survival was accomplished even though one large white-owned company had policies in force on blacks that had a total dollar value greater than that of the top 40 black insurance companies combined.[54]

By 1944 there were 46 black insurance companies that belonged to the National Negro Insurance Association (NNIA), with 43 of them reporting a total of: 3,695,628 black policy holders; more than $630 million worth of policies in force; almost $32.8 million in premium income; and a total income of more than $36 million. The total insurance on blacks held by 262 companies, both white and black, in 1942, however, amounted to $1.685 billion on 9,420,298 black policyholders, with total annual premiums of $67.9 million. Consequently, while white-owned companies carried more than $1 billion worth of policies on blacks and had 5.7 million more black policyholders, black insurance companies had almost 40 percent of the annual premium income from blacks.[55]

By 1946 there were 205 black-owned companies in the insurance business: 23 were legal reserve companies; 39 were miscellaneous (assessment, life, health, accident, and industrial), 91 were burial organizations; and 51 were fraternal benefit societies. By 1963, however, there were some 50 legal reserve insurance companies, but the number of burial associations and fraternal benefit societies that carried insurance declined, holding only $1 million in assets. Then, too, while the 43 NNIA member companies in 1944 held $57.3 million in assets, by 1963 the 20 leading black companies, which held virtually all the assets of black insurance companies, had total assets of $311 million, only 0.23 percent of the $133 billion in assets owned by all life insurance companies. At that time the 20 leading black companies sold $592.3 million of new life insurance policies when overall industry sales amounted to $79.6 billion.

However, 58 percent of the benefits of white insurance companies went to living policyholders in matured endowments, disability, annuity payments, dividends, and policies surrendered for cash. By contrast, death benefits have been the primary form of payment made by black-owned insurance companies, with black performance limited or nonexistent in virtually all areas of the insurance business. In the 1960s black companies were unable to capitalize on two forms of insurance that were expanding the industry. Group life insurance, the fastest growing segment of the industry by 1962, accounted for 31 percent, some $228.5 billion, of all life insurance in force in the United States. Also, black companies did not carry credit life insurance, another fast-growing segment of the industry. By the end of 1963, almost $43.6 billion of credit insurance was in force.

By 1976 there were 41 black insurance companies out of a total of 1,800 American insurance companies. These black companies had $590 million in assets and $9.7 billion insurance in force in an industry with a total of $2.139 trillion of life insurance in force and $289 billion in assets.[56] The number of black insurance companies, however, declined from 42 to 23 between 1973 to 1993. Atlanta Life, headed by Jesse Hill, however, strengthened its position by expanding. Within five years, it purchased three small black-owned insurance companies, including Chicago Metropolitan Life Assurance.[57] Atlanta Life, founded in 1902, is the nation's second-largest black insurance company. Among the 10 leading black insurance companies in 1995, all but one were founded before 1950. The largest, North Carolina Mutual, was founded in 1899.

Simply put, black insurance companies from their founding have had difficulty competing on any level with white companies, except in the case of life insurance.[58] As with other industries in the twentieth-century rise of black corporations, the insurance business, while its assets and policies in force expanded, was unable to compete fully with mainstream insurance companies, underscoring again the persistently low economic condition of almost half the black population. Yet, as one industry analyst said, "As long as black people are getting buried, there will be black insurance companies."[59]

The E. G. Bowman Company, founded in 1954, was the first and remains the largest minority-owned insurance brokerage firm on Wall Street; it is headed by Ernesta Bowman, who established the firm. She and her husband, John Procope, have approximately 2,000 clients, primarily large corporations. PepsiCo was its first commercial client. Government clients include the New York Port Authority, as well as the Fulbright scholarship program. By the mid-1990s sales approached $40 million, but this is considerably less than the $500 million worth of business the company expected to be doing after forty years in business. In 1991, Bowman expanded by forming an investment firm, Bond, Procope Capital Management, with Alan Bond; it has reported managing $315 million in assets.[60]

While the founding of black commercial banks began in 1888, black investment banks are primarily a post–Civil Rights period phenomenon. Only six black banks survived the depression, including Citizen's Trust, the bank founded by Herman Perry. In 1936, Jesse B. Blayton, along with Lorimer D. Milton and Clayton R. Yates, took control of Citizen's Trust. Their first act was to join the Federal Reserve, "the first black bank in the country to do so."[61] At the end of World War II, there were 11 black banks. By 1963 there were 13, with combined assets amounting to $77 million out of the $364 billion in assets held by the 14,079 banks in the country.

By 1978, in the third wave of black corporate America, there were 49 black banks, 40 savings and loans, and 39 insurance companies, which had combined assets that topped $2 billion for the first time. In 1993 their total assets amounted to $4.2 billion, despite a decline in black financial institutions from 123 in 1973 to 76 in 1993. With the contraction of the black financial industry, *Black Enterprise* in 1990 combined its previously separate listings of banks and savings and loans into one category, "B.E. Financial Companies." The list includes 25 financial institutions, 11 of them founded before 1960. In the 1976 *Black Enterprise* listing, there were 50 black banks: 39 were founded in the 1960s and 1970s. At that time, Carver Federal Savings, which became the highest ranked financial institution on the 1995 list, was listed under savings and loans as the leading institution in that category.

In the twentieth century, black commercial banks have been criticized for their limited financial services, especially in providing capital in support of the black business community. Yet, black banks did provide some support, especially in the form of mortgage loans, which was not always the case with white banks established in black communities. In 1955 Congressman Adam Clayton Powell called upon Harlem's blacks to withdraw their funds from white banks because of the "continuing refusal of these banks in the Harlem area to lend any money for mortgages and improvement of property in this area." Emphasizing that he was speaking as head of the Abyssinian Baptist Church, Powell indicated that his church had withdrawn funds from Harlem's white banks. He urged Harlem blacks to do the same and redeposit their funds in either Harlem's Carver Federal Savings or the Tri-State Bank of Memphis.

With support from the local branch of the NAACP, Powell's group produced evidence that showed the extent of New York's discriminatory banking policies, indicating that "in 1949–50, $549 million, was made in out-of state loans, when during the same period nothing was loaned in the Harlem area." At the same time, Powell also noted that in Harlem "black money is being used to finance white business interests."[62] Yet, with so few black banks in the nation, blacks had few alternatives but to use white banks, despite their discriminatory financial policies. Another drawback to black banks was that they had higher losses on loans, 9 percent of total revenue, compared to white banks with only a 3 percent loss. Moreover, black banks had neither the funds on deposit nor the assets to carry these losses, compared to the large white banks, many of whose major depositors were huge corporations.

Still, the third growth period of black corporate America marked a 20-year expansion of the black banking industry in numbers, assets, capital, deposits, and loans. Both the Civil Rights movement and federal affirmative economic policies were significant in contributing to the growth of black banks. In the 1960s the leaders of black economic nationalism called for blacks to control the economy of their communities, which led to a period of rapid bank founding, expansion, and, eventually, contraction.

Chicago's black banking history during the third wave of black corporate America provides an example. Seaway National Bank, established in 1965 and the first black bank founded in the city since the early 1930s, quickly became one of the nation's leading black banks. It was founded by a consortium of black businessmen, including Dempsey Travis, a millionaire real estate broker. He had also founded the first association of black mortgage bankers in 1961, a response to the exclusion of blacks from the white mortgage bankers association.[63] By 1995 Seaway ranked third on *Black Enterprise*'s financial companies listing. Seaway grew by becoming one of Illinois's largest SBA lenders. Also, with Harold Washington as mayor between 1983 and 1987, municipal funds were deposited in Seaway.

In addition, Chicago's Independence Bank, founded in 1964 by black millionaires Alvin Boutte, a drugstore-chain owner, and George H. Johnson, the black hair care products manufacturer, thrived during Washington's term as mayor. Until Boutte took over as president in 1967, however, it appeared that the bank would not survive. He instituted several three-year development plans. The first was to secure deposits from both white and black corporations. With accounts opened by CBS, Chrysler, General Motors, Johnson & Johnson, Delta Airlines, Johnson Publishing, Supreme Life, and Parker House Sausage, the assets of Independence increased in three years from $16 million to $55 million. The development of a black professional staff followed. Both Seaway and Independence had opened with white presidents, but only Seaway's was competent. With Boutte at the helm, however, Independence by 1973 ranked as the nation's leading black bank.[64]

In 1988 Indecorp, the holding company for Independence, acquired Chicago's Drexel National Bank on the South Side. It was the country's first acquisition by a black bank of a financially sound white-owned financial institution. In 1979 Independence had purchased the insolvent white-owned Guaranty Bank and Trust and the Gateway National Bank. With Drexel's purchase, Indecorp's total asset base increased from $113 million to

$230 million. Then, in 1995, with the combined banks' assets at $279 million, Indecorp sold both banks to the white-owned Shorebank Corporation, the holding company of South Shore Bank, located on the South Side. It was expected to increase its assets to $305 million, which would make it one of Chicago's largest banks.[65]

During this time, several other black banks expanded by the acquisition of white financial institutions, but these were primarily failed savings and loans. A federal affirmative action initiative provided this opportunity for black bank expansion. In 1989 the Resolution Trust Corporation (RTC) was created under the Financial Institutions Reform, Recovery, and Enforcement Act (FIRREA). It was charged with liquidating the assets of the nation's failed savings and loans. With pressure from minority lobbyists in the banking industry, the RTC established policies that proved advantageous to blacks. The RTC had six years to liquidate the assets of these savings and loans, which they did by auction. Since black banks could not compete with the large white institution, the RTC initiated a minority preference bidding process. Its primary goal was to forestall the creation of a monolithic banking system had prosperous white banks been allowed to swallow up those failed institutions.

The New York–based Carver Federal Savings, founded in 1948, headed Black Enterprise's 1995 "B. E. Financial Companies" list of financial companies. Carver Federal has eight branch banks located in Brooklyn, Queens, Manhattan, and Long Island, most of which "were branches of white commercial banks fleeing from minority neighborhoods." In 1994 Carver Federal was listed on the NASDAQ, the first and only black bank to go public. In 1996 it expanded its loan capacity to small businesses by up to $100 million. The expansion is a result of partnering with the New York Business Development Corporation, a quasi-public lending institution.[66] Also in 1990 the Consolidated Bank and Trust Company of Richmond, Virginia, the nation's oldest surviving black bank, founded in 1903 as the St. Luke's Penny Savings Bank, purchased and reopened the the 107-year-old Peoples Savings and Loan in Hampton and the 27-year-old Community Savings and Loan in Newport News, both of which were black owned. Consolidated paid the RTC $315,000 to add the two banks to its portfolio, which enabled it to expand to a five-branch banking operation in Virginia.[67]

Perhaps the most exciting event in black banking history in the third wave of black corporate America was the 1992 establishment of the United Bank of Philadelphia, a full-service commercial bank founded by Emma Chappell. In several ways, Chappell's initiative in establishing a bank brings to full circle the history of black women bankers in the twentieth century, which was begun by Maggie Lena Walker who founded the St. Luke's Penny Savings Bank in 1903 and became America's first woman bank president.[68] The founding of United Bank also underscored several trends in contemporary black banking, including that of experienced and knowledgeable blacks moving from white banks to black banks. Before her founding of United Bank, Chappell had spent 35 years at Philadelphia's Continental Bank, advancing to assistant treasurer and then becoming its first black and first female vice president.

Blacks in the Philadelphia community provided more than half of the investment capital for United Bank, which, because of its grass roots funding, has been called "the bank that the people built." Chappell raised 55 percent ($3.3 million) of the amount required by the state department of banking from the black community, often raising funds at several black churches at a time. At one point 220 black ministers held a special Sunday fundraiser, which resulted in the purchase of $400,000 worth of stock in the names of their churches.[69] Pennsylvania also made an exception in its state banking laws to allow Chappell to sell stock in her bank at $10 a share in blocks of 50 and multiples of $500. The other

45 percent, $2.7 million, came from 14 institutional investors. In addition, the bank's 12-member board of directors contributed $600,000 to cover the cost of a business plan and feasibility study.

Since Philadelphia's last black bank went out of business in 1956, the black business and financial community was receptive to a black bank (the Berean Savings Association, founded in 1888, was still in existence). To fill the void, black investment banker Malcolm D. Pryor, CEO of Pryor, McClendon, Counts & Company, had asked Chappell to establish a commercial bank that could provide services to Philadelphia's black business community.[70] Within two years of its founding, United acquired six failed savings and loans from the RTC and converted them into branches. In 1994 the bank had $87.45 million in deposits.[71] In 1995, however, reflecting black-bank trends, deposits dropped to $84.14 million.

One reason for the decline was that the RTC minority bidding process had ended in 1995. Also, in 1994 the Treasury Department had eliminated its system of interest-free overnight deposit revenues, "considered the lifeblood of all financial institutions." The Treasury Department, however, made an exception for banks that serviced "corporations with tax liabilities that exceeded $78 million in 1993." Few, if any, minority banks met this requirement. Indeed, in 1994 there had been only 16 black firms with sales of more than $80 million. In 1995 the number had increased to 18, with 4 of them in New York and 3 in Chicago. What this meant, then, was that "larger nonblack banks [would] gain additional revenue and capital from black banks now excluded from this cash stream."[72]

Black-banking industry analysts saw this change and others in federal banking practices in the 1990s as a turning point for black banks in the twenty-first century. While affirmative government policies had been important in contributing to the improved financial picture of black banks, more recent retrenchment of those policies has had a devastating impact. In 1995, while commercial banks posted a total record profit of $48.8 billion and the earnings of savings and loan associations grew by 1.3 billion, "There was virtually zero growth for the [*Black Enterprise* financial] 25 between 1994 and 1995." Assets grew 1 percent; deposits fell 1 percent.[73] In 1995 Carver Federal, the nation's largest black bank, had assets of $363.2 million. In 1994 its assets were $362.8 million, increasing to $372 million in 1996.

In the post–Civil Rights era, affirmative action benefited black banks in several ways. With the rise of black electoral politics in the 1970s, there had been an increase in large deposits from federal, state, county, and municipal agencies, including school districts, transportation facilities, water utilities, and park districts. Still, those deposits, especially at the county and municipal levels, were contingent on electoral politics, i.e., the party in office. Also, while black banks sought accounts from large nonprofit organizations and institutions, their deposits for the most part were tokens, as were those from large white corporations such as Sears, Kmart, Jewel Foods, and Giant, which have branches in black communities. Yet black banks during this time maintained their historical conservatism, investing in U.S. government securities as opposed to more risky but potentially more profitable investments in tax-free municipal securities.[74]

In the twenty-first century, mergers and acquisitions can strengthen black financial institutions by increasing assets and allowing for expansion of services. For example, the United Bank of Philadelphia increased its deposits from $18 million in 1992 to $87.2 million in 1993 through acquisitions. Mortgage loans constitute 78 percent of United's $63.76 million loan portfolio. Only .5 percent are nonperforming and 2.25 percent are delinquent. In 1995 there was only one bad loan on the books, a $500,000 commercial loan. Small businesses make up 98 percent of all black businesses. Their ability to compete and survive in the mainstream American business community depends on securing capital for development and expansion from commercial banks.

Black investment banks have been critical in securing capital for the rise of black corporate America, but usually they fund only multimillion-dollar enterprises. Beyond providing the capital for this expansion, these investment banks have marked the growth of black financial institutions beyond commercial banks, savings and loans, and insurance companies. Of the 15 institutions on *Black Enterprise*'s investment banks list, most were founded in the 1980s and 1990s, and only one in the 1970s. This reflects the expansion of black businesses that paralleled mainstream American business activity the post–Civil Rights period.

There were two principal factors that accounted for the rise of black investment banks. Although affirmative action initiatives had opened doors for black businesspeople to establish multimillion-dollar enterprises, black entrepreneurs who needed millions in venture capital were limited primarily to federally funded MESBIC loans, which required additional private-sector investment capital to secure. Black banks, with their limited assets, could seldom afford to carry loans in that amount, while white banks created insurmountable obstacles that precluded most blacks from securing funds from them.

The African-American leader in the field of supplying venture capital for minorities was Edward Dugger III, head of UNC Ventures in Boston, an $18-million fund that in 1974 was the largest of the nation's privately run black-owned venture capital firms. From 1974 to 1994, UNC raised $28 million and leveraged more than $1 billion, which was used to finance more than 50 minority businesses. About 57 percent of UNC investments have been in start-up companies and 34 percent for the acquisition of established enterprises. Also, approximately 30 percent of the companies in which UNC has invested are publicly traded, including Envirotest Systems Corporation, which was ranked 11th in *Black Enterprise*'s top 100, with sales of $104.7 million.[75] When Envirotest began public trading on the NASDAQ, opening shares sold at $16 and rapidly rose to $27. UNC was able to buy in at $.77 a share. Since 1984 the average return for UNC investors has been around 15 percent, which compared favorably with Standard & Poor's 500 stock index for the same period.

Investors in UNC's first two funds included Harvard University, Yale University, MIT, Reebok, Peabody Trust, John Hancock, Mobil Oil, the Ford Foundation, and the Rockefeller family. Companies funded by UNC have included Broadcast Enterprises Network, established in 1974 by Ragan Henry. In the 1990s, the company expanded to 60 stations throughout the nation. UNC also leveraged financing for the Boston Bank of Commerce, the only black bank in New England, and also funded $45 million for short-lived Air Atlanta, an airline founded by black entrepreneur Michael Hollis in 1984. It failed because of a shortage of operating capital. From 1974 to 1994, approximately 33 percent of UNC's funds were invested in computers and electronics companies; 23 percent in communications companies; 10 percent in environmental services; 9 percent in transportation; 9 percent in real estate; and 16 percent in miscellaneous companies. UNC's minority investment from 1984 to 1993 was: 61 percent in companies owned by African-Americans; 24 percent in Asian-American firms; 4 percent in Hispanic-American enterprises; and 11 percent in companies owned by other minority groups.

The first annual listing of the *Black Enterprise*'s top black-owned investment banks appeared in 1991. Some twenty years earlier, there had been only two black investment banks, Daniels and Bell, founded by Willie E. Daniels and Travers J. Bell, followed by First Harlem Securities, established by Russell Goings. They were also the first black-owned investment banking firms to be admitted to the New York Stock Exchange in its 178-year history. In 1975 the New Orleans–based Doley Securities became the third black invest-ment firm to trade on the NYSE. Even when black firms were admitted to it they found that "Black entry into corporate trading was blocked."

Daniels and Bell made a lateral move around this obstacle, however, by specializing in public finance. Black mayors made the difference. Ironically, it was the black mayor of Mound Bayou, Mississippi, the most successful town founded by blacks in the late nine-teenth century, that provided Daniels and Bell an entry into public finance. Their company had funded 50 units of public housing in that city. As a result, Daniels and Bell has been credited with creating the municipal bond industry for blacks.[76]

In the third wave of black corporate America, black investment banks leveraged signifi-cant deals in municipal bonds. After its founding in 1979, the San Francisco–based Grigsby Brandford and Company, a fully black-owned company and the oldest black investment banking firm in the nation, with nine offices in major cities, emerged as a lead-ing national (ranked 15th in 1995 by Securities Data.) underwriter of municipal issues. According to Calvin Grigsby, CEO and founder, his firm in that 16-year period managed "over $2 billion for various convention/civic center projects" and "helped provide over $400 billion for basic public infrastructure."[77] The projects included airports and rapid transit, schools and universities, hospitals, housing, and utilities. However, this kind of success was minuscule indeed. According to Grigsby, the 12 to 15 black investment bank-ing firms in 1990 managed less than 1 percent of the nation's total bond business.[78] Nev-ertheless, by 1993 *Black Enterprise*'s investment banks "co-managed bond issues worth $162.7 billion."[79] But Grigsby Brandford, which ranked second on the *Black Enterprise* list of top financial companies for 1995, collapsed in 1996.[80] Its downfall was a reflection of Grisby's failure to mediate new government regulations on tax-exempt and taxable securi-ties, municipal bond and mortgage-backed securities, which since the 1970s have made up the bulk of black investment banking activities.

With the municipal bond and mortgage-backed securities market drying up and with closer scrutiny by the federal government of the nation's investment banking industry, Ray McClendon of Pryor, McClendon, Counts and Company (PMC), on viewing the position of black investment banks in the twenty-first century, said: "We are going to have to con-solidate . . . in order to generate a deeper capital base." In the past, he added, his desire to be in charge of his own operation had prevented consolidation, but he emphasized: "I'd rather have 30 percent of a greater profit base than 100 percent of a small and declining profit base."[81] In 1992 his firm was the lead manager of the $400-million debt offering for the new Denver International Airport, the largest municipal finance deal managed by a black firm in this country. PMC also helped establish Emma Chappell's United Bank of Philadelphia and raised $5.6 million for Maceo Sloan's purchase of a public communica-tion service license.

The new directions and diversification in black investment are reflected in the financial activities of Maceo K. Sloan. He was formerly chief investment officer for North Carolina Mutual Life Insurance, representing the fourth generation of his family to work there, before he bought out its subsidiary, NCM Capital Management in 1991, which he had established in 1985. Both NCM, based in Durham, and New Africa Advisors, with offices in Johannesburg, South Africa, and headed by Justin Beckett, are subsidiaries of the Sloan Financial Group, which also has offices in Atlanta, New York, and San Diego. Sloan is also in partnership with the Calvert Group, which in July 1994, "had $4.6 billion under man-agement in 32 funds." Sloan's senior vice president of finance and investment director,

Clifford D. Mpare, who indicated that from 1992 to 1995 Sloan's "core equity investment performance had an annualized return of 9.15 percent, versus 6.27 percent for the S & P 500."[82]

In 1994 John W. Rogers Jr., formerly with Sloan's Calvert Fund, established the Chicago-based Ariel Capital Management, considered "the first African-American-owned equity mutual fund company." A year earlier, Rogers had bought out his interest from Sloan Financial for "$4 million—or 1% of the assets of the firm's two funds." By 1994 Ariel had "more than $2.1 billion under management," including investments in two Ariel Funds.[83] In 1995 Rogers established a joint venture with his recently formed Ariel Premier Bond Fund and Lincoln Capital Management. Lincoln manages $30 billion for about 90 clients. Minimum investment with Lincoln is $100 million, including "$17.5 billion in three fixed-income portfolios, whose investors include NYC Public Employees Retirement System, Comsat and IBM."[84] In 1995, Litz, Glover & White, founded in 1988, was *Black Enterprise*'s highest ranking investment bank in terms of corporate issues. With offices in five states, it expanded by buying out a white securities firm.[85] In the third wave of black corporate America, as black investment firms became more successful, they expanded by both joint-venture and acquisition activities.

Also during this period, specialized business groups were founded to protect the interests and promote the growth of black banking. The National Association of Urban Bankers, an organization of minority financial institutions and bankers, was founded in 1975. The National Association of Securities Professionals, an organization of minorities and women in the securities industry, was founded in 1985. As a result of the rise of black corporate America, the National Association of Black Accountants (NABA) was created in 1969 by nine black New York accountants.

Although only 1 percent of the nation's accountants are black, there are several prominent black accounting firms. Wall Street's Mitchell, Titus & Company, the nation's largest minority-owned certified public accounting firm, "ranks 37th in the nation among *all* accounting firms." The 16-partner firm with three offices and 210 employees was founded by Brooklyn College graduate Bert Mitchell, the present CEO, and Jamaican-born Robert Titus, a Baruch College graduate. Before establishing the firm in 1972, Mitchell was managing partner of Lucas Tucker & Company, the oldest black-owned CPA firm in the country. Mitchell, Titus, however, took off in the late 1970s, with not-for-profit organizations such as the Ford foundation and the A. Philip Randolph Institute as clients. The firm's Washington office generated accounts from federal agencies and entered into joint-venture projects with Big Eight accounting firms. Also, Mitchell, Titus grew by merging with other black-owned accounting firms, while providing consulting services to its clients, who include the National Urban League, Philip Morris, Time Warner, and PepsiCo. The firm also has a Philadelphia office, and others are planned for Chicago, Atlanta, and Boston, with an increased staff of 500.[86]

The Recording Industry

In the third wave of black corporate America, Motown Records, founded by Berry Gordy in 1959, was the most successful black enterprise in the nation between 1973 and 1983. During that decade, sales exceeded $50 million annually, approaching $100 million in the 1980s, before the company was sold in 1987. The buyers, MCA and Boston Ventures, purchased Motown for $61 million, and they later sold it to PolyGram for $325 million. These developments closely parallel those of two forerunners of Motown Records, the New York-based Pace & Handy Music Company and the Black Swan Phonograph Company, established in the early twentieth century. John H. Johnson said in 1989 that "After Pace put Black artists and Black Record buyers on the business map, White-owned corporations, in moves strikingly similar to the recent acts of White-owned insurance, cosmetics and publishing companies, started issuing 'race catalogs' in a generally successful effort to destroy Black entrepreneurs."[87]

In its inception and development, however, Motown also followed in the tradition of black record companies founded in the second wave of black corporate America after World War II. With the end of Black Swan Records in the late 1920s, black record companies remained on the periphery, as the white companies expanded in the 1930s and 1940s. After World War II, blacks began to establish record companies, primarily prompted by the profits made by white-owned companies from the efforts of black artists. In 1945 the Swing Time Recording Company was established in Los Angeles by Jack Lauderdale. The black-owned company had an interracial staff and its all-time hit, "Hot Biscuits," sold 200,000 records. The company distributed nationally and also in Hawaii, Mexico, France, and England.[88]

In 1946 Gladys Hampton, the wife of jazz great Lionel Hampton, established Hampton Records, becoming the first black woman to own a record company. The announcement of her New York based company said it marked "the first time that colored persons have launched a record company equipped to offer competition to many of the major wax firms." The comment revealed how quickly the Black Swan company of the 1920s had been forgotten. Yet, unlike Black Swan, Hampton Records did not have its own processing plant, but used a white firm to cut its records. With the opening of her company, Gladys Hampton launched a national search for new black talent. She said that her studio would record hot jazz, swing, blues, classics, spirituals, and other forms of folk music. The first cut planned, "Hey Baba Rebop," had been made famous by her husband.[89]

The black-owned Exclusive Record Company, however, was already cutting successful records in 1946. The company, owned by black composer Leon Rene, launched two hits that he wrote, "When the Swallows Come Back to Capistrano" and "The Honeydripper," which sold over one million copies, holding the "No 1 spot on *Billboard*'s music popularity chart for 30 weeks."[90] Also, four World War II veterans, three white and one black, founded the Imperial Music company in 1946. Waverly Ivey was the only black; another partner, music editor of *Billboard*, cowrote "Sleepy-Head," the company's first record.[91]

The 1950s brought a succession of successful, but small and short-lived black record companies. The United Record Corporation, headed by Leonard Allen and Samuel Smith, was established in 1950. By 1953 it had under contract Gene Ammons, the Four Blazes, Memphis Slim, the Caravans, Junior Wells, and the Staples Singers, with distribution in South America and France.[92] In 1958 Zell Sanders started her J & S label after her 15-year-old daughter, Johnnie, was repeatedly turned down for a record contract. Using $5,000 from her savings, Zell Sanders produced "Over The Mountain," recorded by Johnnie and a partner. It sold over 700,000 copies.[93]

The Chicago-based Vee-Jay records, founded in 1953, also put out a string of hits, including "Your Precious Love" in 1958 by the Impressions, whose lead singer was Jerry Butler. The most successful black record company during this period, however, was Dootsie Williams's Dootone Recording Company, which was described as "the largest colored owned and operated business of its kind." Williams, a musician, arranger, and songwriter, not only produced and recorded songs but also discovered, coached, and created music for his recording artists. The Penguins' "Earth Angel" sold more than a million copies and made the Lucky Strike "Hit Parade." In 1955 Dootone also recorded "Don't Take Your Love," which in three months "skyrocketed in sales across the country."[94] When Berry Gordy emerged on the national scene with Motown's first gold record, "Shop Around" by Smokey Robinson and the Miracles in 1960, there was a solid tradition of black participation in the ownership and management of record companies.

Gordy built on this tradition in developing, packaging, marketing, and distributing the music of black America. His Motown sound marked not only the first time that black music crossed over into the mainstream white market but also the first time that mainstream music was black music. Even so, it was not until Michael Jackson's platinum-selling *Thriller* album, released in 1982, that MTV began playing black music. Until he sold Motown, Gordy had placed under contract and developed many of America's leading singers from the 1960s to the 1980s, including the Jackson Five, Stevie Wonder, Gladys Knight and the Pips, Marvin Gaye, and the Temptations. In the 1960s the leading Motown artists were Diana Ross and the Supremes, whose sales totaled over $12 million, second only to the Beatles. In the 1970s the Jackson Five became Motown's most profitable artists, and in the 1980s it was the Commodores, led by Lionel Ritchie. The music of these and many other artists made the Motown sound. Eventually, however, most of the artists whom Gordy discovered and developed moved on and signed with white recording companies. Black songwriters Kenny Gamble and Leon Huff, founded Philadelphia International Records in 1974; they introduced the "Philly sound," but its impact was never as great as Motown's.

Motown was not the only black record company in the third wave of black corporate America. In *Black Enterprise*'s first list of the top 100 black companies, Al Bell's Stax Records, initially owned by whites, and Clarence Avant's Sussex Records were ranked, respectively, 13th and 24th in sales. Dick Griffey Productions, founded in 1974, has been on the list since 1982. The leading black-owned record company in the 1990s has been Rush Communications, founded in 1990 by Russell Simmons. In 1995 it ranked 39th on the *Black Enterprise* list, with sales of $45 million. At the same time, blacks who had established successful record companies in the '70s, such as Sussex Records' Avant, closed their operations to work in the white record industry. In 1993 Avant became chairman of Motown Records, now a PolyGram subsidiary, while Jheryl Busby was appointed Motown's CEO and president. In 1995 Andre Harrell, in a joint venture with MCA Music Entertainment Group, founded and became CEO of Uptown Entertainment, a music, film, and television company. While he had negotiated a seven-year $50 million venture with MCA, Universal Pictures, and Universal Television, Harrell left to head Motown, with rapper Heavy D slated to succeed him at Uptown as CEO.[95]

The participation of blacks in management in white corporate America distinguished the third wave of black corporate America. For more than the past twenty years, the recording industry, more than radio, television, or film, has provided blacks with the best means of advancement into high management positions. Despite their ability to recognize industry trends, however, only a few blacks have sign-off power on record deals.[96] In addition, despite their advancement to powerful positions in the industry and lucrative record contracts, the reality is that "African-Americans remain largely excluded from the profit centers—production and marketing, packaging and distribution of the record business." Leading songwriters and producers Kenneth "Babyface" Edmonds and Antonio Reid, who established LaFace Records and produced over 101 hits, however, have an agreement with Arista Records calling for a 50 percent distribution of profits earned by their titles.[97]

In the third wave of black corporate America, Michael Jackson and the artist formerly known as Prince, as superstar entertainers, have achieved autonomous control of their careers, as have many black sports figures. Jackson used his status as an international superstar to make his own business decisions to promote himself. Also, his videos revolutionized the entertainment world and launched a whole new industry. Prince, on the other hand, developed a multimedia entertainment empire that included artist promotion, record production, and film. But these superstars are the exceptions!

Consequently, despite their contribution in revitalizing the American recording industry and their numerous personal and financial achievements, blacks did not emerge as the principal beneficiaries of the crossover of black music into white markets. Moreover, the expansion of the global economy brought multinationals into the American record industry. The entities that profited most from this development have been the six major recording and distribution companies: the American-owned Warner Elektra Atlantic, BMG Distribution, and CENA/UNI Distribution; the Dutch-owned PolyGram; and MCA and Sony, owned by Matsushita. These six supply 90 percent of the industry's music to wholesale and retail markets, which in 1994 represented more than $12 billion in domestic sales. Blacks make up 13 percent of America's population, but these companies' combined sales of black music—urban contemporary, pop, hip-hop, jazz, and gospel—"account for over 25 percent of all record sales and $3 billion in the U.S."[98] Moreover, the huge profits the industry has earned from black artists have prompted some people to reach back into history for an appropriate term to describe the limited benefits that blacks have received for their contributions and their general status in the industry; and so, one critic has surmised that record industry blacks work under "plantation-like conditions."[99] Simply put, of the $15 paid for a music CD, $1.50 goes to the artist and $.50 to the label, but then only after the major record company recoups its investment, which, at a minimum, is $600,000.[100]

Radio and Television

With the advent of radio in the mid-1920s, many people thought the record industry would collapse and change the way people listened to music. Yet, radio offered many different kinds of programs that went beyond music to capture America's attention, particularly comedy shows and serial stories.

In 1947 during the second rise of black corporate America, there were only 16 black disc jockeys out of 3,000. Yet, by the mid-1950s, there were more than 500, including Chicago's Al Benson, who attracted large numbers of black radio listeners. On the air, Benson was unmistakably black, as compared to some of the other early black djs, whose pronunciation and choice of music led many blacks to think they were white. By the 1950s the increasing number of local black djs was a response to the urbanization of black America. The market potential of black listeners, which was recognized by advertisers, eventually led to the emergence of radio as an important medium for the voice of black America; this outlet was needed to counter the stereotyped images of blacks propagated on national radio.[101]

By 1996, according to the National Association of Black Owned Broadcasters (NABOB), there were "189 Black-owned stations."[102] The first black-owned radio station, WERD in Atlanta, was purchased by Jesse B. Blayton Jr. in 1950.[103] By the 1970s there were only 16 black-owned stations in the country, although there were some 300 stations with black-oriented formats. In 1990, however, there were 206 black-owned stations: 138 AM stations and 68 FM stations.[104]

From the 1950s on, radio listening was changed by new technological advances. The invention of the transistor in the 1950s and headphones in the 1960s took the radio out of the home and into the streets. More recently, the appearance of portable and cellular telephones has revolutionized the way Americans listen to the radio, with more and more of them tuning into talk shows. With increased transportation time to and from work, people are listening to talk radio to alleviate their monotony—and to participate in the actual discussions, which include politics, personal counseling from leading psychologists—electronic versions of Ann Landers—and advice from financial analysts on topics from investments to buying homes. Local and national news topics, especially as they broke each day, gave all Americans an opportunity to become policy analysts. By the 1990s talk radio became as popular, if not more so, than music radio. Some black disc jockeys even syndicated their shows. Several syndicated talk show hosts whose programs are broadcast nationwide have emerged as cult figures, especially for the displaced, demoralized, and disaffected. For white America conservatives, there is Rush Limbaugh. For black America, there is Armstrong Williams. Talk radio, then, has returned the participatory democracy of the colonial New England town meetings to America.

In the third wave of black corporate America, black talk radio, moreover, has had a significant impact on shaping the political views of black America, even launching investigations of government misconduct that were ignored by the white media. In 1996, as a result of black talk radio, a federal investigation was launched into charges "that the CIA helped saturate West Central Los Angeles with crack cocaine in the early '80s to raise money for the Nicaraguan contras."[105]

With each new trend in radio listening, black involvement in the business has increased. One of the largest black-owned radio stations was established in 1972 when Percy Sutton purchased New York's WLIB-AM, which became the basis for Sutton's Inner City Broadcasting Corporation. Sutton also owns radio stations in San Francisco, Berkeley, Los Angeles, and San Antonio. In 1983 he sold his Detroit station to finance a joint venture with the black-owned Unity Broadcasting Network to buy a cable TV system, which was reorganized and renamed as the Queens Inner Unity Cable Systems. The company began operations when it formed a joint-venture partnership with Warner Communications. Each partner invested $3 million, with Warner assuming management responsibilities and establishing bank financing for $60 million.[106]

Dorothy E. Brunson became the first black female owner of a radio station when she purchased Baltimore's WEBB in 1979. She had previously worked for Inner City Broadcasting from 1973 to 1979, where she ran five radio stations and helped "boost the company's sales from $189,000 to $22 million." Before she left radio, Brunson had acquired and sold three other stations, moving on to purchase a Philadelphia television station, WGTV, in 1990.[107]

Brunson's move from radio to television represents the pattern that most other black radio station owners followed in expanding their communications empires. The first black-owned and operated TV station, however, was Detroit's WGPR, purchased in 1975 for $750,000 by William V. Banks, who headed the International Free and Accepted Modern Masons, i.e., the "Black Masons," a group that had subsidized the purchase of WGPR, an FM radio station, in 1964.[108]

In the third growth period of black corporate America, the largest holder of TV stations is Don Cornwell's Granite Broadcasting, founded in 1988 with a white partner, Stuart Beck. Granite, ranked ninth on the *Black Enterprise* top 100 list for 1995, with sales of $119,500 million and a staff of 944, owns nine stations. Cornwell, who holds a Harvard MBA degree and worked at Goldman, Sachs investment firm for 17 years, launched Granite with a business plan that called for buying underperforming stations in small- and medium-sized markets. He soon acquired ABC-affiliated stations in San Jose, California, and Fort Wayne, Indiana; NBC affiliates in Peoria, Illinois, Duluth, Minnesota, and Fresno, California; CBS affiliates in Syracuse, New York, and Kalamazoo, Michigan; and a Fox affiliate in Austin, Texas. The 1978 FCC program giving tax incentives to minorities to encourage their ownership of broadcast stations provided the basis for the Granite acquisitions. Despite its repeal of these programs in 1995, Cornwell is determined to achieve his goal: the acquisition of 14 stations, the maximum allowed for one company by the FCC.

Ironically, it was an attempt by a black-owned company to enter the telecommunications industry that led to the repeal of the FCC program. Actually, the deal involved "big business interests using minorities as fronts to get gargantuan tax breaks." In the early 1990s, Viacom had planned to sell its cable television operations to the black-owned Mitgo Corporation for $2.3 billion. The sale would have given Viacom a tax break of $600 million. Mitgo, however, held only a 21 percent interest in the company actually handling the major financing for the deal, TeleCommunications Incorporated. As the nation's largest owner of cable television systems, it was reported that TCI's involvement "was all the ammunition needed to repeal the tax break incentive."[109] Overall, in the period from 1978 to 1995, minority ownership in the telecommunications industry increased from 1 percent to only 3 percent.

In 1979, Robert L. Johnson founded Black Entertainment Television (BET), the first black-owned cable television network, which, by the mid-1990s, provided 24-hour programming throughout the United States, Puerto Rico, and the Virgin Islands. In broadening its audience appeal, BET introduced a home shopping program.[110] Moreover, BET has moved on to the Internet with a joint venture with Microsoft and is venturing into movie production. For black Americans, who only thirty years earlier saw the purchase of the first black-owned radio station, each advance of BET is important.

In addition to network and cable-TV ownership, blacks have also participated in television syndication ownership, that is, selling programs to networks and stations. Bill Cosby has purchased rights in his own series, and Oprah Winfrey has purchased, produced and syndicated her TV talk show. Increasingly, blacks in television are establishing their own production companies in joint ventures with broadcast and cable-TV stations. When Berry Gordy sold Motown Records, he established the Gordy Company, including its subsidiary Motown Productions, with Suzanne de Passe as CEO. By 1988, Motown had spent $50 million in for-television film production. In 1989 de Passe produced the award-winning *Lonesome Dove* television miniseries. In 1992 she established her own production company, de Passe Entertainment, which produced one of the highest rated TV miniseries of all time, *The Jacksons: An American Dream.* Her company also produced the TV series *On Our Own* and *Sisters Sisters.*[111] In addition, Yvette Lee Bowser, producer for the Cosby-backed sitcom *A Different World* and ABC's *Hangin' With Mr. Cooper*, founded her own company, SisterLee Productions, which in collaboration with the Fox Network and Warner Brothers TV, produced the popular 1990s TV show *Living Single*.

In the third wave of black corporate America, blacks also moved into management-level positions in the television industry. At Walt Disney Productions, Dennis F. Hightower was president of its European, Middle Eastern, and African operations for consumer products from 1991 until 1995, when he was appointed president of Walt Disney Television and Telecommunications, from which he retired in 1996 at age 55.[112] In 1990 Jonathan Rodgers was named president of the CBS Television Stations Division. in 1994 Vaughn Clark, as senior vice president and treasurer at Viacom, was involved in raising the $10 billion for Viacom's takeover of Paramount and its acquisition of Blockbuster Video.[113]

In many ways, television, the "small screen," provided more opportunities for blacks at all levels in the post–Civil Rights era than did the Hollywood film industry. Black production companies were successful because they provided a way for white corporate America to reach a large black consumer market. In 1979, Alex Haley's *Roots*, a television miniseries, captured the largest global TV audience up to that time, demonstrating that there was significant white audience interest in the black experience. The series, based on Haley's book of the same name, also foreshadowed the emergence in the mid-1990s of made-for-TV movies adapted from black books. By the 1990s black production companies capitalized on this trend. Oprah Winfrey's Harpo Films produced both Gloria Naylor's *The Women of Brewster Place* in 1989 and *There Are No Children Here* in 1993 for television. Her future projects include Toni Morrison's *Beloved* and Dorothy West's *The Wedding*. Also, she has a collaboration planned with Quincy Jones's production company to produce Zora Neal Hurston's *Their Eyes Were Watching God* and has agreements with ABC for six films and with Disney for three more. In 1996 Robert Johnson's BET, in a joint venture with Blockbuster Entertainment, released its first film, which is based on a book by black author Clifton Taulbert, *Once upon a Time When We Were Colored*.[114]

The Movie Industry

After Oscar Michaeux, leading black film producer in the early twentieth century, black movies were made primarily by white production companies. In 1955, black bandleader and composer Noble Sissle, who was also president of the Negro Actors Guild of America, pulled together a syndicate of Wall Street bankers and New York businessmen to "finance a million dollar film company to be known as the Ambassador Film Corporation." It planned to produce four pictures a year using black actors who they said had "been denied opportunity in motion pictures, television, radio and the legitimate theater." The financial success of *Carmen Jones* had prompted interest in a black film company, but Sissle said "it would not be the policy of Ambassador Film Corporation to confine its scope of activity to Negro actors only as that would be discriminatory."[115]

Unfortunately the company never moved beyond its planning stage. Also, by the 1960s, white production companies began to exploit the market for black films by producing "blaxploitation" films such as *Shaft* and *Superfly*. The 1960s, however, had also opened Hollywood to black America, beginning with black producers of feature films. Gordon Parks produced *The Learning Tree* in 1969. In 1970 *Cotton Comes to Harlem* was produced by Ossie Davis, and *Watermelon Man* was produced by Melvin Van Peebles. In 1971 Van

Peebles wrote, produced, directed, and distributed *Sweet Sweetback's Baadaass Song,* which grossed $15 million, a first for black films. In 1972 Berry Gordy, who had moved to Los Angeles, also began producing pictures, including *Lady Sings the Blues,* based on the life of Billie Holiday and starring Diana Ross. Yet it was not until almost 20 years later that black films began to enjoy great commercial success.[116]

In the 1990s, the leading black filmmaker in the industry has been Spike Lee, who, with his production company Forty Acres and a Mule, has produced movies that have attracted a mainstream market.[117] His first film, *She's Gotta Have It,* was made in 1986 for $175,000; it grossed $8 million. His most successful film, *Malcolm X,* produced by Warner Brothers for $34 million in 1992, grossed $48.1 million. Also in the early 1990s, the Hudlin brothers, Reginald and Warrington, with their production company Hudlin Brothers, produced *Boomerang,* which grossed over $120 million. In 1991, 24-year-old John Singleton, head of New Deal Productions, was given Academy Award nominations for best director and best screenwriter for *Boyz 'n the Hood,* which grossed over $60 million. He also won success with his 1994 *Higher Learning,* which grossed over $30 million in less than six months, as did *House Party II,* produced by George Jackson's production company, Jackson/McHenry Entertainment.[118]

Yet, as one critic said, black filmmakers such as Spike Lee focus on "Black cultural pathology—moral decay and the demise of the Black family . . . not the operation of global politics and economics . . . the underlying problem for inner-city Blacks."[119] Profits, however, are the sole factor in determining what films will be made and who will make them.[120] In 1991, although 19 black films were released that reached an audience of 40 million people, they accounted for only 4 percent of all American ticket sales that year. In 1993, only 11 of the 469 Hollywood films, which grossed a total of $5 billion, were made by black directors. Their films grossed only $29 million. Also, despite the prominent management positions of many blacks in the movie industry, as of 1994 not one had the power to approve production budgets. Presently, black filmmakers are dependent on white capital for production as well as distribution. Moreover, of the more than 23,000 theaters in the United States as of 1994, only 7 were owned by African-Americans.[121]

Is the question, then, how can the black consumer and black film companies find a way to demonstrate that there is a market for black films beyond those that portray violence?[122] Black film directors have found some success with films such as Mario Van Peebles's *New Jack City,* which depicted the violence in the business organization and urban distribution structures of the black drug trade. Robert Townsend, who made *The Five Heartbeats,* which was an excellent film on a black singing group in the 1950s to the 1970s, but which had low box-office receipts, explained that "Hollywood does not consider most black films marketable unless they include violence." When black female filmmaker Julie Dash took her film *Daughters of the Dust* to the Sundance Film Festival to be marketed, "she was told by a Japanese distributor, 'That's not real black people.' "[123]

The Hollywood film productions of Alice Walker's *The Color Purple* in 1985, and Terry's McMillan's *Waiting to Exhale* and Walter Mosley's *Devil in a Blue Dress,* both released in 1995, demonstrated that there is a market for black movies beyond those depicting urban street-gang violence and the drug trade. Also, black entertainment superstars, such as Whitney Houston, are establishing their own production companies and producing movies by black authors. With his Mundy Lane Entertainment production company, Denzel Washington hopes to produce more films of Walter Mosley's novels in a joint venture with Columbia TriStar Pictures, in addition to buying screen rights for Lawrence Otis Graham's *Member of the Club,* an autobiographical account of a young Harvard-trained lawyer making more than $100,000 a year who left his prestigious position for a year to explore racism while working as a busboy at a white Connecticut country club.[124]

Still, while African-Americans demand black films, they are also as eager as whites to see films such as *Star Wars, Indiana Jones,* and *ET.* At the same time, will the proliferation of books by black authors on diverse topics provide the material for the big screen that has appeal to all Americans? From 1995 to 1996, "at least 15 Black titles have begun their journey to television and theater screens."[125] Perhaps they represent the wave of the future for blacks in film in the twenty-first century and will have as much influence as as did *A Time to Kill* and *The Body Guard.* They featured Hollywood superstars, both black and white, were produced for mainstream audiences, and were box-office successes. A more recent example, which broke box-office records, is the 1996 science fiction action film *Independence Day,* starring former rap singer and TV star Will Smith as a fighter pilot who saves the earth from being destroyed by extraterrestrial invaders.[126]

Hip-Hop Enterprises

Each generation of young blacks in the twentieth century has developed a musical style that became part of mainstream America. Yet only since the 1970s have black artists begun to receive multimillion-dollar royalties from their music. Black music from ragtime to jazz has energized and liberated white America from the constraints of the past, resulting in changes in women's attire that gave them freedom of movement so that they could dance the lindy, which was developed by black Americans and popularized by whites in the 1930s. Then, the zoot suit and beboppers of the 1940s were followed by rhythm and blues and soul in the 1960s, which again marked a crossover of black music into white markets, as did disco in the 1970s. But this latest crossover was different from the one in the 1920s, when whites such as Paul Whiteman took jazz into mainstream American music.

In the third wave of black corporate America, black music revolutionized white music, which had not changed a great deal over the course of several centuries. White artists capitalized on black music by reshaping rock and roll to fit the tastes of their audience, a development that expanded the music industry tremendously. White artists such as Elvis Presley, "the King," and the Beatles enjoyed astonishing audience acclaim and wealth by imitating and capitalizing on several black musical forms. They did, however, give credit to the roots of their music. And a catalogue of many of their songs was purchased for $150 million by Michael Jackson.[127]

Also, while blacks created the blues, it was only in the 1970s and 1980s that whites finally acknowledged and imitated this musical form, ironically, claiming to save it from extinction, since traditional blues was no longer in the mainstream of black music. Yet, as long as racism exists in America, black people will be playing and singing the blues; although, its form continues to change over time. During the Civil Rights era, black music expressed the black-pride sentiments of the time, reflected by James Brown and his "Say It Loud, I'm Black and I'm Proud," Curtis Mayfield, and the Impressions' "Keep on Pushing" and "We're a Winner." Mayfield also did the soundtrack for the movie *Super Fly,* which included hit singles "Freddie's Dead" and "Pusherman." In 1971 Marvin Gay's album *What's Going On* reflected the increasing pessimism of black America with urban life, the Vietnam War, and environmental issues. The black womanist movement in song was expressed in Aretha Franklin's "Respect," and Gloria Gaynor's "I Will Survive" also echoed the same sentiments for white feminists.

In the late twentieth century, hip-hop carried the blues to another level. As black Pulitzer Prize- and Tony Award-winning playwright August Wilson said, hip-hop "is the spiritual fist of African American culture."[128] The music expressed by the hip-hop generation, rap and gangsta rap, reflects the harsh experiences of post-industrial, post–Civil Rights black urban youth. And, it was the hip-hoppers, emerging in the mid-1980s as purveyors of this sound, who became the first black generation to capitalize on its cultural expressions for economic reward beyond the entertainment industry.

The hip-hop generation created its own unique form of wearing apparel, which led to the development of a multimillion-dollar black clothing industry. In the 1990s, young Americans, black and white, put on their baggy and drooping jeans, long T-shirts, combat or work boots, black knit hats or hooded jackets, and dark glasses. While the look was menacing, reinforced by rap's threatening lyrics, mainstream America usurped, modified, and promoted hip-hop attire as the grunge look, which became the casual dress for young white America. The "b-boy look" (hip-hop attire) was represented by the emergence of the first black male superstar model, Tyson Beckford, who was under contract to Ralph Lauren.[129]

The first successful hip-hop enterprises during this time were established in the clothing and shoe industries. In 1990 designer Carl Jones, in his mid-20s, established his Threads 4 Life (also known as Cross Colours) clothing company. Within two years, the company ranked 89th on the Black Enterprise top 100 list, with sales of $15 million. Jones started his career when he and two white partners founded Surf Fetish in 1985. When he left the company four years later, it had sales of $20 million. Jones founded Threads 4 Life to capitalize on the African-oriented urban hip-hop look, which became increasingly popular in the late 1980s. By 1992, the company had five clothing lines, including Cross Colour Classics for older, more conservative buyers. He also expanded by developing Cross Colours Home, a home-furnishing line that emphasized the use of African fabrics and included bedding and table linens, sold in upscale department stores such as Marshall Fields, I. Magnin, and Macys.[130]

The demand was so intense that Threads 4 Life could not fill all of the orders. In 1994 the company shut down its manufacturing operations and began licensing the Cross Colours label to other clothing manufacturers. In the Black Enterprise top 100 list for 1992, the company ranked 10th, with sales of $89 million and in 1993 the company ranked 8th, with sales of $97 million and a staff of 200; it was not on the list for 1994.

Cross Colours's principal designer was Karl Kani, whose men fashion's accounted for 65 percent of Cross Colours's $97 million in sales in 1993. In 1994, however, he left to found his own company, Karl Kani Infinity, with capital of $500,000, which came from his investment in Threads 4 Life. He was 25 years old. Kani had sales of $43 million in 1994 and $59 million in 1995 placing him 25th on the Black Enterprise 100. Jeans, the most popular item in his line, account for 45 percent of revenues, mountain boots, 30 percent and children's wear, 15 percent. His clothes are sold nationally and in 14 countries, including Germany, England, France, the Czech Republic, Japan, and Australia. Kani handles all aspects of his design work, which, along with the high quality of his fabrics, accounts for much of his success.

Using the Calvin Klein company as a model, Kani set up three licensing deals for his leather wear, men's apparel, and children's clothes. He said "The key to success for any designer is that they make the right licensing moves. It's a pure profit gain that can make any designer very rich, very quickly." Kani is also expanding his market and considering a women's line. Initially, his advertising used hip-hop artists, but Kani now wants to appeal to more conservative black tastes represented by such popular figures as TV personality Ed Bradley and sports announcer Ahmad Rashad. Kani plans to run ads in *GQ* and *Ebony Man* and compete with designers such as Armani, whose suits retail for $1,200 to $1,500. His couture line of apparel will be manufactured in Italy. In 1995, Kani launched a big-and-tall line as a response to NBA stars. He also began overseas manufacturing operations which the company notes has reduced the cost of production by 20 percent, with Kani apparel being made in Turkey, Macao, the Philippines, and China, with two main offices in Taiwan and Hong Kong.[131]

The extensiveness and diversity of the company's distribution in a global economy is a first in black clothing manufacturing. Still, most hip-hop apparel enterprises are small businesses but with the potential for growth, such as the Detroit-based Stone Merchant founded by Michael J. Stubblefield. His signature line of hip-hop accessories ranges in price from $34 to $160. In 1993 the firm had sales of $780,000, with expected revenues of $1 million in 1994. His signature backpack is manufactured in Seoul, Korea. In 1996 he was licensed to sell his items carrying the Olympics logo internationally. Also, Foot Locker franchises carry his merchandise, which appeals to young people with its use of "the blue and gold, green, white and black, and red and yellow color schemes associated with the hip-hop trend."[132]

Hip-hop also invaded the comic book industry. In 1989 Roland Laird started Postro Incorporated, publishing both a comic book, *MC Squared: A Man with a Serious Game Plan,* and a comic strip, "The Griots." The hero in *MC Squared* is a 20-year-old Harlem barber and computer designer whose urban adventures provide the basis of the stories. With "The Griots," Postro was the "first independent black publisher to combine hip-hop music with comic books." The characters are a black family. The husband and wife are newspaper publishers with two children, whose main interests are hip-hop music and sports. While Laird's enterprises have produced annual revenues of only $35,000, both the *New York Times* and *Washington Post* have featured "The Griots."[133] Postro's African-American mainstream counterpart is Milestone Media, a black-owned comic-book company with seven titles, all in the top 300 of the 1,600 titles sold monthly. In its first year, the company sold 3.5 million copies, with $5 million in sales. Printing and distribution are handled by DC Comics, Inc.[134]

The hip-hop culture has generated money for a lot of people. Its participants, especially in the music industry and collateral fields, are anxious to further capitalize financially on a phenomenon that is being appropriated by mainstream America. Unlike previous young generations in the entertainment world, hip-hop entrepreneurs are systematically and strategically planning to develop the business side of their music productions, as well as continuing to market the hip-hop culture. They have no intention of repeating the mistakes of the past, which involved rip-offs and the exploitation of black artists. Simply put, the new generation of black performers is as intent on being involved in all the business-related aspects of their enterprises as they are in being recording artists. Rap singer Queen Latifah, who has also emerged as a TV star, established Flavor Unit Record, her label/artist management/record company.

Yet changes in the record industry, especially sublabeling, still have left black artists victims of exploitation. Sublabel deals are described by insiders as "a new system of exploitation," especially those that "add on the ego-stroking tiles president and CEO." When independent black record producers sublabel their companies, they end up as executives in white corporations, and their companies become newly created subsidiaries of the buyout companies. Moreover, most of these transplanted executives lack control not only of their budgets but also of the release dates for their records. Mike Ellis, president of Source Entertainment, said, "It's the most brilliant mind game I've seen."[135] As subsidiaries, black sublabel companies neither own the music they produce nor share in the profits of future sales or reissues.

Why do it, then? One of the reasons is that sublabelling provides capitalization for young artists to get in on the production and management side of the industry. If they have a string of hits, their financial arrangement can be renegotiated to their advantage, enabling them to share in the profits in a joint-venture agreement. This happens, however, to only 10 percent of sublabel companies. With their production and marketing infrastructure in place, companies that own black sublabels reap large financial benefits, because they do not have to share the profits with the sublabel company. Moreover, with sublabeling, research and development costs are minimal. The holding companies can continue to put out top hits, since the product comes to them already developed and with a proven market. Also, the holding company does not have to constantly monitor the market in order to spot new trends in music. Increasingly, however, hip-hop artists are finding ways to produce records without sublabeling. Unlike previous generations, they have numerous black role models who have achieved success in the business end of the entertainment industry.

One model is entertainment mogul Quincy Jones, who, through his *Vibe* magazine, sponsors an annual hip-hop business conference with the focus "Success In The Entertainment Business Is a Science." The fourth annual Hip-Hop/New Jack Power Summit in 1996 was promoted as an "urban entertainment business platform that does what no other conference can do. It effectively links the urban film, fashion, new media, print, and television media with the most common of elements: music." The 1996 conference was entitled "Meet Your Teachers." In addition to Jones, the keynote speaker was Andre Harrell, president and CEO of Motown Records, whose topic was "How to Win." All of the seminars emphasized the technology needed to capitalize on hip-hop culture; participants were encouraged to "Make a Power Move."[136]

While Jones has taken a leadership role in promoting entrepreneurial development in the expansion of the spin-off enterprises from the music, literature, and apparel trends generated from the hip-hop culture, hip-hop entrepreneurs have moved quickly to capitalize on advances in technology that can benefit their companies. Def-Jam Records, a subsidiary of Rush Communications founded by Russell Simmons in 1991, uses XING technology, which enables Internet viewers to simultaneously experience audio and video samples. Def-Jam also promotes the latest hip-hop sounds with a newsletter that provides information on artists' tours as well as their biographies. Def-Jam competes with companies such as the Warner Music Group, which also uses a Web site to promote its black music division. Simmons has also has started a line of clothing, Phat Farm, to compete with Karl Kani. In addition, he has established an advertising agency, Rush Media, that focuses on the urban marketplace.[137] In the *Black Enterprise* 100 for 1996, Rush Communications and its affiliated companies ranked 54th, with sales of $37 million.

Hip-hoppers are the last young black generation of the twentieth century, but their music expresses the same frustrations as other types of music express for other races. Black, white, and brown young Americans have expressed their outrage against a society indifferent to their needs and interests, a society that appears to ignore their future. In the post–Civil Rights period, white youth, outraged by social changes in an America that seemingly no longer guarantees them economic opportunity based on skin color, have expressed their outrage in raucous heavy-metal music, an attempt to drown out the new racial realities that will confront them in the twentieth-first century. On the other hand the hip-hop generation black and brown youths have expressed their outrage to the persistence of racism in America in the raucous and irreverent poetry of hip-hop.[138] Still, the hip-hop generation has an advantage in achieving success in the next century. Through its music enterprises and related businesses, it is developing the ability to capitalize on the technological wave of the future. Its major concern is surviving the twentieth century.[139]

Conclusion

African-American business skyrocketed in the second half of the twentieth century, with numerous megaenterprises developed in hair care products and cosmetics, records, radio, television, and film; and paced by an expansion in black financial services, especially the founding of black investment banks. The enterprises established by S. B. Fuller, Arthur Gaston, John Johnson, and Berry Gordy in the second wave of black corporate America set the pace for black entrepreneurs in post–Civil Rights America. Their enterprises were also symbolically significant in building a bridge over troubled waters, linking traditional enterprises that had relied on a black consumer market with the new black entrepreneurship in the post–Civil Rights period. Those enterprises are distinguished by the acquisition and expansion that parallel mainstream American business activity.

Still, at the end of the third wave of black corporate America, only Johnson Publishing Company and its subsidiaries, with their consumer market composed primarily of blacks, stand wholly intact, the last of the African-American conglomerates that had been established in the second wave of black corporations.

11

BLACKS AND WHITE CORPORATE AMERICA, 1965–1995

The financial warfare of the past 25 years has been fought with an arsenal of MBAs, law degrees, business plans and venture capital. African-Americans led an assault on the financial services industry with this weaponry·

—*Black Enterprise*, 1994

My father used to tell me that this is a wonderful country with great opportunity but that you're going to have to work twice as hard to get half as much.

—James Bruce Llewellyn,
Philadelphia Coca-Cola Bottling Company

The corporate acquisition has become a useful vehicle by which corporations can grow and prosper.

—Reginald F. Lewis,
TLC Beatrice International Holdings

I'm a capitalist. I believe in the system.

—Edward T. Lewis,
Essence Communications Incorporated

Success Runs In Our Race.

—George Fraser, 1994

Introduction

African-American intrapreneurs and entrepreneurs and their business activities in and with white corporate America provide the focus of this chapter. In the third-wave rise of black corporate America, these blacks made significant gains in several ways. As intrapreneurs—creative and innovative corporate managers—they advanced to senior management positions in white corporations. As franchise owners and suppliers, black Americans participated as copartners in the expansion of white corporate America. Through advertising, black sports and entertainment superstars helped sell the products of white corporate America to national and international markets. Also, as entrepreneurs in the third-wave rise of black corporate America, blacks developed businesses that paralleled and competed with mainstream white corporations, especially in the postindustrial rise of the high-tech and telecommunications industries. Black corporate America also expanded internationally.

Blacks also established new forms of business ownership during this time. In the post–Civil Rights period, African-American businesspeople, through acquisitions, joint ventures, leveraged buyouts and mergers, positioned themselves for participation in the mainstream American business community. In a global economy paced by high technology and the economics of managerial capitalism, structural changes in finance capitalism and technological innovations were significant forces in the third wave rise of black corporate America. Moreover, since the 1970s a number of major black corporations secured investment capital from the "cash cows/bulls" of black America's deep pockets—leading entertainers and sports stars.

Significantly, the financial success of black entrepreneurs in the third-wave rise of black corporate America can be attributed to open-door policies in the Civil Rights era promoting racial inclusion in white corporate America. Yet, white corporations have also been reluctant to fully implement these policies. As a result, a new civil rights movement has developed to protest against the recent dismantling of affirmative action initiatives. Federal assistance at the end of the twentieth century remains critical to the future of small black businesses and the ongoing development of black corporate America. In the third-wave rise of black corporate America, federal government affirmative action initiatives did create a climate that fostered white corporate America's support of black corporate America.

Black Corporate Expansion

The third growth period of black corporate America, distinguished by intrusions into mainstream America business, began after the Civil Rights movement, when several new forms of business activity shaped black business expansion and ownership. First, many blacks who owned their own businesses acquired enterprises in white corporate America. In the second wave of black corporate America, S. B. Fuller's pioneering business expansion was based on acquisitions in white corporate America. In the third wave that began in the late 1960s, several black businesspeople made their initial forays in the business world by buying out white corporations, as opposed to establishing their own enterprises from the ground up. The third type of black business expansion and ownership took place through joint ventures. In several ways, the business activities of James Bruce Llewellyn (b.1927), the American-born son of Jamaican immigrants, are representative of the third wave rise of black corporate America.

Llewellyn held several government positions. Although he turned down President Carter's offer to appoint him as secretary of the army, he did accept a position in the Overseas Private Investment Corporation. In 1969, however, Llewellyn entered the private-sector business world with his purchase of Fedco Foods, a white grocery chain of 10 stores in the South Bronx, for $3 million. He sold it 15 years later for $20 million after it had grown to 27 stores with sales of $85 million. In the year before the sale, Llewellyn, as part of a joint venture, purchased a 36 percent minority interest in the Philadelphia Coca-Cola Bottling Company. The consortium held the largest block of shares, but it was not until

1988 that it acquired 100 percent ownership. In another joint venture with Queen City Communication, Llewellyn moved into television, with the purchase of the ABC affiliate, WKBW, in Buffalo, New York, in 1985; in 1989, he entered into a joint venture to purchase the New Jersey–based New York Times Cable Company to buy/form Garden State Cable company.

Llewellyn's purchases from 1969 to 1989 have significance in several ways in the third wave of black corporate America. Foremost, they demonstrate the continuing impact of civil rights protests to the lack of economic opportunities available to blacks in the corporate arena beyond the 1960s. Coca-Cola's sale to Llewellyn was a result of the "moral covenant" policy instituted by Jesse Jackson and Operation PUSH to encourage desegregation of white corporate America. Llewellyn's purchase also underscores the extent to which federal affirmative initiatives promoted black business expansion. In his deal to purchase the television station, Llewellyn offered $65 million, compared to a competitor's bid of $90 million. But in selling to a minority businessperson, the ABC affiliate got "a tax certificate worth $30 million," the result of a 1978 Federal Communications Commission policy to increase minority access to ownership in the communications industry.[1]

Furthermore, the Llewellyn purchases and sales illuminate the new access blacks have to venture capital available from white institutions, also a post–Civil Rights period phenomenon. In the Fedco purchase, Prudential Insurance granted Llewellyn a loan of $2.5 million against the $3 million purchase price. Llewellyn acquired the company in 1969 through a leveraged buyout, which became the corporate takeover strategy of choice in the 1980s. A leveraged buyout, succinctly defined, is "a method of taking over a company by issuing securities backed by the target corporation's assets to finance the purchase."[2] In this instance, Llewellyn put up Fedco's assets as security for Prudential's $2.5 million loan.

The leveraged buyout of Beatrice International for $985 million by Reginald Lewis in 1987 is sometimes viewed as the first such acquisition by a black in American business history. Llewellyn's transaction, however, predated Lewis's by 18 years. There have been other leveraged buyouts by blacks since 1987, but only 4 percent of the *Black Enterprise* top 100 companies have been acquired through such means.

In another instance, the 1994 $6.5 million buyout of the Brooklyn-based Advanced Technological Solutions (ADS) through IBM's Employee Stock Ownership Plan by minority employees perhaps seems financially inconsequential. But it has historic significance beyond that of involving one of the nation's largest minority employee-owned firms. The company was established in 1968 by IBM as one of several firms founded by white corporations in response to black-power mandates calling for the economic development of black communities. ADS has been successful ever since. After the employee purchase, the company has established two new plants, one in Brooklyn and the other in Dallas, with plans for international sales.[3]

Llewellyn's business acquisitions also signaled the increasingly important role wealthy black sports figures and entertainers played in financing black corporations in the late twentieth century. Llewellyn's purchase of the Philadelphia Coca-Cola Bottling Company for $75 million was a joint venture with millionaire entertainer Bill Cosby and basketball great Julius "Dr. J." Erving. The consortium purchased a 36 percent interest in 1983 before Coca-Cola allowed them full ownership. In 1988 they put up the 36 percent minority shares to finance the acquisition, which gave the investors 100 percent ownership. In 1990, in the New York Times Cable purchase for $125 million, Llewellyn's joint investors were Camille Cosby (Bill's wife), Julius Erving, and members of Michael Jackson's family. The consortium put up $25 million, 20 percent of the purchase price.

Llewellyn's purchases also reflected the increasing participation of blacks in joint business ventures with whites. The two corporations that each put up 40 percent of the purchase price for the cable company purchase were white owned, including Prudential. Llewellyn's ownership of several diverse enterprises, acquired through acquisitions and joint ventures, underscores the expansive capital resources of a small group of black businessmen in the third wave of black corporate America. In *Black Enterprise*'s top 100 listing for 1995, the Philadelphia Coca-Cola Bottling Company, with Llewellyn as CEO, was the nation's third largest black business, with sales of $315 million and a staff of 1,000. Queen City Broadcasting, with Llewellyn as CEO, was ranked 59th in the 1994 list, with sales of $29 million. The company was not on the list for 1995.

Llewellyn's diverse holdings marked the rise of the black conglomerate in the post–Civil Rights period. This rise was paced by the diverse activities of Johnson Publishing, whose sales increased from $306.6 million in 1994 to $316.2 million in 1995. Conglomerate building also distinguished H. J. Russell's holdings, *Black Enterprise*'s 4th highest ranking black business in 1995. In addition to his construction company, with its various subsidiaries, Russell owns the Concessions International Corporation. It manages food concessions at major airports, including Chicago's O'Hare. Also, he has investment interest in the Omni Group, including a 10 percent interest in the Atlanta Hawks professional basketball team.[4]

Doubtless, the pioneer in black-conglomerate building in the third wave of black corporate America was New York–based Percy Sutton. Beginning in 1972 with his flagship enterprise, Inner City Broadcasting, Sutton moved into cable TV, video production, and record production with his establishment of the Apollo label. Sutton also owns the Apollo Theater and has extensive international business interests. In 1995, Inner City Broadcasting, headed by Sutton's son, Pierre, as CEO, ranked 76th on the *Black Enterprise* top 100, with sales of $26 million. Sutton's wealth is estimated at $150 million.[5]

The diverse holdings of publisher Earl G. Graves also represent the trend in black conglomerate building. He is CEO of Earl G. Graves, Ltd., the holding company for Earl G. Graves Publishing, which publishes *Black Enterprise,* for Earl G. Graves Marketing and Research, and EGG Broadcasting (which owns AM and FM stations in the Dallas–Fort Worth area). On the *Black Enterprise* top 100 for 1995, Graves, Ltd. ranked 67th, with sales of $29.29 million. Graves is also CEO of Pepsi-Cola of Washington, D.C., purchased for $60 million in 1990 in a joint venture with Earvin "Magic" Johnson. Graves holds two-thirds equity in the company, which was ranked 30th on the *Black Enterprise* list for 1995, with sales of $50.5 million.[6] With combined sales of nearly $63 million, all of Graves's holdings would have ranked 23rd on the list.

In the rise of black corporations in America, buyouts and joint ventures represent, respectively, expansion trends and new forms of business ownership for African-Americans. In the entertainment industry, the road to joint ventures was pioneered by black television performers, whose earnings and success positioned them to either buy into or buy out controlling interest in their shows. The leaders in this kind of venture are Bill Cosby and Oprah Winfrey, one of America's wealthiest women. Both are shrewd businesspeople who profited from television by buying rights in the syndication of their shows. Cosby opted to receive joint profits from the *Cosby Show,* rather than a fixed salary, an arrangement that "netted him a reported $333 million in addition to syndication receipts." In 1988 the show went into syndication for "$500 million."[7]

Winfrey purchased ownership of the *Oprah Winfrey Show,* the most successful daytime TV talk show in history, for $10 million in 1986, the year she took the show into national syndication and established Harpo Productions, which produces the show. Two years later, Winfrey negotiated a deal that gave her rights to 60 percent of all syndication revenues, which in 1993 grossed $180 million. By 1996 the show was syndicated globally to 118 countries. Also, Harpo Productions, worth $20 million, produces movies for television. In 1995 *Forbes* placed Winfrey's earnings at $75 million and her personal wealth at an estimated $340 million.[8] In 1996 *Forbes* placed her wealth at $415 million, ranking her 400th among the nation's wealthiest people.

In expanding her media holdings, as of 1993, Winfrey secured a 45 percent interest in W. Don Cornwell's Granite Broadcasting, a network TV affiliate, ranked 9th on the *Black Enterprise* top 100 for 1995, with sales of $119 million.[9] Also, Winfrey has options to buy an additional 500,000 shares in King World Productions, her distributor/syndicator. The *Oprah Winfrey Show* is such a crucial part of her business empire that when Winfrey hinted that she might give up her show in 1993, King World's stock dropped three points. In 1996, when she did a show on England's so-called mad cow disease, the price of beef dropped on the Chicago Mercantile Exchange.

The joint-venture king in the entertainment world is music genius Quincy Jones, who entered the business side of the industry in 1961. From 1992 to 1995 Jones established numerous enterprises in music, television, film, broadcasting, magazine publishing (*Vibe*), and multimedia. The joint ventures in which Jones holds a 25 percent to 50 percent interest are primarily with white corporations, including Time-Warner, its various subsidiaries, and David Saltzman. The exception is Quest Broadcasting, in which Jones is a partner with Don Cornelius, former host of the TV show *Soul Train;* talk-show host and commentator Geraldo Rivera; and football great Willie Davis. They hold a 55 percent interest in Quest, with 45 percent held by the Tribune Company.[10]

As black corporate America moves into mainstream American business, its success in the twenty-first century will depend on in ability to capitalize on new technologies. A significant development in this regard is the 50–50 joint venture between Black Entertainment Television, headed by Robert L. Johnson, and Microsoft in developing a Web site called BET Networks. The 1996 venture is mutually advantageous and represents an expansion of BET into multimedia. As Bill Gates, Microsoft's founder, chairman, and CEO, said, "It's a great combination of BET's strong leadership and experience in this market and Microsoft's leading-edge technology."[11]

Bob Johnson founded BET, the first black-owned cable-television station, in 1980, with a $15,000 personal loan and $500,000 in investment capital from the cable giant Tele-Communications Inc.[12] BET eventually became the only black-owned cable network. While BET began with a two-hour-a-week programming schedule that reached only 3.8 million cable subscribers in 350 national markets, by 1990 it offered 24-hour programming to 27 million cable households in 2,200 cable systems in the United States, Puerto Rico, and the Virgin Islands. In 1990 Johnson ventured into publishing with *YSB*. He also purchased *Emerge,* black America's answer to the *New Yorker* and the *Atlantic*. In the *Black Enterprise* top 100 companies for 1995, Johnson's BET Holdings was ranked 10th, with sales of $115,000 and a staff of 450.

Envirotest Systems Corporation, an auto emissions testing company, one of the largest in the industry, also has historic significance. It exemplifies the entry of blacks into business through the purchase of an existing company, such as Llewellyn's purchase of Fedco Foods, as opposed to the establishment of one from the ground up. It also reflects how black financial backing can fund a high-tech business ventures. Envirotest secured venture capital through black-owned UNC Ventures, which "put together $57 million in financing" for the company to buy Hamilton Test Systems, a division of United Technologies.[13] Envirotest also bought out its largest competitor, the white-owned Systems Control Inc. In the *Black Enterprise* 100 for 1995, Envirotest ranked 12th, with sales of $107 million and a 1994 "$1.5 billion work backlog." In 1995 the company had emission-testing contracts from New York and Pennsylvania. With a staff of 3,828, Envirotest ranked second among black-owned companies in terms of the number of employees; TLC Beatrice International, with its 4,500 employees, was first

Access to venture and development capital from the private sector, encouraged by federal affirmative action initiatives, was the most important factor that contributed to the third wave of black corporate America. Despite expansion, the earnings of black businesses, when compared to those of white businesses, however, changed little from those that existed before the Civil Rights movement. In the late twentieth century, the pertinacity of American racism remained a challenge to African-Americans in the development and expansion of their business enterprises.

Racism in Financing Black Corporate America

Unlike TLC Beatrice International and other white-owned companies that came under the control and ownership of blacks in the third-wave rise of black corporate America, during most of this century, the financing of nearly all black businesses, including those that grew into multimillion-dollar companies, was undertaken with capital of $500 or less. In 1932, during the second wave of black corporate America, S. B. Fuller's manufacturing empire was founded with $25. John H. Johnson established Johnson Publications in 1942 with $500. The first black company to go public, Johnson Products, was started in 1954 with $250. There was one exception. Berry Gordy began Motown Records with a $700 loan from his family.

In a much different financial context, although the same principal holds, when Reginald Lewis bought McCall Patterns for $23 million in 1984, the deal was also something of a shoestring financial venture. Lewis used only $1 million of his own money, more specifically, a $500,000 MESBIC loan and a $500,000 unsecured personal loan from Morgan Bank.[14] With Lewis's later leveraged buyout of Beatrice International for $985 million, he put up only $15 million of his own money but still acquired 51 percent equity in the company.[15] Legislation passed as a result of the Civil Rights movement and federal policies that mitigated racism in finance capitalism made a difference. Still, throughout the twentieth century, black entrepreneurs suffered from a common plight that distinguished them from their white counterparts: the racism they encountered in building their multimillion-dollar business empires.

In the early 1940s, unable to secure a $500 bank loan to start his publishing company, John Johnson had to borrow it from a loan company. His mother's furniture was used as collateral. In the 1950s, George H. Johnson was refused a $250 business loan to start his company. Several months later, when he returned to that same bank for a $250 vacation loan, his application was approved. Also, Alvin Boutte, founder of Independence Bank, started his first business in 1995, which developed into a million-dollar drugstore chain, with a loan from the Sealtest Dairy, an ice-cream company. At that time, he said, "The banks just didn't have any money to lend a small businessman, if he were black. The assumption was that we didn't know what we were doing. " Boutte added that he was able to get a loan from Sealtest since "They would back you in hopes of getting another outlet for their products." Within 10 years and with four drugstores, Boutte was doing an annual business of $3.5 million.[16]

In negotiating business deals, even in the 1980s, it was often necessary for blacks to hide their race. In the 1950s, after Johnson's bid to purchase a white-owned building was refused, he hired a white to front for him. Already a millionaire, Johnson donned overalls and posed as a janitor of the company proposing to buy the building so he could get in to inspect it. In the early 1960s, public disclosure of Fuller's ownership of a white cosmetic manufacturer, purchased surreptitiously in 1947, brought his company down. John Johnson, a contemporary, said that "Fuller was on his way to a major market share when someone started spreading stories about his racial identity."[17] In addition, Johnson's efforts from the 1940s to the 1960s to secure advertising from white corporations required strategizing personal meetings with company heads to persuade them that black Americans indeed had money to buy their products. Johnson, a member of the *Forbes* 400, summarized the attitudes of such white businesspeople when he said that even in the 1990s, "The closer I get to the top the more I realize that I'm never going to be fully accepted on merit and money alone. And that a different generation of Blacks—and a different generation of Whites—will know the final victory."[18]

Reginald Lewis, however, represents a different generation of black entrepreneurs. In the post–Civil Rights period, their entry into America's mainstream business has come with the end of legal discrimination, a development that opened the doors of Wall Street's negotiating tables to them. Yet racism accounted for the failure of Lewis's first attempted leveraged buyout. Consequently, when he purchased McCall Patterns, Lewis handled the negotiations—inconceivable before the era of civil rights—but as Johnson did thirty years earlier, he did not present himself as the buyer. Rather, Lewis claimed he represented a consortium of investors. As a subsequent review of the negotiations emphasizes, "it is worth noting that he'd gotten a major deal done only after diverting attention away from himself—and his race."[19]

Even though Lewis was the CEO of TLC Beatrice International, a billion-dollar company, his attempts to expand were rebuffed in various ways. Either he was totally ignored or treated as a joke. When he first submitted the $1.3 billion bid to buy the domestic operations of Beatrice, it was "never even acknowledged, by person, letter or phone." In another instance, Lewis's bid to buy a $90 million company was summarily dismissed, and he was treated literally as though he had just walked off the streets with his hat in hand to buy the company. But, as he said, "Here in this country there is a certain conspiratorial desire—regardless of what you do, how much you earn, you're still black. And that's meant to demean. But it only demeans if you allow it."[20]

Racist stereotypes also persisted in the refusal of whites to acknowledge the financial acumen of black entrepreneurs. Just as John H. Johnson had to fight charges that whites were behind the ownership and success of *Ebony*, Lewis, initially, had to refute charges that whites were behind his acquisitions. Yet when Lewis attempted to take Beatrice public in 1989, he was pilloried in the press for being "too greedy" and denounced as "the king of avarice." Labeled a "leveraged buyout artist," Lewis was denigrated and, at the same time, envied, as were white leveraged-buyout maestros. In the 1980s climate of corporate takeovers and leveraged buyouts, Lewis's financial activities were significant in Wall Street, but they were also "a pittance compared with that of Michael Milken, Henry Kravis, and buy-out specialist Ray Chambers, among many others."[21]

Yet it was Michael Milken's support of Lewis that got him to the Drexel Burnham Lambert table to initiate his financial negotiations to acquire Beatrice. But it was only after Lewis, in his leveraged buyout, had sold three Beatrice companies for $430 million, which provided him assets to secure a $450 million line of credit, that Drexel came in to take 34 percent of the deal, secured by Lewis's access to Beatrice's assets.[22] Lewis's financial activities and wealth before he acquired Beatrice were impressive for anyone. Moreover, he acquired ownership of a billion-dollar company with other people's money—Wall Street capital. Lewis, however, was unsuccessful in his 1989 attempt to take TLC Beatrice public on the New York Stock Exchange, with an initial public offering (IPO) of $180 million. Lewis viewed his failure as the "IPO Glass Ceiling."[23]

There were two black companies, however, that preceded Lewis's attempt to go public. And they were successful. Shares of black-owned corporations are also sold on the American Stock Exchange (AMEX) and over the counter (OTC) by the National Association of Securities Dealers Automated Quotations (NASDAQ). In 1970, the Baltimore-based Parks Sausage put its shares on the market with an IPO of $1.5 million on the NASDAQ; while Chicago-based Johnson Products became the first black company to be listed on the American Stock Exchange with a $6.5 million IPO. The company was also listed on the NASDAQ. In 1991 BET became the third black-owned company to be traded publicly, with an IPO of $72.3 million, the first black company listed on the New York Stock Exchange.[24] In 1992 Granite Broadcasting also went public, with a $24 million IPO on the NASDAQ. Phoenix-based Envirotest Systems, founded in 1990, also went public, with a listing on the NASDAQ; by 1994 its stock had increased from $16 to $27 a share. By 1995 there were 11 publicly traded black firms with listings on all the major stock exchanges.

Along with spectacular advances in black business activities and profits, the overall American economy also grew. In 1973 the top 100 black businesses, which included car dealerships, had only $473 million in sales. In 1995 sales reached a combined $13 billion for both the top 100 black businesses and top 100 black dealerships. Indeed, in the third-wave rise of black corporate America, Reginald Lewis had contemplated a leveraged buy-out of Chrysler, but would he have been allowed to by white America? Chrysler, however, was bailed out by the federal government.[25] Despite black economic growth, it is important to note that, at the end of the twentieth century, African-Americans had not approached parity in business receipts with white corporate America. In 1995 the *Black Enterprise* top 100 companies had sales of $13 billion. This includes $7.4 billion by the following: health and beauty aids companies, $239 million; construction, $407 million; manufacturing, $789 million; technology, $877 million; media, $1,073 billion; food and beverage, $3,168 billion; and other enterprises, $846 million. (The $7.4 billion includes $2.1 billion in sales by *Black Enterprise*'s highest ranking business, TLC Beatrice International.) The other $5.7 billion in sales was achieved by black car dealerships—in an industry that has $600 billion in sales.

Yet when these figures are compared to those for businesses owned by white women, affirmative action policies seem to have benefited white women more than they did blacks. Compare the $7.4 billion in total sales of the largest black-owned companies in 1995, which employed 51,057 people, to that of similar businesses owned by American women. In 1994, the top 50 American women business owners, presumably all white except for Oprah Winfrey, had "over $17 billion in revenues and more than 101,000 employees."[26] Moreover, women-owned business employed 35 percent more people in America than the

1994 *Fortune* 500 companies did worldwide. Overall, in the United States, as of 1994, there were 7.7 million businesses owned by women, with nearly $1.4 trillion in sales. Also, women business owners have more than quintupled their revenues since 1984. In Illinois alone, women owned 250,000 businesses in 1995, while in the entire Midwest, there were only 70,239 black businesses. In 1995, there was a total of 424,200 black businesses nationwide, 56 percent of which had receipts of less than $10,000; while the mean sales and receipts for these businesses for 1992 were $52,000.[27]

Also, compare the $7.4 billion in sales made by the *Black Enterprise* top 100 black-owned companies in 1995 to the $1.9 billion made by the 25 highest paid CEOs of white corporations from 1991 to 1995 in salaries, bonuses, perks, and stock gains. Comparing the figures of two distinct economic entities for a one-year period with those of a five-year period may upset some accounting sensibilities. Nevertheless, the figures illuminate the financially dismal standing of black corporations. In 1995 the $66 million in total compensation earned by Lawrence M. Coss, CEO of Green Tree Financial, was equivalent to the $66.6 million in sales achieved by the Stop Shop and Save company, *Black Enterprise*'s 22nd ranked company in 1995, with a staff of 525.[28] Or, since African-Americans compete in a global economy, compare the $7.4 billion in sales to the wealth of just one of the world's 10 richest people. American Kenneth R. Thompson, of the Thompson Corporation, ranked 9th, with $7.4 billion in personal assets.[29] Incidentally, among the world's 447 people worth $1 billion or more in 1996, not one is of acknowledged sub-Saharan African descent. Yet the expansion of the global economy has brought internationals into business competition with blacks, as in the recording industry. Motown Records, for example, is now owned by an international corporation.

As black businesses grew increasingly profitable in the third wave of black corporate America, there was an escalation of activity by whites in buying out successful black businesses. Parks Sausage, Johnson Products, and Indecorp, Inc., parent company of Chicago's Independence Bank and Drexel National Bank, which was once the highest-ranking black bank, were black businesses purchased by whites. Blacks eventually regained control of Parks, which is now again privately owned and listed in the *Black Enterprise* top 100.[30] In 1995, however, Dan Barden, who founded Detroit-based Barden Cablevision, sold his enterprise to whites for $100 million. Is the role of black business in the twenty-first century, then, to become the incubators for white corporate America?

Although the black acquisitions of white corporations distinguished the third-wave rise of black corporate America, black-business participation rates and receipts, compared to those of white businesses, changed proportionately little from those that existed before the Civil War. Indeed systemic racism, a major force that had historically limited black entrepreneurial success and business expansion, persisted into the 1990s. Yet, despite continuing racism and comparatively limited black business profits and participation rates, paradoxically, blacks were again participating in the mainstream American business community not only as entrepreneurs but also as intrapreneurs, a situation similar to what occurred in the period before the Civil War.

Blacks in White Corporate America

The participation of blacks in management positions in white corporations is viewed primarily as a post–Civil Rights period phenomenon. Yet before the Civil War, blacks, many in upper-level positions, served as managers in all areas of the urban, industrial, and agricultural business community in the South. Black intraprenuerial or managerial participation in the white business world, however, virtually disappeared in the century between the Civil War and the Civil Rights movement.

The 1957 appointment of the ex-baseball star Jackie Robinson as a vice president in the Chock Full O' Nuts Corporation is considered as marking the entry of blacks into white corporate America.[31] There were, however, isolated instances from the 1930s to the 1950s when a few blacks were hired in management positions by white companies. In 1934 James "Billboard" Jackson was hired by Esso Standard Oil Company as a special representative. After World War II, he joined the public relations staff of Standard in New York City. By the 1950s, with a slowly increasing number of blacks working in white companies, people considered Jackson "the first of the current crop of Negro salesmen, public relations and sales promotion men."[32]

Yet, California-born Lucius Jenkins, a 1935 University of Hawaii graduate with a degree in civil engineering, was hired at Del Monte in Hawaii in the mid-1930s. While his title was assistant foreman, Jenkins redesigned and installed equipment for Del Monte's juice plant. After World War II, Jenkins was promoted to plant foreman of another division where he managed 200 workers, mainly Asians. One assistant foreman was white, the other Japanese. Explaining the racial composition of the plant, the *Atlanta Daily World* reported: "Naturally, the ordinary employees are not white for the caste system of Mainland 'white supremacy' maintained here opposes the hiring of a haloe [white] in a menial capacity."[33]

In the late 1930s, the board of directors of Pepsi-Cola, the first soft-drink company to employ a black at the management level, elected J. Willard Pikes vice president of its standardization department only eight months after hiring him. Pikes had 20 years of experience in the beverage and bottling industry and was hired by Pepsi to organize the standardization department and train a corps of field representatives to supervise the standardization of practices among Pepsi-Cola's more than 450 franchise bottlers in the United States.[34] Beginning around World War II, white-owned beer, whiskey, and soft-drink companies began hiring blacks as salespeople and also used blacks in their advertisements to promote their products.[35] Also during the war, some national-chain food stores promoted black women cashiers to managers. Those companies explained their decision was a national defense measure in helping "solve the manpower shortage by promoting Negro women."[36]

Still, few blacks were hired in white corporate America after World War II. And those that did get jobs were highly overqualified for their positions. In 1949 the hiring of two blacks, one male, one female, by the Bank of America in Los Angeles was major news. The woman, a Wilberforce University graduate working on a master's degree at UCLA, was hired as a clerk-typist in training for a safe deposit clerk position. The man, a Los Angeles City College student, was a bookkeeper-in-training for a position as bank teller. Bank of America, uneasy about the publicity of its hiring blacks, said, "We do not want this hiring to be treated as a very unusual matter." In response, blacks said their campaign to get Los Angeles white banks to hire them began in 1925, when the Bank of Italy refused to hire blacks for positions as janitors. The bank's response was that the men were overqualified and claimed "if they had asked for white collar positions it would have thought more of them."[37] But would the bank have hired them?

In 1958 white-owned Drexel National Bank on Chicago's South Side appointed two blacks to its board of directors. Arthur B. Knight, vice president of both the Unity Mutual

Life Insurance Company and Unity Funeral Parlor, and Roi Ottley, noted black author and a *Chicago Tribune* journalist, were "the first Negroes to be elected to the board of a national financial institution." With no black-owned banks in Chicago, Drexel, servicing primarily black depositors, perhaps was taking a page from history and considering how the growth of black banks in the past was spurred by the deposits of black insurance companies. Drexel's president, however, emphasized that the appointment of these two black men by no means signaled a "change in the bank's conservative management policies."[38]

A concerted push for blacks in management positions in white corporate America began in the Civil Rights period, as white companies moved, reluctantly, to comply with affirmative action requirements by designating themselves as an "equal opportunity employer." Many of the large corporations did establish special recruitment and training programs to attract blacks. Also blacks were hired in management positions, oftentimes to enhance the politically correct public image of the corporation. Opening the doors to blacks by white corporate America, however, was significant in two ways. On the positive side, it gave blacks the opportunity to become intrapreneurs rather than entrepreneurs.

On the negative side, their entry as intrapreneurs into white corporate America contributed to the drain of blacks who would otherwise have served as entrepreneurs in the third wave of black corporate America. In the post–Civil Rights period, their departure, then, contributed in part to the decline of black business districts. The vacuum was filled, in part, by the nation's new immigrants. Yet the Civil Rights movement had ushered in an era of rising expectations among young and ambitious blacks. Could one really expect them, anymore than young and ambitious whites, both of whom were shaped by the American ideal of managerial and finance capitalism, to enter the American business world by establishing mom-and-pop enterprises? Indeed by 1983, 25 percent of all American college undergraduates, including blacks, were majoring in business.[39]

With the entry of blacks into white corporate America in the 1970s and 1980s, the pages of *Black Enterprise, Ebony, Jet,* and *Essence,* and the black press in general, were filled with articles on blacks employed in managerial positions. Prior to those publications, black newspapers were virtually the only sources of information on black business activities. But by the 1980s, *Forbes, Fortune, Business News,* the *New York Times,* and the *Wall Street Journal* were providing coverage on the third wave rise of black corporate America.

Initially, black hires in white corporate America were for staff positions, such as vice presidents of human resources, community relations, and public affairs, as opposed to line positions with major sign-off powers. By the 1980s, a few even advanced to top management positions. Yet well into the 1990s, the media continued to report news on the "first" or the "only" black who had achieved a significant executive position in white corporate America. At Ben & Jerry's, the socially conscious ice-cream company, Robert Holland was appointed president and CEO in 1995.[40] While Holland instituted changes that improved the company's economic performance, a year later he was out. The Nine West shoe manufactory, which by 1996 dominated the $14 billion retail shoe market, including a third of the department store market, is headed by Noel Hord. With more than 20 years in the industry, Hord was appointed president and CEO in 1995.[41]

It was not until 1987 that an African-American became the first and only head of a *Fortune* 500 company, when Clifton R. Wharton Jr. was appointed CEO of the $70 billion TIAA-CREF (Teachers Insurance and Annuity Association-College Retirement Equities Fund). Under his leadership TIAA-CREF, the world's largest retirement fund, grew to $130-plus billion in assets.[42] Wharton resigned in 1992 to accept an appointment by President Clinton as deputy secretary of state. Before he left, Wharton handpicked Thomas W.

Jones, whom he had recruited earlier, to head the group as president and CEO. Jones had left his position as senior vice president and treasurer at John Hancock Mutual Life Insurance in Boston, where he was on the fast track to become president and CEO. As Jones advanced in his career, he indicated that it had been necessary for him to reestablish his expertise and competency over and over again with not only each new client but also his peers. Racism, however, worked to his advantage, as when, Jones said, his colleagues "weren't looking to do me in.... they completely discounted me."[43]

By the 1990s, the media turned their attention to the highest ranking blacks in white corporate America. Among the first was Kenneth I. Chenault. In 14 years, he rose through the senior managerial ranks at American Express. In 1993 he was appointed president of American Express's Travel Related Services, U.S. Division, and in 1995, vice chairman of American Express.[44] In 1995 Richard D. Parsons, at age 46, became the highest ranking African-American at a *Fortune* 500 company, with his appointment as president of Time-Warner Inc., the nation's largest media conglomerate; he is second in command to Chairman Gerald Levin. Before he left for Time-Warner, Parsons was slated to become chairman and CEO of Dime Bancorp, which became the nation's fourth largest S and L, with $20 billion in assets, through a merger he negotiated.[45]

The 1996 appointment of Roy Roberts as general manager of the newly merged Pontiac-GMC Division, General Motors' second largest unit, placed him as the highest ranked black in the automobile industry. Indeed, he was one of only a few blacks in top management positions in the industry. Roberts had advanced from general manager of GMC, where he was "credited with GMC's record-breaking sales in '93, '94 and '95." Roberts entered white corporate America as a GM management trainee in 1977. After high school, however, he worked on the assembly line in an aerospace parts factory. Despite his success, Roberts, in his mid-50s, today represents a generation of blacks who, before 1964, were without black role models in white corporate America. When Roberts was growing up, unless a black man planned to become a teacher, social worker, lawyer or doctor, education beyond high school seemed unnecessary.

After high school, Roberts also entered a junior college. By the late 1960s, America's involvement in Vietnam motivated many of America's young men, black and white, to continue their education, even those who were not really interested in college. After Roberts was told by the dean when he was getting close to flunking out that, "We have a particular grading system here: A, B, C, and Vietnam," Roberts went on to graduate with honors and then earned a bachelor's degree in business at Western Michigan University.[46] As is often the case with college graduates in business, Roberts was hired in a management position in a industry in which he had no hands-on experience. This was in 1977. In 1985, when he was appointed plant manager of a General Motors assembly facility, another black said, "You're a good guy, but you don't know crap about building a car, do you?" Roberts agreed, so after the plant closed down at night, a few black assembly workers took him through the paces and showed him how to build a car. Roberts's subsequent promotions resulted from his reputation in GM as "car smart and dealer friendly." His present responsibilities include developing marketing strategy, pricing, and repositioning of dealerships.

At the senior management level, blacks in white corporate America often have more employees working under them than the workers employed by most of the *Black Enterprise* top 100. Only 12 black firms in 1995 had more than 1,000 employees. Roberts's management decisions affect not only GMC's 3,736 franchise dealers but also its 78,000 white-collar employees. At the Xerox Corporation, Richard Barton, appointed president of U.S.

customer operation in 1994, heads a 29,000-person workforce, including sales and service personnel, administrators, and suppliers. A 20-year veteran of Xerox, Barton advanced to his new position after 5 years as CEO of Xerox Canada Ltd., with a workforce of 5,000 people; he was the first black American CEO of a major Canadian firm.[47]

As the global economy becomes increasingly important, white corporate America has advanced the role of black managers in their international divisions. With the end of apartheid, South Africa has been the newest target for the placement of African-Americans. By 1996 almost 200 white American companies had established branches in South Africa, some with African-Americans in senior management positions. Carl Ware, a senior vice president at Coca-Cola, is also president of Coca-Cola/Africa, based in Johannesburg. J. Eric Wright, who earned an MBA in finance and management from the Wharton School in 1992, is the manager of international capital markets for Citibank in Johannesburg. In 1995 Frank Coleman was appointed president and managing director of AT&T South Africa. His wife, Roberta, heads AT&T's international public affairs and public relations division for sub-Saharan Africa.[48]

Blacks in white corporate America's international business divisions were put into positions in many regions besides Africa. Belinda Miller, also a graduate of Wharton, works for Swissotel as a marketing advisor. Her assignments have taken her to Turkey, Amsterdam, Zurich, Dusseldorf, and Seoul. Since 1994 she has been director of human resources at Swissotel Beijing, presently training 1,000 Chinese employees. Taran Swan, who holds an MBA from Harvard, was vice president of channel development and international director for Nickelodeon International and was responsible for opening the company's market in Germany from 1993 to 1996; she has since moved on to develop the company's Latin American market.[49]

African-American women employed in the nation's 38,000 EEOC companies outnumber black men 2.77 million to 2.44 million. Yet, despite a 64 percent increase in the number of black women from 1982 to 1992, compared to a 22 percent increase of black men, black men outnumber black women, 146,000 to 113,000, in management positions. Also, the salaries of black women, who constitute 3 percent of all women in corporate management and 5 percent of officers and managers in EEOC companies, are 14 percent less than those for black men.[50] While limited in numbers, black female senior executives can be found in most industries. In 1996 the highest ranking black woman in white corporate America, Ann M. Fudge, was appointed CEO and president of Maxwell House Coffee, the $1.5-billion division of General Foods USA. She heads Maxwell House's three coffee-processing plants employing 2,400 people. Prior to her promotion, Fudge, a Harvard MBA, was executive vice president of General Foods USA, a division of the Philip Morris Companies.[51]

Still, the present corporate culture seems particularly unfavorable for blacks such as GMC's Roberts or John Jacobs to attain the position of CEO, both of whom will be retiring at the turn of the century. Jacobs cracked the "good old-boy network" in white corporate America. In 1994 Jacobs, a former National Urban League president who sat on the board of directors of Anheuser-Busch, accepted the position of executive vice president, one of only two such positions at the $13 billion company. He also remains on the board of directors.[52]

Yet, if the limited number of *Fortune* 500 black senior executives in 1995 represents advancement, what does the future hold for blacks in white corporate America? The federal government is dismantling affirmative action initiatives, its response to the increasing racial hostility of embittered white managers who resent blacks taking their jobs. Yet,

African-Americans have very little input into hiring practices in white corporate America. Where the jobs are and whom they will go to are management decisions made by white senior executives responding to the mandates of their stockholders, most of whom are white and who seek ever-increasing profits on their investments.

With the dismantling of federal affirmative initiatives and the downsizing and restructuring of white corporate America, there will be even fewer blacks in senior management positions, the ultimate model of zero-sum corporate staffing.[53] Moreover, as the numbers show, African-American advancement to senior-level management positions in white corporate America has been comparatively minimal. In the closing decade of the twentieth century, only a few blacks were senior executives positioned for advancement to become CEOs; they include Fudge, Jones, Chenault, Parsons, and Xerox Executive Vice President A. Barry Rand, formerly president of Xerox's U.S. Marketing Group.[54]

Ironically, in 1970, out of 3,000 senior-level *Fortune* 500 executives, only three were black: Clifton Wharton, then at Equitable Life; Thomas Wood at Chase Manhattan; and Robert Weaver at Metropolitan Life. The question for white corporate America at the end of the twentieth century, then, finds a parallel in American politics. Is white corporate America any more ready for a black to head a *Fortune* 500 company than it is for a black to be elected president of the United States?

Racism in White Corporate America

In 1991 the Federal Glass Ceiling Commission, a 20-member group of bipartisan legislators and business leaders was established by President George Bush. The commission was a response to the failure of white corporate America to promote minorities and women to senior management positions.[55] The commission's findings illuminated not only the existence of but also the racial inequities inherent in the glass-ceiling phenomenon. Moreover, the Glass Ceiling Commission documented that blacks were not taking jobs from whites. By 1990, despite affirmative action mandates, from 95 percent to 97 percent of senior managers in the *Fortune* 500 companies and the top 1,000 U.S. industrial firms were white males, whereas of all managers "only 0.6 percent were black, 0.4 percent Latino and 0.3 percent were Asians."[56] The others were white women. As a black banker said in 1995, "Today when I go to corporate America, the treasurers and CFOs that were there in the '70s are retired. Now it's a younger white female."[57]

Even with demographic changes projected for the twenty-first century "browning of America," white corporations reluctantly acknowledge that a multiculturally diverse workforce must be the wave of the future. Moreover, if white America views itself as threatened by black inroads, dismantling affirmative action is not the answer. The ultimate reality for white corporate America is that, with the browning of America, blacks will not be part of the new majorities any more than they are part of the present majority. Rather, with the globalization of the world's economy and because of their national and ethnic origins, the nation's new immigrants, paradoxically, are positioned much better, now and for the future, than are African-Americans to challenge the dominance of white males not only in white corporate America but also in the expanding global economy. In the twenty-first century, according to Joel Kotkin in his comparative assessments of the business activities of the British, Jews, Japanese, Chinese, and Indians, "global tribalism" in the dispersal of ethnic groups will "be the defining factor in the evolution of the global economy."[58]

345

Throughout the 1980s and into the 1990s, moreover, there appeared to be a continual turnover of black talent in white corporate America. Many black managers left after failing to crash the glass ceiling, refusing to continue to expend sweat equity and technical expertise in a no-win situation. Consequently, during the late-twentieth-century era of downsizing, of those blacks who remain, few find themselves in top management positions at the national level. Those who did advance to top positions did so despite racism, and not only because of their exceptional abilities as intrapreneurs but also because they possessed the will and desire to succeed in white corporate America.

By the late twentieth century, several factors were operating, then, that will have an impact on blacks in white corporate America in the next century. For one, only a few blacks survived the racially hostile corporate culture to advance to senior management positions; there were others who chose to leave or who were passed over by failing to negotiate the politics of corporate intrigue.[59] Also, the pool of black candidates for high management positions in white corporate America in the 1990s existed because of federal initiatives that promoted not only equal employment opportunity but also affirmative action support for minorities in higher education.

Many blacks who achieved senior management positions in white corporations were graduates of Ivy League institutions. Based on assessments of the number of blacks at Harvard, it seems that African-Americans are decreasing in numbers in those institutions, which does not bode well for maintaining the flow of black talent into white corporations. The Harvard-Radcliffe graduating class of 1973 had 121 blacks. The 1997 Harvard class had 147 blacks. While this slight increase is in itself reprehensible, for African-Americans, it represents a disastrous decline. Among those of African descent in the 1997 class, "more than half either were not born in the United States or their parents were not." Yet, at the same time, what is significant for the expansion of black corporate America in the twenty-first century is that many of the top African-American scholars are now opting to go to black colleges and universities. Florida A & M University had more black National Merit Scholar winners than Harvard. Under the leadership of Sybil Mobley, dean of the School of Business and Industry since 1974, it has become one of the nation's leading business schools.[60]

With the federal government's assault on affirmative action in higher education, the role of historically black colleges and universities in business education becomes increasingly important. Howard University, Morehouse College, and Hampton University, which also have high-ranked business programs, can produce the next generation of black business leaders for both white and black corporate America. At the end of the twentieth century, then, the significant issue for the future of blacks in white corporate America is: will the federal government's retrenchment in affirmative action carry over to the twenty-first century? Will there be a significant place for blacks in white corporate America by 2019, which will mark four centuries of the economic subordination of black people in this country? I think so! Black Americans survived slavery and a few even rose to the top. Black America will survive white corporate America and more than a few will continue to rise to the top.

Doubtless, black Americans will remain in white corporate America on a quid pro quo basis in which they receive the benefits that accrue from management positions in exchange for white corporate America's access to the enormous consumer power of Black Americans. Also, in the post–Civil Rights period, blacks demonstrated that they know how to make money for white corporate America, which will find itself increasingly forced to share its economic power with people of color. In the final analysis, however, white corporate America will not willingly yield a share of its economic power any more than the Europeans did in the decolonization of Africa.[61] As Frederick Douglass said, "Power concedes nothing without a demand. It never did and it never will.... Men may not get all they pay for in the world, but they certainly must pay for all they get."[62]

Black participation in white corporate America will continue into the twenty-first century. Capitalism proceeds from profits and African-Americans in white corporate America in the late-twentieth-century third-wave rise of black corporate America have demonstrated their profit-making capabilities. Enhancement, augmentation, and expansion, rather than retrenchment, in federal affirmative initiatives are needed to ensure the continued rise of black corporate America in the twenty-first century, as they are needed for the nation's other minorities, if we are all to share in the American dream.

Blacks and Franchising

In the third-wave rise of black corporate America, franchising also provided blacks an entry into white corporate America in five ways: as intrapreneurs in senior management positions in regional and national franchisor offices; as franchise managers; as entrepreneurs in franchise ownership; as food and service suppliers; and as franchisors.[63] In the post–Civil Rights period, blacks intensified their participation in franchising, one of the fastest growing sectors in American business in the late twentieth century, accounting for about 13 percent of the nation's total of sales of goods and services in the early 1990s. In 1994 there were 3,500 franchise companies holding over 550,000 franchise units in 65 different industries with $970 billion in sales, a 12.9 increase from 1993. By 1996, 1 out of every 12 business establishments was franchised.

Even so, black participation rates were not proportionate to their population. By 1994, minorities, including blacks, constituted about 23 percent of the total population, but they owned only 5 percent of all franchises industrywide, which was still an increase from the 2.5 percent ownership in 1990.[64] In 1987 *Black Enterprise* began listing the 50 franchise companies with the most black-owned outlets. In 1993, blacks owned only 4.23 percent of the 75,000 units held by the franchisors listed in the *Black Enterprise* list.

In 1993, of the 9,086 McDonald's franchises, only 658 were owned by blacks. Blockbuster home video rental, with 3,258 units, had only 23 black franchise units, all owned by one company. In 1992, the Atlanta-based NDI Video, Inc., became the nation's only black Blockbuster franchise with the purchase of 23 outlets in the northeast. Start-up costs for a Blockbuster franchise range from $285,000 to $775,000. Among other profitable franchises, of the 5,208 7-Eleven stores, only 1.44 percent, 75 units, were owned by blacks. Start-up costs range from $14,000 to $210,000. In 1995, however, the Convenience Corporation of America (CCA), based in West Palm Beach, Florida, acquired 150 7-Eleven convenience stores and gas stations, thus becoming the "second largest 7-Eleven licensee in the nation." The owners of CCA are a black-owned investment bank and LM Capital Corporation, with Leslie M. Corley as CEO. In 1996, CCA ranked 8th on the *Black Enterprise* 100, with sales of $137.4 million.[65] Typical of the black franchisee is Walter Bridgeforth Jr., who established an IHOP (International House of Pancakes) franchise in downtown Detroit. Because of his initiative, Bridgeforth, who owns the building and the land with a 25-year lease from IHOP and who has plans for full ownership, grossed almost $1.8 million in 1995.[66]

The most successful black franchises are those with multiple units. In 1992, Thompson Hospitality L.P., established by Warren M. Thompson, acquired 31 Bob's Big Boy restaurants for $13.1 million from the Marriott Corporation. He converted 11 of the units to Shoney's restaurants, 10 of which were in the Washington, D.C., area. Thompson ranked fifth in Shoney's list of the largest franchises. In the *Black Enterprise* list of the top 100 for 1995, Thompson ranked 58th, with 2,100 employees and sales of $33.5 million. Indeed, in the rise of black corporate America, most of the black multiple-unit franchise owners are listed on the *Black Enterprise* top 100. In 1992 Larry Lundy of the New Orleans–based Lundy Enterprises purchased 31 Pizza Hut restaurants for $15.5 million, adding to the 4 he already owned. In 1995 Lundy purchased 7 more units. In the *Black Enterprise* list for 1995, Lundy ranked 76th, with 1,000 employees and $26.5 million in sales.

In 1993, the 10-year-old Milwaukee-based V&J Foods, Inc., headed by Valerie Daniels-Carter, who owned 15 Burger King franchises, purchased 17 more units in Detroit. Valerie, a former financial analyst, and her brother, John Daniels, a corporate and real estate lawyer, purchased their first franchise in 1984. The fee was $40,000; more recently, a total site investment costs from $300,000 to $2 million.[67] In 1955, V&J, with 1,300 employees and $33 million in sales, was 59th on the *Black Enterprise* 100. Car dealerships, however, have been the most lucrative and financial rewarding for black franchisees. Albert William Johnson, the first black to secure an Oldsmobile dealership, headed the nation's most successful black-owned auto dealership in 1972, with $14.5 million in sales. In 1995 the highest-ranking *Black Enterprise* auto dealer, Alvin S. Smith, of Brighton, Colorado, had $408.4 million in sales. The 100th ranked dealer, incidentally, had $22.8 million in sales, nearly $8 million more than Johnson's dealership attained in 1972.

In the third wave of black corporate America, almost half of the nation's franchisors had minority franchisee development programs. Also, over half use minority vendors and suppliers, but a general feeling among some insiders is that "these in-house initiatives are nothing but smoke and mirrors."[68] Black franchisees have also claimed that franchisors place them in high-crime areas with high overhead costs in taxes and insurance. Black franchisees in Atlanta "accused Burger King of putting them in depressed areas, then replacing new equipment with faulty machinery."[69] Also, many potential black franchisees have difficulty securing bank loans, with banks typically seeking 60 percent equity in a franchise venture. Most blacks, consequently, buy into franchises with low start-up costs. Business and professional service franchises are gaining in popularity, one of the reasons being that they are not as capital intensive as most other kinds of franchises. Start-up costs for a McDonald's franchise is $500,000; for Coverall, $2,500.

Moreover, African-Americans have been slow to join the ranks of franchisor operations, which enjoy the advantages of cost-effectiveness. Franchisees are responsible for rent or mortgages and hiring employees and are "legally bound to supplier contracts." Yet, franchisor start-up costs are comparatively minimal: $35,000, $65,000, and $95,000, respectively, for establishing local, regional, and national franchisees, compared to a minimum of $200,000, on average, for the cost of building a second store.

While Wallace Amos Jr., who established the Famous Amos Chocolate Chip Cookie Company in 1975, could have been a leading black franchisor, he established only eight franchises under his Famous Amos Retail Development Corporation. After establishing Famous Amos Cookie franchises in the Los Angeles area and then in the upscale department stores Bloomingdales, Neiman-Marcus, and Macy's, Amos was on his way to building a cookie empire. But while he was a great promoter, he had only minimal interest in the management and financial side of his business. He failed to expand his franchising operations, as did his competitors. In 1985, sales approximated $12 million, but his company was in bankruptcy. Mrs. Field's Cookies and David's Cookies, which filled the market niche created by Amos, eclipsed him in sales by establishing franchises nationwide. In 1985 Amos sold the operation, retaining only 8 percent interest. Amos will also be remembered for his flamboyance and high-energy; in 1980 the Smithsonian placed his trademark floral shirt and Panama hat on exhibit in its Business Americana Collection.[70] Like the popcorn mogul Orville Redenbacher and KFC's Colonel Saunders, who also sold the enterprises they founded, Amos remained on as his company's symbol and spokesman, until he lost all equity in his company.[71]

The country's leading black franchisor is Herman Cain, CEO and president of Godfathers's Pizza, which he purchased in a leveraged buyout from Pillsbury in 1988. By 1996 Cain had expanded to 525 franchise units, the same year in which he appeared at a public hearing held by the congressional Joint Economic Committee to present his argument opposing increases in the minimum wage.[72] As franchisors, however, blacks have had only limited success. Ohio-based Claude Patmon established Accent Hair Salons in 1983; in 1996 he had 11 units in 10 major cities with sales of $3.5 million.[73] Liberian-born Chuck Morrison established his Indianapolis-based RACS International, a commercial and industrial cleaning service, in 1990. By 1995 he had 14 units.[74]

Franchisors succeed when the name of the product they sell symbolizes a high-quality product or a dependable and high-quality service. One of the reasons few black franchisors succeeded was that their products or services did not have an opportunity to establish that image. One of the ways for all black entrepreneurs to achieve an image of dependability for their products or services is to get black sports or entertainment superstars to endorse them. At the end of the twentieth century, theirs were the only African-American names that could sell products in both black and white markets in America. Is that because sports and entertainment are the only areas in which white America is willing to concede the excellence of the performers and, consequently, transferring that image of excellence to the products they endorse?

Blacks and Advertising

Advertising sells America. It also supports the mass media. The most successful African-American magazine, *Ebony,* however, was launched in 1945 without advertisements. Within a year of its initial publication, circulation was at 500,000 copies a month, but the magazine still did not have an advertising base. Publisher John H. Johnson envisioned that black America's premier magazine would carry only the sleek half-page and full-page advertisements found in *Life* and the *Saturday Evening Post.* His in-house advertising division was unsuccessful in soliciting ads, as were mainstream advertising agencies. Only when Johnson made personal appeals to CEOs of white corporations was he successful. His first ads were for Chesterfield cigarettes and Kimberly Clark paper products in 1946. By June 1948, *Ebony's* advertising space had increased to 48 pages and carried ads from Zenith, Pepsi-Cola, Beech-Nut, Seagram, Remington Rand, Elgin Watches, and MGM.[75]

Simply put, in the second wave of black corporate America, black consumers were not only taken for granted but also the black consumer market was considered insignificant until the 1940s, when the federal government began releasing figures on the consumer power of black America. While the black newspapers had launched various campaigns to secure ads from white corporate America, prior to World War II, most of them purchased only limited space to promote their products to black America. Even when white companies did advertise in black papers, they were prompted to do so by the publication's sales and public relations staffs, described in a 1948 *Ebony* article as "Brown Hucksters." In black America, the media salesperson was viewed more as "a sales engineer whose job it is to establish contact between the 99 per cent of the country's manufacturers who are non-Negro and the 10 percent of the consuming population that is Negro."[76]

In response to white corporate America's growing awareness of the dollar power of the black consumer, blacks in advertising in the second-wave rise of black corporate America began to professionalize their efforts to attract accounts, especially from manufacturers whose products had a significant black consumer market. In 1948 the New York–based Brandford Advertising agency announced its incorporation. Once it began to secure accounts from white corporate America, Brandford gained recognition as "the first Negro agency with complete facilities, including merchandising and public relations, art, production and model services, for service of any nature for the benefit of manufacturers through newspaper advertising."[77] The agency was founded by Edward Brandford, a commercial artist, who became known for the "Brandford models" he used in his ads.

In 1948 the efforts of the black media and their brown hucksters began to pay off, when several large corporations announced ad campaigns specifically targeted at blacks. Philip Morris launched an advertising campaign based on "Negroes who have taken a leading part in various phases of American business." The selection of businessmen is significant, underscoring the extent to which this group was recognized nationally as leaders and role models for black America. Supreme Liberty Life's Truman Gibson was the first black businessman featured in the ads, which were placed in 17 black newspapers coast-to-coast. The ad copy is interesting, especially in light of recent antismoking campaigns: "No cigarette hang-over when you smoke Philip Morris."[78] Pepsi-Cola's advertising campaign, also launched in 1948, featured "outstanding Negroes from coast to coast," beginning with Dr. Ralph Bunche of the United Nations.[79]

In 1948 Lever Brothers also announced its new advertising campaign in the black press. Its news releases were similar to those made by white corporations in the post–Civil Rights period, when they publicized their support for affirmative action practices. Lever Brothers president Charles Luckman, a member of President Truman's Committee on Civil Rights, was known as an "outspoken champion of justice and opportunity for minority groups." He began his career at Lever Brothers "as a salesman in the Negro section of Chicago." In an address before a conference of the white business leaders in 1948, Luckman said, "Give the members of our minority groups an opportunity and you will find it the best stroke of business you ever pulled. And you'll be helping America to realize more fully the democratic ideal."[80]

After World War II, white corporate America awakened to the fact that it could no longer take the black consumer for granted. By the early 1950s, African-American consumers had purchasing power worth $16 billion, which continued to increase throughout that decade and into the 1960s. As a result of both this development and the Civil Rights movement, blacks in advertising escalated their efforts to break into the advertising major leagues. Their pitch to white companies was that unless advertisements to black consumers were conceived and executed with the specific needs of blacks in mind they would be ineffective. Several black advertising companies were established as specialists in ethnic advertising markets, including Vince Cullers Advertising, Inc., founded in 1956, the first black agency to achieve success in winning accounts from white corporate America.[81]

In the third-wave rise of black corporate America, Barbara Proctor established the first successful advertising agency. She was also the first black woman to found an advertising agency, Chicago-based Proctor and Gardner, Inc. The agency was established in 1970 with an SBA loan of $80,000, with the collateral based on her potential future earnings. In the 1980s Proctor's billings amounted to $13 million from several national companies. Alberto-Culver provided 20 percent of the billings until it withdrew its account. Proctor also had accounts from Sears, Roebuck and the E. J. Gallo winery.[82] The leading black advertising agency from the 1970s, when there were about 13 nationally recognized black firms, until the mid-1990s was another Chicago-based agency. Burrell Advertising was founded in 1971 by Thomas J. Burrell. His clients included Crest toothpaste, Ford, Quaker Oats, Jack Daniels, Coca-Cola, and McDonald's. Burrell's TV commercial "A Family Is" won a coveted CLIO Award for excellence in advertising in 1979. Before establishing his own shop, Burrell worked as a copywriter on both TV and print ads for several white agencies, including Leo Burnett.

Also, blacks in advertising, including Burrell, formed partnerships to start their own agencies, then dissolved the business as each partner branched out alone. In 1977, Frank Mingo, who was a senior vice president at McCann, Erickson, formed a partnership with Caroline Jones, who had been vice president and creative supervisor at BBDO. Within seven years the firm had a multiethnic billing distribution that was: 60 percent African-American; 10 percent Hispanic; and 30 percent general, including ads from Philip Morris, Seagram, Miller Brewing, Goodyear, Liggett & Myers, and Westinghouse Electric. Mingo died in 1988. Jones, however, had left the agency in 1987 to set up Caroline Jones Advertising, Inc., becoming the second black woman to own her own agency.[83] The Mingo Group, under CEO Samuel Chisholm, who succeeded Mingo, ranked 29th on the *Black Enterprise* top 100 list for 1995, with a staff of 35 and sales of $52.3 million.

In the third-wave rise of black corporate America, blacks in advertising changed the face of African-Americans in the media. Rather than present images of African-Americans that placed them in menial service positions such as cooks, maids, and butlers in ads for Aunt Jemima Pancakes, Uncle Ben's Rice, and Hiram Walker's liquor, black agencies showed images of blacks as average Americans with families and in professional and managerial occupations.[84] Advertising campaigns used by white companies to attract black Americans, however, were either directed specifically to the black consumer market, in which case the ads featured all blacks; or they were aimed at the mainstream audience, in which case images of blacks were integrated with whites, but only after market research confirmed that white consumers would not be offended.

Yet, by the 1980s, as African-American culture began to make its mark on the general American culture, white corporate America began using black-based rhythm and blues as background music in many of its ads. Their target market was America's baby boomers. Chevrolet used Martha and the Vandellas and the Four Tops in its ads. Mercury promoted its cars using Brook Benton's "You Are So Beautiful," and Bounce Fabric Softener increased its product recognition and sales with the Pointer Sisters' hit "Jump." Michael Jackson and Lionel Ritchie sang for Pepsi-Cola and Whitney Houston for Diet Coke.

The black entertainer who literally became the voice of many white corporate advertising campaigns was comedian and TV star Bill Cosby. He was the spokesman for Coca-Cola, Ford, Ideal Toys, Kodak, and Texas Instruments; from 1973 to the present, he has been the star of numerous ads for General Foods' Jell-O.[85] The actress and comedian Whoopi Goldberg, after starring in a string of leading movies, including the film adaptation of Alice Walker's novel *The Color Purple,* produced by Stephen Spielberg has been featured in several national TV commercials in the 1990s, including several for MCI Telecommunications.

Yet, while black celebrities have had success in being featured in national mainstream advertising campaigns, several black advertising agencies founded in the 1970s failed in the 1980s. Burrell, however, continued to expand his agency, explaining that he went after clients who "think we can help them, not who are trying to help us." Burrell was the first to introduce "lifestyle" ads that featured blacks in positive roles intended to increase the products' appeal to blacks. In the final analysis, the comparative success of black advertising agencies was minimal, especially when viewed in the light of the gross receipts of white advertising agencies. In the mid-1980s, when the six leading black ad agencies had sales of $155 million, a leading white agency, J. Walter Thompson, had billings of $1.5 billion from its U.S. accounts alone.[86]

With a staff of 141 and sales amounting to $128 million, Burrell Advertising ranked 7th on *Black Enterprise*'s top 100 list for 1995. That same year, Burrell purchased DFA Communications, Inc., a white agency in New York with four subsidiaries.[87] By this time, however, the highest-ranked agency on *Black Enterprise*'s list (in 6th place) had become the New York–based UniWorld Group Inc., founded in 1969 by Byron E. Lewis. After he was turned down for a job by more than 50 white agencies, Lewis launched UniWorld with a $250,000 investment loan from two venture-capital groups. His clients include Burger King, which has been with him for more than decade, AT&T, Kodak, and Ford; in 1995 it had sales of $133.6 million. In the same year, it became the "the first African American advertising agency to snag a major general market account . . . by landing Mars, Inc. [makers of the Three Musketeers candy bar] as a major client."[88]

The leading white agencies, Leo Burnett in Chicago and J. Walter Thompson in New York, however, each had annual billings of $2 billion in a $42.2 billion industry.[89] Moreover, by the 1990s, black advertising agencies were faced with increased competition from white agencies. During the 1970s and 1980s, black advertising firms had expanded with accounts that wanted to appeal to the ethnic market. By the late 1980s, white agencies began to usurp the the influence of black agencies in the ethnic specialty market, even though the profits of the black agencies were minimal. The black owned Mingo-Jones agency developed the slogan "We Do Chicken Right" for Kentucky Fried Chicken's New York market. KFC bought the rights to it to use in their national ad campaign, but gave the account to a white agency.

Moreover, by the late 1980s, with the federal government's relinquishing of its support of affirmative action, white corporate America responded by turning over advertising accounts that were previously held by black agencies to white agencies, which developed or expanded their in-house "special markets" divisions. At BBBO, one of the world's six largest ad agencies, a longtime black employee was made head of the division that handled accounts from white corporate America directed at black consumer markets.[90]

Most ads aimed at black consumers for the products and services of white companies appear on television and in leading black magazines and the mainstream press. In the 1990s, however, while the number of ads in black magazines from white companies increased significantly, the number of people shown in these ads did not match black readership. African-Americans constituted 12 percent of the nation's population and 11.3 percent of all magazine readers, but blacks represented only 3.2 percent of 21,007 people shown in ads.[91] Moreover, in the post–Civil Rights period, newspaper ads aimed at black consumers by white advertisers decreased precipitously, along with the decline of the black press. While the black revolution of the 1960s opened doors for black journalists to the white media, the results were disastrous for the black press. From the 1960s on, the black press suffered declining circulation in both street sales and subscriptions, matched by a consequent loss of advertising revenue. Newspapers in general need at least a 71 percent ad linage to make a profit, but black papers average only a 31 percent to 61 percent ad linage.

The country's first profitable black newspaper, the *Chicago Defender,* founded in 1905 by Robert Abbott, however, built a million-dollar business from street sales and both local and national subscriptions. Even then, Abbott found it difficult to secure advertising. Throughout the 1940s and 1950s, Robert Sengstacke, who succeeded Abbott as publisher of the *Defender,* pushed white companies that manufactured products specifically for the black consumer to increase their advertising in the black media. In 1953 the *Defender* warned the white-owned Galenol Company, whose leading product was Dr. Palmer's Vanishing Cream, that unless it increased its advertising in the black press, the company would face declining sales among blacks. Subsequently, the *Defender* noted that the company promised to increase its ads in the black press.[92]

In the 1930s, with increased competition from local and regional black newspapers, the *Defender* had lost most of its national circulation and also its lead as the country's best-selling black newspaper to the *Pittsburgh Courier.* Only by expanding into other cities did it sustain competition regionally. It maintained its declining local circulation by publishing daily. Also, during the Civil Rights movement, the *Defender,* as did most black newspapers, survived by correcting or interpreting news published on black protest activities in the mainstream press.[93] Notwithstanding, between 1949 and 1976, the black press, with its decline in circulation, not only lost its power as the most influential voice of black America but also much of its advertising base. National companies advertise only in papers audited by the Audit Bureau of Circulation. With declining circulation by the 1980s, few of the more than 300 African-American papers were audited.[94]

In the post–Civil Rights period, the black press was not able to recoup its lost readership, especially among the young generation, whose primary introduction to the news media came during the 1960s from the mainstream press and television. By then, 60 percent of the readers of black newspapers were over 35 years of age. Also, black newspapers were reduced to being little more than community newspapers, as opposed to being a part of the black mainstream media. Black newspapers that survived and were the most successful in generating revenue were responsive not only to the interest of all its readers, especially the younger generation, but also to new developments in advertising. The *St. Louis American* was $400,000 in debt when it was taken over in 1984 by Dr. Donald Suggs. He changed the paper's layout and provided free distribution of nearly 40,000 copies; by 1988 the paper was earning $800,000 annually in advertising. The *Winston-Salem Chronicle,* founded in 1979 by publisher and editor Ernest Pitt, had a weekly circulation of only 7,000. After Pitt began publishing the *Black College Sports Review* as a monthly insert for black newspapers, its circulation climbed to 137,000 and the combined annual gross income to $1 million.

The circulation of the *Miami Times* skyrocketed when its editor and publisher, Garth C. Reeves Jr., modeled its layout after white America's first national newspaper, *USA Today.* In 1987 the *Times* became the first black paper to use full color, with its printing being done at the same plant that prints *USA Today.* Within two years after introducing full color, the paper earned $1 million in advertising revenue from both national and local accounts. Also, similar to the *Defender's* practice early in its existence of publishing news about blacks from various locales throughout the United States, the *Times,* a family-owned paper since its founding in 1922, in response to the diverse black population in Miami, expanded its news coverage to include articles on local events from various West Indies communities.

The National Newspaper Publisher's Organization (NNPA) has been aggressive in securing advertising commitments for the black press from white corporate America. In 1989 Kmart, Chrysler, and Philip Morris committed about $2 million to advertising in black newspapers. Increasingly, in the twenty-first century, the black press will have to tap local black businesses, especially supermarkets and similar enterprises, for advertisements. Supermarkets are among the largest advertisers in the black press, while black hair care product manufacturers, since the early twentieth century, have been the mainstay of the black press. If it is to remain an important force, the black press must also invest in new technologies to reduce costs and increase efficiency, while improving the professionalism of its staff. The black press must also be responsive to the interests of the post–Civil Rights generation, the market advertisers most want to reach.

Black Sports Enterprises

Until the post–Civil Rights period, white corporate America's economic exploitation of black athletes was a national disgrace. First denied the opportunity to play professional sports, then paid salaries gobbled up by unscrupulous agents, few black sports figures left the game with any degree of financial security.[95] In the 1930s and 1940s, Joe Louis was the one black star able to capitalize on his sports prominence to make a mark in the business world, notwithstanding that most of his ventures eventually failed.

In the third-wave rise of black corporate America, one of the most significant advancements by blacks was their move into the business side of the sports industry. In boxing, Don King became a major figure in fight promotion. In one of his most memorable events, he promoted the Muhammed Ali–Joe Frazier "Rumble in the Jungle" in Zaire, Africa, in 1974. Each fighter was guaranteed a $5-million purse out of an estimated $30 million in revenues.[96] In 1994 alone, King promoted 47 championship bouts. He also owns KingVision, a pay-per-view sports and entertainment network that features his fighters. King was also named one of the 40 most influential sports figures for the last 40 years by *Sports Illustrated*.

As Earl G. Graves, publisher of *Black Enterprise* noted, the 1980s signaled "the beginning of the end of a system that pushed Africans to make the shots but refused to let us call them; that profited *wildly* from our athletic skills but dismissed our intellect and management skills; that actually competed to get us on the team but stood strong against our owning the team."[97] In the third wave of black corporate America, black sports figures became increasingly important in both founding and funding black enterprises. In 1974, for example, baseball great Jackie Robinson, the first black to play in a major professional sports league, founded the first black bank in Harlem, Freedom National Bank.[98]

Also, one of the first black franchise owners in the fast-food industry was former professional-football player, Brady Keys. In 1969, his All-Pro Enterprises purchased several Burger King and Kentucky Fried Chicken franchises. In 1990, retaining ownership of his 11 KFC franchises but selling his 12 Burger King franchises, Keys, with two white partners, moved into manufacturing. He held 52 percent ownership in a steel-fabricating company, RMK Steele, that was purchased for $50,000 and a note of $1 million. The company built containers for military tank transmissions and jet engines. In the eight months the group owned the company, sales increased from $300,000 to $3 million; it was sold for "three times the purchase price."[99]

Basketball has proved to be the most financially rewarding professional sport for black athletes. By 1994 African-Americans made up 79 percent of the athletes in the National Basketball Association, 65 percent in the National Football League, and 18 percent in Major League Baseball. The first professional sports team owned by blacks, significantly, was the Harlem Globetrotters. In 1993, former Globetrotter Mannie Jackson and a group of investors purchased the team for $6 million. Blacks also moved into management, even obtaining equity interest in the teams who hired them. When the ex-NBA star Isaiah Thomas became vice president and general manager of an NBA expansion team, the Toronto Raptors, in 1994, he negotiated a contract that gave him 10 percent ownership in the $125 million team.[100] In 1994 "Magic" Johnson bought a 5 percent interest in the ownership of the Los Angeles Lakers for $10 million. Also several black businesspeople purchased interest in professional sports teams.[101]

Black superstars from various sports began to appear in TV ads in the 1980s. Heisman Trophy-winner Herschel Walker advertised McDonald's Big Macs and Adidas sneakers. Former basketball star Julius Erving sold Crest toothpaste and Converse basketball shoes. Baseball great Reggie Jackson promoted Pentax cameras, Panasonic video equipment, and Nabisco cereals.[102] O. J. Simpson, former football great and the "black Golden Boy" of white America until his infamous trial, was the advertising symbol for Hertz Rent-A-Car.[103] The most outrageous black athlete in the mid-1990s has been Dennis Rodman of the Chicago Bulls. With his cross-dressing and other antics, Rodman has emerged as a media superstar, appearing in numerous TV ads.

The preeminent sports figure in American advertising in the 1990s has undoubtedly been Michael Jordan, who is popular because of not only his phenomenal basketball abilities but also his poise and charisma. In 1992 Jordan made $16 million from serving as advertising spokesman for McDonald's, the Quaker Oats's sports drink Gatorade, General Mills's Wheaties, and Ball Park hot dogs. In 1995 he negotiated $30 million in endorsements.[104] By the end of 1997, Jordan's salary, negotiated contract endorsements, and a Nike subsidiary had increased his wealth to over $200 million.

When he turned professional at the age of twenty, the black golfer Tiger Woods signed a $60-million contract for Nike athletic equipment, the largest endorsement contract obtained by any athlete in history. Woods's entry as a pro golf superstar also highlighted the issue of racial discrimination in the sport, which Nike used in its advertising. In commenting on the ad, *Newsweek* noted: "The fact that Woods's first Nike commercial . . . has him looking into a camera and noting that there are (at least) 23 clubs in the United States that will not allow him to play because of the color of his skin is a tip-off to the marketing plans for him."[105] This concept is indeed revolutionary in the history of American advertising. Yet, while black athletes have been successful as spokespersons for the athletic equipment industry, Thomas Burrell, the black advertising executive, said in 1996 that the money has not spilled over to black advertising agencies: "no Black-owned company has been retained and given a free hand to address these products in a major way."[106]

Moreover, advertising campaigns for signature sportswear have been blamed by some criminal-justice authorities for recent increases in juvenile crime, as young blacks have committed violent acts against one another in order to get a pair of signature basketball shoes and other items of clothing valued as status symbols.

The sports apparel industry is indeed lucrative, and so it is no surprise to note the move of African-Americans into it. Drew Pearson, CEO of Drew Pearson Companies, founded in 1985, has sports apparel licenses with four major sports leagues and is the largest licensed head wear dealer in the country. The company ranked 42nd on the *Black Enterprise* top 100 for 1995, with sales of $42 million.[107] Still, black-owned businesses have less than 3 percent of the $27.9 billion sportswear industry, which includes licensed apparel imprinted with names of professional-sports teams.

Yet African-American sports stars are taking control of the marketing of their image. Basketball great Shaquille O'Neal, at age 23, incorporated himself by "establishing his own multi-media conglomerate with an estimated $12 million in endorsements." He owns the Shaq Logo that appears on his signature apparel, which has become the most popular line of NBA clothing. He also secures equity in most of the companies he endorses.[108]

High-Tech and Telecommunications Enterprises

In the third-wave rise of black corporate America, hi-tech and telecommunications enterprises represented a new growth industry providing young African-Americans with a window of opportunity for entry into business. The economic world they face in postindustrial America has been shaped as much by federal affirmative action initiatives as by the revolution in high technology and the growth of global corporations. For the present generation of young black Americans, joint ventures, mergers, acquisitions and leveraged buyouts are as much a part of their business ventures as sole proprietorships were for previous generations of black businesspeople.

For example, within two years of his initial employment at Resource One Computer Systems in 1988, Harvard MBA Stampp W. Corbin had acquired a majority interest in the company; in 1992, at age 31, he acquired 100 percent ownership. The company made *Black Enterprise*'s top 100 in 1993, ranking 88th, with sales of $18.2 million; it advanced to 64th in 1995, with sales of $30.1 million. The Columbus, Ohio-based company specializes in technology acquisition and technical support services. It acquires computer equipment from industry giants such as IBM, Apple, Dell, and Hewlett-Packard and services telecommunications giants, including AT&T, Pacific Bell, Bell Atlantic, and Ameritech.

During the corporate downsizing of the late twentieth century, *Fortune* 1000 companies are restructuring their organizations and streamlining staff. The elimination of middle managers and whole divisions has created outside companies that specialize in providing cost-saving services to maintain and expand corporate growth. Corbin capitalized on the new outsourcing partnerships that developed among phone service providers, and cable companies, and the computer giants.[109] Yet, as white corporate America restructures, it will look more to one or two larger companies, rather than outsourcing to a diversity of small enterprises, to provide these needed services. Indeed, many of these kinds of larger companies, especially computer systems integration firms, are now listed on *Black Enterprise*'s top 100.

The survival of these companies in the twenty-first century, if they intend to compete, will be contingent on expansive growth through mergers. In 1976 *Black Enterprise* did not have any high-tech companies on its list. Since the late 1970s, however, each year has brought an increase in black high-tech companies that have appeared on the list, then moved up, down, and sometimes out of the top 100. In 1995, black high-tech industries accounted for 6.7 percent of the *Black Enterprise* top 100 in total sales, but a year before, high-tech companies listed on the *BE* 100s accounted for 7.5 percent of total sales. Their survival has depended on the extent to which they can compete successfully for private contracts with white corporate America.

Many of these companies, such as Maxima Corporation, founded in 1978 by Joshua Smith, offer a broad range of computer services and are successful. In the *Black Enterprise* top 100 list for 1995, Maxima ranked 38th, with sales of $45 million and a staff of 650. Pulsar Data Systems, a systems integration, office automation, and computer reseller founded in 1982, ranked 5th on the list for 1995, with sales of $165 million; while RMS Technologies, which ranked 6th in1994, with sales of $120 million, dropped to 14th in 1995, with sales of $95 million. RMS also experienced a decline in staff from 1,300 to 1,000. In January 1996, the company announced that it had sold a significant number of its shares to a nonminority interest to secure capital for future growth.[110]

Network Solutions, Inc., which specializes in designing, building, and managing networks for voice, data, and video communications, was also dropped from the *Black Enterprise* list in 1994. The company had been an eight-year participant in the SBA 8(a) federal contract set-aside program until 1990, when it ranked 11th on the *Black Enterprise* list. It had sales of $48.8 million, a staff of more than 300, contracts from AT&T, and an authorized dealership from Digital Equipment Corporation to sell low-end systems and services to both the public and private sector. NSI also had several defense contracts and contracts to monitor the manufacturing of silicon chips in Japan. Two years after NSI left the SBA program, it seems the company was no longer able to compete with comparable high-tech firms. It fell to 66th on the *Black Enterprise* list, with sales of $24.5 million. When it was dropped from the list in 1994, the company had sales of $18.3 million. In 1995 the former SBA 8(a) company was sold.[111]

High-tech by the 1980s was virtually synonymous with telecommunications, a $600-billion industry made up of several different components: telephone services, wired, wireless, and cellular; broadcast, both cable and satellite; and computers, including hardware and software. African-Americans capitalized on the rapidly growing personal communication services (PCS) industry, which included cellular and cordless phone services. In 1994, six *Black Enterprise* top 100 companies and four other black media firms formed a limited partnership to bid for some of the 5,628 narrowband and broadband PCS licenses being auctioned off by the FCC. This financial consolidation was necessary because a PCS license can cost several million dollars, even for a small geographic area. The group, Urban Communications PCS Limited Partnerships, was spearheaded by Sydney L. Small, cochairman of American Urban Radio Networks.[112]

In 1994, Sloan PCS Development Corporation was only one of five companies that acquired licenses to all five FCC regions, therefore acquiring national coverage. Maceo Sloan, in partnership with executive vice president Justin Beckett (who owns 48 percent of Sloan PCS Development) put up $10 million. The capital was acquired from six venture-capital firms, including the Philadelphia-based black investment bank PMC, which raised $5.6 million. There was also government-supported financing. The full price for the five PCS licenses was $151 million. But the FCC granted the African-American firm a 40 percent discount and 10 years to make installment payments because, as Sloan said, "banks will not loan $100 million to a minority no matter how good the idea or deep his or her cash flow."[113]

The telecommunications industry also includes the new media technology, including the Internet, CD-ROMs, and laser discs. African-Americans have established Internet Web sites and related entertainment enterprises, along with white companies in the film, recording, publishing, and video-game industries. NetNoir, a joint venture with American Online, was launched in 1995 by David Ellington and Malcolm Casselle. The black-owned company has 18 departments that digitize and archive Afrocentric cultural information for the Internet. Before Black Entertainment Television established its joint venture with Microsoft, BET's Robert Johnson and Ellington had considered an alliance, with BET as the content provider and NetNoir as the distributor on AOL. While Johnson said that he wanted to partner with a minority-owned company, he also wanted equity in NetNoir, emphasizing that BET does not "do deals for under 49.999 percent of something." The BET/Microsoft venture plans to generate revenues from on-line advertising, subscriptions, and fees for downloading files.[114]

In the 1990s the most successful black high-tech companies provided computer management services and software. Open-Vision Technologies, founded in 1992 by Michael S. Fields, has a client base of 1,000, both government agencies and *Fortune* 1000 companies, including "Wells Fargo Bank, Mercedes Benz and Ford Motor Co." Open-Vision has a staff of 200 employees, consultants, and international distributors in Asia, South America, and Europe. It competes in an industry that in 1998 is expected to operate in a $4 billion market, and industry analysts say Fields's "heavy-weight rivals, including IBM, Computer Associates and Hewlett-Packard could knock Open-Vision out of the ring." The company was established with $68 million in equity investment. Fields did a private placement of $43 million, while E. M. Warburg, Pincus & Co., placed an investment of $25 million.[115] The venture was based on acquisitions of companies in the field of small emerging technologies.

International Business

The 1987 leveraged buyout of the European-based Beatrice International Foods by Reginald Lewis in the third wave of black corporate America did not mark black America's initial entry into international business. But the company did represent the largest international holding by a black-owned company up that time. At its height, before Lewis started selling off its assets, TLC Beatrice International included "64 companies that were located in [31] foreign countries."[116] TLC Beatrice's home office, now in New York City, was located in Paris before Lewis's death. In France its operations are divided into food distribution and grocery products, and it "is the largest wholesale distributor of food and grocery products to supermarkets in the Paris metropolitan areas." TLC Beatrice operates 418 Franprix stores, owning 35 and franchising 383. It also owns 43 LeaderPrice stores, while 46 others are franchises.[117]

On a much smaller scale, the New Orleans–based Le International Imports, founded in 1993, includes as clients Kmart, Wal-Mart, J. C. Penny, and Winn Dixie. It had sales of more than $3 million in imports from China and other Asian countries. In 1996, sales were expected to be $10 million.[118] Black investment firms also leveraged significant international investments in Asia. Calvin Grigsby, CEO and founder of the defunct San Francisco–based Grigsby Brandford and Company, had negotiated multimillion-dollar investment ventures in Beijing.

Also, despite concern for Japan's negative images of blacks, African-Americans have established trade relations with that country. The black publisher of *Japan Watch,* Kathryn

D. Leary, established The Leary Group in 1991. It develops Japanese markets for American products. Items most in demand are sports equipment, home-building supplies, geriatric products, and "especially baggy pants and fancy caps in the young market." Leary admits that, initially, she was reluctant to do business with Japan because of "highly publicized racist and negative remarks made about African-Americans by some of the Japanese," but attributed this to a lack of "one-on-one contacts."[119]

Yet business ventures between the Japanese and African-Americans date to the 1960s, when Seiho Tajiri, a Japanese-born retired oil man who has now lived in the United States for 40 years, "arranged for a major Japanese food company to provide the fish sold in the Nation of Islam's shops and restaurants." In the mid-1990s, Tajiri worked with several black farmers to encourage the cultivation of soybeans; he even found a market for them, the Japanese-based Takan Foods Company. The soybean market can be profitable because agricultural commodities such as soybeans, wheat, and corn are among Japan's top 20 imports from the United States.[120] Also, Brooks Sausage, a long-standing McDonald's supplier in this country, makes a special pork sausage for Japan McDonald's, which represents 35 percent of its international market. Brooks's sales in 1993 were $31.5 million, including $4.4 million in Japan.[121]

Also, black businessman Theodore A. Adams, president and CEO of Pyrocap, contracted with the 130-year-old Japanese trading firm, Cornes & Company for his patented and environmentally safe fire retardant material. In 1993, Adams took Pyrocap public, with a listing on the AMEX. In 1994 he established Saudi Pyrocap, which sells the fire retardant material in Saudi Arabia, and Pyrocap International Bermuda for sales in the Caribbean. On a much larger scale, the African Development Public Investment Corporation, one of the enterprises owned by Dick Griffey, imports African commodities and operates an air travel subsidiary. It also has investments in oil trading. Griffey's holdings ranked 27th on the *Black Enterprise* top 100 list for 1995, with sales of $56 million, half of them generated by African Development and the other by Dick Griffey Productions.[122]

Percy Sutton Intercontinental, a holding company with some 23 subsidiaries, has developed joint ventures in several Southeast Asian, African, and Latin America countries. They include investments in oil and coal and the ownership of a flour mill and macaroni factory in Nigeria. Meat and sugar are imported from Brazil for processing and overseas sales. Sutton moved into international markets in 1978. With a consortium of black businessmen from America and Nigeria, he organized NATRAL (Nigerian-American Tapes and Recordings Associates, Ltd.), a multimillion-dollar enterprise that manufactures tapes and recordings sold in both the United States and Africa. Sutton also owns the only full-time radio station in the Caribbean and services 18 radio stations in Africa and several western European countries.[123]

In the communications industries, the most ambitious international ventures in the third wave of black corporate America have been made by Robert Johnson, BET's founder and CEO. In 1993 he established a subsidiary, BET International (BETI), which includes BET on Jazz: The Cable Jazz Channel, which is carried by satellite. BETI satellite coverage will also extend to South Africa, Botswana, and Zimbabwe. Also satellite systems will provide BETI coverage to central Europe (Germany, Sweden, Austria, Belgium, Luxembourg, and the Czech Republic), North Africa, the Middle East, and the South Pacific (Australia and New Zealand.) BETI began satellite programming in 1985 in the Caribbean. While it expects 20 to 30 percent returns in the next five years, as of 1996 it had "yet to make any money overseas." Moreover, Debra L. Lee, president and CEO of BET Holdings said, "once a country gets cable, they want to produce their own shows."[124]

The African-American health and beauty aids industry first developed international markets in the early twentieth century. In the third wave of black corporate America, the industry expanded its international sales. Fashion Fair cosmetics are sold in West Africa, France, England, Switzerland, the Bahamas, the Virgin Islands, Bermuda, and Canada. John H. Johnson does not reveal how much of the total sales from all his enterprises, $316.2 million in 1995, are from Fashion Fair products. But international sales of American cosmetics in 1994 were $2.4 billion. Considering that people of color make up three-fourths of the world's population, the potential market for ethnic-oriented cosmetics is tremendous.

In the black hair care industry in the 1980s, Soft Sheen launched extensive overseas manufacturing operations. In 1987 it acquired a 66 percent interest in the London-based Dyke and Dryden company, England's largest black business. The company manufactures its own hair care products and is the overseas distributor for Soft Sheen and 40 European and American hair care and cosmetics companies. Before 1987, Soft Sheen was marketing its products in eight African countries, including Nigeria and the Ivory Coast. With its Dyke and Dryden acquisition, the company expected to reach 1.3 million blacks in the United Kingdom and the 3 million blacks living throughout Europe, most of them in France, Germany, Italy, and Belgium. Also, in 1988 Soft Sheen constructed a manufacturing plant in Kingston, Jamaica, in a joint venture with a local businessman, Lasells Chin, in order to tap the Caricom (Caribbean Common Market) island-nations, in addition to expanding its market in various countries in Latin America.

Soft Sheen's overseas strategy and the management of its offshore companies remained in the hands of its local people, while the Chicago office's R and D division developed products specific to the needs of the international markets. In 1995, when Edward Gardner was contemplating the sale of Soft Sheen, with its estimated market value of $70 million to $100 million, industry analysts reported that "Soft Sheen has not been successful in penetrating the international market."[125] This was also the result when Johnson Products sold its products in Liberia, Zaire, and the Ivory Coast. Its international sales never amounted to more than 2.5 percent of the company's total sales.[126] As of 1995, international investments by African-American firms had not resulted in any significant profits, indeed, "the majority of these companies are making little, if any, money."[127]

The American Health and Beauty Aids Institute (AHBAI), however, reported that their 18-member companies in 1995 had international sales of $70 million. Dallas-based Pro-Line, which sells hair products in about 43 counties, has been successful. Pro-Line began developing overseas markets in the mid-1970s and has been systematic in expanding them by using local foreign distributors to market their products. The company also provides technical training in the United States for its international distributors, including hands-on instruction in the use of its products. Pro-Line sales, moreover, are not limited to sub-Saharan Africa, the Caribbean, or Europe. It has also tapped markets in Saudi Arabia, Yemen, the United Arab Emirates, Australia, and Malta. And, by participating in the Department of Commerce's match-maker program, the International Trade Development Center, which pairs U.S. and foreign businesses, the company was provided assistance in developing markets in Jamaica and Brazil. In 1995 Pro-Line's international sales accounted for 10 percent (up 25 percent from the previous year) of the company's total $43 million in sales.[128]

Pro-Line's aggressive marketing ventures can be compared to the Savannah, Georgia-based Carson Products Company, which manufactures Dark & Lovely products. Just over a year after the company was acquired by an investor group led by a former Morehouse College president, it began selling stock on the New York Stock Exchange in 1996. Net sales of $38.7 million were reported for the six months ending September 1996. As part of the company's announced African strategy, it acquired a manufacturing facility in Ghana. Carson's South African subsidiary, including a manufacturing and warehouse facility, is listed on the Johannesburg Stock Exchange. Morehouse College graduate and Harvard MBA John P. Brown Jr. is vice president of strategic planning. In an agreement with the Ghanaian government, Carson was granted "100 percent exemption from duties on products exported from the Ghana facility, and a 60 percent reduction in duties on products sold within Ghana." In South America, the Brazilian government has approved registration of most of Carson's products.[129]

With the end of apartheid, South Africa is seen as the new market of opportunity for African-Americans with international business interests. In the first year following the end of apartheid, approximately 300 blacks from the United States relocated to South Africa to tap its emerging markets. Indeed, the World Bank reclassified South Africa as an emerging, rather than a developed nation, so that it could "qualify for inclusion in lending programs from institutions such as the World Bank, the International Monetary Fund and the African Development Bank." Also, President Clinton's Administration made South Africa eligible for assistance from the Overseas Private Investment Corporation (OPIC). It provides political-risk insurance and finances loans and loan guarantees for U.S. firms operating in developing countries. OPIC appropriated an estimated $100 million for investment capital in South Africa.[130]

One of the first joint African-American/South African firms to establish a business in South Africa was that of Michael Giles and his South African-born wife, Bernadette Moffat, both Columbia University Law School graduates. In 1993, with a $9.3-million approved OPIC loan, they hoped to establish 108 coin-operated laundry centers in the black townships. Soweto, with some four million people, had only one laundromat. By 1996, only 4 had been established, with the Gileses considering franchise operations as a means to expand entrepreneurial opportunities for South African blacks. Californian Dennis Russell, with offices in Capetown and Johannesburg, established a construction firm, one of the industries most critical to the new South Africa. His DLR Construction makes concrete blocks for housing. Russell is not looking for a quick profit. Rather, he envisions he will need five years to train South African blacks as skilled workers and entrepreneurs in the construction industry.[131]

As African-American multinational corporations tap into a new black consumer base in Africa, they face competition from parallel black enterprises developing in those countries. In South Africa, Pro-Line withdrew its products in 1983 in support of economic sanctions against apartheid. In the interim, the South African company Black Like Me was founded. In the new South Africa, faced with a 100 percent tax on imported products, African-American health and beauty aids companies will find it difficult to compete for sales.

Even when African-Americans have launched joint-venture enterprises in South Africa, competition exists. In 1995, Johnson Publishing, with its new subsidiary EBCO International, copartnered the launching of *Ebony South Africa*.[132] Earl Graves's *Black Enterprise* is distributed in South Africa by its counterpart, *Enterprise*. Both publications face stiff competition from South African publications, including *Tribute,* which successfully incorporates the focus of *Ebony, Essence,* and *Emerge*. In the new South Africa, blacks take pride in reading about themselves in their own journals, which also include articles on African-Americans.[133]

One of the most successful international joint business ventures between African-Americans and South African blacks was the South African-owned Pepsi-Cola New Age

Beverages, a $20 million investment. Pepsi put up $5 million while Egoli Beverages, L.P., a consortium of black investors, put up $15 million.[134] South African Khela S. Mthembu is chairman. The goal is for the majority of the company to be owned by South Africa in five years. In turn, Mthembu said, "New Age will also help establish black South Africans in other businesses, such as trucking companies and contracting."[135] In 1997, the venture failed in the face of strong competition from Coca-Cola.

African-Americans, as investors in South Africa, are the same as white Americans—if they are to succeed, they are going to have to bring in heavy investment capital, particularly in joint ventures to areas that need development, rather than investing in established areas with competing business interests.[136] The potential for attractive investment opportunities in a postapartheid Africa prompted the founding of New Africa Advisers in 1990 by CEO Justin F. Beckett, executive vice president of New Africa's parent company, the $4 billion Sloan Financial Group. New Africa Advisers was the first American investment firm to establish offices in the New South Africa.[137] It manages the Calvert New Africa Fund, "the first of its kind with a portfolio devoted primarily to African and African-related investments."[138]

In South Africa, blacks are are pursuing their economic development as a majority people, as opposed to a minority group operating in a dual economy, comparable to African-Americans in the pre–Civil Rights era. Moreover, in the new South Africa white corporations either are allowing blacks to buy majority interests in large enterprises or they are selling out to blacks completely. While South Africa welcomes investments and joint ventures, especially in capital intensive areas, its intent is to develop and control its own infrastructure on all levels, as opposed to relying on internationals to be the prime supplier of its goods and services. The government's hold on AT&T's attempts to take the lead in expanding South Africa's telecommunications network provides only one example.

South African blacks, then, do not operate as minority businesspeople. Yet, while they direct the country's economy, determine trade laws, and contend with foreign-exchange rates, blacks still retain only a minority interest in its business sector. Moreover, when comparing South Africa as an emerging nation to Asia's emerging nations, one has to conclude that, as Michael Giles said, "Aside from the provision of largely unbenefacted natural resources, Africa, including South Africa plays only a minor role in the global economy." Contrasting economic growth in Asia with that in Africa, Giles added that "Forty years ago, Asia was a similarly marginal economic region. Yet, today, it is rapidly becoming the epicenter of the global economy while Africa remains a minor player." Giles then asked "Why? What made the crucial difference? And, do African-Americans have a role in helping South Africa become an important economic power?"[139]

In Asia, however, rapid income growth resulted from employment expansion and opportunities provided by the relocation of manufacturing plants by industrialized Western nations to that region. This led to increased savings in these countries, which released money for investment.[140] As Beckett, of New Africa Advisers said, "emerging markets provide basic, common-sense investment opportunities." In 1995 Beckett was in the process of establishing Sloan International, which is intended to provide specialized advice to pension funds that want to expand their portfolios into global markets.[141]

Yet, as African-Americans increase their participation in the global economy, they are confronted with internal problems in the foreign markets they are attempting to penetrate. Atlanta-based M&M Products, ranked 10th on *Black Enterprise*'s top 100 list in sales for 1987, and Johnson Products abandoned their overseas manufacturing operations. Johnson

Products left Nigeria in 1985, claiming conditions of "political instability and a depressed oil market."[142] In the mid-1980s, Network Solutions, Inc., which provides a global network information center for the Internet and the Defense Data Network, withdrew its business interests in Central Africa. The company found it difficult to resolve problems such as payment issues and the amount of time necessary to close deals.[143]

Does this mean, then, that black American businesspeople who seek international markets are placed in the position of representing neocolonial powers now in "the process of regaining the right of transnational companies to dominate the economies of their former colonies, this time through trade agreements?"[144] In West Africa, some black American businesspeople often found that decolonized nations were more comfortable dealing with their former colonial masters in business than with Americans, white or black. Investment capital for national development is critical for the economic growth of African nations. Until its dissolution in 1996, Pryor, McClendon Counts and Company, for one, was successful with its investments in African financial institutions, including "Ghana's CAL Merchant, the National Merchant Bank of Zimbabwe and Securities Discount Co., a Ghanaian firm that has a wholly owned stock brokerage operation."[145]

In South Africa, Monwabisi Fandeso, president and CEO of New Age Beverages said, "I believe that we have a unique and exciting opportunity to create partnerships with African-Americans who can, through their experience bring useful insights on black economic advancement."[146] African-Americans have worked for South African black firms and a few, such as Sharon Leslie Morgan, have acquired a permanent resident's permit. Morgan initially worked as the joint managing director of Afritel Cellular Systems, Ltd. The company is a joint venture between South African Mark Headbush and African-American entrepreneur Eugene Jackson, "who invested about $1 million . . . for a 25 percent holding in 1993."[147] Morgan, however, moved into the nonprofit sector, founding the South Africa Cultural Renaissance Trust (SACRT). She also organized the African American Alliance with New South Africa (AAANSA) to encourage African-American business investment there.

While most African-Americans with international business interests concentrate on one or two continents, the Chicago-area-based Fuci Metals, USA, founded in 1988 by former professional basketball player Demetrius "Tony" Brown, an international metals trader, has a global market. His London office buys metals, primarily aluminum from Europe and Russia. Brown's company is also the agent for acquiring raw materials for Bratsk Aluminium, the largest aluminum producer in Siberia. In another venture Brown sold four industrial steel furnaces to a Turkish dealer. In the United States, Fuci's domestic customers include Reynolds Aluminum, GMC, and Ford, which awarded him its Q-1 Award for vendor excellence. In its first listing on the *Black Enterprise* top 100 for sales in 1995, Fuci ranked 24th, with $61 million in sales. Fuci also has lines of credit totaling $20 million in various international banks.[148]

On a much smaller scale, Guyanese-born Lex Nigel Barker, a naturalized American citizen, in 1991 established International Aircraft Trading Inc., an aircraft sales, maintenance, operation, and management business, with venture capital of $30,000 in personal loans from family and friends. In 1994 business receipts were almost $2 million. IAT provides "twenty-four/seven" global service. About 90 percent of its business is conducted with China, India, eastern Europe, Africa (Ghana, Zaire, South Africa), Latin America, and various Caribbean countries, where IAT sells used 747 aircraft. In its first year IAT made $500,000, as Barker said, by capitalizing on an untapped market, providing service and parts for single-engine planes: "Government statistics don't always spotlight emerging nations as major markets.... But everyone needs their aircraft to work, so they will find the money to pay for repairs and parts."[149]

Ultimately, the rise of black corporate America in the twenty-first century will require expansion into the global economy. Within a comparative context, moreover, the shoring up of small black businesses in America requires affirmative action assistance in much the same way that comparable small black businesses in Africa and the African diaspora nations in the Americas, such as the West Indies and Brazil, need it. Yet, at the same time, as African-American expatriate Thurlow J. Simmons in South Africa emphasizes, trade relations between Africa and American black business must work both ways:

> Because of the American experience we have a tendency to look at trade initiatives, technology transfer and skill building as uni-directional, that is, from America to South Africa. We should also recognise that there are opportunities to benefit the American market with goods services and technologies from South Africa while providing much needed jobs as a result. As African American businessmen in South Africa our mandate must be clear, the business of freedom and democracy is business.[150]

Africa remains the focus of international business ventures for African-Americans, but in the late twentieth century, African-American trade activities expanded globally. Moreover, in the face of America's balance of trade, if our nation is to sustain a competitive advantage, the full development of all its people must be encouraged. In the rise of black corporate America in the post–Civil Rights era, federal affirmative initiatives precipitated the emergence of a new group of American captains of industry, African-American entrepreneurs. Their entry into the mainstream American business community is only a first step in moving toward the full and equal inclusion of blacks in all areas of the America economy, including the nation's participation in the global economy.

Civil Rights Protest and Black Business

The urban rebellions and racial turmoil of the 1960s, then the 1980s and early 1990s signaled that equality under the Fourteenth Amendment had not been achieved for black Americans. In this bedrock nation of global capitalism, equality of opportunity to create wealth, the area most critical for black equality, eluded blacks. Federal affirmative action guidelines failed. Blacks never achieved parities in employment, income, business participation rates, or business receipts, minimum bread-and-butter prerequisites for full economic freedom. Consequently, while the Civil Rights movement of the 1960s and the black capitalism initiatives of the 1970s brought blacks to the table of America's free-enterprise vast cornucopia of riches, they were served only the most basic provisions. America failed to satisfy the hunger of African-Americans for full economic freedom.

In the post–Civil Rights period, black protest for economic freedom continued on two levels. Demands for equal employment opportunity continued, primarily by individuals in white corporate America, with an occasional class action lawsuit brought against discriminatory employment practices. Protests, led by the NAACP and Operation PUSH, also continued in the efforts to increase black business participation rates. Throughout the

1970s and 1980s, these civil rights organizations were active in promoting business opportunities for blacks.

After Martin Luther King's assassination in 1968, the Reverend Jesse Jackson escalated his Operation PUSH activities in promoting black business by holding trade expositions and business seminars. In his pronouncements Jackson said, "Modern capitalism must become an instrument for a much wider base of participation on the part of the masses in the economic benefits of the nation." In the early 1970s, Operation PUSH initiated a "moral covenant" policy with several franchisors: the Southland Corporation, the holding company for 7-Eleven franchises; Kentucky Fried Chicken; Miller Brewing; Coors Brewing; and Coca-Cola. Agreements with KFC, Anheuser-Busch and Burger King were made, but the Coca-Cola debacle in 1981 symbolized a turning point in white corporate America's response to black boycotts.

Initially successful, Operation PUSH's boycott against Coca-Cola had the national support of black community leaders, politicians, and businesses that depended on black consumers. The boycott resulted in the promise by Coca-Cola of a $34-million package to assist black business and increase black employees. Coca-Cola subsequently rescinded the offer, including its promise to increase the number of black-owned distributorships. A venture capital fund of $1.8 million that Coke had promised was left intact, but Coke stated that any loans granted would be made at high market rates. While the advertising budget for the black media was not doubled as had been promised, it was increased from $1.2 million to $2 million. Doubtless, in its war with Pepsi, Coke was anxious to repair its image in the black community after reneging on its agreement with PUSH.[151] In 1991, however, Coca-Cola ran a full-page ad in the *Wall Street Journal* announcing a five-year program to purchase $1 billion in goods and services from minority- and women-owned businesses: "A Coca-Cola spokesman in 1996 said that: 'the company will meet its goal by the end of the year.' "[152]

In 1982 Heublein, Inc., announced that, in conjunction with Operation PUSH, it would fund a $180-million black-business development program. The plan included $10 million to assist blacks in opening 24 Kentucky Fried Chicken franchises, with plans to open an additional 88 franchises; a 50 percent increase in black advertising agency expenditures; placing 15 percent of the company's group life insurance with a black-owned company; hiring black-owned law and accounting firms; and a $75-million minority purchasing program.[153] The most successful of Operation PUSH's moral covenant initiatives was the one it made with the Burger King Corporation in 1979. By 1994 Burger King had virtually met its initiative agreement to have 15 percent of its franchises minority owned. Of the 14 percent that were minority owned, however, only 3.5 percent were owned by blacks.

In 1983, Jesse Jackson stepped down from his directorship of Operation PUSH to broaden his civil rights agenda in the promotion of human rights. He escalated his political activities nationally through his Rainbow Coalition, seeking the presidency in 1984 and 1988. Jackson also expanded his international reputation in his self-appointed role of America's roving ambassador without portfolio.[154] He also continued his role as a troubleshooter in protesting discriminatory business practices and in promoting black economic expansion and business participation.

In 1990 Operation PUSH launched a boycott against Nike, claiming that, because 30 percent of the company's products were purchased by blacks, which amounted to $669 million of Nike's total annual sales of $2.23 billion, "blacks should receive 30 percent of

Nike's corporate business." Operation PUSH also noted that Nike had no senior level executives and that it did not advertise in black-owned media. Nike's response was that it had an "aggressive minority recruiting effort" and "in two years it would appoint a black vice president." It also stated that 75 percent of its philanthropic budget was given to minority projects, while $30 million was spent on commercials featuring Spike Lee, Michael Jordan, and Bo Jackson. (Jordan was especially important to Nike because of his line of popular Air Jordan sneakers.) The company, however, claimed that black purchases constituted "only 13.6 percent of Nike's sales."[155] The boycott gained some momentum, especially on the West Coast, and then fizzled out.

Along with Operation PUSH and Jackson, the NAACP was also involved in protests to promote black business development and expansion. In 1981 the NAACP launched Operation Fair Share, a five-point initiative aimed at franchisors in order to increase minority participation in franchising at the management, purchasing, and professional levels. By 1994 the NAACP had succeeded in negotiating about "60 fair-share agreements with such companies as Wendy's, McDonalds, United Airlines, Pathmark, Kmart, and Chrysler." The Denny's restaurant chain was a special target.[156] In 1993 it signed a fair-share agreement with the NAACP. The provisions were that Denny's would add 53 new minority-owned restaurants by the year 2000, with plans to refranchise 135 units by 1995. Denny's also hired over 100 minority managers, gave minority ad agencies $1.5 million in business, and signed purchasing contracts with black suppliers for $20 million, 3.3 percent of its total supplier contracts.

Also, in its continuing response to Operation PUSH's moral covenant policy, Burger King set up an eight-point, five-year plan in 1994, backed by a $100-million set-aside fund for developing both minority franchisees and suppliers. The first step was the 1995 joint-venture founding of the Petersburg, Virginia-based Diversity Food Processing LLC, a $20-million meat-processing company to supply beef products to Burger King outlets in an 8- to 10-state area. The deal was put together by African-American Stephen B. Singleteary, president and CEO of Diversity, who sold his 15 Burger King franchise units located in four states to finance his 62-percent share of the deal. Burger King and Hudson Foods, a white-owned poultry products company with 14 processing plants in 10 states, held the remaining share. The white-owned, Miami-based Restaurant Services Inc., a Burger King supplier, not only agreed to purchase beef products from Diversity but also backed Singleteary, who expects annual sales of $124 million, in securing a loan from Chicago's Northern Trust bank.[157]

In the third-wave rise of black corporate America, black business protest was not limited to the activities of Operation PUSH and the NAACP. Black businesses established new organizations to promote their specific interests. In the late 1980s, black manufacturers of health and beauty aids organized to fight off white competitors who were intent on taking control of an industry in which blacks had less than a 25 percent market share. In the late 1970s, when the FTC went after Johnson Products, Revlon, the most aggressive of the white competitors, launched a campaign to destroy black consumer confidence in all hair products made by black manufacturers, highlighted by a Revlon senior executive publicly denouncing the quality of these products.

As Operation PUSH launched a boycott against Revlon products, black manufacturers in the industry formed the American Health and Beauty Aids Institute (AHBAI). It created an AHBAI logo that was used on the labels and packaging of all products that were manufactured by its member companies. This was followed by a $3 million "Black Pride" advertising campaign to inform black consumers of the logo. Also, *Ebony* and *Essence* magazines refused to accept Revlon advertisements. Revlon, along with Alberto-Culver, which had also been targeted, fought back by using prominent black entertainers in their advertising. Nate Bronner Jr., CEO of Bronner Brothers, compared the situation to that of American manufacturers competing with the Japanese: "The Japanese industries to a large degree are government-subsidized, and the white companies that come into the ethnic hair care market are subsidized by their large parent companies. They also have access to both markets and black companies do not have equal access to the white market, just like American companies don't have equal access to the Japanese market."[158]

In the early 1980s, black hair care product firms were growing at a rate of 12 percent annually. By the late 1980s, annual growth had slowed to 6 percent.[159] By 1988 white manufacturers of black hair care products had control of over 50 percent of the more than $1 billion market and were intent on taking it over completely. Indeed, in the 1990s a white manufacturer of black hair care products sued two black-owned companies for their "use of the word 'Africa' and the African colors red, black and green" in their product labeling.[160] By 1995 sales in the black hair care market were approaching $2 billion, but the combined sales of the four leading black manufacturers of these products listed in the *Black Enterprise* top 100 amounted to only $203.7 million.

In 1993 Johnson Products was sold to the white-owned IVAX Corporation. Two years later, Edward Gardner of Soft Sheen, the industry leader and ranked 15th in sales on the *Black Enterprise* list, initiated plans for the sale of his company. In 1993 Soft Sheen had ranked 6th, with sales of $85 million, but from 1993 to 1995, sales dropped from $96.6 million to $92.8 million. In 1996, however, Gardner withdrew his plans to sell. Had he done so, he would have followed a pattern that was developing in the post–Civil Rights period, the selling of black corporate America. Johnson was also one of the founders of Independence Bank, which was also sold to whites in 1995. Despite this troubling development, the multimillion-dollar black businesses that remained, many built from the ground up, symbolizing that blacks had not been defeated totally by racism in the American economy.

By the 1990s African-American business was being assaulted on three fronts. Some of the nation's large black businesses were being purchased by whites. In some industries, especially health and beauty aids, aggressive competition, both nationally and internationally, threatened the continued success of these businesses. Also, the nation's new immigrants were increasing their control of the consumer markets in urban black business districts. These threats to black corporate America have significance beyond black ownership. When companies were black owned, their profits were reinvested in the black community, especially in advancing black electoral politics, and were also directed to higher education programs for black employees. For example, by 1988, the Gordy Foundation, established in 1968 by Berry Gordy, had granted 68 undergraduate scholarships to black students and 12 law school scholarships. But in 1988 Gordy sold Motown. Also before its sale, Johnson Products contributed more than $5 million to virtually all areas of black advancement: politics, civil rights, charities, and scholarships. Johnson personally contributed $1.5 million for college scholarships for 1,600 black students; and the Johnson Foundation granted fellowships to black MBA students.

Edward Gardner of Soft Sheen also supported black politics in Chicago and was the largest single contributor to Harold Washington's successful mayoral campaign. In supporting black institutions, Gardner provided about $5 million to reestablishing Chicago's Regal theater. Johnson Publishing's Ebony Fashion Fair, since its inception in 1958, has raised over $42 million for black charities, institutions, and organizations, including the

United Negro College Fund. In 1990 Comer J. Cottrell, CEO of Pro-Line hair products, advanced $2 million for the relocation of Paul Quinn College, a 118-year-old black institution, from Waco to the Dallas. He also purchased the property of Bishop University, a black school that went bankrupt, for $1.5 million as the new site of Quinn College.[161]

Moreover, blacks who have made money in white corporate America have also contributed significant amounts of money to the black community. Bill Cosby and his family donated $20 million to Spelman College, and their ongoing charitable activities in a variety of causes has run into the tens of millions of dollars. Oprah Winfrey's philanthropy has resulted in about $17 million being contributed to numerous black charities and institutions, including Morehouse College, the United Negro College Fund, Chicago's Harold Washington Public Library, in addition to private charities, including the Desmond Tutu Educational Fund.

Black philanthropy in the third wave of black corporate American, however, has not been limited to America. USA for Africa, the charity established to distribute proceeds from "We Are the World," written by Michael Jackson and Lionel Richie and produced by Quincy Jones, raised approximately $61.8 million between 1985 and 1995. As a result of the song, which sold 7 million copies, "More than 450 charitable organizations in 18 African countries received grants, as well as 250 antipoverty groups in the United States, Canada and Europe."[162] Black philanthropy has also benefited white institutions. Reginald Lewis made a $4 million gift to Harvard.

White corporate America has also contributed to the black community, primarily in return for the profits earned from black America. Frito-Lay, which is wholly owned by PepsiCo Inc., donated $1 million for scholarships to Paul Quinn College. The company's central division president, Lloyd Ward, is a board member of the college.[163] Also, the National Football League, in which African-Americans constitute 65 percent of the players, donated $1 million to the United Negro College Fund. Fifty players contributed $10,000 each and the NFL matched that amount. In addition, foundations have been established by some black athletes to benefit the nation's youth. Doubtless such philanthropy has not been the case with the businesses established in urban black business districts by the new immigrants, despite the profits earned from black consumers.

In addition to their philanthropic activities on behalf of black charities and institutions, black businesses provide numerous benefits to the black community. As well as providing jobs, black-owned businesses are also more inclined to hire blacks without a high school education. Moreover, the larger black businesses provide in-house training and 56.3 percent of them offer tuition loans or grants to employees. Also black businesses "were more likely to have indicated a willingness to participate in programs to assist young people, welfare recipients and individuals from high poverty neighborhoods in making the transition to employment."[164] Consequently, it is not enough that black businesses increase in numbers. Black businesses must also increase in sales. Small businesses, those with fewer than 500 employees, are important for black America. In this nation, more employment is provided by small businesses than by the *Fortune* 1000 companies.

If black America is to achieve parity in business participation rates and business receipts, an aggressive strategy is needed that requires the support of all black Americans. This plan should involve the one area in which blacks do have control, the spending of their consumer dollar. Some of their spending decisions have not always benefited the black community, especially black businesses in urban black business districts.[165] Yet, withholding the black dollar, as in the successful 1956 Montgomery bus boycott, did as much as nonviolent civil disobedience to open doors of integration to black America.

Protest, demonstrations, and boycotts alone, however, will not be enough if one goal for blacks is to control their own business districts. Small black businesses need professionalization and assistance in the form of a private-sector SBA program. Professionalization means careful planning to establish businesses that can compete in providing high-quality consumer goods and services at fair market prices. Obviously, few black consumers consider it their responsibility to subsidize black businesses, an initiative that is part of black nationalist agendas. But African-Americans have shown that they will support those enterprises that provide competitive goods and services and that contribute to the community.

A large share of the black consumer dollar is spent on food. But less than 10 percent of it is spent at black-owned food stores. The establishment of the Richmond, Virginia, Community Pride Food Stores provides a model of how African-Americans in the food industry can capitalize on this sector of the economy. Community Pride, a chain of four stores, was established in 1992 by Boston College graduate Jonathan Johnson. Three years later, the company was ranked 50th on the *Black Enterprise* top 100 list, with sales of $38 million and 363 employees. In establishing this enterprise, Johnson got support from a white competitor, the Ukrop Supermarkets; and a large white-owned food distributor, Rich Foods, served as a cosigner for his $4 million loan to buy the chain.

Community Pride's success is built on providing grade-A quality food products and first-class service to its customers. The company strives to assure customer loyalty in several ways. A fleet of 14 vans is available to drive shoppers home. In cooperation with Coca-Cola and Kraft/General Foods, Community Pride established programs to recognize and reward academically outstanding students, including trips abroad for top-notch performers and a 10 percent food discount to families of other student achievers. For its employees, the company offers share ownership in the business with a plan similar to a 401(k).[166] Community Pride provides a model of black business development and success on three levels: competitive and high-quality service and products, black customer loyalty, and white corporate support leading to venture capital.

Black business expansion, however, should not be limited to producing goods and services only to a black consumer market. In 1995, most of the country's 424,165 black businesses were personal service enterprises, rather than high-tech manufacturers or suppliers.[167] How many of those businesses have been established by blacks in urban ethnic business districts? In order to be viable and profitable, small black businesses must tap both the ethnic consumer market and mainstream consumer market. With the retrenchment in federal affirmative action initiatives, the survival of black business must be maintained on all fronts.

Is now the time for another Civil Rights movement? In 1995 black corporate leaders formed a political action committee (PAC) to challenge the Republican dismantling of federal affirmative action initiatives. The charter PAC organizers represented a cross section of black corporate America in the 1990s: Earl Graves of *Black Enterprise;* Robert Johnson of BET; Don Cornwell of Granite Broadcasting; Emma Chappell of United Bank of Philadelphia; and Calvin Grigsby of Grigsby Brandford and Company. Also, heads of the Chrysler Minority Dealers Association, the Ford Minority Dealers Association, and the highest ranking black executive at General Motors, Richard Davis, participated.[168] A letter from the PAC organizers sent to the heads of black corporate America inviting their support emphasized that affirmative action, set-asides, and minority outsourcing had contributed to the expansion of black corporate America.

Federal assistance was important in contributing to the rise of black corporate America. But it was also supported with funds from private-sector, government-backed investment corporations. MESBIC, for instance, indirectly contributed to the establishment of America's first black billion-dollar corporation, which resulted from Reginald Lewis's TLC's purchase of Beatrice Foods in 1987 for $985 million: "It was a New York City MESBIC, Equico Capital Corp. that helped [Lewis-owned] TLC complete its first major deal, the $25 million buyout of McCall Pattern Co. in 1984, which TLC sold for $63 million in 1987."[169] Profits from that sale provided the basis for Lewis's leveraged buyout of Beatrice.

The Civil Rights movement for African-American equality is not complete. From before the Revolutionary War to the Civil War and from post–Reconstruction America to the post–Civil Rights period, blacks have protested against inequities in American life. And they must do so again. According to BET's Robert Johnson, the nation's largest African-American business owners must be the ones to lead the battle to save affirmative action programs, since they have the most to lose; and he emphasizes that "Everyone's had a chance but black business leaders. This will be the marriage of black business and black economic empowerment with politics."[170]

In the third wave rise of black corporate America in the post–Civil Rights period, African-American business organizations have taken an aggressive lead in attempts to promote and protect black businesses. Individual efforts by black businesspeople to improve their economic condition were accompanied by newly formed professional organizations that actively promoted their interests. On the legal front, the Minority Business Enterprise Legal Defense and Education Fund (MBELDEF) uses the courts to defend against attacks made by both government and the private sector to eliminate government support to black businesses. In the halls of Congress, the Mobilization for Economic Opportunities Political Action Committee (MEOPAC), founded in the 1990s, lobbies to promote black business interests.

Perhaps the most powerful of these groups is the National Minorities Supplier Development Council (NMSDC). By the 1990s it had secured about $20 billion annually in procurement contracts for minority businesses from the nation's megacorporations. Through its efforts, from 1993 to 1994, there was an increase of 18 percent in minority purchasing from $23.3 billion to $27.3 billion.[171] Consequently, despite racial inequities in federal affirmative assistance programs to finance black businesses, there has been a small measure of success, specifically in the improved gross receipts of some large black businesses. The expansion of the big enterprises was a result of strategic alliances not only with other black businesses but also with *Fortune* 500 and 1000 companies in securing profitable procurement contracts.

Conclusion

George Fraser emphasizes that "success runs in our race."[172] In the third-wave rise of black corporate America, African-Americans, through joint ventures, leveraged buyouts, and mergers, established, expanded, and acquired businesses that paralleled mainstream American business. African-Americans, poised at the gates of segregation and discrimination and steeped in a long and established tradition of business activity and entrepreneurship, were poised to continue in the race to succeed in this nation's free-enterprise system. Once the gates of American capitalism were opened by federal affirmative action initiatives, including SBA and MESBIC loans and *Fortune* 1000 minority procurements and outsourcing contracts, black America's Olympic-class entrepreneurs, fortified with business degrees and law degrees, raced off to meet the unique challenges facing black businesses and to establish successful and profitable enterprises. For them, Llewellyn's joint ventures and Lewis's TLC Beatrice leveraged buyouts set the pace in the third-wave rise of black corporate America.

Federal initiatives in affirmative action made a difference in changing the face and pace of black corporate America, as did access to venture capital from white corporate America. As black business moves into capital-intensive, high-tech enterprises, joint ventures with white corporations and public stock offering will become increasingly common, as subsequent generations of young blacks develop an expanded vision of black business success within the context of corporate capitalism.

While there have been numerous wealthy black entrepreneurs since before the Civil War, their number has been relatively low and their influence relatively inconsequential when compared to America's white wealth holders. In 1900, when America's first billion-dollar corporation was established, the total wealth of black America was only $700 million. In contrast, it was only in 1987 when Reginald Lewis formed TLC Beatrice International, that black America acquired its first and only billion-dollar corporation. In the third wave rise of black corporate America, leading black entrepreneurs and superstar entertainers and athletes achieved a degree of wealth that exceeds what had been acquired by black entrepreneurs in the first and second waves of black corporate America.

When one compares the growth of black corporate America since the 1970s with the few successes and numerous defeats black business experienced from 1865 to the 1970s the achievements of black American entrepreneurs in the face of segregation and discrimination are indeed remarkable. Despite the retrenchment in affirmative action programs in the post–Civil Rights period, black entrepreneurship has survived, primarily because it stands on a long tradition of self-sufficiency and self-help. And it will continue to survive in the increasingly competitive climate brought on by corporate efforts to widen America's place in the global economy.

In the final analysis for black America at the close of the century, the more things changed in the nation's economy, the more they remained the same. While the third-wave rise of black corporate America marked a turning point in black business history, economic equality for black America remains as much of an elusive dream at the end of the twentieth century as it did in the first wave of black corporate America. In the twenty-first century, human capital in business formation and expansion, then, must be supported not only by large outlays of both venture and development capital from the private sector but also a federal government supportive of black business expansion.

What the United States must do for African-Americans, specifically the small business sector, is to encourage and support its development through an escalation, rather than a retrenchment, of affirmative action initiatives. Simply put, instead of funding black America as an emerging nation entitled to limited capital aid for development, the federal government should provide black America with a most-favored-nation economic package. In the twenty-first century, during what is hoped is the fourth-wave rise of black corporate America, a major goal for America should be a full and equal inclusion of black business activity in the nation's economy.

Notes

INTRODUCTION

1. Edmund S. Morgan, "Conflict and Consensus in the American Revolution," in *Essays on the American Revolution,* eds. Stephen G. Katz and James H. Hutson (Chapel Hill: University of North Carolina Press, 1973): 289–309.

2. Charles F. Adams, ed., *The Works of John Adams, Second President of the United States* (Boston, 1950–1956), 9: 376.

3. Edward Pessen, *Riches, Class, and Power before the Civil War* (Lexington, Mass.: 1973), 34. In New York City, 1 percent of the 1845 population had wealth above $55,000, which represented 40 percent of the noncorporate wealth, totaling $85.8 million. Some 20 antebellum blacks accumulated wealth exceeding $100,000.

4. E. Franklin Frazier, *Black Bourgeoisie: The Rise of a New Middle Class* (New York: Macmillan Publishing, 1957), 53–55, 153–66, 173. Over time, Frazier's construct was misconstrued by many to suggest that black business was a myth. Rather, Frazier was quite specific in acknowledging the existence of twentieth-century black business because he also said, "The myth of Negro business thrives despite the fact that Negro businessmen can best be described as a 'lumpen-bourgeoisie.'" He acknowledges appropriation of the term to define black businessmen from C. Wright Mills, *White Collar* (New York: Oxford University Press, 1951), 28–33, who used it "to designate the multitude of white firms 'with a high death rate, which do a fraction of the total business done in their lines and engage a considerably larger proportion of people than their quota of business.'" The term *petty capitalist* also has application in describing Frazier's conceptualization of black businesspeople.

5. Frazier, *Black Bourgeoisie,* 165.

6. Nathan Glazer and Daniel Patrick Moynihan, *Beyond the Melting Pot: The Negroes, Puerto Ricans, Jews, Italians and Irish of New York City* (Cambridge: MIT Press, 1963), 30, 33.

7. Ibid., 30, 33. Also see Nathan Glazer, *Affirmative Discrimination: Ethnic Inequality and Public Policy* (New York: Basic Books, 1978).

8. Lawrence M. Friedman, "Law and the Economy: 1776–1850," in *A History of American Law* (New York: Simon and Schuster, 1973, 1985), 177–201. The "invisible hand" described by Adam Smith in his *Wealth of Nations,* 1776, applied to the market as the driving force of the economy, with laissez-faire as governmental noninterference in business, without consideration that in the American free-enterprise system, the factors of production have always included not only land, labor, capital, and management but also government. See, Alfred D. Chandler Jr., *The Visible Hand: The Managerial Revolution in American Business* (Cambridge: Harvard University Press, 1977). Also, Louis Galambos and Joseph Pratt, *The Rise of the Corporate Common Wealth: U.S. Business and Public Policy in the Twentieth Century* (New York, 1988).

9. George Fraser, *Success Runs In Our Race* (New York: William Morrow , 1994).

10. See John W. Handy, "A Theory on the Evolution of Black Business Development," in *A Different Vision: Race and Public Policy*, ed. Thomas D. Boston (London: Routledge Press, 1997), 2: 380–400.

11. Joseph Schumpeter, *The Theory of Economic Development: An Inquiry into Profits, Capital, Credit, Interest and the Business Cycle* (Cambridge: Harvard University Press, 1936), 93.

12. Reginald F. Lewis and Blair S. Walker, *"Why Should White Guys Have All the Fun?": How Reginald Lewis Created a Billion-Dollar Business Empire* (New York: John Wiley and Sons, 1995).

13. Max Rheinstein, ed., *Max Weber on Law in Economy and Society* (Cambridge: Harvard University Press, 1954), 38.

Chapter 1

1. Juliet E. K. Walker, "Trade and Markets in Precolonial West and West Central Africa: The Cultural Foundations of the African-American Business Tradition," in *A Different Vision: African American Economic Thought,* ed. Thomas D. Boston (New York: Routledge Publishers, 1996) 2:206–52.

2. Robin Law, "Slave-Raiders and Middlemen, Monopolists and Free-Traders: The Supply of Slaves for the Atlantic Trade in Dahomey c. 1715–1850," *Journal of African History* 30 (1989): 45.

3. John Barbot, *A Description of the Coasts of North and South Guinea, etc.,* in A. and J. Churchill, *Collections of Voyages and Travels* (1732), 5:420. Also see Elizabeth Donnan, *Documents Illustrative of the History of the Slave Trade to America* (Washington. D.C.: Carnegie Institution, 1930), 1:288.

4. Ray A. Kea, *Settlements, Trade, and Polities in the Seventeenth-Century Gold Coast* (Baltimore: Johns Hopkins University Press, 1982), 32–38. Kea says that the historic tradition that credits the city of Great Accra with from 40,000 to 50,000 people was exaggerated, although admittedly the city was quite populous.

5. Ibid., 40.

6. William Bosman, *A New and Accurate Description of Guinea: Divided into the Gold, the Slave, and the Ivory Coasts* (1704; reprint, London: Frank Cass and Company, 1967), 461.

7. John Adams, *Sketches Taken During Ten Voyages to Africa Between the Years 1786 and 1800; . . . Including Observations on the Country Between Cape Palmas and the River Congo* (London: Hurst, Robinson, and Company; reprint, New York: Johnson Reprint Corporation, 1970), 29. In 1775, the third largest city in America, Boston, had 16,000 people, followed by Charleston with 12,000 and Newport with 11,000. Philadelphia and New York, with respective populations of 40,000 and 25,000, were the two largest cities. One year later, after independence, the populations of America's four largest cities showed a temporary but drastic decline: Philadelphia, 21,767; New York, 5,000; Boston, 3,500; and Newport, 5,299. Charleston, with a large number of slaves, maintained its population size.

8. Lars Sundstrom, *The Exchange Economy of Pre-Colonial Tropical Africa* (Sweden, 1963; reprint, London: C. Hurst and Company, 1974), 50.

9. Kea, *Settlements, Trade, Gold Coast,* 176. Also, Sundstrom, *Exchange Economy,* 47.

10. Ibid., 251.

11. Ibid., 248.

12. Ibid., 252, 264. Also, U. I. Ukwu, "Markets in Iboland," in *Markets in West Africa: Studies of Markets and Trade among the Yoruba and Ibo,* eds., B. W. Hodder and U. I. Ukwu (New York: Africana Publishing Corporation. 1969), 132. An apprenticeship system also existed among the Awka people in Iboland in the Bight of Biafra. The Awka business culture encouraged the early training of young men as traders: "They travelled in troupes of ten to twenty adults, each of whom had with him two to four apprentices aged between five and twelve years."

13. Bosman, *Description of Guinea,* 77.

14. K. B. Dickson, "Trade Patterns in Ghana at the Beginning of the Eighteenth Century," in *An Economic History of Tropical Africa: The Pre-colonial Period,* eds. Z. A. Konczacki and J. M. Konczacki (London: Frank Cass and Company, 1977), 1:145.

15. Sundstrom, *Exchange Economy,* 47.

16. Kwame Yeboa Daaku, *Trade and Politics on the Gold Coast: 1600–1720* (London: Oxford University Press, 1970), 34.

17. Sundstrom, *Exchange Economy,* 36.

18. Ibid., 15, 47.

19. Ibid., 14–15. Also, Kwame Arhin, *West African Traders in Ghana in the Nineteenth and Twentieth Centuries* (London: Longman, 1979), 10.

20. Ibid., 60.

21. Adams, *Sketches,* 43.

22. Bosman, *Description of Guinea,* 352.

23. Robert W. July, *Precolonial Africa: An Economic and Social History* (New York: Charles Scribner's Sons, 1975), 275–79; and A. G. Hopkins, *An Economic History of West Africa* (New York: Columbia University Press, 1973), 264–65.

24. P. L. Wickens, *An Economic History of Africa from the Earliest Times to Partition* (Cape Town: Oxford University Press, 1980), 113.

25. Ibid., 124.

26. Ibid., 112.

27. Ibid., 114.

28. Jeanne K. Henn, "Women in the Rural Economy: Past, Present, and Future," in *African Women South of the Sahara,* eds., Margaret Jean Hay and Sharon Stichter (London: Longman Group Limited, 1984), 5.

29. Hopkins, *Economic History,* 25.

30. Sundstrom, *Exchange Economy,* 127.

31. Daaku, *Trade and Politics,* 50.

32. Loren Schweninger, *Black Property Owners in the South, 1790-1915* (Urbana: University of Illinois Press, 1990), 10.

33. Also see Wickins, *Economic History,* 47–51.

34. Ibid., 48.

35. Basil Davidson, with F. K. Buah, the advice of J. F. Ade Ajayi, *History of West Africa to the Nineteenth Century* (New York: Anchor Books, 1966), 151.

36. Henn, "Women in the Rural Economy," 2.

37. Bosman, *Description of Guinea,* 473.

38. Patrick Manning, *Slavery, Colonialism and Economic Growth in Dahomey* (Cambridge: Cambridge University Press, 1982), 71.

39. July, *Precolonial Africa,* 109

40. Adams, *Sketches,* 54.

41. Bosman, *Description of Guinea,* 140.

42. Manning, *Slavery,* 65.

43. Elliott P. Skinner, "West African Economic Systems," in *Peoples and Cultures of Africa: An Anthropological Reader,* ed. Elliott P. Skinner (Garden City, N.Y.: Doubleday/Natural History Press, 1973), 209–10.

44. S. F. Nadel, *A Black Byzantium* (London: Oxford University Press, 1942), 248.

45. July, *Precolonial Africa,* 102–3.

46. Bosman, *Description of Guinea,* 459.

47. Ibid., 441.

48. Joseph Hawkins, *A History of a Voyage to the Coast of Africa, and Travels into the Interior of that Country; Containing description ... concerning the Slave Trade* (Philadelphia: S. Custik and Company, 1797; reprint, Northbrook, Ill.,: Metro Books, Inc., 1972), 130.

49. Sundstrom, *Exchange Economy,* 148–49.

50. Bosman, *Description of Guinea,* 342.

51. Ibid., 459.

52. Mungo Park, *Travels in the Interior Districts of Africa: Performed in the Years 1795, 1796, and 1797* (London: William Bulmer and Company, 1816) I:11, 275.

53. Sundstrom, *Exchange Economy,* 147–86 for discussion on textile manufacturing.

54. Kea, *Settlements, Trade, Gold Coast*, 220–21.

55. Raymond Mauny, "Essay on the History of Metals in West Africa," in Konczacki and Konczacki, *Economic History*, 1:88–99. Also see Sundstrom, *Exchange Economy*, 122–46, 187–216, 217–51.

56. July, *Precolonial Africa*, 192.

57. Kea, *Settlements, Trade, Gold Coast*, 204.

58. Ibid., 197, 203, 204.

59. Wickins, *Economic History*, 77. For copper, see Sundstrom, *Exchange Economy*, 217.

60. Bosman, *Description of Guinea*, 43, 130, 277–81.

61. Manning, *Slavery*, 71–72, Also, the use of dropped nets was another method to catch fish by two-man canoes that encircled the area.

62. Ibid., 87–88.

63. Bosman, *Description of Guinea*, 80–81.

64. Henn, "Women in the Rural Economy," 7–9.

65. Bosman, *Description of Guinea*, 238, 342, 459.

66. Also, Manning, *Slavery*, 72.

67. Bosman, *Description of Guinea*, 225.

68. July, *Precolonial Africa*, 192.

69. Sundstrom, *Exchange Economy*, 10, 13, 35, 133, respectively for sales tax, death tax, and medieval European road tolls.

70. Ibid., 66: "handing over one commodity directly for another, either according to established rates or by on-the-spot bargaining."

71. Skinner, "West African Economic Systems," 217, 223. The people in the coastal regions of the Gold Coast refused to accept or to use cowries.

72. Visconde de Paiva-Manso, *Historia do Congo* (Lisbon, 1877), 137; also in *The African Past: Chronicles from Antiquity to Modern Times*, ed. Basil Davidson (Boston: Little, Brown, 1964), 194.

73. Richard Hakluyt, *The Principal Navigations, Voyages, Traffiques and Discoveries of the English Nation (1598–1600)*, 6:145; also in Davidson, *African Past*, 197.

74. Sundstrom, *Exchange Economy*, 208.

75. Ibid., 227–28.

76. Ibid., 129, 167.

77. Ibid., 133, 164–78, on geographic differences in precolonial West and West Central African salt and textile exchange rates.

78. Ibid., 13.

79. Bosman, *Description of Guinea*, 460.

80. Ibid., 435.

81. Sundstrom, *Exchange Economy*, 5.

82. Bosman, *Description of Guinea*, 342.

83. Ivor Wilks, *Asante in the Nineteenth Century: The Structure and Evolution of a Political Order* (Cambridge: Cambridge University Press, 1975), 445.

84. Ibid., 430.

85. Bosman, *Description of Guinea*, 434.

86. Ibid., 433.

87. Adams, *Sketches*, 118.

88. Hopkins, *Economic History*, 110.

89. Sundstrom, *Exchange Economy*, 21. Also see Sundiata A. Djata, *The Bamana Empire By The Niger: Kingdom, Jihad and Colonization, 1712–1920* (Princeton, N.J.: Markus Wiener, 1997). Also, Gwendolyn Midlo Hall, *Africans in Colonial Louisiana: The Development of Afro-Creole Culture in the Eighteenth Century* (Baton Rouge: Louisiana State University Press, 1992), 96–118, on the Bambara in Louisiana.

90. Hawkins, *Voyage to the Coast*, 112.

91. Sundstrom, *Exchange Economy*, 254.

92. Phyllis M. Martin, *The External Trade of the Loango Coast, 1576–1870: The Effects of Changing Commercial Relations on the Vili Kingdom of Loango* (Oxford: Clarendon Press, 1972), 167.

93. Adams, *Sketches,* 38–39.

94. C. Duncan Rice, *The Rise and Fall of Black Slavery* (New York: Harper and Row, 1975), 112.

95. Adams, *Sketches,* 38.

96. Robin Law, "Slave-Raiders," 45. Also, Paul E. Lovejoy, *Transformations in Slavery: A History of Slavery in Africa* (Cambridge: Cambridge University Press, 1983), 107.

97. Hawkins, *Voyage to the Coast,* 13–14, 84.

98. Bosman, *Description of Guinea,* 184.

99. Law, "Slave-Raiders," 45.

100. See discussion on African preferences in the next section, (22–24).

101. See Walker, "Trade and Markets," 231–37.

102. Donnan, *Documents Illustrative of Slave Trade,* 1:1.

103. On Arab slavery, see Ralph A. Austen, "The Trans-Saharan Slave Trade: A Tentative Thesis," in *The Uncommon Market: Essays in the Economic History of the Atlantic Slave Trade,* eds. H. A. Gemery and J. S. Hogendorn (New York: Academic Press, 1974), 23–76. Also, Bernard Lewis, "The African Diaspora and the Civilization of Islam," in *The African Diaspora: Interpretative Essays,* eds. Martin L. Kilson and Robert I. Rothberg (Cambridge, Mass.: Harvard University Press, 1976), 19; Allan G. B. Fisher and Humphrey J. Fisher, *Slavery and Muslim Society in Africa: The Institution in Saharan and Sudanic Africa and the Trans-Saharan Trade* (Garden City, N.Y.: Doubleday, 1971).

104. Allan D. Austin, *American Muslims in Antebellum America* (New York: Garland Publishing, 1984). Also Maurice Lombard, *The Golden Age of Islam,* trans. Joan Spencer (Amsterdam, 1975); Reuben Levy, *The Social Structure of Islam* (2d ed. of *The Sociology of Islam*) (Cambridge: Cambridge University Press, 1965); Graham W. Irwin, *Africans Abroad: A Documentary Survey of the Black Diaspora in Asia, Latin America, and the Caribbean during the Age of Slavery* (New York: Columbia University Press, 1977).

105. Hopkins, *Economic History,* 85. Ralph A. Austen, "The Uncomfortable Relationship: African Enslavement in the Common History of Blacks and Jews," *Tikkun: A Bimonthly Jewish Critique of Politics, Culture and Society* 9 (March/April 1994): 86, said: "We Jews, even liberal ones, who justifiably insist that the history of the Nazi Holocaust not be denied, can hardly urge African Americans to suppress the record of the slave trade and the involvement of our own ancestors in it."

106. See Alfred W. Crosby, *The Columbian Exchange: Biological and Cultural Consequences of 1492* (Westport, Conn.: Greenwood Press, 1972); and Philip Curtin, "Epidemiology and the Slave Trade," *Political Science Quarterly* 83 (1968): 190–216. Also, Kirkpatrick Sale, *The Conquest of Paradise* (New York: Knopf, 1991), a revisionist account of Columbus's voyage and its effects on the New World; and "Who Didn't Discover America," *Newsweek,* 22 April 1992, 59, "The National Council of Churches has declared that what some historians have termed a 'discovery' was in reality an invasion and colonization with legalized occupation, genocide, economic exploitation, and a deep level of institutional racism and moral decadence." Also, Eric Williams, *From Columbus to Castro* (New York: Harper and Row, 1970).

107. Philip D. Curtin, *The Atlantic Slave Trade: A Census* (Madison: University of Wisconsin Press, 1969). On the demography of the African slave trade, see Paul E. Lovejoy, "The Volume of the Atlantic Slave Trade: A Synthesis," *Journal of African History* 23 (1982): 473–501.

108. Paul E. Lovejoy, "The Impact of the Atlantic Slave Trade on Africa: A Review of the Literature," *Journal of African History* 30 (1989): 363–73. Also, Walter Rodney, *How Europe Underdeveloped Africa* (Washington, D.C.: Howard University Press, 1974); W. E. B. DuBois, *The Suppression of the African Slave Trade to the United States of America, 1638–1870,* Harvard Historical Studies, no. 1 (New York: Longman, Green, 1896).

109. Patrick S. Manning, "The Impact of Slave Trade Exports on the Population of the Western Coast of Africa, 1700–1850," in *De la traite á l'esclavage,* ed. Serge Daget (Paris/Nantes, 1988), 111–134.

110. Patrick S. Manning, *Slavery and African Life; Occidental, Oriental, and African Slave Trade* (Cambridge: Cambridge University Press, 1990), 84–85.

111. John Smith, *Travels of John Smith,* eds. Edward Arber and A. G. Bradley (Edinburgh: Grant, 1910), 2:541. Also see Susan Myra Kingsbury, ed., *The Records of the Virginia Company of London* (Washington, D.C.: U.S. Government Printing Office, 1933), 3:243.

112. On the initial status of the first Africans in colonial America and the origin of slavery in the 13 colonies, see A. Leon Higginbotham Jr., *In the Matter of Color: Race and the American Legal Process: The Colonial Period* (New York: Oxford University Press, 1978); David Brion Davis, *The Problem of Slavery in Western Culture* (Ithaca, N.Y.: Cornell University Press, 1975); Winthrop Jordan, *White over Black: American Attitudes towards the Negro, 1550–1812* (Chapel Hill: University of North Carolina Press, 1968), 44–98. Oscar and Mary Handlin, "Origins of the Southern Labor System," *William and Mary Quarterly* 7 (1950): 199–222.

113. Abbott Emerson Smith, *Colonists in Bondage: White Servitude and Convict Labor in America, 1607–1776* (Chapel Hill: University of North Carolina Press, 1947), 171.

114. William W. Hening, *Statutes at Large of Virginia* (Richmond: Franklin Press, 1819–1820), 1:226. Even before blacks became a numerically significant group, one of the first legislative acts passed in Virginia, in 1639, only 20 years after the arrival of the first blacks, stipulated that: "All persons except Negroes are to be provided with arms and ammunition or be fined at the pleasure of the governor and council." In 1640, there were only 150 blacks in Virginia and not all were slaves.

115. E. B. O'Callaghan, ed., *Voyages of the Slavers "St. John" and "Arms of Amsterdam," 1659, 1663,* New York Colonial Tracts, no. 111 (Albany, N.Y.: J. Munsell, 1977), xiii.

116. Massachusetts Historical Society *Collections,* 36, 65. Also see "Emanuel Downing to John Winthrop, 1645," in Donnan, *Documents Illustrative of Slave Trade,* 3:8.

117. John Winthrop, *Winthrop's Journal: History of New England, 1634–1649,* ed. James K. Hosmer (New York , 1908), 1:260.

118. Jordan, *White over Black,* 111, where he emphasizes that "[e]very planter knew that the fundamental purpose of the slave laws was prevention and deterrence of slave insurrection."

119. Roi Ottley and William J. Weatherby, eds., *The Negro in New York: An Informal Social History, 1626–1940* (New York: Praeger, 1967), 3.

120. Lorenzo Greene, *The Negro in Colonial New England* (New York: Columbia University Press, 1942), 36–37.

121. Ibid., 36.

122. John Thornton, *Africa and Africans in the Making of the Atlantic World, 1400–1680* (Cambridge: Cambridge University Press, 1992), 135.

123. Peter H. Wood, *Black Majority: Negroes in Colonial South Carolina from 1670 through the Stono Rebellion* (New York: W. W. Norton, 1974), 30–31; and Daniel H. Usner, *Indians, Settlers, and Slaves in a Frontier Exchange Economy* (Chapel Hill: University of North Carolina Press, 1992), 185.

124. Charles Joyner, *Down by the Riverside: A South Carolina Slave Community* (Urbana: University of Illinois Press, 1984), 14.

125. Usner, *Indians, Settlers, and Slaves,* 206–7. Portuguese slave traders brought this grain to West Africa in the sixteenth century. Usner adds that "American corn served as a major food source for the slave trade and quickly entered the cuisine of some societies in present-day Nigeria and Dahomey."

126. William D. Piersen, *Black Yankees: The Development of an Afro-American Subculture in Eighteenth-Century New England* (Amherst: University of Massachusetts Press, 1988), 96–98.

127. Joseph E. Holloway, *Africanisms in American Culture* (Bloomington: Indiana University Press, 1990), 11–16.

128. Ibid.

129. Klaus G. Loewald et al., trans. and eds., "Johann Martin Bolzius Answers a Questionnaire on Carolina and Georgia," *William and Mary Quarterly,* 3d ser., 14 (1975): 259, in Philip D. Morgan, "Work and Culture: The Task System and the World of Low Country Blacks, 1700–1880," *William and Mary Quarterly* 39 (October 1982): 566.

130. Scotus Americanus [pseud.], *Information Concerning the Province of North Carolina, Addressed to Emigrants from the Highlands and Western Isles of Scotland* (Glasgow, 1773), in Morgan, "Work and Culture," 579.

131. Usner, *Indians, Settlers, and Slaves,* 161, 164.

132. Ibid., 43.

133. Evangeline Walker Andrews and Charles McLean Andrews, eds., *Journal of a Lady of Quality* (New Haven: Yale University Press,1923), 176–77, in Morgan, "Work and Culture," 574.

134. Eugene Genovese, *Roll Jordan Roll: The World the Slaves Made* (New York: Vintage, 1972), 539. Also, Sidney Mintz and Douglas Hall, "The Origins of the Jamaican Internal Marketing System," *Yale University Publications in Anthropology* 57 (1960): 15. In their study of the provision ground system and the development of the internal economy in Jamaica, Mintz and Hall seemingly also take the position of Genovese: that food production and marketing activities under the provision ground system provided opportunities for developing skills new and unique to Africans. In their assessment of the Jamaican provision ground system and the marketing and trading activities of slaves in the Caribbean, they state that these economic activities represented a " 'radical breach' in the slave mode of production" since work was performed without supervision, thus transforming a gang slave into a "proto-peasant."

135. Manning, *Slavery,* 73.

136. Usner, *Indians, Settlers, and Slaves,* 161, 164.

137. See Ball Family Account Book, 174, 32, and memorandum of 21 January 1736, South Carolina Historical Society, Charleston; Administration of James Harley's estate, August 1758–July 1760, Inventory Book V, 160–75, South Carolina Archives, Columbia; Henry Ravenel's Day Book, 1763–1767, South Carolina Historical Society, Charleston, in Morgan, "Work and Culture," 572.

138. Usner, *Indians, Settlers, and Slaves,* 161, 164; and Ottley and Weatherby, *Negro in New York*, 25.

139. Piersen, *Black Yankee,* 154.

140. Charles Ball, *Slavery in the United States: A Narrative of the Life and Adventures of Charles Ball [1780—?], A Black Man* (New York, 1837), 194.

141. Benjamin Henry Boneval Latrobe, *Impressions Respecting New Orleans: Diary and Sketches, 1764–1820,* ed. Samuel Wilson Jr. (New York: Columbia University Press, 1951), 21–22.

142. Michael Mullin, *Africa in America: Slave Acculturation and Resistance in the American South and the British Caribbean* (Urbana: University of Illinois Press, 1992), 152–54. Mullin views slave provision ground activities in colonial America insignificant compared to those in the Caribbean. He acknowledges, however, that the underground slave economy in marketing and trading, primarily with pillaged goods and solidly in the hands of men "who were often house servants," was much more extensive than in the Caribbean. The white-consumer market for these goods in the colonial American South was much more expansive than that in the islands.

143. Usner, *Indians, Settlers, and Slaves,* 186.

144. Robert William Fogel, *Without Consent or Contract: The Rise and Fall of American Slavery* (New York: W. W. Norton, 1989).

145. Usner, *Indians, Settlers, and Slaves,* 161, 164.

146. Edgar J. McManus, *Black Bondage in the North* (Syracuse, N.Y.: Syracuse University Press, 1973), 64.

147. Ibid., 63.

148. Ibid.

149. William Read to Jacob Read, 22 March 1800, Read Family Papers, South Carolina Historical Society, Charleston, in Morgan, "Work and Culture," 581.

150. T. H. Breen and Stephen Innes, *"Myne Owne Ground": Race and Freedom on Virginia's Eastern Shore, 1640—1676* (New York: Oxford University Press, 1980), 73–75.

151. Ibid., 74.

152. Edmund S. Morgan, *American Slavery, American Freedom: The Ordeal of Colonial Virginia* (New York: W. W. Norton, 1975), 313.

153. Piersen, *Black Yankees,* 7.

154. Mechal Sobel, *Trabelin' On: The Slave Journey to an Afro-Baptist Faith* (Westport, Conn.: Greenwood, 1979), xxi.

CHAPTER 2

1. Winthrop Jordan, "American Chiaroscuro: The Status and Definition of Mulattoes in the British Colonies," *William and Mary Quarterly*, 3d ser., 19 (April 1962): 183–200.

2. See Higginbotham, *Matter of Color*, 40–47, for a discussion of Virginia laws from the perspective of "White Male Domination and Inter-racial Sexual Relations."

3. McManus, *Black Bondage*, 64, 67, notes, "The growth of a racially mixed population caused much alarm for it threatened and confused the premises of the white hegemony.... [which explains why] Every colony had laws to guarantee white supremacy." Also, Jordan, "American Chiaroscuro," 186–87. In English colonial America, Jordan found only one instance where statutory law distinguished Africans from mulattoes. Even then, the law was never enforced. In 1765 Georgia, vulnerable because of its weak strategic position north of Spanish Florida, with a small white population also threatened by Indians and a large slave population, enacted a law to encourage the migration of mulattoes and mustees. Limited citizenship was promised, but without the vote or the right to sit in the Commons House of Assembly.

4. Helen T. Catterall, *Judicial Cases Concerning American Slavery and the Negro* (Washington, D.C.: Carnegie Institution, 1932), 1: 58, n. 37.

5. Ottley and Weatherby, *Negro in New York*, 12.

6. Ibid., 4 and 17. A conditional grant of land in that same area was made by Judith Stuyvesant to African Francisco Bastiaenz, who was "bound, with his neighbors, to keep in repair the fence of said land."

7. Greene, *Negro in New England*, 290.

8. Robert C. Twombly and Robert H. Moore, "Black Puritan: The Negro in Seventeenth-Century Massachusetts," *William and Mary Quarterly* 24 (April 1967): 224–43, nn. 23–26.

9. Breen and Innes, *"Myne Owne Ground,"* 11.

10. James H. Brewer, "Negro Property Owners in Seventeenth-Century Virginia," *William and Mary Quarterly*, 3d ser., 12 (October 1955): 576–77. The Johnson land was located on the banks of the Pungoteague River on the Eastern Shore. Colonial property deed records in Virginia also show that 10 free African men and 3 free African women also secured land. In 1656, Benjamin Doyle, of Surrey County, was granted 300 acres under the head-rights system for transporting six persons into the colony. In 1667, Emanuel Cambew of James City County was granted 50 acres of land in York County for importing one servant.

11. Breen and Innes, *"Myne Owne Ground,"* 79–80.

12. Ibid., 107–08.

13. Ibid., 90. In protecting their property, the African landholders made use of the courts and also made wills to protect their family's right in their property holdings: "Northampton's free blacks were astute students of the local legal process."

14. Juliet E. K. Walker, *Free Frank: A Black Pioneer on the Antebellum Frontier* (Lexington: University Press of Kentucky, 1983), 195–96, n. 77.

15. Greene, *Negro in New England*, 310.

16. E. Franklin Frazier, *The Negro Family in the United States* (Chicago: University of Chicago Press, 1939), 221–26, 231–34. As a "racial island," Gouldtown provides an example of one of the first distinct concentrations of blacks outside urban areas. Unlike some racial islands founded in the nineteenth century where the inhabitants denied their African ancestry, the Gouldtown community placed itself in the African-American experience.

17. Lerone Bennett Jr., *The Shaping of Black America* (Chicago: Johnson Publishing Company, 1975), 100–101.

18. Thomas A. Meehan, "Jean Baptiste Point Du Sable, The First Chicagoan," *Journal of the Illinois State Historical Society* 56 (Autumn 1963): 439–53. Only in the mid-twentieth century was official recognition given to DuSable for establishing the first permanent settlement at the site of Chicago.

19. Walker, *Free Frank*, 54–59, 93–97.

20. Carter G. Woodson, *The Negro in Our History* (Washington, D.C.: Associated Press, 1962), 39; Frazier, *Negro Family*, 310–11.

21. Also see Carter G. Woodson, *Free Negro Owners of Slaves in the United States in 1830* (Washington, D.C.: Association for the Study of Negro Life and History, 1924. Woodson's thesis has been challenged. See R. Halliburton Jr., "Free Black Owners of Slaves: A Reappraisal of the Woodson Thesis," *South Carolina Historical Magazine* 76 (July 1975): 129–35.

22. Larry Koger, *Black Slaveowners: Free Black Slave Masters in South Carolina, 1790–1860* (Jefferson, N.C.: McFarland and Company, 1985), 101, says that, based on extensive research of slave bills of sale, bills of complaint, marriage settlements, tax books, and wills, "Clearly, the dominant pattern of the commercial use of slaves recorded in these documents indicates that black slaveholding was primarily an institution based on the exploitation of slaves rather than a benevolent system centered upon kinship or humanitarianism."

23. Calvin D. Wilson, "Negroes Who Owned Slaves," *Popular Science Monthly* 81 (November 1912): 484, says: "Moreover, there were in his country tribal differences and antagonism which continued to obtain in America; the 'Guinea nigger' was looked down on by members of superior tribes, and one of a higher race often felt that a Guinea negro was fit only to serve him." Also, Philip J. Schwarz, "Emancipators, Protectors, and Anomalies: Free Black Slaveowners in Virginia," *The Virginia Magazine of History and Biography* 95 (July 1987): 336, notes that "the fraternal form of slaveholding by free blacks in Virginia, a widespread variety of all such ownership, had a few features in common with domestic slavery in some West African tribes, although it was hardly the same thing." Piersen, *Black Yankees*, 93, in his discussion of African retentions in the formation of black families in colonial New England notes that, when free black men purchased their wives from slavery, which was a form of benevolent slave ownership, the practice "may not have seemed particularly alien to Africans acquainted with the custom of making substantial bridewealth payments as part of the bonds of marriage."

24. Breen and Innes, *"Myne Owne Ground,"* 18. Interestingly, the son of Anthony Johnson, who was born in colonial Virginia, named his 44-acre homestead in Somerset, Maryland, established in the 1670s, Angola. Breen and Innes say that his "action, admittedly a small shred of evidence, suggests the existence of a deeply rooted separate culture." The father was one of the first Africans brought to colonial America in 1621.

25. Hening, *Statutes of Virginia*, 2:280.

26. Higginbotham, *Matter of Color*, 202–4.

27. Koger, *Black Slaveowners*, 12–14. Pendarvis had a white wife. Their two daughters married into the white planter class.

28. Ibid., 141–42.

29. Mary Allison Carll-White, "The Role of the Black Artisan in the Building Trades and the Decorative Arts in South Carolina's Charleston District, 1760—1800," (PhD. diss., University of Tennessee, 1982), 67–69. A combination of factors, both economic and social, determined the rate at which a slave was hired, including skill level, the occupation's danger in conjunction with the percentage of the slave's market value, and maintenance costs. General economic factors of supply and demand and the state of the economy also influenced hire rates. Koger, *Black Slaveowners*, 141–42.

30. Twombly and Moore, "Black Puritan," 125; and Greene, *Negro in New England*, 293. There were also colonial free black craftsmen who achieved some distinction because of the quality of their work and the prominence of their customers or clients. Jim Riggs of Framingham, Massachusetts, was a "jobber and basket maker" and his patrons were the leading families of that town; Cato Hanker, also from Framingham, "worked as a shoe-maker, after his liberation."

31. Usner, *Indians, Settlers, and Slaves*, 56; Marcus Wilson Jernegan, *Laboring and Dependent Classes in Colonial America, 1607–1783* (Chicago: University of Chicago Press, 1931), 11–13; Robert E. Perdue, *Black Laborers and Black Professionals in Early America, 1750–1830* (New York: Vantage Press, 1975); and Whittington B. Johnson, *The Promising Years, 1750–1830: The Emergence of Black Labor and Business* (New York: Garland Publishing, 1993).

32. Carll, "Role of the Black Artisans," 41–43.

33. *Bowen's Virginia Gazette and the Winchester Sentinel*, 25 November 1796, p. 4, col. 4, in John Michael Vlach, *The Afro-American Tradition in Decorative Arts* (Cleveland: Cleveland Museum of Art, 1978), 43.

34. Carll, "Role of the Black Artisans," 61–62.

35. Carl Bridenbaugh, *The Colonial Craftsman* (New York: Dover, 1990), 118, 126–28.

36. *City-Gazette and Daily Advertiser*, 9 January 1797; also Koger, *Black Slaveowners*, 116, 167.

37. Carll, "Role of the Black Artisans," 78–82, 189.

38. Bridenbaugh, *Colonial Craftsman*, 121.

39. Ibid., 167–69, 176.

40. Ibid., 139.

41. Ibid., 176.

42. Daniel Horsemanden, *The New York Conspiracy or a History of the Negro Plot* (New York, 1810).

43. *Boston Gazette and the Country Journal*, 18 June 1792. Also see Herbert Aptheker, *American Negro Slave Revolts* (New York: International Publishers, 1943), 211. According to a newspaper account, the leader, a slave named Caleb, was a "favorite servant of his master and had long lived with him in the capacity of overseer."

44. Amos Fortune Papers, Jaffrey Public Library, Jaffrey Center, New Hampshire.

45. Gary Nash, *Forging Freedom: The Formation of Philadelphia's Black Community, 1720–1840* (Cambridge, Mass.: Harvard University Press, 1988), 75.

46. Carl Bridenbaugh, *Cities in Revolt: Urban Life in America, 1743–1776* (New York: Knopf, 1955), 358.

47. Greene, *Negro in New England*, 307–8; Bennett, *Shaping of Black America*, 288. So important did this enterprise become in the social life of the town that Weeden, a historian of Rhode Island, calls it "a way mark of civilization."

48. Greene, *Negro in New England*, 308, 310, notes: "Baroon's establishment served as a model for other Negro caterers who, before the Civil War, entered the business in such northern cities as Newport, New York and Philadelphia." At his death in 1769, he left a house and lot and personal property valued at 539 pounds.

49. Ibid., 307.

50. "An Account Given by Mrs. A. Bustill Smith," in Tinsley L. Spraggins, "The History of Negro Business Prior to 1860" (master's thesis, Howard University, 1936), 5; also Nash, *Forging Freedom*, 204.

51. Ottley and Weatherby, *Negro in New York*, 36–37. Also, Bridenbaugh, *Cities in Revolt*, 158. In his discussion of "first class public houses" which "took pride in the quality and variety of their food and wines," Bridenbaugh notes that "Samuel Francis of the Mason's Arms won fame for his culinary offerings."

52. Bridenbaugh, *Cities in Revolt*, 360.

53. James Weldon Johnson, *Black Manhattan* (New York: Atheneum, 1972; orig. pub., 1930), 44; and Philip S. Foner, *History of Black Americans: From Africa to the Emergence of the Cotton Kingdom* (Westport, Conn.: Greenwood Press, 1975), 544.

54. Ottley and Weatherby, *Negro in New York*, 37. Spraggins, "History of Negro Business," 5, notes that Fraunces "received a vote of thanks from Congress and a gratuity of two hundred pounds 'in consequence of his generous advances and kindness to American prisoners and secret services.'"

55. Spraggins, "History of Negro Business," 5, Appendix A-2.

56. Foner, *History of Black Americans*, 544.

57. Greene, *Negro in New England*, 306; and Bridenbaugh, *Colonial Craftsman*, 67, 111, 145.

58. [Hannah F. S. Lee], *Memoir of Pierre Toussaint* (Boston, Crosby, Nichols and Company, 1854), 34.

59. Henry Binsse, "Pierre Toussaint, a Catholic Uncle Tom," *Historical Records and Studies* 12 (1918) ; while he gave generously, they claim, his charitable contributions were primarily made to whites. Also, Ottley and Weatherby, *Negro in New York*, 65–67.

60. Twombly and Moore, "Black Puritan," 125.

61. Piersen, *Black Yankees*, 80–83.

62. Greene, *Negro in New England*, 306.

63. Piersen, *Black Yankees*, 84.

64. Ibid., 98.

65. Cotton Mather, *The Angel of Bethesda*, as quoted in George Lyman Kittredge, *Some Lost Works of Cotton Mather* (Cambridge: John Wilson and Son, 1912), 431, in Piersen, *Black Yankees*, 40.

66. Foner, *History of Black Americans*, 535–36.

67. Letter from Banneker to Secretary of State; Jefferson to Banneker, 30 August 1791, *Works of Thomas Jefferson*, ed., Worthington Ford (New York: G. P. Putnam Sons, 1904), 6: 309–10.

68. Greene, *Negro in New England*, 242, 294, 306; Piersen, *Black Yankees*, 45–46; and Eileen Southern, *The Music of Black Americans: A History*, 2nd. ed. (New York: W. W. Norton, 1983), 26–27, 44, 64–65, 80–81.

69. *Boston Newsletter,* 7 January 1773.

70. Foner, *History of Black Americans*, 536.

71. Johann D. Schoef, *Travels in the Confederation, 1783–1784*, tr. and ed. by Alfred J. Morrison (Philadelphia: W. J. Campbell, 1911), 2: 221. Also see Leonard Price Stavisky, "Negro Craftsmanship in Early America," *American Historical Review* 54 (January 1949): 315.

72. Greene, *Negro in New England*, 306; George Washington Williams, *History of the Negro Race in America 1619—1880* (New York: G. P. Putnam's Sons, 1883), 200.

73. *Connecticut Courant*, 19 October 1795, in Piersen, *Black Yankees,* 34.

74. William Grimes, *The Life of William Grimes* (New Haven, 1855), 73–82.

75. Mullin, *Africa in America,* 152.

76. J. B. Brissot de Warville, *New Travels in the United States of America, 1788* (Cambridge: Belknap Press of Harvard University, 1964), 1: 239.

77. See T. H. Breen, "Back to Sweat and Toil: Suggestions for the Study of Agricultural Work in Early America," *Pennsylvania History,* 49 (1982): 241–58. Breen rejects the position of James Henretta, "Families and Farms: *Mentalite'* in Pre-Industrial America," *William and Mary Quarterly,* 3d ser., 35 (1978): 3–32, that "an ethic of anti-acquisitiveness, mutuality, and reciprocity as the dominant values of most early Americans." In Innes, "Work and Labor," 11.

78. Edwin J. Perkins and Gary M. Walton, *A Prosperous People: The Growth of the American Economy* (Englewood Cliffs, N.J.: Prentice-Hall, 1985), 24.

79. Joseph C. Pusateri, *A History of American Business* (Arlington Heights, Ill.: Harlan Davidson, 1984), 47. Also see Bernard Bailyn, *The New England Merchants in the Seventeenth Century* (New York: Harper and Row, 1964), 100, who notes, "The all-purpose merchant of the port cities was the central figure in colonial commerce."

80. Perkins and Walton, *Prosperous People*, 18–55.

81. James Rawley, *The Transatlantic Slave Trade: A History* (New York: W. W. Norton, 1981), 363.

82. Bailyn, *New England Merchants*, 135, on merchant family intermarriages.

83. Perkins and Walton, *Prosperous People,* 12. Also see Alice Hanson Jones, *American Colonial Wealth: Documents and Methods* (New York: Arno Press, 1977), 3: 2165–67. Even by the Civil War, family ties persisted as the basis for the accumulation of wealth of the South Carolina rice planters. See Joyner, *Riverside*, 34, who said that in 1860, 29 of the 88 slaveholders in the United States with more than 300 slaves were rice planters, "held together by blood as well as by class . . . [and] were related to one another, with kinship alliances branching out to include politically and socially prominent families elsewhere in the states as well as in England and Scotland."

84. Greene, *Negro in New England*, 28–31.

85. Joseph R. Frese, S. J., and Jacob Judd, eds., *Business Enterprise in Early New York* (Tarrytown, N.Y.: Sleepy Hollow Press and Rockefeller Archive Center, 1979), v; and Perkins and Walton, *A Prosperous People,* 18–55.

CHAPTER 3

1. Buffalo Forge Negro Book, 1850–58; John A. Rex to J. D. Davidson, 25 February 1855, James D. Davidson Papers, McCormick Collection, State Historical Society of Wisconsin, Madison, Wisconsin. Rex was the nephew of the mill owner, William Weaver. See Charles B. Dew, "Disciplining Slave Ironworkers in the Antebellum South," *American Historical Review* 2 (April 1974): 393–418.

2. Greene, *Negro in New England*, 115–18.

3. *South Carolina Gazette*, 31 October 1774.

4. *South Carolina Gazette and Public Advertiser*, 21 May 1785.

5. *Charleston Mercury*, 26 December 1853.

6. Foner, *History of Black Americans*, 543. Also document entitled, "Outline of the Life of Christopher McPherson, as well as can be recollected." Richmond City Legislative Petition, 10 December 1810, Virginia State Library, Richmond; D. Berkeley Jr., "Christopher McPherson, Free Person of Color," *The Virginia Magazine of History and Biography* 77 (April 1969): 181, which quotes McPherson as saying that at one time he was the "Principal Storekeeper whilst 8 to 10 white Gentlemen were under my directions."

7. John Hebron Moore, "Simon Gray Riverman: A slave Who Was Almost Free," *Mississippi Valley Historical Review* 49 (December 1962): 472–84.

8. Frederick Law Olmsted, *The Cotton Kingdom: A Traveller's Observations on Cotton and Slavery in the American Slave States* (New York: Mason Brothers, 1861), 194.

9. Ibid., 69–70.

10. Robert S. Starobin, *Industrial Slavery in the Old South* (New York: Oxford University Press, 1970), 170.

11. Juliet E. K. Walker, "Entrepreneurs, Slave," in *Dictionary of Afro-American Slavery*, eds. Randall M. Miller and John David Smith (Westport, Conn.: Greenwood Press, 1988), 222.

12. Juliet E. K. Walker, "Racism, Slavery, Free Enterprise: Black Entrepreneurship in Antebellum America," *Business History Review* 60 (Autumn 1986): 343–82.

13. Ibid., 353-54.

14. Gowrie Record Book, Hawkins Family Papers, Southern Historical Collection, University of North Carolina; Jemison Letterbooks, 1844–46, Robert Jemison Jr. Papers, University of Alabama; *Journals of the Alabama House and Senate, 1845–46 Session*, in Starobin, *Industrial Slavery*, 30, 107–8, 171–72; also, John N. Ingham and Lynne B. Feldman, *African-American Business Leaders: A Biographical Dictionary* (Westport, Conn: Greenwood Press, 1994), 402–9.

15. James E. Newton, "Slave Artisans and Craftsmen: The Roots of Afro-American Art," in *The Other Slaves: Mechanics, Artisans and Craftsmen*, eds. James E. Newton and Ronald L. Lewis (Boston: G. K. Hall, 1978), 238. Also see Richard K. Dozier, "Black Architects and Craftsmen," *Black World* (May 1974): 5–7. Notable examples of slave architectural style in construction dating from the eighteenth century include not only southern mansions such as Monticello, the home of Thomas Jefferson, but also the Virginia State Capitol Building and the neo-Gothic Chapel of the Cross at Chapel Hill, North Carolina.

16. Kathleen Bruce, "Slave Labor in the Virginia Iron Industry," *William and Mary Quarterly*, ser. 2, vol. 7 (January 1927): 21–23.

17. *Wright v Wright*, Catterall, *Judicial Cases*, 302. [Kentucky, 1822].

18. Edward Shippen to the Reverend George Craig, 13 July 1778, Edward Shippen Letterbooks, Library of the American Philosophical Society, in Jerome H. Wood Jr., "The Negro in Early Pennsylvania: The Lancaster Experience, 1730–1790," in *Plantation, Town, and Country: Essays on the Local History of American Slave Society*, eds. Elinor Miller and Eugene D. Genovese (Urbana: University of Illinois Press, 1974), 450.

19. Walker, *Free Frank*.

20. Ibid., 34–37.

21. After 1817, Free Frank also hired his time to the former owner of his wife, Lucy. See *Free Frank and Lucy v Denham's Administrators*, 5 Littell 330, Ky. (1824); *Free Lucy and Frank v Den-*

ham's Administrator, 4 Monroe 167, Ky. (1827); and Walker, *Free Frank*, 49–54, which show that Free Frank earned $212 in a two-year period in hiring his own time to William Denham. The case was brought to court by Denham's son, who tried to prove the amount was a loan, by suing first Free Frank and then his wife. Denham ultimately lost the 1827 case.

22. Pulaski County Real Estate Conveyances, bk. 4, Pulaski County Courthouse, Somerset, Kentucky, 133–34; the date was 10 August 1815. Also, Walker, *Free Frank*, 39.

23. Pulaski County Real Estate Conveyances, bk. 4, 138; the date was 15 September 1819. Also, Walker, *Free Frank*, 46.

24. Charles White to Hamilton Brown, 20 December 1832, Hamilton Brown Papers, Southern Historical Collection, University of North Carolina, Chapel Hill, North Carolina.

25. This principle of law was upheld throughout the South. See, *Tilly v North*, Catterall, *Judicial Cases*, 106 for a ruling based on law: "A General license, by the master to his slave, to make bargains for work to be done only for the benefit of the slave, and also . . . to borrow money on his own account, would not render the master a *debtor* to a person, who would be so inconsiderate as to run up an account with a slave thus licenced [sic]."

26. On slave holder Plowden Weston's will, see *Record of Wills of Charleston County*, vol. 37, bk. A, 1826–1834, 184–85. On Anthony Weston, also see Koger, *Black Slaveowners*, 36–37, 43–44, 75. Yes, slaves could purchase slaves, but owned them only nominally since, under the law, title to any property owned by a slave rested in the hands of the owner, who had the authority to seize a slave's property at any time. Most owners did not. The more profitable use a slave made of his slave property, the more money the owner could extract or extort from that slave.

27. *Broadhead v Jones,* Catterall, *Judicial Cases*, 258. [Alabama, 1863]

28. Lunsford Lane, *The Narrative of Lunsford Lane, Formerly of Raleigh, N.C.* (Boston, 1842), 15–16.

29. Report of the South Carolina Committee on Colored People, 7 December 1858, South Carolina Archives Division, cited in Richard C. Wade, *Slavery in the Cities: The South 1820—1860* (New York: Oxford, 1964), 52.

30. Olmsted, *Cotton Kingdom*, 186–87.

31. Randall M. Miller, "The Man in the Middle: The Black Slave Driver," *American Heritage* (October–November 1979): 44–45. Ultimately, the slave driver working as a manager had to produce a profit, managing his fellow slaves who were unwilling workers. Given the authority to punish recalcitrant slaves, some drivers went to extremes in pushing for maximum production. See Miller, 42, for an account of an ex-slave denouncing the driver on the Texas plantation where she lived for "all de time whippin' and stroppin' de niggers to make dem work harder."

32. Olmsted, *Cotton Kingdom,* 438; also Miller, "The Man in the Middle," 45.

33. Olmsted, *Cotton Kingdom*, 194.

34. Robert William Fogel and Stanley L. Engerman, *Time on the Cross: The Economics of American Negro Slavery* (Boston: Little, Brown, 1974), 211. Also, Fogel, *Without Consent or Contract*, 44, notes, "The shift from white to slave managers . . . was more or less completed by the beginning of the nineteenth century. . . ." Also, Fogel says that "after 1840 the proportion of large plantations on which slaves were the chief non-ownership managers probably began to decline . . . although even in 1860 slaves were probably still the chief non-ownership managers on about half of all large plantations."

35. Olmsted, *Cotton Kingdom,* 194. Also, Deborah Gray White, *Ar'n't I a Woman?: Female Slaves in the Plantation South* (New York: W. W. Norton & Company, 1985), 129, on plantation female slaves, as "foremen."

36. Spraggins, "The History of Negro Business," 56.

37. Juliet E. K. Walker, "Drivers, Slave," in Miller and Smith, *Dictionary of Afro-American Slavery*, 196–98.

38. Janet Sharp Hermann, *The Pursuit of a Dream* (New York: Random House, 1983), 12.

39. Ibid., 104, 109–10.

40. Ibid., 221.

41. Ibid., 19.

42. Ibid., 21; and Leon F. Litwack, *North of Slavery: The Negro in the Free States, 1790–1860* (Chicago: University of Chicago Press, 1961), 31.

43. Leonard P. Curry, *The Free Black in Urban America, 1800–1850: The Shadow of the Dream* (Chicago: University of Chicago, 1981), 49–146.

44. Dunn Landry Papers, untitled handwritten manuscript, the Amistad Research Center, New Orleans, Louisiana.

45. "Rev. Pierre Landry in the *Donaldsonville Chief*," reproduced by Booker T. Washington in "His College of Life," undated typewritten draft, the Amistad Research Center, New Orleans, Louisiana.

46. Joseph Karl Menn, *The Large Slaveholders of Louisiana, 1860* (New Orleans: Pelican Publishing, 1964), 105, 121–22.

47. "Rev. Pierre Landry in the *Donaldsonville Chief*." After the Civil War, Landry moved to the town of Donaldsonville. In 1868 he was elected to a one-year term as mayor. Later he became justice of the peace, the town's tax collector, and was appointed to a four-year term as postmaster. Landry also served in the Louisiana House of Representative in 1872, 1880–1882, and in the State Senate in 1874 and 1878. He was also a delegate to the 1879 Louisiana State Constitutional Convention.

48. Anna Hoppe, *Negro Slavery* (St. Louis, Mo.: Rudolph Volkening, 1935), 27–28.

49. John Campbell, "As 'A Kind of Freeman'?: Slaves' Market-Related Activities in the South Carolina Up Country, 1800—1860," in *Cultivation and Culture: Labor and the Shaping of Slave Life in the Americas*, eds. Ira Berlin and Philip D. Morgan (Charlottesville: University Press of Virginia, 1993), 137.

50. Ibid., 150.

51. William K. Scarborough, "Mississippi, Slavery In," in Miller and Smith, *Dictionary of Afro-American Slavery*, 493; and Menn, *Large Slaveholders of Louisiana*, 105.

52. Thad W. Tate, *The Negro in Eighteenth-Century Williamsburg* (Williamsburg, Va.: The Colonial Williamsburg Foundation, 1965), 33–45, for discussion of slave occupations in Williamsburg.

53. Juliet E. K. Walker, "Entrepreneurs in Antebellum America," in *Black Women in America: An Historical Encyclopedia*, eds. Darlene Clark Hine, Elsa Barkley Brown, and Rosalynn Terborg-Penn (Brooklyn, N.Y.: Carlson Publishing, 1993), 394–97.

54. On black women purchasing the freedom of slaves, see Suzanne Lebsock, *The Free Women of Petersburg: Status and Culture in a Southern Town* (New York: W. W. Norton, 1984), 96, 282, n. 19; Lebsock indicates that almost half of black emancipators were black women; although, "since women who hired themselves out could not generally earn as much as men could, an increase in self-purchase would have favored men."

55. Walker, "Entrepreneurs," 395.

56. Ann Royall, *Southern Tour* (Washington, 1831), 2: 6–7, 18–19.

57. Elizabeth Keckley, *Behind the Scenes, or, Thirty Years a Slave, and Four Years in the White House* (New York, 1868). Keckley was the dressmaker and confidante of Mrs. Abraham Lincoln.

58. *Knox v Fair*, Catterall, *Judicial Cases*, 174–75. [Alabama, 1850]

59. Olmsted, *Cotton Kingdom*, 94. The Southern medical profession contrived to establish a field of specialization in "diseases peculiar to Negroes," such as "drapetomania," an affliction that was identified as causing slaves to run away. See Todd L. Savitt, *Medicine and Slavery: The Diseases and Health Care of Blacks in Antebellum Virginia* (Urbana: University of Illinois Press, 1978); and Kenneth F. Kiple and Virginia H. King, *Another Dimension in the Black Diaspora: Diet, Disease, and Racism* (Cambridge: Cambridge University Press, 1981).

60. Olmsted, *Cotton Kingdom*, 198.

61. *Aunt Sally; or the Cross the Way of Freedom* (Cincinnati: American Reform Tract and Book Society, 1862), 73–77, 97–98.

62. Loren Schweninger, "A Slave Family in the Antebellum South," *Journal of Negro History* 60 (Jan. 1975):29–44.

63. Delilah L. Beasley, *The Negro Trail Blazers of California* (Los Angeles, 1919; reprint, New York: Negro Universities Press, 1969), 71.

64. See Wade, *Slavery in the Cities*, 330, on urban slave gender distribution. Of the 10 cities listed, only in Richmond, the South's leading industrial center, were male slaves from 1830 to 1860

in the majority; and in 1860 in Mobile, a new industrial city, male slaves were also in the majority. Baltimore's female slave population was 1,541, compared to 671 male slaves; and Washington D.C. had 1,200 female slaves and 574 male slaves. Also, *Harris v. Cooper,* Catterall, *Judicial Cases,* 347.

65. Lebsock, *Free Women of Petersburg*, 96.

66. Beasley, *Negro Trail Blazers*, 71, 109. See the later discussion of her real estate enterprise and philanthropic activities.

67. J. E. Bruce, "A Sketch of My Life," Bruce Manuscripts, Schomburg Collection, New York Public Library, cited in Gerda Lerner, *Black Women in White America: A Documentary History* (New York: Vintage Books, 1973), 33–34. John Bruce was noted for his caustic comments on the post–Civil War "colored aristocracy," light-skinned and dark-skinned blacks who prided themselves on white or Indian ancestry, respectively. See Willard B. Gatewood, *Aristocrats of Color: The Black Elite, 1880–1820* (Bloomington: Indiana University Press, 1990), 55–56, 108.

68. See Deborah G. White, "Female Slaves: Sex Roles and Status in the Antebellum Plantation South," *Journal of Family History* (Fall 1983): 248–60, on the professionalization of three areas of "female work" on plantations of more than 20 slaves: cooking, dressmaking (as opposed to sewing and mending), and midwifery. Regarding the latter, several years of apprenticeship were required. If training included other medical skills, the slave woman was often given the title of "doctor woman" or "herb doctor" if she possessed a superior knowledge of herbs.

69. *Calvert v Wynne et al.*, Catterall, *Judicial Cases*, 20. [Maryland, 1665]

70. Distinctions are made between the conditions of slavery in the lower South and in the upper South, but laws attempting to suppress independent slave economic activities were the same throughout. For the conditions in an upper South state, see Juliet E. K. Walker, "Pioneer Slave Entrepreneurship—Patterns, Processes, and Perspectives: The Case of the Slave Free Frank on the Kentucky Pennyroyal, 1795–1815," *Journal of Negro History* 68 (Summer 1983): 289–308.

71. David J. McCord, ed., *The Statutes At Large of South Carolina*, vol. 10 (Columbia, S.C.: A. S. Johnston, 1841), 352.

72. Ibid., 382.

73. Ibid., 409. See Wood, *Black Majority*, 314–20. Some 20 whites and more than 60 blacks were killed.

74. *Statutes of South Carolina*, 396. Also, see Wade, *Slavery in the Cities*, 125–31, and Ulrich B. Phillips, *American Negro Slavery* (New York: D. Appleton and Company, 1918; Baton Rouge: Louisiana State University Press, 1987), 415–16, for discussion of slave attire.

75. *Statutes of South Carolina*, 396, 412–13.

76. Ibid., 413.

77. Ibid., 423.

78. James Iredell and William H. Battle, *The Revised Statutes of The State of North Carolina, 1836–37* (Raleigh, N.C.: Turner and Hughes, 1837), 1: 703–6, for specific page numbers of slave laws.

79. Lucius Q. C. Lamar, *A Compilation of the Laws of the State of Georgia … Since the Year 1810 to the Year 1819, Inclusive* (Augusta, Ga.: T. S. Hannon, 1821), 809.

80. Ibid.

81. Oliver H. Prince, *A Digest of the Laws of the State of Georgia* (Athens, Ga.: Oliver H. Prince, 1837), 657.

82. *Re Slaves*, Catterall, *Judicial Cases*, 6. [Georgia, 1772]

83. *Patton v Rambo*, Catterall, *Judicial Cases*, 181. [Alabama, 1852]

84. *Hurt v State*, Catterall, *Judicial Cases*, 178. [Alabama, 1851]

85. *Digest of Ordinances of the City Council of Charleston, from the Year 1783 to July 1818* (Charleston, 1818), 182.

86. Phillips, *American Negro Slavery*, 412.

87. Starobin, *Industrial Slavery*, 208. Also see Charles B. Dew, "Black Ironworkers and the Slave Insurrection Panic of 1856," *Journal of Southern History* 30 (May 1964): 143–61; Also Horsemanden, *The New York Conspiracy*. Most of the leaders and many of the participants in the 1741 slaves' conspiracy to burn down New York City and kill all the whites were slave artisans. Some of the leaders and their white allies who had conspired with them were executed.

88. See John Lofton, *Denmark Vesey's Revolt: The Slave Plot That Lit a Fuse to Fort Sumter* (Kent, Ohio: Kent State University Press, 1983); Stephen B. Oates, *The First of Jubilee: Nat Turner's Fierce Rebellion* (New York: Harper & Row, 1975).

89. See Mark V. Tushnet, *American Law of Slavery: Considerations of Humanity and Interest* (Princeton, N.J.: Princeton University Press, 1981); Edward L. Ayers, *Vengeance and Justice: Crime and Punishment in the Nineteenth Century American South* (New York: Oxford University Press, 1984); and Kermit L. Hall, ed., *The Law of American Slavery: Major Interpretations* (New York: Garland Publishing, 1987).

90. In Kentucky, the Slave Code had initially stipulated that slaves who hire their own time were to be sold forthwith out of the state, but the law was changed in 1802 to impose a 10-pound fine on both owner and any hirer of a self-hired slave. For the 1802 law, see William Littell, ed., *The Statute Law of Kentucky, Comprehending Also the Laws of Virginia and the Acts of Parliament in Force in this Commonwealth* (Frankfurt, Ky.: W. W. Hunter, 1809–1819), 1:116–17; and William Littell and Jacob Swigert, eds. *A Digest of the Statute Laws of Kentucky... to the May Session, 1822* 2 vols. (Frankfort, Ky.: Kendall and Russell, 1822), 2:1159–60.

91. Starobin, *Industrial Slavery*, 208.

92. Ibid., 212.

93. Ibid.

94. Phillips, *American Negro Slavery*, 412.

95. Luther Porter Jackson, *Free Negro Labor and Property Holding in Virginia, 1830–1860* (New York: D. Appleton-Century Company, 1942), 180–81. Also Charles H. Wesley, *Negro Labor in the United States, 1850–1925: A Study in American Economic History* (New York: Russell and Russell, 1927), 1–28.

CHAPTER 4

1. Martin R. Delany, *The Condition, Elevation, Emigration and Destiny of the Colored People of the United States* (Philadelphia, 1852; reprint, New York: Arno Press, 1968), 93.

2. John Malvin, *Autobiography of John Malvin: A Narrative* (Cleveland: Leader Publishing Company, 1879), 6; Russell H. Davis, *Memorable Negroes in Cleveland's Past* (Cleveland: Western Reserve Historical Society, 1969), 8–9; and Allen Peskin, ed., *North Into Freedom: The Autobiography of John Melvin, Free Negro, 1795–1880* (Kent, Ohio: Kent State University Press, 1988), 37–40.

3. Melville J. Herskovits, *The Myth of the Negro Past* (Boston: Beacon Press, 1941), 161, notes, "The role of the secret societies in the parts of Africa from which the slaves were derived is well-known." Also Piersen, *Black Yankees*, 151, and Genovese, *Roll Jordan Roll*, 197–201.

4. W. E. B. DuBois, *Economic Co-Operation among Negro Americans*, Atlanta University Publications, no. 12 (Atlanta: Atlanta University Press, 1907), 20–21.

5. Cotton Mather, *Diary*, 1 December 1693, Massachusetts Historical Society, 2 vols. Collection of the Massachusetts Historical Society. (ser. 7) v. 7–8 (pt. 1) 1681—1708.

6. Julian Rammelkamp, "The Providence Negro Community, 1820–1840," *Rhode Island History* (January 1948): 20. Also see Floyd J. Miller, *The Search for a Black Nationality: Black Emigration and Colonization, 1787–1863* (Urbana: University of Illinois Press, 1975), 8–14. Statistics of the births, deaths, and marriages of Newport blacks were also recorded by the organization.

7. Free African Society, "Articles of Association," in DuBois, *Economic Co-Operation*, 21–22. Also see William Douglass, *Annals of the First African Church in the United States of America, Now Styled the African Episcopal Church of St. Thomas* (Philadelphia: King and Baird, 1862), 15–25, 32–47; and John H. Bracey Jr., August Meier, and Elliott Rudwick, *The Afro-Americans: Selected Documents* (Boston: Allyn and Bacon, 1972), 143–56.

8. See "Minutes of the Proceedings of the Fourth American Convention of . . . Abolition Societies, 1797," *Journal of Negro History* 6 (July 1921): 316–22; *Liberator*, 4 August 1832, and 22 November 1861; Curry, *Free Black*, 197. Mutual aid societies and benevolent organizations differed in membership and purpose. Blacks at all economic, societal, and occupational levels, usually the

working poor, joined the former. Benevolent society membership was primarily the province of financially secure blacks, invariably businessmen who provided both mutual aid and built and supported black community institutions, schools, orphan homes, and churches.

9. James H. Browning, "The Beginnings of Insurance Enterprise Among Negroes," *Journal of Negro History* 22 (October 1937): 431–32. Usually $2 per week were paid as sick benefits after a year's membership; widows received $15 for burial expenses and $20 annually in widow's benefits. The Beneficial Society of Free Men of Color of the City of Petersburg, however, required a $10 initiation fee. As with many mutual aid societies, members were required to visit and care for the sick and were fined for failure to do so, as well as fined $1, absent a satisfactory excuse, for not attending members' funerals.

10. DuBois, *Economic Co-Operation*, 98; Richard Bardolph, *The Negro Vanguard* (New York: Vintage Books, 1961), 47.

11. Ira Berlin, *Slaves without Masters: The Free Negro in the Antebellum South* (New York: Pantheon Books, 1974), 310. Also, Browning, "Beginnings of Insurance," 426, 431–32. The Brown Fellowship Society restricted membership to light-skinned blacks, but only those with money or family standing. The Free Dark Men of Color Mutual Aid Society, founded the following year in Charleston, became the Humane Brotherhood in 1843. It provided mutual aid benefits. The tenuous condition of the lives of free blacks was taken into consideration. Families of members unjustly incarcerated received the same benefits as those on sick leave, $1.50 week. The Brown Society continued into the twentieth century; also, Robert L. Harris, "Charleston's Free Afro-American Elite: The Brown Fellowship Society and the Humane Brotherhood," *South Carolina Historical Magazine* 81 (Summer 1981): 289–92. Also, Curry, *Free Black*, 197. Before the Civil War, several hundred mutual aid and benevolent societies had been founded by blacks in both the North and the South.

12. The nation's formal banking history began in 1781 with the Bank of North America. The Post-Revolutionary War period saw the development of two kinds of commercial banks, state-chartered and private investor banks. The national government chartered the First (1791–1811) and Second (1816–1836) BUS [Bank of the United States]. From 1837 to the Civil War, the free-banking system was in operation. When backed with securities on deposit with the state banking authority, anyone could establish a bank, take deposits, and issue banknotes.

13. Howard Holman Bell, ed., *Minutes of the Proceeding of the National Negro Conventions, 1830—1864* (New York: Arno Press and the New York Times, 1969), 7. Article IV of the organization's constitution.

14. *An Address before the New York African Society for Mutual Relief in the African Zion Church, 23 March 1815, Being the Fifth Anniversary of Their Incorporation* (1819), 7.

15. *Record of Wills of Charleston County*, vol. 40, bk. A, 1834–1839, 289–90. Also, *Charleston Inventories, Appraisements & Sales*, vol. H, 1834–1844, 124, cited in Koger, *Black Slaveowners*, 153.

16. Credit report of R. G. Dun and Company, Louisiana Graduate School of Business Administration, Boston. Vol. 11:30, R. G. Dun and Company Collection, Baker Library, Harvard University. Also see, Roulhac Toledano, Sally Kittredge Evans, and Mary Louis Christovich, *New Orleans Architecture: The Creole Faubourgs*, vol. 4 (Gretna, La.: Pelican Publishing Company, 1974), 36.

17. Abram L. Harris, *The Negro as Capitalist: A Study of Banking and Business among American Negroes* (Philadelphia: American Academy of Political and Social Science, 1936), 8.

18. James Freeman Clarke, "A Statistical Inquiry into the Condition of the People of Colour of the United States," *Christian Examiner*, 5th ser. 66 (1859): 252.

19. William Frederic Wormer, "The Columbia Race Riots," *Lancaster County Historical Society* 26 (October 1922): 177.

20. See *A Merchant of Philadelphia, Memoirs and Autobiography of Some of the Wealthy Citizens of Philadelphia with a Fair Estimate of Their Wealth* (Philadelphia, 1846), 12, 44, 50, 58. Only people with wealth in excess of $50,000 were included in this publication. There were four blacks listed, including Robert Purvis; the other three were James Forten, Stephen Smith, and Joseph Cassey.

21. Catterall, *Judicial Cases*, 3: 510. Also, *Boisdere and Goule (f.p.c.) v Bank, Cases Argued and Determined in the Supreme Court of the State of Louisiana* 9: 507–12.

22. Juliet E. K. Walker, "Whither Liberty, Equality, or Legality? Slavery, Race, Property and the 1787 American Constitution," *Journal of Human Rights* 6 (Spring 1989): 307–8. Also see Robert

C. Reinders, "The Free Negro in the New Orleans Economy, 1850–1860," *Louisiana History* 6 (Summer 1965): 283, n. 42: "Citizens' Bank records for 1836 list ten free Negro bank stockholders."

23. Bell, *Minutes*, 34–35.

24. Henry M. Minton, M.D., "Early History of Negroes in Business in Philadelphia" (paper read before the American Historical Society, March 1913, Moorland-Spingarn Research Center, Howard University, Washington, D.C.), 17.

25. Delany, *Colored People*, 95.

26. John Spencer Bassett, *Slavery in the State of North Carolina* (Baltimore, 1899), 44–45.

27. Dun Collection, Louisiana, 11: 30.

28. Delany, *Colored People*, 109.

29. Clarke, "Free Coloured People," 252. Ralph B. Flanders, "The Free Negro in Ante-Bellum Georgia," *North Carolina Historical Review* 9 (July 1932): 270; Dun Collection, Louisiana, 11: 92; and Toledano, Evans, and Christovich, *Creole Faubourgs*, 36.

30. Bell, "Minutes of the Fourth Annual Convention, Philadelphia, 1834," *Minutes*, 34.

31. Bell, "Proceedings of the National Convention of Colored People, Troy, N.Y., 1847," *Minutes*, 42. See Rhoda Golden Freeman, "The Free Negro in New York in the Era Before the Civil War," (Ph.D. diss, Columbia University, 1966), 274, and *Statistical Inquiry into the Condition of the People of Colour of Philadelphia* (Philadelphia: Kite and Walton, 1849), which show that in 1837, free blacks in New York had $50,000–$80,000 on deposit and $200,000 on deposit in Philadelphia banks.

32. Harris, *Negro as Capitalist*, 8.

33. Bell, "Proceedings of the Colored National Convention, Philadelphia, 1855," *Minutes*, 19.

34. On rotating credit unions, see Ivan H. Light, *Ethnic Enterprise in America: Business and Welfare among Chinese, Japanese, and Blacks* (Berkeley: University of California Press, 1972), 20–22, 30–44. Rotating credit unions in the United States have been used by West Indians (the Esusu). Light, 44, notes "that social conditions in the United States extirpated the esusu from the cultural repertoire of blacks in this country."

35. *New York Tribune*, 3 July 1850. Black activist and abolitionist Samuel Ringold Ward was president: vice presidents were Lewis Woodson and Frederick Douglass.

36. Bell, "Proceedings of the Colored National Convention, Philadelphia, 1855," *Minutes*, 19. See also *Anglo-African*, 7 July 1860 for an article calling for a black bank that could provide loans to black businessmen.

37. Delany, *Colored People*, 96, 109.

38. Dun Collection, Louisiana, 11: 92; and Toledano, Evans, and Christovich, *Creole Faubourgs*, 36.

39. William T. Johnson, Diary, vol. 1835–1837, 69, William T. Johnson and Family Memorial Collection, 1793–1937, Special Collections, Hill Memorial Library, Louisiana State University. Interestingly, Johnson indicated in his daybook for December 1836 that $200 was borrowed from his wife to "pay in my Rail Road Stock." His wife, Harriet Battles, at the age of seven, along with her mother, were freed from slavery. Her family also accumulated wealth in property and slaves. The Johnsons had 10 children.

40. Schweninger, *Black Property*, 118, 261. John W. Blassingame, *Black New Orleans, 1860–1880* (Chicago: University of Chicago Press, 1973), 76.

41. Lewis Tappan, *The Life of Arthur Tappan* (1870; reprint, Westport, Conn.: Negro University Press, 1970), 196.

42. William J. Trent, *Development of Negro Life Insurance Enterprises* (Philadelphia: University of Pennsylvania Graduate School of Business, 1932), 8.

43. Deed of sale, 29 December 1817; "Notary Public Statement of Meuillon and Wife for Joint Indebtedness to the Union Bank of Louisiana" 31 May 1833; Receipt to Baptiste Meuillon from, "Bureau d'escompte at de depot de la Banque de l'Union de la Louisiane, 30 mai (fixed) 1839," which read "Votre bond pour mille huit cent soixante quinze piastres . . . ." The bond was for $1,875. Meul-

lion Family Papers, 1776–1906, folder numbers 2 and 3, Special Collections, Hill Memorial Library, Louisiana State University. The interest was 10 percent and the loan had to be repaid in 12 months.

44. Dun Collection, Louisiana, 11: 2.

45. Ibid., 10: 32, 39.

46. Ibid., 11: 92.

47. Curry, *Free Black,* 39.

48. *Plaquemines [Louisiana] Sentinel,* 1859, in *The Condition of the Free People of Colour in the United States of America* (London: Thomas Ward, 1841), 253. Also see Wilson, "Negroes Who Owned Slaves," *Popular Science Monthly* (November 1912): 493; and Menn, *Large Slaveholders,* 99, 112–13. Also, Schweninger, *Black Property,* 116, and Koger, *Black Slaveowners,* 136.

49. Gary Mills, *The Forgotten People: Cane River's Creoles of Color* (Baton Rouge: Louisiana State University Press, 1977), 108. Also, Woodson, "Free Negro Owners of Slaves in the United States in 1830," *Journal of Negro History* 8 (January 1924): 41–85, and *Free Negro Owners of Slaves,* 7. The next largest group of black slave holders lived in South Carolina. In 1830, Angel Justius and Mistress L. Horry owned 84 slaves each, in Colleton County. Also, Michael P. Johnson and James L. Roark, *Black Masters: A Free Family of Color in the Old South* (New York: W. W. Norton, 1984), 129. By 1860, South Carolina's William Ellison ranked as the wealthiest black planter, owning 1,000 acres and 63 slaves. Some 35 of his slaves, on about 200 acres, produced 80 bales of cotton, valued at $3,200.

50. Mills, *Forgotten People,* 111, 137–38, 220. Several Metoyers died in the 1830s. Their estates, in addition to Augustin's holdings, which were valued at $140,958, totaled $405,044. By 1850, the combined real property owned by the family—the second and third generations—each with individual holdings, totaled 5,667 acres of improved land worked by a total of 436 slaves.

51. Francis A. Walker, *A Compendium of the Ninth Census* (Washington, 1872), 639. Mills, *Forgotten People,* 220. Also, H. E. Sterkx, *The Free Negro in Ante-Bellum Louisiana* (Rutherford, N.J.: Farleigh Dickinson University Press, 1972), 202–12. Schweninger, *Black Property,* 33, 34, n. 7, observes, "someone with at least $2,000 worth of real estate was considered relatively prosperous [and] . . . those with $2,000 in realty had reached the upper 13 percent of the population."

52. Menn, *Large Slaveholders*, 246.

53. Clarke, "Free Coloured People," 253. The article confirmed the location of the land "in the rear of Madame C. Ricaud's plantation; and the two plantations, now owned by that family do comprise the number of acres of land and slaves as above stated, making them, doubtless, the richest black family in this or any other country."

54. Ibid., 252.

55. On Soulé, see Dun Collection, Louisiana 11: 19. On D. R. McCarthy, see ibid. 9: 97 and 13: 83b. On Casenave, see ibid. 10: 497. On Pottier, see ibid. 10: 526 and 13: 83a. On the Soulies, see Dun Collection, Louisiana 11: 30.

56. Robert C. Reinders, *End of an Era: New Orleans, 1850–1860* (New Orleans: Pelican Publishing Company, 1964), 40.

57. Menn, *Large Slaveholders,* 99, 112–13. Also, David O. Whitten, "A Black Entrepreneur," and David O. Whitten, "A Black Entrepreneur in Antebellum Louisiana," *Business History Review* 45 (Spring 1971), 201–19.

58. On Free Frank's Kentucky land purchases from 1821 to 1829, see *General Index to the Surveyor's Office Books, Pulaski County Real Estate Conveyances,* Book 7–1, 560, and Book II, 774, Pulaski County Courthouse, Somerset, Kentucky. The two state land-granting systems were the Kentucky Land Treasury Warrant System, initiated in 1815, and the Head Rights Claim System, begun in 1795. With both, the cost of land purchased was $10 per 100 acres. See William Rouse Jillson, *The Kentucky Land Grants* (Baltimore: Genealogical Publishing Company, 1974), 550, and Charles Slaughter Moorehead and Mason Brown, *Digest of the Statute Laws of Kentucky,* 2: 905–1103. The Kentucky Tellico claims, ceded to the U.S. government by the Cherokee nation excluded blacks from acquiring land in this region. The treasury warrant system excluded aliens. The head-rights system applied to any free person. See Walker, *Free Frank,* 49–59, 68.

59. On Free Frank's Illinois land purchases, see *Pike County Tract Index,* Hadley-Berry (T4SR5, 6W), Pike County Courthouse, Pittsfield, Illinois. Also, Walker, *Free Frank*, 94, 155.

60. For New Philadelphia town plat, see *Pike County Deed Record Book*, 9: 183, Pike County Courthouse, Pittsfield, Illinois; Walker, *Free Frank*, 54–58, 68, 94, 155. On town lot sales in New Philadelphia, see *Pike County Deed Record Book*, Town Lot Index, Philadelphia, 46–61, 269–71, Pike County Courthouse. On occupations of New Philadelphia townspeople, see U.S. Bureau of the Census, "Population Schedules of the Seventh of the United States, 1850, Illinois, Pike County." See also, Walker, *Free Frank,* 103–11, 122–46. On black agricultural settlements, see ibid., 114–17, 195–96, n. 77.

61. Walker, *Free Frank,* 133.

62. New Philadelphia first appeared on Illinois maps published for national distribution in 1850. See Joseph Hutchins Colton, *Colton's Traveler and Tourist's Guide Book Through the United States* (New York, 1850). Also, Charles G. Colby, *Handbook of Illinois, Accompanying Morse's New Map of the State* (New York: R. Blanchard, 1854). New Philadelphia also appears on Morse's 1858 revised map. The last map published for national distribution on which New Philadelphia appears was in *Campbell's New Atlas of the State of Illinois* (Chicago, 1870).

63. Bell, "Minutes of the National Convention of Colored Citizens, Buffalo, 1843," *Minutes*, 30–31, 33. Comparisons were also made with the interest earned by black moneylenders, "5 percent," with what could be earned by establishing a farm, particularly in the West, claiming it "would yield at least 25 percent from the commencement, and after a few years (with improvements), it would be found to yield him many hundred percent."

64. Emma Lou Thornbrough, *The Negro in Indiana: A Study of a Minority* (Indianapolis: Indiana Historical Bureau, 1957), 139–40; Benjamin Drew, ed., *A North-Side View of Slavery: The Refugee; Or The Narratives of Fugitive Slaves in Canada Related By Themselves* (Boston, 1856), 272–73. Also see *Illinois General Assembly, Laws. . . . Passed by the Tenth General Assembly, December 1836,* 175, "An Act to change the name of Free Frank." His name was changed to Frank McWorter. The act, a response to his petition, allowed Free Frank "to purchase and convey both real and personal property."

65. On American land laws, U.S. House, *Laws of the United States of a Local or Temporary Character, and Exhibiting the Entire Legislation of Congress upon Which the Public Land Titles in Each State and Territory Have Depended*, 47th Cong., 2d sess., 1881, Misc. Doc. 45, pt. 4; Thomas Donaldson, comp. *The Public Domain: Its History, with Statistics* (Washington D.C., 1884). Also, U.S. Congress, *American State Papers: Public Lands*, vols. 3–6 (Washington, D.C., 1832–1861).

66. See William Loren Katz, *The Black West* (Garden City, N.Y.: Doubleday, 1971); Kenneth W. Porter, *The Negro on the American Frontier* (New York: Arno Press, 1971); and W. Sherman Savage, *Blacks in the West* (Westport, Conn.: Greenwood Press, 1976).

67. For biographical information, see Hubert Howe Bancroft, *History of California* (San Francisco: A. L. Bancroft, 1880–1890), 4: 279, 566, 711, and 5: 566; Delilah Beasley, *The Negro Trail Blazers of California* (Los Angeles: Times Mirror Printing and Binding House, 1919), 107–13; Sue Bailey Thurman, *Pioneers of Negro Origin in California* (San Francisco: Acme Publishing, 1952), 1–5; and Walker, "Racism, Slavery, Free Enterprise," 355–57. Leidesdorff was born in the Danish West Indies. He came to the United States in the 1830s, settled in Louisiana, and became a ship's captain. His mother was variously described as a "negress," "mullatress," or "with a strain of black and Carib blood."

68. James C. Ward, "Extract from my Diary," *San Francisco Argonaut,* 21 September 1878, 10.

69. *Californian,* 18 April 1848. John A. Sutter's New Helvetia Ranch adjoined that of Leidesdorff's Rancho de los Americanos.

70. William A. Leidesdorff, Estate Papers, 1842–52 [accounts and legal papers pertaining to the estate of Leidesdorff], Leidesdorff Collection; Leidesdorff family, Estate Papers, 1846–49, relating J. L. Folsom, administrator of the estate, documents originating in St. Croix, Danish West Indies, securing to Joseph L. Folsom, from the heirs of William A. Leidesdorff; *People ex rel Attorney-General v. Joseph L. Folsom*, 5 Cal. Rep. 373 (1855); Bancroft Court Records, Leidesdorff-Folsom Court Records, Bancroft Library. Also California Legislature, Senate, *Journal of the Sixth*

Session of the Legislature (Sacramento, 1855), 324–26. Also Walker, "Racism, Slavery, Free Enterprise," 355–57.

71. Wesley, *Negro Labor*, 50, and P. F. de Gournay, "The F. M. C.'s of Louisiana," *Lippincott's Monthly Magazine* 53 (April 1894): 513. Figures range from $2.21 million, based on 1850 data, to $4 million, based on 1857 data. See Reinders, "The Free Negro in the New Orleans Economy," 280–81; and Blassingame, *Black New Orleans*, 69.

72. Roulhac Toledano and Mary Louis Christovich, *New Orleans Architecture: Faubourg Treme' and the Bayou Road, North Rampart Street to North Broad Street Canal Street to St. Bernard Avenue*, vol. 6 (Gretna, La.: Pelican Publishing Company, 1980), xv. Faubourg Tremé today encompasses Esplanade Avenue between North Rampart and North Broad, the City Commons, and all the "back of town," dwellings to St. Bernard Avenue, extending into the French Quarter streets. Also see 51, 85–100, 192.

73. Dun Collection, Louisiana, 9: 97.

74. Ibid., 11: 30.

75. Ibid., 11: 19; and Toledano and Christovich, *Faubourg Tremé*, xv.

76. Dun Collection, Louisiana, 9: 140, 12: 39. Also, Toledano and Christovich, *Faubourg Treme'*, 101.

77. Also, Toledano and Christovich, *Faubourg Tremé*, 103, and Blassingame, *Black New Orleans*, 75–76.

78. Dun Collection, Louisiana, 11: 2.

79. Ibid., 10: 32.

80. Ibid., 11: 92.

81. Toledano, Evans, and Christovich, *Creole Faubourgs*, 35.

82. Toledano and Christovich, *Faubourg Tremé*, xv. Also, Toledano, Evans, and Christovich, *Creole Faubourgs*, 32–33, 107. Fouche's "architectural renderings of houses being advertised for sale are preserved in part today in the archival plat books." See New Orleans Notarial Archives, Plat Books.

83. *Journal of the Assembly of the State of New York*, 33d sess. (1810): 118, 156, 237. *Journal of the Senate of the State of New York*, 33d sess. (1810): 99, 100, 110, 129. The organization continued its existence well into the twentieth century.

84. Ottley and Weatherby, *Negro in New York*, 61.

85. George Edmund Haynes, *The Negro at Work in New York City: A Study in Economic Progress* (New York: Columbia University, 1912), 96–97, on leading antebellum New York black businesses in the late 1830s and early 1840s, including "a drug store owned by Dr. Samuel McCune Smith and a cleaning establishment owned by Bennett Johnson [that] were both said to be 'well-known and successful enterprises of the day.' They were boarding houses, a watch and clock maker, two small dry good stores that sold notions owned by B. Bowen and James Green, two pleasure gardens with saloons, a confectionery and fruit store, a bathing establishment, and a coal yard in addition to second-hand clothing shops, barber shops and restaurants."

86. John T. Zuille, *Historical Sketch of the New York African Society for Mutual Relief* (New York, 1892), 20. Also, Daniel Perlman, "Organizations of the Free Negro in New York City, 1800–1860," *Journal of Negro History* 56 (July 1971): 182–84, n. 14, The two buildings purchased in 1820 were still owned by the African Society as late as 1909, according to one source, and into the 1940s, according to another.

87. *Anglo-African*, 31 March 1860.

88. Carter G. Woodson, *A Century of Negro Migration* (Washington, D.C. The Association for the Study of Negro Life and History, 1918), 93.

89. Benezet Joint Stock Association, minutes, 1 January 1861, in Spraggins, "History of Negro Business," 53.

90. Ibid. Also see Roger Lane, *William Dorsey's Philadelphia and Ours: On the Past and Future of the Black City in America* (New York: Oxford University Press, 1991), 108, which indicates that the association was founded by an "enterprising teenager," Jacob White Jr. and that "the stock sold initially for $25.00 a share."

91. Spraggins, "History of Negro Business," 54, notes that the association prospered until the 1870s, "when there was some misunderstanding between members." It remained in existence until 1885 when it dissolved, with each stockholder receiving $30.

92. Delany, *Colored People,* 104; Elizabeth L. Parker, *A Walking Tour of the Black Presence in San Francisco during the Nineteenth Century* (San Francisco: African American Historical and Cultural Society, 1974), 14; and Rudolph M. Lapp, *Blacks in Gold Rush California* (New Haven: Yale University Press, 1977), 99, 188; Beasley, *Negro Trail Blazers,* 146.

93. R. G. Dun & Co. Collection, Pennsylvania, vol. 27, p. 4.

94. Delany, *Colored People,* 104–105; Lapp, *Blacks in California*, 99, 188; Beasley, *Negro Trail Blazers,* 146.

95. See Delany, *Colored People*, 98–99.

96. Carter G. Woodson, "The Negroes of Cincinnati Prior to the Civil War," *Journal of Negro History* 1 (January 1916): 20–23; *Cleveland Gazette,* 1 November, 1887; Davis, *Memorable Negroes in Cleveland's Past,* 13.

97. Delany, *Colored People,* 98, 99.

98. On Boyd, see George Washington Williams, *History of the Negro Race,* 2: 138–40; and Woodson, "Negroes of Cincinnati," 21.

99. Benjamin Bacon, *Statistics of the Colored People of Philadelphia* (Philadelphia: Board of Education of the Pennsylvania Society for the Abolition of Slavery, 1858).

100. Pennsylvania Society for Promoting the Abolition of Slavery, *The Present State and Condition of the Free People of Color, of the City of Philadelphia and Adjoining Districts* (Philadelphia).

101. Wesley, *Negro Labor*, 45, 48; and Schweninger, *Black Property*, 82.

102. John Hope Franklin, "James Boon, Free Negro Artisan," *Journal of Negro History* 30 (April 1945): 150–80. Also see Catherine W. Bisher, "Black Builders in Antebellum North Carolina," *North Carolina Historical Review* 61 (October 1984): 423–58.

103. John Hope Franklin, *The Free Negro in North Carolina, 1790–1860* (1943; reprint, Chapel Hill: University of North Carolina Press, 1994), 45, 142, 144, 160; Franklin, "The Free Negro in the Economic Life of North Carolina," *North Carolina Historical Review,* pt. 1 (July 1942): 255; pt. 2 (October 1942): 370; and Berlin, *Slaves without Masters,* 239–40. Also Thomas H. Clayton, *Close to the Land: The Way We Lived in North Carolina, 1820–1860* (Chapel Hill: University of North Carolina Press, 1983), 63–64. Thomas Day's furniture has been on exhibit at the DuSable Museum of African American History, Chicago, and in Atlanta and Washington, D.C.

104. *Anti Slavery Record,* December 1835.

105. Foner, *History of Black Americans,* 546–47. Also, Charlotte L. Forten, *A Free Negro in the Slave Era: The Journal of Charlotte L. Forten*, ed. Ray Allen Billington (New York: Collier Books, 1953), 13; and *Dictionary of American Biography*, 6 (New York, 1928–1937), 537.

106. Delany, *Colored People*, 94.

107. Henry E. Baker, "The Negro As an Inventor," in D. W. Culp, ed., *Twentieth Century Negro Literature* (New York: Arno Press, 1969), 6.

108. Henry E. Baker, "Negro in the Field of Invention," *Journal of Negro History* 2 (January 1917): 25. Also, J. Carlyle Sitterson, *Sugar Country, The Cane Sugar Industry in the South, 1753–1950* (Lexington: University of Kentucky Press, 1953), 148–50 and R. L. Desdunes, *Nos Hommes et Notre Histoire* (Montreal: Arbour and Dupont, 1911), 102–3.

109. Delany, *Colored People*, 108; Koger, *Black Slaveowners*, 75, 145. Irene Diggs, *Black Innovators* (Chicago: Institute of Positive Education, 1975), 2, notes that there were many slave inventors: "since the mechanical labor of the South was done mostly by slaves, many of the mechanical modifications of the day were made by slaves in their effort to minimize the drudgery."

110. See, Mills, *Forgotten People,* 16, 132, for the price paid for cotton gins by Louisiana's Metoyer family, including $180 for repairs.

111. Johnson and Roark, *Black Masters*, 70, 124, 127. Also, Business Records of William Ellison, MSS. 18, Ellison Family Papers, South Carolina Library, University of South Carolina, cited in Koger, *Black Slaveowners*, 38, 132, 136, 144; Schweninger, *Black Property*, 116. Ellison's slaves were valued at $53,000, his real property at $8,300.

112. *New York Tribune*, 3 July 1850. Frederick Douglass was a vice president, and members included businessmen.

113. *New York Tribune,* 16 April 1851. Also see *Philadelphia, North America, and United States Gazette*, 11 April 1851; and *The Pennsylvanian*, 14 April 1851.

114. Delany, *Colored People,* 128; Baker, "Negro Invention," 26; *New York Tribune*, 16 April 1851.

115. Marcus Bruce Christian, "Genealogy: Creoles of Louisiana Prior to Reconstruction . . . Status in Wealth, Occupations, and Culture," Archives and Manuscripts Department, Earl K. Long Library, University of New Orleans, 102.

116. William E. B. DuBois, *The Philadelphia Negro* (Philadelphia: University of Pennsylvania, 1899), 33–36.

117. *Philadelphia Times*, 17 October 1896.

118. DuBois, *The Philadelphia Negro,* 33–36. Also see Minton, "Early History," and Delany, *Colored People,* 100, 103, 106–7, who ascribes these characteristics to several black caterers.

119. Minton, "Early History," 12. Also see Minton for a poem, "Ode to Bogle," written in 1829 by the president of the Bank of the United States, Nicholas Biddle, in which he describes Bogle as a "Colorless colored man," and "Before his stride the town gives way."

120. Jerome Baptiste, interview by Tinsley Spraggins, Philadelphia, 1935, in Spraggins, "History of Negro Business," 27.

121. Ibid.

122. Ingham and Feldman, *African-American Business Leaders,* 225–27. Another Baptiste daughter married Peter Dutrieuille, who opened a catering business in 1873, which continued in existence until 1974.

123. Lane, *William Dorsey's Philadelphia*, 2, 112.

124. Delany, *Colored People*, 100.

125. Dun Collection, Pennsylvania, vols. 139, 140. Henry Minton was from Virginia and came to Philadelphia in 1830 when he was 19. He first worked as a shoemaker's apprentice, then became a hotel waiter before he opened his own exclusive dining rooms at Fourth and Chestnut. He died in 1883.

126. Dun Collection, New York, vols. 318, 315. Other New York caterers were George Bell, George Alexander, and Thomas M. Jackson, whose specialty was catering elite weddings in that city. See Haynes, *The Negro at Work,* 96. Also, Curry, *Free Black*, 24.

127. Most of the antebellum black caterers were not only leaders of the black community, like the Downings, both father and son, but also active in the abolitionist movement. When he was 12, George joined a literary society that refused to celebrate the Fourth of July, adopting the resolution that "we refrain from participating in the usual festivities of the Fourth of July so long as they are to us a mockery." See *New York Tribune,* 11 May 1858, 5.

128. *Newport Daily News*, 21 July 1848.

129. *Newport Daily News*, 4 April 1850.

130. Dun Collection, Rhode Island, vols. 3, 62. Subsequent entries noted Downing "Has R.E. is taxed $30,500."

131. Genovese, *Roll Jordan Roll,* 541.

132. Luther Porter Jackson, "Free Negroes of Petersburg, Virginia," *Journal of Negro History* 12 (1927): 379–80.

133. See E. Horace Fitchett, "The Traditions of the Free Negro in Charleston, South Carolina," *Journal of Negro History* 25 (April 1940): 139–52; Koger, *Black Slaveowners*, 153–55. Also, Harriet P. Simons and Albert Simons, "The William Burrows House of Charleston," *South Carolina Historical Magazine* 70 (July 1969): 169–71.

134. Berlin, *Slaves without Masters, 243.*

135. Clarke, "Free Coloured People," 252.

136. *California Pioneer Register and Indexes, 1542–1848*, extracted from Hubert Howe Bancroft, *The History of California* (Baltimore: Regional Publishing Company, 1964), 53–54, notes that Beckwourth was also involved in horse rustling. Also see "Black Pioneers in Business," *Pittsburgh*

Courier, 24 February 1979, which adds that he was so highly respected by the Blackfeet and the Crow, that both nations made him a chief.

137. Berlin, *Slaves without Masters*, 235–36, notes that the term used to describe those areas of enterprise dominated by blacks and considered degrading for whites, such as barbering, was "nigger work."

138. Gatewood, *Aristocrats of Color*, 15.

139. Davis, *Memorable Negroes in Cleveland's Past,* 59. Also see David W. Demming, "A Social and Demographic Study of Cuyahoga County Blacks, 1820–1860," (master's thesis, Kent State University, 1976), who lists John Brown as the fourth leading black wealth holder in 1860 with $5,000.

140. *Harris Business Directory for 1839* (Pittsburgh, Pa.), 14.

141. "The Woodson Family," typed manuscript, n.d., Research Collection, The Carnegie Library of Pittsburgh. Also, Frank Bolden, "First 100 Years," *Pittsburgh Courier,* 13 May 1950; and George C. Poole, *Blacks in Allegheny 1850–1920,* Research Collection, The Carnegie Library of Pittsburgh.

142. Woodson was said to be a son of Sally Hemings, allegedly the mistress of Thomas Jefferson. Also, Clarke, "Free Colored People," 252–53; "Condition of the People of Color," report of the Ohio Anti-Slavery Convention, Cincinnati, Ohio, 22–24 April 1835, in Williams, *History of the Negro Race,* 2:137, which states that in 1835, when Cincinnati's black population was 2,500, 1,129 of them had been slaves. Of that number, 476 purchased themselves "at the total expense of $215,522.04."

143. Cyprian Clamorgan, *The Colored Aristocracy of St. Louis* (Alexandria, VA: Chadwyck-Healey, 1987 reprint. Originally published, St. Louis, MO, 1858). Also, Lawrence O. Christensen, "Cyprian Clamorgan, The Colored Aristocracy of St. Louis (1858)," *Bulletin of the Missouri Historical Society* 31 (October 1974): 3–31.

144. Franklin, *Free Negro in North Carolina*, 31–32. Also, Berlin, *Slaves without Masters*, 56. Also, Schweninger, *Black Property*, 82–83., table 6 indicates free black barbers who were property holders. In 1850, in the upper South, 91 black barbers had average property holdings of $1,538. In the lower South, 14 black barbers had average property holdings of $1,293. In 1860, in the upper South, there were 114 black barbers, with average property holdings of $2,866; in the lower South, 18 black barbers, with average property holdings of $1,750. By 1860 in Virginia, there were 236 barbers, including some 50 who owned their shops; in Richmond, there were 18 shops owned by free black barbers. Franklin identifies only 2 free black barbers out of his list of 53 free blacks who owned more than $2,500 in property in North Carolina in 1860.

145. Koger, *Black Slaveowners,* 152–53.

146. William Johnson, Cash Book, November 1828–September 1834, William T. Johnson and Family Memorial Collection, 1793–1937, Special Collections, Hill Memorial Library, Louisiana State University. Also, Charles Sydnor, "The Free Negro in Mississippi before the Civil War," *American Historical Review* 32 (July 1927): 769–88. In 1840, there were 1,366 free blacks. In 1860, there were 733 free blacks (601 were mulattoes) and 400,013 slaves (36,618 mulattoes). Lane, *William Dorsey's Philadelphia*, 115–16, notes that in addition to shampooing hair, shaving "was the backbone of the trade." Prices ranged from five to twenty-five cents. The average price was ten cents.

147. Wesley, *Negro Labor*, 35, 37–38, 43, 45; and "Penna. Analysis of Census," for numbers of free black barbers in 1850. See also Patricia Mae Riley, "The Negro in Cincinnati, 1835–1850," (master's thesis, University of Cincinnati, 1971), 63, which indicates there were 134 black barbers in 1850. Also, Bacon, *Statistics of the Colored People of Philadelphia,* 13–14, indicates that there were 248 black barbers out of 1,637 in Philadelphia in 1859.

148. *Missouri Republican,* 10 June 1845, and *St. Louis Directory for 1859,* 97. Parker, *Walking Tour,* 8, 15; Lapp, *Blacks in California,* 96–97.

149. From unpublished manuscript of Charles Gayarré, 344–46.

150. Dun Collection, Louisiana 9: 140, 149.

151. Christian, "Genealogy," 103.

152. Dun Collection, Louisiana, 10: 329. *Cohen's New Orleans Directory ... for 1853* (New Orleans, 1853), 151.

153. Delany, *Colored People,* 99–100. Also see Schweninger, *Black Property,* 82–83, table 6, which correlates occupations by average real property holding (ARPH), distinguishing the upper

from the lower South. For the lower South he shows: 214 planters, ARPH, $9,708; 17 grocers, ARPH, $9,747; 18 merchants, ARPH, $9,833; 24 tailors, ARPH, $13,954. His figures for grocers, merchants, and tailors in the lower South are skewed, due to the extensive real estate holdings owned by New Orleans merchants and tailors, as opposed to the average profits earned by blacks in those occupations. His ARPH figures for the upper South more realistically reflect the transformation of occupational earning into property ownership: 5 planters, ARPH, $1,200; 8 grocers, ARPH, $1,388; 7 merchants, ARPH, $6,629; 9 tailors, ARPH, $1,689. His findings for storekeepers more accurately reflect the limited earnings of blacks as merchants: (lower South, 4 storekeepers, ARPG $725; upper South, 15 storekeepers, ARPH $1,960), as do his findings for other occupations listed.

154. Delany, *Colored People*, 139–40.

155. Delany, *Colored People*, 102, 139–40; Charles A. Gliozzo, "John Jones: A Study of A Black Chicagoan," *Illinois Historical Journal*," 80 (Autumn 1987): 177–78.

156. *The Rights of All*, 29 May 1829.

157. Ella F. Still, interview in Spraggins, "History of Negro Business," 57–59; Haynes, *The Negro at Work,* 97; Minton, "Early History," 19. See Freeman, "Free Negro in New York," 259, 260, which notes that only three anti-Semitic expressions were found in her examination of New York black newspapers, including the *Colored American,* 10 February 1838, which concerned, she said, "the notorious anti-Negro Major Noah."

158. *The Anglo-African*, 1 (April 1859): 126–28.

159. Spraggins, "History of Negro Business," 23.

160. Clarke, "Free Coloured People," 252.

161. Ibid. On the food-processing enterprises of Georgetown's Alfred Lee, who opened a feed store in 1830 that expanded into a flour-retailing business, see Henry Robinson, "Some Aspects of the Free Negro Population of Washington, D.C., 1800–1862," *Maryland Historical Magazine* 64 (Spring 1969): 52–53.

162. Delany, *Colored People*, 97–98.

163. Delany, *Colored People*, 102.

164. On Lacroix, see Dun Collection, Louisiana 11: 92. Also, Toledano, Evans, and Christovich, *Creole Faubourgs,* vol. 4, 35.

165. On McCarty, see Dun Collection, Louisiana, 9: 97. Louisiana, 10: 328.

166. On Minton, see Dun Collection, Pennsylvania vols. 139, 140; On Gustave Donato Grocers, see Dun Collection, Louisiana, vols., 20, 25; on Metoyer, see, Louisiana 7: 112.

167. Mills, *Forgotten People,* 128–31, 134, 136, 161, 214.

168. See Oscar Dubreuil, Account Book, 1856–1858, Louisiana State University Archives.

169. Mills, *Forgotten People,* 99, 130, 131, 134, 136, 161, 165, 214. Also, Reinders, "The Free Negro in the New Orleans Economy," 283.

170. Dun Collection, Pennsylvania, 207: 4.

171. Charles Colcock Jones, *Suggestions on the Religious Instruction of the Negroes in the Southern States* (Philadelphia, n.d.), 59; and Frederick Law Olmsted, *A Journey in the Seaboard Slave States, with Remarks on Their Economy* (New York: Dix and Edwards, 1856), 24; Wade, *Slavery in the Cities,* 169, 270.

172. A. J. [Absalom Jones] and R. A. [Richard Allen], *A Narrative of the Proceedings of the Black People, during the late awful calamity in Philadelphia, in the year 1793. . . .* (Philadelphia, 1794).

173. *Freedom's Journal,* November 1828.

174. Minton, "Early History, 5.

175. Ibid., 12.

176. Dun Collection, Louisiana, 10:494, for P. Casenave; Ibid., 13: 141 for G. Casenave and Brothers.

177. Reinders, "The Free Negro in the New Orleans Economy," 279. Also see Toledano and Christovich, *Faubourg Treme',* 94. The business was so successful that Casenave even employed a bookkeeper, Francois Boisodore, the son of a builder who was a free man of color.

178. See Greene, *Negro in New England*, 307. Also, Peter Williams Jr., "A Tribute to Captain Paul Cuffe," in Philip S. Foner, ed., *The Voice of Black America: Major Speeches by Negroes in the United*

States, 1797–1971 (New York: Simon and Schuster, 1972), 28–33; Miller, *Search for a Black Nationality,* 23–24; and Lamont D. Thomas, *Rise to be a People: A Biography of Paul Cuffe* (Urbana: University of Illinois Press, 1986).

179. Walker, *Free Frank,* 48, 61–62, 136, 138, for information on Free Frank's arrangements for stone to be quarried on the land that he owned in Pike County. Also, Jackson, *Free Negro Labor,* 80, on Fauquier County, Virginia, where blacks worked as masons and fencers mined the stone and rock quarries.

180. See *The Weekly Herald and Philanthropist,* 13 May 1846, about a free black with a farm and timberland near Cincinnati who refused to sell stave timber to a white cooper who wanted to make whiskey barrels and who said: "Well Sir, I have the time and want the money, but no man can purchase a single stave or hoop pole, or a particle of grain from me for that purpose."

181. Franklin, "Free Negro in North Carolina," pt. 1, 255.

182. *Californian,* 3 July 1847.

183. Delany, *Colored People,* 95–96. Invariably, slave intrapreneurs and entrepreneurs who purchased their freedom continued in those businesses when freed.

184. Delany, *Colored People,* 107–8, and Curry, *Free Black,* 27.

185. Franklin, "Free Negro in North Carolina," pt. 1, 259; William G. Hawkin, *Lane, or Another Helper from North Carolina* (Boston, 1863), 82. Also, Minton, *Early History,* 18, notes that in Philadelphia, when wood was the only fuel,"[n]early all of the horses and carts hauling these were owned by [blacks] the Durhams, Harmons, Clarks, Perkins and Sockums—mostly all related and all originally from Delaware."

186. On California's black miners, see Beasley, *Negro Trail Blazers,* 70–71, 104–5, 114–17.

187. Ibid., 116, 123, 124.

188. Also see Martha S. Putney, "Black Merchant Seamen of Newport, 1803 to 1865: A Case Study in Foreign Commerce," *Journal of Negro History* 57 (July 1972): 160, 162–65, which shows the high percentage of black crewmen in all areas of shipping, except for whaling.

189. Jackson, *Free Negro Labor,* 79, 142; Jackson, "Free Negroes of Petersburg," 368; Luther Porter Jackson, "The Virginia Free Negro Farmers and Property Owners, 1830–1860," *Journal of Negro History* 24 (1939): 423–24. Also, Koger, *Black Slaveowners,* 23, and Schweninger, *Black Property,* 70.

190. Lapp, *Blacks in California,* 99.

191. Delany, *Colored People,* 96, 109.

192. See Greene, *Negro in New England,* 307. Also see, Williams, "A Tribute to Captain Paul Cuffe," 28–33.

193. Edmund Berkeley Jr., "Prophet without Honor: Christopher McPherson, Free Person of Color," *Virginia Magazine of History and Biography* 77 (April 1969): 180.

194. Lorenzo Greene and Carter G. Woodson, *The Negro Wage Earner* (Washington, D.C.: Association for the Study of Negro Life and History, 1930), 6–7.

195. Davis, *Memorable Negroes in Cleveland's Past,* 8–9; Malvin, *Autobiography;* and Peskin, *North into Freedom.*

196. Berlin, *Slaves without Masters,* 218–219. Jackson, *Free Negro Labor,* 219.

197. Jackson, "Free Negroes of Petersburg," 373–75; Tom W. Schick, *Behold the Promised Land: A History of African-American Settler Society in Nineteenth Century Liberia* (Baltimore: Johns Hopkins University Press, 1977), 45–46.

198. Jackson, "Free Negroes of Petersburg," 369, 379; and Jackson, *Free Negro Labor,* 79, n.19.

199. Berkeley, "Prophet without Honor," 180–87.

200. Jackson, *Free Negro Labor,* 221. Also see Koger, *Black Slaveowners,* 156.

201. U.S. House, 41st Cong., 2d sess., in Harris, *Negro as Capitalist,* 10–11. On Knight, see, Delany, *Colored People,* 140–41.

202. *Petersburg Daily Express,* 18 August 1858. Also, Jackson, *Free Negro Labor,* 220–21.

203. Jackson, "Free Negroes of Petersburg," 381; Jackson, *Free Negro Labor,* 221.

204. Charles L. Blockson, *The Underground Railroad* (New York: Prentice Hall, 1987), 82, 88, 91. Also see Davis, *Memorable Negroes in Cleveland's Past,* 11, on a Mr. Greenbrier who was actively involved in the Underground Railroad and used his horses to transport slaves to Canada.

205. *Wilson's Business Directory of New York City, 1857–1858;* Lane, *William Dorsey's Philadelphia,* 111; and Blockson, *Underground Railroad,* 29.

206. *Niles Register,* 22: 163, from *New York Commercial Register.* Also, Harris, "Charleston's Free Afro-American Elite," 289–92; and Kroger, *Black Slaveowners,* 168, for mention of a Samuel Creighton, whose estate was valued at $3,540, but who would not be accepted into the Brown Fellowship Society because he was dark-skinned.

207. Daniel Coker, *Journal of Daniel Coker, A Descendant of Africa, From the Time of Leaving New York . . . On A Voyage for Sherbro, in Africa* (Baltimore: Edward J. Coale, in aid of the funds of the Maryland Auxiliary Colonization Society, 1820).

208. Berlin, *Slaves Without Masters,* 170.

209. Ibid., 170–71.

210. Ibid., 310.

211. Jackson, *Free Negro Labor,* 147.

212. Jackson, "Free Negroes of Petersburg," 373–75; Jackson, *Free Negro Labor,* 146–48; Schick, 45–46.

213. Jackson, *Free Negro Labor,* 147–48; Schick, *Behold the Promised Land,* 45–46. Also, Doris Banks Henries, *The Life of Joseph Jenkins Roberts and His Inaugural Address* (London: Macmillan, 1964).

214. American Colonization Society, *Fifteenth Annual Report* (Washington, D.C., 1832), 43.

215. Jackson, *Free Negro Labor,* 144, 148; and Schick, *Behold the Promised Land,* 46, 50.

216. Nannie Seawell Boyd Collection, Montgomery Bell Papers, 1853–1939, Liberia Project folder No. *. Archives and Manuscripts Section, Tennessee State Library and Archives, in Schick, *Behold the Promised Land,* 33.

217. Schick, *Behold the Promised Land,* 112–13.

218. Charles W. Thomas, *Adventures and Observations on the West Coast of Africa, and Its Islands* (New York, 1860), 154–55, in Schick, *Behold the Promised Land,* 42

219. Franklin, "Free Negro in North Carolina," pt. 1, 257–58.

220. *Baltimore American,* 2 November 1859, p. 1.

221. Bell, "Proceedings of the National Convention of Colored People, Troy, N.Y., 1847," Minutes, 22–24. Also, Rudolph M. Lapp, "The Negro in Gold Rush California," *Journal of Negro History* 49 (April 1964): 82; also see "Black Pioneers in Business," *Pittsburgh Courier,* 24 February 1979, on the business venture of African-American adventurer Barney Ford (1821–1902) in Nicaragua. Ford, a fugitive slave who escaped to Chicago, left for California via Panama. On arriving in Nicaragua, he became sick, saw the need for a first-class hotel, which he constructed and managed. Eventually, Ford made his way to California, then to Colorado and Wyoming, where his various business enterprises proved successful, then failed. Ford was a barber, hotel owner, and post–Reconstruction politician.

222. Mills, *Forgotten People,* 229. Julius Melborne, *Life and Opinion of Julius Melbourne,* cited in Franklin, "Free Negro in North Carolina," pt. 2, 369; Toledano and Christovich, *Faubourg Treme',* 98.

223. Kenneth G. Goode, *California's Black Pioneers* (Santa Barbara, Calif.: McNally and Lofton, 1974), 72–73. Also, Thurman, *Pioneers of Negro Origin,* 50. Gibbs studied law in British Colombia and was the first black elected to the Common Council of the City of Victoria, Vancouver, where he served two terms. From 1897 to 1901, Gibbs served as United States Consul to Madagascar.

224. Parker, *Walking Tour,* 5.

225. Greene, *Negro in New England,* 307. Also, Williams, "A Tribute to Captain Paul Cuffe," 28–33.

226. Jackson, *Free Negro Labor,* 29.

227. Curry, *Free Black,* 16–17.

228. Curry, *Free Black,* 18–19; and Berlin, *Slaves without Masters,* 247–48.

229. Beasley, *Negro Trail Blazers,* 120.

230. *Republican Banner,* October 1859.

231. Delany, *Colored People*, 138.

232. Spraggins, "History of Negro Business."

233. *Macon Telegraph*, 25 May 1832; and Flanders,"Free Negro in Georgia," 271.

234. Clarke, "Free Coloured People," 251.

235. On Boyd, see Delany, *Colored People*, 98; Williams, *History of the Negro Race*, 2: 138–40; and Woodson, "The Negroes of Cincinnati," 21.

236. Dun Collection, Ohio, 80: 73.

237. Wormer, "Columbia Race Riots," 177, 183–84.

238. Woodson, "The Negroes of Cincinnati," 21–22.

239. *Commercial,* 18 January 1871.

240. Jackson, *Free Negro Labor*, 99–100.

241. U.S. House, 41st Cong., 2d sess., in Harris, *Negro as Capitalist*, 10–11.

242. Hawkin, *Lunsford Lane,* 26, 82, 147–55. Lane had been acquitted in a court trial in 1845 for illegally entering the state, although the trial was about his presumed abolitionist activities. Lane had worked for the governor for six months as a messenger.

243. Gayarré, "The Quadroons of Louisiana: Historical Sketch," pp. 6-7.

244. *New York Tribune,* 14 June 1859. Also, 11 June 1859 for paper's comments that the convention: "intimates that if things go on as they have done, doctors, lawyers, and merchants, clerks and newspaper editors and publishers will soon begin to feel the effects of this free Negro competition." Senator James Alfred Pearce, at the convention, opposed removal of free blacks, noting, "It would break up the business and destroy the property of a large number of land owners and land renters."

245. Clarke, "Free Coloured People," 254.

246. Bell, "Proceedings of the Colored National Convention, Philadelphia, 1855," in *Minutes of the Proceedings of the National Negro Conventions, 1830–1864* (New York: Arno Press and the New York Times, 1969), 19.

247. Milton Friedman, *Capitalism and Freedom* (Chicago: University of Chicago Press, 1982), 10.

248. Walker, "Racism, Slavery, Free Enterprise," 345.

249. Joseph A. Schumpeter, *The Theory of Economic Development: An Inquiry into Profits, Capital, Credit, Interest, and the Business Cycle* (Cambridge, Mass.: Harvard University Press, 1936), 93.

CHAPTER 5

1. *Nancy Prince: A Black Woman's Odyssey through Russia and Jamaica* (Boston: 1850; reprint, edited and with an introduction by Ronald G. Walters, New York: Marcus Wiener Publishing, 1990)*, 32.* Nancy's husband, Nero, "was among a small number of blacks employed at the Russian court since the reign of Peter the Great (1682–1725), if not earlier" (xiii). Also, Allison Blakely, *Russia and the Negro: Blacks in Russian History and Thought* (Washington, D.C.: Howard University Press, 1986), 15–19; and, Sterling, *We Are Your Sisters,* 95.

2. Suzanne Lebsock, "Free Black Women and the Question of Matriarchy: Petersburg, Virginia, 1784–1820," *Feminist Studies* 8 (Summer 1982): 271–92; and Jackson, *Free Negro Labor*, 164, 221, on Luraney Butler. W. Sherman Savage, "Colorado Gold Rush," *New Day*, 5 (1947): 12.

3. Dorothy Sterling, ed., *We Are Your Sisters: Black Women in the Nineteenth Century* (New York: W. W. Norton & Company, 1984), 134. Sterling indicates that the "industrial system that permitted women to labor in their homes at piece-work rates was ordinarily denied to blacks." Anna Douglass's important antislavery connections account for this exception.

4. John Wideman, "West of the Rockies," *Black Enterprise* (June 1977): 186.

5. Jackson, "Virginia Free Negro Farmer," 433.

6. Walker, *Free Frank*, 44, 87–88, 141, 162.

7. Dun Collection. Pennsylvania, 156: 267.

8. Frances Whipple Greene McDougall, *Memories of Elleanor Eldridge* (Providence, 1838), cited in Sterling, *We Are Your Sisters*, 89–92. Eldridge was swindled out of her property by white neighbors and the sheriff, but eventually secured it through purchase.

9. *Census of the State of New York for 1855* (Albany, N.Y.: C. Van Benthuysen, 1857). Also, Freeman, "Free Negro in New York City"; and Clarke, "Free Coloured People," 252.

10. Flanders, "Free Negro in Georgia," 267; Jackson, *Free Negro Labor*, 78, 82, 98–99; Franklin, "Free Negro in Carolina," pt. 1, 256.

11. Berlin, *Slaves without Masters*, 220.

12. Curry, *Free Blacks*, 16–17.

13. Christensen, "Cyprian Clamorgan, *The Colored Aristocracy*," notes that she was not listed in the 1850 or 1860 census, but that her daughter married a James Thomas who, according to a July 1871 article in the *New York Tribune,* "was credited with controlling about a half million dollars" (13). Also, Loren Schweninger, ed., *From Tennessee Slave to St. Louis Entrepreneur: The Autobiography of James Thomas* (Columbia: University of Chicago Press, 1984).

14. Stock Certificate, 23 October 1852, folder 4, Meullion Family Papers, 1776–1906 (Parish of St. Landry), Special Collections, Hill Memorial Library, Louisiana State University.

15. Act of Mortgage, 5 July 1836, Municipal Papers, Kuntz Collection Catalogue, Manuscripts Section, Howard-Tilton Memorial Library, Tulane University.

16. Koger, *Black Slaveowners*, 124.

17. Probate Court Records, Natchitoches Parish, Louisiana, Successions, #375, 26 July 1839, in Schweninger, *Black Property*, 265–66.

18. Secretary of State, miscellaneous records, vol. 3Y, 258–60, South Carolina Department of Archives and History, in James W. Hagy, "Black Business Women in Antebellum Charleston," *Journal of Negro History* (Winter/Spring 1987): 43–44. Also see Koger, *Black Slaveowners,* 166, on Daniel Waring, an attorney and subsequently a planter who owned 42 slaves.

19. Sterling, *We Are Your Sisters,* 100.

20. *Macarty et al. v Mandeveille,* 3 La. An, 239–49 (March 1848). Also, Catterall, *Judicial Cases,* 3: 292, 589, 611–12.

21. Woodson, *Free Negro Owners of Slaves,* 11. Woodson also shows that in New Orleans, 752 black heads of household owned 2,354 slaves (9–15).

22. Walker, "Racism, Slavery, Free Enterprise," 354.

23. *Macarty et al. v Mandeveille,* 3 La. An. 239 (March 1848).

24. Mills, *Forgotten People*, 26–49. Also see Gary Mills, "Coincoin: An Eighteenth-Century Liberated Woman," *Journal of Southern History* 42 (1976): 205–22.

25. Mills, *Forgotten People*, 3. By tracing the origin of her name and the order of her birth, Mills concludes that Coincoin's mother and father were from the Gold Cost/Dahomey region: "The name Coincoin is considered the most conclusive clue; its phonetic equivalent, Ko Kwe is the name reserved for second-born daughters by the Glidzi dialect of the Ewe linguistic group which occupied the coastal region of Togo." Also, see Mills for a discussion of Coincoin's woodcarving ability, which he attributes to her African heritage (48, n 92).

26. Ibid., 49, 67.

27. Ibid., 3.

28. Ibid., 208, notes: "Of the 17,462 free nonwhites in Louisiana, only 20 percent were of pure African heritage: 80 percent bore some degree of white ancestry." See Joel Williamson, *New People*: *Miscegenation and Mulattoes in the United States* (New York: Free Press, 1980), and Carl Degler, *Neither White nor Black* (New York: Macmillan, 1971), 101–2. Also, Jordan, "American Chiaroscuro"; Laura Foner, "The Free People of Color in Louisiana and St. Domingue," *Journal of Social History* 3 (Summer 1970): 406–30; Ira Berlin, "The Structure of the Free Negro Caste in the Antebellum United States," *Journal of Social History* 9 (Spring 1976): 297–318; Robert Brent Toplin, "Between Black and White," *Journal of Southern History* 45 (1979): 185–200. Also, James Oliver Horton, *Free People of Color: Inside the African American Community* (Washington, D.C.:

Smithsonian Institution Press, 1993), 122–45, 219 n. 52, discussing light skin and black leadership, indicates that color is not always a basis to determine mulatto heritage, that Dr. Martin Luther King, "was of mixed ancestry, with an Irish grandmother on his father's side of the family."

29. See Reinders, "The Free Negro in the New Orleans Economy," 285, on negative effects of the Americanization of Louisiana and free-black entrepreneurship, which "declined in numbers and prosperity [after] the 1830's—their's was a lost cause." Also, Sterkx, *Free Negro in Ante-Bellum Louisiana*, 160–99.

30. Jackson, "Virginia Free Negro Farmer," 426–27.

31. Jean Baptiste Meullion (1774–1840) was the son of a white planter and his slave, Maria Juana, freed in 1776.

32. Inventory, p. 3, Meullion Family Papers, Special Collections, Hill Memorial Library, Louisiana State University.

33. Wholesale cotton prices were determined by the quality, rating by pound, of cotton, based on five categories. Meuillon's cotton sold on 19 April 1861 was rated at 13¢ a pound, which represented the highest quality categorized as "good to middling," an increase of a quarter point from the previous month. The largest cotton planter in Louisiana, Meredith Calhoun, with 709 slaves, produced 3,800 bales of cotton in 1859. See Menn, *Large Slaveholders of Louisiana*, 111. After the Civil War, as a large landowner, Belazaire was required to take the Amnesty Oath, signed 23 August 1865; but her property was still confiscated by the Union army. The administrator of her estate petitioned for compensation in the amount of $2,780 in December 1869.

34. Sterkx, *Free Negro in Ante-Bellum Louisiana*, 229.

35. Wormer, "Columbia Race Riots," 177.

36. Minton, "Early History," 9.

37. *Frederick Douglass' Paper*, 22 December 1854. Also, Hallie Quinn Brown, ed., *Homespun Heroes and Other Women of Distinctions* (Xenia, Ohio: Aldine Publishing, 1926). In 1920, a New York home for black unwed mothers was named after Ferguson. See William E. Clark, "The Katy Ferguson Home," *Southern Workman* (December 1923).

38. Sterling, *We Are Your Sisters*, 97–98; below on the hair-dressing enterprise of the three Remond sisters. The Remond family, especially Sarah Parker Remond and Charles Lenox Remond, were prominent abolitionists. See Dorothy B. Porter, "The Remonds of Salem, Massachusetts: A Nineteenth-Century Family Revisited," *Proceedings of the American Antiquarian Society,* (October 1986).

39. Wendell Phillips Dabney, *Cincinnati's Colored Citizens; Historical, Sociological, and Biographical* (Cincinnati, Ohio: Dabney Publishing, 1926), 349.

40. Franklin, "Free Negro in North Carolina," pt. 1, 256–57.

41. Koger, *Black Slaveowners*, 38–39, 150–51.

42. Ibid., 154–55.

43. Erastrus Paul Puckett, "The Free Negro in New Orleans to 1860," (Master's thesis, Tulane University, 1907), 47.

44. Franklin, "Free Negro in North Carolina," pt. 1, 257, and pt. 2, 371.

45. Minton, "Early History," 7.

46. Sterling, *We Are Your Sisters*, 103. The great opera singer, actor, and political activist, Paul Bustill Robeson, was Grace's great grandnephew.

47. Minton, "Early History," 7.

48. Carter G. Woodson, *The Education of the Negro Prior to 1861* (New York: Arno Press, 1968), 129–30.

49. Jackson, *Free Negro Labor*, 94, 158.

50. Gayarré, "Quadroons of Louisiana," 7–8.

51. Elizabeth Keckley, *Behind the Scenes*. Keckley designed Mary Todd Lincoln's inaugural gown on display at the Smithsonian Institution. A reproduction is on exhibit at the Black Fashion Museum in Harlem.

52. Correspondence with Mrs. Anne Bustill Smith, March 1935, in Spraggins, "History of Negro Business," 59–60.

53. *Freedom's Journal*, 28 March 1828 and 21 November 1829.

54. *The Anglo-African,* 9 June 1860, and *Weekly Anglo-African,* 21 April 1860.

55. Dorothy Porter, "David Ruggles, 1810–1849: Hydropathic Practitioner," *Journal of the National Medical Association* 49 (January 1957): 67–74.

56. See advertisements from the *Petersburg Republican,* 18 April 1820, 7 July 1820, 23 May 1823, 22 August 1823, in Lebsock, "Free Black Women," 154–55, and *Free Women of Petersburg*, 98–99.

57. Jackson, *Free Negro Labor*, 191, and Lebsock, *Free Women of Petersburg*, 98.

58. Gayarré, "Quadroons of Louisiana," 8. Sterkx, *Free Negro in Ante-Bellum Louisiana*, 231, and Robert C. Reinders, "The Free Negro in the New Orleans Economy," 277.

59. Mills, *Forgotten People*, 137.

60. *The Rights of All*, 12 June 1829, in Hutton, *Early Black Press*, 75.

61. Henry C. Castellanos, *New Orleans as It Was: Episodes of Louisiana Life* (New Orleans, 1905), 100. Also, *New Orleans True Delta,* 29 June 1850, and *Baton Rouge Gazette*, 28 September 1832, on the voodoo participation of whites. Also, Blassingame, *Black New Orleans*, 5–6, and, Blake Touchstone, "Voodoo in New Orleans." *Louisiana History* 13 (1972): 371–86.

62. See David J. Rothman, *The Discovery of the Asylum: Social Order and Disorder in the New Republic* (Boston: Little, Brown, 1971).

63. *New Orleans Daily Delta,* 31 July 1850.

64. On antebellum black health, see Curry, *Free Black*, 136–46; John Duffy, "Medical Practice in the Ante-Bellum South," *Journal of Southern History* 25 (February 1959): 53–72. Also, Kiple and King, *Black Diaspora,* and Savitt, *Medicine and Slavery.*

65. Eliza Potter, *A Hairdresser's Experience in High Life* (Cincinnati: 1859), 158–59. A copy can be found in the Black History Records, Cincinnati Historical Society, Cincinnati, Ohio.

66. Potter, *Hairdresser's Experience*, 158.

67. Dabney, *Cincinnati's Colored Citizens*, 350.

68. "The Woodson Family," manuscript, 8–9.

69. Sterling, *We Are Your Sisters*, 96.

70. July, *Precolonial Africa*, 102–3. Also, Bosman, *Description of Guinea*, 441, and Hawkins, *Voyage to the Coast*, 130.

71. *Freedom's Journal*, 2 May 1828, 13 June 1828. See Sterling, *We Are Your Sisters*, 97.

72. Gayarré, "Quadroons of Louisiana," 9.

73. Sterkx, *Free Negro in Ante-Bellum Louisiana*, 229–30.

74. Potter, *Hairdresser's Experience*, 160.

75. Gayarré, "Quadroons of Louisiana," 8.

76. Toledano and Christovich, *Faubourg Treme'*, xiii.

77. A. E. Perkins, ed., *Who's Who in Colored Louisiana* (Baton Rouge, La.: Douglas Loan Company, 1930), 57. Also, Charles Barthelemy Rousseve, *The Negro in Louisiana; Aspects of His History and His Literature* (New Orleans: Xavier University Press, 1937), 46.

78. Beasley, *Negro Trail Blazer*, 95–97, and Thurman, *Pioneers of Negro Origin in California* (San Francisco: Acme Publishing Company, 1952), 47–50. Also, the *San Francisco Call,* December 1901, and Parker, *Walking Tour*, 2. Pleasant's response was no different from those of antebellum black businessmen who came in contact with wealthy whites: they observed, they listened, and appropriated what they could of financial matters into their own business affairs.

79. Lapp, *Blacks in California* 100. Also, Parker, *Walking Tour,* 2–3, and *Pacific Appeal,* 25 October 1862.

80. Beasley, *Negro Trail Blazer*, 95.

81. Ibid.

82. *Oakland Tribune,* 3 September 1916. The land was sold for $1.8 million by Bell's estate. The title of the article announcing the sale was "The True Story of 'Mammy Pleasant.'" See *San Francisco News-Letter,* August 1904; and Beasley, *Negro Trail Blazer*, 97.

83. Beasley, *Negro Trail Blazer*, 97. Also, Lerone Bennett Jr., "The Mystery of Mary Ellen Pleasant," *Ebony* (April 1979), 74, 76, 82, 86, writes that on arrival in San Francisco, Pleasant worked as a housekeeper, which seems strange for someone with $50,000. On the other hand, Bennett said,

"While working as a housekeeper, she speculated in the stock and money markets ... [and] was sensationally successful in these ventures, partly because she had a genius for financial speculation, partly, because she had developed almost infallible sources of information.... By 1855, she owned a string of laundries." No matter how smart Pleasant was, few housekeepers earned enough to speculate in the stock and money market. Also, Bennett argues that Pleasant opened her first boardinghouse after the Civil War.

84. *San Francisco Call*, 4 January 1904, from her obituary. Her will requested that her tombstone be engraved: "She was a friend of John Brown's."

85. See *Pleasant v. N.B & M.R.R.R.R. Co.*, California Reports, vol. 34, 586. Pleasant won $500 in damages in 1868 after suing the streetcar company for refusing to allow her board a train because she was black.

86. Goode, *California's Black Pioneers*, 87.

87. The San Francisco census of 1860 (ward 10: 31) lists John Pleasant as a servant, with a wife named Ellen; the 1870 census lists him as a ship's cook, with a wife named Marry Ellen. He generally remains an obscure figure, since it appears they lived separate lives. See *San Francisco Elevator,* 4 April 1865, 2, 3, on the marriage of her daughter, Lizie J. Smith, and E. Berry Phillips.

88. Sterkx, *Free Negro in Ante-Bellum Louisiana*, 228.

89. Flanders, "Free Negro in Georgia," 267; Jackson, *Free Negro Labor*, 78, 82, 98–99; Franklin, "Free Negro in North Carolina," pt. 1, 256.

90. Mill, *Forgotten People*, 45.

91. Sterkx, *Free Negro in Ante-bellum Louisiana*, 218.

92. Koger, *Black Slaveowners*, 29, 39, 91–92, 146.

93. Potter, *Hairdresser's Experience,* 158–59. Also, *New Orleans Daily Picayune*, 15 October 1857, and *New Orleans Daily Crescent,* 2 October 1857, contain accounts of the trial of newly freed slave Kate Parker for "nearly beating her slave to death with a cowhide." Among black slave holders, it appears that color made little difference in the treatment of their slaves. See George Rawick, ed., *The American Slave: A Composite Autobiography*, 19 vols. (Westport, Conn.: Greenwood Publishing Company, 1972—), 6: pt. 1, 135, on an Alabama black master, George Wright, described as a "coal black free born nigger," who sold his children; according to former slave, Angie Garrett, "Dey was his own chillun.... De names was Eber, Eli, Ezekiel, Enock, and Ezra, an he sole 'em ter de highes' bidder right yonder ont [the steps] of de Pos' office for cash."

94. Royall, *Southern Tour*, 87–98.

95. Mills, *Forgotten People*, 119. Also, see Olmsted, *Journey in the Seaboard Slave States*, 680, on how slaves viewed the treatment they received from their black masters. Olmsted prompted the following commentary from a slave who he said denounced them as "very hard and cruel, and devoid of feeling.... You might think, master, dat dey would be good to dar own nation; but dey is not.... I'd rather be a servant to any man in de world, dan to a brack man."

96. E. Franklin Frazier, *The Free Negro Family: A Study of Family Origins before the Civil War* (Nashville, Tenn.: Fisk University Press, 1932), 36. This woman had two husbands. The first, a butcher, was killed by one of his slaves. After the Civil War, she refused to salute the American flag, spit on it, and stomped it under her feet. Her descendant claimed she escaped punishment because "she was a woman or because she was a beautiful woman."

97. Jackson, *Free Negro Labor*, 81.

98. Jackson, "Free Negroes of Petersburg," 368.

99. Shane White, " 'We Dwell in Safety and Pursue Our Honest Callings': Free Blacks in New York City, 1783–1810," *Journal of American History* 75 (September 1988): 458. Also, Charles H. Haswell, *Reminiscences of an Octogenarian of the City of New York* (New York: Harper and Brothers, 1897), 35.

100. Reinders, "The Free Negro in the New Orleans Economy," 276, n.15, indicates "[m]ost of the licenses were issued to individuals with German names."

101. Charleston Directory, 1819, 5. On Allergue, see Lebsock, "Free Black Women," 152, 155–56; and Jackson, *Free Negro Labor*, 144 n.

102. Anne Bustill Smith, correspondence with author, March 1935, in Spraggins, "History of Negro Business," 60.

103. Dun Collection, Pennsylvania, 142: 101; also 139: 140 on William H. Minton, owner of Gent's Furnishing Store.

104. Delany, *Colored People*, 109.

105. *Liberator,* 20 November 1857.

106. Secretary of State, miscellaneous records, vol. 30, 165–66, South Carolina Department of Archives and History, in Hagy, "Black Business Women," 43–44. Also see Koger, *Black Slaveowners,* 145–46, 151,191, 198, on several members of the slave-holding Sasportas family.

107. Haynes, *The Negro at Work,* 96–97.

108. *Colored American,* 7 June 1841, in Sterling, *We Are Your Sisters,* 217–18.

109. *National Reformer*, 1 September 1838. The journal lasted one year. It was edited by lumber businessman and community activist William Whipper and published by the American Moral Reform Society.

110. Bell, "Proceedings of the Third Annual Convention, Philadelphia, 1833," *Minutes,* 30.

111. Sterling, *We Are Your Sisters,* 160. Extremely well educated, a noted public speaker on antislavery and equal rights, journalist, internationally known poet and novelist, and peace activist, Frances Ellen Watkins worked first as a seamstress, the only job she could get, and as a baby-sitter for a bookstore owner. See Margaret Hope Bacon, " 'One Great Bundle of Humanity': Frances Ellen Watkins Harper (1825–1911)," *Pennsylvania Magazine of History and Biography* 113 (January 1989): 21–43.

CHAPTER 6

1. Wesley, *Negro Labor,* 142.

2. C. Vann Woodward, *Origins of the New South, 1877–1913* (Baton Rouge: Louisiana State University Press, 1951). Also, Jay R. Mandle, *The Roots of Black Poverty: The Southern Plantation Economy after the Civil War* (Durham, N.C.: Duke University Press, 1978).

3. Wesley, *Negro Labor,* 103–4.

4. *The National Freedman*, 1 April 1865, 90–91.

5. The historical literature on Reconstruction is voluminous. With few exceptions, most of its focus is either on the agricultural labor of blacks or black political participation. For an overview, see William E. B. DuBois, *Black Reconstruction in America, 1860–1880* (New York: Harcourt, Brace and Company, 1935); John Hope Franklin, *Reconstruction* (Chicago: University of Chicago, 1961); Kenneth Stampp, *The Era of Reconstruction, 1865–1877* (New York: Knopf, 1965); Eric Foner, *Reconstruction: America's Unfinished Revolution, 1683–1877* (New York: Harper & Row, 1988); Thomas Holt, *Black over White: Negro Political Leadership in South Carolina during Reconstruction* (Urbana: University of Illinois Press, 1977). Also, Ira Berlin et al., eds., *Freedom: A Documentary History of Emancipation* (New York: The New Press, 1982); Philip S. Foner and Reginald L. Lewis, eds., *The Black Worker: A Documentary History from Colonial Times to the Present,* 8 vols. (Philadelphia: Temple University Press, 1978–1984).

6. Blassingame, *Black New Orleans,* 57–58.

7. B. Byron Johnson, Amnesty Oath of the State of Mississippi, 26 July 1865, Johnson Memorial Collection, 1793–1937, box 2, Special Collections, Hill Memorial Library, Louisiana State University. The oath he signed declared that he "solemnly swear, (or affirm), in the presence of Almighty God, that I will hereafter faithfully support, protect and defend the Constitution of the United States, and the Union of the States there under; and that I will, in like manner, abide by and faithfully support all laws and proclamations which have been made during the existing rebellion with reference to the emancipation of slaves. So help me God."

8. Letter to Dr. N. W. Johnson, 7 December 1934, Johnson Memorial Collection, from the Natchez, Mississippi, Furniture Company regarding the "tract of timber that you have on a planta-

tion in the neighborhood of Anna, Mississippi. We made a cruise of this timber the past spring and found it to be of interest at your prices of $2,250.00."

9. Agreement With Freedmen, 12 February 1869, box 2, folder 12, Johnson Memorial Collection. Also see Roger L. Ransom and Richard Sutch, *One Kind of Freedom* (Cambridge: Cambridge University Press, 1977); and Gerald D. Jaynes, *Branches without Roots: Genesis of the Black Working Class and the American South, 1862–1882* (New York: Oxford University Press, 1986).

10. The Johnson family retained ownership of the land into the 1930s. William Johnson [III] became a doctor. His correspondence dates to the late 1930s. On the loss of property of the large black planters, see Schweninger, *Black Property Owners*, 190–92.

11. See Robert C. Kenzer, "The Black Businessman in the Postwar South: North Carolina, 1865–1880," *Business History Review* (Spring 1989): 61–87, a comprehensive statewide study of 126 post–Civil War black businessmen from R. G. Dun and Company credit reports, collected from 22,500 entries. Dun agents had to be accurate in recording credit information. Incorrect information could lead to financial loss in two ways: if an entry approved a merchant for credit, but was incorrect, creditors could lose money for unpaid debts; if an entry was negative, but the individual was a good credit risk, a prospective creditor could lose a potential customer. After 1859, *The Mercantile Agency Reference Book* was published, which contained codes for credit worthiness and the "pecuniary strength," of the enterprise. Paid subscribers were provided updated information. Businessmen did not pay to be entered in the book.

12. See Schweninger, *Black Property,* 187–94, on decline in wealth of the leading antebellum wealth holders.

13. Dun Collection, Louisiana, 10: 392. Francois, a New Orleans black Reconstruction politician, continued real estate speculation. See David C. Rankin, "The Origins of Black Leadership in New Orleans during Reconstruction," *Journal of Southern History* 40 (August 1974): 431, n. 34: "Lacroix was reportedly a millionaire in 1874 when the state seized a large number of his over 250 different properties in order to pay his tax debt, which dated from before the Civil War and amounted to $75,000." Also, Toledano, Evans, and Christovich, *Creole Faubourgs*, 36, notes that, on his death in 1876, the court-ordered inventory of his estate ran to 115 pages, and it took the notary clerk 11 ten-hour days to list all of his property: "over eighty-one entire squares of undeveloped land in the city's Third District . . . developed rental property, stocks, and accounts receivable." The real estate market was depressed in 1876 and estate sales "did not bring in even as much as the debts owed and in 1878 attorney Alcee' Villere was forced to petition the Second District court to declare the estate insolvent."

14. Dun Collection, Louisiana, 11: 92. Also, Toledano, Evans, and Christovich, *Creole Faubourgs*, 35–36, notes that Julien conveyed 75 properties to his brother in 1857. The inventory of his holdings showed 43 properties, stock in railroads, the Louisiana State Bank, and the Hope Insurance Company. Also, Blassingame, *Black New Orleans,* 74, notes that, on his death in 1868, "the contents of J. A. Lacroix's 'well assorted' grocery store, for instance, were auctioned off for $4,500." Most New Orleans black grocers carried merchandise worth less than $300. Also, 22 of the 35 grocers listed in the 1870 census owned $3,000 or less in property. The leading New Orleans white grocer, Victor Pessou, a wholesaler, who sold to "small retail grocers, coffee houses, restaurants, plantations, and several prominent Orleanians. . . . in 1871 [had] a total of $60,678 due him from his customers, and the contents of his grocery store were valued at $15,818."

15. Dun Collection, Louisiana, 13: 212.

16. Ibid., 10: 497.

17. Ibid., 13: 141.

18. Ibid., 12: 39.

19. Ibid., 12: 38.

20. Ibid., 12: 39. Also, Blassingame, *Black New Orleans*, 36, 39, 72, 212–13; and Rankin, "Black Leadership," 425, 437.

21. Beth L. Savage, ed., *African-American Historic Places: National Register of Historic Places* (Washington, D.C.: Preservation Press, 1994), 295–96, for information on the Mississippi China Grove plantation purchased by former slaves August and Sarah Mazique in 1869 from the heirs of

their former owner when the plantation was put up for sale at public auction. They became large post–Reconstruction planters. In 1874, former slaves Charlie and Charity Rounds purchased the Adam County Glen Aubin plantation.

22. Dun Collection, Mississippi, 21: 81E, 82.

23. Hermann, *Pursuit of a Dream,* 156–58. Also, Dun Collection, Mississippi, 21: 170, 198, on the Vicksburg store, W. T. Montgomery & Co., opened by Benjamin's son, William Thornton, in 1874 with capital of $10,000. It failed in 1877 and the Davis Bend store, Montgomery & Sons, failed in 1879. See Hermann, *Pursuit of a Dream*, 199–201, 207.

24. Ibid., 148–49, 202–3, 205, 211–12.

25. Ransom and Sutch, *One Kind of Freedom*, 345, n. 23, and Hermann, *Pursuit of a Dream*, 161.

26. Dun Collection, South Carolina 12: 123.

27. Ibid., 12: 104. Also see the same page on a Jewish merchant, a dry-goods grocer, new in Orangeburg and described as "considered good & respons. for a small cr."

28. Ibid., 12: 141.

29. See J. H. Harmon, A. G. Lindsay, and C. G. Woodson, *The Negro as a Business Man* (Washington, D.C.: Association for the Study of Negro Life and History, 1929; reprint, College Park, Md.: McGrath Publishing Company, 1969), 7, for an explanation of the difficulties encountered by postwar blacks attempting to establish stores: "the few who thus set themselves up in communities where neither others nor their own people had observed Negroes operating in this field, did not easily succeed. They could hardly expect whites to abandon their former connections to patronize novices in business; and the freedmen themselves could not easily abandon the thought that the white business man was more reliable and could give the most in return for one's money."

30. Dun Collection, South Carolina, 12: 105. Most entries for blacks in the South noted "colored," which was not always the case in Louisiana or the North, especially after the war. Some Dun reporters had ethnic and racial biases, but financial information in credit entries had to be accurate. See, Dun Collection, Mississippi, vol. 3, Bolivar County, 3, on Jewish slave owners and dry-good merchants with two stores described as "[c]alled good and appear to be making money," while one partner was described as "buy and sell everything. would to go the Devil for a Dollar, own Negroes & R.E." Another entry said, "He is a Jew who has made a fortune in 12 years trading first as pedler [sic] & then as merchant at Greenville Miss, He stands well in Washington Co." Also, Dun Collection Louisiana, 10: 564 a, on an importer of French wines, described as "An honest Frenchman."

31. *New York Tribune*, 11 December 1869, and *New York Times*, 14 March 1876.

32. F. W. Loring and C. F. Atkinson, *Cotton Culture and the South Considered with Reference to Emigration* (Boston: A. Williams and Company, 1869), 75. Also, Gavin Wright, *The Political Economy of the Cotton South* (New York: W. W. Norton, 1978).

33. Also, W. E. B. DuBois, *The Negro Artisan* (Atlanta: Atlanta University Press, 1902), 150–53, for information on black artisans in three categories: those reported to be " 'gaining' in number and efficiency," "losing," and "holding their own."

34. Dun Collection, Pennsylvania, 145: 354.

35. Minton, "Early History"; Lane, *William Dorsey's Philadelphia,* 111–12, 115, 132–33; Schweninger, *Black Property*, 204; and, Harmon, Lindsay, and Woodson, *Negro as a Business Man,* 9.

36. Harmon, Lindsay, and Woodson, *Negro as a Business Man*, 9. Also, Schweninger, *Black Property Owners,* 210, 211, 296, 298, 299, on Tate and Johnson, with an estimated estate of $20,000 to $50,000, and on Harris, with an estimated estate of more than $100,000.

37. Booker T. Washington, *The Negro in Business* (1907; reprint Chicago: Afro-Am Press, 1969), 21–22, 25–27; and Schweninger, *Black Property*, 297, 299–300. On Jackson, see Monroe N. Work, *Negro Year Book: An Annual Encyclopedia of the Negro* (Tuskegee, Al.: Negro Year Book Publishing Company, 1912), 167; and Schweninger, *Black Property,* 298, who lists Deal Jackson with an estimated estate of $50,000 to $100,000; Ibid., 210, lists other large black fruit and vegetable farmers in the South who shipped boxcar loads of produce to eastern markets.

38. Washington, *Negro in Business,* 34.

39. Still interview, in Spraggins, " History of Negro Business," 59; Horace Fitchett, "The Oldest Sawmill in the South: The Story of a Unique Negro Family," *Opportunity* (May 1932):

138–39; and Harmon, Lindsay, and Woodson, *Negro as a Business Man*, 11. Also, Washington, *Negro in Business,* 161. In Savannah, Georgia, blacks raised and invested $50,000 in a land and lumber enterprise that failed.

40. *New York Times*, 11 February 1864.

41. Harris, *Negro as Capitalist*, 27.

42. On the Freedmen's Bank, see Walter L. Fleming, *The Freedmen's Bank: A Chapter in the Economic History of the Negro Race* (Chapel Hill: University of North Carolina Press, 1927); and Harris, *Negro as Capitalist*, 25–45. The 35 branches of the Freedmen's Bank, including those in St. Louis, Philadelphia, New York, and Washington, were located in southern cities: Huntsville, Mobile, and Montgomery, Alabama; Little Rock, Arkansas; Jacksonville and Tallahassee, Florida; Atlanta, Augusta, Macon, and Savannah, Georgia; Lexington and Louisville, Kentucky; Alexandria, New Orleans, and Shreveport, Louisiana; Baltimore, Maryland; Columbus, Natchez, and Vicksburg, Mississippi; New Bern, Raleigh, and Wilmington, North Carolina; Beaufort and Charleston, South Carolina; Chattanooga, Columbia, Memphis, and Nashville, Tennessee; and Lynchburg, Norfolk, and Richmond, Virginia.

43. See *Congressional Globe*, 38th Cong., 2d sess., Part II, p. 1403, for Lincoln's remarks when signing the Freedmen's Bank Act, including the statement: "This bank is just what the freedmen need."

44. Senate, 62d Cong., 2d sess., Doc. 759, p. 4. Also, Harmon, Lindsay, and Woodson, *Negro as a Business Man*, 48; and Harris, *Negro as Capitalist*, 28.

45. Fleming, *Freedmen's Bank*, 39–40, 76–77. Also, Harris, *Negro as Capitalist*, 185–89 on Freedmen's Bank loans to the white managers and their business partners.

46. Ibid., 57.

47. See U.S. Senate, 43d Cong., 2d sess., Bruce's Report, S. Misc. Doc. 88; U.S. House, 44th Cong., 1st sess., Douglass Report in House Report 502, serial 1710; and U.S. House, 44th Cong., 2d sess., Misc. Doc. 16, serial 1653, 6. Also see U.S. Senate, *The Freedmen's Bank and Trust Company, An Act to Incorporate*, 46th Cong., 2d sess., 1865, Rept. 440, 1880, serial 1895.

48. Harris, *Negro as Capitalist*, 44–45, in reference to William E. B. DuBois, *The Souls of Black Folk* (Chicago: A. C. McClurg, 1903), 36; and Booker T. Washington, *Story of the Negro: The Rise of the Race from Slavery* (New York: Doubleday, Page and Company, 1909), 2:124. Also see Frederick Douglass, *Life and Times of Frederick Douglass* (Hartford, Conn.: Park Publishing, 1881), 487–88, for comments on the Freedmen's Bank and his circular statement made after his appointment as bank president to persuade blacks to retain their confidence in the bank.

49. Harmon, Lindsay, and Woodson, *Negro as a Businessman*, 61.

50. Harris, *Negro as Capitalist*, 67, 73. Also, DuBois, "Economic Co-Operation," 139; and W. P. Burrell and D. E. Johnson, *Twenty-five Years of the Grand Fountain of the United Order of True Reformers, 1881–1905* (Richmond, n.p., 1909).

51. Washington, *Negro in Business,* 162.

52. *The Washington Morning News*, 22 September 1869; *National Freedman*, 1, 15 August 1865, 242; and, N. B. Scudder, *Barnard Freedmen's Aid Society of Dorchester*, 31 January 1869.

53. Harris, *Negro as Capitalist*, 104, notes: "The forerunner of the Capital Savings Bank was the Industrial Building and Savings Company, a building and loan society, organized in May, 1885. After the bank was organized the two institutions, although run separately, were closely associated."

54. Bettye C. Thomas, "A Nineteenth-Century Black Operated Shipyard, 1866–1884: Reflections upon Its Inception and Ownership," *Journal of Negro History* 59 (January 1974): 4. Also Wesley, *Negro Labor*, 145, 199–200, who emphasizes that racism in the shipyards, where white carpenters and caulkers refused to work with blacks in those trades, was the precipitating factor that led to the organization of the company, with its purpose to provide employment for black caulkers.

55. DuBois, "Economic Co-Operation," 161.

56. Harold Rabinowitz, *Race Relations in the Urban South, 1865–1890* (New York: Oxford University Press, 1978), 80; and Harmon, Lindsay, and Woodson, *Negro as a Business Man*, 10.

57. DuBois, "Economic Co-Operation," 153, indicates the reasons for the failure of the company: "Desertion of the white boss carpenter . . . followed by his men and colored caulkers . . . loss

of a number of patrons; the desertion of the colored manager, Samuel Dogherty, with his followers." Also, the larger of the two railways used for docking ships became run down, but repairs by a white company, which were flawed and took one year at a cost of $6,000, contributed to the company's loss of prestige and customers, especially when "[s]hips in several instances, were wedged in the tract and extricated only at a great cost and delay."

58. Thomas, "Nineteenth Century Shipyard," 12. His critics, however, took other positions: "Black business leaders themselves had connived with whites, or had permitted themselves to be deceived by whites, or blacks, at the cost of exploiting the black community, not in the inception of the Company but also in its operation as well." Also, Wesley, *Negro Labor*, 145, 199–200, on Frederick Douglass, who said the positive outcome of the Chesapeake Marine Railway and Dry Dock Company was that black caulkers were allowed to join the caulkers' union, which accomplished the initial purpose for organizing the company.

59. Ibid., 8–12. See Schweninger, *Black Property*, 300, who lists Thomas, with the occupation of a shipping merchant, in the group of black wealth holders with more than $100,000.

60. Ingham and Feldman, *African-American Business Leaders*, 156–62.

61. Harmon, Lindsay, and Woodson, *Negro as a Business Man*, 10; Rabinowitz, *Race Relations*, 81; DuBois, "Economic Co-Operation" ; Woodson, 148, 250.

62. Washington, *Negro in Business*, 161.

63. William E. Bittle and Gilbert Geis, "Racial Self-Fulfillment and the Rise of an All-Negro Community in Oklahoma," *Phylon* 18 (1975): 247–60. Also, Kenneth Hamilton, *Race and Profit: Black Town Promotion and Development in the Trans-Appalachian West, 1877–1915* (Urbana: University of Illinois Press, 1991). Also, William Cohen, *At Freedom's Edge: Black Mobility and the Southern White Quest for Racial Control, 1861–1915* (Baton Rouge: Louisiana State University Press, 1991); and Thomas Knight, *Sunset on Utopian Dreams: An Experiment of Black Separatism on the American Frontier* (Washington, D.C.: University Press of America, 1977): 93.

64. Sundiata Cha Jua, "Founded by Chance/Sustained by Courage: Black Power, Class, and Dependency in Brooklyn, Illinois, 1830–1915" (Ph.D. diss., University of Illinois, 1993), provides the first study of the impact of industrialization on a black town, Brooklyn, located near East St. Louis.

65. Work, *Negro Year Book*, 165–66. Many of the agricultural settlements were established before the Civil War. See Frazier, *The Negro Family*, 221–26, 231–34. The earliest, the Gouldtown settlement established in the mid-1760s in New Jersey, was listed as a black town in the *Negro Year Book* with a population of 250 in 1910.

66. Nell Painter, *Exodusters: Black Migration to Kansas after Reconstruction* (New York: Knopf, 1977).

67. Arthur Lincoln Tolson, "The Negro in Oklahoma Territory, 1889–1907: A Study in Racial Discrimination" (Ph.D. diss., University of Oklahoma, 1966), 59–75, on black towns founded in Oklahoma.

68. *Langston (Okla.) City Herald*, 15 June 1893.

69. Kenneth M. Hamilton, "The Origin and Early Development of Langston, Oklahoma." *Journal of Negro History* 62, 3 (July, 1977): 275–76. Also see Bittle and Geis, "Racial Self-Fulfillment," 247–60. See the *Daily Oklahoma State Capitol*, 27 September 1893, for information on a Santa Fe Railroad depot established at Liberty, a town founded by McCabe. It notes that the town was to be settled by blacks from Texas and Mississippi.

70. See August Meier, "Booker T. Washington and the Town of Mound Bayou," *Phylon* 15 (1954): 397–401; Hermann, *Pursuit of a Dream*, 219–36; DuBois, "Economic Co-Operation," 171–72; Washington, *Negro in Business*, 88–93. Also, "Charles Banks, Benjamin Thornton Montgomery and Isaiah T. Montgomery," in Ingham and Feldman, *African-American Business Leaders*, 37–54, 701.

71. Frederick C. Luebke, "Ethnic Group Settlement on the Great Plains," *Western Historical Quarterly* 8 (1977): 428. Also, Willard B. Gatewood Jr., "Katie D. Chapman 'Reports on the Yankton Colored People,' 1889," *South Dakota History* 7 (1967): 28–35; George H. Wayne, "Negro Migrations and Colonization in Colorado, 1870–1930," *Journal of the West* 15 (1976): 110–15.

72. On Boley, see Savage, *African-American Historic Places,* 402. *Dallas Express,* 5 September 1914, on Muskogee.

73. *Savannah Tribune*, 5 April 1913.

74. *New York Age,* 28 March 1912.

75. *Dallas Express,* 24 January 1914.

76. *Indianapolis Freeman*, 31 January 1914.

77. Linda Krane Ellwein, "The Negroes in Cincinnati: The Black Experience, 1870–1880," (master's thesis, University of Cincinnati, 1970).

78. Schweninger, *Tennessee Slave to St. Louis Entrepreneur*, 14. He died in 1913, virtually penniless.

79. Ingham and Feldman, *African-American Business Leaders*, 708–11; Gatewood, *Aristocrats of Color,* 44, 66; and Schweninger, *Black Property Owners*, 204, 300.

80. Haynes, *The Negro At Work*, 68, 97.

81. Ingham and Feldman, *African-American Business Leaders*, 225–28, and Lane, *Dorsey's Philadelphia*, 111–113

82. DuBois, *Philadelphia Negro*, 32, 119; Lane, *William Dorsey's Philadelphia*, 114. Gatewood, *Aristocrats of Color*, 110, and photo, first page of illustrations following p. 84.

83. *Newport (R.I.) Journal*, 25 July 1903. Downing's three sons, however, worked for the government: Thomas, as a Boston post-office administrator; Philip worked in the Boston Customs House; and John worked in the New York Customs House.

84. Washington, *Negro in Business*, 41–53.

85. Haynes, *The Negro at Work*, 69, and Washington, *Negro in Business,* 40–41. The Fossett family continued its catering business into the 1920s.

86. Washington, *Negro in Business*, 54–67, and Work, *Negro Year Book,* 166.

87. Harmon, Lindsay, and Woodson, *Negro as a Business Man*, 7.

88. Work, *Negro Year Book,* 180.

CHAPTER 7

1. See W. E. B. DuBois, *Darkwater: Voices from within the Veil* (New York: Harcourt, Brace and Howe, 1920), 13, 137, views the business activities of America's captains of industry resting upon a code of "honor among thieves."

2. Eric D. Walrond, "The Largest Negro Commercial Enterprise in the World: Amazing Story of Herman E. Perry, Commercial BookerWashington, Founder $30,000,000 Standard Life Insurance Company," *Forbes*, 2 February 1924. To assure his readers that his report on Perry's financial holdings were correct, Walrond added, "(These figures, let me assure you, I did not get from Mr. Perry himself or from any one in his organization, but from disinterested white men in Atlanta whose business it is to know these things.)"

3. Booker T. Washington, *Up From Slavery: An Autobiography* (New York: Doubleday, Page and Company, 1901), 218–25. For DuBois's critique of Washington, see W. E. B. DuBois, "Of Mr. Booker T. Washington and Others," in William E. B. DuBois, *The Souls of Black Folk* (Chicago: A. C. McClurg, 1903), 42–54.

4. W. E. B. DuBois, *The Negro in Business: Report of a Social Study Made under the Direction of Atlanta University* (Atlanta: Atlanta University Press, 1898).

5. Ibid., 50.

6. Albon L. Holsey, "The National Negro Business League," in *Progress of a Race: On the Remarkable Advancement of the American Negro,* eds. J. L. Nichols and Wiliam H. Grogman (Naperville, Ill.: J. L. Nichols, 1920), 211–29. Booker T. Washington, "The National Negro Business League," *World's Work*, 4 (October 1902): 271–75.

7. Louis R. Harlan, *Booker T. Washington: The Wizard of Tuskegee, 1901–1915* (New York: Oxford University Press, 1983), 266–94.

8. *Ilanga Lase Natal*, 30 October 1903. The quote was from Washington's 1895 Atlanta speech. See an article in the same newspaper, 19 June 1903, noting that Washington, on the advice

of President Theodore Roosevelt, declined an invitation from Lord Earl Gray to visit South Africa. Also, Harlan, *Washington*, 273. Washington's most fervent South African admirer was the Reverend John Langalabele Dube, who in 1901 established the Zulu Christian Industrial School and also the Bantu Business League, modeled after the NNBL. While Dube was called the Booker T. Washington of South Africa, he was also one of the founders of the African National Congress in 1914.

9. *Umteleli wa Bantu*, 4 September 1920.

10. Booker T. Washington, "Industrial Education for the Negro," in *The Negro Problem: A Series of Articles by Representative American Negroes of Today*, Booker T. Washington et al. (New York: James and Company, 1903), 13.

11. W. E. B. DuBois, "The Talented Tenth," in Washington, *The Negro Problem*, 33–34.

12. W. D. Allison, "The Science of the Booker T. Washington Theory," *Champion* 1 (November 1916): 141. The *Champion* had absorbed an earlier black business publication, the *Business Men's Bulletin*. The Chicago Business League was founded in 1919.

13. DuBois, *Souls of Black Folk*, 43.

14. Ray Stannard Baker, "An Ostracized Race in Ferment," *American Magazine* 66 (May 1908): 65.

15. *Indianapolis Freeman*, 7 September 1901, indicated that of the 200 delegates present in addition to businesspeople, there were: "the teacher, doctor, lawyer, to the ripe scholar, skilled surgeon and diplomat." Also, *Report of the Eleventh Annual Convention of the National Negro Business League*, (Nashville: A.M. E. Sunday School Union, 1911), 78–85.

16. *New York Age*, 11 September 1920 and 5 March 1921; *Raleigh Independent*, 16 June 1917; *Negro Year Book, 1931–1932* (Tuskegee, Ala.: Negro Year Book Publishing Company, 1932), 134.

17. *Indianapolis Freeman*, 7 September 1901.

18. *New York Age*, 18 April 1912. Also *New York Age*, 18 June 1916, indicates that in 1916 there were 11 black saloons (3 with cabarets) in Harlem, compared to 57 saloons owned by whites. Also, *New York Age*, 5 October 1916 and 23 September 1916, notes that there were only 30 to 40 members. The Colored Business Men's Association also published a journal, *The Commercial Outlook*. Also, *New York Age*, 11 September 1920.

19. *The Atlanta Independent*, 1915.

20. W. E. B. DuBois, "The Niagara Movement," *Voice of the Negro* 2 (September 1905): 619–22.

21. W. E. B. DuBois, "Negro and Socialism," *Horizon* 1 (February 1907), 7–8. This was the short-lived journal published by the Niagara Movement, an organization of blacks opposed to Washington's accomodationist politics. The movement ended in 1909.

22. Herbert Aptheker, ed., *A Documentary History of the Negro People in the United States: From the Reconstruction Era to 1910* (New York: The Citadel Press, 1951), 917. This 31 May–1 June, 1909 conference provided the basis for the subsequent founding of the National Association for the Advancement of Colored People in May 1910.

23. W. E. B. DuBois, *The Crisis Writings*, ed. Daniel Walden (Greenwich, Conn.: Fawcet Publications, 1972).

24. *Crisis*, August 1917, 168, and December 1919, 48, 50. Eventually, five stores were established that served 75,000 people.

25. Harlan, *Washington*, 271–73. W. E. B. DuBois, "Segregation in the North," *Crisis*, April 1934, 115–17. Also, W. E. B. DuBois, *Dusk of Dawn* (New York: Harcourt, Brace and Company, 1940), 97.

26. Harmon, Lindsay, and Woodson, *Negro as a Business Man*, 57–58. Other banks established by fraternal orders were the Mutual Aid and Banking Company, New Bern, North Carolina; the Bank of Galilean Fishermen, Hampton, Virginia; Sons and Daughters of Peace, Penny, Nickel and Dime Bank, Newport News, Virginia.

27. M. S. Stuart, *An Economic Detour: A History of Insurance in the Lives of American Negroes* (New York: Wendell Mallett and Company, 1940). Also, Monroe N. Work, "Secret Societies as Factors in the Social and Economic Life of the Negro," in *Democracy in Earnest*, ed. James E. McCul-

loch (Washington, D.C.: Southern Sociological Congress, 1918); Carter G. Woodson, "Insurance Business among Negroes," *Journal of Negro History* 14 (April 1929): 202–26; J. H. McConico, "The Business Side of Fraternal Orders," in *Report of the Fifteenth Annual Convention*, National Negro Business League (Nashville, 1914); W. P. Burrell, "Report of the National Negro Insurance Association," in *Annual Report of the Sixteenth Session and the Fifteenth Anniversary Convention*, National Negro Business League (Nashville, 1915).

28. DuBois, *Economic Co-Operation*, 137.

29. Harmon, Lindsay, and Woodson, *Negro as a Business Man*, 67, 69, 74. John Mitchell Jr., its president, was also editor of the *Richmond Planet*.

30. Ibid., 67, 69.

31. Ibid., 97–98.

32. Harmon, Lindsay, and Woodson, *Negro as a Business Man*, 96. Also, Brown, *Economic Cooperation*, 37, indicates that the success of the Standard Life Insurance Company, founded by Perry, was a significant factor that accounted for leading white companies to begin to accept black policyholders.

33. Stuart, *Economic Detour*, 9, provides the example of the Union Central Relief Association, founded in 1894 in Birmingham, Alabama, by Rev. T. W. Walker, as a response to the "discrimination and discourtesies" to blacks holding health and accident policies in the white Southern Mutual Aid Company. The company survived until it was incorporated into the Atlanta Life Insurance Company.

34. DuBois, *Economic Co-Operation*, 100.

35. Ibid., 99, indicates the department store was incorporated, capitalized at $25,000, and its 1907 gross receipts amounted to $28,340. See Elsa Barkley Brown, "Womanist Consciousness: Maggie Lena Walker and the Independent Order of St. Luke," *Signs: Journal of Women in Culture and Society* 14, no. 3 (1989): 610–33; Charles Willis Simmons, "Maggie Lena Walker and the Consolidated Bank and Trust Company," *Negro History Bulletin* 38, no. 2 (1975): 345–49.

36. Harmon, Lindsay, and Woodson, *Negro as a Business Man*, 62–64; Ingham and Feldman, *African-American Business Leaders*, 670–80.

37. "First Negro Woman Banker Urges Sex to Enter Business—Says Opportunities in Commercial Life Never Were Better than Now," *Philadelphia Press*, 21 August 1920.

38. Stuart, *Economic Detour*, 116–17. Bethune is noted for her work in education as founder of a school in 1904 that became Bethune-Cookman College in 1924; she also worked in the federal government as director of the National Youth Administration's Division of Negro Affairs, and in black women's organizations as a member and officer of the National Association of Colored Women (NACW) and as founder of the National Council of Negro Women (NCNW) in 1935.

39. Ibid., 288–89; Willard B. Gatewood, "Theodore Roosevelt and the Indianola Affair," *Journal of Negro History* 53 (January 1968): 48–69; Ingham and Feldman, *African-American Business Leaders*, 415, 418, 656, 659.

40. Ingham and Feldman, *African-American Business Leaders*, 533–47. Perry, born in Houston, Texas, was educated formally up to the seventh grade, informally in business by working in his father's several small enterprises. In Texas, Perry was a cotton sampler and ran a cotton farm; before he was twenty, he worked as an attendant in a Turkish bath in Cincinnati. In New York from the 1890s until he relocated to Georgia in 1908, he was a solicitor for Equitable, Manhattan Life, Fidelity Mutual, and Mutual Reserve.

41. *Forbes*, 2 February 1924; Stuart, *Economic Detour*, 310–12; and Alexa Benson Henderson, "Herman E. Perry, 1908–1925," *Business History Review* 61 (Summer 1987): 216–42. Most black insurance companies were organized as industrial enterprises and required few reserves or little capital. Organized as an ordinary life insurance company, Standard, under Georgia state law, was required to have a $100,000 capitalization before a charter was granted. Perry's first attempt in 1908 to raise the money failed. His second succeeded, with a $50,000 loan from a white bank and investments by leading black businessmen, including Herndon of Atlanta Mutual. Standard's board of directors read like a virtual who's who in the 1913 black financial world, including Morehouse College president John Hope and Emmett Scott, private secretary to Booker T. Washington.

42. *Forbes,* 2 February 1924; Stuart, *Economic Detour*, 310–12; Henderson, "Herman E. Perry"; and Ingham and Feldman, *African-American Business Leaders*, 533–47.

43. Stuart, *Economic Detour*, 308.

44. Harmon, Lindsay, and Woodson, *Negro as a Business Man*, 110–11. The Citizens Trust became Citizens Bank in 1924. J. E. Walker, who had left Mississippi Life, established his own insurance company in 1923, the Universal Life Insurance Company in Memphis.

45. Ingham and Feldman, *African-American Business Leaders*, 553, comparing Perry to William Durant, founder of General Motors, note: "like Perry, a man of enormous vision and gigantic dreams. Durant was a marvelous salesman, promoter, and organizer who, because of his inability or disinterest in the mundane, day-to-day details of running a massive empire lost control of General Motors twice, and ultimately died a nearly forgotten man." Also, Henderson, "Herman E. Perry."

46. Walter B. Weare, *Black Business in the New South: A Social History of the North Carolina Mutual Life Insurance Company* (Urbana: University of Illinois Press, 1973), and Stuart, *Economic Detour*, 195–215. Also, Ingham and Feldman, *African-American Business Leaders*, 451–57, 387–90, on Merrick and Spaulding.

47. *Black Enterprise,* June 1996, 173.

48. Alexa Benson Henderson, *Atlanta Life Insurance Company: Guardian of Black Dignity* (Tuscaloosa: University of Alabama, 1990), 120–21, and Stuart, *Economic Detour*, 117.

49. Henderson, *Atlanta Life*, 90. In 1922 Atlanta Mutual also became the first black insurance company to provide in-house training in life insurance salesmanship.

50. Stuart, *Economic Detour*, 120, indicates Herndon defeated a bill "allegedly" promoted by his white competitors that would have made it illegal for black barbers to serve white patrons in their shops.

51. Ingham and Feldman, *African-American Business Leaders*, 324.

52. Harmon, Lindsay, and Woodson, *Negro as a Business Man*, 75–76.

53. Ibid.

54. Ibid., 55–56; Washington, *Negro in Business*, 133.

55. *New York Age,* 2 January 1913.

56. Harmon, Lindsay, and Woodson, *Negro as a Business Man*, 69–70.

57. Harris, *Negro as Capitalist*, 163.

58. Ibid., 153–64; Carl Osthaus, "The Rise and Fall of Jesse Binga, Black Banker," *Journal of Negro History* 58 (January 1973): 39–60; Allan H. Spear, *Black Chicago: The Making of a Negro Ghetto* (Chicago: University of Chicago Press, 1967), 74–75, 112–13, 184, 192, 227. Also, Ingham and Feldman, *African-American Business Leaders*, 75–80.

59. Harris, *Negro as Capitalist*, 144–53. Also, Ingham and Feldman, *African-American Business Leaders*, 497.

60. See "Some Chicagoans of Note," *Crisis,* September 1915, 242; J. H. Harmon Jr., "The Negro as a Local Business Man," *Journal of Negro History* 14 (April 1929): 116–55; Dewey R. Jones, "Chicago Claims Supremacy," *Opportunity* 7 (March 1929): 93; Spear, *Black Chicago*, 184; Joseph J. Boris, ed., *Who's Who in Colored America, 1928–1929: A Biographical Dictionary of Notable Living Persons of African Descent in America* (New York, 1929), 282.

61. Harris, *Negro as Capitalist*, 152. The National Baptist Convention had a loan of $11,000, the Knights of Pythias, a loan of $22,000, and the Chicago African Methodist Episcopal Conference owed $18,000.

62. Ibid., 48.

63. See Richard Kluger, *Simple Justice: The History of the Brown Decision and Black America's Struggle for Equality* (New York:. Knopf, 1976), and Richard Bardolph, ed., *The Civil Rights Record: Black Americans and the Law, 1849–1970* (New York: Thomas Y. Crowell, 1970). The earlier 1876 *U.S. v Reese* and *U.S. v Cruikshank* decisions made the distinction between public-sector and private-sector acts of discrimination, establishing that the Fourteenth Amendment only guaranteed that the federal government would require the states to provide "equal protection of the law" in the public sector, while also neutralizing the amendment's privileges and immunities clause. The 1883

civil rights cases provided constitutional sanction for private-sector acts of discrimination in places of public accommodation, including hotels, restaurants, theaters, and places of amusement. *Plessy v Ferguson*, however, sanctioned state discrimination and segregation under the "separate but equal" mandate of that decision. States segregated but did not provide for "equal" accommodations.

64. DuBois, *Economic Co-Operation*, 165.

65. *New York Post*, 21 November 1905. Washington, *Negro in Business*, 213–15. Also, Schweninger, *Black Property*, 223.

66. Ingham and Feldman, *African-American Business Leaders*, 138–39. The orchestra was headed by W. C. Handy, who became nationally known as the creator of the blues, one of America's distinct music forms.

67. DuBois, *Economic Co-Operation*, 164–65. Also, *Christian Index*, 16 January 1908.

68. Ingham and Feldman, *African-American Business Leaders*, 106. Also, DuBois, *Economic Co-Operation*, 164.

69. *Indianapolis Freeman*, 14 November 1914.

70. Washington, *Negro in Business*, 209.

71. *New York Age*, 21 March 1912.

72. *The (Cincinnati) Union*, 11 June 1912.

73. See Helen Buckler, *Doctor Dan: Pioneer in American* Surgery (Boston: Little, Brown, 1954). Also, Spear, *Black Chicago, 74.*

74. Savage, *African-American Historic Places*, 121.

75. *Christian Recorder*, 15 March 1915.

76. *Negro World*, 1931–1932.

77. *Crisis*, November 1923, 76–78. Also, *Negro Year Book*, 1931–1932, 134–35. By 1930 Roberts had moved his dealership to Chicago, which also sold new cars. In Baltimore, Albert A. French, who also owned a car dealership in Philadelphia, was "a direct Ford dealer."

78. *The East Tennessee News*, 27 March 1920. The park was renamed the Booker Washington Park. In 1920, owners of black baseball teams organized the National Negro Baseball League.

79. Washington, *Negro in Business*, 166–70.

80. *Indianapolis Freeman*, 1 July 1912. Also, Booker T. Washington, "Negro Rises in Business," *Christian Science Monitor*, June 1914; and *Philadelphia North American,* June, 1914. Also, Savage, *African-American Historic Places*, 92.

81. Washington, "Negro Rises in Business," *Christian Science Monitor*, June 1914; and *Philadelphia North American*, June 1914.

82. *Baltimore Afro-American*, 26 November 1920.

83. *Chicago Bee*, 27 June 1914.

84. *Negro Year Book, 1931–1932*, 135–36. On Archie Alphonson Alexander (1888–1958), see Ingham and Feldman, *African-American Business Leaders*, 17–24.

85. Savage, *African-American Historic Places,* 150–51. Whitelaw was also the founder of the Industrial Savings Bank and the National Mutual Improvement Association of America.

86. *Indianapolis Freeman,* 23 November 1912; and *New York Age,* 18 September 1912.

87. *Christian Recorder*, 6 May 1915.

88. *New York Age*, 5 December 1912.

89. Ingham and Feldman, *African-American Business Leaders*, 521–22.

90. Washington, *Negro in Business*, 277.

91. Ibid., 198, 204.

92. Gilbert Osofsky, *Harlem: The Making of a Ghetto: Negro New York, 1890–1930,* 2d. ed. (New York: Harper and Row, 1971), 92–104; and Ingham and Feldman, *African-American Business Leaders*, 522–23.

93. "Million Dollar Deal," *New York Age,* 30 March 1911. Also, *New York Age,* 5 December 1912. On Nail, see Ingham and Feldman, *African-American Business Leaders*, 476–83.

94. Spear, *Black Chicago,* 11–27, 91–110, on the creation of the physical and institutional black ghetto. Also, Osofsky, *Harlem*, 113.

95. *New York City Evening World*, 1 April 1920. Also, *New York Age*, 23 March 1918, for information on the $1,500,000 purchase, in which the Payton Apartments Corporation asked white tenants to move.

96. *Amsterdam News*, 11 July 1917. Payton named the six properties after black heroes: (Crispus) Attucks Court; (Toussainte) L'Ouverture' Court; (Phillis) Wheatley Court; (Paul Laurence) Dunbar Court; (Frederick) Douglass Court; and (Booker T.) Washington Court. These were luxury three-, four-, five-, and six-room apartment buildings, which covered two acres—33 full city lots. The buildings were fireproof and contained 306 apartments with "beautiful gas and electrical fixtures," along with "[h]ardwood trim floors and French doors with Florentine glass."

97. *New York Age,* 19 March 1918. Brown was president of the Brown Savings Bank of Norfolk and a member of the firm of Brown and Stevens, bankers. Stevens, a prominent real estate broker and president of the Home Extension Life Insurance Company was vice president, and Emmett J. Scott, secretary of Tuskegee Institute, was secretary and treasure of the company. With the real estate boom in Harlem, wealthy blacks from all over the country invested in property there.

98. *New York Age*, 14 August, 1920.

99. *Report of the Thirteenth Annual Convention of the National Negro Business League* (Washington, D.C., n.d.), 52. Also, Washington, *Negro in Business*, 160, noted that in 1907 "there was organized in Indian Territory a company for owning and operating oil wells."

100. Savage, *African-American Historic Places*, 118.

101. DuBois, *Economic Co-Operation*, 161.

102. "Miss Proctor's Wealth Increasing," *(Howard University) Commercial College Outlook*, 5 November 1913, 45.

103. Savage, *African-American Historic Places*, 405; *Oklahoma City Black Dispatch*, 12 November 1920.

104. Woodson, *Negro in Our History* , 297–98. Also, Sidney Kaplan, "Jan Earnst Matzeliger and the Making of the Shoe," *Journal of Negro History* 40 (January 1955): 8–33. Also, McKinley Burt Jr., *Black Inventors of America* (Portland, Ore.: National Book Company, 1969).

105. Baker, "The Negro in the Field of Invention," 21–36. Joseph Rossman, "The Negro Inventor," *Journal of the Patent Office Society* 12, no. 4 (1930): 549–53. Also, Burt, *Black Inventors;* Robert C. Hayden, *Eight Black Inventors* (Reading, Mass.: Addison Wesley, 1972); Louis Haber, *Black Pioneers of Science and Invention* (New York: Harcourt, Brace and World, 1970).

106. Portia James, *The Real McCoy: African-American Invention and Innovations, 1619–1930* (Washington, D.C.: Smithsonian Institution Press, 1989), 46–55 on slaves who were inventors, including Benjamin Montgomery, who invented a steamboat propeller. But in 1858 the U.S. attorney general held that "machines invented by slaves could not be patented." Montgomery was the slave of the brother of Jefferson Davis, who, when he became president of the Confederacy, pushed for a law that would allow the owner of a slave who created an invention to patent it. Under the Confederate Patent Act, the owner was given "all the rights to which a patentee is entitled by law."

107. United States Patent Office, patent no. 252,386 issued to Lewis H. Latimer and assigned to the United States Electric Lightning Company, 17 January 1882. Application filed 19 February 1881.

108. *Lewis Howard Latimer: A Black Inventor* (Southfield, Mich.: Thomas Alva Edison Foundation, 1979). Also, James Michael Brodies, *Created Equal: The Lives and Ideas of Black American Inventors* (New York: William Morrow, 1993). Latimer also wrote one of the first textbooks on electricity, *Incandescent Electric Lighting* (1896). Also, Glennette Tilly Turner, *Lewis Howard Latimer* (Englewood Cliffs, N.J.: Silver Burdette, 1991), for juvenile readers.

109. See United States Patent Office, patent no. 463,020 issued to Elijah McCoy, 10 November 1891. The application, filed 31 August 1891, said: "The object of this invention is to construct a cheap, simple, and efficient electric-railway system adapted as well for existing lines of street-railways, as for new lines and which entirely dispenses with overhead wires or with exposed feeders and does not require conduits or openings in the street for the purpose of connecting with the main feeder. The system, briefly stated, provides for placing the main feeder ... in the road-bed."

110. See United States Patent Office, patent no. 371,655 to Granville T. Woods and assigned to the Woods Electric Company for an "Electro-Magnetic Brake Apparatus," 18 October, 1887; the application was filed 2 October, 1886.

111. John E. McWorter's patents were no. 1,115,710, 20 October 1914. The application, however, was filed 26 June 1911; whereas, his application for patent 1,114,167 was filed 9 May 1913 and granted 20 October 1914. His 1922 application for patent 1,438,929 was filed 18 July 1921 and assigned to the Airplane Company of America. See United States Patent Office, patent no. 1,438,929 to John E. McWorter and assigned to Autoplane Company of America for a "Flying Machine," 12 December 1922; application filed 18 July 1921. Also, Walker, *Free Frank,* 170. As early as 1900, black inventors secured patents for "airships." See United States Patent Office, for patent no. 643,975 issued to John F. Pickering, 20 February 1900; application filed 19 July 1899. The patent was for a dirigible.

112. See United States Patent Office, patent no. 1,475,024 issued to Garrett A. Morgan, 20 November 1923. For a traffic signal; application filed 27 February 1922. On Morgan's invention of the gas mask, see below, 435–36.

113. See "The Patterson-Greenfield Automobile in Evidence at the State Colored Fair," *Negro Review,* 10 November 1916. Also, Beverly Rae Kimes and Henry Austin Clark Jr., *Standard Catalogue of American Cars, 1905–1942* (Iola, Wis.: Krause Publications, 1989), 1116–17; "Patterson-Greenfield Automobile Sales Bulletin," The National Automotive History Collection. The Detroit Public Library. Both sources have pictures.

114. Harmon, Lindsay, and Woodson, *Negro as a Business Man,* 20–21. Also, William Newton Hartshorn, *An Era of Progress and Promise, 1863–1910* (Boston: Priscilla Publishing, 1910), and George Reason and Sam Patrick, *They Had a Dream,* vol. 3 (Los Angeles: Los Angeles Times Syndicate, 1971).

115. James, *The Real McCoy,* 48, 89–91 on the Ripley, Ohio, Parker Machine and Foundry Company founded before the Civil War by self-hired slave John Parker (1827–1900), who purchased his freedom in 1850 for $1,800. Parker invented a tobacco screw press, which his company manufactured until the company closed in 1918. Also, the Chicago-based Howard Manufacturing Company, which made shoe polishes, and the Brooklyn-based Scottron Manufacturing Company, which made lamp pedestals and columns, were successful. Both were established in the early 1900s.

116. See United States Patent Office, patent for a "Heating Furnace," issued to Alice H. Parker 23 December 1919; application filed 9 July 1918. Also, Patricia Carter-Ives, "Patent and Trademark Innovations of Black Americans and Women," *Journal of the Patent Office Society* 62 (February 1980), and Autumn Stanley, "From Africa to America: Black Women Inventors," in *The Technological Woman: Interfacing With Tomorrow,* ed. Jan Zimmerman (New York: Praeger, 1985).

117. "Prospectus of the Cotton Seed Oil Mill—To Be Located at—Mound Bayou—Fostered by—Mississippi Negro Business League," William Johnson Papers, Special Collections, Hill Memorial Library, Louisiana State University. Charles Banks, who had been a resident of Mound Bayou since 1903, was involved in the development of many of the town's businesses, including the Mound Bayou State Bank, the Mound Bayou Supply Company, and the Banks' Cotton Company. He was also one of the founders of Peace, Arkansas, a black sawmill town.

118. Stock certificate for the Mound Bayou Oil Mill & Manufacturing Company, William Johnson Papers, Special Collections, Hill Memorial Library, Louisiana State University.

119. *New York Age,* 19 June 1912.

120. *Tuskegee Student,* 14 December 1912.

121. Ingham and Feldman, *African-American Business Leaders,* 49.

122. From a letter by Charles Bank to the editor, *New York Age,* 28 February 1920.

123. *New York Age,* 10 August 1916.

124. Ibid.

125. Ibid.

126. *Chicago Defender,* 10 May 1919.

127. Ibid., 5 April 1919, for advertisements of "Colored Dolls," which sold from $.29 for a "10 in. Colored Boy, dressed in rompers," to $3.50 for a girl doll, "16 in., with long flowing curls, beau-

tifully dressed." While Berry & Ross advertised that their dolls would "teach RACE-PRIDE," their ads indicated that their dolls had "nice straight hair," "wavy hair," and "Buster Brown style hair." Also, Berry & Ross made a "Soldier Boy in Full Uniform" doll.

128. Ibid., 26 April 1919.

129. Ibid., 10 May 1919, and *Norfolk Journal and Guide,* 28 August 1920.

130. *Chicago Defender*, 24 July 1920.

131. *Dallas Express*, 14 February 1920.

132. *Norfolk Journal and Guide*, 28 August 1920.

133. Ibid., 11 December 1920.

134. *Negro Year Book, 1931–32*, 135.

135. Vishnu V. Oak, *The Negro's Adventure in General Business* (Yellow Springs, Ohio: Antioch Press, 1949; reprint, Westport, Conn.: Negro Universities Press, 1970), 59.

136. Savage, *African-American Historic Places,* 402–3. Also, Ingham and Feldman, *African-American Business Leaders*, 452, on John Merrick, founder of North Carolina Mutual Insurance, who in the 1890s, while a barber, also ventured into the manufacturing of hair preparations, producing one that he claimed cured dandruff and advertised as "Merrick's Dandruff Cure. No greec, no fussy oder, its quick efect is cooling and clensing Power make it wonderful." Merrick had little formal education, but few would match his stature as an American entrepreneur at the turn of the century.

137. *New York Age*, 4 December 1920.

138. Ibid.

139. *Pittsburgh Courier*, 5 May 1927; *Chicago Defender*, 3 September 1927.

140. Ingham and Feldman, *African-American Business Leaders*, 634–40.

141. *Chicago Defender,* 14 June 1919, for a copy of Walker's will.

142. Ingham and Feldman, *African-American Business Leaders*, 680–91. Also see entries Kathy Peiss, "Beauty Culture," and A' Leila Perry Bundles, "Walker, Madame C. J. (Sarah Breedlove)," in Hine, Brown, and Terborg-Penn, *Black Women in America*, 100–104, 1209–14.

143. The first of Walker's conventions was held in August 1917. See *Norfolk Journal and Guide*, 1 September 1917. Also see *Chicago Defender,* 3 November 1917, on the Poro College annual convention that met in Chicago in 1917.

144. United States Patent Office, patent no. 1,693,515 issued to Marjorie S. Joyner and assigned to the Madame C. J. Walker Manufacturing Company For a "Permanent-Waving Machine," 27 November 1928; application filed 16 May 1928.

145. Ingham and Feldman, *African-American Business Leaders*, 689–90.

146. *Chicago Defender*, 6 March 1915.

147. Ingham and Feldman, *African-American Business Leaders*, 493–94.

148. *Norfolk Journal and Guide*, 30 August 1919.

149. *Indianapolis Freeman*, 12 July 1913. Also see, Marianna W. Davis, ed., *Contributions of Black Women to America* (Columbia, S.C.: Kenday Press, 1982), 342–43.

150. *Oklahoma City Black Dispatch*, 12 November 1920.

151. *Savannah Tribune,* 4 November 1920.

152. *New York Age*, 14 January 1915.

153. *Negro Year Book, 1917–1918*, 4.

154. *New York News*, 10 December 1914. As a basis for validating Trotman's expertise, the paper noted that he had recently "purchased the finest apartment house owned by any colored man anywhere in the country. The property is a large four-story apartment house located on Bedford Avenue, in the heart of the aristocratic St. Mark's section . . . and one block from the new building erected by Henry Ford, the millionaire automobile manufacturer."

155. *Tulsa Star*, 13 March 1915.

156. *Negro World*, 1918–1919.

157. "Colored Inventor Makes Fortune," *(Howard University) Commercial College Outlook,* 5 November 1913, 46. Also, United States Patent Office, patent issued to Garrett A. Morgan and assigned to the National Safety Device Company for a "Breathing Device," 24 March 1914; application filed 21 September 1912.

158. *Negro Year Book, 1917–1918,* 5. Other patented inventions by blacks included bombs, an antiaircraft gun, submarine detector, torpedo-catcher, and mine destroyer. See page 6 on black inventor Isaiah Williams of Jacksonville, Florida, who claimed that "the 'mystery gun' which bombarded Paris at a distance of 74 miles was the exact duplicate of the model of a gun which he offered the United States Government a few years ago." Later, black inventor Thomas W. Harold of Portsmouth, Virginia, claimed that he had invented a gun that "will throw a shell ninety miles." Both inventions were rejected by the government.

159. *Norfolk Journal and Guide*, 1 September 1917.

160. *Chicago Defender*, 26 April 1919; also 3 May 1919.

161. *Raleigh Independent*, 12 June 1920.

162. *New York Women's Wear*, 27 March 1918. Also, *Norfolk Journal and Guide*, 24 April 1920, for a reprint of the article, but with no reference to St. Louis; the reprint noted that "Our trade is becoming more valuable and should be corralled by our own group.... If our trade is worth so much to the other fellow, it is worth doubly that amount to ourselves. Who will be the next one to enter business in Norfolk?"

163. *New York City Mail*, 30 January 1919.

164. James Grossman, *Land of Hope: Chicago, Black Southerners, and the Great Migration* (Chicago: University of Chicago Press, 1989).

165. John Sibley Butler, *Entrepreneurship and Self-Help among Black Americans: A Reconsideration of Race and Economics* (Albany: State University of New York Press, 1991), 175–84. Also, Booker T. Washington, "Durham, North Carolina: A City of Negro Enterprises," *Independent* 70 (30 March 1911): 642, and E. Franklin Frazier, "Durham: Capital of the Black Middle Class," in *The New Negro*, ed. Winold Reiss (New York: Albert and Charles Boni, 1925), 333–34.

166. Butler, *Entrepreneurship*, 205–23. Also, Scott Ellsworth, *Death in a Promised Land* (Baton Rouge: Louisiana University Press, 1982).

167. *Atlanta Independent*, 24 October 1914.

168. Spear, *Black Chicago*, 11–28, 91–110.

169. Osofsky, *Harlem*, and David Levering Lewis, *When Harlem Was in Vogue* (New York: Oxford University Press, 1989).

170. *New York News*, 2 March 1914.

171. *Voice of the People*, 26 August 1915. Also, *New York Age*, 5 March 1921.

172. *New York Age*, 10 January 1920.

173. Ibid., 3 March 1916.

174. Ibid., 23 March 1916.

175. Ibid., 11 September 1913.

176. *Norfolk Journal and Guide*, 24 April 1920. The Brown Savings and Banking Company and the Southern Aid Society, a Virginia insurance company, were located on Queen's street.

177. *New York News,* 25 January 1917.

178. *New York Age*, 30 May 1912. This was an extraordinary proposal at the time. In the 1990s, the People's Liberation Army in China, with its investments in factories, construction, transportation, hotels, and casinos, in addition to providing workers, is viewed as the leading capitalist organization in that country.

179. *Negro World*, 30 April 1920.

180. Oak, *Negro's Adventure in Business*, 202–3.

181. *Atlanta Daily World*, 27 May 1919.

182. *Philadelphia North American*, 1 February 1920. Also see Oak, *Negro's Adventure in Business,* 52–57, for information on various stock schemes and wildcat business ventures put before the black public.

183. DuBois, *Economic Co-Operation,* 167.

184. *Negro Year Book, 1914–1915.*

185. *New York Age*, 5 March 1921.

186. *Chicago Defender*, 11 September 1920.

187. *Norfolk Journal and Guide*, 2 January 1919.

188. Amy Jacques-Garvey, *Garvey and Garveyism* (New York: Collier, 1970), 86. Also, Robert A. Hill, ed., *The Marcus Garvey and Universal Negro Improvement Association Papers,* 7 vols. (Los Angeles: University of California Press, 1983–1991).

189. *New York City Herald*, 31 October 1919.

190. *New York Age*, 18 December 1920.

191. "See What Garvey Has Done," *Crisis*, 24 (1922): 34–36. Garvey was found guilty, fined $1,000, and sentenced to five years in jail, but released in 33 months and deported from the United States.

192. Harlan, *Washington: The Wizard*, 280–81.

193. See Edmund D. Cronon, *Black Moses: The Story of Marcus Garvey and the UNIA* (Madison: University of Wisconsin Press, 1955); Tony Martin, *Race First: The Ideological and Organizational Struggles of Marcus Garvey and the Universal Negro Improvement Association* (Westport, Conn.: Greenwood Press, 1976). Garvey was controversial in many ways. He met with the Ku Klux Klan. He denounced both the light-skinned "mulatto" leadership of black America and dark-skinned blacks, such as the *Chicago Defender's* Robert Abbott, who encountered color prejudices from light-skinned blacks, and A. Philip Randoph. Both men opposed Garvey, while light-skinned Rev. Adam Clayton Powell said Garvey was the first to make him feel ashamed of his color. Also, that the UNIA in Harlem seemed to attract more West Indian immigrants than it did African-Americans was a point of contention. Some black Americans felt West Indians dismissed the African-American experience, were clannish, and more interested in retaining cultural ties with their colonial masters than in assimilating with them. Whatever the differences, few blacks anywhere could deny that what Garvey said about white racial oppression and exploitation was the truth. The post–World War I racial violence demonstrated that white America would not relent in its efforts to subordinate blacks "by any means necessary." It was Garvey's voice, more than any other, that articulated the frustrations and despair of blacks.

194. *Crisis*, 24 (1922): 120–22.

195. Stuart, *Economic Detour*, 75–77, and Ingham and Feldman, *African-American Business Leaders*, 502–3. In 1904, DuBois, investing $1600, along with Ed Simmons, a printer, launched the Memphis-based weekly magazine *Moon Illustrated Weekly*. Harry Pace was managing editor, while DuBois, the editor, remained in Atlanta. Disappointed with the magazine's quality, DuBois appealed to white bankers Jacob Schiff and Isaac Seligman for a $10,000 subsidy. Failing to secure the money, DuBois left the magazine to Pace, who attempted to save it.

196. *Norfolk Journal and Guide*, 3 August 1914; *Negro Year Book, 1925–1926,* and Walter Weare, "Charles Clinton Spaulding: Middle-Class Leadership in the Age of Segregation," in *Black Leaders of the Twentieth Century,* eds. John Hope Franklin and August Meier (Urbana: University of Illinois Press, 1982), 167–76.

197. Woodson, *Negro in Our History*, 371; this was perhaps a slap to both Garvey and DuBois's Pan-Africanism. Also, John Henrik Clark, ed., *Marcus Garvey and the Vision of Africa* (New York: Vintage Books, 1974).

198. *Crisis,* November 1921, 5–10, emphasized at the Second Pan-African Conference. The African-American church, however, stood in the vanguard, in not only extending missionary support to but also establishing schools in Africa. See DuBois, *Economic Co-Operation*, 59, 81, 83, for schools established by black churches before 1907.

199. Harlan, *Washington: The Wizard*, 271–73.

200. Ibid.; W. E. B. DuBois, "Segregation in the North," *Crisis,* April 1934, 115–17. Also, DuBois, *Dusk of Dawn*, 97.

201. *Negro Year Book, 1931–32*, 133.

202. E. Franklin Frazier, *Black Bourgeois*, 153–73.

CHAPTER 8

1. Bureau of the Census, *Retail Business—Negroes in the United States, 1920–1932* (Washington, D.C., 1934). Also, Vishnu V. Oak, "Business Opportunities for Negroes," *Crisis,* April 1938, 108–9, 126; and *Norfolk Journal and Guide,* 30 December 1939.

2. Gunnar Myrdal, *An American Dilemma*: *The Negro Problem and Modern Democracy* (New York: Harper and Brothers, 1944), 307.

3. St. Clair Drake and Horace A. Cayton, *Black Metropolis: A Study of Negro Life in a Northern City,* rev. and enl. ed. (Chicago: University of Chicago, 1993), 437–38.

4. Joseph A. Pierce, *Negro Business and Business Education: Their Present and Prospective Development* (New York: Harper and Brothers, 1947), 32; also Florence Murray, ed., *The Negro Handbook, 1946–1947* (New York: A. A. Wyn, 1947), 320, on 1939 population.

5. Drake and Cayton, *Black Metropolis,* 432, 438. Also, Harris, *Negro as Capitalist,* 183–84, on blacks and anti-Semitism in New York, where, despite limited black business profits, Harris states, "If there is exploitation of the black masses in Harlem, the Negro business man participates in it as well as the Jews, while both the Jewish business man and the Negro are governed by higher forces that are beyond control." Also, Pierce, *Negro Business,* 23.

6. Drake and Cayton, *Black Metropolis,* 430–32. See *Amsterdam News,* 18 August 1941, for Rev. O. Clay Maxwell, pastor of Mt. Olive Baptist Church in Harlem, who spent most of a Sunday sermon urging blacks to support Joe Louis's Brown Bomber Baking Company, explaining, "Economic strength is needed if we ever hope to make a place for ourselves in the sun." Also, *Amsterdam News,* 3 May 1941, for an account of a sermon given by the pastor of St. Martin's Episcopal Church, Rev. John H. Johnson, urging black support of black business, with Robert Chapman, general manager of the baking company, speaking at the service.

7. Myrdal, *American Dilemma,* 313, 802–3, 816. Most campaigns were led by ad hoc organizations, such as the Colored Clerks Circle in St. Louis; although in some cities, local NAACP and Urban League branches participated.

8. *Amsterdam News,* 20 July 1940. See Claude McKay, *Harlem: Negro Metropolis* (New York, E. P. Dutton 1940), 188–96. Also, Lewis, *Harlem in Vogue,* 301–2. In 1934, Bishop Amiru Al-Minin Sufi Abdul Hamid, who founded the Universal Holy Temple of Tranquillity in Harlem in 1930, led boycotts against white merchants there. His earlier Chicago boycotts against white merchants had some success. Later he joined with Father Divine to protest black unemployment.

9. William Jones, "Trade Boycotts," *Opportunity* 18 (August 1941): 239. Also, William Muraskin, "Harlem Boycott of 1934," *Labor History* 13 (Summer 1972): 361–73.

10. See *Amsterdam News,* 7 and 14 May 1938. At the same time, under the leadership of Adam Clayton Powell Jr. (1908–1973), the Harlem Job Committee in 1938 initiated a mass boycott of New York's gas, electric, and telephone companies in addition to large department stores such as Macy's, Bloomingdale's, Gimbels and Saks. Powell, then pastor of the Abyssinian Baptist Church, was elected to Congress in 1945. Also, Aptheker, *Documentary History,* 316–18. A. Philip Randolph was one of the founders of the committee.

11. John A. Davis, "We Win The Right to Fight for Jobs," *Opportunity* 16 (August 1928): 230–37.

12. Jones, "Trade Boycotts, 240–41, and Pierce, *Negro Business,* 26–28.

13. Vere S. Johns and George S. Schuyler, "To Boycott or Not to Boycott," *Crisis,* September 1934, 274. Also, Harris, *Negro as Capitalist,* 181, notes one consequence of the Don't Buy Where You Can't Work, campaign could be "a retaliatory movement of whites demanding that Negroes be employed only by those white capitalists whose income is mainly derived from Negro patronage." Of course, considering that white American business captures most of the black consumer dollar, that demand would be advantageous to blacks. Also, Myrdal, *American Dilemma,* 313, 802–3, 816.

14. See *New Negro Alliance v Sanitary Grocery Co.,* 303 U.S. 552 (1938), in which white Harlem merchants, in an effort to stop Don't Buy Where You Can't Work campaigns, secured a federal district court injunction to stop black boycotts as a violation of restraint of trade. The charge was upheld by the court of appeals but reversed by the Supreme Court, which found that boycotts

were labor disputes protected under the Norris-LaGuardia Act. Federal courts were thus denied jurisdiction to issue injunctions against nonviolent picketing. Also, Derrick A. Bell Jr., *Race, Racism, and American Law* (Boston: Little, Brown, 1980), 314–15. This 1935 injunction was a factor precipitating the 1935 Harlem race riot.

15. Murray, *Negro Handbook, 1946–1947* , 320–21 for a summary of black retail business activity from 1929 to1939. The decline in black retail service enterprises was primarily in the southern states, where 80 percent of the blacks lived, although 50 percent of them lived in urban areas. In all three periods, the South Atlantic region led in the number of stores, sales, proprietors, and employees. Also in 1939, Texas had the largest number of unincorporated black businesses, 2,679 (9 percent), displacing Georgia, which ranked first in 1929 and 1935. In 1939, New York led in sales (8.8 percent), followed by Texas (7.5 percent), and Illinois (6.1 percent). Also, New York led in payroll, with $480 million (8.9 percent); then Illinois, with $455 million (8.4 percent); and Ohio, with $417 million (7.7 percent).

16. Also, Beatrice Webb, *The Co-Operative Movement in Great Britain* (London: Swan Sonnenschein, 1910). The first cooperative was founded in England in 1843 and 1844—the Rochdale Cooperative by 28 textile workers, who established a grocery store/consumer cooperative. Eventually, the cooperative had 300,000 members, 800 stores, and owned 3 factories.

17. *Crisis*, July 1931, 225.

18. *Baltimore Afro American*, 22 August 1919.

19. *St. Louis Star,* 18 March 1920.

20. *Chicago Defender*, 2 May 1920.

21. *Louisville News*, 18 September 1920.

22. *Savannah Tribune*, 18 September 1920, and *Savannah Journal*, 20 September 1920.

23. Harris, *Negro as Capitalist*, 178

24. *Negro Year Book, 1931–1932*, 133.

25. Pierce, *Negro Business*, 210–11.

26. Harris, *Negro as Capitalist*, 178.

27. *Pittsburgh Courier*, 21 February 1931.

28. Ibid., 17 December 1932.

29. Oak, *Negro's Adventure in Business*, 64–65.

30. Harris, *Negro as Capitalist,* 178.

31. Florence E. Parker, *Consumers' Credit and Productive Cooperation in 1933*, Bulletin no. 612, Department of Labor, Bureau of Labor Statistics (Washington, D.C.:, 1935), 2; and Pierce, *Negro Business*, 164–78.

32. *Amsterdam News,* 12 July 1941. C. Lowell Turner, the co-op's marketing agent, said that the Florida Farmer's Cooperative was "a well-planned movement on the part of the Negro farmers in Florida of sharecropping and low-income status to become more self-sustaining, to improve their homes and living conditions in general through cultivation of their own products."

33. *Chicago Defender,* 1 June 1946. The cooperative was founded and headed by Simpson P. Dean, who also established a study club to encourage active participation in decision making among all of its members.

34. Ibid., 26 October 1946. Writing in his column in the *Defender,* Samuel Hayakawa compared some of the plans of the Tyrrell Cooperative with those made by the Cooperative Commonwealth group in Gary, Indiana, founded in 1941. See Pierce, *Negro Business*, 164–78, on consumer cooperatives. Also, *Chicago Defender*, 16 October 1948, on the Heth, Arkansas, Black Fish Cooperative, a cotton gin cooperative with 82 members and 15 directors founded by the family of wealthy black entrepreneur Scott Bond. Whites were among the customers; also see *Norfolk Journal and Guide*, 8 January 1944, on the Ayden, North Carolina, Bright Leaf Credit Union founded in 1941, which established a co-op exchange that sold feeds, seeds, produce, and groceries.

35. *Butler (Ga.) Herald*, 3 June 1943. Also see *East Tennessee News*, 19 January 1939, on the Dillard University Cooperative Stores, which sold books and school supplies and paid five percent dividend to its members, both students and faculty. Also Pierce, *Negro Business*, 167–69.

36. *Chicago Defender*, 16 November 1946. After the war, new co-ops were started on the South Side by the Chicago Consumers Cooperative.

37. Ibid., 1 and 14 September 1946. He notes that the Altgeld Gardens co-op was "the biggest demonstration project, not only in this area, but in the nation, of how far Negroes can go in governing their own economic destinies." Also see *Atlanta Daily World*, 16 April 1953, on the city's University–John Hope Homes Co-op Food Store founded in 1947.

38. *Norfolk Journal and Guide*, 8 April 1944. One of the founders, George Edmund Haynes (1880–1960) earned a Ph.D., and was a sociologist, university professor, cofounder of the National Urban League in 1910, founder of the Association of Negro Colleges and Secondary Schools in 1910, and special assistant to the secretary of the Department of Labor from 1918 to 1920.

39. *People's Voice*, 6 March 1943. Also, *Pittsburgh Courier*, 2 March 1946, on a black St. Paul, Minnesota, co-op, a supermarket, and a member of the St. Paul Co-op, Inc.; and the *Des Moines (Iowa) Bystander*, 6 May 1948, on the black Wise Buyers, Inc., co-op, founded in Kansas City, Missouri, by members of the Negro Employees Credit Union, which was organized in 1935 by the Kansas City Council of Negro Employees as a mutual benefit organization to "help members solve their financial problems." The Wise Buyers co-op started with a membership of 400 and $11,000.

40. *Chicago Bee*, 30 May 1943.

41. Joseph Demarco, "The Rationale and Foundation of DuBois's Theory of Economic Cooperation," *Phylon* 35 (March 1974): 5–15; George. S. Schuyler, "Consumers' Cooperation: The American Negro's Salvation," *Cooperation* 17 (August 1931): 144–45, and George. S. Schuyler, "The Young Negro Cooperative League," *Crisis*, January 1932, 456, 472. Also, "Cooperative Movement Offers Best Solution to Race's Economic Problems," *Miami (Fla.) Whip*, 8 July 1944; *Pittsburgh Courier*, 15 January 1944, on an article promoting black cooperatives; and *Houston Informer*, 23 September 1944, on the need for black manufacturing cooperatives to provide goods to black consumer cooperatives. Also, E. Franklin Frazier, "Cooperatives: The Next Step in the Negro's Business Development," *Southern Workman* 53 (November 1924): 505–9.

42. Pierce, *Negro Business*, 74, 165, 203, on the "high correlation" between the gross volume of black-owned businesses and the level of business education their owners received; blacks with a college-based business education: "have been established longer, employ more persons, and have larger volumes of business than those operated by persons with no business education."

43. See Emmer M. Lancaster, *First, Second and Third Annual Reports of Banking Institutions Owned and Operated by Negroes*, Department of Commerce, 17 April 1943, 28, on black bank resources that showed the following increases: 1939, $6,497,000; 1940, $7,404,476; 1941, $8,636,543; and 1942, $111,041,974. Also see *Afro-American*, 17 April 1943. On black credit unions, see *Louisiana Weekly*, 22 February 1946, and *Chicago Defender*, 26 October 1946.

44. *Daily Norfolk*, 3 February 1948. In 1933 there were some 5,000 cooperatives with almost a million members. In 1943 there were 35,000 cooperatives with 2.5 million members in addition to 100 co-op factories, 300 co-op oil wells, 10 co-op gasoline refineries, 1,000 miles of a co-op-owned pipeline, and a co-op coal mine. At that time co-ops were doing an annual business of almost a billion dollars, which included $235 million earned by cooperative stores. By 1948 co-op membership dropped and the number of enterprises declined to 3,000.

45. *Chicago Tribune*, 9 May 1944, noted several large corporations charged co-ops as being "Breeders of Socialism."

46. DuBois, *Dusk of Dawn*, 216.

47. Light, *Ethnic Enterprise*, 141–51; Jill Watts, *God, Harlem USA: The Father Divine Story* (Berkeley: University of California Press, 1992), 104–6, 137; Ottley and Weatherby, *Negro in New York*, 252–54; and Robert Weisbrot, *Father Divine and the Struggle for Racial Equality* (Urbana: University of Illinois Press, 1983). Father Divine also referred to his movement as the Righteous Government. Also, Robert Allen Parker, *The Incredible Messiah: The Deification of Father Divine* (Boston: Little, Brown, 1937), 78–107; Arthur Huff Fauset, *Black Gods of the Metropolis* (Philadelphia: University of Pennsylvania Press, 1944), 9–10; John Hoshor, *God in a Rolls Royce: The Rise of Father Divine, Madman, Menace, or Messiah* (New York: Hillman-Curl, 1936), 36, 46–47, 139. Marcus Bach, *Strange Sects and Curious Cults* (New York: Dodd, Mead, 1961), 126–32.

48. Sara Harris, *Divine Husband: Holy Husband* (Garden City, N.Y.: Doubleday and Company, 1953), 55.

49. Watts, *God, Harlem USA*, 58. Much of Divine's philosophy and his model for communal economic activity were derived from Charles Fillmore's Unity School, which by the 1920s was based on a farm outside of Kansas City, Missouri. Watts, 115, also suggests that Marcus Garvey's UNIA movement in its promotion of business reflected New Thought principles of the 1920s.

50. McKay, *Harlem*, 66.

51. Parker, *Incredible Messiah*, 228–29. Also, Ottley and Weatherby, *Negro in New York*, 265, 267, indicate that Harlem blacks reluctantly turned to relief, with a few chanting "Jesus will Lead me and the Welfare will Feed me." Relief allotted eight cents a meal, but during the early 1930s, Divine fed people ten-course meals. The Peace Mission also provided housing, and Langston Hughes noted, "I wish the rent Was Heaven Sent."

52. See Dennis Kimbro and Napoleon Hill, *Think and Grow Rich: A Black Choice* (New York: Ballantine Books, 1991). The book provides success principles and strategies for leading blacks but does not mention Divine.

53. Drake and Cayton, *Black Metropolis*, 470–94; J. Saunders Redding, "Playing the Numbers," *North American Review* 238 (December 1934): 533–43.

54. Rufus Schatzberg, *Black Organized Crime in Harlem: 1920–1930* (New York: Garland Publishing, 1993), 11, 21; *Newsweek*, 1 August 1938, 7–8. Criminal investigations in New York showed close ties between Dutch Schultz's numbers racket activities and The Tammany Hall political machine.

55. *Kansas City (Mo.) Call*, 6 September 1940.

56. Drake and Cayton, *Black Metropolis*, 487–88.

57. *Chicago Bee*, 26 February 1939. Also, Drake and Cayton, *Black Metropolis*, 488. In his speech, Robinson said: "Really, I don't know what you people want. . . . You have Jesse Owens, the fastest track man of all times; Joe Louis, the greatest fighter in the world. You even have God—Father Divine. . . . Now, you have the Jones Brothers with one of the finest stores in the world. Patronize them."

58. Drake and Cayton, *Black Metropolis*, 487. Also, Lewis, *Harlem in Vogue*, 221, on black policy king Caspar Holstein, "a Talented Tenth gangster . . . as distressed by guns and violence as Countee Cullen would have been."

59. Drake and Cayton, *Black Metropolis*, 486–89; Spear, *Black Chicago*, 76–77, on how Mushmouth Johnson established the Old Peoples Home. Also, Harold F. Gosnell, *Negro Politician: The Rise of Negro Politics in Chicago* (Chicago: University of Chicago Press, 1935), 125–27, 131–35, on Chicago's black vice lord and gambling king Daniel M. Jackson, who, before his death, contributed thousands of dollars to black charities, the NAACP, and homes for underpaid women employed in the formal economy. Compared to policy, vice would not seem as rewarding. See "Prostitutes in New York," *Nation*, 25 March 1936, which notes that black prostitutes were paid from $.25 to a $1, while white prostitutes made $1to $5; less than three percent of the "high-class" brothels were owned by blacks. See Hendrix de Leeuw, *Sinful Cities of the Western World* (New York: J. J. Messner, 1934), 266.

60. Drake and Cayton, *Black Metropolis*, 481. Also, W. Lloyd Warner, Buford H. Junker, and Walter A. Adams, *Color and Human Nature: Negro Personality Development in a Northern City* (Washington, D.C.: American Council on Education, 1941), 19, notes that "The game gives employment to more than 4,000 people and maintains a weekly payroll of $40,000 in salaries and commission. No other business in the Negro community is so large or so influential."

61. Drake and Cayton, *Black Metropolis*, 478.

62. See "Harlem," *Fortune*, July 1939, 170, and Drake and Cayton, *Black Metropolis*, 474–78, on peripheral businesses developed in urban centers in response to policy, especially occult enterprises, fortune-tellers, spiritualists, astrologers, merchants selling dream books, incense, candles, and holy oil, all of which were promoted to reveal lucky numbers. Also, black newspapers profited from publishing the advertisements of these enterprises.

63. Philip Harding and Richard Jenkins, *The Myth of the Hidden Economy: Towards a New Understanding of Informal Economic Activity* (Philadelphia: Open University Press, 1989), 16. National balance of payments accounts and estimates of the gross domestic or national product

(GNP and GDP) are recognized as underestimates of the actual level of a nation's economic activity. Also see J. I. Gershundy, *Social Innovation and the Division of Labour* (Oxford: Oxford University Press, 1983), 34–36, who categorizes informal economic activity into household, communal, and underground or ("hidden"); in the latter, he includes occupational theft and tax evasion.

64. Drake and Cayton, *Black Metropolis,* 485–87. Also, Spear, *Black Chicago*, 75–76, 113. Binga married in 1912. Johnson, in addition to his gambling enterprises, initiated policy in Chicago in the late 1890s in partnership with white crime kingpin Patsy King and the Chinese crime boss King Foo, who even attended Johnson's funeral in 1907. The funeral of his contemporary, gambling king Robert Motts, who built the showcase Pekin Theater, was attended by 4,000 people. Despite the violence, there was greater economic opportunity for blacks in America's underworld enterprises than in the formal economy, where blacks were denied equal opportunity.

65. Drake and Cayton, *Black Metropolis*, 487, note: "Many ministers, civic leaders, and politicians have eschewed any discussion of policy, purely on the ground that the game is a business, employing many people, and that the policy men have also opened legitimate business places."

66. Ibid. on the financial impact of the policy kings: "They have even given some reality to the hope of erecting an independent economy within the Black Metropolis."

67. See Lawrence Gordon, "A Brief Look at Blacks in Depression Mississippi, 1929–1934: Eyewitness Accounts," *Journal of Negro History* 64 (Fall 1979): 380–82. One eyewitness said: "most of us were really struggling, but . . . Barber Jones drove a Rolls Royce. We didn't know how he got the money because he only serviced Negroes in his barber shop." Another black, who worked at a fertilizer plant "for twelve and a half cent an hour, ten hours a day," said, "I made up my mind to try my hand at a little moonshining, cause I knowed no matter how bad things got, folks was gonna always find a little drinking money. . . . I musta been making about five or six hundred dollars a month." Some blacks on relief got as little as $10 a month.

68. T. Arnold Hill, "The National Negro Business League—Forty Years in Review," *Crisis,* April 1941, 104–5.

69. *Oklahoma City Black Dispatch*, 7 September 1940, and *Philadelphia Tribune*, 5 September 1940. Also see *Kansas City (Kan.) Plaindealer*, 23 August 1940. The meeting also signaled an upswing in interest in the NNBL, which had shown an increase in the number of local business leagues. Carlton W. Gaines was president of the Detroit organization.

70. *Oklahoma City Black Dispatch*, 18 January 1941.

71. *Nashville Globe and Independent*, 24 July 1942; *Baltimore Afro-American*, 5 September 1942; and *Atlanta Daily World*, 30 August 1942. Also, Oak, *Negro's Adventure in Business*, 100–102, on the Housewives League organized in 1930 by the National Negro Business League, whose membership was open to anyone who advocated "A belief in the future of Negro Business and a desire to assist in every way by patronizing and encouraging the same."

72. *New York PM,* 19 March 1943.

73. *Kansas City (Mo.) Call,* 10 September 1943.

74. *Baltimore Afro-American,* 11 September 1943.

75. *Chicago Defender,* 5 September 1942, and *Chicago Crusader,* 19 September 1942. Also, *Atlanta Daily World,* 31 August 1943. By 1943, the NNBL had had only four presidents: Booker T. Washington, its founder; R. R. Moton; C. C. Spaulding; and Dr. Walker, who was elected in 1939 and was in his fifth term. Spaulding had attended the first meeting of the NNBL when it was founded in 1900.

76. *Baltimore Afro-American*, 11 September 1943.

77. *New York Age*, 16 March 1940.

78. *Kansas City (Mo.) Call*, 13 October 1944, based on an article by David J. Sullivan, "Export Market at Home," in the *Negro Digest* (September 1944). Moreover, by 1943, when the black gross national income reached an all-time high of $10,290,000,000, it was emphasized that it was "far greater than Canada's 1943 total of $8,800,000,000."

79. *Atlanta Daily World*, 8 June 1942. The article noted the members of the committee who "arranged" the banquet for Spaulding's installation to the Chamber of Commerce, including Frederick H. Ecker, president, Metropolitan Life Insurance Company; Walter S. Gifford, president, American Telephone and Telegraph Company.; Sydney G. McAllister, president, International Har-

vester Company; J. Pierpont Morgan, J. P. Morgan and Company; John M. Schiff, Kuhn Loeb and Company; Walter C. Teagle, chairman of the board, Standard Oil Company of New Jersey; Perry H. Johnson, chairman of the board, Chemical National Bank.

80. *Kansas City (Mo.) Call*, 27 August 1943. Also, *Amsterdam News,* 28 August 1943.

81. *Atlanta Journal*, 1 May 1941.

82. Booker T. Washington Papers, doc. N-843, box 9, Hollis Burke Frissell Library-Archives, Special Collections, Tuskegee University, Tuskegee, Alabama. This campaign was tied in with the fourth war bond drive.

83. *Pittsburgh Courier*, 17 April 1943. An important issue dealt with at the conference was the "prevalence of absenteeism among employees recently integrated into war production enterprises." Also "spending orgies and dissipation following pay days" were condemned. It was decided that black organizations, including the NNBL, sororities, fraternities, churches, and schools should embark on a campaign to "to improve the serious condition created by such conduct." Blacks and whites from 11 states attended the conference.

84. See Paula F. A. Pheffer, *A. Philip Randolph, Pioneer of the Civil Rights Movement* (Baton Rouge: Louisiana State University Press, 1990). Also, Bardolph, *Civil Rights Record*, 41–42 and 301–2. There were three sections to Executive Order 8802. The most important for black workers was: "All contracting agencies of the Government of the United States shall include in all defense contracts hereafter negotiated by them a provision obligating the contractor not to discriminate against any worker because of creed, color, or national origin." Also, a committee on fair employment practices in the Office of Production Management was established.

85. See Jacques S. Gansler, *The Defense Industry* (Cambridge: Harvard University Press, 1980); Gerald T. White, *Billions for Defense: Government Financing by the Defense Plant Corporations during World War II* (University, Ala.: University of Alabama Press, 1979); Francis Walton, *Miracle of World War II: How American Industry Made Victory Possible* (New York: Macmillan, 1956).

86. *Atlanta Daily World,* 14 November 1940, indicated that California Senators Hiram Johnson and Sheridan Downey supported the bid. Defense contract bids were handled through the Army Quartermaster General in Philadelphia. Also see *Washington (D.C.) Tribune,* 23 November 1940, and *Savannah Journal*, 16 November 1940.

87. *Chicago Defender*, 14 March 1942. The unemployment situation of Toledo's blacks also underscores the extent to which many blacks during World War II, despite the nation's need for increasing numbers of workers in industry, were still receiving relief through the NYA and the WPA. During the war, there were more than 10,000 complaints.

88. *Atlanta Daily World*, 12 July 1944.

89. *Chicago Defender*, 28 August 1943. Howard Smith worked first in air shows as a parachute jumper, making 154 jumps. His partner was another young black man, Mark Gravelly; they were known as "Skip and Skippy." After Gravelly died in a jump, Smith began working at the Standard Parachute Company, the largest in the nation. He convinced Standard's owner, Colonel Fauntleroy, to subcontract the manufacturing of 18-inch pilot canopies to his company. At the time, however, Smith had no company and only $250. Financial support came from entertainer Eddie "Rochester" Anderson. Also, *Baltimore Afro-American,* 9 June 1945.

90. *Baltimore Afro-American*, 17 August 1946.

91. *Atlanta Daily World*, 1 April 1952.

92. *Chicago Defender*, 21 October 1950. *Tulsa Eagle*, 3 June 1954. Washington's employees, all of whom were black, worked two shifts because of space limitations, which also hindered production and resulted in his turning down orders.

93. *Atlanta Daily World*, September 1944.

94. *Oklahoma City Black Dispatch*, 20 December 1941. Also see *Atlanta Daily World*, 30 August 1942: "Mose McKissack [sic] noted contractor of Nashville, who holds a million-dollar government contract," was given the Spaulding Award for national achievement in business.

95. *Amsterdam Star-News*, 1943. Williams came to America in 1917 to join his older brother, Rupert, who had studied chemistry at New York University and who "became the first Negro consulting chemist in the country." During World War I, Rupert established the Hellenic Color and

Chemical Company and was said to have "attained great prominence by supplying the government with the pigment green used in the ink by the U.S. Mint."

96. *Baltimore Afro-American*, 10 September 1944, and *Nashville Globe and Independent*, 14 July 1944. The Kerfords owned the caves since 1887, when George Kerford established his quarrying business, which produced crushed rock, limestone, ballast sand, and gravel. On his death, the business was inherited by his two sons, Lloyd and George. In June 1944, Lloyd "was the first delegate-at-large ever named from Kansas to the Republican convention."

97. Ibid. Also, *Birmingham Age-Herald*, 12 February 1950, and *Kansas City (Mo.) Call*, 5 December 1950. See also *Chicago Defender*, 14 July 1945. At that time it was announced that the government was going to abandon the Kerford caves. Opposition to the use of the caves for food storage was said "to come from Warehouse association officials." Also at the House subcommittee hearings on the War Food Administration Agency, "it was charged that the government was being overcharged for the lease." The subcommittee recommended that the mine project be abandoned.

98. *Pittsburgh Courier*, 17 April 1943.

99. Pierce, *Negro Business*, 68–69. Percentage increases ranked from 1 to 400, with the average 34.5 percent. Pierce indicates the following showed the greatest increase: "building and loan associations, jewelry stores, accounting offices, optical stores, cosmetic manufacturing establishments, apparel shops, and potato chip factories . . . over 100 percent." The greatest decrease was shown by electrical appliance stores, electrical contractors, poolrooms and music studios.

100. Ibid., 31–74, on black businesses and their owners' motivation, capital outlays, location, types of ownership, record keeping, management policies and methods, and operating and financial analysis. Also see Butler, *Entrepreneurship and Self-Help*, 154–64, on his review of Pierce's findings.

101. Pierce, *Negro Business*, 32–34. An intensive study was made of 384 of these businesses. Also, Myrdal, *American Dilemma*, 301–10.

102. Pierce, *Negro Business*, 193.

103. Ibid., 70–71.

104. *Montgomery Advertiser*, 26 March 1944.

105. See *Daily World*, 6 August 1939, and "Million Dollar Casket Industry Possible Thru Co-Operative Effort," *Cincinnati Union*, 3 April 1941.

106. Pierce, *Negro Business*, 224.

107. *People's Voice*, 29 May 1943.

108. *Detroit Chronicle*, 10 August 1946, noted that "A large number of the women worked in war plants during the war, but most of them are housewives now."

109. *Baltimore Afro-American*, 13 January 1945, where the black presence dated back to the nineteenth century. The migration of blacks to Alaska escalated during World War II, although there were black sourdoughs who arrived there before the building of the Alaskan railroad.

110. Ibid., 10 July 1944. War correspondent Herbert M. Frisby wrote a piece entitled "SOMEWHERE IN ALASKA Aboard Army Transport Plane." Impressed by the business-minded attitude of Alaska's black women pioneers, he said, "if our men could see and appreciate what these colored women have done up here, they would feel that women should rule the world." See "Frisby Finds More Pioneers to Alaska," *Baltimore Afro-American*, 14 October 1944. The *Norfolk Journal and Guide*, 23 January 1954, showed that blacks lived in Anchorage, Fairbanks, and Juneau. In Anchorage, 40 businesses were owned by blacks, which differed little from those in the lower 48 states." There were restaurants, barber and beauty shops, a dry cleaners, grocery, electrical appliance store, cab company, and four real estate brokers. Former Chicagoan Franklin G. Dandridge was in real estate and brokered oil securities. In 1952 the black newspaper *Alaska Spotlight* was founded by George C. Anderson.

111. Ulysses Lee, *The Employment of Negro Troops: United States Army in World War II* (Washington, D.C.: Office of the Chief of Military History, U.S. Army, Government Printing Office, 1966) Russell Buchanan, *Black Americans in World War II* (Santa Barbara, Calif.: Clio Book, 1977); Richard M. Dalfiume, *Fighting on Two Fronts: Desegregation of the U.S. Armed Forces, 1939–1953* (Columbia, Mo.: University of Missouri Press, 1969); Morris J. MacGregor Jr., *Integration of the Armed Forces, 1940–1965* (Washington, D.C.: Center of Military History, U.S. Army, Government

Printing Office, 1981); Mary Penick Motley, *The Invisible Soldiers: The Experience of the Black Soldier in WWII* (Detroit: Wayne State University Press, 1975).

112. *Oklahoma City Black Dispatch*, 8 March 1947.

113. W. A. Caudill, *Negro GIs Come Back* (Chicago: American Council on Race Relations, 1945). Also see *New York Peoples' Voice*, 13 October 1945, and *Pittsburgh Courier*, 20 March 1948, on two disabled black veterans who established a successful leather craft business in Hollywood, California.

114. Pierce, *Negro Business,* 293, based on his survey of the median initial capital of 278 business in nine cites.

115. *Baltimore Afro-American*, 3 April 1950.

116. Ibid., 4 March 1939.

117. *(Des Moines) Bystander*, 2 November 1944; *Atlanta Daily World,* 2 November 1944, for a picture of the Union Air Lines flagship, *Mary Bethune*. A florist by trade, he was involved in various business ventures, including real estate. His application also included a request to operate three air routes among the following cities after the war: (1) Washington-Baltimore-Philadelphia-New York-Buffalo-Cleveland-Chicago-Indianapolis-Cincinnati-Memphis-New Orleans; (2) Chicago-St. Paul-Minneapolis-Fargo-Butte-Seattle-Tacoma-Portland-San Francisco-Los Angeles; and (3) Washington-Louisville-St. Louis-Kansas City-Omaha-Denver-Salt Lake City-Los Angeles.

118. *Chicago Defender*, 24 August 1946. One of the backers was Lionel Hampton. Also, Pierce, *Negro Business,* 223 notes that, in the 1940s, a group of black airmen founded a commercial aviation company to operate in South America.

119. *Pittsburgh Courier*, 7 January 1939. See, *Baltimore Afro-American,* 21 June 1947. In 1947 the International Merchandising Corporation, an import-export firm, was founded and incorporated with $20,000 capital stock and with ownership "99% by colored—with 1% in the hands of a white man who is married to a colored woman." The company planned to import West Indian rum, fruits, and sugar; spices and silk from India; and whiskey from Scotland. Plans were also being made for "a promotion campaign that will touch 37 countries of the world."

120. *Atlanta Daily World*, 9 April 1944.

121. *Amsterdam Star-News*, 1943.

122. *Chicago Defender*, 19 April 1947.

123. *Baltimore Afro-American*, 17 February 1951. In Mexico City, the journalist Carl Murphy interviewed the mother, wife, and 15-year-old son of Edward Jones. Mrs. Edward Jones Jr. said that "Her husband was away. She did not know when he would return ('Next week maybe or next month.')."

124. *Oklahoma City Black Dispatch*, 8 March 1947.

125. *Atlanta Daily Worker*, 5 November 1948.

126. Ingham and Feldman, *African-American Business Leaders*, 17–24. Also, *Chicago Defender,* 27 April 1946. Alexander also built the Moton airfield at the Tuskegee Institute. Also, *Kansas City (Mo.) Call*, 27 October 1950.

127. Jonathan Greenberg, *Staking a Claim: Jake Simmons Jr. and the Making of an African-American Oil Dynasty* (New York: Penguin Group, 1991), 2–6, 160–75, 196–97, 199. A business associate recalled: "I remember Jake telling me that he owed me something for the fact that I had let him in on the opening to a two- or three- or ten-million-dollar deal—that much which he made out of the Phillips Petroleum deal."

128. *Kansas City (Mo.) Call*, 15 May 1942.

129. *Atlanta Daily World*, 25 November 1955, and *Oklahoma City Black Dispatch*, 3 December 1955. Blind since the age of seven, John Randolph Smith owned and operated the Smith Music and Appliance Company in Atlanta, with gross sales of $100,000; he also owned and operated the Club Ponciana, the first black nightclub in downtown Atlanta. In 1950, Smith was appointed as a consultant to the Special Services for the Blind branch of the Federal Office of Vocational Rehabilitation. Although he was based in Washington, D.C., Smith's responsibilities resulted in his traveling to some 34 states.

130. Also see *Chicago Defender*, 14 September 1946, on the opening of Joe Louis's Harlem nightclub and restaurant.

131. *Houston Informer*, 31 May 1952.

132. *Chicago Defender*, 16 October 1954.

133. See *Baltimore Afro-American*, 2 October 1948. In New Jersey, John H. Rudd opened the Rudd Diary in 1945, buying his products from a processing plant. Rudd had owned a landscape business until World War II but noted that "Uncle Sam drafted his workers and forced him out of business because it was not essential to the war effort." For several years, Rudd worked in a "war plant."

134. *Chicago New Crusader*, 12 March 1955.

135. *Amsterdam News,* 1 February 1942.

136. *Chicago Defender,* 8 July 1939. Fifty percent of sales were for sweet-potato pies; 20 percent for apple pies,; 10 percent for peach pies; and 20 percent for cherry, lemon-cream, raisin, pineapple, and coconut-cream pies.

137. *Pittsburgh Courier*, 30 March 1946, and *Detroit Chronicle*, 3 August 1946. Alexander was considered one of the nation's leading black businesswomen in the early 1940s. In 1941, her Nanette Candy company grossed $60,000, but wartime restrictions on sugar limited production after that.

138. *Baltimore Afro-American*, 5 August 1950. The Chicago-based Baldwin Ice Cream Company was established in 1939 and incorporated in 1946 by Kit Baldwin, a 1911 graduate of Tuskegee Institute. In 1947 the company built a new plant, and in 1950 his company became the first black food manufacturer to sell its product in two national chains, A & P and Kroger.

139. *Chicago Defender*, 7 October 1950. Blacks were also involved in the wholesale food business. See *Los Angeles Tribune*, 31 July 1944, on the Petty Produce Company, established in 1944 by Edwin Petty, who did a six-figure annual business, buying produce from 150 farmers. He had 6 trucks and employed 18 blacks, 1 Filipino, and 1 white. Petty got his start in 1932, when he was hired by a Japanese merchant after being rejected by whites. In 1935 he became a salesman and then general manager, supervising 35 people. It was after his Japanese employers "were picked up by the FBI (their business was the first alien one closed in Los Angeles)" that Petty became a general broker, then a state-licensed wholesale broker in 1942, later obtaining a commission license.

140. *Miami Herald*, 10 December 1954.

141. *Pittsburgh Courier,* 6 September 1941. At the 1941 meeting of the NNBL, Wright won the Spaulding Award. Also see *Kansas City (Mo.) Call*, 12 September 1941, and *Nashville Globe and Independent*, 19 September 1941.

142. *Chicago Bee*, 29 March 1942.

143. *Durham Herald*, 14 April 1944.

144. *Seattle Northwest Enterprise*, 5 June 1946. Also, the black drivers would become members of the local AFL taxicab drivers union.

145. *Orlando Morning Sentinel*, 10 September 1946, and *Ft. Pierce(Fla.) News and Tribune*, 24 July 1946. This was the first time the Orlando city council had approved an application for a black taxi company. Support for the application came from the city's Negro Chamber of Commerce and the Negro American Legion post. Opposition from the white owner of a taxi company was based on his claim that he "was equipped to give the Negro population of Orlando adequate taxi service."

146. *Oklahoma City Black Dispatch*, 20 September 1947.

147. *Pittsburgh Courier*, 1 March 1947, and 26 December 1959. While Owl Cab failed, "The Negro-owned cab firm's hiring of Negro drivers broke the color ban against Negro drivers which AFL-CIO Taxicab Drivers Union had rigidly maintained against Negroes up to that time." Also, *Amsterdam News*, 24 January 1948, which reported that in St. Louis "Race franchise owners who operate about 350 cabs saw a serious threat to their business." New amendments to the city's taxicab law increased liability insurance from $2,500 to $5,000, raised the bond for companies to $60,000, and required taxicab permit fees. Meters were required, ending the zone-rate system.

148. *Pittsburgh Courier*, 18 July 1948. The cab companies included Liberty, the largest, with 34 cabs; City, with 19 cabs; Dependable, with 18 cabs; Lincoln and Kentucky each had 16 cabs; Central, with 12 cabs; and Avenue, with 7 cabs. Also, the black cab companies required their drivers to pay them $.20 for each mile they drove.

149. *Chicago Tribune*, 10 May 1958. Roberts was born in 1924. In 1954, to meet the entertainment needs of Chicago's blacks, he opened Roberts Show Club, which by 1958 was a $250,000 oper-

ation with seating for 1,000 people; also was the site of black social functions, including church teas, fashion shows, and dinners, as well as meetings held by black sororities and fraternities.

150. *Chicago Defender*, 1 May 1954. Hall was progressive in the development of his enterprise. All profits were immediately reinvested in the purchase of new cabs. To encourage good customer relations, he provided training for his drivers, a 20-hour course in courtesy and how to serve the public offered by the Savannah Vocational School. Also, to keep employee morale high, Hall opened a bank account for each driver, with deposits made by his wife in the accounts of drivers too busy to so for themselves.

151. *Pittsburgh Courier*, 25 May 1940; *Norfolk Journal and Guide*, 5 April 1945; and *Chicago Defender*, 10 July 1943. Also see *Oklahoma City Black Dispatch*, 5 June 1948, on the black-owned bus company in Baton Rouge that was ordered off the streets but continued to run. The company served both blacks and whites and was said to "have reduced racial friction on the city busses." Also, *Norfolk Journal and Guide*, 24 July 1948, on the Mississippi Public Service Commission, which in 1948 voted unanimously to give a permit to a black man, John Payton, to operate a bus company that would run between the Gulf Coast and Jackson. Payton said that his line would be "confined to colored traffic."

152. *Houston Informer*, 27 December 1958, and *Norfolk Journal and Guide*, 25 February 1959. See *Browder v Gayle*, 142 F. Supp. 707 Ala. (1956), aff'd curiam, 352 U.S. 903 (1956).

153. *Norfolk Journal and Guide*, 4 November 1950.

154. *Chicago Defender*, 2 July 1955.

155. *Baltimore Afro-American*, 28 August 1943. Wisconsin, Montana, and New Hampshire each had only one black hotel.

156. *Chicago Defender*, 28 December 1946.

157. *Pittsburgh Courier*, 31 July 1954.

158. Ibid., 5 November 1955. Also see *New Orleans Weekly*, 5 February 1955, on the expansion of the "new luxurious Marsalis Tourist Motel" in suburban New Orleans and owned by Mr. and Mrs. E. L. Marsalis. Openings of black motels and hotels were community events, with black and white leaders attending the ceremony. In this instance, an AME minister was on hand to bless the hotel, with the key speaker being the Most Powerful Sovereign Grand Commander George Longe of the Ancient and Accepted Scottish Rite Free Masons of Louisiana.

159. *Pittsburgh Courier*, 18 September and 10 November 1951, on the opening of the newly constructed $100,000 Ben Moore Hotel and the Parkway Hotel in Nashville, owned by Lemuel A. Bowman.

160. *Birmingham News*, 30 June 1954. The Gaston Motel had 32 air-conditioned units with telephones in every room. Its opening coincided with the black Baptist convention, and it had the endorsement of R. A. Hester, Supreme Chancellor of the Knights of Pythias, with black leaders stating that it was a "wonderful step [that] we hope will encourage the opening of other all-Negro motels and hotels over the southeast."

161. *Baltimore Afro-American*, 18 September 1954.

162. *Pittsburgh Courier*, 13 February 1954.

163. *New Orleans Weekly*, 8 October 1955.

164. *Argus*, 11 March 1955.

165. *Miami Herald*, 2 July 1957.

166. Ibid., 12 May 1955.

167. *Pittsburgh Courier*, 23 May 1953. Did the owner see the handwriting on the wall with the Brown case in the lower courts in Missouri? Or was he losing white customers and saw that opening his motel and restaurant to blacks would keep him from going under?

168. *Norfolk Journal and Guide*, 3 September 1955, and *Pittsburgh Courier*, 10 August 1955.

169. *Pittsburgh Courier*, 11 June 1955. Also see *Baltimore Afro-American*, 21 May 1955, which notes that the Moulin Rouge had encountered difficulty securing a license from the Nevada State Tax Commission to open the hotel and to allow gambling.

170. *Pittsburgh Courier*, 5 March 1955, added that with the Moulin Rouge using blacks at their gaming tables, "it might mean the white clubs will loosen their racial bars and not only hire race

gaming men, but admit Negroes to play at their tables." The Moulin Rouge was owned by Louis Rubin, Alexander Bison, and Will Max Schwartz.

171. *Baltimore Afro-American,* 21 May 1955, and 4 June 1955; Rubin was the well-known owner of New York's Chandler's Restaurant, "which featured the liberal Barry Gray late-night radio program." Bison was a Los Angeles real estate man. In addition to 24-hour gambling, the Moulin Rouge introduced a new concept in Las Vegas entertainment, all-night floor shows that began at 2:15 A.M. Also, black showgirls were featured. At its opening, the first scheduled artists were Wild Bill Davis, the Ahmad Jamal Trio, and Louis Jordan.

172. *Baltimore Afro-American,* 7 April 1956. Also, *Pittsburgh Courier,* 20 October 1956, ran the headline "Atomic Energy Commission May Buy Padlocked Hotel." The Dunes and the Riviera hotels were also closed at that time. The *Baltimore Afro-American,* 22 November 1955, noted that the Moulin Rouge had some 250–300 employees with a $50,000 a week payroll. The closing was forced by an investment company's attempt to recover $271,928 in defaulted notes. Despite the bankruptcy petition, the owners and investors had to "pay off all debts incurred by the operation," which resulted in the Moulin Rouge being put up for auction to pay off a total of $1,500,000 in debts.

173. *Birmingham Record,* 6 October 1953. Brown was father of the first black secretary of commerce, Ronald Brown.

174. *Pittsburgh Courier,* 3 January 1959.

175. Ibid.

176. *New York World-Telegram,* 21 September 1960. See *Washington (D.C.) Evening Star,* 29 September 1960, which noted "Castro Hotel Bill Paid Each Day—by Request." Also, *Baltimore Afro-American,* 1 November 1960, for a brief history of the Hotel Theresa and a statement that indicates that policy was still alive and strong in Harlem; it was noted that Castro's room number, 929, was the "Favored number played in Harlem last week," with the comment that "people DO play the numbers in spite of hell, high water—Commissioner Kennedy and Adam Powell." Also, *Atlanta Daily World,* 22 November 1960. The Hotel Theresa was owned by South Carolina-born Love B. Woods, who operated for more than 40 years as a hotel and real estate owner in Harlem. He had been the owner of the Woodside Hotel, which was "made famous by Count Basie in 'Jumpin' At the Woodside.' " It was the headquarters for black baseball teams and entertainers, as well as noted for its ladies of the evening. Woods took over the Hotel Theresa in the late 1950s after the city "purchased the Woodside, demolishing it along with other tenements in the area to make way for a housing project." In Havana, Cuba. the swank Riviera Hotel was renamed Theresa in honor of Castro's Harlem accommodations.

177. *Pittsburgh Courier,* 30 May 1959. There were blacks who felt that they could withstand competition from white hotels, especially for the weekend trade; blacks continued to build motels for blacks. In Los Angeles, black attorney Sherman Smith and his wife, Dr. Helen Guenveur Smith, constructed the two-story $175,000 Palm Vue Motel.

178. *Baltimore Afro-American,* 28 February 1959.

179. *Miami Herald,* 10 December 1954.

180. *Baltimore Afro-American,* 21 January 1932.

181. *Amsterdam News,* 7 December 1935.

182. *Atlanta Daily World,* 28 April 1950. Abraham and Company also employed another black, Dennis Barron, who sold investment trust securities.

183. *Kansas City (Mo.) Call,* 6 July 1956. Also, Chicago *Defender,* 24 September 1960. In 1960, the Hooper, Bowers and Hilliard, Inc. investment firm was opened in the Drexel National Bank building on the South Side. Earl Hooper, president of the firm, had previously worked for McGhee. The two partners, Nathaniel H. Bowers and William H. Hilliard were registered pharmacists who worked as store managers for Walgreen Drugs before each opened his own business. Hooper announced that the purpose of the investment firm was to "assist Chicago's Negroes to become active owners of shares in American industry."

184. *Nashville Globe and Independent,* 24 October 1958.

185. *New York Times,* 22 July 1955. Also see *Nashville Globe and Independent,* 22 July 1955. The board of directors included whites, although blacks had the controlling vote. Jenkins had a diversi-

fied career in finance and investments, working as an account executive for B. G. Phillip and Company. He was also on the board of the Mutual Investment Company of America and manager of the mutual fund department of Baruch Brothers and Company. In the 1930s Jenkins worked at the NNBL-sponsored National Colored Merchants Association (CMA), in addition to the highly successful black real estate firm Nail and Parker.

186. *Saturday Evening Post*, 29 October 1955.

187. *Montgomery Advertiser*, 12 December 1954. The Merrill Lynch representative stated that while his company preferred opening accounts at a minimum of $500, "people do invest as little as $15 to $20 in stocks under investment houses despite the cost of handling the account of the commission involved. Often they will place a regular amount each month into a stock plan." He also indicated that several Montgomery store chains had instituted a stock plan for their employees to purchase stock in the companies where they worked.

188. *Miami Herald*, 10 December 1954.

189. *Kansas City (Mo.) Call*, 29 April 1955. Also, *Business Week*, January 1955, which stated that the black business population was "the fastest changing part of the U.S. market and the U.S. labor force."

190. *Atlanta Daily World*, 15 April 1955.

191. *Jackson (Miss.) Advocate*, 8 November 1955.

192. "Race Problems," *Fortune* (March 1959). Union discrimination in American industry was a major contributing factor in the black economic picture, according to the magazine.

193. *Pittsburgh Courier*, 16 April 1960.

194. Ibid., 9 April 1960.

195. Ibid., 12 March 1960. In the same column, to emphasize that even small sums could be used for investment, McGhee stated that members of his investment class had purchased five shares of a stock for $4 each, which increased to $12 within the year.

196. *Oklahoma City Black Dispatch*, 12 July 1957.

197. *Pittsburgh Courier*, 13 February 1960.

198. Ibid., 23 July 1960.

199. *Norfolk Journal and Guide*, 18 June 1960, and the *Baltimore Afro-American*, 9 July 1960.

200. *Pittsburgh Courier*, 1 March 1960.

201. Ibid., 14 February 1959.

202. Ibid., 1 January 1960.

CHAPTER 9

1. Timothy Bates, "Black Entrepreneurship and Government Programs," *Journal of Contemporary Studies* 4 (Fall 1981): 59–70.

2. Nathan Glazer, *Affirmative Discrimination, Ethnic Inequality and Public Policy* (New York: Basic Books, 1975). Also, Ronald Takaki, "Reflections on Racial Patterns in America: An Historic Perspective," *Ethnicity and Public Policy* 1 (1982): 1–23, who notes, "Glazer spear-headed the intellectual assault on affirmative action."

3. Mansel G. Blackford, *A History of Small Business in America* (New York: Twayne Publishers; Macmillan Publishing, 1991), xii–xiii, 107.

4. United States Commission on Minority Business Development, *Historically Underutilized Business (HUBs): Final Report* (Washington, D.C., 1992), 28–29, is based on census reports of sole proprietorships, partnerships, and Subchapter S corporations. Many of the largest black businesses are organized as Subchapter C corporations. Their business earnings are not included in census figures on black businesses. See Margaret C. Simms, "How the Census Bureau Devalues Black Business," *Black Enterprise*, June 1996, 223–24, 226–28. The differences between Subchapters S and C corporations is that, with the former, shareholders report their shares of corporate profit or loss in their individual tax returns: with the latter, the corporation pays its own taxes and shareholders pay taxes only on dividends. Nonminority businesswomen are not included in this report.

5. See Dinesh D'Souza, *The End of Racism: Principles for a Multiracial Society* (New York: Free Press, 1995), 235–37. Also, Commission on Minority Business, *Historically Underutilized Business*. Racial and ethnic groups identified as minorities by the federal government include not only African-Americans but also Hispanic-Americans, Native-Americans /native Alaskans, and Asian-Pacific-Americans. Small businesses owned by members of these groups are classified by the government as "disadvantaged" minority business enterprises. Firms recognized as *historically underutilized businesses* are: "a for-profit business enterprise, at least 51 percent of which is owned and controlled by one or more individuals who are identified as belonging to a racial or ethnic group that has been subjected historically to prejudice, due to factors beyond the group's control, resulting in an underrepresentation of such enterprises in a particular field of commercial endeavor."

6. Blackford, *History of Small Business*, 70, 74–76, notes that from 1933 to 1942, Congress considered 390 bills to protect small businesses but enacted only 26 that pertained primarily to retail establishments. The 1936 Robinson-Patman Act and the 1937 Miller-Tydings Act were enacted to protect small businesses against competition from retail chains, who secured quantity discounts in their purchases from manufacturers and wholesalers. There was also the precedent of the World War II Smaller War Plants Division (SWPD) and the Smaller War Plants Corporation (SWPC).

7. Ibid., 69–70, 77. The banking activities of the RFC were transferred not only to the SBA but also to the Export-Import Bank, the Federal National Mortgage Association, and the Commodity Credit Corporation.

8. Ibid.

9. The SBA was established by the Small Business Act of 1953, Public Law 85–536, as amended, and codified as Title 15, United States Code Section 631.

10. *Norfolk Journal and Guide,* 11 September 1954. Members of the association, located in 20 states and 30 cities, displayed a red-white-and-blue emblem. Also, *Oklahoma City Black Dispatch,* 3 July 1954, which noted some of the financial success of Kansas City black real estate dealer Robert Williams, who capitalized on the benefits paid World War II veterans as a "broker for the Veterans Administration in the appraising and reselling of repossessed property." He was an established businessman, having purchased the city's landmark black Street's Hotel from its black owner for $250,000 and making $75,000 in renovations. The hotel had 38 two- and three-room suites, 6 single rooms, a cocktail lounge, restaurant, and barbershop. He employed more than 100 blacks, including 33 full-time in the hotel, while his real estate business had 60 full-time employees.

11. *Pittsburgh Courier*, 23 February, 22 July, and 17 August 1957. Also, *Oklahoma City Black Dispatch,* 11 June 1955, for commentary that presages the Civil Rights movement and role of the NAACP as the legal arm of black protest in the 1960s. In response to the building of the integrated Moulin Rouge hotel and casino in Las Vegas, an editorial denounced laws that prohibited whites and blacks from dwelling in the same lodging places : "[T]he NAACP should immediately break up this sort of sectional viciousness, and we believe it could be clearly shown that the Negroes are denied a property right by such deprivation of normal trade, and thus a violation of the 14th Amendment to the Constitution."

12. *Atlanta Daily World*, 13 December 1958. Also, Flournoy A. Coles Jr., "Financial Institutions and Black Entrepreneurship," *Journal of Black Studies* 3 (March 1973): 332–33.

13. "SBA Probes 'Black Fronts' Charges," *Baltimore Afro-American,* 16 July 1977.

14. On 22 June 1963, President Kennedy issued Executive Order 11114, entitled "Equal Employment Opportunity," which required fair employment in any institution given federal monies or construction companies with federal contracts. Kennedy's Executive Order 10925, 6 March 1961, established the Committee on Equal Employment Opportunity by combining the President's Committee on Government Contracts and the President's Committee on Government Employment Policy. No special provisions were made for black business. Also see *Race Relations Law Reporter* (Nashville: Vanderbilt University School of Law, 1956–1967): 1: 9, 3: 793.

15. See United States Commission on Civil Rights, *Special Bulletin: Summary of the Civil Rights Act of 1964* (Washington, D.C, 1964.)

16. Gerald David Jaynes and Robin M. Williams Jr., *A Common Destiny: Blacks and American Society* (Washington, D.C.: National Academy Press, 1989), 255–56, on the SBA: "The impetus

for the federal initiative in this area appears to have come from the National Urban League. Whitney Young, then the league's executive director, made black business opportunity a centerpiece of his "Marshall Plan for the Cities" proposal in 1963. See "Whitney M. Young, Jr.: For a Federal 'War on Poverty,' " in *Black Protest Thought in the Twentieth Century*, eds. August Meier, Elliott Rudwick, and Frances L. Broderick (New York: Macmillan Publishing, 1971), 430–37, for Young's statement made before the House Committee on Education and the Labor Ad Hoc Subcommittee on the War on Poverty Program.

17. See Arnold Schuchter, *White Power/Black Freedom: Planning for the Future of Urban America* (Boston: Beacon Press, 1968), 321–45; he notes, "the EOL program was not designed especially to help Negro businessmen make greater use of the public and private resources available to assist business." Also, Timothy Bates, "Government as Financial Intermediary for Minority Entrepreneurs," *Journal of Business* 48 (October 1975): 541–47; and Timothy Bates, "Small Business Viability in the Urban Ghetto," *Journal of Regional Science* 29 (1989): 625–43. Also, Flournoy A. Coles Jr., *Black Economic Development* (Chicago: Nelson Hall, 1975), 169–75, on "Federal Government Programs for Black Entrepreneurs," listed under the following: Departments of Agriculture; Commerce; Defense; Health, Education and Welfare; Housing and Urban Development; Labor, in addition to the General Services Administration, SBA, and the Veteran's Administration.

18. Leon H. Sullivan, *Build Brother Build* (Philadelphia: Macrae Smith Company, 1969), 69, 76, 77. Also, David J. Garrow, *Bearing the Cross: Martin Luther King Jr., and the Southern Christian Leadership Conference* (New York: Random House, 1988), 223, 462, 489, 538, 568.

19. See Gary Massoni, "Perspectives on Operation Push," in *Chicago 1966: Open Housing Marches, Summit Negotiations, and Operation Breadbasket*, ed. David J. Garrow (Brooklyn, N.Y.: Carson Publishing, 1989); Barbara J. Reynolds, *Jesse Jackson: The Man, the Movement, the Myth* (Chicago: Nelson, Hall, 1975). Also, Robert B. McKersie, "Vitalize Black Enterprise," *Harvard Business Review* 46 (September/October, 1968): 88–99, provides an example of Operation Breadbasket's success: the black-owned Argia B's Food Products company grew "from virtually zero sales to a volume in six figures," with a "10 percent to 15 percent penetration in the entire Chicago market."

20. *New York Review of Books*, 22 September 1968. Also, Floyd B. Barbour, ed., *The Black Power Revolt* (Boston: Porter Sargent, 1968). See Al Ulmer, "Cooperatives and Poor People in the South," in *Black Business Enterprise: Historical and Contemporary Perspectives*, ed. Ronald W. Bailey (New York: Basic Books, 1971), 243–50, describes 40 people's cooperatives in the South in 1969: credit unions, farm-marketing and farm machinery co-ops, buying clubs, sewing co-ops, handicraft production groups, bakers, candy-making businesses, gas and oil retailers, wholesalers, grocery stores, and a fish-processing association with an outreach of 15,000 people. As the black revolution of the 1960s moved from civil rights to the black power movement, CORE and SNCC pushed whites out. See "Chicago Office of SNCC, 'We Must Fill Ourselves With Hate For All White Things,' " in Meier, Rudwick, and Broderick, *Black Protest Thought*, 484–90, from a 1967 SNCC leaflet, "WE WANT BLACK POWER."

21. Shelley Green and Paul Pryde, *Black Entrepreneurship in America* (New Brunswick: Transaction Publishers, 1990), 23. Also see Andrew Brimmer and Henry Terrell, "The Economic Potential of Black Capitalism," *Public Policy* 19 (Spring 1971): 289–308.

22. C. Eric Lincoln, *The Black Muslims in America* (Boston: Beacon Press, 1961); Elijah Muhammad, "The Muslim Program," *Muhammad Speaks*, 31 July 1962, in *Black Nationalism in America*, eds. John H. Bracy Jr., August Meier, and Elliot Rudwick (Indianapolis: Bobbs-Merrill, 1970), 404–7; C. Eric Lincoln, *The Black Church since Frazier* (New York: Schocken Books, 1974), 155–57. The Nation of Islam, founded in 1930, was given momentum under Elijah Muhammad, who assumed control in 1934. Its business ventures were centered in real estate, farm ownership, and apartment complexes, in addition to restaurants, dry cleaners, newspapers, and personal health care product manufacturing. National attention was directed to the organization in the 1960s for its separatist position and especially its denunciation of white America. Also, African-American critics denounced the Nation for failing to participate in the Civil Rights movement. See E. U. Essien-Udom, *Black Nationalism: The Search For an Identity* (Chicago: University of Chicago Press, 1962). Also, Martha F. Lee, *History of the Nation of Islam* (Lewiston, N.Y.: Edwin Mellon Press, 1988).

23. See Harold Cruse, "Black Economy—Self-Made Myth and "Capitalism Revisited," *Crisis of the Negro Intellectual* (New York: William Morrow, 1967), who views Garvey's economic program as a failure but emphasizes the merits of DuBois's economic program based on a "cooperative commonwealth." DuBois, by the 1960s, had given up on American capitalism and racism and emigrated to Ghana.

24. Earl Ofari, *The Myth of Black Capitalism* (New York: Monthly Review Press, 1970), 59.

25. In the 1960s, militant blacks representing black economic nationalism placed the economic problems of black America within the context of the Third World, emphasizing that black Americans existed in a colonial relationship to white America. A significant influence was Franz Fanon, *The Wretched of the Earth* (New York: Grove Press, 1963).

26. Floyd B. McKissick, *Three-Fifths of a Man* (New York: Macmillan Publishing, 1969), 145, 164; and Floyd B. McKissick, "Black Business Development with Social Commitment to Black Communities," in Bracy, Meier, and Rudwick, *Black Nationalism in America*, 492–503; and Robert L. Allen, *Black Awakening in Capitalist America: An Analytic History* (Garden City, N.Y.: Doubleday and Company, 1969), 68–70. Also, Nathan Wright Jr., *Black Power and Urban Unrest* (New York: Hawthorn, 1967), 63.

27. Martin Luther King Jr., *Where Do We Go From Here: Chaos or Community?* (New York: Harper and Row, 1967).

28. David Levering Lewis, "Martin Luther King Jr. and the Promise of Nonviolent Populism," in Franklin and Meier, *Black Leaders*, 277–303.

29. Malcolm X, "Liberation by Any Means Necessary," in *Afro-American History: Primary Sources*, ed. Thomas R. Frazier (Belmont, Calif: Wadsworth, 1988), 384. This statement was made in a speech given by Malcolm X in April 1964, less than a month after he left the Black Muslims. Also, Malcolm X, "The Black Revolution," *Two Speeches by Malcolm X* (New York: Merit, 1966).

30. "The Black Panther Party Program," in Bracy, Meier, and Rudwick, *Black Nationalism in America*, 527. Also see Richard F. America Jr., "What Do You People Want?" *Harvard Business Review* (March–April 1969): 103–22; it can also be found in Bailey, *Black Business Enterprise*, 124, 127. In 1969, America, a black economist, was director of the Urban Programs Division of the Graduate School of Business, University of California at Berkeley; to achieve black the economic empowerment, he said "a workable mechanism is required for the transfer of some major national corporations to Black Control." Also, Dunbar S. McLaurin, "Ghetto Economic Development and Industrialization Plan (Ghedi-plan)," in Bailey, *Black Business Enterprise*, 184–92. McLaurin was also an economist and international businessman.

31. James Forman, "The Black Manifesto: Total Control as the Only Solution to the Economic Problems of Black People," in Bailey, *Black Business Enterprise*, 324.

32. *Commonweal*, 30 May 1969, 308.

33. *The Christian Century*, 21 May 1969, 701. Also see Lester Thurow, "Affirmative Action in a Zero-Sum Society," in *The Zero-Sum Society: Distribution and the Possibilities for Economic Change* (New York: Basic Books, 1980).

34. Robert S. Lecky and H. Elliott Wright, *Black Manifesto: Religion, Racism, and Reparations* (New York: Sheed and Ward, 1969), 7, 13, 114–28, 141, 157–62. Also James Forman, *The Making of Black Revolutionaries* (New York: Macmillan, 1972), 545, 548–49.

35. Allen, *Black Awakening*, 211.

36. "Why Few Ghetto Factories Are Making It," *Business Week*, 16 February 1987, 86–87. Also, Allen, *Black Awakening*, 215–26. Also see Theodore L. Cross, *Black Capitalism: Strategy for Business in the Ghetto* (New York: Atheneum, 1969), 227–54, for a survey of black businesses developed from community organizations, coalitions of white corporate America, and government agencies in coalition with black organizations; Coles, *Black Economic Development*, 177–82; and Raymond L. Hoewing and Lawrence J. Finkelstein, *Minority Entrepreneurship . . . A Status Report* (Washington, D.C.: Public Affairs Council, 1969). The Interracial Council for Business Opportunity (ICBO), founded in 1963 in New York by the Urban League and the American Jewish Congress, was nationally based, with locals in Newark, Washington D.C., St. Louis, New Orleans, and Los Angeles.

37. Also see *U.S. News & World Report*, 30 September 1968, on Nixon's black capitalism agenda.

38. Frederick D. Sturdivant, "The Limits of Black Capitalism," *Harvard Business Review* (January–February 1969): 122–28, on the Community Self-Determination bill introduced in the U.S. Senate in July 1968, which was drafted by CORE and the Harvard Institute of Politics. It called for the creation of federally chartered community-owned and community-directed corporations (CDCs) that "would acquire, create, and manage all businesses in its areas." Sturdivant viewed the bill as detrimental to black entrepreneurship and black capitalism and surmised that it would fail in surmounting racial barriers, explaining: "Any legislation that ignores this objective and enforces a concept of 'separate but equal' economic development moves the nation toward apartheid."

39. Robert F. Kennedy, "A Business Development Program for Our Poverty Areas," in *The Ghetto Marketplace,* ed. Frederick D. Sturdivant (New York: Free Press, 1969), 193–209. Also, "Community Development Corporations: A New Approach to the Poverty Problem," in Bailey, *Black Business Enterprise,* 269–89; and "Is Black Capitalism the Answer?" *Business Week,* 3 August 1968, 60–61. Also, *Black Enterprise,* November 1994, 216.,

40. Green and Pryde, *Black Entrepreneurship*, 39–42, on the SBA. See Grayson Mitchell, "Maryland's Most Maverick Mitchell," *Black Enterprise,* July 1977, 26–33, 54. Also, Timothy Bates, "Impact of Preferential Procurement Policies on Minority Businesses, *Review of Black Political Economy* 14 (Summer 1985): 51–65; and Bates, "Black Entrepreneurship," 59–70. Also, Cross, *Black Capitalism*; Timothy Bates, *Black Capitalism: A Quantitative Analysis* (New York: Praeger, 1973); and George E. Berkner, *Black Capitalism and the Urban Negro* (Tempe: Arizona State University Press, 1979).

41. "Minority Enterprise and the Carter Administration," *Black Enterprise,* June 1977, 85, 87–89, 91, 182–83.

42. Commission on Minority Business, *Historically Underutilized Business,* xii, 7. Also, Bates, "Government as Financial Intermediary"; and William L. Scott, "Financial Performance of Minority- Versus Non-minority-Owned Businesses," *Journal of Small Business Management* 21 (January 1983): 42–48. Also on government assistance to black business, see Green and Pryde, *Black Entrepreneurship*, 39–42.

43. Drew S. Days III, "Turning Back the Clock: The Reagan Administration and Civil Rights," *Harvard Civil Rights-Civil Liberties Law Review* 19 (Summer 1984): 309–47.

44. Commission on Minority Business, *Historically Underutilized Business,* xii, 7, for the commission's recommendation that the term *HUB* should be used in all government laws and regulations in lieu of the term *socially and economically disadvantaged small business concern*. The consensus was that the latter term "stressed the status of discrimination rather than the effects of discrimination on the nation's economic system."

45. In 1963 President Kennedy appointed black economist Andrew F. Brimmer as a deputy-assistant secretary of commerce for economic policy. Under President Johnson, Brimmer was appointed assistant secretary for economic affairs in 1965.

46. Earl G. Graves, "NAFTA's Promise," *Black Enterprise,* December 1993, 11.

47. Joyce Jones, "The Best Commerce Secretary Ever," *Black Enterprise,* June 1996, 90–92, 96, 98; "America's Top Business Advocate," *Black Enterprise,* June 1993; "What's Up at the MBDA," *Black Enterprise,* June 1994, 43–46; "Ron Brown: 'Requiem for a Hero Who Went Out into the Deep Water with the Big Boats,' " *Ebony,* June 1996, 28–29, 32, 34. Brown served in the military, was a lawyer in both the private and public sector, worked as a lobbyist for the National Urban League, served as Senator Edward Kennedy's campaign manager, and also managed Jesse Jackson's 1988 presidential campaign. In 1989, he was elected chairman of the national Democratic Party and was a significant force in the election of President Clinton, who considered Brown his closest advisor. The author met Brown in Washington, D.C. and again in South Africa where he led a trade mission. At that time, the author was a senior Fulbright fellow. When she reintroduced herself to him at the American ambassador's house in Pretoria, he said, "Of course I remember you, Professor Walker, you are working on the history of African-American business."

48. Matthew S. Scott and Carolyn Brown, "The State of Black Business," *Black Enterprise*, November 1995, 82. Also, Michael K. Frisby, "The Unsinkable Ron Brown," *Black Enterprise,*

December 1995, 26, briefly mentions the special-counsel investigation of Brown's private business deals.

49. Rev. Leon Sullivan, "The Sullivan Principles," in *The Anti-Apartheid Reader: The Struggle against White Racist Rule in South Africa,* ed. David Mermelstein (New York: Grove Weidenfeld, 1987), 383–86. Also, Richard W. Hull, *American Enterprise in South Africa: Historical Dimensions of Engagement and Disengagement* (New York: New York University Press, 1990), 303, 311, 351.

50. Elizabeth Schmidt, "The Sullivan Principles: A Critique," in Mermelstein, *Anti-Apartheid Reader,* 399; and Hull, *American Enterprise,* 304, 308, 310–11, 329–36, 344, for discussion on the impact of the Sullivan principles.

51. Shlomo Katz, ed., *Negro and Jew: Encounter in America* (New York: Macmillan Publishing, 1967). Also, Harold J. Sheppard, "The Negro Merchant: A Study of Negro Anti-Semitism," *American Journal of Sociology* 53 (September 1947): 96–99.

52. Ira De A. Reid, *The Negro Immigrant* (New York: Columbia University Press, 1939).

53. Wendy Manning and William O'Hare, "The Best Metros for Asian-American Businesses," *American Demographics* 10 (August 1988): 35–37, 59; Dinker Raval, "East Indian Small Businesses in the U.S.: Perceptions, Problems, and Adjustments," *American Journal of Small Business* 7 (January–March 1983): 39–44; William O'Hare, "Best Metros for Hispanic Businesses," *American Demographics* 9 (November 1987): 31–33; William O'Hare, "Best Metros for Black Businesses," *American Demographics* 9 (July 1987): 38–41. For exceptions, see March Beauchamp, "Welcome to Teheran, Calif.," *Forbes,* 12 December 1988, 61, 62, 66, who notes, "The top 1% of Iran's population now resides in California," with most involved in multimillion-dollar mainstream business enterprises. Also, Dan Fost, "Iranians in California," *American Demographics* 12 (May 1990): 47–49, notes their racial, ethnic, and religious diversity: "Muslims, Jews, Armenians, Bahais, Assyrians, and Zoroastrians are all part of L.A.'s Iranian culture."

54. Bank of Korea, *Han'guk ui Oehwan Kwalli,* Korean Exchange Controls, (Seoul 1981), and Korea Exchange Bank, *Oegukhwan Kwallibop kwa Tongbop Sihaengnyong,* Exchange Control Law and Order of Its Implementation (Seoul: Korea Exchange Bank, 1987), from In-Jin Yoon, "The Changing Significance of Ethnic and Class Resources in Immigrant Businesses: The Case of Korean Immigrant Businesses in Chicago," *International Migration Review* 25, no. 2 (1991): 325–26. Also, Ronald Takaki, ed., *From Different Shores: Perspectives on Race and Ethnicity in America,* 2d ed. (New York: Oxford University Press, 1994,), 225–26, notes that in 1973, "65 percent of the Korean immigrants had been professionals, technicians, and managers in their home countries."

55. Ivan Light, *Ethnic Enterprise,* 21–44. Also, William Mitchell, *Mishpokhe: A Study of New York City Jewish Family Circles* (New York: Mouton, 1978). Also, Green and Pryde, *Black Entrepreneurship,* 138–42, who also note that the West Indian *susu* has been institutionalized, as in the D.C. Council of Caribbean Businessmen.

56. Matthew Schifrin, "Horatio Alger Kim," *Forbes,* 17 October 1988, 93–94. Also, Yoon, "Korean Immigrant Businesses," 303.

57. See Butler, *Entrepreneurship and Self-Help,* 1–33, which reviews theories (e.g., middlemen, minorities, enclaves, ethnic solidarity, dual economies) constructed to explain immigrant ethnic-group business success in America. Also, Edna Bonacich, "A Theory of Middleman Minorities," *American Sociological Review* 38 (October 1972): 583–94; Edna Bonacich and John Modell, *The Economic Basis of Ethnic Solidarity: Small Business in the Japanese-American Community* (Berkeley: University of California Press, 1980); Scott Cummmings, ed., *Self-Help in Urban America: Patterns of Minority Business Enterprise* (New York: National University Publications, 1980); Alejandro Portes and Leif Jensen, "What's an Ethnic Enclave? The Case of Conceptual Clarity," *American Sociological Review* 52 (December 1987): 768–71; Victor Neu and Jimy M. Sanders, "The Limits of Ethnic Solidarity in the Enclave Economy," *American Sociological Review* 52 (December 1987): 745–73. Also, Yoon, "Korean Immigrant Businesses," 303–31, rejects prevailing theories that explain post-1965 Korean-immigrant business success.

58. Thomas Sowell, "West Indian Immigrants," in *American Ethnic Groups* (n.p.: The Urban Institute, 1978), 41–48.

59. William Julius Wilson, *The Declining Significance of Race* (Chicago: University of Chicago Press, 1978).

60. See Takaki, *Different Shores*, 225–26, on Asian and white income patterns.

61. Ibid., 226, emphasizes the business resources of Asian's "education, employable skills, and finances—which underclass blacks do not have." For these reasons Takaki notes, "the need for scholars and journalists to become more restrained in asking blacks to copy Asian Americans and shun government intervention and structural economic changes in favor of conservative strategies of self-help and ethnic enterprise."

62. Schifrin, "Horatio Alger Kim," 92–94, 96, indicates that Korean Americans "are rarely innovators," but rather "masters at revitalizing sleepy, small businesses," and they also show a "willingness to adopt new lifestyles." Most are Christian, and "the glue that holds the Korean community together in the U.S. is its churches." Also, T. W. Kang, *Is Korea the Next Japan: Understanding the Structure, Strategy, and Tactics of America's Next Competitor* (New York: Free Press, 1989), 11: "In Korea there are still some people who go to work in a company without pay because they need somewhere to go to save face socially and with their families."

63. See Sowell, "West Indian Immigrants," 45–46, compares the achievement of African-Americans with West Indian immigrants and their descendants, emphasizing demographics and the history of economic independence to the explain success of the latter. Sowell explains that in the West Indies, blacks were the majority and slave rebellions were more frequent and more successful so "blacks were not psychologically crushed by a sense of the futility of resistance to whites." He also notes that during slavery West Indians "had generations of experience in individual reward for individual effort, in at least part of their lives, as well as experience in marketing their surplus, and in managing their own food needs and monetary returns." Sowell fails to acknowledge the internal economy of African-American slave communities, slave entrepreneurship, and free-black enterprises, which have a historic continuity in business ventures beyond petty trading activities.

64. Ellis Cose, *The Rage of a Privileged Class* (New York: HarperCollins, 1993), 1, notes, "Despite its very evident prosperity, much of America's black middle class is in excruciating pain." Also, Cornell West, *Race Matters* (Boston: Beacon Press, 1993).

65. See, D'Souza, *End of Racism*, 1–24, on examples of contemporary white violence, white backlash, and white anti-immigration attitudes. He claims that "clear evidence of racism has declined," but he says, "black cultural pathology has contributed to a new form of discrimination, rational discrimination"; also, that "liberal antiracism," as opposed to racism, "is the main problem for blacks." D'Souza, a member of an immigrant minority group, is a champion of white America and denies that slavery was a white institution in that it existed globally in every society, including China, India, Europe, the Arab world, and throughout Africa. Even in America, blacks owned slaves. The issue of black slave ownership does not negate white racism in American life. In America, only people of African descent were enslaved. By law, whites could not be made slaves, and laws made it illegal for blacks to enslave whites. In America, then, no whites were ever slaves. In America, to be a slave was a matter of race, a condition that invalidates the specious premises, subsequent faulty analysis, and inconsistency of D'Souza's arguments throughout his book, which attempts to disprove the reality of racism in America. As he indicates, the purpose of the book is to destroy the argument that "Racism is the main obstacle facing African Americans today, and the primary explanation for black problems." See, Alphonso Pinkney, *White Hate Crimes* (Chicago: Third World Press, 1994).

66. Andrew Hacker, *Two Nations: Black and White, Hostile, Unequal* (New York: Scribner's 1992); West, *Race Matters*; Douglas S. Masey and Nancy A. Denton, *American Apartheid: Segregation and the Making of the Underclass* (Cambridge: Harvard University Press, 1993); Derrick Bell, *Faces at the Bottom of the Well: The Permanence of Racism* (New York: Basic Books, 1992); and Charles Lawrence, "The Id, the Ego, and Equal Protection: Reckoning With Unconscious Racism," *Stanford Law Review* 39 (January 1987): 330, who notes that as a result of the influence of the American cultural "belief system," "we are all racists."

67. Fost, "Iranians in California," 49, emphasizes Iranian business success and cultural assimilation (86 percent know English on immigration), but still Iranians encounter American racism.

Each year, Iranians, as a group, protest the Khomeni regime, "[a]nd each year, they are heckled by American bystanders who exhort them to leave the country."

68. Washington, *Up from Slavery*, 221–27.

69. Norman L. Zucker and Naomi Flink Zucker, *Crossings to America: Refuge, Asylum, and Mass Escape* (Armonk, N.Y.: M. E. Sharpe, Incorporated, 1996), includes costs of resettlement of Cuban, Haitian, and Central American immigrants.

70. *Miami Times*, 23 February and 22 June 1989. Also see Harold M. Rose, "Blacks and Cubans in Metropolitan Miami's Changing Economy," *Urban Geography* 10 (September/October 1989): 464–86; Raymond A. Mohl, "On the Edge: Blacks and Hispanics in Metropolitan Miami since 1959," *Florida Historical Quarterly* 69 (July 1990): 37–56. Cuban threats to black economic progress were recognized soon after the first wave of immigrants in 1959. See "Miami's Cuban Refugee Crisis," *Ebony* 18 (June 1963): 96–104. Also, Kenneth L. Wilson and W. Allen Martin, "Ethnic Enclaves: A Comparison of the Cuban and Black Economies in Miami," *American Journal of Sociology* 88 (July 1982): 135–60.

71. *New York Times*, 13 May 1992. Also, *Newsweek*, 18 May 1992, 41; and *U. S. News & World Report,* 18 May 1992, 25, 34.

72. Andrew F. Brimmer, from a statement before the House Select Committee on Small Business, U.S. 25 July 1969, in Bailey, *Black Business Enterprise*, 164–72.

73. Also see *Wall Street Journal*, 8 May 1992, B1; and Yoon, "Korean Immigrant Businesses," 309–10, notes in Chicago's black business districts Korean merchants are concentrated in five types of businesses: "general merchandise (26%), apparel (38%), shoes (12%), beauty supplies (10%), and wigs (9%)." The commonality is that they are cheap, easily liquidated consumer goods; and by specializing in cheap product lines, capital requirements are small: "one half of them started with less than $40,000." Also, Yoon notes that Korean business success in black business districts "depends on the economic condition of local black residents." Most are poor and many are on welfare, and Korean businesses are said "to experience a 'brief sales boost' shortly after blacks receive welfare checks."

74. Schifrin, "Horatio Alger Kim," 92–94, 96, indicates that Korean-Americans locate in "impoverished sections," "distressed communities," and "worst sections," of inner cities, i.e., black business districts. In Los Angeles, Koreans own most of the liquor stores. In Atlanta, they dominate the inner-city grocery business, and in New York in 1988 "own 85% of the $500 million retail green-grocery businesses," many dry cleaners, nail salons, fish markets, and "a good chunk of the garment industry." Also, Yoon, "Korean Immigrant Businesses," 310.

75. See Dinesh D'Souza, *Iliberal Education* (New York: Macmillan Publishing, 1991). Also, Arthur M. Schlesinger Jr., *The Disuniting of America: Reflections of a Multicultural Society* (Knoxville, Tenn.: Whittle, 1991).

76. See Peter K. Eisinger, "Black Mayors and the Politics of Racial Economic Advancement," in *Readings in Urban Politics: Past, Present and Future*, eds. Harlan Hahn and Charles Levine (New York: Longman, 1984). Also, Timothy Bates, "Impact of Preferential Procurement," 51–65. In 1967, Carl Stokes of Cleveland and Richard Hatcher of Gary, Indiana, were the first blacks elected mayors in northern cities. In 1973, Coleman Young was elected in Detroit, and Thomas Bradley in Los Angeles, followed by Maynard Jackson in Atlanta in 1974. In 1983, Wilson Goode became mayor of Philadelphia and Harold Washington mayor of Chicago; and in 1989 David Dinkins won the election in New York City. Since 1967, Washington, D.C., has had three black mayors, Walter Washington, Sharon Pratt Dixon, and Marion Berry. Other black women mayors, Lottie Shackleford of Little Rock and Carrie Perry of Hartford, Connecticut, were elected in 1987. In 1994, Sharon Sayles Belton was elected mayor of Minneapolis, one of several cities with white majorities that elected black mayors.

77. Frank McCoy, "Black Power in City Hall," *Black Enterprise,* August 1990, 150. Also, Andrew Brimmer, "A Battleplan for Fairness," *Black Enterprise,* November 1990, 46.

78. Timothy Bates, *Banking on Black Enterprise: The Potential of Emerging Firms for Revitalizing Urban Economies* (Washington, D.C.: Joint Center for Political and Economic Studies, 1993), 93–106.

79. "Six Hot Cities for Black Business," *Black Enterprise,* May 1994, 49, notes that in cities with black mayors, minority and women business owners were awarded the following in municipal contract procurement dollars: Cleveland, $96 million out of $247 million; Denver, $100 million out of $391 million; Minneapolis, $11 million out of $74 million; Rochester, New York, $3 million out of $38 million.

80. Margaret C. Simms, "Expectations of Empowerment," *Black Enterprise,* December 1993, 33. Also, Frank McCoy, "Can Clinton's Urban Policies Really Work?" *Black Enterprise,* June 1994, 178–80, 182, 184, 186. Also, Bates, *Banking on Black Enterprise*, 119–21.

81. *City of Richmond v J.A. Croson & Company*, 448 U.S. 469 (1989). The Supreme Court required that a state or local government must meet the following tests before granting set-asides: (1) produce specific evidence of racial or ethnic discrimination against the group targeted for assistance, and (2) that the remedy selected must be "narrowly tailored" to address the types of discrimination found to exist in the jurisdiction.

82. McCoy, "Black Power in City Hall," 150. Also, Brimmer, "Battleplan for Fairness, 46.

83. Tyrone D. Press, memorandum, The Effect of *Richmond v Croson* and Similar Attacks on Federal, State, and Local MBE, and DBE Programs Nationwide, (Washington, D.C.: MBELDEF, 1 March 1991), 37–38. Also, United States Commission on Minority Business, *Historically Underutilized Business*, 97–99.

84. "Consultant Finds Bias in St. Petersburg," *Tampa Tribune,* 24 May 1990, 1, 6.

85. Bates, *Banking on Black Enterprise,* 107–14.

86. "Trumark Acquires CMS Corp," *Black Enterprise,* November 1993, 16.

87. Fonda Marie Lloyd, "Plastic Joins Steel," *Black Enterprise*, September 1994, 15.

88. *Black Enterprise,* August 1990, 24.

89. Theodore Philip Kovaleff, *Business and Government during the Eisenhower Administration: A Study of the Antitrust Policy of the Antitrust Division of the Justice Department* (Athens: Ohio University Press, 1980).

90. Ofari, *Myth of Black Capitalism.* Also, Manning Marable, *How Capitalism Underdeveloped Black America: Problems in Race, Political Economy and Society* (Boston: South End Press, 1983); and Alphonso Pinkney, *The Myth of Black Progress* (New York: Cambridge University Press, 1984).

91. See Joseph G. Conti and Brad Stetson, *Challenging the Civil Rights Establishment: Profiles of a New Black Vanguard* (Westport Conn.: Praeger, 1993), which reviews the economic thought of four black libertarian thinkers, including Thomas Sowell, "unquestionably, the father of this intellectual rebellion against civil rights orthodoxy"; Shelby Steele; Robert L. Woodson; and Glenn C. Loury, who, unlike his supporters on the right, acknowledges the legacy of racism and its residual effects on black America. Also included for discussion are Walter Williams, William Julius Wilson, Stanley Crouch, and Clarence Thomas. Also, Murray Friedman, "The New Black Intellectuals," *Commentary,* June 1980, 46, notes that they "do not share a common social and political philosophy. At important points, they differ sharply from one another. What permits them to be classed together, however, is that in their work on poverty they have avoided generalized indictments of American society and eschewed purely racial explanations of the plight of the poor." See Martin Kilson, "Anatomy of Black Conservatism, *Transition* 59 (1993): 4–18.

92. Wilson, *Declining Significance of Race*, 1. The salient issue for blacks, however, is not the "day-to-day encounters with whites," but the persistence of institutional racism that limits their life chances to advance to the middle class.

93. See Nora K. Moran, " 'The Importance of Being Excellent': Human Relations and 'Corporate Culture,' 1930–1995," *Essays in Economic and Business History* 14 (1996): 229–48, which examines the literature on excellence and corporate culture. Despite the country's increasingly multiethnic corporate culture, the author does not include a discussion of any books that place blacks or other minorities into America's corporate culture. Only the Japanese are mentioned. Even in the best companies that have demonstrated a commitment to diversity, racism continues as a part of the corporate culture. See *AT&T Focus,* September 1993, an in-house magazine in which a cartoon depicting AT&T's international network showed a globe connecting people of the world, some in traditional dress representing their respective continents. For Africa, however,

instead of an African in traditional dress, a monkey was depicted. See *Black Enterprise,* December 1993, 20.

94. Thomas Sowell, *The Economics and Politics of Race: An International Perspective* (New York: William Morrow, 1963), 163. How these rights might benefit the larger society is an even more valid issue.

95. Shelby Steele, *The Content of Our Character: A New Vision of Race in America* (New York: St. Martin's, 1990), 123, attributes racial conflict today to affirmative action. His remedy to make whites comfortable and to stop racial violence is for middle-class blacks to relinquish their demands for affirmative action; and instead of preferential treatment, the federal government should "go back to its original purpose of enforcing equal opportunity." Steele would achieve credibility if he demanded that America go forward and move to enforce equality of opportunity, since equal opportunity has yet to be operative for blacks in American life.

96. Green and Pryde, *Black Entrepreneurship*, 171, considers that "Sustained economic progress throughout the black community will require blacks to overcome negative beliefs based on lessons of the past. Whether and how much they achieve will depend to a large degree on what they believe achievable."

97. Clarence Page, *Showing My Color: Impolite Essays on Race and Identity* (New York: Harper-Collins, 1996), 224.

98. Terry Eastland, *Ending Affirmative Action: The Case for Colorblind Justice* (New York: Basic Books, 1996).

99. See Randall L. Kennedy, "Black Conservatism's Would-Be Spokesmen," *QBR: The Black Book Review* 3 (November/December 1995): 12–13. Kennedy, a Harvard Law professor and editor of *Reconstruction*, reviews radio commentator Armstrong Williams's *Beyond Blame: How We Can Succeed by Breaking the Dependency Barrier* (New York: Free Press, 1996), and public television commentator Tony Brown's *Black Lies, White Lies: The Truth according to Tony Brown* (New York: William Morrow, 1995). Kennedy explains why black conservative thought remains on the periphery of African-American political culture. He notes, however, that "Glenn C. Loury is the outstanding voice among black conservative intellectuals." See Glenn C. Loury, *One by One from the Inside Out: Essays and Reviews on Responsibility in America* (New York: Free Press, 1995).

100. *Black Enterprise,* April 1996, 20.

101. Udayan Gupta, "Cash Crunch: For Black Entrepreneurs, Raising Money Is Often the Biggest Hurdle," *Wall Street Journal*, 19 February 1993, R4. The findings were based on a 1992–1993 Roper Organization survey of 500 black business owners throughout the continental United States. The sample was randomly chosen from the SBA's lists of black-owned businesses with annual revenues from $100,000 to $17 million and with fewer than 500 employees. According to Roper, had the entire list of black businesses been surveyed, the findings would differ by no more than five percentage points. Also, "The Republican Years: Minority Enterprise Grew Its Strongest during the Nixon Presidency," *Black Enterprise,* June 1977, 75–76 79, 83.

102. Simms, "Census Bureau Devalues Black Businesses," 222–24, 226, 228. Also, Eric L. Smith, "Is Black Business Paving the Way?" *Black Enterprise,* June 1996, 196, 198, 200. Also, each June *Black Enterprise* provides a board of economists report that has included leading economists such as Andrew Brimmer, Board of Reserve, Phillis Wallace, and Sir Arthur Lewis, who in 1979 won the Nobel Prize in economic science.

103. Faith Ando, "Capital Issues and Minority-Owned Business," *Review of Black Political Economy* 16 (Spring 1988): 77–109.

104. Smith, "Paving the Way?" 194.

105. Ibid., 206.

106. Commission on Minority Business, *Historically Underutilized Business*, 33.

CHAPTER 10

1. *Pittsburgh Courier*, 17 October 1959, for a picture of Fuller with Rodman C. Rockefeller, son of New York's governor, who attended a New York reception for the black entrepreneur.

2. *Chicago Defender,* 3 September 1955. Also, "Fuller," *African-American Business Leaders*, 244–49; "A Man and His Products," *Black Enterprise,* August 1975; and Kimbro and Hill, *Think and Grow Rich,* 82–85, 134, 156.

3. John H. Johnson, *Succeeding against the Odds: The Inspiring Autobiography of One of America's Wealthiest Entrepreneurs* (New York: Warner Books, 1989), 89.

4. *Chicago Defender*, 22 September 1955, for pictures of Fuller's Land Index Division and Records of Business Corporations offices.

5. On the third annual convention in 1955 see *Chicago Defender,* 3 September 1955. It was attended by 1,500 of his salespeople, and top performers were awarded gold and silver pins, dotted with diamonds, sapphires, and rubies. The main speaker was Napoleon Hill of *Think and Grow Rich* fame. The article said that "Fuller's fair play employment policy has resulted in an interracial firm which is years ahead of most companies in the demonstration of democracy in action." Also, *Chicago Defender*, 3 August 1957, on that year's convention, where top sales people were awarded with, in addition to cash, a Cadillac Fleetwood, a Ford, and a Plymouth. Fuller paid transportation and hotel expenses, totaling about $56,000, for 1,000 of his salespeople.

6. Leonard Wiener, "S. B. Fuller's Downfall Tied to Race Tension," *Chicago Daily News*, 15 August 1988.

7. See "A Negro Businessman Speaks His Mind," *U.S. News & World Report*, 19 August 1963, and "NAACP Raps Negro's Attack on Own Race," *New York Times*, 8 December 1971.

8. Ingham and Feldman, *African-American Business Leaders*, 268.

9. *Black Enterprise*, June 1996, 108. See Brimmer, "Battleplan for Fairness," 46.

10. Stuart, *Economic Detour*, 72–86. The Supreme Liberty Life Insurance Company was established in Chicago in 1929, from the merger of the Liberty Life Insurance Company, founded in 1919 by Frank L. Gillespie; the Supreme Life and Casualty Company of Columbus, Ohio; and the Northeastern Life Insurance Company of Newark, New Jersey. The merger was engineered in 1929 by Harry Herbert Pace, founder and president of the latter company. Pace also became president of Supreme Liberty, which in 1920 had a combined capital of $400,000, insurance in force of $25 million, and 1,090 employees. Truman Kella Gibson Sr., one of the cofounders, took the position of chairman and treasurer of Supreme Liberty Life. Also, Ingham and Feldman, *African-American Business Leaders*, 198–208, 511–17, on Pace, who taught Latin and Greek at Lincoln University from 1906 to 1908, worked as a cashier at the Solvent Savings Bank in Memphis; its president, Robert R. Church Sr., increased the bank's assets from $50,000 in 1908 to $600,000 in 1912. Pace then joined Herman E. Perry as secretary of Standard Life Insurance Company, professionalizing the business operations of the company. From 1920 to 1925, he was in the music business, having established the successful Black Swan record company. Bousfield's earned his medical degree from Northwestern University in 1907. His interest in insurance developed during his hiatus from medicine in 1911, when he worked as a railroad barber and counterman and also as secretary to the railway's International Benevolent Association. In 1929 he became associate director for the Julius Rosenwald Fund.

11. Johnson, *Succeeding Against the Odds*, 94–96. Also, Ingham and Feldman, *African-American Business Leaders*, 366–79.

12. Johnson, *Succeeding Against the Odds*, 68.

13. Ibid., 95.

14. Ibid., 19.

15. Ibid., 70.

16. Ingham and Feldman, *African-American Business Leaders*, 188.

17. Derek T. Dingle, "Not Business as Usual," *Black Enterprise*, June 1996, 108. The figures include both the *Black Enterprise* "Industrial/Service 100" and "Auto Dealer 100."

18. *Baltimore Afro-American*, 4 and 11 April 1953; 19 and 23 May 1953.

19. *Chicago Defender*, 1 May 1957.

20. *Norfolk Journal and Guide*, 23 May 1957. Also, *Chicago Defender*, 11 August 1956, for information on Murray's wife, who had to fight to retain control of the company after her husband's death.

21. *Christian Index*, 4 March 1948. The Meridian, Mississippi-based E. F. Young Jr. and his family also owned a chain of hotels, including the $100,000 Young Hotel in Meridian, beauty schools, a taxi company, the Holbrook Benevolent Association, a newspaper, and vocational schools.

22. *Kansas City (Kan.) Plaindealer*, 17 November 1939. Also see, *Norfolk Journal and Guide*, 28 January 1939; *Pittsburgh Courier*, 28 January 1939; and *Baltimore Afro-American*, 28 January 1939, in which Overton stated that the only change his company would have to make was "in a minor label to meet the requirements on statement of the net contents of the packages."

23. Research Company of America, *The New Philadelphia Story: A Report on the Characteristics of the Philadelphia Negro Market . . . Its Buying Habits and Brand Preferences* (Baltimore: The Afro-American Company, 1946), 4. Philadelphia had the third largest black population in the United States. In 1940 there were 250,880 blacks (a total of 64,728 families) out of a total population of 1,931,334. While the black populations in Chicago and New York were larger, 277,731 and 458,444, respectively, in Chicago only 8 out of every 100 people were black, and in New York, only 6 in every 100 people were black. In Philadelphia, 13 out of every 100 people were black.

24. Ingham and Feldman, *African-American Business Leaders*, 689–90.

25. *Baltimore Afro-American*, 11 April 1953, magazine section. Washington's death, presumably due to diabetes, created controversy. Instead of following doctor's orders, Washington relied on prayer to cure her. Some attributed her belief to her involvement with Father Divine, whose movement she supported with substantial contributions. In doing so, "she violated her rule about buying property with mortgages and her name appeared on the cult's real estate transactions." Also, she flirted with Christian Science.

26. *Baltimore Afro-American*, 6 April 1946.

27. *Pittsburgh Courier*, 9 November 1957.

28. *Baltimore Afro-American*, 20 August 1949.

29. *Chicago Defender*, 2 April 1949. The founders, owners, and investors were black and included Rose Morgan, attorney Oscar C. Brown, and I. Wesley Brown, owner of the Continental Casket Company and president of Mary Ann Morgan, Inc. The company had a sales force of about 40 people. Also, *Black Enterprise*, October 1993, 14. The Morgan company never took off, but the Atlanta-based Bronner Brothers, Inc., was successful. It was founded in 1947 by Morehouse College graduate Nathaniel H. Bronner Sr. and his brother with money they made from sales of their products in their sister's beauty shop. A *Black Enterprise* top 100 company for over a decade, Bronner Brothers in 1995 ranked 79th, with sales of $25 million and a 250-employee staff.

30. *Chicago Defender*, 14 August 1954.

31. Ibid., 13 August 1955. By mid-century, the Walker Company was into its third generation of family control, with management still in the hands of the Walker family: A'Lelia Mae Perry, Madame Walker's granddaughter was president.

32. *Nashville Globe and Independent*, 12 February 1960. Also see *Baltimore Afro-American*, 20 February 1960.

33. *Los Angeles Tribune*, 5 February 1960.

34. Ingham and Feldman, *African-American Business Leaders*, 590–97.

35. Ibid., 250–58.

36. Ibid., 362.

37. Ibid.

38. Derek T. Dingle, "Soft Sheen's Triangle of Trade," *Black Enterprise*, June 1989, 222–26, 228, 230, 232.

39. "So Much for Family Ties," *Newsweek*, 23 March 1992, 18.

40. Alfred D. Chandler Jr., *The Visible Hand: The Managerial Revolution in American Business* (Cambridge: Harvard University Press, 1977), 1–12.

41. "Chicago's Top 100 Businesses," *Chicago Tribune*, 19 May 1991, sec. 20, 42.

42. "So Much for Family Ties," 49. Also, *Black Enterprise,* September 1990, 18.

43. *Baltimore Afro-American*, 1 January 1949. In 1946 the company changed leadership and was headed by Anthony Overton's only son, Everett Vann Overton, who had held the position of vice president and general manager of the plant for 18 years. At that time, the company had a 50-item product line that included not only face powder but also perfumes, hair pomades, colognes, and lotions. In 1949 Overton-Hygienic Company celebrated 50 years of operations.

44. *Atlanta Daily World*, 15 August 1947.

45. *Pittsburgh Courier,* 9 November 1957.

46. *Chicago Defender,* 2 April 1949.

47. *Chicago Defender*, 15 March 1947.

48. *Atlanta World*, 23 March 1960.

49. Christina F. Watts and Lloyd Gite, "Emerging Entrepreneurs," *Black Enterprise,* November 1995, 106. Jackson Mouyiaris, with a master's degree in human relations from New York University and a J. D. degree from Boston University, created her products with a black dermatologist, Dr. Cheryl Burgess, a fact that is emphasized in advertisements for Black Opal products.

50. *Newsweek*, October, 1986.

51. Lloyd Gite, "Iman Fashions Cosmetics Business," *Black Enterprise,* November 1994, 47.

52. See product advertising in *Essence*, including the front- and back-inside cover and the back cover for its May 1996 issue. In the 190-page issue, there were 50 pages of advertisements for health, cosmetics, hair, and personal care products. Only 3 pages carried ads for black skin and cosmetic companies: Iman had 2 pages, and Black Opal had 1. Of the white companies, Cover Girl had 5 pages; Revlon, 4; Avon and Maybelline, 2; Palmer and Nivea, 2 1/3 pages each; Clairol and Estee Lauder, 1 page each. Also see *Essence*, March 1996, in which there were no advertisements for black skin care and cosmetic products. Of the white owned companies, Lancome, Nivea, L'Oreal, Clinique, Clarins, Clairol, Flori Roberts, and Noxzema each had 1 page. Avon ran a special 8-page advertisement. Interestingly, *Emerge*, whether by editorial policy or a failure to secure advertising, does not appear to carry much advertising aimed at black women, although articles including or focusing on black women are often featured. Of the February, March, and August 1996 issues of *Emerge*, only the February issue carried an ad aimed at black women: Avon, in a salute to Black History Month, featured a full-page ad with pictures of four black saleswomen.

53. Johnson, *Succeeding against the Odds*, 91, indicates, "Supreme was a sound business, and it was a sound *Black* business. It emphasized the double-duty dollar, telling Blacks that a dollar invested in Supreme provided insurance protection *and* employment for Black men and women. 'Spend Your Money Where You Can Work' was the company's theme."

54. Light, *Ethnic Enterprise*, chaps. 3 and 8.

55. Murray, *Negro Handbook: 1946–1947*, 314. The 1942 figures on the 262 companies were provided by Asa T. Spaulding of the North Carolina Mutual Insurance Company.

56. Winfred Bryson, "Insurance Companies: An Overview," *Black Enterprise,* June 1977, 121.

57. Robert E. Weems Jr., *Black Business in the Black Metropolis: The Chicago Metropolitan Assurance Company, 1925–1985* (Bloomington: Indiana University Press, 1996), 119–24.

58. "Fortify or Die," *Black Enterprise*, June 1989, 285–86, 288.

59. Gracian Mack, "Dogged, Defiant, and Determined," *Black Enterprise*, June 1995, 160.

60. Shelly Branch, "A Premium Asset on Wall Street," *Black Enterprise*, December 1993, 100–102, 104–5. Also, *Black Enterprise*, August 1974,

61. Ingham and Feldman, *African-American Business Leaders*, 84–91. Blayton was a leading entrepreneur in Atlanta and the first black CPA in Georgia who opened his accounting firm in 1928. He was also a professor of accounting at Morehouse College. In 1925 he was one of the founders of the Mutual Federal Savings and Loan Association. Both financial institutions were important in financial housing development for blacks in Atlanta and in loan support to black businesses.

62. *Pittsburgh Courier*, 12 March 1955. Also, John Vaughn, "Banks Cash Out of the Ghetto," *Business and Society Review* (Summer 1989): 40–42, on the denial of banking services to minorities in East Harlem in the late 1980s. The application made by a Puerto Rican merchant was denied despite the fact that he "had equity, a sound business plan, business experience, and sufficient cash flow to repay his loan request for $150,000." The loan officer based in midtown Manhattan said, "Sorry, but we do not provide loans that small."

63. Ingham and Feldman, *African-American Business Leaders*, 631–32.

64. Ibid., 91–97.

65. See "Black Banks: An Overview," and Beverly Jensen, "Independence Bank of Chicago," *Black Enterprise,* June 1977, 92–95, 105–8, 109–10; Melodye McDowell, "Banking on New Territory," *Black Enterprise,* June 1989, 256–58, 260; and Debbie Ann McGann, "The Second Bid Gets the Bank," *Black Enterprise,* December 1995, 19–20. Had Detroit's black-owned Omnibanc Corporation purchased Indecorp, it would have emerged as the nation's largest black-owned bank. Both Omnibanc and Shorebank were cautious because of Indecorp's low CRA rating (Community Reinvestment Act), in which banks are graded by "how well they serve minority borrowers." The CRA, a federal affirmative initiative, was created in 1977 as an inducement for nonblack banks to provide credit, services, and investment opportunities to low- and moderate-income communities.

66. Juliette Fairley, "A New Lease on Banking," *Black Enterprise,* June 1996, 174, 176, 180–81; and *Black Enterprise,* December 1996, 20.

67. *Black Enterprise,* November 1990, 22. Also, on black banks, see Charles Moses, "Avoiding the Day of Default," and on S & Ls, see Alfred Edmonds, "Enduring the Industry's Rebirth," *Black Enterprise,* June 1990, 173–74, 193–94. In 1990, Freedom National Bank in Harlem was shut down and liquidated by the Federal Deposit Insurance Corporation. Also see Matthew Scott, "A Black Bank's Failure: What Price Freedom?" *Black Enterprise,* February 1991, 15, where questions of a "double standard" in the procedures used to close a bank were raised by Harlem Congressman Charles Rangel. Also, Andrew Brimmer, "How Safe Are Black Banks?" *Black Enterprise,* March 1991, 31–32.

68. On Chappell, see Carolyn M. Brown, "A Bank Grows In Philly," *Black Enterprise,* June 1995, 166–68, 170, 172–74. Also, "The First Lady Bank President," *The Commercial College Outlook* 3 (October 1915): 5–7, on a Japanese woman, Mrs. Kin Seno, who established the Seno Bank of Tokyo in 1913 "with a capital of 500,000 yen." The source for the article was the Japanese magazine, *Muyako*. Interestingly, notwithstanding that Maggie Lena Walker founded her bank in 1903 and was also its president, the article in the Howard University publication said: "Mrs. Seno is the first woman to organize and manage a bank and assume the office of its president, either in Japan or probably in any other country." While Walker's contribution to both her local and national black community is well known, Chappell, her late-twentieth-century counterpart, has also been a community leader. Chappell was a founder of the Delaware Valley Mortgage Plan, which helped low- and moderate-income families buy homes with small down payments and below-market interest rates; she also founded the Philadelphia Commercial Development Corporation, an organization formed to rebuild the inner city through commercial development. In 1986 she took a leave of absence from Continental Bank to serve as national treasurer for Jesse Jackson's presidential campaign. She was a founding vice president of the National Rainbow Coalition and chairperson of the board of Operation PUSH.

69. Ingham and Feldman, *African-American Business Leaders*, 85, note the importance of the black church in contributing to the survival of Atlanta's Citizen's Trust Bank during the 1930s: "Around 11:00 the lobby would be full of nothing but preachers. And the people, seeing their preacher deposit God's money from the churches in Citizens Trust, put their money into it and helped put it over, in a great way."

70. Brown, "A Bank Grows In Philly," 170. Chappell incorporated her master's thesis, "A Banking Strategy for Minority Business Development," which she did at Rutgers University's Stonier Graduate School of Banking, into the bank's development plan. Chappell's daughter Verdaynea, who holds an MBA from the Wharton School in international economic development, helped in the founding of the United Bank.

71. Ibid.

72. Mack, "Dogged, Defiant, and Determined," 157–58.

73. Matthew Scott and Wendy C. Pelle, "Must Black Banks Merge or Be Purged?" *Black Enterprise,* June 1996, 160–62, 164, 166, 168.

74. "Black Banks: An Overview," June 1977, 92–95, 185; and Scott and Pelle, "Must Black Banks Merge or Be Purged?"

75. Mark Lowery, "Capitalists on a Mission," *Black Enterprise,* November 1994, 166, 170–71. Also, Gracian Mack, "The Soft Walk Yields the Big Bucks," *Black Enterprise,* June 1995, 236–38, 242, 244, on blacks in private equity financing, i.e., African-American-run private equity funds, that are capitalized primarily by insurance companies and also public and private pension funds.

76. Sharon King, "The Tough Get Going," *Black Enterprise,* June 1995, 179. In December 1994, Daniels and Bell closed, "unable to make payments to lease the New York Stock Exchange seat," in part as a result of the "wave of conservative Republicans" who challenged affirmative initiatives for minorities.

77. *Black Enterprise*, June 1996, 102. Grigsby Brandford was lead manager in underwriting renovations for the Oakland Coliseum ($202 million); the Oceanside Civic Center ($34 million); the Los Angeles Convention and Exhibition Center ($503 million); and the Sacramento Center ($25 million).

78. Eleanor Branch, "How High Is Up?" *Black Enterprise,* October 1990, 96–100.

79. See "25 Years of Blacks in Financing," *Black Enterprise,* October 1994, 146–49.

80. *Black Enterprise,* December 1996, 17.

81. King, "The Tough Get Going," 178–80, 182, 184, 186. Also, Ylonda Gault, "Now That the Smoke Has Cleared," *Black Enterprise,* June 1997, 218, on McClendon, who left FMC for Mesirow Financial, "which handles nearly $3 billion in diversified assets."

82. Frank McCoy, "The Nonstop from Durham," *Black Enterprise,* May 1995, 88–92. Sloan, a Morehouse College graduate and holder of a J.D. degree from North Central University Law School, is a direct descendant of Dr. Aaron McDuffie Moore, a cofounder of the country's leading black-owned insurance company, North Carolina Mutual, and nephew of William Kennedy, former North Carolina Mutual CEO. Beckett, Sloan's executive vice president is from Boston, a Duke University graduate and former Dallas Cowboys football player. He was an account executive at E. F. Hutton before he was hired by Sloan to join the firm. In 1989 Beckett, then 25 years old, was the originator and developer of New Africa Advisers. Also see Kelvin Boston, *Smart Money Moves for African Americans* (New York: G. P. Putnam's Sons, 1996), 224. Boston is a director of the Calvert New Africa Mutual Fund.

83. Sharon King, "Preparing for a Muni-less Future," *Black Enterprise,* June 1996, 188.

84. Frank McCoy, "A $100 Million Manager for $1,000," *Black Enterprise*, November 1995, 64. With the Lincoln joint venture, small investors in the Ariel Premier Bond Fund with as little as $1,000, as well as small or midsize businesses with a 401(k) plan, can have "access to Lincoln's investment expertise." Also, Frank McCoy, "Mature and Independent," *Black Enterprise,* October 1994, 23. Rogers is the son of leading black Republican Jewel LaFontant Rogers, who in 1960 seconded the nomination of Richard Nixon for president when he ran against Kennedy. She has held distinguished government positions: from 1970 to 1972, as a member of the President's Council on Minority Business Enterprise, and in 1973 as the first woman deputy solicitor general; in 1972, she was a U.S. delegate to the United Nation.

85. King, "Muniless Future," 190.

86. Matthew S. Scott, Rhonda Reynolds, and Cassandra Hayes, "Twenty-Five Years of Blacks in Financing," *Black Enterprise,* October 1994, 146. Also, Matthew S. Scott, "Two Decades in the Black," *Black Enterprise,* October 1994, 150, 152. 154, 156.

87. Johnson, *Succeeding against the Odds,* 87.

88. *Pittsburgh Courier,* 28 January 1950.

89. *Memphis World,* 10 May 1946; *Chicago Defender,* 11 May 1946; and *Washington Tribune,* 14 May 1946. Also, *Baltimore Afro-American*, 8 June 1946. Hampton was under contract to Decca Records and was only involved in the company in an unofficial way. See the *Afro-American* for company advertisement.

90. *Los Angeles Tribune*, 7 September 1946. Also see *Baltimore Afro-American*, 19 May 1945, on "Handy Brothers Nearing Half Century as Music Publishers." The company was founded in 1907 when Handy went into partnership with Harry H. Pace.

91. *Kansas City (Mo.) Call*, 25 October 1946. The New York-based company was first temporarily housed in the offices of Gene Krupa's orchestra. Also see *Baltimore Afro-American*, 16 November 1946, on when the company was given the Award of Merit by the Young Citizen's Political Action Committee of New York for promoting racial unity.

92. *New Orleans Weekly*, 26 September 1953.

93. *Baltimore Afro-American*, 1 February 1958.

94. Ibid., 15 October 1955. The company also recorded the Medallions and Meadowlarks.

95. Eric L. Smith, "Familiar Face on Old Label," *Black Enterprise*, December 1995, 20.

96. Matthew S. Scott and Tarik K. Muhammad, "Top 50 Black Powerbrokers in Entertainment," *Black Enterprise*, December 1994, 58–60, 62. Even before the 1980s, many white companies appointed blacks as presidents or vice presidents of their black music divisions. Most ranged in age from the early 20s to the late 30s when they assumed these positions. The president of MCA's black music division, Ernie Singleton, with a $100-million budget, produced Patti LaBelle and Bobby Brown. Epic Records has Lamont Boles, senior vice president of black music who has a staff of 24 and a $40-million operating budget. He has recorded superstars Luther Vandross and Sade, and had Michael Jackson under contract before the latter signed a $65 million deal with Sony in 1991. Since Sylvia Rhone's appointment as chair and CEO of Elektra/EastWest Records in 1991, she signed En Vogue and rappers Das EFX.

97. Muriel L. Whetson, "Who Are the Top Record Sellers, *Ebony,* June 1996, 116–18, 120. Also, Tarik K. Muhammad, "The Real Lowdown on Labels," *Black Enterprise,* December 1995, 75.

98. Muhammad, "The Real Lowdown on Labels," 75.

99. Ibid., 76.

100. Rhonda Reynolds and Ann Brown, "A New Rhythm Takes Hold," *Black Enterprise,* December 1994, 84. Also see Diane Weathers, "Managing the Muses: The Business Side of Black Music," *Black Enterprise,* December 1976, 23, for an account of when managers got 15 percent to 20 percent, the booking agent 10 percent, the accountant 3 to 5 percent, in addition to legal fees, all of which amounted to almost 40 percent of the artist's income.

101. Nelson George, *The Death of Rhythm and Blues* (New York: E. P. Dutton, 1989), 41–42. The two most popular radio shows in the 1930s were *Amos and Andy*, which was as television show in the 1950s with whites playing the black-faced comedy roles, and *The Jack Benny Show*, in which Eddie Anderson was cast in the role of Benny's incompetent black servant. "The Black Man Distorted: A Gallery of Twisted Images," *Emerge*, October 1995, 42–44, notes that "many early media images of Black men were of happy-go-lucky buffoons and dullards. That old tradition continues." The article provides examples from the contemporary media.

102. Trevor W. Coleman, "Black Talk," *Emerge,* November 1996, 54.

103. *Atlanta Constitution*, 18 September 1949. Also, Ingham and Feldman, *African-American Business Leaders*, 84–91.

104. John Downing, "Ethnic Minority Radio in the USA," *Howard Journal of Communication*, 1, no. 4 (1989): 135–48. Black colleges and universities own 32 public FM stations. In 1980 Howard University established the first black-owned public broadcast television station, WHMM. Also see Hal Bennett and Lew Roberts, "National Black Network: Black Radio's Big Brother," *Black Enterprise,* June 1977, 141–47.

105. Coleman, "Black Talk," 54.

106. Ingham and Feldman, *African-American Business Leaders*, 603–14.

107. Rhonda Reynolds, "Twenty-Five Black Women Who Have Made a Difference in Business," *Black Enterprise,* August 1994, 77. Also, Joyce Jones, "Keeping It in the Black," *Black Enterprise,* May 1994, 22, on Cathy Hughes, African-American woman who purchased her first station, WOL-AM in Washington, D.C., in 1980. Since it was a distressed sale, Hughes got an FCC price break. By 1995, her company, Hughes Radio One, owned seven stations after the $34 million purchase of WKYS-FM from Albimar Communications. At the time of the sale, Albimar's principal partners included "U.S.

Commerce Secretary Ron Brown and Jim Kelly, husband of former D.C. Mayor Sharon Pratt Kelly." For its sale to a minority, Albimar secured a tax credit. Hughes Radio One's earnings for 1994 were $17.6 million. Hughes said, "We are the first black corporation in America to attempt all-talk, news and information." About 195 of her 210 employees are African-American. Until she launched her own station, Hughes was general manager of Howard University's WHUR-FM.

108. Claude L. Matthews, "Detroit's WGPR: Struggling Start for Black TV," *Black Enterprise,* November 1976, 63, 65, 73, 75–77.

109. Mark Lowery, "Solid as a Rock," *Black Enterprise,* June 1995, 122–24, 128, 130, 132.

110. Cassandra Hayes, "Cashing In on the Home Shopping Boom," *Black Enterprise,* February 1995, 120.

111. Alfred Edmond Jr., "Companies to Watch in the 1990s," *Black Enterprise,* June 1989, 300–302. Also, Mark Mussari, *Suzanne de Passe: Motown's Boss Lady* (New York: Garrett Educational Corporation, 1992); and *Black Enterprise,* December 1994, 92–94, 96, 98, 100.

112. Matthew S. Scott, "Wonderful at Disney," *Black Enterprise,* December 1995, 58–60, 64. Hightower is a Howard University graduate. His appointment reflected Disney's push to capitalize on its expanding global market. Hightower headed the unit responsible for the production of films such as *The Lion King,* which "grossed $3.6 billion of Disney's $12 billion revenues in 1994"; the unit also includes the Disney Channel, and pay TV, worldwide home video and interactive-media ventures. Also, *Black Enterprise,* July 1996, 18.

113. Gracian Mack, "Inside the Viacom-Paramount Deal, *Black Enterprise,* December 1994, 114–16, 118.

114. TaRessa Stovall, "From Page to Screen," *Emerge,* March 1996, 38–40, 42.

115. *Pittsburgh Courier,* 14 May 1955.

116. Lindsay Patterson, ed., *Black Films and Filmmakers: A Comprehensive Anthology* (New York: Dodd, Mead, 1975). Also, Thomas Cripps, *Black Film as Genre* (Bloomington: Indiana University Press, 1978); Donald Bogle, *Toms, Coons, Mulattoes, Mammies and Bucks* (New York: Viking Press, 1973); and Thomas Cripps, *Slow Fade to Black: The Negro in American Film, 1900–1942* (New York: Oxford University Press, 1977).

117. See Stuart Mieher, "Spike Lee's Gotta Have It," *New York Times Magazine,* 9 August 1987, 26, on Lee's "She's Gotta Have It." Also, Mark Landler, "Spike Lee Does a Lot of Things Right," *Business Week,* 6 August 1990, 62; and Jerome Christensen, "Spike Lee, Corporate Populist," *Critical Inquiry* 17 (Spring 1991): 588–89.

118. Jesse Algernon Rhines, *Black Film/White Money* (New Brunswick, N.J.: Rutgers University Press, 1996), 167.

119. Ibid., 134. Also, Jim Merod, "A World without Whole Notes: The Intellectual Subtext of Spike Lee's Blues," *Boundary* 18 (Summer 1991): 239–51.

120. David F. Prindle, *Risky Business: The Political Economy of Hollywood* (San Francisco: Westview Press, 1993). Also, Thomas R. King, "Cut! Hollywood's Budget-Mindedness Sets Black Filmmakers Back Again," *Wall Street Journal,* 19 February 1993, R12. Also, Jesse Jackson, "A 31-Year Struggle for Fairness and Inclusion in the American Dream," *Black College Today* (May/June 1996): 10–11, on inequities in the film industry.

121. Evettte Porter, "Black Marketing," *Village Voice,* 13 September 1994, 2.

122. Thomas Cripps, *Making Movies Black* (New York: Oxford University Press, 1993).

123. Mark Lowery and Nadirah Z. Sabir, "The Making of Hollywood," *Black Enterprise,* December 1994, 112. Also, *Black Enterprise,* June 1989, 120, 122, on the films *Lean on Me* and *Colors,* which depict black gang violence. Also, Julie Dash, *Daughters of the Dust* (New York: New Press, 1992), a story of African-American family life on the Carolina Sea Islands.

124. Stovall, "From Page to Screen," 40. Both *The Color Purple* and *Waiting to Exhale* were viewed by some blacks, primarily males, as doing violence to their image, while many black females refused to accept that the male images in the films perpetuated stereotypes.

125. Stovall, "From Page to Screen," 43.

126. Lynn Norment, "Will Smith," *Ebony,* August 1996, 34–34b, 34f, 126–27. Smith starred in the hit TV series *The Fresh Prince of Bel Air.*

127. George, *Death of Rhythm and Blues*, 62, 92, 195, notes that Presley even used the black hair product Royal Crown to slick back his hair and also traces the influence of Chuck Berry on the Beatles. Jackson also purchased the Sly Stone song catalog.

128. "Power Moves," *Vibe*, September 1996, 160. Also, Ronin Ro, *Gangsta: Merchandising Rhymes of Violence* (New York: St. Martin's Press, 1996).

129. Diane Weathers, "And Along Came Tyson," *Essence*, August 1996, 64–66, 126, 130–33.

130. Shelly Branch, "How Hip-Hop Fashion Won Over Mainstream America," *Black Enterprise*, June, 1993, 111–14, 116, 118, 120.

131. Kevin D. Thompson, "The Freshman Class of '95," *Black Enterprise*, June 1995, 145–46, 148; and Tarik K. Muhammad, "From Here to Infinity, Karl Kani," *Black Enterprise*, June 1996, 140–42, 144, 146–47.

132. Donna Mitchel, "Next Stop—Atlanta," *Black Enterprise*, November 1994, 48–49.

133. *Black Enterprise*, September 1994, 22.

134. Carolyn M. Brown, "Marketing a New Universe of Heroes," *Black Enterprise*, November 1994, 80–81, 84–86. The comics books are *Blood Syndicate* (on a multiethnic super-powered street gang); *Hardware* (the hero is a technological genius who challenges a corrupt and racist employer who exploits him and his inventions); *Icon* (the hero is an extraterrestrial alien who becomes a slave on earth, but who then becomes an attorney and superhero); *Kobalt*; *Shadow Cabinet*; *Static*; and *Xombi*. Black fans of these comic books include Supreme Court Justice Clarence Thomas and filmmaker John Singleton. The Association of Black Comic Book Publishers, however, does not consider Milestones "an authentically black-owned company," because of its relationship to DC Comics, which is owned by Time Warner. Milestones claims it is a black business.

135. Muhammad, "The Real Lowdown on Labels," 76.

136. *Vibe*, August 1996, 78–79.

137. *Black Enterprise*, June 1996, 32.

138. Tricia Rose, *Black Noise: Rap Music and Black Culture in Contemporary America* (Hanover, N.H.: Wesleyan University Press, 1994).

139. "The Year 2000: A Look into the Future of the Hip Hop Generation," *Source*, August 1996, 39–61. Also, in the fight against AIDS, hip-hop artists have collaborated on a 1996 multimedia production, "America Is Dying Slowing," which is in contrast to the somewhat optimistic Quincy Jones/Michael Jackson 1985 production, "We Are the World."

CHAPTER 11

1. Ingham and Feldman, *African-American Business Leaders*, 445–47. Also, *Black Enterprise*, November 1990, 31, on federal laws and Supreme Court decisions to increase minority ownership in the broadcast industry. In October 1986 black Representatives Mickey Leland and Cardiss Collins introduced the Diversity in Media Act and the Anti-Discrimination in Advertising Act. Also in 1978 the FCC established distress sale polices that required broadcast license holders "facing FCC disciplinary proceedings to sell out to a minority business at a price not exceeding 75 percent of the fair market value." Only 12 stations were sold under these policies. With the FCC tax certification policy that allowed the deferring of capital-gains taxes to sellers of properties, 233 stations were sold to minorities. The tax certification policy was eliminated in 1995, an action that is viewed as a conservative attack on minorities in the media.

2. John N. Ingham and Lynne B. Feldman, "*Contemporary American Business Leaders: A Biographical Dictionary* (Westport, Conn.: Greenwood Press, 1990), 362.

3. Danyielle L. Peebles, "Workers Use a Buyout To Buy In," *Black Enterprise*, January 1994, 19. The company employs 240 African-Americans and Hispanic. ATS began as a computer-refurbishing and maintenance business. With the buyout, it was expected to expand production, beginning with a $100 million contract from IBM, which continues to provide technical assistance.

4. Ingham and Feldman, *African-American Business Leaders*, 575–76. Russell also owns City Beverage Company, a beer distributor. Until 1966, he owned Russell-Rowe Communications,

which operated WGXA-TV, an ABC affiliate in Macon, Georgia. In May 1996. Also see Michael Barrier, "Entrepreneurs Who Excel," *Nation's Business,* August 1996, 18–19.

5. Ingham and Feldman, *African-American Business Leaders*, 603–14.

6. Fred Martin, "The Big Three in D.C.: Graves, Pepsi, Johnson," *Black Enterprise,* October 1990, 111, 114. At the time of purchase, the company had accounts for servicing the White House, the U.S. Capital Building, and Air Force One. Of Pepsi-Cola's 900 company-operated and franchised bottling plants worldwide, it was the second African-American franchise. The first, located in Michigan, is owned by Dr. William R. Harvey, president of Hampton University. Graves also holds interest in an international Pepsi-Cola venture. Also, Ingham and Feldman, *African-American Business Leaders*, 287–93.

7. Matthew S. Scott and Tarik K. Muhammad, "Top 50 Black Powerbrokers," *Black Enterprise,* August 1990, 126.

8. Barbara Grizutti Henderson, "The Importance of Being Oprah," *New York Times Magazine,* 11 June 1989, 28–30; Also, Peter Newcomb and Lisa Gubernick, "The Top 40," *Forbes,* 27 September 1993, 97, which reported that Winfrey topped Cosby and Spielberg in earnings that year. Winfrey made her screen debut in Spielberg's production of Alice Walker's *The Color Purple.* Also, Nellie Bly, *Oprah!: Up Close and Down Home* (New York: Kensington Publishing, 1993).

9. See Lowery, "Solid as a Rock," 122–23. Also, Rhines, *Black Film/White Money,* 71–74. While the focus is on "white money" in the financing of *Malcolm X,* released in 1992 by Warner Brothers, black investors Oprah Winfrey, Michael Jordan, Magic Johnson, Janet Jackson, and Bill Cosby, among other blacks, provided the last $5 million to finance completion of the film. See Elizabeth Lesley and Maria Mallory, "Inside the Black Business Network," *Business Week,* 29 November 1993, 70–74.

10. *Black Enterprise,* February 1995, 25. The group purchased WATL in Atlanta for $150 million and paid $17 million for New Orleans station WNOL.

11. Joyce Jones, "Bob and Bill's Excellent (Ad)venture," *Black Enterprise,* May 1996, 24. See "Microsoft vs. Netscape: Round One," and Marc Gunther, "CNN Envy," *Fortune,* 8 July 1996, 70, 120–22, 124–26, on the 1995 joint venture between Microsoft and NBC that produced the MSNBC cable network and Internet operation. The alliance "came into focus during a meeting at NBC's Rockefeller Center headquarters last October, on the day of the Million Man March." Initially Microsoft and CNN's Ted Turner had considered a joint venture. With $18.5 billion, Gates was described by *Forbes* as the wealthiest person in America.

12. *Black Enterprise,* October 1990, 18.

13. Lowery, "Capitalists on a Mission," 171. Envirotest was founded by Slivy Edmonds and Chester Davenport, CEO and president.

14. Lewis and Walker, *Why Should White Guys Have All the Fun?*, 153. The statement was the introduction to Lewis's paper, "Defenses to Takeover Bids," for his class on securities regulation at Harvard Law School under Professor Louis Loss. See, ibid., 58.

15. Ibid., 236.

16. Ingham and Feldman, *African-American Business Leaders*, 92.

17. Johnson, *Succeeding against the Odds*, 89.

18. Ibid., 21. Also, Hans J. Massaquoi, "The New Racism," *Ebony,* August 1996, 56–58, 60; Carl T. Rowan, *The Coming Race War in America: A Wake up Call* (Boston: Little, Brown, 1996).

19. Lewis and Walker, *Why Should White Guys Have All the Fun?*, 137, 155. Lewis was born in Baltimore and attended Virginia State University and Harvard Law School. After three years at a white law firm, he became a partner in the first black law firm on Wall Street in 1970. In 1973 Lewis founded his own firm, specializing in MESBIC venture capital investments with minority firms. In 1983, Lewis founded TLC and subsequently purchased McCalls, increasing profits to $14 million in a company with prior average annual sales of $6.5 million. Innovations, such as using McCalls printing facilities to make greeting cards and knitting patterns for international sales, boosted profits. He sold McCalls for $95 million ($63 million in cash and an absorption of $32 million).

20. Lewis & Walker, *Why Should White Guys Have All the Fun?*, 253 and 269–270.

21. Ibid., 266. Also, *Black Enterprise,* August 1994, 28; and Tom Lowery, "Former Trader Gets to Tell SEC His Side," *USA Today,* 20 May 1996, on Joseph Jett, black Harvard MBA, fired from his

position at Kidder, Peabody & Company, "accused of manipulating his investment banking firm's computer system to book $350 million in phantom profits." Jett, 1993 Kidder employee of the year, was paid more than $11 million in bonuses in 1992 and 1993; his supervisor, $20 million. The supervisor, previously censured and fined by the NASDAQ, remained, along with six suspended white employees. Only Jett was fired. The white press castigated him, creating an "image of a black man blundering into a position above his ability, covering his short-comings with bluster and crying racism when found out." Insiders say he was set up to distract attention from his white supervisor's incompetency and $80 million losses. In 1995 Jett filed a $50-million lawsuit against Kidder and GE, its parent company at the time of his firing.

22. Lewis and Walker, *Why Should White Guys Have All the Fun?*, 205–6. Also, Jolie Solomon, "Operation Rescue," *Working Woman*, May 1996, 58–59, on the suit brought against TLC Beatrice by Drexel Burnham Lambert and Michael Milken, who, with 22 percent of the stock, "charges that RFL paid himself $22.1 million in undeserved compensation and milked Beatrice for millions more to cover personal expenditures." Lewis's widow and Beatrice CEO and president disclaims the charges and views the basis of the suit as racist: "She's convinced the plaintiff's ardor dates back to arguments during the 1987 negotiations, with this emphasis: 'A black man (was) saying harsh words to a white man.' " A TLC attorney said the basis of the suit is that the plaintiffs "just don't want their money tied up for the long haul."

23. Lewis and Walker, *Why Should White Guys Have All the Fun?*, 265–69. Before an IPO, a company would have to show at least two years of increased earnings before it can go public, an equity-financing process to raise capital, but only 10,000 American corporations offer shares for public trading. Also, Boston, *Smart Money Moves*, 71. Boston, formerly a financial planner with IDS/American Express, is CEO of Boston Media, which produces *The Color of Money* for PBS and cable television and publishes the journals *Color of Money* and *Corporate Detroit*. Karen Gibbs, who holds an MBA from the University of Chicago, has been a financial analyst and anchorwoman for CNBC. Also, *Black Enterprise*, June 1996, 70, indicates that in 1995, 583 companies went public and raised $30 billion.

24. Alfred Edmond Jr., "Milestones in Black Business, 1970–1971," *Black Enterprise*, August 1994, 100. Also, *Black Enterprise*, September 1994, 42, on BET filing "for a public offering of up to 100,000 shares of previously restricted Class A common stock . . . the proposed offering is slated to generate between $1.5 and $1.6 million in new cash." Proceeds were slated to be used to establish the nonprofit Geron P. Johnson Educational Fund in memory of the Johnsons' son. Also, Rhonda Reynolds, "Knowing the S.C.O.R.," *Black Enterprise*, June 1995, 252–54, 256. The usual amount to set up an IPO is $500,000. With SCOR (Small Corporate Offering Registration), set up by the SEC in 1996, outside capital can be raised without going public and costs only about $20,000.

25. Lewis and Walker, *Why Should White Guys Have All the Fun?*, 271. Also, Peter F. Drucker, *Innovation and Entrepreneurship: Practice and Principles* (New York: Harper and Row, 1985), 79.

26. *Black Enterprise*, July 1995, 31.

27. See Carolyn M. Brown, "The Hottest Industries for New Business Opportunities," *Black Enterprise*, March 1995, 65–67, 70–73. In 1995, in addition to the Midwest, the regional breakdown for black businesses was: the Northeast, 103,694; the South, 152,256; the Southwest, 39,773; the West, 54,013; and the Northwest, 4,190. Also, Smith, "Paving the Way?" *Black Enterprise*, June 1996, 198.

28. Eric S. Hardy, "America's Highest Paid Bosses," *Forbes*, 20 May 1996, 189, who also indicates that, while the average salary of the top people in white corporations was $1.5 million, $609,000 was in salary and $440,000 was in bonuses. Coss's salary was only $434,000, and the rest, $65.1 million, was a bonus of two million shares of Green Tree stock and cash, a reward for Coss's business acumen: "He made mortgages available to buyers of mobile homes, a class of buyers most lenders shirked. He proved they were good risks."

29. Graham Button, "The Superrich: The World's Richest People," *Forbes*, 15 July 1996, 124–25. In the United States, the richest is Microsoft's Bill Gates, worth $18 billion. There were 123 Asian billionaires on the list, including 41 Japanese, in 1995. As indicated, "Asia, largely a back-

ward area at the end of WWII, is home to more than one in four of the world's great fortunes—those worth $1 billion or more." While African decolonization began after World War II, political liberation did not bring economic liberation during the rise of neocolonialism. Yet Africa has the same kinds of resources for development as Asia does, but "much of the big new money comes from such businesses as property development, energy and natural resources. In this respect, Asia mirrors the U.S. of a few decades black."

30. Alfred Edmond Jr., "Milestones in Black Business. 1970-1971, *Black Enterprise*," August 1994, 100.

31. *Pittsburgh Courier*, 2 September 1957. Also, *New York Times,* 9 March 1958. The company, with a 27-store restaurant chain, a Brooklyn coffee plant, and a New Jersey bakery, grossed $30 million in sales in 1957. It employed about 1,000 people, 80 percent of whom were black. Robinson worked in the personnel department. He had been the first black player to play major league baseball: "Branch Rickey, then the Dodgers' general manager, broke an unwritten baseball law in 1945, when he signed Robinson as the first Negro to play in organized baseball."

32. *Pittsbugh Courier*, 8 May 1954, 13 March 1954. In the early 1950s, Clary Multiplier Corporation, a leading business machine manufacturer, employed William T. Phillips in Detroit; for several years he was honored as one of the company's leading salespeople.

33. Frank Marshall Davis, "Democracy: Hawaiian-Style, Del Monte's Negro Foreman," *Atlanta Daily World*, 18 March 1949.

34. *Pittsburgh Courier*, 21 October 1939. Pike's hiring was taken to the Pepsi-Cola board of directors, which held a vote as to whether he should be given the position; it announced that "it had elected" him to assume that position.

35. *Birmingham Weekly Review,* 3 December 1948.

36. *New York Daily Worker*, 20 June 1944.

37. *Seattle Northern Enterprise*, 16 February 1949. Several groups, the Independent Progressive Party, the NAACP, and Urban League took credit for the hiring, with the Bank of America claiming it had "conferred for years" with these groups before making a decision to hire blacks. Also, *Atlanta Daily World,* 28 April 1949, which two months later reported that Security First National Bank promoted a black man to the position of teller and placed him in a branch bank "where 75 per cent of the patronage is colored."

38. *Chicago Crusader*, 18 January 1958.

39. Ivan Light, "Self-Help for the Urban Poor," *The American Enterprise* (July/August 1996): 50–52. Considering the success of these immigrant enterprises, especially in providing venture capital to move into the mainstream American business community, and considering the restructuring and downsizing in corporate America and the existence of chronic unemployment, these enterprises and their financing, often by rotating-credit unions, provide a model for any American who seeks self-employment but lacks the prerequisites for participation in other business activities. Also, Andrew Hacker, "The Decline of Higher Education," *New York Review of Books,* 13 February 1986, 36.

40. Mark Lowery, "Sold on Ice Cream," *Black Enterprise,* April 1995, 60–62, 64.

41. Eric L. Smith, "Walking Tall," *Black Enterprise*, February 1996, 130–32, 134. In 1995, Nine West in a $600 million deal acquired U.S. Shoe's Footwear Group. Holt left Nine West to become president of the group before returning to Nine West. Black corporate leader Brenda J. Lauderback was president of U.S. Shoe's Footwear Wholesale Group.

42. Caroline V. Clarke, "The $70 Billion Man," *Black Enterprise,* June 1989, 100–102, 104. Wharton (b. 1926), a Harvard graduate and holder of Ph.D in economics from the University of Chicago, was the first black to head a predominantly white university when he became president of Michigan State University and then chancellor of the entire SUNY system. He was also the first black director of Equitable Life Assurance. He is the son of the country's first African-American ambassador, Clifton Wharton Sr.

43. Caroline V. Clarke, "#2 at the World's Largest Retirement Fund," *Black Enterprise,* June 1994, 252–54, 256, 258, 260. Jones, son of a black nuclear physicist who was also a minister, was one of the Cornell University students, armed with rifles and giving black power salutes, blazoned across the the cover of *Newsweek* in April 1969. Jones has bachelor's and master's degrees in public health from Cornell

and an MBA from Boston University. He is a CPA, one of the few Americans who ever passed all five parts of the exam the first time at one sitting. He had been with the Arthur Young & Co. accounting firm in Boston. At TIAA-CREF, Jones quickly gained a Triple-A rating for the company, its first; it is now only one of four insurance companies in America with a Triple-A rating from all four rating agencies.

44. *Black Enterprise*, October 1993, 14.

45. Mark Lowery, "Second in Command at Time Warner," *Black Enterprise*, January 1995, 15. Time-Warner, a $15 billion *Fortune* 500 company, owns *Time* and *Sports Illustrated*, HBO, and Warner Brothers. See Fonda Marie Lloyd and Mark Lowery, "The Man behind the Merger, *Black Enterprise*, October 1994, 69–70, 72, 76. Parsons, a graduate of the University of Hawaii, with a 1971 J.D. from Union University's Albany Law School, ranked first in his class. He was assistant counselor to Nelson Rockefeller, when he was governor of New York and deputy counsel for him when he was vice president. Parsons's father was an electrician.

46. Caroline V. Clarke, "Delivering High Performance," *Black Enterprise*, June, 1996, 214–16, 218, 220. Roberts quickly moved up GM's corporate ladder but left one year after he was promoted in 1987 to vice president for personnel. GM asked him back in 1988, but he did not return until 1992 when he was moved to operations as GM general manager. Roberts was the 9th of 10 children, all of whom earned college degrees. His father was a Detroit factory worker.

47. Richard Prince, "Reinventing Xerox," *Black Enterprise*, June 1994, 262–64, 266. Also, *Ebony*, May 1966, 9.

48. Cassandra Hayes, "Can a New Frontier Boost Your Career?" *Black Enterprise* May 1995, 72–73, and "On The Move," *Black Enterprise*, May 1995, 56. Initially, AT&T hoped to play a role in developing the telecommunications infrastructure, which would have put it in competition with South Africa's government-owned telephone system, Telekom. By 1996, with South Africa's increasing concern that control of their system could be usurped by American corporations, AT&T's input was limited to that of a primary technology supplier. Also, Sven Lunsche, "Dollars Down South," *Tribune*, September 1995, 66–68, in this Johannesburg publication notes, "80 odd African American businessmen and women" are in Johannesburg. See Eric L. Smith, "Traveling Rocky Roads," *Black Enterprise*, May 1996, 108–9. IBM, Dell Computers, Chrysler, Ford, Levi Strauss, Duracell, Coca-Cola, and Silicon Graphics are some companies that have placed African-American executives in their South African divisions.

49. Cassandra Hayes, "The Intrigue of International Assignments," *Black Enterprise*, May 1996, 98–100, 105. Nickelodeon is a subsidiary of Viacom, one of the world's largest international entertainment and publishing companies. Also, Tonia L. Shakespeare, "From Star to Team Player," *Black Enterprise*, January 1996, 50, on Jerry Florence, Wichita State University grad and former Chicago White Sox baseball player from 1966 to 1971. In 1993 he was hired by Nissan Motors as its first African-American vice president, with a position in Nissan's U.S. marketing division, where he was credited with "the successful launch of the 1995 Maxima and 20SX," increasing their sales by 30 percent and 10 percent, respectively. Florence credits his American sports team experience for his ability to adapt to the Japanese corporate culture, *kaisan*, and its *nimiwashi* management style, which requires each proposal to be thoroughly analyzed before a decision is reached. At General Motors from 1983 to 1993, he worked as a sales, marketing, and business planner, and then as general director in marketing and product planning for the Cadillac division in international sales, developing and negotiating contracts with the former Soviet Union and Japan.

50. Sheryl Hilliard Tucker, "Black Women in Corporate America: The Inside Story," *Black Enterprise*, August 1994, 60–63. Also, Carolyn Odom Steele, "Setting a New Agenda for Women's Networks," *Black Enterprise*, October 1994, 126–28, 130, 132.

51. Rhonda Reynolds, "Ann M. Fudge: Brewing Success," *Black Enterprise*, August 1994, 68–70. Also see, Ernest Holsendolph, "More Minorities and Women in Key Jobs," *Emerge*, August 1996, 22. Also, *Black Enterprise*, August 1974, its first issue focusing on African-American women in business. See *Jet*, 20 May 1996, 8, on Karen Sock, who in 1996 was appointed general manager of Harrah's Tunica Casino in Mississippi, a $59 million operation with 500 employees.

52. Matthew S. Scott, "Climbing Jacob's Ladder," *Black Enterprise*, September 1994, 128–31. Also see *Black Enterprise*, November 1995, which notes that "African Americans make up only 2%

of the board members of Fortune industrial and service corporations." Also, corporations usually seat the same black people: "On average African directors are active on three boards whereas other directors sit on only two."

53. Lester C. Thurow, *The Zero Sum Solution: Building a World-Class American Economy* (New York: Simon and Schuster, 1985), 11, 317, describes aspects of unemployment in America as "pictures of a national disgrace."

54. Caroline V. Clarke, "Meeting the Challenge of Corporate Leadership," *Black Enterprise,* August 1995, 156–57. Also slated for advancement to a CEO position are Richard Nanula, president of Disney Stores Worldwide, and Lloyd Ware, central division president at Frito-Lay, a subsidiary of PepsiCo.

55. Fonda Marie Lloyd, "Assault on Texaco's Glass Ceiling," *Black Enterprise,* August 1994, 19, on a class action lawsuit by 1,500 black executives at Texaco who claim they have been passed over for promotions, including one woman who said that "a white male without proper qualifications was promoted over her, and then she was asked to train him." Texaco in 1993 had 11,277 management employees, 554 of whom were black. The suit was settled in 1996 for $176 million.

56. Frank McCoy, "Shattering Glass Ceilings," *Black Enterprise,* September 1995, 22, which also summarizes the findings of Rutgers University law professor Alfred W. Blumrosen in his "Employment Discrimination Report" done for the Bureau of National Affairs in 1995; it is based on his review of 3,000 federal district and appeals courts decisions made from 1990 to 1994 in discrimination cases. Only 100 of those decisions involved reverse discrimination cases, but "reverse discrimination was established legally in only six cases." As an aside, charges of reverse discrimination frequently start with personnel officers. In turning down white males for a position or explaining their failure to be promoted, personnel managers will frequently lie by telling the applicants that they were qualified, but affirmative action guidelines require that a minority be hired. Also, Sylvester Monroe, "America's Most Feared: The State of African America Men," *Emerge,* October 1995, 25. Also, *Black Enterprise,* August 1995, 124, on Harvard graduate Alphonse Fletcher, who, at age 26, won a $1.3 million lawsuit against Kidder, Peabody, for giving him a bonus lower than he thought he deserved. Fletcher established Fletcher Asset Management. A 1993 SEC filing showed the black Wall Street firm with $46 million in assets and $3.6 million in equity. "On a good day, his firm is responsible for as much as 5 percent of all trades executed at the New York Stock Exchange."

57. *Black Enterprise,* June 1995, 158.

58. Joel Kotkin, *Tribes: How Race, Religion and Identity Determine Success in the New Global Economy* (New York: Random House, 1992), 4.

59. See, Lesley and Mallory, "Black Business Network," 73, on a black Xerox employee in a line management position in the 1970s who helped blacks negotiate the corporate culture but found he could no longer conform to it himself, an early black casualty of white corporate America.

60. Rhonda Reynolds, "Black Women Who Have Made a Difference," 76; and *Black Enterprise,* October 1994, 179. Florida A & M's business school professional development program "models corporate America with 23 in-house 'companies,' such as an investment firm, insurance company and television station."

61. Martin Khor, "Colonialism Redux," *The Nation,* 15/22 July 1996, 18–20, views new trade policies by the West as actions for "reconquering the third world with protocols instead of gunboats."

62. Foner, *Voice of Black America,* 200, from a speech made by Frederik Douglass on 4 August 1857, often identified as the "If there is no struggle, there is no progress" speech.

63. See Valencia Roner, "The Dynamic Duo of Franchising," *Black Enterprise,* September 1995, 68–78. Also, "The Dean of 'Fast-Food's Harvard,'" *Black Enterprise,* September 1994, 52. McDonald's Hamburger University, established for the training of franchisee candidates, owner/operators, and managers from 72 countries, is headed by Shirley Rogers, an African-American.

64. Carolyn M. Brown, "B.E. Franchise 50: More Than Window Dressing," *Black Enterprise,* September 1994, 103–4, 106, 108, 112.

65. Derek T. Dingle, "Pursuing a Strategic Vision," *Black Enterprise*, June 1997, 122, 124.

66. Carolyn M. Brown, "All Talk, No Action," *Black Enterprise*, September 1995, 60–61.

67. Cassandra Hayes and Rhonda Reynolds, "25 Years of Blacks in Franchising," *Black Enterprise*, September 1994, 126. In 1986 Arnold Whitmore and five investors purchased 25 Church's Chicken franchise units. In 1987 Lonear Heard purchased her seventh Los Angeles-area McDonald's. Also, Caroline V. Clarke, "Giant Steps for Black Franchisees," *Black Enterprise*, September 1993, 44–50.

68. Brown, "B.E. Franchise 50," 104. Also, Valencia Roner, "Going For a Denny's Grand Slam," *Black Enterprise*, September 1995, 75, 78, on Denny's Fast Track Ownership Program. A Denny's franchise grosses $1.2 million in annual sales.

69. Brown, "B.E. Franchise 50," 103–4, 106, 108, 112. In 1989 black franchisees filed a $500 million class action suit against Burger King. Also, Joan Delaney, "Ten Danger Signs to Look for When Buying a Franchise," *Black Enterprise*, September 1994, 118–21; Rhonda Reynolds, "Black Franchise Hopefuls Beware," *Black Enterprise*, September 1995, 81–82, 84, 86.

70. See Wally Amos, with Leroy Robinson, *The Famous Amos Story: The Face That Launched a Thousand Chips* (Garden City, N.Y.: Doubleday, 1983). Also, Ingham and Feldman, *African-American Business Leaders*, 24–31.

71. *Black Enterprise*, January 1995, 22. The company went through four owners from 1985 to 1988, when Amos lost ownership in the company. In 1992 he lost ownership of his trademark cookie name. In 1994 he established another cookie enterprise, The Uncle Noname Cookie Company.

72. Herman Cain, "Bad Solution for the Wrong Problem," *The American Enterprise*, July/August 1996, 53–54.

73. See Maria Mallory, "Claude Patmon's Accent on Growth," *Black Enterprise*, September 1990, 66–68, 70. Patman, who had an MBA from the University of Miami, was a Burger King vice president for 10 years and also worked for Ponderosa, Inc.

74. Tonia L. Shakespeare, "So You Want to Be a Franchisor?," *Black Enterprise*, September 1995, 88–91. Morrison was in the industry for 20 years. Unable to pay a $100,000–$500,000 fee to establish a regional franchise, Morrison established himself as a franchisor. Also, Hayes and Reynolds, "Twenty-Five Years of Blacks in Franchising," 126–27; and *Black Enterprise*, September 1990, 47, on the sale of black franchisor Fatburger Corp. to Keith Warlick and Forest Hamilton.

75. Johnson, *Succeeding against the Odds*, 161, 172–73, 179–91.

76. *Ebony*, "Brown Hucksters," May 1948. Pepsi Cola had employed its first black sales rep in the mid-1930s.

77. *Norfolk Journal and Guide*, 31 January 1948. Brandford supplied his "famous Brandford Models," and in this instance was recognized as "establishing a new mode in advertising for manufacturers."

78. *Pittsburgh Courier*, 10 July 1948.

79. Ibid. In 1948 Bunche mediated the Palestinian-Israeli conflict. In 1950 he became the first Nobel Peace Prize winner of African descent.

80. *Norfolk Journal and Guide*, 17 April 1948. Under what was known as "the progressive Lever policy," a black navy veteran was hired as a salesman for the New York division, joining the other black, a long-time employee. The black press also reported that "Negroes are also employed in the six plants where Lever's fine soap and shortening products are manufactured." Lever brands were Lux, Lifebuoy, Rinso, and Swan.

81. *Black Enterprise*, February 1971, 15–22.

82. Ricki L. Francki, "Success Story Good News: Proctor Takes a Gamble and Hits the Jackpot," *Working Woman*, August 1979, 19. Also, Nancy Ryan, "Equality Shelved," *Chicago Tribune*, 10 May 1992, 17; Kevin Klose, "In the Spirit of Enterprise," *Washington Post*, 27 January 1984. Also, Ingham and Feldman, *African-American Business Leaders*, 564–69, includes sources. Until she lost the Alberto-Culver account, Proctor had refused to write ads for liquor, beer, and wine companies. She has been an outspoken critic of racism in the advertising industry.

83. Ken Smikle, "The Image-Makers," *Black Enterprise*, December 1985, 44–55.

84. Herbert Allen, "Product Appeal: No Class," *Advertising Age*, 1 May 1981. Quaker Oats, parent company for Aunt Jemima, introduced a stereotyped image of a black woman as a smiling

domestic in 1893 at the Columbia World's Fair in Chicago. The image was changed in 1991. Yet in 1995 criticism erupted from some in the African-American community when black female singer Gladys Knight, a glamorous grandmother, was used in an Aunt Jemima TV ad. Until the 1960s blacks featured in ads for white products invariably were light-skinned with Caucasian features and straight hair. In the Civil Rights period, ads for white products featured dark-skinned black models with African features and Afro hairstyles. In the 1970s dark-skinned blacks with Caucasian features were popular. By the 1990s white corporate America had decided that tan was the appropriate color for black models, especially if they also appeared to be Hispanic, which might appeal to two markets at the same time. In general, the image presented depended on the product advertised. By the 1990s blacks of all colors, sizes, features, hairstyles and hair textures, including perms, short Afros, braids, and wigs, were depicted in ads for products from both black and white companies.

85. John Revett, "Cosby Top Star Presenter of 1978," *Advertising Age, 17* July 1978, 1. Also, Gary Dub, "The Ever-Popular Cosby," *Dallas Morning Star*, 16 March 1985; Ronald L. Smith, *Cosby* (New York: St. Martin's, 1986).

86. Irvin Friend and J. B. Kravis, "New Light on the Consumer Market," *Business History Review* 31 (January–February 1957): 112–15; Sylvia Applebaum, "On Desegregating Advertising," *Crisis* 69 (June–July 1962): 313–17; Rich Blake, "Minorities: Reaching the World's Ninth Largest Market," *Public Relations Journal* 41 (January 1985): 31. Also, Janette L. Dates and William Barlow, eds., *Split Image: African Americans in the Mass Media,* 2d. ed. (Washington, D.C.: Howard University Press, 1992).

87. Ernest Holsendolph, "Burrell Ads Up to Commercial Success," *Emerge,* March 1996, 20. With this acquisition, Burrell added Citicorp/Citibank, Dow-Jones, and the American Association of Retired Persons to his roster of clients, including Mobil OIl, NYNEX, Kmart, and Polaroid, while giving him access to the New York ad market since nationally "25 to 30 percent of billings are originated from New York." Also, Ingham and Feldman, *African-American Business Leaders*, 120–29, includes sources.

88. *Chicago Defender*, 7 March 1996. In March 1996, a black business leadership conference was held in Durham, North Carolina. Lewis was one of the principal speakers. He was also noted for having "generated combined annual revenues of approximately $1 billion." The issues discussed at the conference were "the impact of current market shifts, layoffs and cutbacks on the African American professional entrepreneurs and the strategies they must employ to remain competitive globally."

89. Cassandra Hayes, "Marketing to the World," *Black Enterprise,* January 1995, 94–95, 98–99.

90. Smikle, "The Image Makers," 4–5; and Marianne Paskowski, "Cover Story: Shades of Grey," *Marketing and Media Decisions,* 21 (March 1986): 30–40.

91. "Twenty-Five Years of Blacks in Advertising," *Black Enterprise,* January 1995, 92–93.

92. *Chicago Defender*, 7 February 1953. Only limited expenditures were made by white manufacturers of black hair and beauty aids products for advertising in the black press. According to the *Defender*, the Dr. Palmer line of products was a leader in field of cosmetics for black women.

93. Juliet E. K. Walker, "The Promised Land: The *Chicago Defender* and the Black Press in Illinois," in *The Black Press in the Middle West, 1865–1985,* ed. Henry Lewis Suggs (Westport, Conn.: Greenwood Press, 1996): 9–50. Robert Sengstacke died in 1997. The *Defender* was put on sale, and whites have expressed interest.

94. Margaret Bernstein, "Pressing On," *Black Enterprise,* June 1989 142–44, 146, 148. Also, James D. Williams, "The Black Press: How Power Can Slip Away," *Black Enterprise,* June 1977, 148–49, 151, 153–54, 156–57. In 1976 the *Chicago Defender* was a *Black Enterprise* 100 company, with sales of $6.5 million.

95. Eric L. Smith, "Negotiating the Deals," *Black Enterprise,* July 1995, 94–96, 98. Today, player unions limit agents to only 4 percent to 5 percent of contract deals, with increasing numbers of black professionals, lawyers, and financial advisers representing black sports stars as agents. Also, NFL Hall of Famer Gene Upshaw, as executive director of the NFL Players Association, was instrumental in raising player salaries. Also, Bobby Clay, "Eight Great Careers in the Sports Industry, *Black Enterprise,* February 1995, 158.

96. *Black Enterprise,* December 1995, 33, on the Silver Springs, Maryland, Muhammad Ali Rotisserie Chicken restaurant that opened in 1994 with plans for expansion as a franchise.

97. *Black Enterprise,* July 1995, 11, 62. Also, J. R. Richard, a top major league pitcher in the 1970s, was found homeless living under a freeway in 1993.

98. Ingham and Feldman, *African-American Business Leaders*, 444. In 1971 Llewellyn took over as CEO and then as bank chairman in 1973 to reestablish the bank's financial standing, which he accomplished in 1975, then stepped down. The bank, however, closed in 1991.

99. *Black Enterprise,* October 1990, 22. Two whites held 48 percent interest in RMK steel.

100. Tarik K. Muhammad and Matthew S. Scott, "The 30 Most Valuable Professionals in the Business of Sports," *Black Enterprise,* July 1995, 76, 80. In 1997, Thomas left the Toronto Raptors to become a television commentator.

101. Merlisa Lawrence Corbett, "Building the Champions," *Black Enterprise,* July 1995, 84–87. Some of the black businesspeople who are part owners of professional sports teams include Comer Cottrell, Pro-Line CEO, who has ownership in the Texas Rangers; and Edward Garner, CEO of Soft Sheen, and his wife, who have ownership in the Chicago Bulls. The Lee-Bynoe 1989 deal for the purchase of the Denver Nuggetts fizzled out by 1992. Deron Cherry has a share in the Jacksonville Jaguars and Bill Sims has part ownership in the Carolina Panthers. Herman J. Russell is a member of the Omni Group that purchased the National Hockey League franchise that became the Atlanta Flames before the team was sold. The group owns the Omni, the 17,000-seat sports and convention center where the Atlanta Hawks play (Russell's ownership was $1.8 million of the $12 million package).

102. Brian Burwell, "Super Deals for Superstars: Top Jocks Put On the Hard Sell for Big Bucks," *Black Enterprise,* July 1984, 37–57; Sundiata Djata, "Madison Avenue Blindly Ignores the Black Consumer," *Business and Society Review* 60 (Winter 1987): 9–13. Also, Raymond Bauer and Scott M. Cunningham, "The Negro Market," *Journal of Advertising Research* 10 (April 1970): 2–13.

103. Lewis R. Gordon, "A Lynching Well Lost"; Lisa M. Anderson, "Presumed Guilty: Or, I Thought This Was the Movie of the Week"; James B. Stewart, "Race, Science, and 'Just-Us': Understanding Jurors: Reasonable Doubt in the O. J. Simpson Trial"; and Stanley O. Gaines Jr., "O. J. Simpson, Mark Fuhrman, and the Moral 'Low Ground' of Ethnic/Race Relations in the United States," *Black Scholar* 25 (Fall 1995): 37–42, 43–47, provide a black perspective.

104. Jim Naughton, *Taking to the Air: The Rise of Michael Jordan* (New York: Warner Books, 1992). Also, Muhammad and Scott, "The 30 Most Valuable Professionals," 77; Jeffrey E. Walker, "Sports," in *Encyclopedia of African-American Business History* (Westport, Conn.: Greenwood, forthcoming 1998).

105. John Feinstein, "Tiger by the Tail," *Newsweek,* 9 September 1996, 58.

106. Holsendolph, "Burrell Ads Up to Commercial Success," 20.

107. Eleanor D. Branch, "Marketing the Games," *Black Enterprise,* July 1995, 89–90, 92. Also see *Black Enterprise,* July 1995, 22, on the sports apparel company HCBU (Historically Black College and Universities), founded by six blacks whose black-college signature apparel is sold by Foot Locker and J. C. Penney. Some 6 percent to 8 percent of the company's profits are given to historically black colleges.

108. Muhammad and Scott, "The 30 Most Valuable Professionals," 78. Since 1995, both Michael Jordan and Shaquille O'Neal have starred in big-screen movies.

109. Matthew S. Scott, "Tapping into the Telecommunications Industry," *Black Enterprise,* February 1995, 177.

110. *Black Enterprise,* March 1995, 66. Also, "RMS Strikes Deal for Growth Capital," *Black Enterprise,* January 1996, 19.

111. Cliff Hocker, "Graduating with Honors, *Black Enterprise,* November 1990, 88–89, 92, 94. Also, *Black Enterprise,* January 1991, 23, where new regulations for 8(a) contracts have resulted in a decline in bidding for contracts by 21 percent ; and Alfred Edmond Jr., "Evolution Not Revolution," *Black Enterprise,* June 1995, 90. Network Solutions Inc. was sold to San Diego-based Science Applications International.

112. Fonda Marie Lloyd, "Black Media Firm Rides the Information Highway," *Black Enterprise,* August 1994, 16. The *Black Enterprise* top 100 companies with investments in Urban Communications OCS Limited Partnership are: Inner City Broadcasting, Burrell Communications, Granite Broadcasting, and UniWorld Group, in addition to Motown Records.

113. McCoy, "Nonstop from Durham," 88–91; King, "Muni-less Future," 188. Also, *Black Enterprise,* June 1995, 55, indicates that Sloan paid $91 million for five PCS licenses.

114. Jones, "Bob and Bill's," 24.

115. Watts and Gite, "Emerging Entrepreneurs," 102.

116. Lewis and Walker, *Why Should White Guys Have All the Fun?*, 203, 217. Lewis sold off the Canadian assets for $235 million. The Australian assets were also sold. TLC companies are located in Italy, Spain, Portugal, Netherlands, Belgium, Germany, Denmark, Latin America, and Thailand.

117. Ibid., 251–52. TLC is the major supplier for ice cream in western Europe, operates soft-drink bottling plants in several countries and is "the No.1 maker of potato chips and snacks in Ireland."

118. *Black Enterprise,* July 1996, 26.

119. *Black Enterprise,* September 1994, 110. Also, Matthew S. Scott, "CBC [Congressional Black Caucus] on Japanese Slur: Bush Must Speak Out," *Black Enterprise,* December 1990, 17, notes that in the 1980s some Japanese advertising used gross stereotyped images of African-Americans. One company produced a line of Black Sambo dolls, toys, and beach towels, with the Black Sambo character saying "When I'm hungry there's no stoppin' me. I'll be up a palm pickin' coconuts before you can count to three. (An' I can count way past three, too!)." In stores, black mannequins were depicted "with bulging eyes and enormous lips." The CBC protested and the items were taken off the market. Also, from 1986 to 1988, three Japanese government officials made racial slurs. One said blacks ruined residential areas in the same way that Japanese prostitutes ruin neighborhoods. Another blamed the decline of America on "the inferiority of African-Americans and Hispanics," while another said blacks are "financially irresponsible."

120. Frank McCoy, "Black Business Courts the Japanese Market," *Black Enterprise,* June 1994, 216. There are at least 7,000 African-Americans living in Japan, with the 13-year-old Japan Afro-American Friendship Association (JAFA) helping to build bridges. Black filmmaker Regge Life has a Tokyo residence. His documentary, "Struggle and Success: The African-American Experience in Japan," showed that Commodore Perry brought American racism to Japan in 1853 when he forced that nation to open its doors to American trade and then "entertained Japanese dignitaries with minstrel shows."

121. Ibid., 216, 218, 222. African-Americans have established small businesses in Japan, including Kyle Sexton who established a bakery with loans from his father and several Japanese friends. A Japanese exchange student who studied African-American history with the author at the University of Illinois at Urbana exhibited no racial prejudices toward her, or her African-American or white classmates. Also, Lewis and Walker, *Why Should White Guys Have All the Fun?*, 107, in which Lewis contrasts the lack of racism he encountered in Japan and the Philippines while on his honeymoon, with the looks of "condescension and disapproval" that he got from white American tourists in Hawaii. Also, since the 1990s, Japanese automakers have increased their number of black employees and dealerships.

122. In the 1970s and 1980s, blacks made several ventures in the oil refinery business. See Herschel Johnson, "First Black-Owned Refinery: Record Investment to Yield Record Sales," *Black Enterprise,* November 1976, 47, 49–50, on the New York-based Wallace & Wallace Chemical & Oil Corporation, which in 1976 had a fleet of 16 trucks, 60 employees, and $17 million in gross sales. The Tuskegee air base was selected as the site of the refinery. The company was started in 1968 with an SBA loan of $350,000. There were five black fuel oil companies listed on the *Black Enterprise* top 100 list for 1976.

123. Ingham and Feldman, *African-American Business Leaders*, 612. Also, Lewis and Walker, *Why Should White Guys Have All the Fun?*, 127–31, on Lewis's short-lived Caribbean Basin Broadcasting radio network, which he established in 1982 and sold in 1986.

124. Marjorie Whigham-Desir, "Forging New Frontiers," *Black Enterprise,* May 1996, 74, 76.

125. Tonia L. Shakespeare, "Is Soft Sheen Products Being Sold?" *Black Enterprise,* September 1995, 16.

126. Edmond, "Companies to Watch," 302, 304.

127. Whigham-Desir, "Forging New Frontiers," 71.

128. Ibid., 72, 74.

129. "Carson Reports Record Second Quarter Sales," *Public Relations Newswire,* 11 November 1996, The PointCast Network.

130. "South Africa Inc.: The Quest for Gold," *Black Enterprise,* August 1994, 15. Also, Andrew F. Brimmer, "Africa Wants Your Money," *Black Enterprise,* October 1994, 26; and Gracian Mack, "Getting in on the Ground Floor," *Black Enterprise,* May 1995, 78–82.

131. Frank McCoy, "Doing Business in South Africa," *Black Enterprise,* May 1995, 61–62; Eric L. Smith, "Traveling Rocky Roads," 108; and Frank McCoy, "Tapping into Emerging Markets," *Black Enterprise,* May 1996, 86.

132. "Forging New Frontiers," *Black Enterprise,* 76, 78. Johnson holds 51 percent interest. His five South African partners hold 49 percent. See *Ebony South Africa* 1 (November/December 1995). Some of the articles included are: "The South African Revolution Goes to America: Franklin Sonn is the First Black South African Ambassador in Washington D.C."; "Denzel Washington Opens Up about Stardom, Family and Sex Appeal"; "At Home with Daphney Hlomuka: South Africa's Most Watched TV Actress"; "Hugh Masekela is Back"; "Pamela Bridgewater: First Black Woman Counsel General"; "Basketball: South Africa's Fastest-Growing Sport"; and "Why Almost Everybody Loves Colin Powell." D. Michael Cheers, an *Ebony/Jet* photographer and managing editor of *Ebony South Africa*, was the force behind the launching of the new Johnson publication while he was a 1995 Fulbright fellow in South Africa.

133. See *Tribute,* September 1995, which included the following articles on African-Americans: "Keep Ya Head Up," on now-deceased black hip-hop artist Tupac Shakur; "The Sounds of Music City," on the New Orleans Jazz Festival; and "Dollars Down South," on African-American business activities in South Africa. Its world focus section included "Waging Peace," on Vietnam's General Vo Nguyen Giap. *Tribute* also carried ads from Revlon, IVAX's Flori Roberts, and black-owned M & M Products, in addition to those for Christian Dior and Toyota Camrys. Other South African periodicals are *Bona* and *Pace*. Also, *Thandi,* March 1995, for articles that target the female market: "Sexual Jealousy"; "Married Women with 'Extra-Marital Affairs' "; "75 Ways to De-Stress"; "Zindzi Mandela Pours Her Heart Out"; "Viva Generation Gap"; and "Do You Want Him to Use a Condom?" Also, *Thandi,* August 1995, on "Women Who Yield Power" and an "A-Z Guide for Working Women."

134. Michael J. Goodman, "For the Defence," *Tribute,* November 1995, 78–81, on Johnnie Cochran, described as "the superb lawyer who is a defender of all African Americans, and the shrewd businessman whose investments include a substantial stake in a black South African business."

135. Mark Lowery, "Blacks Invest $15 Million in Pepsi Venture," *Black Enterprise*, December 1994, 22, including Earl Graves, Calvin Grigsby, Shaquille O'Neal, Clarence Avant and Jheryl Busby of Motown Records, Danny Glover, Whitney Houston, attorney Johnnie Cochran, Dr. William R. Harvey, and Percy Sutton. See "Dollars Down South," *Tribute,* 67.

136. *Enterprise,* May 1995, 37, 119, published in South Africa. The editor is Thambi Mazwai. Within one year of the New South Africa, 11 South African black companies were listed on the Johannesburg Stock Exchange. However, there are also about 800,000 SMMEs (small, medium, and micro enterprise), in addition to 2.5 million informal "survival enterprises" that parallel the black-American small business sector. Also, Mack, "Getting in on the Ground Floor," 79–83.

137. McCoy, "Nonstop from Durham," 89–92; McCoy, "Doing Business in South Africa," 59, 62, 64; and Smith, "Traveling Rocky Roads," 106–8. Beckett is recognized as one of the foremost authorities on African investment panels. Also, "Dollars Down South," 67, notes the Sloan financial group in 1995 was "the largest African American investor to date."

138. McCoy, "Nonstop from Durham," 92. Also, "Dollars Down South," 67, notes that Calvert invests in 15 African stock markets, and "60 percent of its total value is the Johannesburg Stock Exchange."

139. Michael Giles, "Forging Links," in the program for the conference, Forging Links: Business Enterprise, Entrepreneurship and Development, African Americans and South African Blacks, held by the Wits Business School, University of Witwatersrand, Johannesburg, 19 October 1995, 6; also 4, 7. This was the first international African-American/black South African forum on black business held in South Africa at the university level. The author was the conference convener while she was a senior Fulbright scholar in 1995 in the history department at the University of Witwatersrand (Wits) researching South African business history. The conference was sponsored in part by Wits University, the United States Information Agency, *Tribute,* and the African American Institute.

140. See Andrew Tanzer, "The Pacific Century," *Forbes,* 15 July 1996, 108–13, who attributes Asia's phenomenal growth to those countries that "maintain high savings and investment rates, practice fiscal and monetary discipline, educate their work forces, tax lightly. They eschew income redistribution and social welfare systems and are hotbeds of entrepreneurism." Malaysia, a country racked by race riots, he notes "was completely remade by foreign direct investment and in ten years moved from palm oil to exporting disk drives."

141. McCoy, "Nonstop from Durham," 92.

142. Edmond, "Companies to Watch," 302, 304.

143. *Black Enterprise*, August 1994, 24.

144. Khor, "Colonialism Redux," 18–20.

145. King, "The Tough Get Going," 180.

146. Monwabisi Fandeso, "Forging Links," 5. Other South African Blacks who participated in the conference were: Rev. Godfrey Mandla Gamede, CEO, ZikLife Funeral Benefit Fund; Professor Malegapuru William Makgoba, vice chancellor, University of Witwatersrand, 1993–1996; Dr. David Sepo Molapo, managment consultant and motivational speaker; Philip Machaba, general secretary of NAFCOC; Dr. Mohale Manhanyale, chairman of National Sorghum Breweries; and Professor Fred Ahwireng-Obeng, Wits Business School.

147. "Dollars Down South," 67. Also, "Forging Links," 7.

148. Derek Dingle, "The Freshman Class of '96," *Black Enterprise,* June 1996, 156, 158. After graduating from Indiana University, where he played on the basketball team that won the 1981 NCAA championship, Brown played professional basketball in Italy. Having become fluent in Italian, Brown worked in the off-season for Nuova Fucinati, an Italian firm that manufactured alloyed metal for the car industry. Fuci was started in partnership with Nuova, with Brown having 51 percent. In 1989, with $250,000 of his savings, Brown bought out Nuova and has 100 percent ownership.

149. "Lex Nigel Barker: Flying High," *Black Enterprise*, 16; and Rhonda Reynolds and Marjorie Whigham-Desir, "Four Challenges to Growing Your Business," *Black Enterprise,* November 1995, 98. Also, Thompson, "The Freshman Class of '95," 148, 152, on the Red River Shipping Company, founded in 1983 by an African-American admiralty-law professor, John P. Morris Sr. (1928–1993), who taught in Chicago and at Arizona State University. His son is president and CEO. The company owns two U.S. flagships (America has only 300). It has transported soybean oil to Karachi, Pakistani, for the United States Agency for International Development. Red River also hauls military cargo. In the Gulf War, the company conducted two military supply runs in 1990. Red River Shipping was ranked 100th on *Black Enterprise*'s top 100 list for 1996, with sales of $20.5 million.

150. Thurlow J. Simmons, "Forging Links," 9. Simmons is founder and managing director of the Johannesburg-based United States Business Development Group and formerly head of Soft Sheen's international division; he is presently director of the Ideal Diamond Company, which he indicates "is the first diamond company to be owned by a black in South Africa."

151. William Raspberry, "Coke Deal: Reciprocity Rather Than Generosity," *Miami Times*, 3 September 1981; and Tony Brown, "The Newest Twist in the Coke Deal," *Pensacola Voice,* 26 September and 2 October 1981.

152. April W. Klimley, "Minority Vending," *Black Enterprise,* June 1996, Special Advertising Supplement, 310.

153. Also, "Heublein Plan on Blacks," *New York Times,* 17 March 1982,

154. John H. Franklin and Alfred A. Moss Jr., *From Slavery to Freedom: A History of African Americans,* 7th ed. (New York: McGraw Hill, 1994), 539–43; Also, Adolph L. Reed Jr., *The Jesse Jackson Phenomenon: The Crisis of Purpose in Afro-American Politics* (New Haven: Yale University Press, 1986); Roger D. Hatch and Frank E. Watkins, eds., *Reverend Jesse L. Jackson, Straight from the Heart* (Philadelphia: Fortress Press, 1987); and Marshall Frady, *Jesse: The Life and Pilgrimage of Jesse Jackson* (New York: Random House, 1996).

155. *Black Enterprise,* November 1990, 17.

156. Brown, "B.E. Franchise 50," 104. In 1994 a $54 million class-action racial discrimination lawsuit by African-Americans was settled with Denny's restaurant chain, a subsidiary of Flagstar Companies (which also holds the El Pollo Loco and Hardee's franchises) for actions such as refus-

ing to seat blacks, refusing to serve blacks, reneging on reservations made by blacks, and two instances of requiring blacks to pay for their food before being served.

157. Mark Lowery, "Burger King Backs Meat Processing Plant, " *Black Enterprise,* November 1994, 26. There are several black business listed in the *Black Enterprise* top 100 for 1995, including the oldest African-American business in the nation, 68th ranked C. H. James & Sons, founded in 1883 in West Virginia. A wholesale food distribution and produce-processing enterprise, it had $28.4 million in sales in 1995. Also see Ingham and Feldman, *African-American Business Leaders,* 339–51.

158. Ingham and Feldman, *African-American Business Leaders,* 254.

159. *Black Enterprise,* June 1989, 22–26.

160. "The Return of an Empire: What Will It Take to Restore the Black Hair Care Industry to Its People?" *Class,* August 1994, 31. Shark Products, makers of African Pride, was the white company that initiated the suit.

161. *Black Enterprise,* September 1990, 18.

162. *Black Enterprise,* May 1995, 24.

163. Lloyd Gite, "Playing above the Rim," *Black Enterprise*, June 1995, 217. Scholarship recipients in turn must spend two hours a week tutoring high-school students.

164. Simms, "How the Census Bureau Devalues Black Businesses," 224, 226, 228. The findings were based on a Joint Center for Politics and Economics survey, which was sent to over 2,000 African-American, Hispanic, and Asian-American companies and 2,000 nonminority firms. Only 21.9 percent responses from minority firms were used for analysis.

165. Tony Brown has been a leading contemporary proponent of the campaign to "Buy Black." His public-affairs talk show, *Tony Brown's Journal,* has been shown on PBS since 1968. Also see Tony Brown, *Black Lies, White Lies: The Truth according to Tony Brown* (New York: William Morrow, 1996). Also, Kennedy, "Black Conservatism's Would-Be Spokesmen," 12, an account of Brown as a conservative.

166. Dingle, "Freshman Class of 96," 154–56.

167. Brown, "Hottest Industries for New Business Opportunities," 65–67, 70–73.

168. "A New Entrant in the War," *Black Enterprise,* June 1995, 34.

169. B. Wright O'Connor, "What's Next For the SBA?" *Black Enterprise,* June 1989, 138.

170. *Black Enterprise,* June 1995, 34.

171. Udayan Gupta, "Affirmative Buying," *Wall Street Journal*, 19 February 1993, R-12. Also, Klimley, "Minority Vending," 310.

172. George C. Fraser, *Success Runs in Our Race: The Complete Guide to Effective Networking in the African-American Community* (New York: William Morrow, 1994). Also see George Fraser, *Race for Success: The Ten Best Business Opportunities for Blacks in America* (New York: William Morrow, 1998), and Earl G. Graves, *How to Succeed in Business without Being White: Straight Talk on Making It in America* (New York: HarperBusiness, 1997). On the most recent United States Census Bureau's information on black American business, see http://www.census.gov/Press-Release/cb95-219.txt, which indicates that African-American-owned businesses increased 46 percent during a five-year period, from 424,165 in 1987 to 620,912 in 1992, with a 63 percent increase in business receipts during this same period, from $19.8 billion to $32.2 billion. The total number of the nation's businesses increased 26 percent, 13.7 million in 1987 to 17.3 million in 1992, while business receipts for all American firms increased 67 percent, from $2 trillion to $3 trillion. In 1992, African-American-owned firms averaged $52,000 in business receipts, compared to all United States firms, which averaged $193,000 in receipts. Yet, 56 percent of African-American businesses had receipts of less than $10,000, while only 3,000 black firms out of 620,912 had sales of $1 million or more. On population figures, see http://www.census.gov/population/estimates/nation/infile3-1.txt, which indicates that on 1 November 1997, there were an estimated 34 million African-Americans, constituting 12.7 percent of the population. Also, see http://www.census.gov/Press-Release/cb97-55.html, which indicates that in 1997, 6 percent (2 million) of blacks in the United States were foreign born. Also, on black business history in the United States, see Juliet E. K. Walker, *Encyclopedia of African American Business History* (Westport, Conn.: Greenwood Publishing Group, forthcoming 1998).

Index

INTRODUCTORY NOTE: *Italicized* page references indicate information located in tables.

The Author

Juliet E. K. Walker is professor of history at the University of Illinois at Urbana-Champaign. She received her Ph.D from the University of Chicago, did postdoctoral work at Harvard University, and served as research associate at the W. E. B. DuBois Institute, Harvard University. Walker has taught at the University of Witwatersrand in Johannesburg, South Africa, as a senior Fulbright professor. She is the author of *Free Frank: A Black Pioneer on the Antebellum Frontier* (1983) and *War, Peace, and Structural Violence: Peace Activism and the African American Experience* (1992) and is editor of the *Encyclopedia of African American Business History* (1998) and guest editor of *African Americans in Business: The Path towards Empowerment.* In addition to a Fulbright Fellowship for research in South African black business history, she has won a Newberry Library Fellowship for the Study of State and Local History, an American Historical Association Albert J. Beveridge Grant for Research in American History, a Rockefeller Fellowship, a National Endowment for the Humanities (NEH) Fellowship for Independent Study and Research, an American Historical Association Beveridge Research Award, a Berkshire Fellowship at the Radcliffe Bunting Institute, and a Princeton University Shelby Cullom Davis Center Fellowship for Historical Studies. Her publication awards include a Karl E. Mundt Educational and Historical Foundation Prize; an Otto A. Rothert Award; the Carter G. Woodson Award for the best article published in the *Journal of Negro History,* 1983 –1987; and the Newcomen Society Prize for the best article published in the *Harvard Business History Review,* "Racism, Slavery, and Free Enterprise: Black Entrepreneurship in the United States before the Civil War," which also won the Association of Black Women Historians Brown Publication Prize.

The Editor

Dr. Kenneth J. Lipartito is associate professor of history at the University of Houston, Houston, Texas. He holds a Ph.D. in history from the Johns Hopkins University and has published extensively in the field of economic and business history. He is the author of *The Bell System and Regional Business: The Telephone in the South* and *Baker and Botts in the Development of Modern Houston*. His work has appeared in leading journals, including the *American Historical Review*, the *Journal of Economic History*, the *Business History Review*, and *Industrial and Corporate Change*. Dr. Lipartito was appointed Newcomen Fellow at the Harvard Business School for the years 1989 to 1990. In 1995 he was awarded the IEEE Life Members Award for the best article in the history of electrical technology, as well as the Newcomen Society Award for Excellence in Business History Research and Writing by the Business History Conference.